INFORMING
AND EDUCATING
ANTI-FRAUD
PROFESSIONALS
WORLDWIDE

FRAUD EXAMINERS MANUAL

VOLUME I

2005 US EDITION

©1990-2005 by the Association of Certified Fraud Examiners, Inc.

The original purchaser of this volume is authorized to reproduce in any form or by any means up to 50 pages contained in this work for nonprofit, educational, or private use. Such reproduction requires no further permission from the Authors or Publisher and/or payment of any permission fee as long as proper credit is given.

Except as specified above, no portion of this work may be reproduced or transmitted in any form or by any means electronic or mechanical, including photocopying, recording, or by any information storage and retrieval system without the written permission of the Association.

ISBN 1-889277-11-8

ACFE
Association of Certified Fraud Examiners

The Gregor Building
716 West Avenue
Austin, Texas 78701
(800) 245-3321
(512) 478-9000
www.cfenet.com

DISCLAIMER

Every effort has been made to ensure that the contents of this publication are accurate and free from error. However, it is possible that errors exist, both typographical and in content. Therefore, the information provided herein should be used only as a guide and not as the only source of reference.

The author, advisors, and publishers shall have neither liability nor responsibility to any person or entity with respect to any loss, damage, or injury caused or alleged to be caused directly or indirectly by any information contained in or omitted from this publication.

Printed in the United States of America

Table of Contents

FRAUD EXAMINERS MANUAL

TABLE OF CONTENTS

VOLUME I

SECTION 1
FINANCIAL TRANSACTIONS AND FRAUD SCHEMES

OCCUPATIONAL FRAUDS

ACCOUNTING CONCEPTS
Accounting Basics	1.101
Financial Statements	1.104
Generally Accepted Accounting Principles (GAAP)	1.107

MANAGEMENT'S AND AUDITORS' RESPONSIBILITIES
Management	1.201
Certified Fraud Examiners	1.203
External Auditors	1.205
Internal Auditor Responsibilities	1.222
GAO Auditing Standards	1.231
Sarbanes-Oxley Act of 2002	1.240
Private Securities Litigation Reform Act	1.251

FINANCIAL STATEMENT FRAUD
What is Financial Statement Fraud?	1.303
The Cost of Financial Statement Fraud	1.303
Why Financial Statement Fraud is Committed	1.304
The COSO Study on Financial Statement Fraud	1.305
Effect of Fraud on Financial Statements	1.307
What Red Flags are Associated with Financial Statement Fraud Generally?	1.326
Detection of Fraudulent Financial Statement Schemes	1.326
Financial Statement Analysis	1.329
Interviews in Fraudulent Financial Statement Cases	1.337
Prevention of Financial Statement Fraud	1.347

FRAUD EXAMINERS MANUAL

FINANCIAL TRANSACTIONS AND FRAUD SCHEMES

ASSET MISAPPROPRIATION: CASH THEFT
Skimming	1.401
Cash Larceny	1.419

ASSET MISAPPROPRIATION: FRAUDULENT DISBURSEMENTS
Register Disbursement Schemes	1.501
Check Tampering	1.509
Billing Schemes	1.533
Payroll Fraud	1.552
Expense Reimbursement Schemes	1.569

ASSET MISAPPROPRIATION: INVENTORY AND OTHER ASSETS
Misuse of Inventory and Other Assets	1.601
Theft of Inventory and Other Assets	1.602
Detection	1.612
Prevention	1.616

BRIBERY AND CORRUPTION
Bribery	1.701
Methods of Making Illegal Payments	1.714
Detection	1.716
Conflicts of Interest	1.730
Prevention	1.739

INTELLECTUAL PROPERTY
Competitive Intelligence (CI) Versus Espionage	1.802
Open Sources of Information	1.803
The Intelligence Pyramid	1.806
Building Financial Statements	1.812
Nontraditional Sources	1.815
A Closer Look at Databases	1.817
A Corporate Spy Uses Open Sources: What of It?	1.819
Favorited Targets	1.820
How Information is Lost	1.821
Basic Principle of Spying	1.827
Infiltration Techniques	1.833
Transactional Intelligence	1.840
Telling Good Lies	1.842
Visual Surveillance Against People	1.844

FRAUD EXAMINERS MANUAL

FINANCIAL TRANSACTIONS AND FRAUD SCHEMES

INTELLECTUAL PROPERTY (CONT.)

E-Mail	1.845
Social Engineering	1.846
Cloaking and Misdirection	1.849
Technical Surveillance	1.859
Investigating an Information Theft Case	1.873
Program for Safeguarding Proprietary Inforamtion (SPI)	1.875
Technical Surveillance Countermeasures (TSCM) Survey	1.881
Preventing Employee Theft of Propietary Information	1.883
Protecting the Trade Sectrets of Others	1.885
Legal Issues Related to Theft of Intellectual Property	1.887
Bibliography	1.887

OTHER FRAUDS

FINANCIAL INSTITUTION FRAUD

Embezzlement Schemes	1.901
Loan Fraud	1.903
Real Estate Fraud	1.913
New Account Fraud Schemes	1.919
Money Transfer (Wire) Fraud Schemes	1.922
Automated Teller Machine (ATM) Fraud	1.926
Advanced Fee Fraud	1.926
Letter-of-Credit Fraud	1.927
Inside/Outside Frauds	1.928
Prevention	1.928
Suspicious Activity Reports	1.931
Applicable Federal Statutes	1.931

CHECK AND CREDIT CARD FRAUD

Check Fraud	1.1001
Check Fraud Rings	1.1007
Check Fraud Detection	1.1008
Check Fraud Prevention and Investigation	1.1009
Credit Card Fraud	1.1013
Magnetic Stripe Diagram	1.1019
Prevention and Detection of Credit Card Fraud	1.1020

FRAUD EXAMINERS MANUAL

FINANCIAL TRANSACTIONS AND FRAUD SCHEMES

INSURANCE FRAUD
Types of Insurance Policies 1.1101
Agent/Broker Fraud 1.1102
Underwriting Irregularities 1.1103
Vehicle Insurance Schemes 1.1105
Property Schemes 1.1107
Life Insurance Schemes 1.1108
Liability Schemes 1.1108
"Red Flags" of Insurance Fraud 1.1108
Computer-Generated Detection Reports 1.1112
Workers Compensation Fraud 1.1113

HEALTH CARE FRAUD
Laws Relating to Health Care Fraud 1.1201
Fraud by the Insurance Company 1.1205
Employee Claims Fraud 1.1207
Agent Fraud 1.1209
Provider Fraud 1.1210
Fraud by the Medical Staff 1.1217
Kickbacks in the Health Care Industry 1.1217
Inflated Billings 1.1218
Insured Fraud 1.1222
Criminal Rings 1.1223
Collusion 1.1223
Detection of External Fraud 1.1224
Fraud by Medical Institutions 1.1225
Nursing Homes 1.1229
Psychiatric Hospital Fraud 1.1230
Other Frauds in the Institutional Setting 1.1232
Managed Care 1.1233
Electronic Claims Fraud 1.1235
Health Care Compliance Programs 1.1239

BANKRUPTCY FRAUD
Introduction 1.1301
The Bankruptcy Code 1.1304
Trustees 1.1305
Creditors' Rights and Remedies 1.1309
Bankruptcy Crime Statutes 1.1312

FRAUD EXAMINERS MANUAL

FINANCIAL TRANSACTIONS AND FRAUD SCHEMES

BANKRUPTCY FRAUD (CONT.)
Bankruptcy Schemes 1.1318

TAX FRAUD
Introduction 1.1401
Hallmarks (Badges) of Fraud 1.1402
Civil vs. Criminal 1.1404
Taxpayer Penalties 1.1405
Tax Preparer Penalties 1.1407
Defenses for Tax Fraud 1.1409
Evidence of Tax Fraud 1.1411
Other Legal Elements of Fraud 1.1412

SECURITIES FRAUD
Introduction 1.1501
Federal Regulation 1.1501
The NASD and Other Regulatory Organizations 1.1513
State Regulation 1.1515
What Constitutes a Security? 1.1517
Commodity Futures, Exchange-Traded Options, and OTC Options 1.1525
Investigation of Securities Fraud 1.1526
Exchange-Traded Options 1.1528
Securities Fraud Schemes 1.1531
Investigative Tips 1.1543
Securities Fraud and the Internet 1.1545

MONEY LAUNDERING
Introduction 1.1601
Federal and State Law 1.1607
State Laws 1.1630
Enforcement and Prevention Strategies 1.1631
Special Problems for Insurance Companies 1.1634

FRAUD EXAMINERS MANUAL

FINANCIAL TRANSACTIONS AND FRAUD SCHEMES

CONSUMER FRAUD
Con Schemes 1.1702
Telemarketing Fraud 1.1707
Ponzi and Pyramid Schemes 1.1728
Franchise Fraud 1.1738
Identity Theft 1.1744

COMPUTER AND INTERNET FRAUD
Computer Fraud vs. Computer Crime 1.1803
Computer Hacking 1.1805
Electronic Mail 1.1814
Computer Viruses 1.1816
Internet Fraud 1.1825
Electronic Commerce 1.1828
Insider Threats 1.1832
Computer Security 1.1833
Internal Controls in the Data Center 1.1836
Internal Controls in Computer Applications 1.1840
Conducting an Investigation Regarding Computer Crimes 1.1843
Computer Crime Laws 1.1857
Government Information on Cybercrime 1.1862

PUBLIC SECTOR FRAUD
Government Fraud Auditing Standards 1.1901
Summary of GAO Standards Relating to Fraud 1.1902
False Claims and Statements 1.1927
Beneficiary Fraud 1.1931
Government Initiatives to Reduce Fraud 1.1934
Prosecution: The Government Employee's Role 1.1936
Interviewing Government Officials 1.1938
Assigning the Inteview 1.1938
The Warning Dilemma 1.1939
Requirement to Cooperate 1.1940
Criminal Investigations 1.1941
Declination of Prosecution 1.1941
Legal Counsel 1.1942
Obstructing the Investigation 1.1943
Rules of Procedure 1.1943

FRAUD EXAMINERS MANUAL

FINANCIAL TRANSACTIONS AND FRAUD SCHEMES

CONTRACT AND PROCUREMENT FRAUD
Elements of a Contract 1.2001
Presolicitation Phase 1.2001
Solicitation and Negotiation Phase 1.2003
Contract Performance and Administration Phase 1.2005

FRAUD EXAMINERS MANUAL

VOLUME II

SECTION 2
LAW

OVERVIEW OF THE UNITED STATES LEGAL SYSTEM
Constitutional, Statutory, and Common Law	2.101
Substantive and Procedural Law	2.102
The Court System	2.103
Civil and Criminal Actions for Fraud	2.109

THE LAW RELATED TO FRAUD
Definition of Fraud	2.201
Principal Types of Fraud	2.201
Federal Legislation Related to Fraud	2.211
Fines Under Title 18	2.284
Qui Tam Suits and the False Claims Act	2.288
Federal "Whistleblower" Statutes	2.290

INDIVIDUAL RIGHTS DURING EXAMINATIONS
Employee's Duty to Cooperate	2.301
Employee's Rights During the Investigation	2.301
Interviews	2.303
Searches and Surveillance	2.310
Polygraph Examinations	2.325
Obtaining Information About Employees	2.327
Discharging a Suspected Wrongdoer	2.330

CRIMINAL PROSECUTIONS FOR FRAUD
Basic Principles of Criminal Law	2.401
Arrest and Interrogation	2.402
The Charging Process	2.404
The Trial Process	2.414
Sentencing	2.419
Appeal	2.423

THE CIVIL JUSTICE SYSTEM
Civil Litigation	2.501
Alternative Dispute Resolution	2.506
Trial of a Civil Case	2.507

FRAUD EXAMINERS MANUAL

LAW

THE CIVIL JUSTICE SYSTEM (CONT.)
Fidelity Bond Claims	2.509

BASIC PRINCIPLES OF EVIDENCE
Definition of Evidence	2.601
Three Types of Evidence	2.601
Direct Versus Circumstantial Evidence	2.602
Relevance	2.603
Special Problems Concerning Some Types of Circumstantial Evidence	2.604
Exhibits	2.606
Hearsay	2.610
Excluding Illegally Seized Evidence	2.614

TESTIFYING AS AN EXPERT WITNESS
Introduction	2.701
Pre-Trial Preparation	2.703
Conflicts of Interest	2.703
Qualifying as an Expert Witness	2.707
Preparing to Testify	2.710
Direct Examination	2.713
Cross-Examination	2.715
Expressing an Opinion on Guilt	2.719
Summary	2.720

APPENDIX

FEDERAL RULES OF CIVIL PROCEDURE
I. Scope of Rules—One Form of Action	2.801
II. Commencement of Action; Service of Process, Pleadings, Motions and Orders	2.801
III. Pleadings and Motions	2.808
IV. Parties	2.818
V. Depositions and Discovery	2.825
VI. Trials	2.846
VII. Judgment	2.857

FRAUD EXAMINERS MANUAL

LAW APPENDIX

FEDERAL RULES OF CIVIL PROCEDURE (CONT.)
VIII. Provisional and Final Remedies	2.863
IX. Special Proceedings	2.867
X. District Courts and Clerks	2.871
XI. General Provisions	2.873

FEDERAL RULES OF CRIMINAL PROCEDURE
I. Scope, Purpose, and Construction	2.901
II. Preliminary Proceedings	2.901
III. The Grand Jury, the Indictment and the Information	2.904
IV. Arraignment and Preparation for Trial	2.909
V. Venue	2.920
VI. Trial	2.922
VII. Post-Conviction Procedures	2.926
VIII. Supplementary and Special Proceedings	2.935
IX. General Provisions	2.938

FEDERAL RULES OF EVIDENCE
Article I. General Provisions	2.1001
Article II. Judicial Notice	2.1002
Article III. Presumptions in Civil actions and Proceedings	2.1003
Article IV. Relevancy and Its Limits	2.1003
Article V. Privileges	2.1008
Article VI. Witnesses	2.1008
Article VII. Opinions and Expert Testimony	2.1011
Article VIII. Hearsay	2.1013
Article IX. Authentication and Identification	2.1018
Article X. Contents of Writings, Recordings, and Photographs	2.1020
Article XI. Miscellaneous Rules	2.1022

FRAUD EXAMINERS MANUAL

VOLUME III

SECTION 3
INVESTIGATION

ANALYZING DOCUMENTS

Chain of Custody	3.101
Obtaining Documentary Evidence	3.102
Examining Fraudulent Documents	3.104
Early Consultation with an Expert can Prove Valuable	3.105
Types of Forensic Document Examinations	3.105
Handling Documents as Physical Evidence	3.106
Identifying Writings	3.108
The Document Expert's Findings	3.111
How to Obtain Handwriting Samples	3.112
Typewriters and Computer Printers	3.114
Photocopies	3.116
"Dating" a Document	3.118
Indented Writings	3.119
Counterfeit Printed Documents	3.120
Fingerprints	3.121
Sources for Expert Document Examinations	3.123

INTERVIEW THEORY AND APPLICATION

Preparation	3.201
Characteristics of a Good Interview	3.201
Characteristics of a Good Interviewer	3.202
Question Typology	3.202
Legal Elements of Interviewing	3.204
Elements of Conversations	3.204
Inhibitors of Communication	3.206
Facilitators of Communication	3.208
Introductory Questions	3.211
Informational Questions	3.217
Assessment Questions	3.233
Admission-Seeking Questions	3.245
Kinesic Interview and Interrogation	3.268
Criteria-Based Statement Analysis	3.271
The Cognitive Interview Technique	3.276

FRAUD EXAMINERS MANUAL

INVESTIGATION

COVERT OPERATIONS
Covert Examinations	3.301
Establishing an Identity	3.302
Objectives	3.303
Problems in Covert Operations	3.304
Entrapment	3.305
Surveillance	3.305
Sources and Informants	3.311
Uses of Operatives	3.319

SOURCES OF INFORMATION
Rules Governing Public Record Information	3.401
City Government	3.407
County Government	3.409
State Government	3.413
Federal Government	3.417
Commercial Sources	3.431
Credit Records	3.433
Commercial Databases and Research Reference Services	3.435
Directories	3.436
Banks and Financial Institutions	3.448
Investigative and Law Enforcement Information Centers and Databases	3.451

ACCESSING INFORMATION ON-LINE
Accessing Information Through Computer Databases	3.501
Using an On-Line Service to Find Information	3.503
The Internet	3.514
A Guide to Successful Searching	3.518
Websites Table	3.520

DATA ANALYSIS AND REPORTING TOOLS
Data Analysis Software Functions	3.601
Data Analysis Software	3.611
Other Fraud-Related Software	3.639

FRAUD EXAMINERS MANUAL

INVESTIGATION

TRACING ILLICIT TRANSACTIONS
Comprehensive Guidelines for Information to be Collected in Financial Interviews	3.701
Direct Methods of Tracing Financial Transactions	3.705
Indirect Methods of Tracing Financial Transactions	3.722
Locating Hidden Assets	3.740

REPORTING STANDARDS
Preparation	3.801
Accuracy of Reports	3.801
Clarity	3.802
Impartiality and Relevance	3.802
Timeliness	3.802
Reporting Mistakes	3.803
Effective Note-taking	3.804
Organization of Information	3.805
Analyzing the Reader	3.805
Outlining	3.807
Report Structure	3.811
Signed Statements	3.815
Visual Aids	3.818
Engagement Contracts	3.822

FRAUD EXAMINERS MANUAL

INVESTIGATION

APPENDIX

FRAUD EXAMINATION CHECKLIST
Fraud Examination Checklist 3.901

SAMPLE REPORT
Bailey Books, Incorporated 3.1001

FORMS
Consent to Search 3.1101
Telephone Recording Consent 3.1103
Consent to Record 3.1104
Customer Consent and Authorization for Access to Financial Records 3.1105
Evidence Control Log 3.1106

ENGAGEMENT CONTRACTS AND OPINION LETTERS
Engagement Letters 3.1201
Fraud Examination Opinion Letters 3.1205

FRAUD EXAMINERS MANUAL

SECTION 4
CRIMINOLOGY AND ETHICS

INTRODUCTION TO CRIMINOLOGY/ UNDERSTANDING HUMAN BEHAVIOR
Applying Behavioral Theory to a Fraud Case 4.102
Why People Obey the Law 4.121

THEORIES OF CRIME CAUSATION
Classical Criminology 4.201
Routine Activities Theory 4.202
Biological Theories 4.203
Pyschological Theories 4.204
Social Structure Theories 4.205
Social Process Theories 4.206

WHITE-COLAR CRIME
What is White-Collar Crime? 4.301
Public Perceptions of White-Collar Crime 4.303
Crimes of the Middle Classes—A Look at White-Colar Crime 4.305
Varieties of White-Collar Crime? 4.315

ORGANIZATIONAL CRIME
Corporate Organization and Criminal Behavior 4.402
Types of Violations 4.405
Causes of Organizational Crimes 4.407
Opportunities for Unlawful Organizational Behavior 4.409
Criminogenic Organizational Structures 4.416
Corporate Executives and Criminal Liability 4.419
Management Behavior 4.422
Controlling Organizational Crime 4.423

OCCUPATIONAL CRIME
Research in Occupational Fraud and Abuse 4.501
Edwin H. Sutherland 4.501
Donald R. Cressey 4.502
Dr. Steve Albrecht 4.513
Richard C. Hollinger 4.517
The 2004 Report to the Nation on Occupational Fraud and Abuse 4.524

FRAUD EXAMINERS MANUAL

CRIMINOLOGY AND ETHICS

FRAUD PREVENTION PROGRAMS

Responsibility for Fraud Prevention	4.601
Corporate Sentencing Guidelines	4.607
Implementing an Effective Compliance Program Under the Corporate Sentencing Guidelines	4.614
Fraud Prevention Standards Under Sarbanes-Oxley	4.626
Fraud Prevention Policy	4.631
Ethics Programs	4.636
Sample Corporate Compliance Program	4.639
Sample Fraud Policy	4.650
Fraud Policy Decision Matrix	4.654
Sample Code of Business Ethics and Conduct	4.655

PUNISHMENT AND THE CRIMINAL JUSTICE SYSTEM

The Police and Regulatory Inspectors	4.702
Processing Offenders	4.706
The Court System	4.708
Sentencing Options	4.712
Corrections	4.718
Crime Statistics	4.725
Public Attitudes Toward the Criminal Justice System	4.733

ETHICS FOR FRAUD EXAMINERS

What is Ethics?	4.801
Morality, Ethics, and Legality	4.803
Values and Principles	4.806
Some Concluding Remarks	4.817

ACFE CODE OF ETHICS

Commitment to Professionalism and Diligence	4.902
Legal and Ethical Conduct and Conflict of Interest	4.905
Integrity and Competence	4.908
Professional Skepticism	4.910
Court Orders and Testimony	4.911
Reasonable Evidential Basis for Opinions	4.912
Evidential Basis for Opinions	4.912
Guilt and Innocence	4.914

FRAUD EXAMINERS MANUAL

CRIMINOLOGY AND ETHICS

ACFE CODE OF ETHICS (CONT.)
Confidential Information	4.915
"Blowing the Whistle"	4.919
Complete Reporting of Material Matters	4.920
Professional Improvement	4.921
Professional Standards and Practices	4.922
Predication Standards	4.925

ACFE CODE OF PROFESSIONAL STANDARDS
CFE Code of Professional Standards	4.1001

PREFACE

Over ten years ago, the First Edition of the *Fraud Examiners Manual* postulated that "...fraud will be the crime of choice for the 21st century."

The truth of that prophetic prediction has been borne out in the events of the last years. According to estimates by the Association of Certified Fraud Examiners, occupational fraud and abuse in the United States alone may exceed six hundred billion dollars annually. If we add together the various confidence schemes, check and credit card frauds and securities swindles, the total may run as much as ten percent of global economic output — trillions of dollars world-wide. Enron, WorldCom, Adelphia, and the rest of a rougue's gallery — as devastating as these frauds were — are only a microcosm of the problem.

As I wrote in the Third Edition, one difficult aspect of fraud and white-collar crime is that it is hidden — we only know about the ones that surface. Whatever the true cost of this problem, it is a staggering social and economic sum. But there is hope.

When the First Edition of the *Fraud Examiners Manual* was released, there were less than a thousand Certified Fraud Examiners. The Association is now fast approaching 35,000 members in 120 countries on five continents. These members bring true hope to understanding and eventually controlling the problem of white-collar crime. It will not be easy, and will not be accomplished quickly.

This new version of the *Fraud Examiners Manual* is but one weapon to fight fraud. Like all weapons, it means nothing except in the hands of someone trained to use it. You, the individual fraud examiner, are the real key. Study the enclosed information carefully, then add this knowledge to your arsenal. It represents the common body of knowledge in the fraud examination field. But auditors, forensic accountants, attorneys, law enforcement personnel, regulatory examiners, investigators, and other anti-fraud professionals will find much useful information too.

Like the three other editions of the *Manual*, this one is organized into four sections. The first section has been renamed Financial Transactions and Fraud Schemes. It describes hundreds of fraud schemes as well as providing information about basic accounting concepts and managers' and auditors' responsibilities to detect fraud. The section is divided into two subsections: occupational fraud and other fraud. Occupational fraud schemes include three types of asset misappropriation (cash, inventory, and fraudulent disbursements), corruption, and fraudulent financial statements. These chapters follow a standard taxonomy originally

PREFACE

developed for the book *Occupational Fraud and Abuse*. The section also details a number of other fraud schemes ranging from financial institution fraud to government fraud.

The Investigation Section provides the basic tools and techniques necessary to develop information and evidence when conducting a fraud examination and identifying the perpetrators. It describes how to gather evidence through the examination of documents and through interview techniques. It also contains information about using data analysis techniques and how to locate information through the Internet and other on-line sources.

The Law Section focuses on the statutes and common law principles involved in prosecuting fraudsters through both the criminal and civil systems, as well as the legal pitfalls you may encounter in conducting an investigation. It also contains information about how to succeed as an expert witness, as well as the complete text of the Federal Rules of Civil and Criminal Procedure and the Federal Rules of Evidence.

The Criminology and Ethics Section discusses why people commit crime and what can be done to stop them including developing corporate compliance programs. It also includes fraud statistics and analyses of organizational and occupational crime. The Ethics portion discusses current professional and ethical issues facing the Certified Fraud Examiner.

We would like to acknowledge the assistance of the following experts in contributing material to this edition: Bob Bauman, Neil Bebbington, Charlotte J. Bell, Tasha Bollinger, Dick Brodfuehrer, Chris Campos, Larry Cook, Dave Cotton, Tom Creelman, Don Dame, Joe Dervaes, Ron Durkin, Dennis Dycus, Bryan Farrell, John Francolla, Mason Haynesworth, Jim Healy, Steve Hendrix, Dick Hollinger, Frank Howatt, Mike Kline, Mike Lawrence, Frank Leggio, Jim Lile, Bob Lindquist, Kathleen Lower, Tony Maceo, Judge Frank Maloney, Walt Manning, John McLaren, Bob Miller, Frank Nasuti, Dick Nossen, Joan Norvelle, Brett Holloway-Reeves, Ric Rowe, William N. Rudman, Mike Ryman, Ken Sibley, Craig Starr, Bill Thornhill, Don Wall, and John Fisher Weber.

Final thanks go to the staff of the Association of Certified Fraud Examiners. We are especially appreciative of the efforts of John Warren, DeAnn Holzman, Tony Rolston, Cynthia Gomez, Andi McNeal, Juliana Morehead, Kathie Lawrence, and Jeanette LeVie.

PREFACE

The following pages will provide you with detailed references. But remember, no procedure can replace good judgement. The detection and deterrence of fraud is difficult. But if you learn the information in this book, your task will be immeasurably easier.

Authors:
Joseph T. Wells, CFE, CPA
Toby J.F. Bishop, CFE, CPA, FCA
Nancy S. Bradford, CFE, CPA, CIA
Gilbert Geis, Ph.D.
John D. Gill, J.D., CFE
W. Michael Kramer, J.D., CFE
James D. Ratley, CFE
Jack Robertson, Ph.D., CFE, CPA

Introduction

INTRODUCTION

Fraud Examination Defined

Fraud examination is a methodology for resolving fraud allegations from inception to disposition. More specifically, fraud examination involves obtaining evidence and taking statements, writing reports, testifying to findings, and assisting in the detection and prevention of fraud.

Obtaining Evidence and Taking Statements

Evidence of fraud usually takes the form of documents or statements by witnesses. Accordingly, the fraud examiner must know how to properly and legally obtain evidence, as well as how to conduct interviews of witnesses and related parties.

Writing Reports

Once evidence has been obtained and the appropriate witnesses have been interviewed, the fraud examiner is responsible for writing clear, accurate, and unbiased reports reflecting the fraud examination results. These reports ultimately might be used by management, attorneys, prosecutors, and others to determine the facts. The fraud examiner is a gatherer of evidence—not the ultimate judge thereof. Opinions in fraud examination matters are generally avoided.

Testifying to Findings

Once a fraud examination has been completed, the evidence assembled, and the written report prepared, the fraud examiner often is called upon to testify before judicial authorities regarding the findings. Fraud examiners are expected to testify truthfully to matters relevant to the examination and to do so in a clear, and succinct manner.

Assisting in the Detection and Prevention of Fraud

The responsibility for the prevention of fraud lies with management or other appropriate authority. However, the fraud examiner is expected to actively pursue and recommend appropriate policies and procedures to prevent fraud.

The detection of fraud within organizations is the primary responsibility of internal and external auditors. However, once evidence of fraud is presented, the fraud examiner is expected to perform sufficient procedures, as set forth in this manual, to resolve the issue. Allegations must be resolved in a legal and professional manner.

INTRODUCTION

Many fraud examiners have an accounting background. Indeed, some fraud examiners are employed primarily in the audit function of their organizations. Although fraud examination and auditing are related, they are not the same discipline. The following table lists some of the principal differences.

Auditing vs. Fraud Examination

Issue	Auditing	Fraud Examination
Timing	**Recurring** — Audits are conducted on a regular, recurring basis	**Non Recurring** — Fraud examinations are non recurring. They are conducted only with sufficient predication.
Scope	**General** — The scope of the audit is a general examination of financial data.	**Specific** — The fraud examination is conducted to resolve specific allegations.
Objective	**Opinion** — An audit is generally conducted for the purpose of expressing an opinion on the financial state-ments or related information.	**Affix Blame** — The fraud examination's goal is to determine whether fraud has/is occurring, and to determine who is responsible.
Relationship	**Non Adversarial** — The audit process is non-adversarial in nature.	**Adversarial** — Fraud examinations, because they involve efforts to affix blame, are adversarial in nature.
Methodology	**Audit Techniques** — Audits are conducted primarily by examining financial data.	**Fraud Examination Techniques** — Fraud examinations are conducted by (1) document examination; (2) review of outside data such as public records; and (3) interviews.
Presumption	**Professional Skepticism** — Auditors are required to approach audits with professional skepticism.	**Proof** — Fraud examiners approach the resolution of a fraud by attempting to establish sufficient proof to support or refute an allegation of fraud.

Techniques for the examination of fraud issues differ considerably from other disciplines. Because of fraud's fundamental elements, several axioms must be considered, regardless of the nature or extent of the fraud.

INTRODUCTION

Axioms of Fraud Examination

Fraud is Hidden
Unlike other offenses, part of the method of fraud is to conceal its existence. A bank robber uses threats or force, while a bank embezzler not only steals money, but also covers up the theft. As a result, *no opinion should be given to any person that fraud does or does not exist within a specific environment.* The methods for concealing fraud are so numerous and sometimes ingenious that almost anyone—even the examiner—might be defrauded. Offering opinions might leave the examiner personally vulnerable to legal problems.

Reverse Proof
The examination of fraud matters is approached from two perspectives. To prove that a fraud *has* occurred, the proof must include attempts to prove it has *not* occurred. The reverse is also true. In attempting to prove fraud *has not occurred*, that proof must also attempt to prove that it *has*. The reason is that both sides of fraud must be examined. *Under the law, proof of fraud must preclude any explanation other than guilt.*

Existence of Fraud
The existence of fraud is solely the purview of the courts and juries. *The examiner must not express opinions on the guilt or innocence of any person or party.* In resolving fraud issues, the examiner must postulate a theory —guilt or innocence—in order to attempt to prove that theory. Any discussion of guilt or innocence is only a part of that theory; the examiner must not make statements that could be construed to be conclusive in regard to the theory.

Assembling the Fraud Team
Fraud examinations usually require a cooperative effort among different disciplines. A typical investigation team might include the following:

Certified Fraud Examiners
A CFE is trained to conduct a complex fraud case from inception to conclusion.

Auditors
Internal auditors often are used to review internal documentary evidence, evaluate tips or complaints, schedule losses, and provide assistance in technical areas of the company's operations.

INTRODUCTION

Security

Security department investigators often are assigned the "field work" stage of the investigation, including interviewing outside witnesses and obtaining public records and other documents from third parties.

Human Resources Personnel

The human resources department should be consulted to ensure that the laws governing the rights of employees in the workplace are not violated. Such involvement will lessen the possibility of a wrongful discharge suit or other civil action by the employee. Advice from a human resources specialist might also be needed. Normally this person would not directly participate in the investigation.

Management Representative

A representative of management, or in significant cases, the audit committee of the Board of Directors, should be kept informed of the progress of the investigation, and be available to lend the necessary assistance. A sensitive employee investigation has virtually no hope of success without strong management support.

Outside Consultant

In some cases, particularly when the suspect employee is particularly powerful or popular, it might be useful to employ outside specialists who are relatively immune from company politics or threats of reprisals. Such experts might also have greater experience and investigative contacts than insiders.

Legal Counsel

It is necessary to have counsel involved in, and in most cases, "directing" the investigation, at least as far as the legal aspects are concerned.

Characteristics of a Fraud Examiner

Fraud examiners should have unique abilities. In addition to technical skills, the successful examiner has the ability to elicit facts from numerous witnesses in a fair, impartial, lawful, and accurate manner, and to report the examination results accurately and completely. The ability to ascertain the facts and to report them accurately are of equal importance. The fraud examiner is part lawyer, part accountant, part criminologist, and part detective or investigator.

INTRODUCTION

Allan Pinkerton, one of the first successful private investigators, stated what qualities a detective should possess:

The detective must possess certain qualifications of prudence, secrecy, inventiveness, persistency, personal courage, and above all other things, honesty; while he must add to these the same quality of reaching out and becoming possessed of that almost boundless information which will permit of the immediate and effective application of his detective talent in whatever degree that might be possessed.

The ability to deal effectively with people is paramount for fraud examiners. The examiner typically meets people for a short period of time and with a specific purpose: to obtain information. Ideally, the examiner has the personality to attract and motivate people to be helpful.

The examiner's attitude toward others affects their attitude toward him. A hostile attitude will create anxiety in the respondents, thereby causing them to become withdrawn and protective, even if there is no reason to do so. Contrary to lore, the successful investi-gator is rarely "tough," except when the need arises and toughness has been carefully planned and evaluated.

Art Buckwalter says, "The secret is for each private investigator to be the kind of person others will want to deal with." Examiners who mislead others will often themselves be misled. For each guilty person an examiner encounters, he will deal with many innocent witnesses. Those innocent witnesses, and the examiner's ability to draw them out, are indispensable to fraud examination methodology. Because an examiner deals with people from all walks of life, being able to establish rapport with strangers is vital.

Because no two people are alike, the fraud examiner must be able to communicate in the respondent's language. A college graduate will not be questioned exactly the same way as a ninth-grade dropout; someone with a technical vocabulary won't respond in the same manner as a person with an artistic background. As each case differs, so will the examiner's approach.

The fraud examiner must have the technical ability to understand financial concepts, and the ability to draw inferences from them. A unique feature of fraud cases is that, unlike traditional property crimes, the perpetrator's identity usually is known. In a bank robbery, for

INTRODUCTION

example, the issue is not whether a crime was committed, but rather who committed the crime. In fraud cases, the issue usually is not the identity of the culprit, but whether or not the conduct constitutes fraud.

It is important that the examiner be able to simplify financial concepts so that others comprehend them. Fraud cases often involve issues that appear complicated, but in reality most fraud is rather simple; the concealment methods make it appear complex.

Fraud Examination Methodology

Fraud examination methodology requires that all fraud allegations be handled in a uniform, legal fashion and be resolved on a timely basis. Assuming there is sufficient reason (predication) to conduct a fraud examination, specific examination steps usually are employed. At each step of the fraud examination process, the evidence obtained and the fraud theory approach continually is assessed. That is to say, the suspect (subject) of the inquiry typically would be interviewed last, only after the fraud examiner has obtained enough general and specific information to address the allegations adequately.

The fraud examination methodology gathers evidence from the general to the specific. Because of the legal ramifications of fraud examiners' actions, the rights of all individuals must be observed throughout.

Predication

Investigation of fraud consists of the multitude of steps necessary to resolve allegations of fraud—interviewing witnesses, assembling evidence, writing reports, and dealing with prosecutors and the courts. The investigation of fraud, because it deals with the individual rights of others, must be conducted only with adequate cause or predication.

Predication is the totality of circumstances that would lead a reasonable, professionally trained, and prudent individual to believe a fraud has occurred, is occurring, and/or will occur. Predication is the basis upon which an examination is commenced. Fraud examinations should not be conducted without proper predication.

Fraud Theory Approach

Each fraud examination begins with the proposition that all cases will end in litigation. To solve a fraud without complete evidence, the examiner must make certain assumptions. This is not unlike

INTRODUCTION

the scientist who postulates a theory based on observation and then tests it. In the case of complex fraud, fraud theory is almost indispensable. Fraud theory begins with the assumption, based on the known facts, of what might have occurred. Then that assumption is tested to determine whether it is provable. The fraud theory approach involves the following steps, in the order of their occurrence:

- Analyze available data
- Create a hypothesis
- Test the hypothesis
- Refine and amend the hypothesis

A case study on internal fraud that is based on an actual incident, and one that is common in the commercial and governmental environment, illustrates the concepts involved in the fraud examination process. The names and certain other facts have been changed for purposes of illustration.

LINDA REED COLLINS CASE STUDY

Linda Reed Collins is purchasing manager for Bailey Books Incorporated in St. Augustine, Florida. Bailey, with $226 million in annual sales, is one of the country's leading producers of textbooks for the college and university market as well as technical manuals for the medical and dental professions.

Bailey's headquarters consists of 126 employees, plus numerous sales personnel in the field. Because of the competitive nature of the textbook business, their profit margins are quite thin. Bailey's purchases average about $75 million annually, consisting mostly of paper stock and covering used in the manufacturing process. The great majority of the manufacturing is done in Mexico through contracts with the Mexican government.

The purchasing function is principally handled by three purchasing agents. Linda Reed Collins is the purchasing manager and has two other buyers who report to her, plus another 18 clerical and support personnel.

Because Bailey Books is required by investors and lenders to have audited annual financial statements, Bailey employs a large regional CPA firm to conduct its annual audit, and has a staff of five internal auditors. All internal fraud matters within the company are referred to Loren D. Bridges, a Certified Fraud Examiner. The typical internal frauds at Bailey involve

INTRODUCTION

defalcations by their cashiers, as well as a constant stream of complaints concerning alleged fraud by Bailey Books' salespeople and distributors.

On January 28, Bridges was referred a telephone call. The male caller advised that he did not wish to disclose his identity. However, he claimed to have been a "long-term" supplier to Bailey in the area of books and sundries, and magazines. The caller said that ever since Linda Collins took over as purchasing manager for Bailey several years ago, he has been systematically "squeezed out" of doing business with Bailey. Although Bridges queried the caller for additional information, the person hung up the telephone.

There could be many legitimate reasons why a vendor would feel unfairly treated. To use the fraud theory approach, the Certified Fraud Examiner, in this case Bridges, must analyze the available data before coming to any preliminary hypothesis as to what has occurred.

Analyzing Available Data

If an audit of the entire purchasing function is deemed warranted, it would be conducted at this time and would specifically keep in mind the possibility of fraud resulting from the anonymous allegation.

Creating a Hypothesis

The hypothesis is invariably a "worst-case" scenario. That is, based on the allegation, what is the worst possible outcome? In this case, for Bailey Books, it would be that one of its purchasing agents was accepting kickbacks to steer business to a particular vendor. A hypothesis can be created for any specific allegation, i.e., a bribery or kickback scheme, embezzlement, conflict of interest, financial statement fraud, and so forth. In furtherance of the hypotheses, fraud examiners know that each specific scheme has its own unique characteristics that constitute the badges or "red flags" of fraud.

Testing the Hypothesis

Testing a hypothesis involves creating a "what-if" scenario. If, as part of the hypothesis, a bribery of a purchasing agent existed, the fraud examiner likely would find some or all of the following facts:
- A personal relationship between the buyer and vendor
- Ability of the purchasing agent to steer business toward a favored vendor
- Higher prices and/or lower quality for the product or service being purchased
- Excessive spending by the purchasing agent

INTRODUCTION

In the hypothetical case of Linda Reed Collins, the Certified Fraud Examiner—using Bailey Books' own records—can readily establish whether or not one vendor is receiving a larger proportional share of the business than similar vendors. Bridges could ascertain whether or not Bailey Books was paying too much for a particular product, such as paper, by simply calling other vendors and determining competitive pricing. A personal relationship with any suspected vendor and the buyer could be confirmed by discreet observation or inquiry. Whether or not a particular purchasing agent had the ability to steer business toward a favored vendor could be determined by reviewing the company's internal controls to ascertain who is involved in the decision-making process. The purchasing agent's lifestyle could be discreetly determined through examination of public documents such as real estate records and automobile liens.

Refining and Amending the Hypothesis

In testing the hypothesis, the fraud examiner might find that all facts do not fit a particular scenario. If such is the case, the hypothesis should be revised and retested. (Obviously, if the known facts are tested with negative results, it could be that a fraud is not present, or it could indicate that the fraud cannot be proved.) In the Linda Reed Collins example, a discreet inquiry might determine that Collins did not have an excessive lifestyle but rather significant personal indebtedness. The fraud theory could then be appropriately revised.

Following is a flow chart setting forth how the fraud examination process is used to resolve allegations.

INTRODUCTION

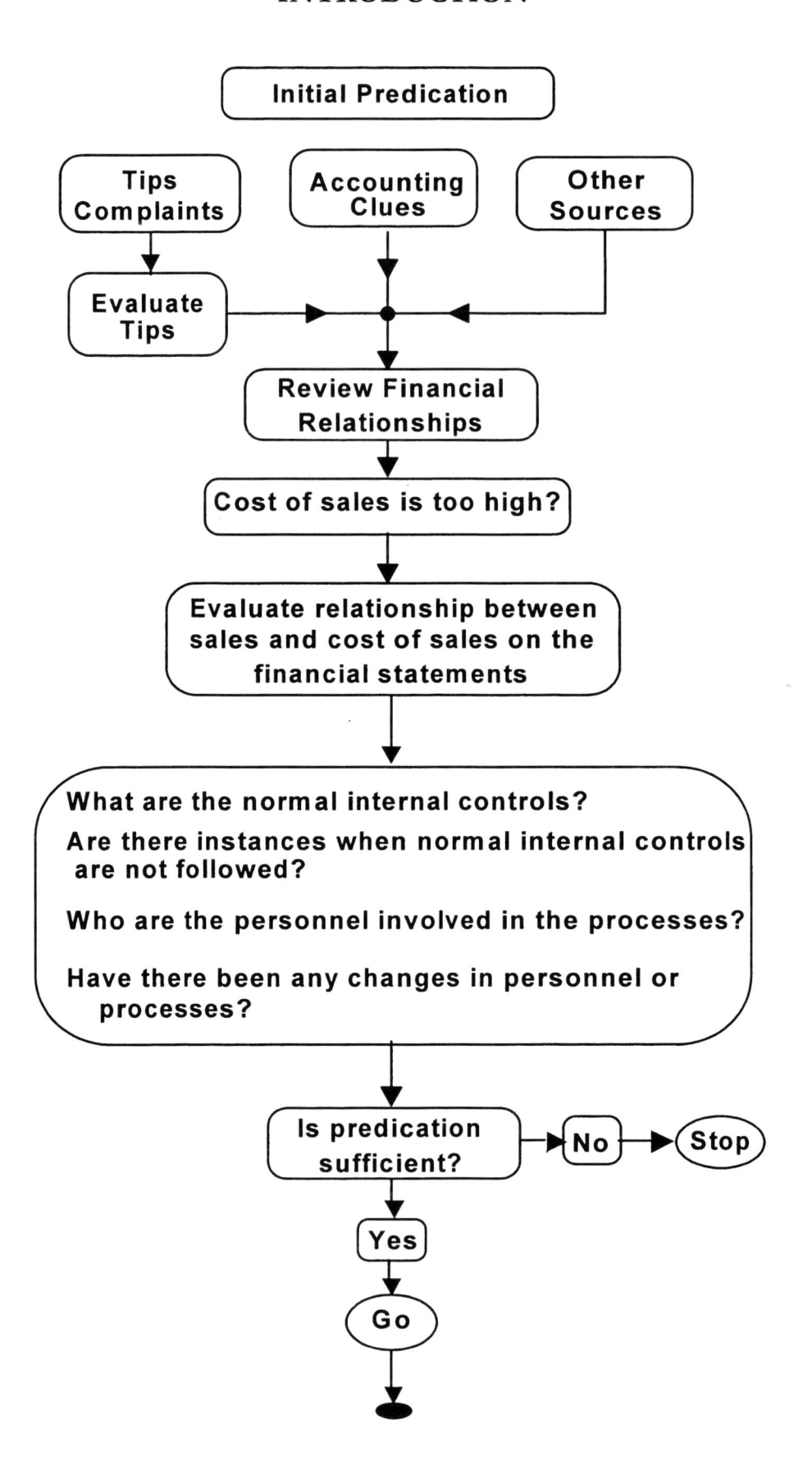

```
                    ┌──────────────────┐
                    │ Initial Predication │
                    └──────────────────┘

   ┌──────────┐      ┌──────────┐      ┌──────────┐
   │   Tips   │      │Accounting│      │  Other   │
   │Complaints│      │  Clues   │      │ Sources  │
   └──────────┘      └──────────┘      └──────────┘
         │                │                 │
         ▼                │                 │
   ┌──────────┐           │                 │
   │ Evaluate │──────────►●◄────────────────┘
   │   Tips   │           │
   └──────────┘           ▼
                 ┌──────────────────┐
                 │ Review Financial │
                 │  Relationships   │
                 └──────────────────┘
                          │
                          ▼
                 ┌──────────────────┐
                 │ Cost of sales is too high? │
                 └──────────────────┘
                          │
                          ▼
              ┌────────────────────────────┐
              │ Evaluate relationship between │
              │ sales and cost of sales on the │
              │    financial statements    │
              └────────────────────────────┘
                          │
                          ▼
```

- What are the normal internal controls?
- Are there instances when normal internal controls are not followed?
- Who are the personnel involved in the processes?
- Have there been any changes in personnel or processes?

```
                  ┌──────────────┐       ┌────┐      ┌──────┐
                  │ Is predication │────►│ No │────►│ Stop │
                  │  sufficient?   │      └────┘      └──────┘
                  └──────────────┘
                          │
                          ▼
                       ┌─────┐
                       │ Yes │
                       └─────┘
                          │
                          ▼
                       ┌─────┐
                       │ Go  │
                       └─────┘
                          │
                          ▼
                          ●
```

INTRODUCTION

Develop fraud theory:
- Who might be involved?
- What might have happened?
- Why might the allegation be true?
- Where are the possible concealment places or methods?
- When did this take place (past, present, or future)?
- How is the fraud being perpetrated?

Determine where the evidence is likely to be:
- On-book vs. Off-book
- Direct or circumstantial
- Identify potential witnesses

What evidence is necessary to prove intent?
- Number of occurrences
- Other areas of impropriety
- Witnesses

Revise fraud theory

Prepare chart linking people and evidence

Determine defenses to allegations

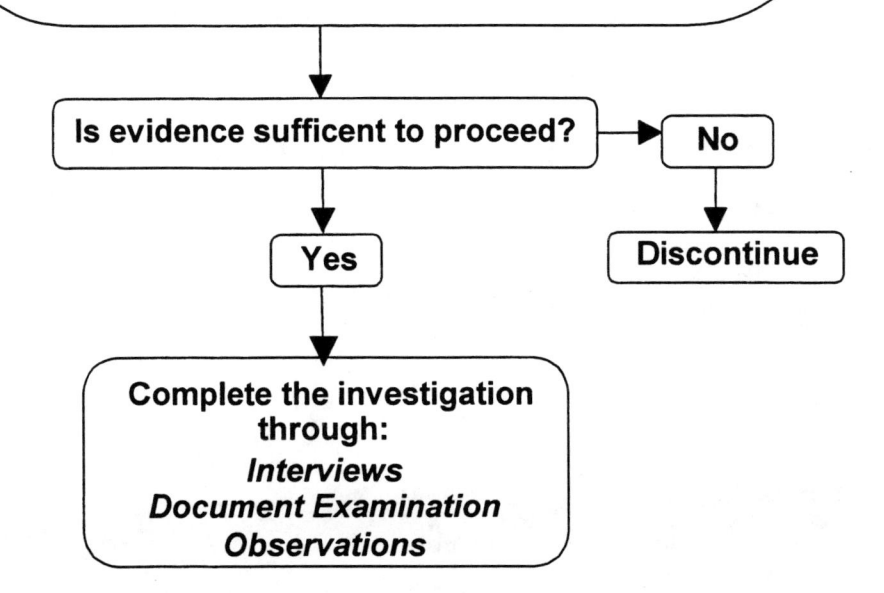

Is evidence sufficent to proceed? → **No** → **Discontinue**

↓ **Yes**

Complete the investigation through:
Interviews
Document Examination
Observations

2005 Fraud Examiners Manual

INTRODUCTION

The Fraud Examiner's Tool Kit

Essentially three tools are available to the fraud examiner regardless of the nature of the fraud examination. First is interviewing, which is the process of obtaining relevant information about the matter from those with knowledge of it. For example, in developing information about Linda Reed Collins, it might be necessary to interview her co-workers, superiors, and subordinates.

Second, the fraud examiner must be skilled in the examination of financial statements, books and records, and supporting documents. The examiner must know the legal ramifications of evidence and how to maintain the chain of custody over documents. For example, checks and other financial records to prove the case must be lawfully obtained, analyzed, and conclusions must be drawn, if it is determined that Linda Reed Collins was taking payoffs from a supplier.

Finally, fraud examiners are often placed in a position where they must observe behavior, search for displays of wealth, and in some instances, observe specific offenses. A Certified Fraud Examiner, for example, might recommend a video surveillance of a company's cashiers department to witness a defalcation being committed. Or, the fraud examiner might establish a visual surveillance in a public place to determine the patterns or activities of the subject.

Interviewing

If it appears that the fraud theory is still applicable after the fraud examiner analyzes the documents, the examiner proceeds to the next step: interviews of neutral third-party witnesses.

Neutral Third-Party Witnesses

A neutral third-party witness is a person not involved in a specific instance of fraud. For example, if the fraud examination of Linda Reed Collins progressed past the stage of analyzing documents, it would be common for the fraud examiner to interview the personnel officer at Bailey Books Incorporated regarding Collins' personnel file.

Corroborative Witnesses

Corroborative witnesses are those who can corroborate facts relating to a specific offense. These witnesses might be cooperative or uncooperative, but they are not directly related to

INTRODUCTION

the offense involved. Collins' co-workers or subordinates at Bailey Books Inc. could be corroborative witnesses. Interviews with witnesses to corroborate facts should be done after interviewing neutral third-party witnesses.

Co-Conspirators

If after examining documents, neutral third-party witnesses, and corroborative witnesses, it still appears that further work is warranted, the fraud examiner typically would interview co-conspirators to the alleged offense. In the case of Linda Reed Collins, if it were determined that a vendor was paying Collins kickbacks, that vendor typically would be interviewed prior to contacting Collins. People suspected of complicity generally are interviewed in the order of those thought to be least culpable to those thought to be most culpable. In criminal prosecutions, law enforcement officers and prosecutors can sometimes promise leniency to co-conspirators in return for their cooperation. These individuals are called "inside witnesses" and will be discussed in detail later. Such promises by private sector fraud examiners are not permitted, and might legally invalidate any admissions that are made.

Subject

In general, the subject (also called the suspect or accused) is interviewed last, after all facts necessary to resolve the allegation are obtained. Even if it is felt that the subject will not offer a confession, an interview is usually scheduled; in many instances it can be used later for impeachment. An interview might also give the examiner a good idea of what defenses the subject might raise.

Purpose of the Fraud Examination

The purpose of the fraud examination is to prove or disprove the legal elements of the offense. Each and every element must be proven (1) beyond a reasonable doubt in criminal cases, and (2) by a preponderance of the evidence in civil cases. To do this, it is necessary to understand certain objectives common to white-collar cases. Because investigations of fraud often involve an extensive array of information, the fraud examiner can lose sight of the objectives. According to Herbert Edelhertz:

> *One of the characteristics that most distinguishes the investigation of white-collar crime from that of common crimes is the necessity for the investigator to establish the intent and underlying motives of the subject by placing together jigsaw puzzle pieces of apparently legitimate activities*

INTRODUCTION

to add up to a picture of illegitimacy—rather than by a simple showing of one event which by itself flatly demonstrates wrongful intent.

Elements of White-Collar Offenses

While it is not possible or necessary to list every variation of white-collar crime and fraud, all have common elements, such as:
- Intent—knowingly to commit a wrongful act or to achieve a purpose inconsistent with law or public policy
- Disguise of purpose—falsities and misrepresentations employed to accomplish the scheme
- Reliance—by the offender on the ignorance or carelessness of the victim
- Voluntary victim action—to assist the offender
- Concealment—of the offense

Intent

Intent must be shown in fraud matters. Intent rarely is self-evident, but must rather be demonstrated by showing a pattern of activity. Some of the more common ways to show intent include proof that the accused:
- Had no legitimate motive for the activities
- Repeatedly engaged in the same or similar activity of an apparent wrongful nature
- Made conflicting statements
- Made admissions
- Acted to impede the investigation of the offense
- Made statements the offender clearly knew to be false

Disguise and Misrepresentation

Misrepresentation usually is shown by the facts that the representation was made and that it was false, either by omission or commission.

Voluntary Victim Action to Assist the Offender

Proof that the victim assisted the offender usually is not difficult to obtain from the victim. It is important for the fraud examiner to ascertain the exact circumstances regarding the fraud from the victim, clearly drawing out what made the fraud possible. In the case of employee thefts, for example, the victim (the company) entrusted the care of assets to the subject. That fiduciary capacity must be established.

INTRODUCTION

Concealment

Concealment is a cornerstone of fraud. As opposed to traditional crimes, where there is no effort to conceal, fraud perpetrators take steps to keep the victim ignorant. Acts in fraud schemes designed to conceal include committing offenses too small to be recognized as fraud by the victim. In embezzlement cases, for example, the amount of money taken at any one time usually is small relative to the total company assets. By demonstrating a continuing pattern of thefts, the concealment aspect can be shown.

To hide their actions, fraud perpetrators often create complex financial trails. The more obscure the act, the greater likelihood that it will not be detected. Some fraud cases involve fraudulent invoices and journal entries. Concealment in these types of cases often can be proven by the fact that the entries made had no purpose other than to conceal.

Proof Stages in Fraud Cases

Proof in most complex white-collar cases usually proceeds through three basic stages. First, the fraud examiner builds the circumstantial case through interviews of cooperative witnesses and review of available documentation. Then the examiner uses the circum-stantial evidence to identify and persuade an inside witness who can provide direct evidence against the defendant. Then the case is sealed, defenses are identified and rebutted, and intent is proved through examination of the subject.

Stage One: Building the Circumstantial Case

As used here, *circumstantial evidence* means all proof other than direct admission of wrongdoing by the subject or a co-conspirator. In a fraud case, it is the proof of the defendant's representations, evidence of their falsity and intent. In a corruption case, it is evidence of the standard behavior, the defendant's breach, and the illegal payments. The circumstantial case also might include "similar act evidence" to show a common scheme or plan, lack of mistake or accident, *modus operandi*, and most commonly, intent.

Circumstantial evidence might be all that is available. It must be complete with no gaps, consistent (tending to prove a single point), and must exclude all explanations other than guilt. Collecting this type of evidence can be very difficult. Many complex cases lose direction during the circumstantial stage when the examiner becomes overwhelmed by the mass of accumulated detail and documents. To avoid getting bogged down, consider the following:

INTRODUCTION

Keep an Eye on the Ball

Examiners must remember the importance of the fraud theory and keep in mind exactly what they are attempting to prove at all times. If examiners lose track of the objective, they should review and reorganize the evidence, develop an alternate theory, and refocus efforts. The examiner always is trying to prove or disprove something—even if merely a hunch—but never merely collecting information.

Simplify the Case

If the case starts to sink under its own weight, the fraud examiner might look for a less demanding legal theory, break the case down into smaller components (e.g., prove one set of charges against one set of defendants before pursuing the other), or look for an informant or inside witness. The objective in every complex case is to break it down to its essentials and make it as simple and clear as possible.

Stage Two: Obtaining Direct Evidence

In many cases cooperation from a co-conspirator or other insider is a necessity, either because the case is so complicated that it is otherwise unmanageable, or a key element—such as cash payments in a corruption case or the full extent of wrongdoing or intent in a fraud case—cannot be proved circumstantially. In some cases, the objective of the circumstantial stage is not so much to obtain evidence to convict the ultimate defendant, but rather to identify and turn an inside witness.

Ideally, the least culpable witness should be approached first. In a corruption case, this might be the "bag man," a subordinate. Or, if the only choice is the payer or taker, usually the payer is the better choice. A jury will react negatively if its members believe that the witness is more culpable than the defendant. A decision must also be made about how to convince the witness to assist. Ideally, to preserve the witness' credibility, the fewer concessions the better. Remember that immunity might be given only with the consent of the court.

Remember, too, that even the most self-incriminating testimony of a co-conspirator must be corroborated. Testimony from the insider should mesh with and augment the circumstantial evidence, not replace it. The credibility of a turned witness can become the central issue in the case and distract the jury from the strength of the circumstantial evidence. If nonessential testimony from a co-conspirator cannot be corroborated, don't use it.

INTRODUCTION

Be aware that cooperating, culpable witnesses in a white-collar case often minimize their role to avoid embarrassment, even if protected from legal consequences, and are prone to describe themselves more as observers than participants. This is very damaging to credibility, and must be overcome before such witnesses can be perceived as believable.

Stage Three: Sealing the Case through Examination of the Subject
Circumstantial evidence might be explained away, and direct testimony impeached or rebutted. The best witness against the suspect might be himself. The suspect's admissions might provide otherwise missing elements. "False exculpatories"—lies offered to explain or justify conduct—might be the best evidence of intent. False denials of cash deposits in a corruption case might indicate an illicit source; false explanations for fraudulent representations might help prove that the original misstatements were intentional.

To be effective, impeachment must show real, not apparent or explainable contradictions, and must focus on central, not tangential or trivial points. Attempted impeachment fails many times because the plaintiff has not laid a sufficient foundation to show that the defendant's statements were knowingly false.

To adequately prepare the fraud examiner to understand and respond to the complex nature of fraud, the remaining material is divided into four sections: Financial Transactions and Fraud Schemes, Law, Investigation, and Criminology and Ethics.

Section 1
Financial Transactions and Fraud Schemes

FINANCIAL TRANSACTIONS AND FRAUD SCHEMES

TABLE OF CONTENTS

OCCUPATIONAL FRAUDS

ACCOUNTING CONCEPTS

Accounting Basics	1.101
Accounts and the Accounting Cycle	1.102
Financial Statements	1.104
Users of Financial Statements	1.107
Generally Accepted Accounting Principles (GAAP)	1.107
GAAP Hierarchy	1.107
Basic Underlying Accounting Principles	1.108
Historical Cost	1.108
Revenue Recognition	1.108
Matching	1.108
Consistency	1.109
Full Disclosure	1.109
Objectivity	1.109
Separate Entity Assumption	1.109
Going Concern—Continuity Assumption	1.109
Unit of Measure	1.109
Periodicity—Time Period Assumption	1.110
Departures from GAAP—Modifying Conventions	1.110
Conservatism	1.110
Industry Practices and Peculiarities	1.110
Substance over Form	1.110
Application of Judgment	1.110
Materiality	1.111
Cost-Benefit	1.111

MANAGEMENT'S AND AUDITORS' RESPONSIBILITIES

Management	1.201
The Treadway Commission	1.201
Mandatory Independent Audit Committee	1.201
Written Charter	1.202
Resources and Authority	1.202
Informed, Vigilant, and Effective Audit Committees	1.202
The COSO Report	1.202
Certified Fraud Examiners	1.203
Help Resolve Allegations of Fraud	1.203
Obtain Evidence	1.203
Take Statements	1.204

FINANCIAL TRANSACTIONS AND FRAUD SCHEMES

MANAGEMENT'S AND AUDITORS' RESPONSIBILITIES (CONT.)

Write Reports	1.204
Testify to Findings	1.204
Assist in the Detection and Prevention of Fraud	1.204
External Auditors	1.205
Prior SAS Treatment of Fraud	1.205
SAS No. 99 — *Consideration of Fraud in a Financial Statement Audit*	1.205
Description and Characteristics of Fraud	1.206
Importance of Exercising Professional Skepticism	1.207
Discussion among Engagement Personnel Regarding Risk of Material Misstatement Due to Fraud	1.207
Obtaining Information Needed to Identify Risks of Material Misstatements Due to Fraud	1.208
Identifying Risks That May Result in Material Misstatements Due to Fraud	1.209
Assessing the Identified Risks after Taking into Account an Evaluation of the Entity's Programs and Controls	1.209
Responding to the Results of the Assessment	1.210
Evaluating Audit Evidence	1.213
Communicating About Possible Fraud to Management, the Audit Committee, and Others	1.215
Documenting the Auditor's Consideration of Fraud	1.216
SAS No. 96 — *Audit Documentation*	1.216
PCAOB Auditing Standard No. 2 —	1.218
Performing an ICOFR Audit	1.219
Fraud Considerations	1.220
Forming an Opinion on the Effectiveness of ICOFR	1.221
Internal Auditor Responsibilities	1.222
1210 – Proficiency	1.223
1210.A2	1.223
1220 – Due Professional Care	1.228
1220.A1	1.228
1220.A3	1.228
2130 – Governance	1.228
2130.A1	1.229
GAO Auditing Standards	1.231
Applicability	1.231
Roles and Responsibilities	1.232
Management	1.232
Auditors	1.232
Types of Government Audit Engagements	1.233
Financial Statement Audits and Financial-Related Audits	1.233
Performance Audits	1.234
Audit Standards	1.234

FINANCIAL TRANSACTIONS AND FRAUD SCHEMES

MANAGEMENT'S AND AUDITORS' RESPONSIBILITIES (CONT.)
General Standards	1.234
Field Work Standards for Financial Audits	1.236
Reporting Standards for Financial Audits	1.237
Field Work Standards for Performance Audits	1.238
Reporting Standards for Performance Audits	1.239
Sarbanes-Oxley Act of 2002	1.240
Public Company Accounting Oversight Board	1.240
Officers and Directors	1.241
Certification Obligations	1.241
Internal Controls	1.242
Code of Ethics	1.244
Audit Committee	1.246
Composition of the Audit Committee	1.246
Responsibilities Relating to External Auditors	1.248
Procedures for Handling Complaints	1.249
Authority to Engage Outside Advisors	1.249
Funding	1.250
External Auditors	1.250
Reports to the Audit Committee	1.250
Report over Internal Controls	1.250
Whistleblower Protection	1.250
Civil Liability	1.250
Criminal Sanctions	1.251
Civil and Criminal Penalties for Noncompliance	1.251
Private Securities Litigation Reform Act	1.251

FINANCIAL STATEMENT FRAUD
What is Financial Statement Fraud?	1.303
The Cost of Financial Statement Fraud	1.303
Why Financial Statement Fraud is Committed	1.304
The COSO Study on Financial Statement Fraud	1.305
Effect of Fraud on Financial Statements	1.307
Fictitious Revenues	1.308
Sales with Conditions	1.310
What Red Flags are Associated with Fictitious Revenues?	1.310
Timing Differences (Including Premature Revenue Recognition)	1.310
Premature Revenue Recognition	1.310
Long-Term Contracts	1.312
Channel Stuffing	1.313
Recording Expenses in the Wrong Period	1.314

FINANCIAL TRANSACTIONS AND FRAUD SCHEMES

FINANCIAL STATEMENT FRAUD (CONT.)

What Red Flags are Associated with Timing Differences
    (Including Premature Revenue Recognition)? 1.314
  Improper Asset Valuation 1.314
    Inventory Valuation 1.315
    Accounts Receivable 1.316
    Business Combinations 1.316
    Fixed Assets 1.317
    Understating Assets 1.318
    Capitalizing Nonasset Cost 1.318
    Misclassifying Assets 1.318
    What Red Flags are Associated with Improper Asset Valuation? 1.318
  Concealed Liabilities and Expenses 1.319
    Liability/Expense Omissions 1.319
    Capitalized Expenses 1.321
    Returns and Allowances and Warranties 1.322
    What Red Flags are Associated with Concealed Liabilities and Expenses? 1.322
  Improper Disclosures 1.322
    Liability Omissions 1.323
    Subsequent Events 1.323
    Management Fraud 1.323
    Related-Party Transactions 1.324
    Accounting Changes 1.324
    What Red Flags are Associated with Improper Disclosures? 1.325
What Red Flags are Associated with Financial Statement Fraud Generally? 1.326
Detection of Fraudulent Financial Statement Schemes 1.326
Financial Statement Analysis 1.329
  Percentage Analysis—Horizontal and Vertical 1.329
    Vertical Analysis Discussion 1.331
    Horizontal Analysis Discussion 1.331
    Financial Ratios in Detail 1.331
  Tax Return Review 1.335
  Fraudulent Financial Statement Red Flags 1.336
Interviews in Fraudulent Financial Statement Cases 1.337
  Interviewing Techniques 1.338
    The Interview 1.340
Prevention of Financial Statement Fraud 1.347
  Auditors 1.347
  Management 1.347
    Reduce the Situational Pressures that Encourage Statement Fraud 1.347
    Reduce the Opportunity to Commit 1.348
    Reduce Rationalization of Fraud—Strengthen Employee Personal Integrity 1.348

FINANCIAL TRANSACTIONS AND FRAUD SCHEMES

ASSET MISAPPROPRIATION: CASH THEFT

Skimming	1.401
Sales Skimming	1.402
Register Manipulation	1.404
Skimming During Nonbusiness Hours	1.405
Skimming of Off-Site Sales	1.405
Poor Collection Procedures	1.406
Understated Sales	1.407
Theft of Checks Received through the Mail	1.409
Check for Currency Substitutions	1.411
Skimming Receivables	1.412
Forcing Account Balances or Destroying Transaction Records	1.412
Lapping	1.413
Stolen Statements	1.414
False Account Entries	1.415
Inventory Padding	1.416
Detection of Skimming Schemes	1.417
Receipt or Sales Level Detection	1.417
Journal Entry Review	1.417
Detecting Lapping of Sales or Receivables	1.417
Prevention of Skimming Schemes	1.418
Receipt or Sales Level Control	1.418
General Controls	1.418
Skimming Controls	1.418
Cash Larceny	1.419
Incoming Cash	1.420
Theft of Cash from the Register	1.420
Other Larceny of Sales and Receivables	1.423
Cash Larceny from the Deposit	1.424
Deposit Lapping	1.428
Deposits in Transit	1.428
Detection of Cash Larceny	1.428
Receipt Recording	1.428
Control Objectives	1.429
Analytical Review	1.429
Register Detection	1.430
Cash Account Analysis	1.430
Prevention of Cash Larceny	1.431
Segregation of Duties	1.431
Assignment Rotation and Mandatory Vacations	1.431
Surprise Cash Counts and Procedure Supervision	1.431
Physical Security of Cash	1.431

FINANCIAL TRANSACTIONS AND FRAUD SCHEMES

ASSET MISAPPROPRIATION: FRAUDULENT DISBURSEMENTS

Register Disbursement Schemes	1.501
False Refunds	1.501
Fictitious Refunds	1.503
Overstated Refunds	1.503
Credit Card Refunds	1.503
False Voids	1.504
Concealing Register Disbursements	1.506
Small Disbursements	1.507
Destroying Records	1.507
Detection of Register Schemes	1.507
Fictitious Refunds or Voided Sales	1.507
Review and Analysis of Decreases in Gross Sales and/or Increases in Returns and Allowances	1.508
Register Scheme Red Flags	1.508
Prevention	1.509
Check Tampering	1.509
Forged Maker Schemes	1.510
Obtaining the Check	1.510
To Whom is the Check Made Payable?	1.511
Forging the Signature	1.513
Converting the Check	1.514
Forged Endorsement Schemes	1.515
Intercepting Checks Before Delivery	1.515
Theft of Returned Checks	1.517
Re-Routing the Delivery of Checks	1.518
Converting the Stolen Check	1.518
Altered Payee Schemes	1.519
Altering Checks Prepared by Others: Inserting a New Payee	1.519
Altering Checks Prepared by Others: "Tacking On"	1.521
Altering Checks Prepared by the Fraudster: Erasable Ink	1.521
Altering Checks Prepared by the Fraudster: Blank Checks	1.522
Converting Altered Checks	1.522
Authorized Maker Schemes	1.522
Overriding Controls through Intimidation	1.522
Poor Controls	1.523
Concealment	1.525
The Fraudster Reconciling the Bank Statement	1.526
Re-Alteration of Checks	1.527
Miscoding Fraudulent Checks	1.527
Re-Issuing Intercepted Checks	1.528
Bogus Supporting Documents	1.529
Detection	1.529

FINANCIAL TRANSACTIONS AND FRAUD SCHEMES

ASSET MISAPPROPRIATION: FRAUDULENT DISBURSEMENTS (CONT.)

Account Analysis through Cut-Off Statements	1.529
Bank Reconciliations	1.529
Bank Confirmation	1.530
Check-Tampering Red Flags	1.530
Prevention	1.531
Check Disbursement Controls	1.531
Bank-Assisted Controls	1.532
Physical Tampering Prevention	1.532
Check Theft Control Procedures	1.533
Billing Schemes	1.533
Invoicing Via Shell Companies	1.534
Forming a Shell Company	1.534
Submitting False Invoices	1.536
Self-Approval of Fraudulent Invoices	1.536
"Rubber Stamp" Supervisors	1.537
Reliance on False Documents	1.537
Collusion	1.538
Purchases of Services Rather than Goods	1.538
Pass-Through Schemes	1.539
Invoicing Via Nonaccomplice Vendors	1.539
Pay-and-Return Schemes	1.539
Overbilling with a Nonaccomplice Vendor's Invoices	1.540
Personal Purchases with Company Funds	1.541
Personal Purchases through False Invoicing	1.541
Personal Purchases on Credit Cards or Other Company Accounts	1.544
Detection	1.545
Analytical Review	1.547
Computer-Assisted Analytical Review	1.547
Statistical Sampling	1.548
Vendor or Outsider Complaints	1.548
Site Visits—Observation	1.548
Sample Audit Program	1.548
Prevention	1.550
Education (Training)	1.550
Compensation	1.550
Proper Documentation	1.551
Proper Approvals	1.551
Segregation of Duties	1.551
Hotlines	1.551
Competitive Bidding	1.551
Prevention Checklist	1.551
Payroll Fraud	1.552

FINANCIAL TRANSACTIONS AND FRAUD SCHEMES

ASSET MISAPPROPRIATION: FRAUDULENT DISBURSEMENTS (CONT.)

Ghost Employees	1.552
Adding the Ghost to the Payroll	1.553
Collecting Timekeeping Information	1.554
Issuing the Ghost's Paycheck	1.556
Delivery of the Paycheck	1.557
Falsified Hours and Salary	1.558
Manually Prepared Timecards	1.558
Timeclocks and Other Automated Timekeeping Systems	1.561
Rates of Pay	1.562
Commission Schemes	1.562
Fictitious Sales	1.562
Altered Sales	1.564
Altering Commission Rates	1.564
Detection of Payroll Schemes	1.564
Independent Payroll Distribution	1.564
Analysis of Payee Address or Accounts	1.565
Duplicate Identification Numbers	1.565
Overtime Authorization	1.565
Commissions	1.565
Analysis of Deductions from Payroll Checks	1.566
Prevention of Payroll Schemes	1.566
Segregation of Duties	1.566
Periodic Review and Analysis of Payroll	1.567
Indicators of Payroll Fraud	1.567
Expense Reimbursement Schemes	1.569
Mischaracterized Expense Reimbursements	1.569
Overstated Expense Reimbursements	1.571
Altered Receipts	1.571
Overpurchasing	1.573
Overstating Another Employee's Expenses	1.573
Orders to Overstate Expenses	1.574
Fictitious Expense Reimbursements	1.574
Producing Fictitious Receipts	1.574
Obtaining Blank Receipts from Vendors	1.576
Claiming the Expenses of Others	1.576
Multiple Reimbursements	1.576
Detection of Expense Reimbursement Schemes	1.577
Review and Analysis of Expense Accounts	1.577
Detailed Review of Expense Reports	1.577
Prevention of Expense Reimbursement Schemes	1.578
Detailed Expense Reports: Submission and Review	1.578

FINANCIAL TRANSACTIONS AND FRAUD SCHEMES

ASSET MISAPPROPRIATION: FRAUDULENT DISBURSEMENTS (CONT.)

Misuse of Inventory and Other Assets	1.601
The Costs of Inventory Misuse	1.601
Theft of Inventory and Other Assets	1.602
Larceny Schemes	1.602
The False Sale	1.605
Asset Requisitions and Transfers	1.605
Purchasing and Receiving Schemes	1.606
Falsifying Incoming Shipments	1.607
False Shipments of Inventory and Other Assets	1.608
Concealing Inventory Shrinkage	1.610
Altered Inventory Records	1.611
Fictitious Sales and Accounts Receivable	1.611
Write Off of Inventory and Other Assets	1.612
Physical Padding	1.612
Detection	1.612
Statistical Sampling	1.612
Perpetual Inventory Records	1.613
Shipping Documents	1.613
Physical Inventory Counts	1.613
Analytical Review	1.613
Computer-Generated Trend Analysis	1.614
Detailed Audit Program	1.615
Prevention	1.616
Proper Documentation	1.616
Segregation of Duties	1.617
Independent Checks	1.617
Physical Safeguards	1.617

BRIBERY AND CORRUPTION

Bribery	1.701
Kickback Schemes	1.702
Diverting Business to Vendors	1.702
Overbilling Schemes	1.704
Bid-Rigging Schemes	1.706
The Presolicitation Phase	1.707
The Solicitation Phase	1.711
The Submission Phase	1.712
Economic Extortion	1.713
Illegal Gratuities	1.713
Methods of Making Illegal Payments	1.714
Gifts, Travel, and Entertainment	1.714

FINANCIAL TRANSACTIONS AND FRAUD SCHEMES

BRIBERY AND CORRUPTION (CONT.)

Cash Payments	1.714
Checks and Other Financial Instruments	1.714
Hidden Interests	1.715
Loans	1.715
Payment of Credit Card Bills	1.715
Transfers at Other than Fair Market Value	1.715
Promises of Favorable Treatment	1.715
Detection	1.716
Red Flags of Bribery Schemes	1.716
The Corrupt Recipient	1.716
The Corrupt Payer	1.716
General Purchasing	1.717
Presolicitation	1.717
Bid Solicitation	1.718
Bid Submission or Contract Acceptance	1.719
Methods of Proving Corrupt Payments	1.719
The Business Profile—Analysis	1.720
Sources of Information for the Business Profile	1.722
Proving On-Book Payments	1.722
Fictitious Disbursement Schemes	1.722
Ghost Employee Schemes	1.726
Overbilling Schemes	1.726
Proving Off-Book Payments	1.727
Indirect Evidence of Unrecorded Sales on the Suspect Company's Books and Records	1.727
Unbalanced Ratios of Costs to Sales	1.727
Investigation in the Marketplace	1.728
Proving Payments in Cash	1.728
Conflicts of Interest	1.730
Purchase Schemes	1.732
Unique Assets	1.734
Turnaround Sales	1.735
Sales Schemes	1.735
Underbillings	1.735
Writing Off Sales	1.736
Other Schemes	1.736
Business Diversions	1.736
Resource Diversions	1.736
Financial Interest in Companies Under Perpetrator's Supervision	1.737
Financial Disclosure	1.737
Appearance of Conflict of Interest	1.737
Detection	1.738

FINANCIAL TRANSACTIONS AND FRAUD SCHEMES

BRIBERY AND CORRUPTION (CONT.)

Tips and Complaints	1.738
Comparison of Vendor Addresses with Employee Addresses	1.738
Review of Vendor Ownership Files	1.738
Review of Exit Interviews and Comparisons of Vendor Addresses to Addresses of Subsequent Employers	1.738
Interviews of Purchasing Personnel for Favorable Treatment of One or More Vendors	1.738
Prevention	1.739

THEFT OF INTELLECTUAL PROPERTY

Competitive Intelligence (CI) Versus Espionage	1.802
Open Sources of Information	1.803
Why do Companies Resort to Corporate Espionage?	1.804
The Bootstrap Effect	1.805
The Intelligence Pyramid	1.806
Fundamental Research Techniques	1.807
Basic Sources	1.807
Government Sources	1.808
Industry Analyst Reports	1.809
Electronic Sources	1.810
Creative Sources	1.810
Classified Ads	1.811
Environmental Impact Statements	1.811
UCC Filings	1.811
Proxies	1.812
Posing as a Customer	1.812
Building Financial Statements	1.812
How Income Statements are Calculated	1.813
Revenue Estimates	1.813
Costs of Goods Sold	1.814
Overhead	1.814
How Balance Sheets are Calculated	1.815
Nontraditional Sources	1.815
InfoTrac	1.816
A Closer Look at Databases	1.817
First Tier Databases	1.817
Second Tier Databases	1.817
Third Tier Databases	1.818
Newsgroups	1.818
Dun & Bradstreet and Lexis/Nexis	1.818
i2	1.818

FINANCIAL TRANSACTIONS AND FRAUD SCHEMES

THEFT OF INTELLECTUAL PROPERTY (CONT.)

Competitive Intelligence Websites	1.818
A Corporate Spy Uses Open Sources: What of It?	1.819
Favorite Targets	1.820
Research and Development	1.820
Marketing	1.820
Manufacturing and Production	1.821
Human Resources	1.821
How Information is Lost	1.821
Accident	1.821
Poor Information Security Procedures	1.822
On-site Materials that are Targeted	1.822
Guarding Manual Systems	1.824
Guarding Information Stored in Electronic Format	1.825
Basic Principles of Spying	1.827
Recruited Spies	1.827
False Flag Recruitment	1.827
Recruiting by Justification	1.827
Trapping Recruits	1.828
Counter-Recruitment Training	1.828
After Recruitment	1.829
Targeted Information	1.829
Methods for Safely Collecting Data	1.829
Communications between the Employee and the Control	1.830
Security Measures for the Recruit	1.831
Planting Bugs	1.831
Deception Techniques	1.831
Employment Advertisements	1.831
Headhunter Scams	1.832
Market Research Scams	1.832
Phony Contract Bids	1.832
Infiltration Techniques	1.833
Posing as an Employee or Contract Laborer	1.833
Stealing Badges	1.834
Moles and Sleepers	1.834
Places Where Spies Snoop	1.835
Mailroom	1.835
Loading Docks	1.836
Storage Areas	1.836
Hotels	1.837
Warning Signs of Infiltrations	1.838
Countermeasures	1.839
Transactional Intelligence	1.840

FINANCIAL TRANSACTIONS AND FRAUD SCHEMES

THEFT OF INTELLECTUAL PROPERTY (CONT.)

Informants	1.840
Decoy Websites	1.842
Telling Good Lies	1.842
Visual Surveillance Against People	1.844
Pre-Recruitment Surveillance	1.844
Briefing Files on the Subject	1.844
Moving Surveillance	1.845
Fixed Surveillance	1.845
E-Mail	1.845
Social Engineering	1.846
The Neophyte	1.846
The Power Broker	1.847
The Systems Administrator	1.847
Fraudulent Surveys	1.847
Fake Prizes	1.847
Reverse Social Engineering	1.848
Countering Social Engineering	1.848
Cloaking and Misdirection	1.849
Intelligence Needs	1.849
Print Media	1.850
Database Searches	1.850
Networking	1.851
Existing Staffing	1.851
Security Surveys	1.851
Cloaking Operations	1.853
Trash and Waste Disposal	1.854
Deliveries and Shipments	1.854
Hours of Operation and Power Consumption	1.854
Emissions	1.854
Food Deliveries	1.854
Computer Emanations	1.855
Travel Plans	1.855
Misdirection	1.855
Spotting False Suitors	1.856
Vendors and Suppliers	1.857
Technical Articles and Publications	1.857
Consultants	1.858
Dealing with Employees who are Leaving	1.858
Hackers	1.859
Technical Surveillance	1.859
Aerial Photography	1.861
Bugging and Wiretapping	1.862

FINANCIAL TRANSACTIONS AND FRAUD SCHEMES

THEFT OF INTELLECTUAL PROPERTY (CONT.)

The Insertion Point	1.862
The Technology	1.862
Warning Signs of Bugging	1.865
Preliminary Search Procedures	1.867
Video Surveillance	1.870
Photographic Cameras	1.870
Minicameras	1.870
Digital Cameras	1.871
Infrared Film	1.871
35mm Cameras	1.871
Cellular Telephones	1.872
Monitoring Computer Emanations	1.872
Tape Recorders	1.873
Computer System Penetrations	1.873
Investigating an Information Theft Case	1.873
Program for Safeguarding Proprietary Information (SPI)	1.875
Task Force	1.875
Employee Awareness	1.876
Nondisclosure Agreements	1.876
Document Classification	1.877
Visitors	1.877
Offices	1.877
Maintenance Workers	1.877
Meeting Rooms	1.877
Quiet Rooms	1.878
Communications Equipment	1.878
Electronic Mail and Voice Mail	1.878
Computer Systems	1.878
Faxing Documents	1.880
Video Encryption	1.880
Corporate Telephone Exchanges	1.880
Trade Shows and Public Events	1.881
Foreign Travel	1.881
Technical Surveillance Countermeasures (TSCM) Survey	1.881
Preventing Employee Theft of Proprietary Information	1.883
Employee Awareness	1.883
Nondisclosure and Noncompetition Agreements	1.884
Make Sure Employees Know When Not to Speak	1.885
Exit Interviews	1.885
Protecting the Trade Secrets of Others	1.885
Legal Issues Related to Theft of Intellectual Property	1.887
Bibliography	1.887

FINANCIAL TRANSACTIONS AND FRAUD SCHEMES

OTHER FRAUDS

FINANCIAL INSTITUTION FRAUD

Embezzlement Schemes	1.901
Types of Embezzlement Schemes	1.901
False Accounting Entries	1.902
Unauthorized Withdrawals	1.902
Unauthorized Disbursement of Funds to Outsiders	1.902
Paying Personal Expenses from Bank Funds	1.902
Theft of Physical Property	1.902
Moving Money from Customers' Dormant or Inactive Accounts	1.902
Unauthorized, Unrecorded Cash Payments	1.903
Theft and Other Unauthorized Use of Collateral	1.903
Detection Methods	1.903
Loan Fraud	1.903
Financial Institution Failures as a Result of Real Estate Loan Fraud	1.903
Common Loan Fraud Schemes	1.903
Loans to Nonexistent Borrowers	1.903
Sham Loans with Kickbacks and Diversion	1.904
Double-Pledging Collateral	1.904
Reciprocal Loan Arrangements	1.904
Swapping Bad Loans—Daisy Chains	1.904
Linked Financing	1.904
False Applications with False Credit Information	1.904
Single-Family Housing Loan Fraud	1.904
Construction Loans	1.905
Red Flags of Loan Fraud	1.908
Nonperforming Loans	1.908
High Turnover in Developer's Personnel	1.909
High Turnover in Tenant Mix	1.909
Increased Change Orders	1.909
Missing Documentation	1.909
Loan Increases or Extensions, Replacement Loans	1.911
Cash Flow Deficiencies	1.912
Change in Ownership Makeup	1.912
Disguised Transactions	1.912
Real Estate Fraud	1.913
Appraisal Fraud	1.913
The Role of the Appraiser	1.913
Fundamentals of Real Estate Appraisals	1.913
Determining "Value"	1.914
Valuation Methods	1.915

FINANCIAL TRANSACTIONS AND FRAUD SCHEMES

FINANCIAL INSTITUTION FRAUD (CONT.)

Fraudulent Appraisals	1.916
Uses for Fraudulent Appraisals	1.916
Red Flags of "Made-as-Instructed" Appraisals	1.917
Detecting Fraudulent Appraisals	1.917
Mortgage-Backed Securities	1.918
Equity Skimming	1.918
Land Flips	1.918
Nominee or Strawman Loans	1.919
Mortgage-Pulling	1.919
New Account Fraud Schemes	1.919
False Identification	1.919
Business Accounts Using Stolen Checks	1.919
Personal Accounts Using Fraudulent Checks	1.920
Prevention	1.920
Personal Accounts	1.920
Business Accounts	1.921
Detection	1.922
Money Transfer (Wire) Fraud Schemes	1.922
Instantaneous Transfer	1.922
Common Schemes	1.923
Dishonest Bank Employees	1.923
Misrepresentation of Identity	1.923
System Password Security Compromised	1.923
Forged Authorizations	1.923
Unauthorized Entry and Interception	1.923
Preventing and Detecting Wire Transfer Fraud	1.923
Business Audits	1.924
Bank Audits	1.924
Automated Teller Machine (ATM) Fraud	1.926
Detection	1.926
Advanced Fee Fraud	1.926
Red Flags	1.927
Brokered Loans	1.927
Letter-of-Credit Fraud	1.927
Inside/Outside Frauds	1.928
Account Information Frauds	1.928
Trading Activities	1.928
Prevention	1.928
Loan Origination, Underwriting, Closing, Disbursement, and Servicing Segregation	1.928
Committee Approval of all Large or Unusual Transactions	1.929
Transfer Journal Entries and Orders Review	1.929

FINANCIAL TRANSACTIONS AND FRAUD SCHEMES

FINANCIAL INSTITUTION FRAUD (CONT.)

Independent Review of Loans	1.929
Management Review of Write-Offs	1.929
Routine Examination of Officers' Accounts	1.929
Proper Lending Policies	1.929
Document Requirements for Standard Transactions	1.930
Information Verification (for example, Loan Applications)	1.930
Employee Training	1.930
Standardized Procedures	1.930
Suspicious Activity Reports	1.931
Applicable Federal Statutes	1.931
Bank Fraud	1.932
Financial Institutions Reform, Recovery and Enforcement Act (FIRREA)	1.932
Crime Control Act of 1990	1.932
Financial Institution Anti-Fraud Enforcement Act of 1990	1.932
Continuing Financial Crime Enterprise Statute	1.933
Embezzlement, Misapplication, and False Entries	1.933
Participation in the Affairs of a Financial Institution by a Convicted Felon	1.933
Offer of Loan or Gratuity to a Bank Examiner	1.933
Receipt of Commissions or Gifts for Procuring Loans	1.934
Other Federal Statutes	1.934

CHECK AND CREDIT CARD FRAUD

Check Fraud	1.1001
Counterfeiting Checks	1.1002
Signs of Counterfeit and Forged Checks	1.1002
Check Fraud Vulnerabilities	1.1003
Check Theft	1.1003
Check Fraud Schemes	1.1004
"Paperhangers"	1.1004
Stop Payment Orders	1.1004
Check Kiting	1.1004
Demand Drafts	1.1005
Third-Party Bill Paying Services	1.1005
Travelers' Checks	1.1005
Payroll Check Fraud	1.1006
Dumpster Diving	1.1006
Scanning	1.1006
System Password Security Compromised	1.1007
Check Fraud Rings	1.1007
Check Fraud Detection	1.1008
FBI Profile of Check Fraud Activity	1.1008

FINANCIAL TRANSACTIONS AND FRAUD SCHEMES

CHECK AND CREDIT CARD FRAUD (CONT.)

Detection Techniques	1.1008
Check Fraud Prevention and Investigation	1.1009
Check Fraud Investigations	1.1010
Check Fraud Prevention Tools	1.1012
Fingerprint Identifiers	1.1012
Forensic Document Examination	1.1012
Signature	1.1012
Handwriting	1.1013
Video Spectral Comparator	1.1013
Electrostatic Detection Apparatus	1.1013
Credit Card Fraud	1.1013
Online Credit Card Fraud	1.1014
Credit Card Schemes	1.1014
Unauthorized Use of a Lost or Stolen Card	1.1014
Organized Crime Rings	1.1015
Advance Payments	1.1015
Shave and Paste	1.1015
De-Emboss/Re-Emboss	1.1015
Counterfeit Cards	1.1016
Telephone/Mail Order Fraud	1.1016
False Applications	1.1017
Credit "Doctors"	1.1017
True Name Fraud	1.1017
Non-Receipt Fraud	1.1017
Key-Enter Counterfeiting	1.1017
Creditmaster	1.1018
Probing	1.1018
Skimming	1.1018
Merchant Scams	1.1019
Magnetic Stripe Diagram	1.1019
Prevention and Detection of Credit Card Fraud	1.1020
Prevention	1.1022
Education Programs	1.1022
Liaison with Law Enforcement	1.1022
Physical Security Features	1.1022
Activation of Cards	1.1025
Computer Edits	1.1025
Card Scrutiny at Point of Sale	1.1026
Internet/Telephone Orders	1.1026
Financial Institution Measures	1.1026
Smart Cards	1.1027

FINANCIAL TRANSACTIONS AND FRAUD SCHEMES

INSURANCE FRAUD

Types of Insurance Policies	1.1101
Agent/Broker Fraud	1.1102
Cash, Loan, and Dividend Checks	1.1102
Settlement Checks	1.1102
Premium Fraud	1.1102
Fictitious Payees	1.1103
Fictitious Death Claims	1.1103
Underwriting Irregularities	1.1103
Equity Funding	1.1103
Misrepresentation	1.1104
False Information	1.1104
Fictitious Policies	1.1104
Surety and Performance Bond Schemes	1.1104
Sliding	1.1105
Twisting	1.1105
Churning	1.1105
Vehicle Insurance Schemes	1.1105
Ditching	1.1105
Past Posting	1.1105
Vehicle Repair	1.1106
Vehicle Smuggling	1.1106
Phantom Vehicles	1.1106
Staged Accidents	1.1106
Two Vehicle Accident	1.1106
Three or More Vehicle Accident	1.1106
Other Staged Accidents	1.1106
Inflated Damages	1.1107
Vehicle Identification Number (VIN)-Switch	1.1107
Rental Car Fraud	1.1107
Property Schemes	1.1107
Inflated Inventory	1.1107
Phony or Inflated Thefts	1.1107
Paper Boats	1.1108
Life Insurance Schemes	1.1108
Fraudulent Death Claims	1.1108
Murder for Profit	1.1108
Liability Schemes	1.1108
"Red Flags" of Insurance Fraud	1.1108
Computer-Generated Detection Reports	1.1112
Address Similarity Report	1.1112
Downloading of Files	1.1112
Electronic Confirmations	1.1113

FINANCIAL TRANSACTIONS AND FRAUD SCHEMES

INSURANCE FRAUD (CONT.)
    Exception or Manual Override Reports 1.1113
Workers Compensation Fraud 1.1113
    Common Schemes 1.1113
        Premium Fraud 1.1113
        Agent Fraud 1.1115
        Claimant Fraud 1.1116
        Organized Fraud 1.1117
    Red Flags 1.1118
    Investigation Tips 1.1120
        Premium Fraud 1.1120
        Claimant Fraud 1.1121

HEALTH CARE FRAUD
Laws Relating to Health Care Fraud 1.1201
    HIPAA 1.1201
    Other Federal Statutes 1.1202
        False Claims and Statements 1.1202
        Computer Fraud 1.1203
        Money Laundering 1.1203
    Civil Remedies 1.1203
    State Statutes 1.1204
        Regulatory Boards 1.1204
        "Running" and "Capping" Legislation 1.1205
Fraud by the Insurance Company 1.1205
    Submission of False Documents 1.1205
    Mishandling Claims 1.1205
    Failure to Pay Legitimate Claims 1.1206
    Charging Unapproved Rates 1.1206
    Requesting Rate Increases Based on Fraudulent Data 1.1206
    Deceptive or Illegal Sales Practices 1.1206
    Failure to Give "Fee Breaks" 1.1206
    Patient Screening 1.1207
    Detection 1.1207
Employee Claims Fraud 1.1207
    Claims Fraud Using the Employee's Contract 1.1207
    Claims Fraud Using Another Insured's Contract Number 1.1208
    Claims Payment Using a Relative's Contract 1.1208
        Claims Adjustment System 1.1208
    Payment for Canceled Contracts or Deceased Insureds 1.1208
    Improper Payee 1.1208
    Detection 1.1208

FINANCIAL TRANSACTIONS AND FRAUD SCHEMES

HEALTH CARE FRAUD (CONT.)

Agent Fraud	1.1209
Phony Groups	1.1209
Phony or Nonexistent Policies	1.1209
Medical Underwriting Fraud	1.1209
Eligibility Fraud	1.1209
ERISA Fraud	1.1209
Payment Inducements	1.1210
Switching Policies	1.1210
Provider Fraud	1.1210
Rolling Labs	1.1210
Clinical Labs	1.1211
Suppliers	1.1211
Ambulance Transportation	1.1211
Infusion Care	1.1211
Durable Medical Equipment Suppliers	1.1211
Home Health Companies	1.1212
Pharmacy	1.1212
Chiropractors	1.1212
Chiro-Shenanigans	1.1213
Patients for Life	1.1213
Patient Recruiting	1.1213
Treatment for Nonspinal Conditions	1.1214
Other	1.1214
Red Flags	1.1214
Podiatrists	1.1214
Ophthalmologists	1.1215
Psychiatrists and Psychiatric Clinics	1.1215
Anesthesiologists	1.1215
Dental Fraud	1.1215
Allergists	1.1215
Infertility Treatment	1.1215
Impostor Provider	1.1215
Investigation Tips	1.1215
False Diagnoses	1.1216
Red Flags of Provider Fraud	1.1216
Fraud by the Medical Staff	1.1217
Kickbacks in the Health Care Industry	1.1217
Payment for Referral of Patients	1.1218
Waiver of Deductibles and Co-payments	1.1218
Payment for Insurance Contracts	1.1218
Payment for Vendor Contracts	1.1218
Payments to Adjusters	1.1218

FINANCIAL TRANSACTIONS AND FRAUD SCHEMES

HEALTH CARE FRAUD (CONT.)

Inflated Billings	1.1218
Alterations	1.1219
Detection	1.1219
Adding Services	1.1219
Code Gaming	1.1219
Unbundling Charges/Fragmentation	1.1220
Mutually Exclusive Procedures	1.1221
Global Service Period Violations	1.1221
Upcoding	1.1222
Misuse of "New Patient" Codes	1.1222
Insured Fraud	1.1222
Doctor/ER Shopping	1.1222
Misrepresentation on Application	1.1222
Third-Party Fraud	1.1222
Death of Insured	1.1222
Investigation Tips	1.1223
Criminal Rings	1.1223
Collusion	1.1223
Detection	1.1223
Divorce	1.1224
Foreign Insured	1.1224
Investigation Tips	1.1224
Detection of External Fraud	1.1224
Fraud by Medical Institutions	1.1225
False Cost Reports	1.1226
Inclusion of Unallowable Items	1.1226
DRG Creep	1.1226
Billing for Experimental Procedures	1.1226
Improper Relationships with Physicians	1.1227
Revenue Recovery Firms	1.1227
Changing Codes	1.1227
Adding Items	1.1228
Kickbacks	1.1228
Billing for Expensive Treatments	1.1228
Altering Records	1.1228
Donating Organs	1.1228
Additional Anesthesia Time	1.1228
Nursing Homes	1.1229
Failure of the Nursing Facility to Monitor Outside Providers	1.1229
Excessive Reimbursements	1.1230
Psychiatric Hospital Fraud	1.1230
Abuse in the Admissions Process	1.1230

FINANCIAL TRANSACTIONS AND FRAUD SCHEMES

HEALTH CARE FRAUD (CONT.)

    Fraud in the Treatment Process 1.1230
    Abusive Marketing Practices 1.1231
    Financial Rewards for Referrals 1.1231
    Red Flags for Psychiatric and Substance Abuse Claims 1.1231
Other Frauds in the Institutional Setting 1.1232
    Write-Off of Patient Accounts 1.1232
    Credit Balances 1.1232
    Theft of Pharmaceuticals and Supplies 1.1233
Managed Care 1.1233
    Modified Traditional Coverage 1.1233
    HMOs 1.1233
    PPOs 1.1234
    How Managed Care Alters the Potential for Fraud 1.1234
    Types of Managed Care Frauds 1.1234
    Red Flags 1.1235
Electronic Claims Fraud 1.1235
    The Effects of Prosecution in an Electronic Environment 1.1239
Health Care Compliance Programs 1.1239

BANKRUPTCY FRAUD

Introduction 1.1301
    Bankruptcy Court 1.1301
    Office of the United States Trustee 1.1301
    Examiners 1.1302
    Debtors 1.1302
    Creditors 1.1303
        Secured Creditors 1.1303
        Unsecured Creditors 1.1303
        Adjusters 1.1304
The Bankruptcy Code (Title 11, United States Code) 1.1304
    Chapter 1 — General Provisions 1.1304
    Chapter 3 — Case Administration 1.1304
    Chapter 5 — Creditors, Debtors, and the Estate 1.1305
    Chapter 7 — Liquidation of Debtor's Assets 1.1305
    Chapter 11 — Reorganization 1.1305
Trustees 1.1305
    Grounds for the Appointment of a Trustee 1.1305
    The Role of the Trustee in Bankruptcy Fraud Matters 1.1306
    Statutory Authority 1.1307
    Investigation by the Trustee 1.1307
    Sources of Information 1.1308

FINANCIAL TRANSACTIONS AND FRAUD SCHEMES

BANKRUPTCY FRAUD (CONT.)
    Investigative Procedures 1.1309
Creditors' Rights and Remedies 1.1309
    Creditors' Committees 1.1310
    Involuntary Petitions 1.1310
    Investigations by Creditors 1.1312
Bankruptcy Crime Statutes 1.1312
    Title 18, U.S. Code, Section 151 .... 1.1313
    Title 18, U.S. Code, Section 152 .... 1.1313
        Paragraph 1 — Concealment of Property 1.1313
        Paragraph 2 — False Oath or Account 1.1313
        Paragraph 3 — False Declarations 1.1314
        Paragraph 4 — False Claims 1.1314
        Paragraph 5 — Fraudulent Receipt of Property 1.1314
        Paragraph 6 — Extortion and Bribery 1.1315
        Paragraph 7 — Fraudulent Transfer or Concealment 1.1315
        Paragraph 8 — Fraudulent Destruction or Alteration of Documents 1.1315
        Paragraph 9 — Fraudulent Withholding of Documents 1.1315
    Embezzlement Against the Estate 1.1316
    Adverse Interest and Conduct of Officers 1.1316
    Knowing Disregard of Bankruptcy Law or Rule 1.1317
    Bankruptcy Fraud 1.1317
    Bankruptcy-Related Violations 1.1317
Bankruptcy Schemes 1.1318
    Concealed Assets 1.1318
    The Planned "Bustout" 1.1318
        Detection 1.1319
        Prevention 1.1319
    Multiple Filings 1.1319
    Credit Card Bustout 1.1319
    Forged Filings 1.1320
    "Typing Services" or "Petition Mills" 1.1320

TAX FRAUD
Introduction 1.1401
    Fraudulent Intent 1.1401
    Objectively Reasonable "Good Faith" Misunderstanding of the Law 1.1401
Hallmarks (Badges) of Fraud 1.1402
    Fraud is More Than a Mistake in Judgment 1.1402
    False vs. Fraudulent 1.1402
        Definitions of False 1.1402
        Corporate Fraud 1.1403

FINANCIAL TRANSACTIONS AND FRAUD SCHEMES

TAX FRAUD (CONT.)

Burden of Proof	1.1403
Fraud	1.1404
Civil vs. Criminal	1.1404
Taxpayer Penalties	1.1405
Civil	1.1405
Negligence	1.1405
Frivolous Return	1.1405
Fraud	1.1405
Criminal	1.1405
Tax Evasion	1.1405
Making a False Return (Tax Perjury)	1.1406
Failure to File and Pay	1.1406
Conspiracy to Commit Offense Against the United States or to Impair and Impede the Department of Treasury	1.1406
Tax Preparer Penalties	1.1407
Negligence	1.1407
Understatement of Taxpayer's Liability	1.1407
Criminal Fraud	1.1407
Fraud and False Statements	1.1407
Defenses for Tax Fraud	1.1409
No Deficiency	1.1409
Avoidance not Evasion	1.1409
Objectively Reasonable Position	1.1409
Claim of Right Doctrine	1.1409
Other Defenses	1.1410
Mental Illness	1.1410
Incompetent Bookkeeper	1.1410
Ignorance of the Law	1.1410
Innocent Spouse	1.1410
Reliance on an Attorney or Accountant	1.1410
Inappropriate Defenses	1.1411
Amended or Delinquent Return	1.1411
Statute of Limitations	1.1411
Death of Taxpayer	1.1411
Bankruptcy	1.1411
Evidence of Tax Fraud	1.1411
Direct Evidence	1.1411
Unexplained Bank Deposits	1.1411
False Documents	1.1412
False Explanations for Prior Conduct	1.1412
Participation in Illegal Business	1.1412
False Claims of Extra Withholding Exemptions	1.1412

FINANCIAL TRANSACTIONS AND FRAUD SCHEMES

TAX FRAUD (CONT.)
    Circumstantial Evidence 1.1412
        Illicit Income 1.1412
        Income in Excess of Deposits 1.1412
    Other Legal Elements of Tax Fraud 1.1412

SECURITIES FRAUD
Introduction 1.1501
Federal Regulation 1.1501
    Securities Act of 1933 .... 1.1501
    Securities Exchange Act of 1934 .... 1.1502
    Investment Advisor Act of 1940 .... 1.1503
    Investment Company Act of 1940 .... 1.1503
    The Sarbanes-Oxley Act 1.1504
        Certification Obligations for CEOs and CFOs 1.1504
        New Standards for Audit Committee Independence 1.1506
        Enhanced Financial Disclosure Requirements 1.1507
        Protections for Corporate Whistleblowers under Sarbanes-Oxley 1.1509
        Other Criminal Penalties 1.1511
The NASD and Other Regulatory Organizations 1.1513
    Municipal Securities Rule Making Board (MSRMB) 1.1514
    National Futures Association (NFA) 1.1514
    Regional Exchanges 1.1514
    Commodities Futures Trading Commission (CFTC) 1.1515
State Regulation 1.1515
    National Securities Markets Improvement Act of 1996 .... 1.1516
What Constitutes a Security? 1.1517
    "Traditional" Securities 1.1517
        Stocks 1.1517
        Bonds 1.1517
        Certificates of Deposit 1.1517
        Futures 1.1517
        Options 1.1517
    Investment Contracts 1.1518
        The Howey Test 1.1518
        Risk Capital Test 1.1519
        Examples of Investment Contracts 1.1519
Commodity Futures, Exchange-Traded Options, and OTC Options 1.1525
    Commodity Futures Primer 1.1526
        The Principle of Offset 1.1527
        Trading on Margin 1.1527
        Trading Basics 1.1528

FINANCIAL TRANSACTIONS AND FRAUD SCHEMES

SECURITIES FRAUD (CONT.)

    Options Primer 1.1528
  Exchange-Traded Options.. 1.1528
      Relationship of the Underlying to an Option 1.1529
      Option Values and Premiums 1.1530
  Over-the-Counter (OTC) Options... 1.1530
  Securities Fraud Schemes 1.1531
    Securities Fraud by Registered Persons and Entities.. 1.1531
      Churning.. 1.1531
      Unsuitable Recommendations 1.1532
      Failure to Supervise 1.1533
      Failure to Report Client Complaints 1.1534
      Parking... 1.1534
      Front Running - Dual Trading.. 1.1534
      Bucket Shops 1.1535
      Excessive Markups 1.1535
      Misuse or Misappropriation of Customer's Securities 1.1535
      Unauthorized Trading 1.1535
      Systematically Trading Accounts Against Each Other............................... 1.1536
      Block Order Schemes 1.1537
      Market Manipulation 1.1538
      Insider Trading.. 1.1538
      Disclosures (Misrepresentations and Omissions) 1.1540
    Securities Fraud by Unregistered Persons.. 1.1542
      Exemptions... 1.1542
  Investigative Tips... 1.1543
    Promotional Materials.. 1.1543
    Is it a Security or an Investment? 1.1544
    Investigative Resources.. 1.1544
  Securities Fraud and the Internet... 1.1545
    Same Old Frauds, New Medium 1.1546
      Newsletters... 1.1546
      Online Trading 1.1546

MONEY LAUNDERING

Introduction 1.1601
  Placement... 1.1601
  Integration.. 1.1601
  Using a Legitimate Business to Launder Funds 1.1603
    Overstatement of Reported Revenues... 1.1603
    Overstatement of Reported Expenses.. 1.1603
    Depositing Cash and Writing Checks in Excess of
      Reported Revenues and Expenses (Balance Sheet Laundering) 1.1604

FINANCIAL TRANSACTIONS AND FRAUD SCHEMES

MONEY LAUNDERING (CONT.)

Favorite Businesses for Hiding or Laundering Money	1.1604
Bars, Restaurants, and Night Clubs	1.1605
Vending Machines	1.1605
Wholesale Distribution	1.1605
Real Estate Purchases	1.1606
ATMs	1.1606
Calling in a Specialist	1.1606
Federal and State Law	1.1607
USA PATRIOT Act of 2001	1.1607
Anti-Money Laundering Programs	1.1607
Identification and Verification of Accountholders	1.1608
Prohibition Against Foreign Shell Bank Accounts	1.1608
Suspicious Activity Reporting by Broker-Dealers	1.1609
Special Due Diligence for Foreign Accounts	1.1609
Currency Reports by Non-financial Businesses	1.1610
Sharing Information Between Financial Institutions	1.1610
New Government Access to Financial Information	1.1611
Office of Foreign Assets Control (OFAC)	1.1612
The Bank Secrecy Act	1.1612
Title I — Recordkeeping	1.1613
Title II — Reporting and Recordkeeping	1.1614
Suspicious Activity Reports (SARs)	1.1618
Unregistered Investment Firms	1.1623
Other Federal Laws Related to Money Laundering	1.1624
Structuring Transaction to Evade Reporting Requirements	1.1624
Bulk Cash Smuggling Into or Out of the United States	1.1624
Money Laundering Statutes	1.1624
Prohibition of Illegal Money Transmitting Businesses	1.1626
1961–1968 Racketeer Influenced and Corrupt Organizations (RICO)	1.1627
Seizures and Forfeitures	1.1627
False Statements	1.1629
Conspiracy to Defraud the United States	1.1630
1952 Travel Act	1.1630
State Laws	1.1630
Enforcement and Prevention Strategies	1.1631
Bank Secrecy Act Compliance Programs	1.1631
Minimum Standards	1.1631
Compliance Officer	1.1631
Policy Statement	1.1632
"Know Your Customer" Programs	1.1632
Special Problems for Insurance Companies	1.1634
Red Flags	1.1635

FINANCIAL TRANSACTIONS AND FRAUD SCHEMES

MONEY LAUNDERING (CONT.)
    Detection 1.1635

CONSUMER FRAUD
Con Schemes 1.1702
    Advance Fee Swindles and Debt Consolidation Schemes 1.1702
    Directory Advertising Schemes 1.1703
    Merchandising Schemes 1.1703
    Personal Improvement Frauds 1.1703
    Diploma Mills 1.1703
    Modeling Schools 1.1704
    Direct Debit from Checking Accounts 1.1704
    Equity-Skimming Schemes 1.1704
    Fundraising, Non-profits, and Religious Schemes 1.1704
    Home-Based Businesses 1.1704
    Home Improvements 1.1704
    Money Manager or Financial Planner 1.1705
    Phone Card Schemes 1.1705
    Scavenger or Revenge Scheme 1.1705
    Sweepstakes, Giveaways, and Prizes 1.1705
    College Scholarship Services 1.1705
    Credit Repair 1.1705
    Other Con Schemes 1.1705
        Block Hustle 1.1705
        Pigeon Drop 1.1705
        Bank Examiner Swindle 1.1706
        Jamaican Handkerchief or Envelope Switch 1.1706
        The Obituary Hustle 1.1706
        Three-Card Monte 1.1706
        Poker Bunco 1.1706
        Missing-Heir Scheme 1.1706
        Gold Mine Swindle 1.1707
        Spanish Prisoner Game 1.1707
        Murphy Game 1.1707
        Badger Game 1.1707
        Goat Pasture Scam 1.1707
Telemarketing Fraud 1.1707
    Top Ten Telemarketing Schemes of 2003 and 2002 .... 1.1708
    Telemarketing Terminology 1.1708
        Boiler Room Staff 1.1709
        Fronters 1.1709
        Closers 1.1709

2005 Fraud Examiners Manual

FINANCIAL TRANSACTIONS AND FRAUD SCHEMES

CONSUMER FRAUD (CONT.)

Verifiers	1.1709
Staff Exploitation	1.1709
Telemarketing Suppliers	1.1710
Turnkeys	1.1710
Independent Service Organizations	1.1711
Factoring Companies	1.1711
International Factoring Companies	1.1711
Check-Cashing Establishments	1.1712
Common Telemarketing Scams	1.1712
Senior Scams	1.1712
Targeting the Unemployed	1.1713
Affinity Fraud	1.1713
Consolation	1.1714
800 Numbers	1.1714
Automatic Debits	1.1715
Business Opportunities (Biz Ops)	1.1715
Work-at-Home Schemes	1.1715
Fly and Buy	1.1716
Vending Machine and Payphone Scams	1.1716
Entrepreneurial Enterprises	1.1717
Inventions Schemes	1.1717
Employment Services	1.1718
Credit Services	1.1718
Credit Repair Scams	1.1719
Prime-Rate Credit Cards	1.1719
Gold Cards	1.1719
Lotteries/Lottery Clubs	1.1719
Buyers Clubs	1.1720
Travel/Vacation Schemes	1.1720
Telephone Slamming	1.1721
Real Estate	1.1721
Timeshares	1.1722
Art/Rare Items	1.1722
Collectibles and Memorabilia	1.1723
Precious Stones	1.1723
Precious Metals	1.1724
900 Numbers/800 Numbers/International Calls	1.1724
International Calls	1.1725
Selling Free Information	1.1725
Scholarship Services	1.1725
Charity Fronts	1.1726
Door-to-Door Promotions	1.1726

FINANCIAL TRANSACTIONS AND FRAUD SCHEMES

CONSUMER FRAUD (CONT.)

Prizes, Sweepstakes, Discount Services	1.1726
Magazine Subscriptions	1.1727
Office and Household Supplies	1.1727
Recovery Rooms	1.1727
Ponzi and Pyramid Schemes	1.1728
Definition	1.1728
Illegal Pyramid or Ponzi Scheme?	1.1728
Pyramid Schemes, Legal and Illegal	1.1728
What's the Difference between an Illegal Pyramid and a Ponzi Scheme?	1.1729
Categories of Ponzi Schemes	1.1731
Pure Cash Schemes	1.1732
Product Fronts	1.1734
Spotting Pyramid Schemes	1.1736
Franchise Fraud	1.1738
Franchise Regulation	1.1738
The FTC Franchise Rule	1.1738
State Laws	1.1740
Other Remedies	1.1740
Overview of Franchising	1.1740
Trademark	1.1740
Significant Control or Assistance	1.1741
Required Payment	1.1741
Disclosure Issues	1.1741
Earnings Claims	1.1741
Success Rates	1.1742
Relationship Issues	1.1742
Termination Issues	1.1743
Identity Theft	1.1744
The Profile	1.1745
Common Ways of Obtaining Information	1.1745
Sorting Through Discarded Trash	1.1746
Shoulder Surfing	1.1746
Rifling Through Co-Worker's Desk Drawers	1.1746
Theft of Mail — Incoming or Outgoing	1.1747
Using an Accomplice within the Organization	1.1747
Soliciting Identifiers through False Job Application Schemes	1.1747
Utility Companies, Health Clubs, and Schools	1.1747
Certifications, Diplomas, Licenses Placed On Workplace Walls	1.1748
Using Pretext, Ruse, or Gag Calls	1.1748
Rental and Loan Applications	1.1748
Public Records	1.1748
The Internet	1.1749

FINANCIAL TRANSACTIONS AND FRAUD SCHEMES

CONSUMER FRAUD (CONT.)

Tracking Down the Thief 1.1750
Confronting the Fraudster 1.1750
Federal Statutes 1.1750
    Identity Theft and Assumption Deterrence Act 1.1750
    Gramm-Leach-Bliley Act 1.1751
State Laws 1.1752
Preventing False Identity Fraud 1.1753
What to Do If Your Identity Is Stolen 1.1754

COMPUTER AND INTERNET FRAUD

Computer Fraud vs. Computer Crime 1.1803
    Computer Crime 1.1804
    Computer-Assisted Crime 1.1804
    Information Crime 1.1805
Computer Hacking 1.1805
    Definition 1.1805
    Social Engineering 1.1806
    Hacker Computer Manipulation 1.1807
        War-Dialers 1.1807
        Trojan Horse 1.1807
        Trap Doors 1.1807
        Salami Techniques 1.1807
        Logic Bombs 1.1808
        Data Diddling 1.1808
        Scavenging and Dumpster Diving 1.1808
        Data Leakage 1.1808
        Piggybacking/Impersonation 1.1808
        Simulation and Modeling 1.1808
        Wire Tapping 1.1809
        Network Weaving 1.1809
        Altering the Way a System Generates Passwords 1.1809
        Buffer Overflow Exploits 1.1810
        Privilege Escalation Exploits 1.1810
        Backdoors 1.1810
        HTTP Exploits 1.1811
    Anti-Hacker Measures 1.1811
    Hacker Detection Measures 1.1813
    Hacking Insurance 1.1813
Electronic Mail 1.1814
    E-Mail Security Concerns 1.1815
        E-mail Ownership 1.1815
        Organizational Liability 1.1815

FINANCIAL TRANSACTIONS AND FRAUD SCHEMES

COMPUTER AND INTERNET FRAUD (CONT.)

Computer Viruses 1.1816
    Hoaxes 1.1817
    Types and Terminology of Computer Viruses 1.1817
        Macro Virus 1.1817
        Boot Sector Viruses 1.1818
        Parasitic Viruses 1.1818
        TSRAM Viruses 1.1819
        Application Software Viruses 1.1819
        Polymorphic Viruses 1.1820
        Stealth Viruses 1.1820
        Mutation Engine Viruses 1.1821
        Network Viruses 1.1821
        Worms 1.1821
    Virus Carriers 1.1822
    Virus Indicators 1.1822
    Virus Protection 1.1823
    Antivirus Software Operation 1.1823
        Traditional Scanners 1.1823
        Heuristic Scanners 1.1824
        Behavior Blocking Scanners 1.1824
        Change Detection Scanners 1.1824
    Investigating Virus Infections 1.1824
Internet Fraud 1.1825
    Typical Internet Schemes 1.1825
        Modem Hijacking 1.1825
        Internet Commerce 1.1825
        Get Rich Quick 1.1826
        Pyramid Schemes 1.1826
        Foreign Trusts 1.1826
        Chain Letters 1.1827
        Investment and Securities Fraud 1.1827
        Spamming 1.1827
    Combating Internet Fraud 1.1827
Electronic Commerce 1.1828
    Applying Encryption to E-Commerce Security 1.1830
        Smart Cards 1.1831
Insider Threats 1.1832
    Characteristics 1.1833
Computer Security 1.1833
    Effective Security 1.1833
        Securing the Communications Network 1.1834
        Passwords 1.1834

FINANCIAL TRANSACTIONS AND FRAUD SCHEMES

COMPUTER AND INTERNET FRAUD (CONT.)

Other Network Security	1.1834
The Risk Assessment Process	1.1836
Internal Controls in the Data Center	1.1836
Systems Maintenance	1.1837
Implementation Controls	1.1837
Computer Operations	1.1837
System Software	1.1838
Data Files	1.1838
Access and Telecommunication Controls	1.1838
Separation of Duties	1.1839
Logs and History Files	1.1839
Security Software	1.1840
Internal Controls in Computer Applications	1.1840
Control Techniques	1.1841
Control Objectives	1.1841
Evaluating Application Controls	1.1842
End-User Computing Internal Control	1.1842
Conducting an Investigation Regarding Computer Crimes	1.1843
Handling the Evidence	1.1844
Integrity of Evidence	1.1845
Search & Seizure—Expectation of Privacy	1.1845
Pre-Search Preparation	1.1846
Search Warrant Affidavit Construction	1.1846
Processing Evidence for Removal	1.1848
Evidence Storage	1.1853
Possible Threats to Magnetic Media	1.1853
Evidence Analysis	1.1853
Understanding the Terms	1.1854
Evidence Inventory	1.1854
"Mirror" Copies	1.1855
Virus Detection	1.1855
Keyword Search	1.1855
"Hidden" and "Deleted" Files	1.1855
File Slack Area	1.1856
File Signatures	1.1856
Encrypted Files	1.1856
Computer Crime Laws	1.1857
International Law	1.1857
Federal Laws	1.1857
Computer Fraud and Abuse Act	1.1857
Electronic Communications Privacy Act	1.1859
Unlawful Access to Stored Communications	1.1859

FINANCIAL TRANSACTIONS AND FRAUD SCHEMES

COMPUTER AND INTERNET FRAUD (CONT.)
    Wire Fraud 1.1859
        Limitations on Exclusive Rights: Computer Programs 1.1860
        Criminal Infringement of a Copyright 1.1860
        Copyright Infringement: Criminal Offenses 1.1860
        Electronic Fund Transfers: Criminal Liability 1.1861
    State Laws 1.1862
Government Information on Cybercrime 1.1862

PUBLIC SECTOR FRAUD
Government Fraud Auditing Standards 1.1901
Summary of GAO Standards Relating to Fraud 1.1902
    Field Work Standards for Financial Audits — Chapter 4 .... 1.1902
        Detecting Material Misstatements Resulting from
            Violations of Contract Provisions or Grant Agreements, or from Abuse 1.1902
        Developing Elements of a Finding 1.1905
        Audit Documentation 1.1905
    Field Work Standards for Performance Audits — Chapter 7 .... 1.1907
        Designing the Audit to Detect Violations of Legal and
            Regulatory Requirements 1.1907
        Obtaining Information About Laws, Regulations,
            and Other Compliance Requirements 1.1909
        Abuse 1.1910
        Evidence 1.1911
        Tests of Evidence 1.1912
        Audit Documentation 1.1915
    Reporting Standards for Financial Audits — Chapter 5 .... 1.1917
        Reporting Auditors' Compliance with GAGAS 1.1917
        Reporting on Internal Control and on Compliance with Laws,
            Regulations, and Provisions of Contracts or Grant Agreements 1.1918
        Reporting Deficiencies in Internal Control, Fraud, Illegal Acts,
            Violations of Provisions of Contracts or Grant Agreements, and Abuse 1.1919
        Reporting Fraud, Illegal Acts, Violations of Provisions of Contracts
            or Grant Agreements, and Abuse 1.1921
        Direct Reporting of Fraud, Illegal Acts, Violations of
            Provisions of Contracts or Grant Agreements, and Abuse 1.1922
        Reporting Views of Responsible Officials 1.1923
        Reporting Privileged and Confidential Information 1.1924
        Report Issuance and Distribution 1.1924
    Reporting Standards for Performance Audits — Chapter 7 .... 1.1924
        Fraud, Illegal Acts, Violations of Provisions of Contracts or
            Grant Agreements, and Abuse 1.1924
        Direct Reporting of Fraud, Illegal Acts, Violations of

FINANCIAL TRANSACTIONS AND FRAUD SCHEMES

PUBLIC SECTOR FRAUD (CONT.)

Provisions of Contracts or Grant Agreements, and Abuse	1.1925
False Claims and Statements	1.1927
Federal Laws Prohibiting False Claims	1.1927
Examples of False Claims	1.1928
False Statements Concerning Employees	1.1928
Fictitious Transactions	1.1928
False Documentation	1.1929
Detection	1.1929
Failure to Produce Documents in a Timely Manner	1.1929
Failure to Respond to Inquiries in a Timely Manner	1.1930
Inadequacies in Reporting Requirements	1.1930
Failure to Have Adequate Information Gathering and Retrieval Systems	1.1930
Altered or Missing Documents	1.1930
Photocopied or Duplicate Documents	1.1930
Failure to Have Adequate Supporting Documentation for Reports and Summary Data	1.1930
Beneficiary Fraud	1.1931
Schemes	1.1931
Social Security Frauds	1.1931
False Claims For Benefits	1.1932
Supplemental Security Income Fraud	1.1932
Fraudulent Social Security Numbers	1.1932
Improper Billing Procedures	1.1933
False Medicare Claims	1.1933
Kickbacks	1.1933
Detection	1.1934
Government Initiatives to Reduce Fraud	1.1934
The Department of Defense (DoD)	1.1934
Defense Contract Audit Agency (DCAA)	1.1934
Defense Logistics Agency (DLA)	1.1935
The Justice Department	1.1935
Criminal Division	1.1936
Voluntary Disclosure	1.1936
Prosecution: The Government Employee's Role	1.1936
Common Problems of Investigators	1.1937
Lack of Familiarity with Terminology	1.1937
Wide Variety of Case Assignments	1.1937
Case Loads	1.1937
Reluctance of Government Prosecutors	1.1937
Key Issues Facing Investigators	1.1937
Overcoming the Reluctance to Investigate	1.1938
Interviewing Government Officials	1.1938

FINANCIAL TRANSACTIONS AND FRAUD SCHEMES

PUBLIC SECTOR FRAUD (CONT.)
Assigning the Interview 1.1938
The Warning Dilemma 1.1939
Requirement to Cooperate 1.1940
    Administrative Warnings 1.1940
Criminal Investigations 1.1941
Declination of Prosecution 1.1941
Legal Counsel 1.1942
Obstructing the Investigation 1.1943
Rules of Procedure 1.1943

CONTRACT AND PROCUREMENT FRAUD
Elements of a Contract 1.2001
Presolicitation Phase 1.2001
    Determining Needs 1.2002
    Bid Specifications 1.2002
Solicitation and Negotiation Phase 1.2003
    Bid Submission Schemes 1.2003
    Bid-Rigging Schemes 1.2004
    Defective Pricing Schemes 1.2005
Contract Performance and Administration Phase 1.2005
    Product Substitution 1.2006
    Mischarges 1.2007

The material in this Financial Transaction section is divided into three principal topic areas. First, general accounting concepts are illustrated, including the basics of debits and credits as well as the contents of financial statements. Second, employee defalcation schemes are detailed. This section includes discussion on management's, auditors', and fraud examiners' responsibilities regarding financial transaction fraud, fraudulent financial statement schemes, asset misappropriation schemes, and bribery and corruption. Finally, other fraud schemes, primarily external frauds, ranging from securities violations to health care frauds, are covered and explained.

ACCOUNTING CONCEPTS

Fraudulent acts are usually of a financial nature. The fraud examiner must understand the essential nature of financial transactions and how they affect records. The fraud examiner should have a grasp of financial terminology as well as accounting theory.

Accounting Basics

Accounting can be defined as the identification, accumulation, measurement, and communication of economic data about an enterprise for decision-makers and other interested parties. The measurement and recording of this data are accomplished through keeping a balance of the accounting equation. The *accounting model* or *accounting equation*, as shown below, is the basis for all double-entry accounting:

$$Assets = Liabilities + Owners'\ Equity$$

By definition, the *Assets* side of the equation consists of the net resources owned by an entity. Examples of assets include cash, receivables, inventory, property, and equipment as well as intangible items of value such as patents, licenses, and trademarks. To qualify as an asset, an item must be (1) owned by the entity and (2) provide future benefit.

Liabilities are the obligations of an entity or an outsider's claim against a company's assets. Liabilities are generally incurred through the acquisition of assets or by operational expenses.

Owners' Equity represents the investment of the owners in the company plus accumulated profits (revenues less expenses). Owner's equity is equal to assets minus liabilities.

This equation has been the cornerstone of accounting since 1494, when Luca Pacioli invented it. The balance of the equation is the key. If a company borrows from a bank, cash (an asset) and notes payable (a liability) increase to show the receipt of cash and an obligation owed by the company. Since both assets and liabilities increase by the same amount, the equation stays in balance.

Accounts and the Accounting Cycle

The major items of the accounting equation are made up of numerous detail accounts. An account is nothing more than a specific accounting record that provides an efficient way to categorize similar transactions. All transactions are recorded in accounts that are categorized under assets accounts, liability accounts, owners' equity accounts, revenue accounts, and expense accounts. Account format occurs in a number of ways. The simplest, most fundamental format is to use a large letter T, often referred to as a *T account*.

Entries to the left side of an account are *debits* (dr) and entries to the right side of an account are *credits* (cr). Debits increase assets and expense accounts, while credits decrease them. Conversely, credits increase liabilities, owners' equity, and revenue accounts; debits decrease them. Every transaction recorded in the accounting records will have both a debit and a credit; thus the term *double-entry accounting*. The accounting equation, in the form of T accounts, looks like the following:

$$\underline{\text{Assets}} \quad = \quad \underline{\text{Liabilities}} \quad + \quad \underline{\text{Owner's Equities}}$$
$$\text{dr} \mid \text{cr} \qquad \text{dr} \mid \text{cr} \qquad \text{dr} \mid \text{cr}$$

Fraud investigation often requires an understanding of the debit-and-credit process. For example, a fraud examiner who is searching for a mysterious $5,000 disappearance of cash finds a debit in the legal expense account and a corresponding credit in the cash account for $5,000 and cannot find genuine documentation for the charge. He can then reasonably suspect that a perpetrator may have attempted to conceal the theft by labeling the stolen $5,000 as a legal expense.

Discovering concealment efforts through review of accounting records is one of the easier methods to detect internal fraud. Usually, one need only look for weaknesses in the various steps of the accounting cycle. Legitimate transactions leave an audit trail. They start with a source document such as an invoice, a check, a receipt, or a receiving report. These source documents become the basis for journal entries that are chronological listings of transactions with their debit and credit amounts. Entries are made in various accounting journals. Then, entries are posted to the appropriate general ledger account. The summarized account amounts become the basis for financial statements for a particular period.

Illustrated below is this flow of transaction information through the accounting records followed by examples of typical accounting transactions to help in understanding how transactions affect the balance sheet:

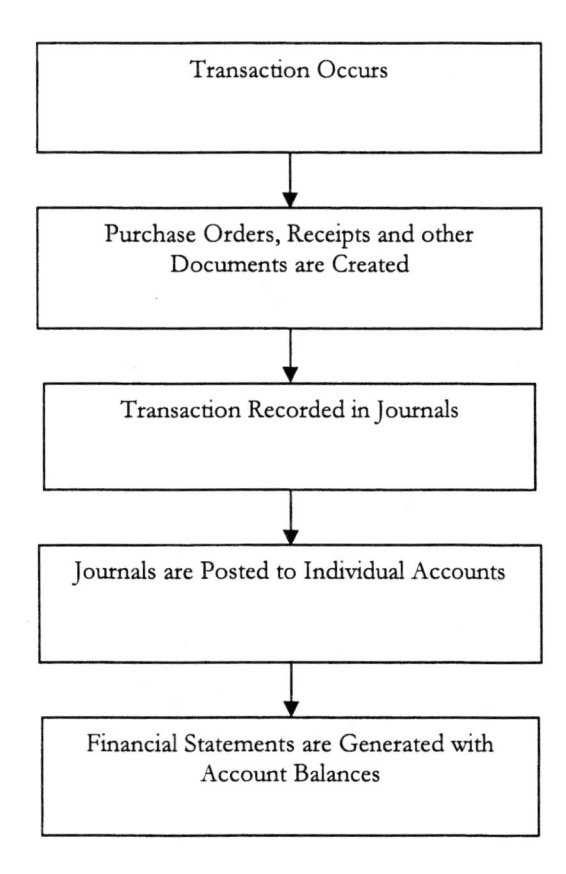

```
┌─────────────────────────────────┐
│       Transaction Occurs        │
└─────────────────────────────────┘
                │
                ▼
┌─────────────────────────────────┐
│ Purchase Orders, Receipts and   │
│     other Documents are Created │
└─────────────────────────────────┘
                │
                ▼
┌─────────────────────────────────┐
│  Transaction Recorded in Journals│
└─────────────────────────────────┘
                │
                ▼
┌─────────────────────────────────┐
│ Journals are Posted to Individual│
│             Accounts            │
└─────────────────────────────────┘
                │
                ▼
┌─────────────────────────────────┐
│ Financial Statements are        │
│ Generated with Account Balances │
└─────────────────────────────────┘
```

| Transaction | Analysis | Journal Entry | | | Balance Sheet Effect | | |
| | | | | | Assets = Liabilities + Owners Equity | | |
		Account	Debit	Credit	Assets	Liabilities	Equity
Enterprise established, Owner invests $192,000	Cash increased Liabilites no effect Equity increased	Cash Common Stock	192,000	192,000	192,000		192,000
Cummulative Balance.........			192,000	192,000	192,000	-	192,000
Owner borrowed $80,000 on a note payable	Cash increased Liabilities increased Equity no effect	Cash Notes Payable	80,000	80,000	80,000	80,000	
Cummulative Balance.........			272,000	272,000	272,000	80,000	192,000
Purchase business equipment for $70,000	Cash decreased Assets increased Liab & Equity no effect	Equipment Cash	70,000	70,000	70,000 (70,000)		
Cummulative Balance.........			342,000	342,000	272,000	80,000	192,000
Services rendered to client $40,000, $15,000 collected in advance	Cash increased A/R increased Equity increased	Cash Accounts Receivable Owners Equity	15,000 25,000	40,000	15,000 25,000		40,000
Cummulative Balance.........			382,000	382,000	312,000	80,000	232,000
Operating expeses incurred $25,000, 14,000 paid in cash	Cash decreased Liabilities increased Equity decreased	Operating Expenses Cash Accounts Payable	25,000	14,000 11,000	(14,000)	11,000	(25,000)
Cummulative Balance.........			407,000	407,000	298,000	91,000	207,000
Paid $5,000 on Note Payable	Cash decreased Liabilities decreased	Notes Payable Cash	5,000	5,000	(5,000)	(5,000)	
Cummulative Balance.........			412,000	412,000	293,000	86,000	207,000
Depreciated equipment for 1 yr, estimated life 10yr ($70,000/10) = $7,000	Asset decreased Equity decreased	Depreciation expense Accum. Depreciation	7,000	7,000	(7,000)		(7,000)
Cummulative Balance.........			419,000	419,000	286,000	86,000	200,000

Financial Statements

The results of accounting are reports or financial statements concerning the assets, liabilities, and operating results of an entity. The *balance sheet* of a company is an expansion of the accounting equation. That is, it lists all assets on one side of the page and all liabilities and owners' equity on the other side. While assets and liabilities are easy to understand, owners' equity requires more explanation.

The owners' equity in a firm usually represents amounts from two sources—from undistributed earnings (usually referred to as *retained earnings*) and from owner contributions (usually referred to as *common* or *capital stock*). The balances in the capital stock account increase only when the owners invest in a company. The retained earnings balance increases when a company has earnings and decreases when a company has losses or when distributed earnings go to the owners in the form of dividends. Thus, the basic accounting equation expands to look like the following:

```
        Assets  =  Liabilities + Owners Equity
                            /          \
                 Common Stock      Retained Earnings
```

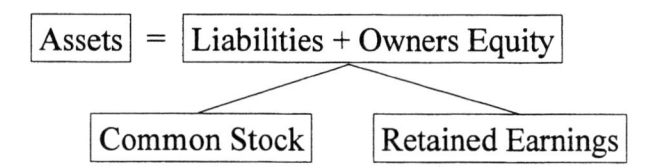

In addition to the balance sheet, the *income statement* is another major corporate financial statement. While a balance sheet shows total assets, liabilities, and owners' equities at a specific point in time (usually the last day of a fiscal year); an income statement details how much income (or loss) a company had during a period of time, such as a year. The accounts comprising the income statement are temporary and at the end of each fiscal year, they are reduced to a zero balance (closed), with the resulting net income (or loss) being added to retained earnings on the balance sheet.

Two basic types of accounts are reported on the income statement—*revenues,* or gross amounts received from the sale of goods or services, and *expenses,* or costs incurred to generate correlating revenues. For example, a sporting goods store would have revenues from the sale of skis, guns and other items. It also would have expenses for amounts paid to purchase the skis and guns (inventory) as well as utilities, wages, taxes, telephone expense and other operating costs. The format for an income statement is:

```
        Revenue - Expenses  =  Net Income
```

At the end of each period revenues and expenses are closed or brought to a zero balance and the difference, net income (loss), is added to retained earnings on the balance sheet. The income statement ties to the balance sheet through the retained earnings account as follows:

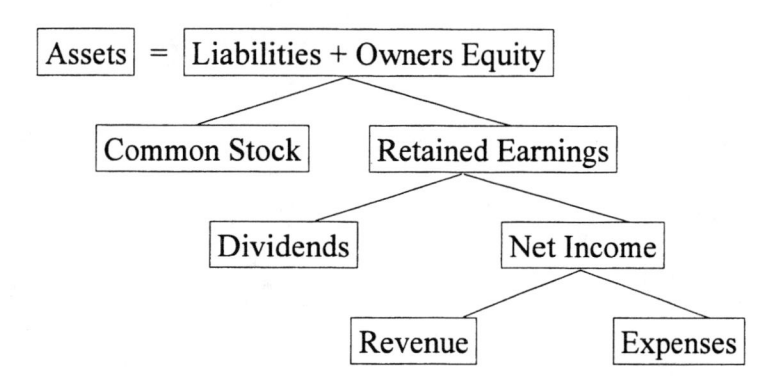

```
        Assets  =  Liabilities + Owners Equity
                            /          \
                 Common Stock      Retained Earnings
                                      /        \
                                Dividends    Net Income
                                                /    \
                                          Revenue    Expenses
```

According to the Statement on Auditing Standards No. 62, promulgated by the AICPA Auditing Standards Board, financial statements include presentations of financial data and accompanying notes prepared in conformity with either generally accepted accounting principles or some other comprehensive basis of accounting. The following is a list of such financial statements:

- Balance sheet
- Statement of income or statement of operations
- Statement of retained earnings
- Statement of cash flows
- Statement of changes in owners' equity
- Statement of assets and liabilities that does not include owners' equity accounts
- Statement of revenue and expenses
- Summary of operations
- Statement of operations by product lines
- Statement of cash receipts and disbursements

Although not specifically noted in SAS No. 62, financial statements may also include other financial data presentations, such as:

- Prospective financial information (forecasts)
- Proxy statements
- Interim financial information (for example, quarterly financial statements)
- Current value financial presentations
- Personal financial statements (current or present value)
- Bankruptcy financial statements
- Registration statement disclosures (Securities Act of 1933)

Other comprehensive bases of accounting, according to SAS No. 62, include:

- Government or regulatory agency accounting
- Tax basis accounting
- Cash receipts and disbursements, or modified cash receipts and disbursements
- Any other basis with a definite set of criteria applied to all material items, such as the price-level basis of accounting

Consequently, the term *financial statements* includes almost any financial data presentation prepared according to generally accepted accounting principles or in accord with another comprehensive basis of accounting. Throughout this section, the term financial statements will include the above forms of reporting financial data, including the accompanying footnotes and management's discussion. Financial statements are the vehicles through which fraud occurs.

Users of Financial Statements

Financial statement fraud schemes are most often perpetrated by management and against potential users of the statements. These users of financial statements include company ownership and management, lending organizations, and investors. The accurate production of financial statements plays an important role in the continued success of an organization. Fraudulent statements are used for a number of reasons. The most common is to increase the apparent prosperity of the organization in the eyes of potential and current investors.

Generally Accepted Accounting Principles (GAAP)

Fraud examiners, certified public accountants, and other accountants and auditors are charged with following measurement and reporting practices regarding financial statements known as *generally accepted accounting principles* (GAAP). These accounting practices are included in GAAP through the accumulation of authoritative accounting pronouncements. These pronouncements include Accounting Research Bulletins, APB Opinions, and Financial Accounting Standards Board (FASB) Statements and Interpretations. Statements on Accounting Standards (SAS) No. 69, issued by the Accounting Standards Board in 1992, gives a hierarchy of GAAP which organizes and gives higher level pronouncements precedence over lower level principles.

GAAP Hierarchy

Level A	FASB Statements of Financial Accounting Standards
	FASB Interpretations
	APB Opinions
	Accounting Research Bulletins
Level B	FASB Technical Bulletin
	AICPA Industry Audit and Accounting Guides
	AICPA Statements of Positions
Level C	AICPA Practice Bulletins
	Emerging Issues Task Force consensus positions
Level D	AICPA accounting interpretations
	"Qs and As" published by FASB
	Practices widely recognized and prevalent in an industry
Other Accounting Literature	FASB Statements of Financial Accounting Concepts
	APB Statements
	AICPA Issues Papers

	International Accounting Standards Committee Statements
	GASB Statements, Interpretations and Technical Bulletins
	Pronouncements of other professional associations or regulatory agencies
	AICPA Technical Practice Aids
	Accounting textbooks, handbooks, and articles

Basic Underlying Accounting Principles

Basic accounting principles, referred to as the generally accepted accounting principles, are the rules by which resources and obligations are recorded into their appropriate account classifications. These principles have evolved over time and are expected to change in response to changes in social and economic conditions, advancements in technology, and demand by users for more useful or productive standards. The following is a list of the basic underlying principles on which accountants should base their practices.

Historical Cost

Historical cost is the proper basis for the recording of assets, expenses, equities, etc. For example, a piece of operational machinery should be shown on the balance sheet at initial acquisition cost and not at current market value or an estimated replacement value.

Revenue Recognition

In general, revenue is recognized or recorded when it becomes realized, measurable, and reasonably collectable. The second criterion for recognition is that the revenue be earned, that is that the entity has substantially accomplished what it must do to be entitled to the benefits represented by the revenues. Revenue should not be recognized for work that is to be performed in subsequent accounting periods, even though the work may currently be under contract. The revenue should be recognized in the period in which the work is performed.

Matching

The matching concept requires that revenue and expenses related to generating the corresponding revenue be recorded in the same accounting period. Estimates, accruals, and allocations are often required to meet this requirement. As a sale is made, the appropriate charges for cost of goods sold or other expenses directly corresponding to the sale should be recorded in the same accounting period.

Consistency

Entities should employ consistent accounting procedures from period to period. Variations or changes in accounting policy and procedures must be justifiable. Standards used to value inventory, depreciate assets, or accrue expenses should be consistent from one accounting period to the next.

Full Disclosure

The financial statements of an entity should include all information necessary for the formation of valid decisions by the users. The statements should not include too much information but are required to include enough information so that the user is not misled. Supplemental notes to the financial statements are often required to meet these criteria.

Objectivity

Accounting records should be designed and kept on objective, rather than subjective evidence. Underlying verifiability must exist for the information contained in the statements. For example, assets are carried at historical cost and not at an estimated current value. This historical cost should be verifiable through legitimate proof of purchase.

Separate Entity Assumption

Economic activity of an entity should be kept separate from other personal or business entities. For example, personal business transactions of the entity's owners or operators should not be included in the financial reports of the entity.

Going Concern—Continuity Assumption

There is an assumption that the life of an entity will be long enough to fulfill its financial and legal obligations. Any evidence to the contrary must be reported in the financial statements of the entity.

Unit of Measure

All financial reports are based on the monetary unit, the dollar for U.S. entities. This assumption recognizes that the monetary unit is an effective means of communicating financial information. Adjustments for inflationary trends are not shown in the financial statements of the entity.

Periodicity—Time Period Assumption

The life of an entity is divided into short economic time periods on which reporting statements are fashioned. These reporting periods vary but a year is the most common. Some companies follow the calendar year, while others use a business year that ends near the lowest point of business activity in a 12-month cycle, disregarding its relation to the calendar year.

Departures from GAAP—Modifying Conventions

As with rules for most things, variations from GAAP are sometimes required. The following modifying conventions give guidance and should be considered when departing from what is generally acceptable.

Conservatism

When considering an accounting matter in which there are two alternatives that equally satisfy conceptual and implementation principles for a transaction, the accountant should take the conservative approach, and follow the alternative that will have the least favorable impact on the net income of the entity.

Industry Practices and Peculiarities

The peculiarities and practices of an industry (such as banking, investment, insurance, etc.) may warrant selective exceptions to accounting principles. Some differences in accounting also occur in response to legal requirements, such as those entities subject to regulatory controls.

Substance over Form

The economic substance of a transaction determines the accounting treatment, even when the legal aspects of the transaction indicate otherwise. For example, although a lease contract may not transfer property rights, if the true substance of the transaction is a sale, then the lessee may capitalize the property as a sale by the lessor and as an acquisition.

Application of Judgment

An accountant may depart from GAAP if the results of departure appear reasonable under the circumstances, especially when the strict adherence to GAAP will produce unreasonable results.

Materiality

The amount of an item is material if its omission would affect the judgment of a reasonable person who is relying on the financial statements. The materiality threshold does not mean that immaterial items do not have to be recorded. Rather, strict adherence with GAAP is necessary only when the item has a significant impact on the financial statements of the entity. In addition, the aggregate effect of immaterial items must also be considered.

Cost-Benefit

A departure from GAAP is permitted if the expected cost of reporting something in compliance with GAAP exceeds the expected benefits of compliance.

MANAGEMENT'S, AUDITORS' AND FRAUD EXAMINERS' RESPONSIBILITIES

Management

Although financial statements are the responsibility of management, fraud frequently is investigated by members of management or, at least, by people under the direction and control of management. This can present obvious potential conflicts.

An organization's board of directors and senior management generally set the code of conduct for the company. This code of conduct is often referred to as the company's "ethic" and is the standard by which all other employees are expected to conduct themselves. If the company's ethic is one of high integrity, it is anticipated that the employees will tend to be more honest. If, on the other hand, the ethic is corrupt, the employees will view that as a license to be corrupt. "Ethical leadership has to come from inside, and from the top. Ethical considerations have got to be on senior management's agenda. And they have to set the tone by example, not by sending memos," says J. Gregory Dees, a professor at Harvard Business School.

An unimpeachable company ethic does not, in and of itself, assure that financial statement fraud will not occur. Other measures are required for management to discharge its responsibilities to prevent and detect fraudulent financial reporting.

The Treadway Commission

The National Commission on Fraudulent Financial Reporting was formed in the United States in 1987 to better define the responsibilities of the auditor in detecting and preventing fraud. The professional auditing organizations—the American Institute of CPAs, the Institute of Internal Auditors, and the National Association of Accountants, among others—established the Commission to underwrite a study and make recommendations. In an effort to curb fraudulent financial reporting, the Treadway Commission offered four recommendations that, when combined with other measures, might help reduce the probability of fraudulent financial reporting. These recommendations are addressed to the board of directors' audit committee.

Mandatory Independent Audit Committee

The board of directors oversees the conduct of management. The Treadway Commission recommended that each board of directors have an audit committee with outside directors comprising its membership.

Written Charter

The Treadway Commission also suggested that companies develop a written charter setting forth the duties and responsibilities of the audit committee. The board of directors should periodically review, modify, and approve this written charter.

Resources and Authority

According to the Commission, the existence of an audit committee and a written charter is not enough. The committee also must have adequate resources and authority to carry out its responsibilities.

Informed, Vigilant, and Effective Audit Committees

The audit committee should be comprised of members who are informed, vigilant, and effective.

The COSO Report

In addition, in 1987, the Treadway Commission recommended that *management* of publicly held companies include with their management reports an acknowledgement of responsibility for internal controls and an assessment of its effectiveness in meeting those controls. It formed the Committee on Sponsoring Organizations (COSO) to actualize Treadway's recommendations. COSO issued *Internal Control – Integrated Framework,* with a later issued addendum, which provided the following definition:

> *Internal Control is a process...designed to provide reasonable assurance regarding the achievement of objectives in the following categories:*
> *a) reliability of financial reporting,*
> *b) effectiveness and efficiency of operations, and*
> *c) compliance with applicable laws and regulations.*

COSO also identified, for management, five interrelated components of internal control:
- The Control Environment sets the tone of an organization, influencing the control consciousness of the organization and providing a foundation for all other control components.
- Risk Assessment is an entity's identification and assessment of risks relevant to achieving control objectives.
- Control Activities are an entity's control policies and procedures.
- Information and Communication is the exchange of information in a way that allows employees to carry out their responsibilities.

- Monitoring is the process that assesses the control environment over time.

These components combined form an integrated system of controls.

People other than management also are responsible for the detection and deterrence of fraudulent financial reporting. These people include external auditors, internal auditors, and Certified Fraud Examiners. Following is a discussion of the professional responsibilities of these people.

Certified Fraud Examiners

A Certified Fraud Examiner normally is not responsible for the initial detection of fraud; instead, the Certified Fraud Examiner usually becomes involved after sufficient predication exists. Certified Fraud Examiners commonly supervise or direct the fraud examination or investigation. The responsibilities of the Certified Fraud Examiner are to:

- Help resolve allegations of fraud, from inception to disposition
- Obtain evidence
- Take statements
- Write reports of fraud examinations
- Testify to findings
- Assist in fraud detection and prevention

Help Resolve Allegations of Fraud

Allegations of fraud often are based on insufficient evidence. They must be resolved through lawful evidence-gathering methods. The Certified Fraud Examiner Professional Code of Ethics requires the Certified Fraud Examiner to assist in that resolution. The disposition of a case might be a settlement or some other form of agreement, rather than trial and conviction or acquittal.

Obtain Evidence

The Certified Fraud Examiner is responsible for gathering and maintaining custody of evidence that will either confirm or refute a fraud allegation. The available evidence might demonstrate that the fraud allegation is without merit. Such evidence is equally as important as evidence that might prove the commission of fraud.

Take Statements

Certified Fraud Examiners use the skills of interviewing. These skills are invaluable in obtaining statements from witnesses as well as securing admissions of guilt from perpetrators.

Write Reports

Report writing is an important step in fraud examinations. The report is the narration of the series of events that has occurred, the witnesses who will testify to the facts, and, if appropriate, the signed admission of the perpetrator.

Testify to Findings

The Certified Fraud Examiner might testify to the findings of the examination. Although this step is not always necessary (for example, in cases which do not proceed to trial), it is important that all examinations be conducted under the premise that the case will go to trial and testimony will be required. Keeping this premise in mind helps the fraud examiner remember to take the time to perform the examination scrupulously.

Assist in the Detection and Prevention of Fraud

Because of their education, experience, and training, Certified Fraud Examiners are uniquely qualified to assist companies with proactive fraud prevention and detection programs. Certified Fraud Examiners assist in the investigation of fraud allegations and also aid management with designing and implementing internal control systems so that fraud schemes will be less common and not go undetected.

It is common for a Certified Fraud Examiner to hold another designation, such as Certified Public Accountant, Certified Protection Professional, or Certified Internal Auditor. Dealing with accounting and auditing matters often requires the opinions of these professionals. Although the Certified Fraud Examiner might hold another designation, he is bound by the Certified Fraud Examiner Code of Professional Ethics, which specifically states in part:

> *A Certified Fraud Examiner, when conducting examinations, will obtain evidence or other documentation to establish a reasonable basis for any opinion required. No opinion shall be expressed regarding the guilt or innocence of any person or party.*

This article means that the Certified Fraud Examiner will not express an opinion, even if personally convinced of the guilt of an individual. Determining the guilt or innocence of an individual is reserved for a judge and jury; the Certified Fraud Examiner is a gatherer of facts, not the ultimate judge of them.

External Auditors

Prior SAS Treatment of Fraud

In 1996, the Auditing Standards Board issued SAS No. 82, *Consideration of Fraud in a Financial Statement Audit*, in response to questions and criticisms of the auditing and accounting profession's lack of adequate addressing of the subject of fraud. In response to the high-profile financial frauds that occurred in 2001 and 2002, the Auditing Standards Board of the AICPA replaced SAS 82 with SAS 99 to give expanded guidance to auditors for detecting material fraud. Per the AICPA, the standard was part of an effort to "restore investor confidence in U.S. capital markets and re-establish audited financial statements as a clear picture window into Corporate America."

The standard is effective for audits of financial statements for periods beginning on or after December 15, 2002.

SAS No. 99 — *Consideration of Fraud in a Financial Statement Audit*

Statement on Auditing Standards (SAS) No. 1 states, "The auditor has a responsibility to plan and perform the audit to obtain reasonable assurance about whether the financial statements are free of material misstatement, whether caused by error or fraud."

The purpose of SAS 99 is to "establish standards and provide guidance to auditors in fulfilling that responsibility."

It is divided into ten main sections:
- Description and characteristics of fraud
- Importance of exercising professional skepticism
- Discussion among engagement personnel regarding risk of material misstatement due to fraud
- Obtaining information needed to identify risks of material misstatements due to fraud
- Identifying risks that may result in material misstatements due to fraud
- Assessing the identified risks after taking into account an evaluation of the entity's programs and controls
- Responding to the results of the assessment
- Evaluating audit evidence

- Communicating about fraud to management, the audit committee, and others
- Documenting the auditor's consideration of fraud

Following is a brief description of each of these sections. Practitioners in this area should review SAS 99 in its entirety for more detailed information. A copy of the entire standard can be obtained from the AICPA (www.aicpa.org).

Description and Characteristics of Fraud

This section emphasizes that while auditors do not make legal determinations about the existence of fraud, they should be interested in all acts that result in a material misstatement of the financial statements. Such misstatements can be the result of either fraud or error, depending on whether the misstatement was intentional or unintentional.

Two types of misstatements are considered relevant for audit purposes:
- Misstatements arising from fraudulent financial reporting, and
- Misstatements arising from misappropriation of assets.

MISSTATEMENTS ARISING FROM FRAUDULENT FINANCIAL REPORTING

This category is defined as intentional misstatements or omissions of amounts or disclosures in financial statements that are "designed to deceive financial statement users."

Fraudulent financial reporting may be accomplished by the following:
- Manipulation, falsification, or alteration of accounting records or supporting documents
- Misrepresentation in or intentional omission of events, transactions, or other significant information
- Intentional misapplication of accounting principles relating to amounts, classification, manner of presentation, or disclosure

MISSTATEMENTS ARISING FROM MISAPPROPRIATION OF ASSETS

Also referred to as theft or defalcation, this category includes the theft of an entity's assets where the effect of the theft causes the financial statements, in all material respects, not to be in conformity with GAAP.

This section goes on to remind the auditor that, by definition, fraud often is concealed, and management is in a position to perpetrate fraud more easily because they are in the position of being able to directly or indirectly manipulate accounting records. Auditors cannot obtain absolute assurance that material misstatements are not present, but auditors should be aware of the possibility that fraud may be concealed and that employees may be in collusion with each other or outside vendors. If the auditor notices records or activities that seem unusual, the auditor should at least consider the possibility that fraud may have occurred.

Importance of Exercising Professional Skepticism
SAS No.1 states that performing an audit with due professional care requires the auditor to exercise professional skepticism throughout the engagement. Because of the characteristics of fraud, the auditor should conduct the audit "with a mindset that recognizes the possibility that a material misstatement due to fraud could be present." It also requires an "ongoing questioning" of whether information the auditor obtains could suggest a material misstatement due to fraud.

Discussion among Engagement Personnel Regarding Risk of Material Misstatement Due to Fraud
Prior to or in conjunction with the information-gathering procedures discussed below, the members of the audit team should discuss the potential for material misstatements due to fraud.

The discussion should include "brainstorming" among the audit team members about the following:
- How and where they believe the entity's financial statement might be susceptible to fraud;
- How management could perpetrate or conceal fraud; and
- How assets of the entity could be misappropriated.

This discussion should also include a consideration of known external and internal factors affecting the entity that might:
- Create incentives/pressures for management and others to commit fraud;
- Provide the opportunity for fraud to be perpetrated; and
- Indicate a culture or environment that enables management and others to rationalize committing fraud.

The discussion should also emphasize the need to maintain "a questioning mind" in gathering and evaluating evidence throughout the audit and to obtain additional information if necessary.

Obtaining Information Needed to Identify Risks of Material Misstatements Due to Fraud

SAS No. 22 provides guidance on how the auditor obtains knowledge about the entity's business and industry. As part of that process, the auditor should perform the following procedures to obtain information to use in identifying the risks of material misstatement due to fraud:

- Make inquiries of management and others within the entity to obtain their views about the risks of fraud and how they are addressed
- Consider any unusual or unexpected relationships that have been identified in performing analytical procedures in planning the audit
- Consider whether one or more fraud risk factors exist
- Consider other information that may be helpful in the identification of risks of material misstatement due to fraud

MAKING INQUIRIES OF MANAGEMENT AND OTHERS WITHIN THE ENTITY TO OBTAIN THEIR VIEWS ABOUT THE RISKS OF FRAUD AND HOW THEY ARE ADDRESSED

This step involves asking management about a number of issues, including:

- Whether management has knowledge of fraud or suspected fraud
- Management's understanding of the risk of fraud
- Programs and controls the entity has established to help prevent, deter, or detect fraud
- Whether and how management communicates to employees its views on business practices and ethical behavior

The auditor should also question the audit committee directly about its views concerning the risk of fraud and whether the committee has knowledge of fraud or suspected fraud. The same should be done with the company's internal audit department.

Additionally, the auditor may need to conduct similar inquiries of the entity's other personnel if the auditor believes they may have additional information about the risks of fraud.

CONSIDERING THE RESULTS OF ANALYTICAL PROCEDURES PERFORMED IN PLANNING THE AUDIT

SAS No. 99 requires that analytical procedures be performed in planning the audit with an objective of identifying the existence of unusual transactions or events, and amounts, ratios, and trends that might indicate matters "that have financial statement and audit planning implications." If the results of these procedures yield unusual or unexpected relationships, the auditor should consider the results in identifying the risks of material misstatement due to fraud.

CONSIDERING FRAUD RISK FACTORS

As discussed above, even though fraud is concealed, the auditor may identify events or conditions that indicate incentives or pressures to commit fraud, opportunities to carry out fraud, or attitudes and rationalizations to justify fraudulent conduct. These events and conditions are referred to as "fraud risk factors." The auditor should consider whether one or more of the fraud risk factors are present and should be considered in identifying and assessing the risks of material misstatement due to fraud. The Appendix to SAS No. 99 contains a list of examples of fraud risk factors.

CONSIDERING OTHER INFORMATION THAT MAY BE HELPFUL IN IDENTIFYING RISKS OF MATERIAL MISSTATEMENT DUE TO FRAUD

Finally, the auditor should also consider any other information that he or she may feel would be helpful in identifying the risks of material misstatement.

Identifying Risks That May Result in Material Misstatements Due to Fraud

After gathering the information as discussed above, the auditor should consider the information in the context of the three conditions present when fraud occurs – incentives/pressures, opportunities, and attitudes/rationalizations.

Auditors should consider:
- The *type* of risk that may exist, i.e. whether it involves fraudulent financial reporting or misappropriation of assets.
- The *significance* of the risk, i.e. whether it is of a magnitude that could result in a possible material misstatement.
- The *likelihood* of the risk, i.e. the likelihood that it will result in a material misstatement.
- The *pervasiveness* of the risk, i.e. whether the potential risk is pervasive to the financial statement as a whole or is specifically related to a particular assertion, account, or class of transactions.

Assessing the Identified Risks after Taking into Account an Evaluation of the Entity's Programs and Controls

SAS No. 55 requires the auditor to obtain an understanding of each of the five components of internal controls sufficient to plan the audit. As part of this step, the auditor should evaluate whether the entity's programs and controls that address identified risks of fraud have been suitably designed and placed in operation. These programs and controls may involve:

- Specific controls designed to mitigate specific risks of fraud (e.g., controls to prevent misappropriation of particular, susceptible assets), and
- Broader programs designed to prevent, deter, and detect fraud (e.g., ethics policies).

Exhibit I of SAS No. 99 provides examples of programs and controls an entity might implement to create a culture of honesty and to prevent fraud (see also the chapter on "Fraud Prevention" in the Criminology section of *The Fraud Examiners Manual*).

Responding to the Results of the Assessment

Once the auditor has gathered the information and assessed the risk of fraud, he or she must determine what impact the assessment will have on how the audit is conducted. For example, the auditor may need to design additional or different audit procedures to obtain more reliable evidence in support of account balances, transactions, etc., or to obtain additional corroboration of management's explanations and representations concerning material matters (such as third-party confirmation, documentation from independent sources, use of a specialist, analytical procedures, etc.).

OVERALL RESPONSES TO THE RISK OF MATERIAL MISSTATEMENT

Judgments about the risk of material misstatement due to fraud have an overall effect on how the audit is conducted in several ways:

- Assignment of personnel and supervision. The auditor may need to consult with specialists in a particular field.
- Accounting principles. The auditor should consider management's selection and application of significant accounting principles, particularly those related to subjective measurements and complex transactions.
- Predictability of auditing procedures. The auditor should incorporate an "element of unpredictability" in the selection of auditing procedures to be performed, such as using differing sampling methods at different locations or at locations on an unannounced basis.

RESPONSES INVOLVING THE NATURE, TIMING, AND EXTENT OF PROCEDURES TO BE PERFORMED TO ADDRESS THE IDENTIFIED RISKS

This section notes that the auditing procedures performed in response to identified risks will vary depending on the type of risks identified. Such procedures may involve both substantive tests and tests of the operating effectiveness of the entity's internal controls.

However, because management may have the ability to override controls that may otherwise appear to be operating effectively, it is unlikely that the audit risk can be reduced appropriately by performing only tests of controls.

Therefore, the auditor's response to specifically identified risks of fraud should include the following:

- Changing the *nature* of the auditing procedures to obtain more reliable or additional corroborative information (such as through independent sources or physical inspection).
- Changing the *timing* of substantive tests. For example, the auditor may conduct substantive tests at or near the end of the reporting period.
- The *extent* of the procedures should also reflect the assessment of the risk of fraud, such as increasing the sample sizes or performing analytical procedures at a more detailed level.

<u>EXAMPLES OF RESPONSES TO IDENTIFIED RISKS OF MISSTATEMENTS ARISING FROM FRAUDULENT FINANCIAL REPORTING</u>

SAS No. 99 provides a number of examples of responses the auditor may take in regard to risks of misstatements arising from both fraudulent financial reporting and asset misappropriation.

Some of the examples concerning fraudulent financial reporting include:

- Revenue recognition — performing substantive analytical procedures relating to revenue using disaggregated data (for example, comparing revenue reported by month and by product line during the current reporting period with comparable prior periods); confirming with customers relevant contract terms; or questioning staff about shipments near the end of a period.
- Inventory quantities — examining inventory records to identify locations or items that require specific attention during or after the physical inventory count; more rigorous examination of the count such as examining contents of boxed items; additional testing of count sheets, tags, or other records.
- Management estimates — depending on the situation, the auditor may wish to engage a specialist or develop an independent estimate for comparison to management's estimate. Gathering further information may help the auditor evaluate the reasonableness of management's estimates and underlying assumptions.

EXAMPLES OF RESPONSES TO IDENTIFIED RISKS OF MISSTATEMENTS ARISING FROM MISAPPROPRIATIONS OF ASSETS

If the auditor identifies a risk of material misstatement due to fraud relating to misappropriation of assets, the auditor may wish to include additional procedures. For example, if a particular asset is highly susceptible to misappropriation, the auditor may wish to conduct further testing of the controls to prevent and detect such misappropriation.

RESPONSES TO FURTHER ADDRESS RISK OF MANAGEMENT OVERRIDE OF CONTROLS

Because management is in a unique position to override existing controls, if such a risk is identified, the auditor may need to perform further procedures to further address the risk of management override of controls.

EXAMINING JOURNAL ENTRIES AND OTHER ADJUSTMENTS FOR EVIDENCE OF POSSIBLE MATERIAL MISSTATEMENT DUE TO FRAUD

Material misstatements of financial statements often involve recording inappropriate or unauthorized journal entries or making adjustments to amounts reported in the financial statements that are not reflected in journal entries (such as consolidating adjustments or reclassifications). Therefore, the auditor should design procedures to test the appropriateness of journal entries recorded in the general ledger and other adjustments (such as entries posted directly to financial statement drafts).

REVIEWING ACCOUNTING ESTIMATES FOR BIASES THAT COULD RESULT IN MATERIAL MISSTATEMENT DUE TO FRAUD

In preparing financial statements, management is responsible for making a number of judgments or assumptions that affect significant accounting estimates. Fraudulent financial reporting is often accomplished through intentional misstatement of these estimates. In performing the audit, the auditor should consider whether the differences between estimates supported by the audit evidence and the estimates included in the financial statements indicate a possible bias on the part of management. If so, the auditor should perform a retrospective review of significant accounting estimates of the prior year. This should provide the auditor with additional information about whether management may have a bias in presenting the current-year estimates.

EVALUATING THE BUSINESS RATIONALE FOR SIGNIFICANT UNUSUAL TRANSACTIONS

During the course of the audit, the auditor may become aware of significant transactions that are outside the normal course of the entity's business or appear unusual given the auditor's understanding of the entity's operations. The auditor should gain an understanding of the business rationale for these transactions and whether the rationale (or lack thereof) suggests the transactions may have been entered into to engage in fraudulent financial reporting or to conceal misappropriation of assets.

Some factors the auditor should consider include:
- Are the transactions are overly complex?
- Has management discussed the transactions with the board of directors and audit committee?
- Has management placed more emphasis on the need for a particular accounting treatment than on the underlying economics of the particular transaction?
- Do the transactions involve unconsolidated, unrelated parties (including special purposes entities), or parties that do not have the substance to or financial strength to support the transaction?

Evaluating Audit Evidence
ASSESSING RISKS OF MATERIAL MISSTATEMENT DUE TO FRAUD THROUGHOUT THE AUDIT

During the performance of the audit, the auditor may identify conditions that either change or support a judgment regarding the assessment of risks.

Examples include:
- Discrepancies in the accounting records (such as transactions that are not recorded, unsupported or unauthorized balances or transactions, or last minute adjustments).
- Conflicting or missing evidential matter (such as missing or altered documents/records, unexplained items or reconciliations, or missing inventory).
- Problematic or unusual relationships between the auditor and management (such as denial of access to records, facilities, employees, customers; complaints by management about the conduct of the audit team; unusual delays in providing information; or unwillingness to add or revise disclosures).

EVALUATING WHETHER ANALYTICAL PROCEDURES PERFORMED INDICATE A PREVIOUSLY UNRECOGNIZED RISK OF FRAUD

Analytical procedures performed during the audit may result in identifying unusual or unexpected relationships that should be considered in assessing the risk of material misstatement due to fraud. Determining whether a particular trend or relationship is a risk of fraud requires professional judgment. Unusual relationships involving year-end revenue and income often are particularly relevant and might include (1) uncharacteristically large amounts of income reported in the last week or two of the reporting period from unusual transactions and (2) income that is inconsistent with trends in cash flow from operations.

Analytical procedures are useful because management or employees generally are unable to manipulate all the information necessary to produce normal or expected relationships. SAS No. 99 provides several examples, including:

- The relationship of net income to cash flows from operations may appear unusual because management recorded fictitious revenues and receivable but was unable to manipulate cash.
- Changes in inventory, accounts payable, sales, or costs of sales from the prior period to the current period may be inconsistent, indicating a possible theft of inventory because the employee was unable to manipulate all of the related accounts.
- An unexpected or unexplained relationship between sales volume as determined from the accounting records and production statistics maintained by operations personnel (which is more difficult for management to manipulate) may indicate a possible misstatement of sales.

EVALUATING RISKS OF MATERIAL MISSTATEMENT AT OR NEAR THE COMPLETION OF FIELDWORK

At or near the completion of fieldwork, the auditor should evaluate whether the accumulated results of auditing procedures and other observations affect the assessment of risk of material misstatements due to fraud made earlier. Such an evaluation may identify whether there is a need to perform further audit procedures.

RESPONDING TO MISSTATEMENTS THAT MAY BE THE RESULT OF FRAUD

If the auditor believes that misstatements are or may be the result of fraud, but the effect of the misstatements is not material to the financial statements, the auditor nevertheless should evaluate the implications, especially those dealing with the "organizational position" of the person involved, which may require a reevaluation of the assessment of the risk of material misstatement. The example provided involves theft of cash from a small petty cash fund. The amount of the theft generally would not be of significance to the auditor, but if the theft was perpetrated by higher-level management, it may be indicative of a more pervasive problem such as management integrity.

If the auditor believes that a misstatement is or may be the result of fraud, and either has determined that the effect of the misstatement is material to the financial statements, or has been unable to evaluate whether the effect is material, the auditor should:

- Attempt to obtain additional evidence to determine whether material fraud occurred and its effect on the financial statements.
- Consider the implications for other aspects of the audit.
- Discuss the matter and the approach for further investigation with an appropriate level of management that is at least one level above those involved, and with senior management and the audit committee.
- If appropriate, suggest the client consult with legal counsel.

Communicating About Possible Fraud to Management, the Audit Committee, and Others

SAS No. 99 states, "Whenever an auditor has determined that there is evidence that fraud may exist, the matter should be brought to the attention of an appropriate level of management." It is considered appropriate to do so even if the matter might be considered inconsequential. Fraud involving senior management and fraud (by anyone) that causes a material misstatement should be reported directly to the audit committee.

If the auditor has identified risks of material misstatement due to fraud that have continuing control implications, the auditor should also consider whether these risks should be communicated to senior management and the audit committee. Conversely, the auditor should also consider whether the absence of controls to deter, detect, or prevent fraud should also be reported.

The disclosure of possible fraud to parties other than the client's senior management and its audit committee is ordinarily not part of the auditor's responsibility and may be precluded by the auditor's legal or ethical obligations of confidentiality unless the matter is reflected in the auditor's report.

However, SAS 99 points out that there may be a duty to disclose the information to outside parties in the following circumstances:

- To comply with certain legal and regulatory requirements (such as SEC rules);
- To a successor auditor pursuant to SAS No. 84;
- In response to a subpoena;
- To a funding agency or other specified agency in accordance with the requirements for audits of entities that receive governmental financial assistance.

Documenting the Auditor's Consideration of Fraud

SAS No. 99 concludes by requiring that auditors document the following:

- Discussion among engagement personnel regarding the susceptibility of the entity's financial statements to material misstatement due to fraud (including how and when the discussion occurred, the team members who participated, and the subject matter discussed);
- Procedures performed to obtain information necessary to identify and assess the risks of material misstatement due to fraud;
- Specific risks of material misstatement due to fraud that were identified;
- If the auditor has not identified improper revenue recognition as a risk, the reasons supporting the auditor's conclusion;
- The results of the procedures performed to further address the risk of management override of controls;
- Other conditions and analytical relationships that caused the auditor to believe that additional auditing procedures or other responses were required to address such risks; and
- The nature of the communication about fraud made to management, the audit committee, or others.

SAS No. 96 — *Audit Documentation*

Statement on Auditing Standards (SAS) No. 96, *Audit Documentation* provides general guidance on the content and extent of audit documentation. It also adds specific documentation guidance to certain other standards. The new standard supersedes SAS No. 41, *Working Papers*.

SAS No. 96 reaffirms the objectives in SAS No. 41 that audit documentation serves mainly to provide the "principal support for the auditor's report," and to help the auditor conduct and supervise the audit. Although SAS No. 96 retains much of the guidance in SAS No. 41, it provides more specific guidance and requirements than SAS No. 41. Specifically, SAS No. 96:

- Contains a list of factors that the auditor should consider in determining the nature and extent of the documentation for a particular audit area or auditing procedure. Additionally, audit documentation now is required to include: (a) abstracts or copies of significant contracts or agreements that were examined to evaluate the accounting for significant transactions and (b) for tests of operating effectiveness of controls and substantive tests of details that involve inspection of documents or confirmation, an

identification of items tested. The identification of the items tested may be satisfied by indicating the source from which the items were selected and the specific selection criteria.
- Contains a new requirement for auditors to document audit findings or issues that in their judgment are significant, actions taken to address them (including any additional evidence obtained), and the basis for the final conclusions reached. Significant audit findings or issues include the following:
  - Matters that both (a) are significant and (b) involve issues regarding the appropriate selection, application, and consistency of accounting principles with regard to the financial statements, including related disclosures. Such matters often relate to (a) accounting for complex or unusual transactions or (b) estimates and uncertainties and, if applicable, the related management assumptions.
  - Results of auditing procedures that indicate that (a) the financial statements or disclosures could be materially misstated or (b) auditing procedures need to be significantly modified.
  - Circumstances that cause significant difficulty in applying auditing procedures the auditor considered necessary.
  - Other findings that could result in modification of the auditor's report.
- Retains much of the ownership/record-retention guidance of SAS No. 41. However, in recognition of rapid changes in technology, SAS No. 96 now requires that the record-retention procedures enable the auditor to access electronic audit documentation throughout the retention period. Additionally, SAS No. 96 replaces the "safe custody" provision of SAS No. 41 with a requirement for the auditor to adopt reasonable procedures to maintain the confidentiality of confidential client information contained in audit documentation.

SAS No. 96 also contains amendments adding specific documentation requirements to the following SASs:
- SAS No. 47, *Audit Risk and Materiality*
- SAS No. 56, *Analytical Procedures*
- SAS No. 59, *The Auditor's Consideration of an Entity's Ability to Continue as a Going Concern*

As amended, SAS No. 47 now requires an auditor to document the nature and effect of aggregated misstatements and his or her conclusion as to whether they cause the financial statements to be materially misstated.

The amended SAS No. 56 now requires auditors to document the factors they considered in developing the expectation for a substantive analytical procedure. They also have to document the expectation, if it is not apparent from the documentation of the work that they performed. The auditor also should document (a) the results of his or her comparison of that expectation to the recorded amounts or ratios that he or she developed from recorded amounts and (b) any additional auditing procedures he or she performed in response to significant unexpected differences arising from the analytical procedures as well as the results of such additional procedures.

The amendment to SAS No. 59 requires the auditor to document:
- The conditions or events that led him or her to believe that there is substantial doubt about the entity's ability to continue as a going concern.
- The work performed in connection with the auditor's evaluation of management's plans.
- The auditor's conclusion as to whether substantial doubt about the entity's ability to continue as a going concern for a reasonable period of time remains or is alleviated.
- The consideration and effect of that conclusion on the financial statements, disclosures, and the audit report.

PCAOB Auditing Standard No. 2 — *An Audit of Internal Control over Financial Reporting Performed in Conjunction with An Audit of Financial Statements*

Auditing Standard No. 2 provides guidance for auditors on performing an audit of internal control over financial reporting (referred to as an audit of ICOFR) as required by section 404 of the Sarbanes-Oxley Act. Following is a description of some of the requirements laid out in the Standard. Practitioners in this area should review Auditing Standard No. 2 in its entirety for more detailed information. A copy of the entire standard can be obtained from the PCAOB (www.pcaobus.org).

Section 404 mandates that management must assess and report on the effectiveness of the company's internal controls over financial reporting, and that the external auditor must attest to management's internal control assessment. (See section on the Sarbanes-Oxley Act later in this chapter for more information on management's responsibilities under Section 404.) An auditor performing an audit of ICOFR must therefore express two opinions as a result of the engagement: one on the effectiveness of the company's internal controls and one on management's assessment of the effectiveness of the internal controls.

Performing an ICOFR Audit

To perform an audit of ICOFR, the Standard asserts that the auditor must "obtain sufficient competent evidence about the design and operating effectiveness of controls" (paragraph 27). In doing so, an auditor must:

- Apply the general, fieldwork, and reporting auditing standards;
- Evaluate management's internal control assessment process by evaluating management's consideration of the following elements in forming their assessment:
  - Which internal controls to test in performing the assessment;
  - Whether the failure of a control could result in a misstatement to the financial statements, the magnitude of the resulting misstatement, and whether other controls are in place to mitigate this occurrence;
  - Which locations or business units to include in the assessment, if applicable.
  - How effectively the internal controls are designed;
  - How effectively the internal controls are operating;
  - Whether any internal control deficiencies identified are of such magnitude and likelihood that they constitute material weaknesses (any deficiency where the likelihood of potential misstatement is more than remote) or significant deficiencies (any deficiency where the likelihood of potential misstatement is more than remote and the magnitude is more than inconsequential);
  - The communication of the assessment findings to the auditor and other applicable parties;
  - Whether management's documentation of findings provides reasonable support for its assessment;
- Obtain an understanding of the design of the company's internal controls through:
  - Evaluating the effectiveness of the audit committee's oversight by examining factors such as the level of independence of the audit committee from management, the clarity with which the audit committee's responsibilities are laid out, the audit committee's interaction with external and internal auditors, and the audit committee's involvement with key financial officers;
  - Identifying significant accounts using both qualitative and quantitative factors such as the size, nature, and composition of the account; the susceptibility of the account to losses from errors or fraud; the volume, complexity, and uniformity of transactions processed within the account; and the existence of related party transactions within the account;
  - Identifying which of the financial statement assertions (existence or occurrence, completeness, valuation or allocation, rights and obligations, and presentation and

disclosure) is relevant for each significant account balance or disclosure by evaluating the nature of the assertion, the volume of transactions related to the assertion, and the nature and complexity of the systems used to process and control information relating to the assertion;
- Identifying major classes of transactions based on the level of inherent risk and associated level of management supervision for each transaction class
- Identifying significant processes, obtaining an understanding of the flow of transactions within those processes, identifying any weaknesses within the processes that may result in a misstatement, and identifying controls that management has implemented to address such risks;
- Understanding the period-end financial reporting process, which is always considered a significant process, through an evaluation of the inputs, processes, outputs, technology, participants, locations, entries, and oversight involved in the process;
- Performing a walkthrough for each major class of transactions by tracing a transaction from origination to ultimate reflection in the financial statements; and
- Identifying which of the internal controls to test by evaluating where errors or fraud are likely to occur, the nature of the controls, the significance of each control in achieving the internal control objectives, and the risk that the controls are not operating effectively.

- Test and evaluate whether the internal controls are designed effectively to meet the control objectives using procedures such as inquiry, observation, walkthroughs, and document inspection;
- Test and evaluate whether the internal controls are operating effectively and being performed by individuals with adequate authority and qualifications to ensure their effectiveness by using procedures such as inquiries, document inspection, observation, and reperformance; and
- Evaluate the results of these tests while retaining an attitude of professional skepticism.

Fraud Considerations

The auditor must specifically evaluate all of the internal controls that are intended to detect and prevent any fraud that has a "reasonably possible likelihood of having a material effect on the company's financial statements" (Paragraph 24). Among those factors that should be evaluated are:
- Controls addressing misappropriation of company assets that could result in materially misstated financial statements;

- The company's risk assessment processes;
- The company's code of ethics or code of conduct, specifically those provisions relating to conflicts of interest, related-party transactions, and illegal acts;
- The adequacy of the internal audit function and activities;
- The extent of the audit committee's involvement with the internal audit function; and
- The adequacy of the company's procedures for handling complaints and concerns about questionable accounting or auditing issues.

Further, if the auditor discovers any deficiencies in these controls, he or she should adjust the nature, timing, and extent of testing performed during the financial statement audit as a response.

Forming an Opinion on the Effectiveness of ICOFR

In developing the auditor's opinion over the ICOFR, an auditor must consider all evidence obtained from all sources including the adequacy of management's assessment of the controls, the results of the auditor's evaluation of the design and operating effectiveness of the controls, the contents of reports issued by internal audit during the year that pertain to internal controls, and any pertinent information discovered during the performance of the financial statement audit. The auditor must then evaluate any control deficiencies revealed and determine whether they, individually or aggregated, could result in a material misstatement of an account balance or disclosure, and thus constitute significant deficiencies or material weaknesses. A lack of documentation on either the design of the controls or the evidence to support management's assessment is considered a control deficiency that should be included in the evaluation and opinion formation. Deficiencies in the following areas are usually considered significant deficiencies in ICOFR:

- Controls pertaining to the selection and application of accounting policies;
- Controls and programs pertaining to the prevention and detection of fraud;
- Controls over non-routine or non-systematic transactions; and
- Controls over the period-end financial reporting process.

The Standard lists many other factors, such as restatements of previously issued financial statements and ineffective oversight of the financial reporting and internal control processes by the audit committee, which may indicate the presence of significant deficiencies or material weaknesses in ICORF. The issuance of an unqualified opinion is precluded if any material weaknesses are identified or if the scope of the auditor's work has been restricted.

Likewise, an auditor must either withdraw from the engagement or disclaim an opinion if management does not provide the auditor with certain written representations, including:

- An acknowledgement of management's responsibility for establishing and maintaining effective ICOFR;
- A statement that management has performed an assessment of the effectiveness of the company's ICOFR and specifying the control criteria used in that assessment;
- A statement that management did not use the auditor's procedures performed during the audit of ICOFR or during the audit of the financial statements in performing their assessment of ICOFR;
- A statement of management's conclusion about the effectiveness of ICOFR;
- A statement that management has disclosed all identified deficiencies in the design and operating effectiveness of the controls to the auditor;
- A description of any material fraud or immaterial fraud that involves senior management or other employees who have a significant role in the company's ICOFR;
- A statement as to whether control deficiencies previously identified and communicated to the auditor have been resolved, with specific identification of those that have not; and
- A statement as to whether there have been any changes made to the ICOFR, such as corrections to deficiencies, since the report date.

Auditing Standard No. 2 provides that an auditor may audit a company's financial statements without also conducting an audit of ICOFR. However, when an auditor performs an audit of ICOFR, he or she must also audit the company's financial statements. When both audits are to be undertaken, the auditor should plan and perform the engagement to achieve the objectives of both audits. An interesting result of performing such an integrated audit is the possibility for an auditor to issue different types of opinions for each objective. For example, an auditor may issue an unqualified opinion on both the company's internal controls and management's assessment, but may simultaneously issue a qualified or adverse opinion on the company's financial statements.

Internal Auditor Responsibilities

Internal auditors play a key role in helping organizations prevent and detect fraudulent activity. Because of their proximity to and understanding of the inner workings of the organization, internal auditors are in a unique position to uncover potential unscrupulous acts. In fact, the 2004 Report to the Nation of Occupational Fraud and Abuse showed that the internal audit function was second only to tips in detecting occupational frauds, accounting for the detection of 23.8% of the 508 cases included in the study.

The Institute of Internal Auditors (IIA) has developed the International Standards for the Professional Practice of Internal Auditing. This section contains a description of those IIA Standards that pertain to the internal auditor's responsibilities for preventing and detecting fraud within an organization. Additionally, as an organization's ethical tone is a vital component of its fraud prevention program, the IIA Standards relating to responsibilities for ethical culture are discussed. More detail on these and all other IIA Standards can be found at the IIA's website (www.theiia.org).

1210 – Proficiency

Internal auditors should possess the knowledge, skills, and competencies needed to perform their individual responsibilities. The internal auditing activity collectively should possess or obtain the knowledge, skills, and competencies needed to perform its responsibilities.

1210.A2

The internal auditor should have sufficient knowledge to identify indicators that fraud may have been committed. This requires that the internal auditor knows the characteristics of fraud, the techniques used to commit fraud, and the types of frauds associated with the activities audited. The internal auditor is not expected to have the expertise of a person whose primary responsibility is detecting and investigating fraud.

PRACTICE ADVISORY 1210.A2-1: IDENTIFICATION OF FRAUD

1. Fraud encompasses an array of irregularities and illegal acts characterized by intentional deception. It can be perpetrated for the benefit of or to the detriment of the organization and by persons outside as well as inside the organization.
2. Fraud designed to benefit the organization generally produces such benefit by exploiting an unfair or dishonest advantage that also may deceive an outside party. Perpetrators of such frauds usually accrue an indirect personal benefit. Examples of frauds designed to benefit the organization include:
   - Sale or assignment of fictitious or misrepresented assets.
   - Improper payments such as illegal political contributions, bribes, kickbacks, and payoffs to government officials, intermediaries of government officials, customers, or suppliers.
   - Intentional, improper representation or valuation of transactions, assets, liabilities, or income.
   - Intentional, improper transfer pricing (e.g., valuation of goods exchanged between related organizations). By purposely structuring pricing techniques improperly,

management can improve the operating results of an organization involved in the transaction to the detriment of the other organization.
– Intentional, improper related-party transactions in which one party receives some benefit not obtainable in an arm's-length transaction.
– Intentional failure to record or disclose significant information to improve the financial picture of the organization to outside parties.
– Prohibited business activities such as those that violate government statutes, rules, regulations, or contracts.
– Tax fraud.
3. Fraud perpetrated to the detriment of the organization generally is for the direct or indirect benefit of an employee, outside individual, or another organization. Some examples are:
– Acceptance of bribes or kickbacks.
– Diversion to an employee or outsider of a potentially profitable transaction that would normally generate profits for the organization.
– Embezzlement, as typified by the misappropriation of money or property, and falsification of financial records to cover up the act, thus making detection difficult.
– Intentional concealment or misrepresentation of events or data.
– Claims submitted for services or goods not actually provided to the organization.
4. Deterrence of fraud consists of those actions taken to discourage the perpetration of fraud and limit the exposure if fraud does occur. The principal mechanism for deterring fraud is control. Primary responsibility for establishing and maintaining control rests with management.
5. Internal auditors are responsible for assisting in the deterrence of fraud by examining and evaluating the adequacy and the effectiveness of the system of internal control, commensurate with the extent of the potential exposure/risk in the various segments of the organization's operations. In carrying out this responsibility, internal auditors should, for example, determine whether:
– The organizational environment fosters control consciousness.
– Realistic organizational goals and objectives are set.
– Written policies (e.g., code of conduct) exist that describe prohibited activities and the action required whenever violations are discovered.
– Appropriate authorization policies for transactions are established and maintained.
– Policies, practices, procedures, reports, and other mechanisms are developed to monitor activities and safeguard assets, particularly in high-risk areas.

- Communication channels provide management with adequate and reliable information.
- Recommendations need to be made for the establishment or enhancement of cost-effective controls to help deter fraud.

6. When an internal auditor suspects wrongdoing, the appropriate authorities within the organization should be informed. The internal auditor may recommend whatever investigation is considered necessary in the circumstances. Thereafter, the auditor should follow up to see that the internal auditing activity's responsibilities have been met.

7. Investigation of fraud consists of performing extended procedures necessary to determine whether fraud, as suggested by the indicators, has occurred. It includes gathering sufficient information about the specific details of a discovered fraud. Internal auditors, lawyers, investigators, security personnel, and other specialists from inside or outside the organization are the parties that usually conduct or participate in fraud investigations.

8. When conducting fraud investigations, internal auditors should:
    - Assess the probable level and the extent of complicity in the fraud within the organization. This can be critical to ensuring that the internal auditor avoids providing information to or obtaining misleading information from persons who may be involved.
    - Determine the knowledge, skills, and other competencies needed to carry out the investigation effectively. An assessment of the qualifications and the skills of internal auditors and of the specialists available to participate in the investigation should be performed to ensure that engagements are conducted by individuals having appropriate types and levels of technical expertise. This should include assurances on such matters as professional certifications, licenses, reputation, and the fact that there is no relationship to those being investigated or to any of the employees or management of the organization.
    - Design procedures to follow in attempting to identify the perpetrators, extent of the fraud, techniques used, and cause of the fraud.
    - Coordinate activities with management personnel, legal counsel, and other specialists as appropriate throughout the course of the investigation.
    - Be cognizant of the rights of alleged perpetrators and personnel within the scope of the investigation and the reputation of the organization itself.

9. Once a fraud investigation is concluded, internal auditors should assess the facts known in order to:

- Determine if controls need to be implemented or strengthened to reduce future vulnerability.
- Design engagement tests to help disclose the existence of similar frauds in the future.
- Help meet the internal auditor's responsibility to maintain sufficient knowledge of fraud and thereby be able to identify future indicators of fraud.

10. Reporting of fraud consists of the various oral or written, interim or final communications to management regarding the status and results of fraud investigations. The chief audit executive has the responsibility to report immediately any incident of significant fraud to senior management and the board. Sufficient investigation should take place to establish reasonable certainty that a fraud has occurred before any fraud reporting is made. A preliminary or final report may be desirable at the conclusion of the detection phase. The report should include the internal auditor's conclusion as to whether sufficient information exists to conduct a full investigation. It should also summarize observations and recommendations that serve as the basis for such decision. A written report may follow any oral briefing made to management and the board to document the findings.

11. Section 2400 of the *Standards* provides interpretations applicable to engagement communications issued as a result of fraud investigations. Additional interpretive guidance on reporting of fraud is as follows:
    - When the incidence of significant fraud has been established to a reasonable certainty, senior management and the board should be notified immediately.
    - The results of a fraud investigation may indicate that fraud has had a previously undiscovered significant adverse effect on the financial position and results of operations of an organization for one or more years on which financial statements have already been issued. Internal auditors should inform senior management and the board of such a discovery.
    - A written report or other formal communication should be issued at the conclusion of the investigation phase. It should include all observations, conclusions, recommendations, and corrective action taken.
    - A draft of the proposed final communications on fraud should be submitted to legal counsel for review. In those cases in which the internal auditor wants to invoke client privilege, consideration should be given to addressing the report to legal counsel.

12. Detection of fraud consists of identifying indicators of fraud sufficient to warrant recommending an investigation. These indicators may arise as a result of controls established by management, tests conducted by auditors, and other sources both within and outside the organization.

13. In conducting engagements, the internal auditor's responsibilities for detecting fraud are to:
    - Have sufficient knowledge of fraud to be able to identify indicators that fraud may have been committed. This knowledge includes the need to know the characteristics of fraud, the techniques used to commit fraud, and the types of frauds associated with the activities reviewed.
    - Be alert to opportunities, such as control weaknesses, that could allow fraud. If significant control weaknesses are detected, additional tests conducted by internal auditors should include tests directed toward identification of other indicators of fraud. Some examples of indicators are unauthorized transactions, override of controls, unexplained pricing exceptions, and unusually large product losses. Internal auditors should recognize that the presence of more than one indicator at any one time increases the probability that fraud may have occurred.
    - Evaluate the indicators that fraud may have been committed and decide whether any further action is necessary or whether an investigation should be recommended.
    - Notify the appropriate authorities within the organization if a determination is made that there are sufficient indicators of the commission of a fraud to recommend an investigation.
14. Internal auditors are not expected to have knowledge equivalent to that of a person whose primary responsibility is detecting and investigating fraud. Also, audit procedures alone, even when carried out with due professional care, do not guarantee that fraud will be detected.

PRACTICE ADVISORY 1210.A2-2: RESPONSIBILITY FOR FRAUD DETECTION

1. Management and the internal audit activity have differing roles with respect to fraud detection. The normal course of work for the internal audit activity is to provide an independent appraisal, examination, and evaluation of an organization's activities as a service to the organization. The objective of internal auditing in fraud detection is to assist members of the organization in the effective discharge of their responsibilities by furnishing them with analyses, appraisals, recommendations, counsel, and information concerning the activities reviewed. The engagement objective includes promoting effective control at a reasonable cost.
2. Management has a responsibility to establish and maintain an effective control system at a reasonable cost. To the degree that fraud may be present in activities covered in the normal course of work as defined above, internal auditors have a responsibility to exercise "due professional care" as specifically defined in *Standard 1220* with respect to

fraud detection. Internal auditors should have sufficient knowledge of fraud to identify the indicators that fraud may have been committed, be alert to opportunities that could allow fraud, evaluate the need for additional investigation, and notify the appropriate authorities.

3. A well-designed internal control system should not be conducive to fraud. Tests conducted by auditors, along with reasonable controls established by management, improve the likelihood that any existing fraud indicators will be detected and considered for further investigation.

1220 – Due Professional Care

Internal auditors should apply the care and skill expected of a reasonably prudent and competent internal auditor. Due professional care does not imply infallibility or extraordinary performance.

1220.A1

The internal auditor should exercise due professional care by considering the:
- Extent of work needed to achieve the engagement's objectives;
- Relative complexity, materiality or significance of matters to which assurance procedures are applied;
- Adequacy and effectiveness of risk management, control, and governance processes;
- Likelihood of material irregularities or noncompliance; and
- Cost of assurance in relation to potential benefits.

1220.A3

The internal auditor should be alert to the significant risks that might affect objectives, operations, or resources. However, assurance procedures alone, even when performed with due professional care, do not guarantee that all significant risks will be identified.

If controls do not mitigate these risks and exposures, the auditor should investigate further for the existence of fraud. If sufficient indicators of fraud are detected, internal auditors should recommend an investigation to the appropriate individuals.

2130 – Governance

The internal audit activity should assess and make appropriate recommendations for improving the organization's governance process over:
- Promoting appropriate ethics and values within the organization.

- Ensuring effective management and accountability for organizational performance.
- Effectively communicating risk and control information to appropriate areas within the organization.
- Effectively coordinating the activities of and communicating information among the board, the external and internal auditors, and management.

2130.A1

The internal auditor activity should evaluate the design, implementation, and effectiveness of the organization's ethics-related objectives, programs, and activities.

PRACTICE ADVISORY 2130-1: ROLE OF THE INTERNAL AUDIT ACTIVITY AND INTERNAL AUDITOR IN THE ETHICAL CULTURE OF AN ORGANIZATION

1. This Practice Advisory underscores the importance of organizational culture in establishing the ethical climate of an enterprise and suggests the role that internal auditors could play in improving that ethical climate. Specifically, the Practice Advisory:
   - Describes the nature of the governance process;
   - Links it to the ethical culture of the organization;
   - States that all people associated with the organization, and specifically internal auditors, should assume the role of ethics advocates; and
   - Lists the characteristics of an enhanced ethical culture.

GOVERNANCE AND ORGANIZATIONAL CULTURE

2. An organization uses various legal forms, structures, strategies, and procedures to ensure that it:
   - Complies with society's legal and regulatory rules;
   - Satisfies the generally accepted business norms, ethical precepts, and social expectations of society;
   - Provides overall benefit to society and enhances the interests of the specific stakeholders in both the long- and short-term; and
   - Reports fully and truthfully to its owners, regulators, other stakeholders, and general public to ensure accountability for its decisions, actions, conduct, and performance.

   The way in which an organization chooses to conduct its affairs to meet those four responsibilities is commonly referred to as its governance process. The organization's governing body (such as a board of directors or trustees or a managing board) and its senior management are accountable for the effectiveness of the governance process.

3. An organization's governance practices reflect a unique and ever-changing culture that affects roles, specifies behavior, sets goals and strategies, measures performance, and

defines the terms of accountability. That culture impacts the values, roles, and behavior that will be articulated and tolerated by the organization and determines how sensitive — thoughtful or indifferent — the enterprise is in meeting its responsibilities to society. Thus, how effective the overall governance process is in performing its expected function largely depends on the organization's culture.

SHARED RESPONSIBILITY FOR THE ORGANIZATION'S ETHICAL CULTURE

4. All people associated with the organization share some responsibility for the state of its ethical culture. Because of the complexity and dispersion of decision-making processes in most enterprises, each individual should be encouraged to be an ethics advocate, whether the role is delegated officially or merely conveyed informally. Codes of conduct and statements of vision and policy are important declarations of the organization's values and goals, the behavior expected of its people, and the strategies for maintaining a culture that aligns with its legal, ethical, and societal responsibilities. A growing number of organizations have designated a chief ethics officer as counselor of executives, managers, and others and as champion within the organization for "doing the right thing."

INTERNAL AUDIT ACTIVITY AS ETHICS ADVOCATE

5. Internal auditors and the internal audit activity should take an active role in support of the organization's ethical culture. They possess a high level of trust and integrity within the organization and the skills to be effective advocates of ethical conduct. They have the competence and capacity to appeal to the enterprise's leaders, managers, and other employees to comply with the legal, ethical, and societal responsibilities of the organization.

6. The internal audit activity may assume one of several different roles as an ethics advocate. Those roles include chief ethics officer (ombudsman, compliance officer, management ethics counselor, or ethics expert), member of an internal ethics council, or assessor of the organization's ethical climate. In some circumstances, the role of chief ethics officer may conflict with the independence attribute of the internal audit activity.

ASSESSMENT OF THE ORGANIZATION'S ETHICAL CLIMATE

7. At a minimum, the internal audit activity should periodically assess the state of the ethical climate of the organization and the effectiveness of its strategies, tactics, communications, and other processes in achieving the desired level of legal and ethical compliance. Internal auditors should evaluate the effectiveness of the following features of an enhanced, highly effective ethical culture:

- Formal Code of Conduct, which is clear and understandable, and related statements, policies (including procedures covering fraud and corruption), and other expressions of aspiration
- Frequent communications and demonstrations of expected ethical attitudes and behavior by the influential leaders of the organization
- Explicit strategies to support and enhance the ethical culture with regular programs to update and renew the organization's commitment to an ethical culture
- Several, easily accessible ways for people to confidentially report alleged violations of the Code, policies, and other acts of misconduct
- Regular declarations by employees, suppliers, and customers that they are aware of the requirements for ethical behavior in transacting the organization's affairs
- Clear delegation of responsibilities to ensure that ethical consequences are evaluated, confidential counseling is provided, allegations of misconduct are investigated, and case findings are properly reported
- Easy access to learning opportunities to enable all employees to be ethics advocates
- Positive personnel practices that encourage every employee to contribute to the ethical climate of the organization
- Regular surveys of employees, suppliers, and customers to determine the state of the ethical climate in the organization
- Regular reviews of the formal and informal processes within the organization that could potentially create pressures and biases that would undermine the ethical culture
- Regular reference and background checks as part of hiring procedures, including integrity tests, drug screening, and similar measures

GAO Auditing Standards

Standards for government auditors are fundamentally based on the generally accepted auditing standards set by the AICPA. However, for audits of government organizations, programs, activities, functions, and funds, the requirements of Government Auditing Standards, also known as the *Yellow Book,* go beyond the AICPA standards.

Applicability

Federal legislation requires that the federal inspectors general comply with the *Yellow Book* standards for audits of federal organizations, programs, activities, and functions. The legislation further states that the inspectors general are to ensure that nonfederal auditors comply with these standards when they audit federal organizations, programs, activities, and functions. Other federal auditors must also follow these standards. The Office of Management and Budget included these standards in OMB Circular A-73 as basic audit criteria for federal executive departments and agencies. The Chief Financial Officers Act of 1990 requires that these standards be followed in audits of federal departments and agencies.

Additionally, the Single Audit Act Amendments of 1996 require that these standards be followed in audits of state and local governments and nonprofit entities that receive federal awards. Some state and local laws and regulations may require auditors of state and local governments to comply with the standards, as well. Finally, the terms of a contract or program may require an organization to be subject to an audit under the *Yellow Book* standards.

Many auditors that are not required to follow the standards may find it useful to do so in performing audits of federal, state, and local government programs and government awards administered by contractors, nonprofit entities, and other nongovernment entities.

Roles and Responsibilities

Generally accepted government auditing standards (GAGAS), as promulgated in the *Yellow Book*, include explicit roles and responsibilities for many parties involved in the undertaking of government audits.

Management

The *Yellow Book* states that the management of an organization or program required to undergo a government audit is responsible for:

- Efficiently, economically, effectively, and legally using the organization's resources to achieve its designated purposes;
- Complying with all applicable laws and regulations;
- Establishing and maintaining an effective internal control system;
- Providing appropriate reports to oversight bodies and the public;
- Addressing the findings and recommendations of the auditors; and
- Following sound procedures when contracting for audits and attestation engagements, including establishing clear objectives and scope for the engagement.

Auditors

Under GAGAS, all auditors performing government audit engagements must:

- Observe the principles of serving the public interest and maintaining the highest degree of integrity, objectivity, and independence;

- Act in way that will serve the public interest, honor the public trust, and uphold the auditing profession;
- Make decisions that are consistent with the public interest in the organization or program under audit;
- Maintain professional, objective, fact-based, nonpartisan, and non-ideological relationships with the audited entities and the users of the auditor's reports, including being honest and candid with all parties involved and using all information gathered in a prudent manner;
- Observe both the form and spirit of all technical and ethical standards such that service and the public trust do not become subordinated to personal gain and advantage;
- Remain impartial, intellectually honest, free of conflicts of interest, and independent in both fact and appearance;
- Using professional judgment when establishing scope and methodologies of the engagement, determining the tests and procedures to be performed, conducting the work, and reporting the results; and
- Helping management and other report users understand the auditor's responsibilities under GAGAS.

Additionally, the *Yellow Book* provides that while management is responsible for addressing any audit findings and recommendations and following the status of their resolution, audit organizations are responsible for establishing follow-up policies and procedures to determine whether previous significant findings and recommendations have been addressed and should be considered in planning future audit engagements.

Types of Government Audit Engagements

The *Yellow Book* describes and promulgates standards for two types of audits that government and non-government audit organizations conduct: *financial audits* (including financial-related audits) and *performance audits*. The *Yellow Book* also contains standards covering attestation engagements, such as examinations and reviews, and other non-audit services performed on government organizations and programs.

Financial Statement Audits and Financial-Related Audits

Financial audits are defined as those audits that are "primarily concerned with providing reasonable assurance about whether financial statements are presented fairly in all material respects in conformity with generally accepted accounting principles (GAAP), or with a comprehensive basis of accounting other than GAAP." The *Yellow Book* also includes in this category those engagements for:

- Providing special reports for specified elements, accounts, or items of a financial statement;
- Reviewing interim financial information;
- Issuing letters for underwriters or other requesting parties;
- Reporting on the processing of transactions by service organizations; and
- Auditing compliance with regulations relating to federal award expenditures and other governmental financial assistance.

Performance Audits

Performance audits are described in the *Yellow Book* as audits that "provide information to improve program operations and facilitate decision making by parties with responsibility to oversee or initiate corrective action, and improve public accountability." These audits include the assessment of a wide variety of objectives, including those related to program effectiveness and results; economy and efficiency; internal control; compliance with legal or other requirements; and objectives related to providing prospective analyses, guidance, or summary information.

Audit Standards

The *Yellow Book* sets out three types of government audit standards: general standards, field work standards, and reporting standards. The general standards apply to both financial and performance audits. However, GAGAS provide a separate set of field work and reporting standards for each type of government audit.

General Standards

The general standards provide the underlying framework that is critical to properly perform audit engagements under GAGAS. The *Yellow Book* mentions that it is the responsibility of the audit organization to ensure compliance with each of these standards throughout the engagement.

INDEPENDENCE

The auditor must remain independent in both fact and appearance throughout the engagement so that all opinions, conclusions, judgments, and recommendations made by the auditor will be impartial and will be viewed as impartial by knowledgeable third parties. In determining independence, auditors must consider three types of potential impairments — personal impairments, such as family relationships and financial interests; external impairments arising from pressures from the audited organization's management or employees; and organizational impairments due to overlap in the places within the governmental structure of both the organization performing the audit and the organization being audited. If the auditor is deemed not to be independent, he or she should decline the work, or if the auditor is precluded from declining the work due to legislative or other reasons, he or she must disclose the impairment in the audit report.

PROFESSIONAL JUDGMENT

The auditor must use professional judgment in determining the scope of the engagement, the methodology to employ, the type and amount of evidence to gather, and the tests and procedures to perform. Professional judgment must also be applied in performing the tests and procedures and in reporting the results of the work. In applying professional judgment, an auditor must exercise reasonable care and diligence, and observe the principles of serving the public interest and maintaining the highest degree of integrity, objectivity, and independence. Additionally, auditors must retain an attitude of professional skepticism and should not assume that management is either inherently honest or inherently dishonest. Thus, auditors must approach the engagement with a questioning mind and a critical assessment of all evidence.

COMPETENCE

The staff assigned to an engagement must collectively possess adequate professional knowledge, skills and experience to properly conduct the audit. The necessary competence includes knowledge of applicable GAGAS; general knowledge of the organization's operating environment; skills to communicate clearly and effectively, both orally and in writing; and any specific skills appropriate to the work being performed, such as statistical sampling skills or information technology skills. In order to maintain their professional competence, all auditors performing governmental audits must meet the continuing professional education requirements under GAGAS. It is the responsibility of the audit organization to ensure that the auditors fulfill these educational requirements. Audit organizations may also need to use external or internal specialists for certain engagements to conform to the competence standard.

QUALITY CONTROL AND ASSURANCE

Audit organizations performing government audits must have an internal quality control system in place. This system is comprised of the organization's structure and its policies and procedures established to provide reasonable assurance that the organization is complying with all applicable audit standards. As part of the system, organizations should establish procedures for continuous monitoring of whether the quality control policies and procedures are effectively designed and applied. Additionally, audit organizations conducting audits under GAGAS should have an independent, external peer review of their internal quality control system at least once every three years to determine whether the system is adequately designed and effectively applied. The results of the peer review should be made available to any parties contracting for an audit, the appropriate oversight bodies, and the public.

Field Work Standards for Financial Audits

GAGAS field work standards for financial audits include the three generally accepted standards of fieldwork established by the AICPA, as well as five additional fieldwork standards. Any new AICPA standards relevant to financial statement audits are incorporated into GAGAS unless the General Accounting Office excludes them by formal announcement.

The three AICPA standards of fieldwork are as follows:
- The audit work must be adequately planned and any assistants must be properly supervised.
- The auditor must obtain a sufficient understanding of internal control to plan the audit and to determine the nature, timing, and extent of tests to be performed.
- The auditor must obtain sufficient competent evidential matter, through inspection, observation, inquiries, and confirmations, to provide a reasonable basis for issuing an opinion on the financial statements under audit.

The five additional fieldwork standards prescribed by GAGAS are as follows:
- Auditors should communicate information about the nature, timing, and extent of planned testing and the level of assurance provided by the engagement to the officials of the audited organization, the individuals contracting for or requesting the audit services, and the audit committee. This communication should specifically address the auditors' responsibilities for testing and reporting on internal control over financial reporting and on compliance with laws and regulations.
- Auditors should consider the results of previous engagements and follow up on known material findings and recommendations that directly relate to the objectives of the current audit.
- Auditors should design the audit to provide reasonable assurance of detecting material misstatements resulting from violations of contract provisions or grant agreements that have a direct and material effect on the determination of financial statements amounts. Auditors should also remain alert to situations that could indicate the existence of abuse

that significantly affects the financial statement amounts. If the auditors discover evidence of material misstatements from violations or abuse, they should apply procedures specifically designed to determine whether such violations or abuse has occurred.
- When auditors identify problems such as internal control deficiencies, fraud, illegal acts, violations of provisions of contracts or grant agreements, or abuse, they should plan audit procedures to develop an explanation of the criteria, condition, effect, and cause of the problem to facilitate developing the auditors' report.
- Audit documentation should contain sufficient information to enable an experienced auditor, having no previous connection with the audit, to ascertain from the documentation the evidence that supports the auditors' significant judgments and conclusions. The documentation should contain support for the auditors' findings, conclusions, and recommendations prior to the issuance of the auditors' report.

Reporting Standards for Financial Audits

For reporting standards for financial statement audits, GAGAS incorporates the following four AICPA generally accepted standards of reporting:

- The auditors' report must state whether the financial statements are presented in accordance with generally accepted accounting principles (GAAP).
- The auditors' report must identify any circumstances in which GAAP was not consistently applied in the current period in relation to the preceding period.
- Informative disclosures in the financial statements are considered reasonably adequate unless otherwise stated in the auditors' report.
- The auditors' report must contain either an expression of opinion regarding the financial statements, taken as a whole, or an assertion that such an opinion cannot be expressed. If an overall opinion cannot be expressed, the reasons should be stated.

GAGAS prescribe six additional reporting standards for government financial audits. They are:

- The auditors' report should specifically state that the audit was performed in accordance with GAGAS.
- The auditors' report should either (1) describe the scope of the auditors' testing of compliance with laws and regulations and internal control over financial reporting and present the results of those tests or an opinion, if sufficient work was performed, or (2) refer to separate reports containing that information. If a separate report is used, the

auditors' report should state that the separate report is an integral part of the audit and should be considered in assessing the results of the audit.
- Auditors should report (1) significant deficiencies in internal control, (2) all material instances of fraud and illegal acts, and (3) significant violations of contract provisions or grant agreements and abuse. In some situations, the auditors should report the occurrence of these problems directly to parties outside of the audited organization.
- If the auditors' report contains any disclosures regarding deficiencies in internal control, fraud, illegal acts, violations of contract provisions or grant agreements, or abuse, the report should also include the views of the organization's responsible officials concerning the findings, conclusions, and recommendations, as well as any planned corrective actions.
- If any pertinent information about the audited organization or program is prohibited by law or regulation from being disclosed to the general public, the auditors' report should state the nature of the omitted information and the reason for its omission.
- Government auditors should submit their audit reports to the appropriate officials of the audited organization, the parties requiring or arranging for the audit, officials with oversight authority for the organization, and the public unless legal or regulatory restrictions prevent it. Nongovernment auditors should distribute the report according to the agreement reached with the party contracting the audit.

Field Work Standards for Performance Audits

GAGAS has adopted the following four field work standards for conducting performance audits:
- Work must be adequately planned. This includes obtaining an understanding of the organization or program to be audited and defining, documenting, and continuously adjusting as necessary, the audit objectives, scope, and methodology. Additionally, auditors are required to:
  - Design the audit to provide reasonable assurance about compliance with laws and regulations that are significant to audit objectives.
  - Assess the risk that material fraud, abuse, significant illegal acts, or violations of contract provisions or grant agreements could occur.
  - Be alert for situations or transactions that could be indicative of fraud, abuse, or illegal acts, and if detected, extend the audit steps and procedures to determine if they have or are likely to occur and their effect on the audit results.
  - Exercise due professional care in pursuing indications of possible illegal acts so as not to interfere with potential investigations, legal proceedings, or both.

- Staff must be properly supervised.
- Sufficient, competent, and relevant evidence must be obtained to provide a reasonable basis for the auditors' findings and conclusions.
- Auditors should prepare and maintain audit documentation related to planning, conducting, and reporting on the audit. This documentation should provide sufficient information to enable an experienced auditor, having no previous connection with the audit, to ascertain the evidence that supports the auditors' significant judgments and conclusions. The documentation should contain support for the auditors' findings, conclusions, and recommendations prior to the issuance of the auditors' report.

Reporting Standards for Performance Audits

The *Yellow Book* contains four reporting standards for performance audit engagements:

- Auditors should prepare audit reports communicating the results of each audit. The report should be written or in some other retrievable form, and should be appropriate for its intended use.
- The auditors' report should contain:
  - the audit objectives, scope, and methodology;
  - the audit results, including findings, conclusions, and recommendations;
  - a reference to compliance with GAGAS;
  - the views of responsible officials; and
  - the nature of any privileged and confidential information omitted, if applicable.
- The reported findings should include any significant deficiencies in internal control, all material instances of fraud and illegal acts, significant violations of provisions of contracts or grant agreements, and significant abuse.
- The auditors' report should be timely, complete, accurate, objective, convincing, clear, and as concise as the subject of the audit permits.
- Government auditors should submit their audit reports to the appropriate officials of the audited organization, the parties requiring or arranging for the audit, officials with oversight authority for the organization, and the public unless legal or regulatory restrictions prevent it. Nongovernment auditors should distribute the report according to the agreement reached with the party contracting the audit.

In addition to these standards, auditors should refer to *SAS No. 74 (AU 801) - Compliance Auditing Applicable to Governmental Entities and Other Recipients of Governmental Financial Assistance* that superseded SAS Nos. 63 and 68. This standard incorporates a discussion of responsibilities under certain laws and government bulletins, and auditors should know these requirements. A thorough review of this statement will provide additional guidance.

More information about *The Yellow Book* and government auditing is contained in the chapter on "Public Sector Fraud." The full text of all of the Government Auditing Standards is also available at the Government Accountability Office's website (www.gao.gov).

Sarbanes-Oxley Act of 2002

On July 30, 2002, President Bush signed the Sarbanes-Oxley Act. This law significantly changes the laws of corporate governance and the rules and regulations under which accounting firms and corporations must operate. Additionally, certain provisions considerably increase the responsibilities of management and the accounting profession with regard to fraud. Since the enactment of Sarbanes-Oxley, the Securities and Exchange Commission (SEC) has issued numerous SEC Releases that support and expand the Act's requirements. Below is a summary of some of the most important provisions of Sarbanes-Oxley and the corresponding SEC Releases that relate to fraud detection and prevention. More information about Sarbanes-Oxley can be found in the chapter on "The Law Related to Fraud" in the Law Section of the *Manual*.

Public Company Accounting Oversight Board

Moving to a different private sector regulatory structure, the new Public Company Accounting Oversight Board (PCAOB) will be appointed and overseen by the SEC. The PCAOB, made up of five full-time members, will establish auditing, quality control, and independence standards, and sanction both firms and individuals for violations of laws, regulations, and rules.

Additionally, Section 104 of the Act requires the PCAOB to conduct quality reviews of public accounting firms to assess the firm's level of compliance with all laws, regulations, and professional standards during the performance of audits. Accounting firms that audit more than 100 public companies are subject to these inspections annually. Firms that audit between one and 100 public companies must undergo a quality inspection once every three years. These regular inspections will include a review of selected audit and review engagements performed by different employees and at different locations of the firm and an evaluation of the sufficiency, documentation, and communication of the firm's quality control system. The PCAOB also has the authorization to conduct special inspections regarding specific issues whenever it, or the SEC, deems such an inspection necessary. At the conclusion of the inspection, the PCOAB must make a draft report available to the firm for review and response. Thereafter, a final report must be issued, made available to the firm for review, and transmitted to the SEC and each appropriate state regulatory agency. The accounting firm then has 12 months to prove to the PCAOB that it has sufficiently addressed any deficiencies identified during the inspection. Those defects that are not satisfactorily corrected within 12 months will be made known to the public. If during an inspection the PCAOB discovers a violation of laws, rules, or professional standards, it has the option to report the violation to appropriate regulatory authorities or to conduct its own investigation.

Officers and Directors

The Act includes several new responsibilities for the officers and directors of public companies.

Certification Obligations

The Chief Executive Officer and Chief Financial Officer of public companies must personally certify annual and quarterly SEC filings.

Section 302 of the Act requires that the CEO and CFO personally certify the following:
- They have personally reviewed the report;
- Based on their knowledge, the report does not contain any material misstatement that would render the report misleading;
- Based on their knowledge the financial statements and information in the report fairly presents in all material respects the financial condition and results of operations of the company;
- They are responsible for establishing and maintaining internal controls and have designed such controls to ensure that material information relating to the company and its consolidated subsidiaries is made known to them; they have evaluated the effectiveness of internal controls within 90 days prior to the report; and they have presented their conclusions about the effectiveness of those controls in the report;
- They have disclosed to their auditors and the audit committee any significant deficiencies in the controls that could adversely affect the company's ability to record, process, summarize, and report financial data and they have identified for their auditors any material weaknesses in internal controls. Further, they have disclosed to their auditors any fraud, whether material or not, that involves management or other employees who have a significant role in the company's internal controls; and

- They have indicated in their report whether there have been significant changes in the company's internal controls since the filing of the last report including any corrective actions with respect to previously identified significant deficiencies and material weaknesses.

Internal Controls

Under Section 404 of the Act, SEC Release Nos. 33-8238 and 34-47986, and PCAOB Auditing Standard No. 2, management's responsibility pertaining to the company's internal control over financial reporting has been increased substantially.

DEFINING INTERNAL CONTROL

Internal control over financial reporting (ICOFR) is defined as:

"A process designed ... to provide reasonable assurance regarding the reliability of financial reporting and the preparation of financial statements for external purposes in accordance with generally accepted accounting principles..."

Additionally, ICOFR is deemed to include all policies and procedures that:
- *"Pertain to the maintenance of records that in reasonable detail accurately and fairly reflect the transactions and dispositions of the assets of the [company];*
- *Provide reasonable assurance that transactions are recorded as necessary to permit preparation of financial statements in accordance with generally accepted accounting principles, and that receipts and expenditures of the [company] are being made only in accordance with authorizations of management and directors of the [company]; and*
- *Provide reasonable assurance regarding prevention or timely detection of unauthorized acquisition, use or disposition of the [company's] assets that could have a material effect on the financial statements."*

Examples of internal controls covered by Section 404 and the related Releases and Standard include, but are not limited to:
- Controls over initiating, authorizing, recording, processing, reconciling, and reporting significant account balances, transactions, and disclosures included in the financial statements
- Controls related to the prevention, identification, and detection of fraud
- Controls related to initiating and processing of non-routing and non-systematic transactions
- Controls related to the selection and application of appropriate accounting policies

MANAGEMENT'S REPORT ON INTERNAL CONTROL

The provisions of Section 404 require management to acknowledge its responsibility for the ICOFR of the company and to assess the operating effectiveness of those controls. As a result, public companies must issue an additional internal control report within their annual report containing:

- A statement of management's responsibility for establishing and maintaining adequate ICOFR;
- A statement identifying the framework that management used in conducting the assessment of the effectiveness of the company's ICOFR;
- Management's assessment of the effectiveness of the company's ICOFR as of the end of the company's most recent fiscal year, including disclosure of any material weaknesses identified in the company's ICOFR and an explicit statement as to whether the or not the ICOFR is effective; and
- A statement that the company's independent auditor has issued an attestation report covering management's assessment of the company's ICOFR. The auditor's attestation report must also be filed with the annual report.

MANAGEMENT'S ASSESSMENT OF INTERNAL CONTROL

In performing the ICOFR assessment, management must choose a suitable internal control framework against which to evaluate the design and effectiveness of the company's ICOFR. The most commonly used model in the United States is the Internal Control — Integrated Framework established by the Committee of Sponsoring Organizations ("COSO") of the Treadway Commission, which provides five components of effective internal controls:

- Control Environment
- Control Activities
- Risk Assessment
- Information and Communication
- Monitoring

The COSO framework is discussed in more detail in the "Fraud Prevention" chapter of the Criminology section of the manual. Further detail on the Internal Control — Integrated Framework is also available at the COSO website (http://www.coso.org).

Additionally, management must:
- Determine which internal controls to test in performing the assessment, considering the significance of each control, both individually and in the aggregate;

- Evaluate whether the failure of a control could result in a misstatement to the financial statements, the likelihood and magnitude of any resulting misstatement, and whether other controls are in place to mitigate this occurrence;
- Determine which locations or business units to include in the assessment, if applicable;
- Evaluate the design and operating effectiveness of the internal controls using the internal control framework chosen as a guide;
- Evaluate the probability of occurrence and the size of potential misstatements resulting from the internal control deficiencies identified and determine whether they, either individually or in the aggregate, constitute material weaknesses (any deficiency where the likelihood of potential misstatement is more than remote) or significant deficiencies (any deficiency where the likelihood of potential misstatement is more than remote and the magnitude is more than inconsequential);
- Provide sufficient documentation to support the assessment of ICOFR, including documenting the design of the internal controls and the results of management's testing and evaluation; and
- Communicate the assessment findings to the independent auditor and any other applicable parties.

Recognizing that each company differs with regard to internal control structure, the rules state that the nature of the testing performed by management will depend on the specific circumstances of the company and the significance of the control being tested. However, the rules also assert that inquiries alone are generally not a sufficient basis for management's assessment.

Code of Ethics

As required by Section 406 of the Act and SEC Release No. 33-8177, public companies must disclose in their annual report whether they have adopted a code of ethics for senior financial officers, and if they have not, they must explain their reasoning.

DEFINING "CODE OF ETHICS"

The rules define a "code of ethics" as a set of written standards that are designed to deter wrongdoing and to promote:
- Honest and ethical conduct, including the ethical treatment of actual or apparent conflicts of interest between personal and professional interests;
- Full, fair, accurate, timely, and understandable disclosure in all documents filed with the SEC and all other public communications;

- Compliance with all applicable governmental laws, rules, and regulations;
- The prompt reporting to the appropriate person or persons within the company of violations of the code; and
- Accountability for adherence to the code.

The SEC believes that the establishment of provisions beyond this definitional outline is best left to the discretion of the company. Therefore, the rules do not specify any detailed requirements, particular language, compliance procedures, or sanctions for violations that must be included in the code of ethics. The SEC does, however, explicitly encourage the adoption of codes that are broader and more comprehensive than necessary to meet the new disclosure requirements.

SENIOR FINANCIAL OFFICERS

The senior financial officers that must be covered by the company's code of ethics include the principal executive officer, principal financial officer, principal accounting officer or controller, and persons performing similar functions. While the rules state that a company must have a specialized code of ethics that applies to senior financial officers, the company does not need to adopt a separate code of ethics for these officers. However, if it does not, the company's general code of ethics should expressly state that it applies to all senior financial officers.

DISCLOSURE REQUIREMENTS

In addition to the disclosure of the existence of the code of ethics in the annual report, the rules require that companies make publicly available the portions of their code of ethics that address the ethical considerations contained within the definition of "code of ethics" and that apply to the senior financial officers. To do so, the SEC permits companies to employ one of three alternative methods:

- Filing the code of ethics that applies to the senior financial officers as an exhibit in the company's annual report;
- Posting the code of ethics that is relevant to the senior financial officers on its website, and disclosing the Internet address and the fact that the code is posted in this manner within the annual report; or
- Providing a copy of the code of ethics to any person upon request, and without charge, provided the annual report contains an undertaking to do so and an explanation of how a person can make such a request.

Public companies must also make known, either on a Form 8-K or on their website, any changes in and any waivers of the code of ethics relating to the senior financial officers. The nature of the change or waiver must be disclosed within five business days of its occurrence and, if disclosed on a website, must remain posted for 12 months.

EXAMPLES OF CODES OF ETHICS

The following are some examples of organizations that have adopted codes of ethics that meet the SEC's guidelines. Additionally, the ACFE's sample code of ethics is contained in the "Fraud Prevention" chapter in the criminology section.
- FEI (http://www.fei.org/about/ethics.cfm)
- Exxon Mobil (http://www.exxonmobil.com/corporate/files/corporate/ExxonMobilAR2003.pdf)
- Neiman Marcus
- (http://media.corporate-ir.net/media_files/nys/nmg.a/reports/nmg_coefp.pdf)
- McDonald's (http://www.mcdonalds.com/corp/invest/gov/officer_ethics.html)
- Safeway, Inc. (http://media.corporate-ir.net/media_files/IROL/64/64607/governance/CodeofConductSrOffrsFinal.pdf)

Audit Committee

The audit committee of a company is a committee established by the board of directors for the purpose of overseeing the accounting, financial reporting, and auditing processes. Sections 301 and 407 of the Act and SEC Release Nos. 33-8177, 33-8220, 34-47235, and 34-47654 set out specific requirements for audit committees of public companies.

Composition of the Audit Committee
INDEPENDENCE

Each member of the audit committee must be a member of the board of directors and must be "independent," as evaluated by two criteria:
- Fees - Audit committee members may only be compensated for their services on the board and any board committee. They cannot be paid by the company, or any of its subsidiaries, for any other consulting or advisory work, including indirect payments made by the company to a party related to the committee member. Audit committee members may receive any fixed retirement benefits they are entitled to for prior service with the company without violating this provision, as long as the benefits are not contingent upon the member's continued service.

- Affiliation - Audit committee members cannot be "affiliated persons" of the company or any other company related to it. This precludes executive officers, director/employees, general partners, and managing members of the company, or its parent, subsidiary, or sister company, from serving on the audit committee. There is a safe harbor provision that excludes members from being considered an affiliated person as long as they are not an executive officer of the company or any of its subsidiaries, and they are not a shareholder of 10% or more of any class of voting stock of the company or any of its subsidiaries.

The SEC permits three exemptions from the independence standards. The first provides a one-year phase in period for public non-investment companies, whereby there must be at least one fully independent member when the company goes public, a majority of independent members within 90 days, and a fully independent committee within one year. The second exemption allows a committee member to simultaneously sit on the board of directors of the company and of an affiliated company (i.e. a parent, subsidiary, or sister company) without being considered an affiliated person, provided the member otherwise meets the independence criteria. The final exemption exists to provide a number of accommodations for "foreign private issuers", or listed companies that are incorporated outside of the United States. The SEC has stated that beyond these three exemptions, no additional exemptions will be granted, nor will it consider exemptions or waivers for particular relationships on a case-by-case basis.

FINANCIAL EXPERT

The board of directors must include a disclosure in the company's annual report stating whether or not there is at least one member of its audit committee that qualifies as an "audit committee financial expert". If there is, the company must also include the name of the expert, and whether the expert is independent from management. If there is not, an explanation must be given as to why the committee does not have such an expert. Additionally, the board is permitted, but not required, to disclose that it has more than one audit committee financial expert on its audit committee.

To qualify as an "audit committee financial expert", an individual must possess:
- An understanding of generally accepted accounting principles and of financial statements;
- The ability to evaluate the application of accounting principles used in the accounting for estimates, accruals, and reserves;

- Experience in preparing, auditing, analyzing, or evaluating financial statements containing accounting issues that are "generally comparable" to those expected to be raised in the company's financial statements, or experience supervising someone engaged in such activities;
- An understanding of internal controls and financial reporting procedures; and
- An understanding of the functions of an audit committee.

The rules state that the audit committee financial expert must have acquired these attributes through education and experience from serving as or actively supervising a principal financial officer, principal accounting officer, controller, public accountant or auditor, or other similar position, or through the oversight or assessment of companies or public accountants regarding the preparation, audit, or evaluation of financial statements. The SEC also recognizes that individuals that do not meet any of these requirements but have "other relevant experience" may qualify as an audit committee financial expert. However, any board of directors that qualifies an expert under this category are required to provide a brief listing of that person's experience with the disclosure in the annual report.

In determining whether an individual qualifies as an audit committee financial expert, the board of directors should consider all relevant facts and circumstances including, but not limited to, certain qualitative factors such as the level of the person's accounting or financial education, whether the person is a CPA, whether the person has previously served as a CFO or controller of a public company, the person's past or current membership on other audit committees, and any other relevant qualifications or experience that would assist in understanding and evaluating the company's financial statements. The SEC emphasizes that such factors are merely examples and should be considered only as part of an evaluation of the person's knowledge and experience as a whole.

To dissuade hesitancy to serve as an audit committee financial expert, the SEC has expressly stated that the duties, obligations, and liability of the member serving as the expert are no greater than the duties, obligations, and liability of all other members of the audit committee. Similarly, the designation of an audit committee member as a financial expert does not change the duties, obligations, or liability of any other board or audit committee members.

Responsibilities Relating to External Auditors
The audit committee has sole responsibility for hiring, paying, retaining, overseeing, and, if necessary, firing the company's outside auditors, as well as the ultimate authority to approve all audit engagement fees and terms. As a result, the external auditors must report directly to

the audit committee. The committee is also charged with resolving any disputes that arise between the external auditors and management regarding financial reporting issues.

All audit and permitted non-audit services, other than *de minimis* services, provided by the external auditor must be pre-approved by the audit committee. The audit committee can accomplish this either by approving all services separately prior to each engagement or by establishing a detailed set of pre-approval policies and procedures covering all engagements, as long as the audit committee is informed on a timely basis of each service and the responsibility of pre-approval can not be shifted to management. If the committee chooses to implement a set of pre-approval policies and procedures, then either a clear description or copy of those policies and procedures must be included with the company's proxy statement.

Procedures for Handling Complaints

The audit committee is required to establish procedures (such as a hotline) for receiving, retaining, and dealing with complaints, including confidential or anonymous employee tips, regarding irregularities in the company's accounting methods, internal controls, or auditing matters.

The SEC does not require any specific procedures for handling complaints, but rather allows the audit committee to determine the most appropriate procedures for the company's circumstances. Included in this flexibility is the ability of the audit committee to defer the receipt and screening of the complaints to another party, such as a messaging service. However, when complaints are received by a party outside of the audit committee, the procedures should dictate that the tips are ultimately directed to the audit committee for resolution. Further, the procedures should be designed such that management is not exclusively responsible for receiving and screening the complaints, to prevent unscrupulous managers from mishandling complaints or retaliating against employee complainants. Ultimately, the enactment of formal procedures should encourage the disclosure of concerns and promote proper conduct throughout the organization. The established procedures should also allow the audit committee to be alerted to potential problems before serious consequences arise.

Authority to Engage Outside Advisors

In certain situations, audit committees may want to consult experts other than those hired by management, especially when faced with possible conflicts of management interests. The rules provide that audit committees are allowed to engage any outside advisors, such as experts in specific accounting issues, that may be necessary to properly carry out their duties.

Funding

The audit committee is entitled to receive appropriate funding from the company for:

- Fees paid to the external auditors for performance of any audit, review or attestation engagements;
- Payments to any outside advisors retained by the audit committee; and
- Any administrative expenses necessary for the audit committee to carry out its duties.

External Auditors

Reports to the Audit Committee

Auditors must report directly to the audit committee – not management – and must make timely reports on the following:

- All critical accounting policies and practices used;
- Alternative GAAP methods that were discussed with management, the ramifications of the use of those alternative treatments, and the treatment preferred by the auditors; and
- Any other material written communications between the auditors and management, such as any management letter or the schedule of unadjusted audit differences.

Report over Internal Controls

Auditors must also now attest to and issue a report on management's assessment of internal controls over financial reporting under Section 404 of Sarbanes-Oxley. This requirement is covered in more detail in the section on External Auditors' Responsibilities, PCAOB Audit Standard No. 2.

Whistleblower Protection

In addition to requiring the audit committee to establish procedures to handle employee tips and complaints, the Sarbanes-Oxley Act includes two provisions that create broad protections for corporate whistleblowers.

Civil Liability

Section 806 creates a civil liability for an employer who, out of retaliation, fires, demotes, suspends, threatens, harasses, or discriminates against an employee who provided information or otherwise assisted in an investigation of fraudulent activity. Employees are also protected against retaliation for filing, testifying, participating, or otherwise assisting in a proceeding filed or about to be filed relating to an alleged violation of securities laws and regulations. Employees that were retaliated against in such a manner are entitled to compensatory damages under Section 806, including reinstatement with back pay and interest and compensation for legal fees. It should be noted, however, that this provision does not provide protection to all whistleblowers as it only covers employees of publicly traded companies.

Criminal Sanctions

Section 1107 of the Act establishes criminal sanctions for anyone who intentionally retaliates against another party for providing information regarding an alleged Federal offense to a law enforcement officer. Punishments for violating the provision include fines of up to $250,000 and up to 10 years in prison for individuals and fines of up to $500,000 for corporations. Unlike the civil liability, the protection provided under Section 1107 applies to all individuals, regardless of where they work.

The whistleblower protection provisions are discussed in more detail in the "Law Related to Fraud" chapter of the Law section of the manual.

Civil and Criminal Penalties for Noncompliance

Depending on which particular provision of Sarbanes-Oxley is violated, the penalties can be severe. In addition to creating new criminal offenses (such as the whistleblower retaliation crime discussed above), it increases the jail term for existing crimes such as mail fraud and wire fraud from five to twenty years. It also makes it a crime to destroy documents and requires auditors of public companies to keep work papers for at least five years.

The Act also authorizes the SEC to freeze questioned assets during an investigation and allows courts to order the disgorgement of any bonuses received by a CEO or CFO resulting from the company having to restate its financials due to misconduct.

Private Securities Litigation Reform Act

The Private Securities Litigation Reform Act of 1995 drastically changed the procedures and proof required in securities fraud cases. It also included new responsibilities for independent auditors of public companies. Under the Act, each audit of the financial statements of a public company must include the following:

- Procedures designed to provide reasonable assurance of detecting illegal acts that would have a direct and material effect on the determination of financial statement amounts.
- Procedures designed to identify related-party transactions that are material to the financial statements or otherwise require disclosure therein.
- An evaluation of whether there is substantial doubt about the ability of the issuer to continue as a going concern during the ensuing fiscal year.

The term *illegal act* is defined to mean any act or omission "that violates any law, rule, or regulation having the force of law."

Additionally, if in the course of an audit, an auditor "detects or otherwise becomes aware that an illegal act (whether or not perceived to have a material effect on the financial statements of the issuer) has or might have occurred," the auditor must then:

- Determine whether it is likely that an illegal act has occurred, and if so
- Determine and consider the possible effect of the illegal act on the financial statements of the company, including any contingent monetary effects such as fines, penalties, and damages, and
- Inform the appropriate level of management "as soon as practicable," and assure that the audit committee (or the board of directors in the absence of an audit committee) is adequately informed of the illegal acts that have been detected unless such acts are "clearly inconsequential."

The Reform Act provides further that the auditor must take notice of what, if any, action is taken by the company in response. If the auditor concludes that the illegal act has a material effect on the financial statements of the company, the auditor must then determine:

- Whether senior management has taken "timely and appropriate remedial actions," and
- Whether the failure to take remedial action is "reasonably expected to warrant departure from a standard report of the auditor, when made, or warrant resignation from the audit engagement."

If the answer to these questions is "yes," then the auditor must report his/her conclusions to the board of directors. If the board receives such a report, the board is then required to notify the SEC within one business day and send a copy of the SEC notice to the auditor. If the auditor does not receive a copy of this notice before the one-day deadline, then the auditor is required to furnish the SEC with a copy of his/her report to the board.

The auditor is provided with some protection, however. The Act expressly provides that the auditor cannot be liable in a private action for any statements contained in the auditor's report to the SEC.

FINANCIAL STATEMENT SCHEMES

Financial statement schemes are one of a large category of frauds that fall under the heading of *Occupational Fraud and Abuse*, which is defined as "the use of one's occupation for personal enrichment through the deliberate misuse or misapplication of the employing organization's resources or assets." Simply stated, occupational frauds are those in which an employee, manager, officer, or owner of an organization commits fraud to the detriment of that organization. The three major types of occupational fraud are: Corruption, Asset Misappropriation, and Fraudulent Statements (which include financial statement schemes). The complete classification of Occupational Fraud is shown below:

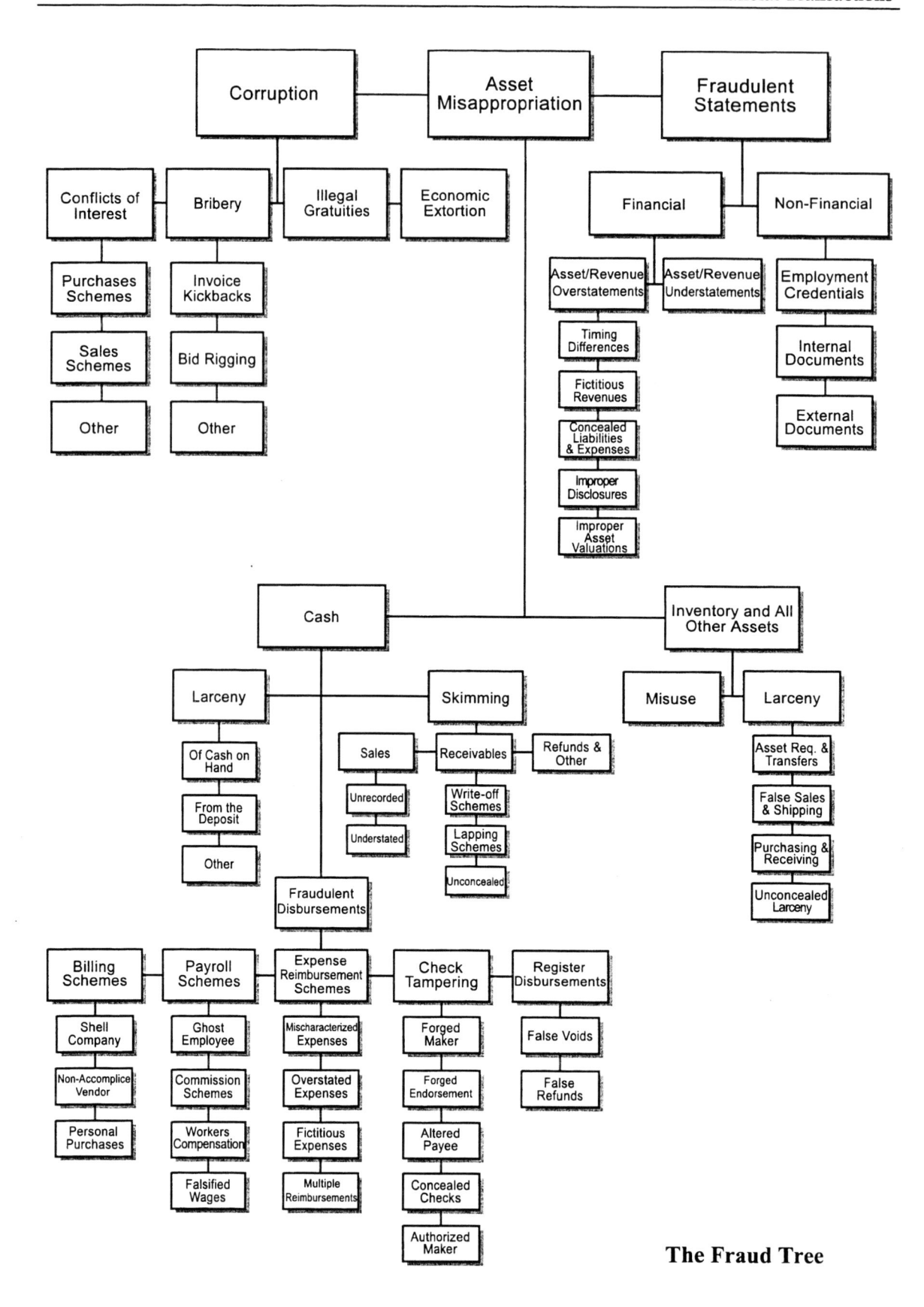

Financial Statement Schemes / Financial Transactions

The Fraud Tree

- **Corruption**
  - Conflicts of Interest
    - Purchases Schemes
    - Sales Schemes
    - Other
  - Bribery
    - Invoice Kickbacks
    - Bid Rigging
    - Other
  - Illegal Gratuities
  - Economic Extortion

- **Asset Misappropriation**
  - Cash
    - Larceny
      - Of Cash on Hand
      - From the Deposit
      - Other
    - Skimming
      - Sales
        - Unrecorded
        - Understated
      - Receivables
        - Write-off Schemes
        - Lapping Schemes
        - Unconcealed
      - Refunds & Other
    - Fraudulent Disbursements
      - Billing Schemes
        - Shell Company
        - Non-Accomplice Vendor
        - Personal Purchases
      - Payroll Schemes
        - Ghost Employee
        - Commission Schemes
        - Workers Compensation
        - Falsified Wages
      - Expense Reimbursement Schemes
        - Mischaracterized Expenses
        - Overstated Expenses
        - Fictitious Expenses
        - Multiple Reimbursements
      - Check Tampering
        - Forged Maker
        - Forged Endorsement
        - Altered Payee
        - Concealed Checks
        - Authorized Maker
      - Register Disbursements
        - False Voids
        - False Refunds
  - Inventory and All Other Assets
    - Misuse
    - Larceny
      - Asset Req. & Transfers
      - False Sales & Shipping
      - Purchasing & Receiving
      - Unconcealed Larceny

- **Fraudulent Statements**
  - Financial
    - Asset/Revenue Overstatements
      - Timing Differences
      - Fictitious Revenues
      - Concealed Liabilities & Expenses
      - Improper Disclosures
      - Improper Asset Valuations
    - Asset/Revenue Understatements
  - Non-Financial
    - Employment Credentials
      - Internal Documents
      - External Documents

What is Financial Statement Fraud?

Financial statement fraud is the *deliberate misrepresentation* of the financial condition of an enterprise accomplished through the *intentional misstatement* or *omission* of amounts or disclosures in the financial statements to *deceive* financial statement users.

Financial statement fraud is usually a means to an end rather than an end in itself. When people "cook the books" they may be doing it to "buy more time" to quietly fix business problems that prevent their company from achieving its expected earnings or complying with loan covenants. It may also be done to obtain or renew financing that would not be granted, or would be smaller, if honest financial statements were provided. People intent on profiting from crime may commit financial statement fraud to obtain loans they can then siphon off for personal gain or to inflate the price of the company's shares, allowing them to sell their holdings or exercise stock options at a profit. However, in many past cases of financial statement fraud, the perpetrators have gained little or nothing personally in financial terms. Instead the focus appears to have been preserving their status as leaders of the organization — a status that might have been lost had the real financial results been published promptly.

Financial statement fraud usually involves overstating assets, revenues and profits and understating liabilities, expenses and losses. However, the overall objective of the manipulation may sometimes require the opposite action, e.g., concealing over-budget results in a good year in order to help the subsequent year that is expected to be tougher.

The Cost of Financial Statement Fraud

Financial statement fraud typically has a devastating impact on the reputation and the financial position of organizations and people involved. The stock market capitalization of companies affected by financial statement fraud may fall substantially almost overnight, losing billions of dollars for investors. A 2002 report by the United States General Accounting Office (GAO-03-138) found that in the three trading days surrounding the initial announcement of a restatement, the companies studied lost $100 billion in market capitalization. According to a 1999 study by the Committee of Sponsoring Organizations of the Treadway Commission (COSO), *Fraudulent Financial Reporting: 1987-1997, An Analysis of U.S. Public Companies,* 51% of the companies studied ended up in bankruptcy or experienced an ownership change.

Many jobs may be lost as companies restructure to try to restore profitability. As media interviews of former Enron employees showed, financial statement fraud can exert a high toll on the well-being of employees, who may lose their jobs, their pensions, their savings invested in their employer's stock, and health care and other benefits. The company's auditors are likely to be sued for the amount of investors' losses, which these days may mean tens of billions of dollars for large public companies. For large and small companies alike, financial statement fraud can be hugely costly and potentially a corporate deathblow.

Why Financial Statement Fraud is Committed

There are a number of reasons why individuals commit financial statement fraud. Most commonly, financial fraud is used to make a company's earnings look better on paper. It sometimes covers up the embezzlement of company funds. Financial fraud occurs through a variety of methods, such as valuation judgments and fine points of timing the recording of transactions. These more subtle types of fraud often are dismissed as either mistakes or errors in judgment and estimation. Some of the more common reasons why people commit financial statement fraud include:

- To encourage investment through the sale of stock
- To demonstrate increased earnings per share or partnership profits interest, thus allowing increased dividend/distribution payouts
- To cover inability to generate cash flow
- To dispel negative market perceptions
- To obtain financing, or to obtain more favorable terms on existing financing
- To receive higher purchase prices for acquisitions
- To demonstrate compliance with financing covenants
- To meet company goals and objectives
- To receive performance-related bonuses

However, in government contracts, just the opposite may be true:
- Assets and revenues are understated
- Liabilities and expenses are overstated

Why? As explained by government auditors, entities may rely on understated revenues or overstated expenses to get more money for a project or contract.

This limited list of reasons shows that the motivation for financial fraud does not always involve personal gain. Sometimes, the cause of fraudulent financial reporting is the combination of situational pressures on either the company or the manager and the opportunity to commit the fraud without the perception of being detected. These pressures are known as "red flags." That is to say, if red flags (situational pressures and opportunity) are present, then the risk of financial reporting fraud increases significantly.

Examples of situational pressures include:
- Sudden decreases in revenue or market share experienced by a company or an industry
- Unrealistic budget pressures, particularly for short-term results (the pressures become even greater with arbitrarily established budgets that are without reference to current conditions)
- Financial pressures resulting from bonus plans that depend on short-term economic performance (these pressures are particularly acute if the bonus is a significant component of the individual's total compensation)

Opportunities to commit fraud most often arise gradually. Generally, these opportunities can stem from the lack of adequate oversight functions within the company. The existence of an oversight function does not, in and of itself, guarantee the detection of fraudulent acts; the oversight functions also must respond effectively. The perception of detection, not internal control per se, is arguably the strongest deterrent to fraud.

Some of the more obvious opportunities for the existence of fraud are:
- The absence of, or improper oversights by, the board of directors or audit committee; or, the neglectful behavior of the board or committee
- Weak or nonexistent internal controls, including an ineffective internal audit staff and a lack of external audits
- Unusual or complex transactions (an understanding of the transactions, their component parts, and their impact on financial statements is paramount to fraud deterrence)
- Financial estimates that require significant subjective judgment by management

The COSO Study on Financial Statement Fraud

In 1999, the United States Committee of Sponsoring Organizations for the Treadway Commission (COSO) published a follow-up study to its 1987 report. The report, entitled *Fraudulent Financial Reporting: 1987-1997, An Analysis of U.S. Public Companies*, examined a random sample of 204 financial statement fraud cases that were the subject of SEC enforcement.

Among the highlights of the report are the following:
- The most common methods used to misstate financial statement fraud were improper revenue recognition, overstatement of assets, and the understatement of expenses, in that order. With respect to revenue frauds, recording fictitious revenues was the most common and recording revenues prematurely was the second most common. With respect to overstating assets, overstating existing assets was most common, recording fictitious assets or assets not owned was second most common, and capitalizing items that should have been expensed was third most common.
- The assets most often misstated were accounts receivable, inventory, property, plant and equipment, loans/notes receivable, cash, investments, patents, and natural resources, in that order.
- The mean cumulative financial statement misstatement was $25 million while the median cumulative misstatement was $4.1 million; however, the mean was disproportionally increased by several very large frauds.
- The Chief Executive Officer (CEO) was the person most often named as the perpetrator (72% of cases). Other positions, in descending order, were Chief Financial Officer (CFO), Controller, Chief Operating Officer, other Vice Presidents, members of the Board of Directors, and lower level personnel. In 29% of the cases, the external auditor was also named in the enforcement action.
- Most companies either had no audit committee or a committee that met less than twice per year.
- The boards of directors were generally insiders or "gray" directors (outsiders with special ties to the company or management) with significant equity ownership and apparently little experience. In nearly 40% of the companies, the proxy provided evidence of family relationships among the officers and/or directors. The founder was on the board or the original CEO/President was still in place in nearly half of the companies. In nearly 20%, there was evidence of officers holding incompatible job functions such as CEO and CFO.
- Pressures of financial strain or distress may have been an incentive for some companies to commit fraud. The lowest quartile of companies indicate that they were in a net loss position, and the median company had a net income of only $175,000 in the year preceding the first year of the fraud period. Some companies were experiencing downward trends in net income in the preceding periods, while others were experiencing

upward trends. This means that some companies may have committed fraud to reverse a downward spiral or to preserve an upward trend for others.
- The majority of companies were relatively small. The typical size ranged well below $100 million in total assets. Seventy-eight percent were not listed on the New York or American Stock Exchanges.
- Most frauds were not isolated to a single period. Most overlapped at least two fiscal periods. The average fraud period extended over 23.7 months. Only 14% of the sample companies engaged in fraud fewer than 12 months.

The report also gives some excellent advice to auditors on what they can do to prevent such frauds. Among the recommendations are the following:
- The relatively small size of the companies suggests they may be unwilling or unable to implement cost-effective internal controls. Auditors need to challenge management to ensure that a baseline of internal control is present.
- Given that some companies experienced financial strain the periods preceding the fraud, auditors need to monitor an organization's going-concern status, especially with new clients.
- Because frauds so often run over many reporting periods, auditors need to consider interim reviews of quarterly financial statements as well as the possible benefits of continuous auditing strategies.
- Auditors need to consider and test internal controls related to transaction cutoff and asset valuation. They should design testing procedures to reduce audit risks to an acceptable level. Procedures affecting transaction cut-off, transaction terms, and account valuation for end-of-period accounts and transactions may be particularly pertinent.
- Companies with weak boards and audit committees present an audit challenge. Auditors should assess the substance and quality of client boards and be alert for boards dominated by insiders or others with strong ties to the company or its management.

Effect of Fraud on Financial Statements

Fraud in financial statements typically takes the form of:
- Overstated Assets or Revenue
- Understated Liabilities and Expenses

Overstating assets and revenues falsely reflects a financially stronger company by inclusion of fictitious asset costs or artificial revenues. Understated liabilities and expenses are shown through exclusion of costs or financial obligations. Both methods result in increased equity and net worth for the company. This overstatement and/or understatement results in increased earnings per share or partnership profit interests or a more stable picture of the company's true situation.

To demonstrate these over/understatements, the schemes typically used have been divided into five classes. Because the maintenance of financial records involves a double-entry system, fraudulent accounting entries always affect at least two accounts and, therefore, at least two categories on the financial statements. While the areas described below reflect their financial statement classifications, keep in mind that the other side of the fraudulent transaction exists elsewhere. It is common for schemes to involve a combination of several methods. The five classifications of financial statement schemes are:
- Fictitious Revenues
- Timing Differences
- Improper Asset Valuations
- Concealed Liabilities and Expenses
- Improper Disclosures

Fictitious Revenues

Fictitious or fabricated revenues involve the recording of goods or services sales that did not occur. Fictitious sales most often involve fake or phantom customers, but can also involve legitimate customers. For example, a fictitious invoice can be prepared (but not mailed) for a legitimate customer although the goods are not delivered or the services are not rendered. At the beginning of the next accounting period, the sale might be reversed to help conceal the fraud, but this may lead to a revenue shortfall in the new period, creating the need for more fictitious sales. Another method is to use legitimate customers and artificially inflate or alter invoices reflecting higher amounts or quantities than actually sold.

In December 1999, the Securities and Exchange Commission issued Staff Accounting Bulletin No. 101, *Revenue Recognition in Financial Statements* (SAB 101) to give additional guidance on revenue recognition and to rein in some of the inappropriate practices that had been observed. SAB 101 indicates that revenue generally is realized or realizable and earned when all of the following criteria are met:
- Persuasive evidence of an arrangement exists;
- Delivery has occurred or services have been rendered;
- The seller's price to the buyer is fixed or determinable; and
- Collectibility is reasonably assured.

SAB 101 concedes that revenue may be recognized in some circumstances where delivery has not occurred, but sets out strict criteria that limit the ability to record such transactions as revenue.

EXAMPLE OF FICTITIOUS REVENUES

In one recent case, a foreign subsidiary of a U.S. company recorded several large fictitious sales to a series of companies. They invoiced the sales but did not collect any of the accounts receivable, which became severely past due. The manager of the foreign subsidiary arranged for false confirmations of the accounts receivable for audit purposes and even hired actors to pretend to be the customers during a visit from U.S. management. Background checks on the customers would have revealed that some of the companies were fictitious while others were either undisclosed related parties or operated in industries that would have no need of the goods supposedly supplied. An investigation revealed that the manager of the foreign subsidiary directed the scheme to record fictitious revenues in order to meet unrealistic revenue goals set by U.S. management.

In some cases, companies go to great lengths to conceal fictitious sales. A sample journal entry from this type of case is detailed below. A fictional entry is made to record a purported purchase of fixed assets. This entry debits fixed assets for the amount of the alleged purchase and the credit is to cash for the payment:

Date	Description	Ref.	Debit	Credit
12/01/03	Fixed Assets	104	350,000	
	Cash	101		350,000

A fictitious sales entry is then made for the same amount as the false purchase, debiting accounts receivable and crediting the sales account. The cash outflow that supposedly paid for the fixed assets is "returned" as payment on the receivable account, though in practice the cash might never have moved if the fraudsters didn't bother to falsify that extra documentary support.

Date	Description	Ref.	Debit	Credit
12/01/03	Accounts Rec	120	350,000	
	Sales	400		350,000
12/15/03	Cash	101	350,000	
	Accounts Rec	120		350,000

The result of the completely fabricated sequence of events is an increase in both fixed assets and revenue. The debit could alternatively have been directed to other accounts, such as inventory or accounts payable, or simply left in accounts receivable if the fraud were committed close to year end and the receivable could be left outstanding without attracting undue attention.

Sales with Conditions

Sales with conditions are those that have terms that have not been completed and the rights and risks of ownership have not passed to the purchaser. They do not qualify for recording as revenue. These types of sales are similar to schemes involving the recognition of revenue in improper periods since the conditions for sale may become satisfied in the future, at which point revenue recognition would become appropriate. These are discussed further in the next section.

What Red Flags are Associated with Fictitious Revenues?

- Rapid growth or unusual profitability, especially compared to that of other companies in the same industry.
- Recurring negative cash flows from operations or an inability to generate cash flows from operations while reporting earnings and earnings growth.
- Significant transactions with related parties or special purpose entities not in the ordinary course of business or where those entities are not audited or are audited by another firm.
- Significant, unusual, or highly complex transactions, especially those close to period end that pose difficult "substance over form" questions.
- Unusual growth in the number of days sales in receivables.
- A significant volume of sales to entities whose substance and ownership is not known.
- An unusual surge in sales by a minority of units within a company, or of sales recorded by corporate headquarters.

Timing Differences (Including Premature Revenue Recognition)

Financial statement fraud might also involve timing differences, that is, the recording of revenue and/or expenses in improper periods. This can be done to shift revenues or expenses between one period and the next, increasing or decreasing earnings as desired.

Premature Revenue Recognition

Generally, revenue should be recognized in the accounting records when the four criteria set out in SEC Staff Accounting Bulletin No. 101 have been satisfied:

- Persuasive evidence of an arrangement exists;
- Delivery has occurred or services have been rendered;
- The seller's price to the buyer is fixed or determinable; and
- Collectibility is reasonably assured.

One or more of these criteria is typically not met when managers recognize revenues prematurely. Examples of common problems with premature revenue recognition are set out below.

PERSUASIVE EVIDENCE OF AN ARRANGEMENT DOES NOT EXIST:
- No written or verbal agreement exists.
- A verbal agreement exists but a written agreement is customary.
- A written order exists but is conditional upon sale to end users (such as a consignment sale).
- A written order exists but contains a right of return.
- A written order exists, but a side letter alters the terms in ways that eliminate the required elements for an agreement.
- The transaction is with a related-party, which fact has not been disclosed.

DELIVERY HAS NOT OCCURRED OR SERVICES HAVE NOT BEEN RENDERED:
- Shipment has not been made and the criteria for recognizing revenue on "bill-and-hold" transactions set out in SEC Staff Accounting Bulletin No. 101 have not been met.
- Shipment has been made not to the customer but to the seller's agent, an installer, or to a public warehouse.
- Some but not all of the components required for operation were shipped.
- Items of the wrong specification were shipped.
- Delivery is not complete until installation and customer testing and acceptance has occurred.
- Services have not been provided at all.
- Services are being performed over an extended period and only a portion of the service revenues should have been recognized in the current period.
- The mix of goods and services in a contract has been misstated in order to improperly accelerate revenue recognition.

THE SELLER'S PRICE TO THE BUYER IS NOT FIXED OR DETERMINABLE:
- The price is contingent upon some future events.

- A service or membership fee is subject to unpredictable cancellation during the contract period.
- The transaction includes an option to exchange the product for others.
- Payment terms are extended for a substantial period and additional discounts or upgrades may be required to induce continued use and payment instead of switching to alternative products.

COLLECTIBILITY IS NOT REASONABLY ASSURED:
- Collection is contingent upon some future events, e.g., resale of the product, receipt of additional funding, or litigation.
- The customer does not have the ability to pay, e.g., it is financially troubled, it has purchased far more than it can afford, or it is a shell company with minimal assets.

EXAMPLE

ABC, Inc. sells products that require engineering and adapting work before they are acceptable to customers. However, the company records sales revenue before completing the engineering, testing, evaluation, and customer acceptance stages of production. In some cases, sales do not take place for weeks or months. In other cases, the sales are specifically contingent upon the customer's trial and acceptance of the product.

EXAMPLE

Another company is engaged in the design, development, manufacture, marketing, and servicing of computer peripheral subsystems. The company recognized revenue prior to a time when collection of the sales price was reasonably assured and at a time prior to completion of the underlying sales transaction.

It was the company's policy to recognize revenue when the products were shipped. However, the sales are not complete as of the time of shipment because customers were not obligated to pay for the equipment until it had been installed; the company had substantial obligations to the customers for installation and adjustments; and there remained major uncertainties concerning the customers' true willingness to complete the transaction because of the volatile nature of the high-tech product.

Long-Term Contracts

Long-term contracts pose special problems for revenue recognition. Long-term construction contracts, for example, use either the completed contract method or the percentage of completion method, depending partly on the circumstances. The completed contract method does not record revenue until the project is 100% complete. Construction costs are held in an inventory account until completion of the project. The percentage of completion method recognizes revenues and expenses as measurable progress on a project is made, but this method is particularly vulnerable to manipulation. Managers can often easily manipulate the percentage of completion and the estimated costs to complete a construction project in order to recognize revenues prematurely and conceal contract overruns.

Channel Stuffing

A difficult area of revenue recognition that is attracting the SEC's attention is "channel stuffing," which is also known as "trade loading." This refers to the sale of an unusually large quantity of a product to distributors, who are encouraged to overbuy through the use of deep discounts and/or extended payment terms. This practice is especially attractive in industries with high gross margins (cigarettes, pharmaceuticals, perfume, soda concentrate, and branded consumer goods) because it can increase short-term earnings. The downside is that by stealing from the next period's sales, it makes it harder to achieve sales goals in the next period, sometimes leading to increasingly disruptive levels of channel stuffing and ultimately a restatement. Although orders are received, the terms of the order might raise some question about the collectibility of accounts receivable and there may be side agreements that grant a right of return, effectively making the sales into consignment sales. There may be a greater risk of returns for certain products if they cannot be sold before their shelf life expires.

This is particularly a problem for pharmaceuticals because retailers will not accept drugs with a short shelf life remaining. As a result, "channel stuffing" should be viewed skeptically as in certain circumstances it may constitute fraud. The SEC's complaint against Bausch & Lomb indicated that the company's internal estimates showed that it might take distributors up to two years to sell the quantity of contact lenses the company was trying to get them to purchase in the last two weeks of its 1993 fiscal year. The SEC's complaint against the former Chairman and CEO and the former CFO of Sunbeam Corporation included that they failed to disclose that Sunbeam's 1997 revenue growth was in part achieved at the expense of future results, by offering discounts and other inducements to customers to sell merchandise immediately that would otherwise have been sold in later periods, i.e., channel stuffing. As recently as December 2002, the SEC staff indicated this was an issue they were focusing on closely.

Recording Expenses in the Wrong Period

The timely recording of expenses is often compromised due to pressures to meet budget projections and goals, or due to lack of proper accounting controls. As the expensing of certain costs is pushed into periods other than the ones in which they actually occur, they are not properly matched against the income that they help produce. For example, revenue may be recognized on the sale of certain items, but the cost of goods and services that went into the items sold might intentionally not be recorded in the accounting system until the subsequent period. This might make the sales revenue from the transaction almost pure profit, inflating earnings. In the next period, earnings would be depressed by a similar amount.

What Red Flags are Associated with Timing Differences (Including Premature Revenue Recognition)?

- Rapid growth or unusual profitability, especially compared to that of other companies in the same industry.
- Recurring negative cash flows from operations or an inability to generate cash flows from operations while reporting earnings and earnings growth.
- Significant, unusual, or highly complex transactions, especially those close to period end that pose difficult "substance over form" questions.
- Unusual increase in gross margin or margin in excess of industry peers.
- Unusual growth in the number of days sales in receivables.
- Unusual decline in the number of days purchases in accounts payable.

Improper Asset Valuation

Under the "lower of cost or market value" rule, where an asset's cost exceeds its current market value (as happens often with obsolete technology), it must be written down to market value. With the exception of certain securities, asset values are not increased to reflect current market value. It is often necessary to use estimates in accounting. For example, estimates are used in determining the residual value and the useful life of a depreciable asset, the uncollectible portion of accounts receivable, or the excess or obsolete portion of inventory. Whenever estimates are used, there is an additional opportunity for fraud by manipulating those estimates.

Many schemes are used to inflate current assets at the expense of long-term assets. The net effect is seen in the current ratio. The misclassification of long-term assets as current assets can be of critical concern to lending institutions that often require the maintenance of certain financial ratios. This is of particular consequence when the loan covenants are on unsecured or under-secured lines of credit and other short-term borrowings. Sometimes these misclassifications are referred to as "window dressing."

Most improper asset valuations involve the fraudulent overstatement of inventory or receivables. Other improper asset valuations include manipulation of the allocation of the purchase price of an acquired business in order to inflate future earnings, misclassification of fixed and other assets, or improper capitalization of inventory or start-up costs. Improper asset valuations usually take the form of one of the following classifications:

- Inventory Valuation
- Accounts Receivable
- Business Combinations
- Fixed Assets

Inventory Valuation

Since inventory must be valued at the acquisition cost except when the cost is determined to be higher than the current market value, inventory should be written down to its current value, or written off altogether if it has no value. Failing to write down inventory results in overstated assets and the mismatching of cost of goods sold with revenues. Inventory can also be improperly stated through the manipulation of the physical inventory count, inflating the unit costs used to price out inventory, failure to relieve inventory for costs of goods sold, and by other methods. Fictitious inventory schemes usually involve the creation of fake documents such as inventory count sheets, receiving reports, and similar items. Companies have even programmed special computer reports of inventory for auditors that incorrectly added up the line item values so as to inflate the overall inventory balance. Computer assisted audit techniques can significantly help auditors to detect many of these inventory fraud techniques.

In some instances, a friendly co-conspirator claims to be holding inventory for the company in question, or a large value of inventory in transit is created, perhaps conveniently in the middle of the Pacific Ocean where it is hard for auditors to observe it. "Bill and hold" items that have already been recorded as sales might be included in the physical inventory count, as might goods owned by third parties but held by the company on consignment or for storage. Companies have even made up pallets of inventory with hollow centers, placed bricks in sealed boxes instead of high value products, or shuttled inventory overnight between locations being observed by auditors on different days, so as to double count the inventory.

Finally, it is also common to insert phony count sheets during the inventory observation or change the quantities on the count sheets.

Accounts Receivable

Accounts receivable are subject to manipulation in the same manner as sales and inventory, and in many cases, the schemes are conducted together. The two most common schemes involving accounts receivable are fictitious receivables and failure to write off accounts receivable as bad debts (or failure to establish an adequate allowance for bad debts). Fictitious receivables commonly arise from fictitious revenues, which were discussed earlier. Accounts receivable should be reported at net realizable value, that is, the amount of the receivable less amounts expected not to be collected.

FICTITIOUS ACCOUNTS RECEIVABLE

Fictitious accounts receivable are common among companies with financial problems, as well as with managers who receive a commission based on sales. The typical entry under fictitious accounts receivable is to debit (increase) accounts receivable and credit (increase) sales. Of course, these schemes are more common around the end of the accounting period, since accounts receivable are expected to be paid in cash within a reasonable time. Fraudsters commonly attempt to conceal fictitious accounts receivable by providing false confirmations of balances to auditors. They get the audit confirmations because the mailing address they provide for the phony customers is typically either a mailbox under their control, a home address, or the business address of a co-conspirator. Such schemes can be detected by using business credit reports, public records, or even the telephone book, to identify significant customers with no physical existence or no apparent business need for the product sold to them.

FAILURE TO WRITE DOWN

Companies are required to accrue losses on uncollectible receivables when the criteria in Financial Accounting Standards Board Statement No. 5 are met, and to record impairment of long-lived assets under SFAS 144 and of goodwill under SFAS 142. Companies struggling for profits and income may be tempted to omit the recognition of such losses because of the negative impact on income.

Business Combinations

Companies are required to allocate the purchase price they have paid to acquire another business to the tangible and intangible assets of that business. Any excess of the purchase price over the value of the acquired assets is treated as goodwill. Changes in goodwill accounting have decreased the incentive for companies to allocate an excessive amount to purchased assets, to minimize the amount allocated to goodwill that previously was required to be amortized and which reduced future earnings. However, companies may still be tempted to over-allocate the purchase price to in-process research and development assets, in order to then write them off immediately. Or they may establish excessive reserves for various expenses at the time of acquisition, intending to quietly release those excess reserves into earnings at a future date.

Fixed Assets

Bogus fixed assets can be created by a variety of methods. They are subject to manipulation through several different schemes. Some of the more common schemes are Booking Fictitious Assets, Misrepresenting Asset Valuation, and Improperly Capitalizing Inventory and Start-up Costs.

BOOKING FICTITIOUS ASSETS

One of the easiest methods of asset misrepresentation is in the recording of fictitious assets. This false creation of assets affects account totals on a company's balance sheet. The corresponding account commonly used is the owners' equity account. Because company assets are often physically found in many different locations, this fraud can sometimes be easily overlooked. One of the most common fictitious asset schemes is to simply create fictitious documents. In other instances, the equipment is leased, not owned, and the fact is not disclosed during the audit of fixed assets. Bogus fixed assets can sometimes be detected because the fixed asset addition makes no business sense.

MISREPRESENTING THE VALUE OF FIXED ASSETS

Fixed assets should be recorded at cost. Although assets may appreciate in value, this increase in value should not be recognized on company financial statements. Many financial statement frauds have involved the reporting of fixed assets at market values instead of the lower acquisition costs, or at even higher inflated values with phony valuations to support them. Misrepresentation of asset values frequently goes hand in hand with other schemes.

EXAMPLE

In October 2002, the SEC filed a civil enforcement action against former Enron CFO Andrew S. Fastow, who also faced criminal charges relating to an alleged a self-enriching scheme to defraud Enron's security holders through use of certain off-balance-sheet entities. One of the six transactions in the SEC's complaint against Andrew Fastow was Raptor I/Avici. According to the complaint, Enron and Fastow-controlled partnership LJM2 engaged in complex transactions with an entity called Raptor I. Raptor I was used to manipulate Enron's balance sheet and income statement and to generate profits for LJM2 and Fastow at Enron's expense. In September 2000, Fastow and others used Raptor I to effectuate a fraudulent hedging transaction and thus avoid a decrease in the value of Enron's investment in the stock of a public company called Avici Systems Inc. Specifically, Fastow and others back-dated documents to make it appear that Enron locked in the value of its investment in Avici in August of 2000, when Avici's stock was trading at its all time high price.

Understating Assets

In some cases, as with some government-related or regulated companies, it is advantageous to understate assets. Additional funding is often based on asset amounts. This understatement can be done directly or through improper depreciation.

Capitalizing Nonasset Cost

Excluded from the cost of a purchased asset are interest and finance charges incurred in the purchase. For example, as a company finances a capital equipment purchase, monthly payments include both principal liability reduction and interest payments. On initial purchase, only the original cost of the asset should be capitalized. The subsequent interest payments should be charged to interest expense and not to the asset. Without reason for intensive review, fraud of this type can go unchecked.

Misclassifying Assets

In order to meet budget requirements, and for various other reasons, assets are sometimes misclassified into general ledger accounts in which they don't belong. The manipulation can skew financial ratios and help comply with loan covenants or other borrowing requirements.

What Red Flags are Associated with Improper Asset Valuation?

- Recurring negative cash flows from operations or an inability to generate cash flows from operations while reporting earnings and earnings growth.
- Significant declines in customer demand and increasing business failures in either the industry or overall economy.

- Assets, liabilities, revenues, or expenses based on significant estimates that involve subjective judgments or uncertainties that are difficult to corroborate.
- Non-financial management's excessive participation in or preoccupation with the selection of accounting principles or the determination of significant estimates.
- Unusual increase in gross margin or margin in excess of industry peers.
- Unusual growth in the number of days sales in receivables.
- Unusual growth in the number of days purchases in inventory.
- Allowances for bad debts, excess and obsolete inventory, etc. that are shrinking in percentage terms or are otherwise out of line with industry peers.
- Unusual change in the relationship between fixed assets and depreciation.
- Adding to assets while competitors are reducing capital tied up in assets.

Concealed Liabilities and Expenses

Understating liabilities and expenses is one of the ways financial statements can be manipulated to make a company appear more profitable. Because pre-tax income will increase by the full amount of the expense or liability not recorded, this financial statement fraud method can have a significant impact on reported earnings with relatively little effort by the fraudster. It is much easier to commit than falsifying many sales transactions. Missing transactions can also be harder for auditors to detect than improperly recorded ones because there is no audit trail.

There are three common methods for concealing liabilities and expenses:
- Liability/Expense Omissions
- Capitalized Expenses
- Failure to Disclose Warranty Costs and Liabilities

Liability/Expense Omissions

The preferred and easiest method of concealing liabilities/expenses is to simply fail to record them. Multi-million dollar judgments against the company from a recent court decision might be conveniently ignored. Vendor invoices might be thrown away (they'll send another later) or stuffed into drawers rather than being posted into the accounts payable system, thereby increasing reported earnings by the full amount of the invoices. In a retail environment, debit memos might be created for chargebacks to vendors, supposedly to claim permitted rebates or allowances but sometimes just to create additional income. These items may or may not be properly recorded in a subsequent accounting period, but that does not change the fraudulent nature of the current financial statements.

Often, perpetrators of liability and expense omissions believe they can conceal their fraud in future periods. They often plan to compensate for their omitted liabilities with visions of other income sources such as profits from future price increases.

Just as they are easy to conceal, omitted liabilities are probably one of the most difficult to uncover. A thorough review of all post-financial-statement-date transactions, such as accounts payable increases and decreases, can aid in the discovery of omitted liabilities in financial statements, as can a computerized analysis of expense records. Additionally, if the auditor requested and were granted unrestricted access to the client's files, a physical search could turn up concealed invoices and unposted liabilities. Probing interviews of accounts payable and other personnel can reveal unrecorded or delayed items too.

EXAMPLE

In July 2002, the SEC filed suit in the United States District Court for the Southern District of New York charging major cable television producer Adelphia Communications Corporation; its founder John J. Rigas; his three sons, Timothy J. Rigas, Michael J. Rigas, and James P. Rigas; and two senior executives at Adelphia, James R. Brown and Michael C. Mulcahey, in one of the most extensive financial frauds ever to take place at a public company. The SEC charges that Adelphia, at the direction of the individual defendants: (1) fraudulently excluded over $2.3 billion in liabilities from its consolidated financial statements by hiding them in off-balance sheet affiliates; (2) falsified operations statistics and inflated Adelphia's earnings to meet Wall Street's expectations; and (3) concealed rampant self-dealing by the Rigas Family, including the undisclosed use of corporate funds for Rigas Family stock purchases and the acquisition of luxury condominiums in New York and elsewhere.

With respect to the concealed liabilities, the complaint alleges that between mid-1999 and the end of 2001, John J. Rigas, Timothy J. Rigas, Michael J. Rigas, James P. Rigas, and James R. Brown, with the assistance of Michael C. Mulcahey, caused Adelphia to fraudulently exclude from the Company's annual and quarterly consolidated financial statements over $2.3 billion in bank debt by deliberately shifting those liabilities onto the books of Adelphia's off-balance sheet, unconsolidated affiliates. Failure to record this debt violated GAAP requirements and precipitated a series of misrepresentations about those liabilities by Adelphia and the defendants, including the creation of: (1) sham transactions backed by fictitious documents to give the false appearance that Adelphia had actually repaid debts when, in truth, it had simply shifted them to unconsolidated Rigas-controlled entities, and (2) misleading financial statements by giving the false impression through the use of footnotes that liabilities listed in the Company's financials included all outstanding bank debt.

Capitalized Expenses

Capitalizing expenses is another way to increase income and assets since capitalized items are depreciated or amortized over a period of years rather than expensed immediately. If expenditures are capitalized as assets and not expensed during the current period, income will be overstated. As the assets are depreciated, income in subsequent periods will be understated.

EXAMPLE

In November 2002, the SEC filed an amended complaint against WorldCom, Inc., broadening its charges to allege that WorldCom misled investors from at least as early as 1999 through the first quarter of 2002. The complaint states that the company has acknowledged that during that period WorldCom materially overstated the income it reported on its financial statements by approximately $9 billion, mainly using two methods. First, WorldCom reduced its operating expenses by improperly releasing as a credit to operating expenses certain provisions previously established for line costs and for taxes. Second, it improperly reduced its operating expenses by recharacterizing certain expenses as capital assets. Much of the $9 billion related to improper accounting for "line costs," which were among WorldCom's major operating expenses. The SEC complaint alleges that in a scheme directed and approved by members of senior management, WorldCom concealed the true extent of its "line costs." By improperly reducing provisions held against "line costs" and by transferring certain "line costs" to its capital asset accounts, WorldCom falsely portrayed itself as a profitable business when it was not, and concealed large losses. These improper accounting practices were designed to and did inflate income to correspond with estimates by Wall Street analysts and to support the price of WorldCom's stock.

Former WorldCom Controller David F. Myers and former Director of General Accounting Buford "Buddy" Yates, Jr. pled guilty to criminal charges prosecuted by the U.S. Attorney's Office for the Southern District of New York. At time of writing, they have not yet been sentenced. They were also permanently enjoined from acting as an officer or director of any public company and were suspended from practicing before the SEC as an accountant, under Rule 102(2) of the Commission's Rules of Practice. The SEC also brought civil actions against former members of the WorldCom General Accounting Department, Betty L. Vinson, CPA, and Troy M. Normand. Both were permanently enjoined from securities violations. Vinson was suspended from appearing or practicing before the SEC as an accountant. All four face civil money penalties. Civil and criminal actions against one or more additional WorldCom executives are widely anticipated.

EXPENSING CAPITAL EXPENDITURES

Just as capitalizing expenses is improper, so is expensing costs that should be capitalized. The organization may want to minimize its net income due to tax considerations, or to increase earnings in future periods. Expensing an item that should be depreciated over a period of time would help accomplish just that—net income is lower and so are taxes.

Returns and Allowances and Warranties

Improper returns and allowances liabilities occur when a company fails to accrue the proper expenses and related liabilities for potential product returns or warranty repairs. It is inevitable that a certain percentage of products sold will, for one reason or another, be returned. It is the job of management to try to accurately estimate what that percentage will be over time and provide for it. In warranty liability fraud, the liability is usually either omitted altogether or substantially understated. Another similar area is the liability resulting from defective products (product liability).

What Red Flags are Associated with Concealed Liabilities and Expenses?

- Recurring negative cash flows from operations or an inability to generate cash flows from operations while reporting earnings and earnings growth.
- Assets, liabilities, revenues, or expenses based on significant estimates that involve subjective judgments or uncertainties that are difficult to corroborate.
- Non-financial management's excessive participation in or preoccupation with the selection of accounting principles or the determination of significant estimates.
- Unusual increase in gross margin or margin in excess of industry peers.
- Allowances for sales returns, warranty claims, etc., that are shrinking in percentage terms or are otherwise out of line with industry peers.
- Unusual reduction in the number of days purchases in accounts payable.
- Reducing accounts payable while competitors are stretching out payments to vendors.

Improper Disclosures

Accounting principles require that financial statements include all the information necessary to prevent a reasonably discerning user of the financial statements from being misled. The notes should include narrative disclosures, supporting schedules, and any other information required to avoid misleading potential investors, creditors, or any other users of the financial statements.

Management has an obligation to disclose all significant information appropriately in the financial statements and in management's discussion and analysis. In addition, the disclosed information must not be misleading. Improper disclosures relating to financial statement fraud usually involve the following:
- Liability Omissions
- Subsequent Events
- Management Fraud
- Related-Party Transactions
- Accounting Changes

Liability Omissions
Typical omissions include the failure to disclose loan covenants or contingent liabilities. Loan covenants are agreements, in addition to or as part of a financing arrangement, which a borrower has promised to keep as long as the financing is in place. The agreements can contain various types of covenants including certain financial ratio limits and restrictions on other major financing arrangements. Contingent liabilities are potential obligations that will materialize only if certain events occur in the future. A corporate guarantee of personal loans taken out by an officer or of a private company controlled by an officer is an example of a contingent liability. The company's potential liability, if material, must be disclosed.

Subsequent Events
Events occurring or becoming known after the close of the period may have a significant effect on the financial statements and should be disclosed. Fraudsters typically avoid disclosing court judgments and regulatory decisions that undermine the reported values of assets, that indicate unrecorded liabilities, or that adversely reflect upon management integrity. Public record searches can reveal this information.

Management Fraud
Management has an obligation to disclose to the shareholders significant fraud committed by officers, executives, and others in positions of trust. Withholding such information from auditors would likely also involve lying to auditors, an illegal act in itself.

Related-Party Transactions

Related-party transactions occur when a company does business with another entity whose management or operating policies can be controlled or significantly influenced by the company or by some other party in common. There is nothing inherently wrong with related-party transactions, as long as they are fully disclosed. If the transactions are not conducted on an arm's-length basis, the company may suffer economic harm, injuring stockholders. The financial interest that a company official might have may not be readily apparent. For example, common directors of two companies which do business with each other, any corporate general partner and the partnerships with which it does business, and any controlling shareholder of the corporation with which he/she/it does business may be related parties. Family relationships can also be considered related-parties, such as all lineal descendants and ancestors, without regard to financial interests. Related-party transactions are sometimes referred to as "self-dealing." While these transactions are sometimes conducted at arm's-length, they often are not.

EXAMPLE

In September 2002, the SEC charged former top executives of Tyco International Ltd., including former CEO L. Dennis Kozlowski, with violating the federal securities laws by failing to disclose to shareholders hundreds of millions of dollars of low interest and interest-free loans they took from the company, and in some cases, never repaid. The SEC complaint, which also charged former Tyco CFO Mark H. Swartz and chief legal officer Mark A. Belnick, alleges that the three former executives also sold shares of Tyco stock valued at millions of dollars while their self-dealing remained undisclosed. The complaint alleges numerous improper transactions, including Kozlowski's use of $242 million of loans for impermissible and unauthorized purposes including funding an extravagant lifestyle. With these undisclosed loans, Kozlowski allegedly amassed millions of dollars in fine art, yachts, and estate jewelry, as well as a $31 million Park Avenue apartment and a palatial estate in Nantucket. Kozlowski and Swartz allegedly engaged in undisclosed non-arm's-length real estate transactions with Tyco or its subsidiaries and received undisclosed compensation and perquisites including forgiveness of multi-million dollar loans, rent-free use of large New York apartments, and use of corporate aircraft for personal purposes at little or no cost.

Accounting Changes

Accounting Principles Board (APB) Opinion No. 20 describes three types of accounting changes that must be disclosed to avoid misleading the user of financial statements:

accounting principles, estimates, and reporting entities. Fraudsters may fail to restate financial statements or disclose the cumulative effect of a change in accounting principle they have made simply to boost earnings. They may fail to disclose significant changes in estimates such as the useful lives and estimated salvage values of depreciable assets, or the estimates underlying the determination of warranty or other liabilities. They may even secretly change the reporting entity, by adding entities owned privately by management, or excluding certain company-owned units, in order to improve reported results.

What Red Flags are Associated with Improper Disclosures?

- Domination of management by a single person or small group (in a nonowner-managed business) without compensating controls.
- Ineffective board of directors or audit committee oversight over the financial reporting process and internal control.
- Ineffective communication, implementation, support, or enforcement of the entity's values or ethical standards by management or the communication of inappropriate values or ethical standards.
- Rapid growth or unusual profitability, especially compared to that of other companies in the same industry.
- Significant, unusual, or highly complex transactions, especially those close to period end that pose difficult "substance over form" questions.
- Significant related-party transactions not in the ordinary course of business or with related entities not audited or audited by another firm.
- Significant bank accounts or subsidiary or branch operations in tax-haven jurisdictions for which there appears to be no clear business justification.
- Overly complex organizational structure involving unusual legal entities or managerial lines of authority.
- Known history of violations of securities laws or other laws and regulations, or claims against the entity, its senior management, or board members alleging fraud or violations of laws and regulations.
- Recurring attempts by management to justify marginal or inappropriate accounting on the basis of materiality.
- Formal or informal restrictions on the auditor that inappropriately limit access to people or information or the ability to communicate effectively with the board of directors or audit committee.

What Red Flags are Associated with Financial Statement Fraud Generally?

Red flags associated with particular financial statement fraud schemes have been discussed above. There are many red flags associated with financial statement fraud generally. An extensive list of such red flags can be found in an appendix to SAS No. 99, where they are called "risk factors." Some red flags indicate increased vulnerability to financial statement fraud. Others indicate a greater likelihood that financial statement fraud has occurred.

Some of the more significant red flags listed in SAS No. 99 are:
- Domination of management by a single person or small group (in a nonowner-managed business) without compensating controls.
- A practice by management of committing to analysts, creditors, and other third parties to achieve aggressive or unrealistic forecasts.
- Ineffective communication, implementation, support, or enforcement of the entity's values or ethical standards by management or the communication of inappropriate values or ethical standards.
- Recurring negative cash flows from operations or an inability to generate cash flows from operations while reporting earnings and earnings growth.
- Rapid growth or unusual profitability, especially compared to that of other companies in the same industry.
- Significant, unusual, or highly complex transactions, especially those close to period end that pose difficult "substance over form" questions.
- Significant related-party transactions not in the ordinary course of business or with related entities not audited or audited by another firm.
- Recurring attempts by management to justify marginal or inappropriate accounting on the basis of materiality.
- Formal or informal restrictions on the auditor that inappropriately limit access to people or information or the ability to communicate effectively with the board of directors or audit committee.

Detection of Fraudulent Financial Statement Schemes

To better understand basic accounting concepts and to show how an analysis of accounting records and procedures can reveal a fraud, consider the following example:

EXAMPLE

Jackson Hardware Supply is a medium-sized plumbing and electrical wholesale distributor. On December 31, the balance sheet and income statement were as follows:

Jackson Hardware Supply
Balance Sheet
As of December 31

Assets		Liabilities & Owners' Equities	
Cash	$2,427,000	**Liabilities**	
Accounts Receivable	300,000	Accounts Payable	$ 300,000
Inventory	300,000	Salaries Payable	70,000
Supplies	11,000	Rent Payable	50,000
Prepaid Insurance	44,000	Deferred Taxes Payable	438,000
Equipment	440,000	Total Liabilities	858,000
		Owners' Equities	
		Common Stock	$2,000,000
		Retained Earnings	664,000
		Total Owners' Equity	$2,664,000
Total Assets	$3,522,000	Total Liabilities & Owners' Equity	$3,522,000

Jackson Hardware Supply
Income Statement
For the year ending December 31

Revenues

Sales Revenue	$3,470,000	
Cost of Goods Sold	2,100,000	
Gross Profit from Sales	1,370,000	
Rent Revenue	10,000	
Gross Profit	$ 1,380,000	
Total Revenue		$3,480,000

General and Administrative Expenses

Insurance Expense	4,000	
Salary Expense	220,000	
Supplies Expense	14,000	
Rental Expense	40,000	
Total Expense		$2,378,000
Net Income Before Taxes		$1,102,000
Income Taxes		438,000
Net Income		$ 664,000

An anonymous tip was received that the paymaster is stealing cash from the company. Lately, he has been seen driving a new BMW and has taken expensive vacations. The president of the company wants to follow up on the tip. Although the paymaster is a longtime, trusted employee, the president asks the fraud examiner to determine if the paymaster has been stealing. Although there are several ways to proceed with the investigation, the fraud examiner with accounting knowledge decides to first compare this year's total salary expense with last year's balance. He theorizes that if the paymaster is dishonest, he might be concealing the theft in the salaries expense account. Past experience has taught the fraud examiner to look in the most obvious place first.

The examiner notes that the balance of $220,000 in the salary expense account this year is significantly larger than the $180,000 balance last year. He asks the owner if there is an increase in the number of employees and how large across-the-board raises were this year. He discovers that the work force has not increased and all employees, including the owner, received 10 percent raises. He recalculates this year's salaries by increasing last year's salaries 10 percent and determines that the balance in the salary expense account should be approximately $198,000 ($180,000 × 1.10 = $198,000). He now believes that excess salaries went to someone.

The next step is to follow the overstatement in salary expense backwards from the income statement through the accounts and journal entries to the source documents—the payroll checks in this case. He finds that there are 12 checks payable to John Doe, an employee who quit in January of last year. He compares the endorsements on John Doe's checks with those on the paymaster's checks and notices distinct similarities in the signatures. Armed with this evidence, he interviews the paymaster who confesses that he has stolen $22,000 and concealed the theft by issuing payroll checks to a nonexistent employee, checks which he subsequently endorsed and cashed.

Obviously, this example is relatively simple; but most fraud schemes are simple, especially for an examiner who understands concealment techniques and accounting.

Other detection techniques are available for determining if the paymaster is stealing. These include running a computer listing of all employees who do not elect insurance coverage and other payroll withholdings (withholdings on fictitious employees create additional concealment problems for perpetrators), having someone else distribute the checks, and checking Social Security numbers of all active employees. Any of these methods might have revealed the spurious paychecks to John Doe. The approach shows, however, how an understanding of accounting can be invaluable for detecting fraud.

Financial Statement Analysis

Comparative financial statements provide information for current and past accounting periods. Accounts expressed in whole dollar amounts yield a limited amount of information. The conversion of these numbers into ratios or percentages allows the reader of the statements to analyze them based on their relationship to each other, as well as to major changes in historical totals. In fraud detection and investigation, the determination of the reasons for relationships and changes in amounts can be important. These determinations are the red flags which point an examiner in the direction of possible fraud. If large enough, a fraudulent misstatement will affect the financial statements in such a way that relationships between the numbers become questionable. Many schemes are detected because the financial statements, when analyzed closely, do not make sense. Financial statement analysis includes the following:

- Vertical Analysis
- Horizontal Analysis
- Ratio Analysis

Percentage Analysis—Horizontal and Vertical

There are traditionally two methods of percentage analysis of financial statements. *Vertical analysis* is a technique for analyzing the relationships between the items on an income statement, balance sheet, or statement of cash flows by expressing components as percentages. This method is often referred to as "common sizing" financial statements. In the vertical analysis of an income statement, net sales is assigned 100%. For a balance sheet, total assets is assigned 100% on the asset side, and total liabilities and equity is expressed as 100%. All other items in each of the sections are expressed as a percentage of these numbers.

Horizontal analysis is a technique for analyzing the percentage change in individual financial statement items from one year to the next. The first period in the analysis is considered the base, and the changes to subsequent periods are computed as a percentage of the base period. Like vertical analysis, this technique will not work for small, immaterial frauds.

The following is an example of financial statements that are analyzed by both horizontal and vertical analysis:

BALANCE SHEET	Vertical Analysis				Horizontal Analysis	
	Year One		Year Two		Change	%Change
Assets						
Current Assets						
Cash	45,000	14%	15,000	4%	(30,000)	-67%
Accts Receivable	150,000	45%	200,000	47%	50,000	33%
Inventory	75,000	23%	150,000	35%	75,000	100%
Fixed Assets (net)	60,000	18%	60,000	14%	-	0%
Total	330,000	100%	425,000	100%	95,000	29%
Acc'ts Payable	95,000	29%	215,000	51%	120,000	126%
Long-term Debt	60,000	18%	60,000	14%	-	0%
Stockholder's Equity						
Common Stock	25,000	8%	25,000	6%	-	0%
Paid-in Capital	75,000	23%	75,000	18%	-	0%
Retained Earnings	75,000	23%	50,000	12%	(25,000)	-33%
Total	330,000	100%	425,000	100%	95,000	29%

INCOME STATEMENT	Vertical Analysis				Horizontal Analysis	
	Year One		Year Two		Change	%Change
Net Sales	250,000	100%	450,000	100%	200,000	80%
Cost of Goods Sold	125,000	50%	300,000	67%	175,000	140%
Gross Margin	125,000	50%	150,000	33%	25,000	20%
Operating Expenses						
Selling Expenses	50,000	20%	75,000	17%	25,000	50%
Administrative Expenses	60,000	24%	100,000	22%	40,000	67%
Net Income	15,000	6%	(25,000)	-6%	(40,000)	-267%

Additional Information

Average Net Receivables	155,000	210,000
Average Inventory	65,000	130,000
Average Assets	330,000	425,000

Vertical Analysis Discussion

Vertical analysis is the expression of the relationship or percentage of component part items to a specific base item. In the above example, vertical analysis of the income statement includes total sales as the base amount, and all other items are then analyzed as a percentage of that total. Vertical analysis emphasizes the relationship of statement items within each accounting period. These relationships can be used with historical averages to determine statement anomalies.

In the above example, we can observe that accounts payable is 29% of total liabilities. Historically we may find that this account averages slightly over 25%. In year two, accounts payable total rose to 51%. Although the change in the account total may be explainable through a correlation with a rise in sales, this significant rise might be a starting point in a fraud examination. Source documents should be examined to determine the rise in this percentage. With this type of examination, fraudulent activity may be detected. The same type of change can be seen as selling expenses decline as a part of sales in year two from 20 to 17%. Again, this change may be explainable with higher volume sales or another bona fide explanation. But close examination may possibly point a fraud examiner to uncover fictitious sales, since there was not a corresponding increase in selling expenses.

Horizontal Analysis Discussion

Horizontal statement analysis uses percentage comparison from one accounting period to the next. The percentage change is calculated by dividing the amount of increase or decrease for each item by the base period amount. The resulting percentages are then studied in detail. It is important to consider the amount of change as well as the percentage in horizontal comparisons. A 5% change in an account with a very large dollar amount may actually be much more of a change than a 50% change in an account with much less activity.

In the above example, it is very obvious that the 80% increase in sales has a much greater corresponding increase in cost of goods sold, which rose 140%. These accounts are often used to hide fraudulent expenses, withdrawals, or other illegal transactions.

Financial Ratios in Detail

Ratio analysis is a means of measuring the relationship between two different financial statement amounts. The relationship and comparison are the keys to the analysis. Many professionals, including bankers, investors, and business owners, as well as major investment firms use this method. Ratio analysis allows for internal evaluations using financial statement data. Traditionally, financial statement ratios are used in comparisons to an entity's industry average. They can be very useful in detecting red flags for a fraud examination.

As the financial ratios present a significant change from one year to the next, or over a period of years, it becomes obvious that there may a problem. As in all other analysis, specific changes are often explained by changes in the business operations. As a change in specific ratios is detected, the appropriate source accounts should be researched and examined in detail to determine if fraud has occurred. For instance, a significant decrease in a company's current ratio may point to an increase in current liabilities or a reduction in assets, both of which could be used to cover fraud.

In the analysis of financial statements, each reader of the statements will determine which portions are most important. Like the statement analysis discussed previously, the analysis of ratios is limited by its inability to detect fraud on a smaller, immaterial scale. Some of the types of financial ratio comparisons are shown below.

Many of the possible ratios are used in industry-specific situations, but the nine comparisons mentioned below are ratios that may lead to discovery of fraud. The following calculations are based on the example financial statements presented earlier:

INTERPRETATION OF FINANCIAL RATIOS

CURRENT RATIO

$$\frac{\text{Current Assets}}{\text{Current Liabilities}}$$

The current ratio, current assets to current liabilities, is probably the most-used ratio in financial statement analysis. This comparison measures a company's ability to meet present obligations from its liquid assets. The number of times that current assets exceed current liabilities has long been a quick measure of financial strength.

In detecting fraud, this ratio can be a prime indicator of manipulation of accounts involved. Embezzlement will cause the ratio to decrease. Liability concealment will cause a more favorable ratio.

In the case example, the drastic change in the current ratio from year one (2.84) to year two (1.70) should cause an examiner to look at these accounts in more detail. For instance, a check-tampering scheme will usually result in a decrease in current assets, cash, which will in turn decrease the ratio.

QUICK RATIO

$$\frac{Cash + Securities + Receivables}{Current\ Liabilities}$$

The quick ratio, often referred to as the acid test ratio, compares assets that can be immediately liquidated. This calculation divides the total of cash, securities, and receivables by current liabilities. This ratio is a measure of a company's ability to meet sudden cash requirements. In turbulent economic times, it is used more prevalently, giving the analyst a worst-case look at the company's working capital situation.

An examiner will analyze this ratio for fraud indicators. In year one of the example, the company balance sheet reflects a quick ratio of 2.05. This ratio drops in year two to 1.00. In this situation, a closer review of accounts receivable shows they are increasing at an unusual rate which could indicate fictitious accounts receivable have been added to inflate sales. Of more concern perhaps is the increase in accounts payable which might require, at a minimum, a closer review to determine why.

RECEIVABLE TURNOVER

$$\frac{Net\ Sales\ on\ Account}{Average\ Net\ Receivables}$$

Receivable turnover is defined as net sales on account divided by average net receivables. It measures the number of times accounts receivable is turned over during the accounting period. In other words, it measures the time between on-account sales and collection of funds. This ratio is one that uses both income statement and balance sheet accounts in its analysis. If the fraud is caused from fictitious sales, this bogus income will never be collected. As a result, the turnover of receivables will decrease, as in the example.

COLLECTION RATIO

$$\frac{365}{Receivable\ Turnover}$$

Accounts receivable aging is measured by the collection ratio. It divides 365 days by the receivable turnover ratio to arrive at the average number of days to collect receivables. In general, the lower the collection ratio, the faster receivables are collected. A fraud examiner may use this ratio as a first step in detecting fictitious receivables or larceny and skimming schemes. Normally, this ratio will stay fairly consistent from year to year, but changes in billing policies or collection efforts may cause a fluctuation. The example shows a favorable reduction in the collection ratio from 226.3 in year one to 170.33 in year two. This means that the company is collecting its receivables more quickly in year two than in year one.

INVENTORY TURNOVER

$$\frac{\text{Cost of Goods Sold}}{\text{Average Inventory}}$$

The relationship between a company's cost of goods sold and average inventory is shown through the inventory turnover ratio. This ratio measures the number of times inventory is sold during the period. This ratio is a good determinant of purchasing, production, and sales efficiency. In general, a higher inventory turnover ratio is considered more favorable. For example, if cost of goods sold has increased due to theft of inventory (ending inventory has declined, but not through sales), then this ratio will be abnormally high. In the case example, inventory turnover increases in year two, signaling the possibility that an embezzlement is buried in the inventory account. An examiner should look at the changes in the components of the ratio to determine a direction in which to discover possible fraud.

AVERAGE NUMBER OF DAYS INVENTORY IS IN STOCK

$$\frac{365}{\text{Inventory Turnover}}$$

The average number of days inventory is in stock ratio is a restatement of the inventory turnover ratio expressed in days. This rate is important for several reasons. An increase in the number of days inventory stays in stock causes additional expenses, including storage costs, risk of inventory obsolescence, and market price reductions, as well as interest and other expenses incurred due to tying up funds in inventory stock. Inconsistency or significant variance in this ratio is a red flag for fraud investigators. Examiners may use this ratio to examine inventory accounts for possible larceny schemes. Purchasing and receiving inventory schemes can affect the ratio. As well, understating the cost of goods sold will result in an increase in the ratio. Significant changes in the inventory turnover ratio are good indicators of possible fraudulent inventory activity.

DEBT TO EQUITY RATIO

$$\frac{\text{Total Liabilities}}{\text{Total Equity}}$$

The debt to equity ratio is computed by dividing total liabilities by total equity. This ratio is one that is heavily considered by lending institutions. It provides a clear picture of the relative risk assumed by the creditors and owners. The higher the ratio, the more difficult it will be for the owners to raise capital by increasing long-term debt. Debt to equity requirements are often included as borrowing covenants in corporate lending agreements. The example displays a year one ratio of 0.89. This is very favorable. However, Year 2 shows a ratio of 1.84; this means that debt is greatly increasing. In this case, the increase in the ratio corresponds with the rise in accounts payable. Sudden changes in this ratio may signal an examiner to look for fraud.

PROFIT MARGIN

$$\frac{\text{Net Income}}{\text{Net Sales}}$$

Profit margin ratio is defined as net income divided by net sales. This ratio is often referred to as the efficiency ratio, in that it reveals profits earned per dollar of sales. This percentage of net income to sales relates not only the effects of gross margin changes, but also charges to sales and administrative expenses. As fraud is committed, net income will be artificially overstated, and the profit margin ratio will be abnormally high. False expenses and fraudulent disbursements will cause an increase in expenses and a decrease in the profit margin ratio. Over time, this ratio should be fairly consistent.

ASSET TURNOVER

$$\frac{\text{Net Sales}}{\text{Average Assets}}$$

Net sales divided by average operating assets is the calculation used to determine the asset turnover ratio. This ratio is used to determine the efficiency with which asset resources are utilized. The case example displays a greater use of assets in year two than in year one.

By performing an analysis of the financial statements, the examiner may be directed toward the direct evidence to resolve an allegation of fraud. After performing a financial statement analysis, the examiner can select statistical samples in the target account and eventually examine the source documents. If an irregularity of overstatement is suspected, begin the examination with the financial statements. If, however, an irregularity of understatement is suspected, begin the examination with a review of the source documents. This rule of thumb is of particular effectiveness in the area of omission of liabilities, such as litigation, contingent liabilities, leases, and some product warranties.

Tax Return Review

Tax returns are good sources of additional and comparative information on the operations of the business. A complete review and comparison to the financial statement may provide information unknown to the lender, or disclose unexplained discrepancies. Again, the lack of properly prepared or timely filed tax returns may be a method of stalling or not providing the required information. Most perpetrators of fraud are reluctant to continue the deception and falsify a tax return. Year-after-year extensions and filing of the tax returns on the last possible date could be a ploy to cover up financial statement and tax return differences.

Fraudulent Financial Statement Red Flags

A survey of large accounting firm auditors identified and ranked potential warning signs of financial statement fraud and their relative importance. The survey revealed a pattern of auditors perceiving attitude factors to be more important warning signs of fraud than situational factors.

Auditors' Ranking   *Fraud Warning Signs*

1. Managers have lied to the auditors or have been overly evasive in response to audit inquiries.

2. The auditor's experience with management indicates a degree of dishonesty.

3. Management places undue emphasis on meeting earnings projections or other quantitative targets.

4. Management has engaged in frequent disputes with auditors, particularly about aggressive application of accounting principles that increase earnings.

5. The client has engaged in opinion shopping.

6. Management's attitude toward financial reporting is unduly aggressive.

7. The client has a weak control environment.

8. A substantial portion of management compensation depends on meeting quantified targets.

9. Management displays significant disrespect for regulatory bodies.

10. Management's operating and financial decisions are dominated by a single person or a few persons acting in concert.

11. Client managers display a hostile attitude toward the auditors.

12. Management displays a propensity to take undue risks.

13.5 There are frequent and significant difficult-to-audit transactions.

13.5 Key managers are considered highly unreasonable.

15. The client's organization is decentralized without adequate monitoring.

16. Management and/or key accounting personnel turnover is high.

17. Client personnel displays significant resentment of authority.

18. Management places undue pressure on the auditors, particularly through the fee structure or the imposition of unreasonable deadlines.

19. The client's profitability is inadequate or inconsistent relative to its industry.

20. The client is confronted with adverse legal circumstances.

21. Management exhibits undue concern with the need to maintain or improve the image/reputation of the entity.

22. There are adverse conditions in the client's industry or external environment.

23. Accounting personnel exhibit inexperience or laxity in performing their duties.

24. The client entered into one or a few specific transactions that have a material effect on the financial statements.

25. Client management is inexperienced.

26.5 The client is in a period of rapid growth.

26.5 This is a new client with no prior audit history or insufficient information from the predecessor auditor.

28. The client is subject to significant contractual commitments.

29. The client's operating results are highly sensitive to economic factors (inflation, interest rates, unemployment, etc.).

30. The client recently entered into a significant number of acquisition transactions.

[Heiman-Hoffman, Morgan, and Patton, "The Warning Signs of Fraudulent Financial Reporting," *Journal of Accountancy*, October 1996.]

Interviews in Fraudulent Financial Statement Cases

For in-depth interviewing techniques, please refer to the Interview Theory and Application segment in the Fraud Examination section of this *Manual*.

Financial statement fraud does not occur in an isolated environment. People in organizations who have both motive and opportunity are the prime candidates to commit fraudulent misstatement. In the overwhelming majority of situations, two key managers most often participate actively in the fraud: the chief executive officer and the chief financial officer.

From there, others become involved largely out of necessity. Those who are not directly involved most often are not aware that anything is wrong.

Investigations of financial statement frauds are unique in that it is almost always necessary to interview the executive management of the organization. To detect or deter financial statement fraud, it is absolutely necessary that top management be interviewed by a competent and experienced fraud examiner who possesses the ability to solicit honest answers to tough—but vital—questions about whether anyone has tampered with the books.

Interviewing Techniques

Situations in which accountants are tempted to misstate financial statements most often involve pressure connected with financial performance. The following is a fictitious conversation between upper management of a corporation. The example shows how the pressure to commit financial statement fraud can greatly affect the actions of accounting personnel.

> *CFO: (To CEO) "Boss, it looks like we will not have a good year financially. We told the shareholders (or bank) that our earnings would be $4 a share, and it looks like we'll be very lucky to make $3."*
> *CEO: "Well, what are we going to do about it? If we miss the earnings projections (or don't get the loan) our gooses will be cooked; we'll both lose our jobs. We must get those earnings up to where they should be."*
> *CFO: "What do you mean?"*
> *CEO: "What I mean is that it is your job to bring in the numbers. You're going to have to find a way to get them up. I'm sure we can probably make up the difference next year, but for now, you get our earnings/assets/equity up however you have to. All financial statements are essentially estimates anyhow. So you figure out how to 'estimate' the numbers more in our favor. I don't know how to do it, and I don't want you to tell me. But get it done."*

The CFO faces a dilemma: cook the books or lose his job. The actions of the CFO are very hard to predict. If the CFO steps over the edge, chances are he will need to enlist the aide of accounting and clerical personnel to carry out the details, even if these employees do not know what they are actually doing. For example, the CFO may tell the chief accountant to book certain receivables and income, which has the needed effect—pumping up the equity. In some instances, though, that is only apparent to the real insiders.

In order to detect financial statement frauds through interviews, management as well as key support staff must be interviewed. The following issues should be considered by fraud examiners when conducting interviews:

- There is generally no liability in asking a question in which one has a legitimate interest, no matter how insulting someone might find it. A fraud examiner therefore has the legal right to be fearless in asking questions, as long as the questions are asked privately and under reasonable circumstances. That doesn't extend to accusations—only questions. Example: "Are you still cooking the books?" is an accusation. "Are you cooking the books?" is a question. It is important to know the difference, and frame questions accordingly.

- All interviews should be conducted one person at a time. Groups of people should not be interviewed because members tend to influence each other. Interviews should always be conducted under private conditions, which permit the respondent to answer candidly.

- A good interviewer will be nonthreatening in approach. It stands to reason that the less threatening one appears, the less reluctant someone will be to answer questions. An interviewer should not show surprise, disgust, or be judgmental; those actions will inhibit the flow of information.

- An interviewer should warm up the respondent thoroughly before asking sensitive questions. This means that fraud should usually be the last thing discussed in an interview; get all the procedural information and internal control questions out of the way first.

- An interviewer can almost always ask tough questions without offending if it is done right. There are two things one can do to make the process easier. The first is to explain the nature of interest before asking the question. Example: "As you know, we as auditors are required to actively look for fraud. That means we must ask you some direct questions about the subject. Do you understand?" After obtaining a positive response, one should proceed with questions, from the easiest to the hardest.

- The second thing an interviewer can do to make tough questions more palatable is to phrase them hypothetically. For example, if one is interviewing the chief financial officer, one might start—instead of end—with the most direct question, "Have you committed fraud?" The common response of course would be "no," whether that person actually has or not. It would also be common for the respondent to either laugh at the question or be offended by it.

- A better approach is to start with: "Suppose someone in the position of chief financial officer decided to pump up the financials. How would he do it?" One can easily see the first question, although legal and direct, is not as likely to elicit specific information as would the latter.

- Before one ends an interview with a highly placed executive, the executive should be asked specifically if he or she has committed fraud. The question may be phrased something like this: "Mr. Smith, my professional responsibilities require me to ask you one particularly sensitive direct question. Have you committed fraud or illegal acts against the company?"

As stated, the vast majority of respondents will answer "no" without hesitation, whether they have or not. Simply asking this question will give the fraud examiner a much more favorable posture if attacked professionally for not detecting the fraud. The fraud examiner will be able to tell the court or any other authority that he or she did not shirk professional responsibilities, asking all persons interviewed in connection with the audit or examination if they were involved in the fraud, and that they lied.

The Interview

With the above as a predicate, there is a series of questions you can ask which are designed to elicit the most specific information in a professional manner.

THE CHIEF EXECUTIVE OFFICER

Generally, the CEO should be interviewed first in any proactive or reactive fraud situation. There are several good reasons for this approach. First of all, the auditor or fraud examiner must have a thorough understanding with management as to what his responsibilities in this area are. Second, it is unwise to conduct sensitive inquiries within any organization without first advising the CEO. If he learns from some other source that you are making discreet fraud-related inquiries without telling him, he is more likely to misunderstand your objectives and take the inquiry as a personal affront. Third, as stated, if there is any significant diddling with the books, the Chief Executive Officer is almost always involved. The fraud-related questions you should ask in connection with a regular audit should include, as a minimum, the following. Note how the questions are for "set up" purposes.

- Mr. CEO, as you know we are required to assess the risk that material fraud exists in every company, not just yours. This is sort of a sensitive area for everyone, but our professional responsibilities dictate that we address this area. Do you understand? (Wait for an affirmative response before proceeding).

- Do you have any reason to believe that material fraud is being committed at any level within the organization?

- Mr. CEO, one trend in fraud is that small frauds are committed by employees with little authority, which means that the largest ones are usually committed with the knowledge of upper management. Do you understand that? (Wait for an affirmative response before proceeding.)

- Because of that, we are required to at least look at the possibility that all CEOs, including you, might commit significant fraud against customers, investors, or shareholders. Do you understand our situation? (Wait for an affirmative response.)

- So during this audit (examination) I need to ask direct questions about this subject with you and your staff. As a matter of fact, we will at least discuss the possibility of fraud with every employee we talk with in connection with this audit/examination. Do you have any trouble with that? (Wait for a negative response. If the CEO protests, satisfy his objections. If he cannot be satisfied, assess the risk of whether the CEO is attempting to obstruct the audit or examination.)

- First, let's look at your CFO position. Can you think of a reason he might have to get back at you or the company by committing fraud?

- Has the CFO ever asked you to approve any financial transaction you thought might be improper or illegal?

- Do you know whether the CFO has any outside business interests that might conflict with his duties here?

- Does the CFO employ any friends or relatives in the company? (Look for possible conflicts or sweetheart deals.)

- What information do you have about the CFO's lifestyle? (Look for expensive homes, cars, toys, and habits.)

- What is your general impression of how the CFO gets along with his staff? (Look for abuses of authority, etc., that would motivate employees directly below the CFO to participate in fraud.)

- How do you think fraud in your company compares with others in the same industry?

- Of course, Mr. CEO, I must ask you many of the same questions about yourself. Is there any reason that anyone below you might claim you are committing fraud against the company?

- I must also ask you some personal financial questions. Does that give you any problem? (Wait for negative response.)

- Please give me a current estimate of your personal assets, liabilities, income, and expenses. (List) What percentage of your net worth is tied directly to this company? (Look for highly leveraged individuals whose company holdings are the significant portion of their net worth.)

- Are you currently experiencing any personal financial problems? (Look for lawsuits, liens, judgments, or other indicators.)

- Do you have friends or relatives working for this company? (Look for conflicts of interest.)

- Do you have friends or relatives working for major suppliers or vendors to your company? (Look for conflicts.)

- Do you own any portion of a company that does business with this organization? (Look for conflicts.)

- Hypothetically, if you wanted to pump up your company's profits, what would be the easiest way to do it?

- As I said, we will be required to ask many questions of your staff. Is there any reason why someone who works for you would say you are at risk to commit significant fraud against the company or its shareholders?

- Mr. CEO, this is the last question, and it should be obvious why I have to ask it. Have you committed fraud or other illegal acts against the company? (Do not apologize for asking the question; it's your job.)

THE CEO'S TOP STAFF

Chief Executive Officers of corporations, large and small, are busy individuals. Because they tend to be "big picture" people by nature, they rely heavily on their staffs—principally their personal assistants—to take care of the details. But personal assistants do not usually get closely tied with the boss without a demonstrated history of loyalty and discretion. In short, if you make the boss's assistant mad, your fraud-related questions are going to be interpreted in the worst possible light, thereby making your job much more difficult.

So the key to interviewing the CEO's top staff is to approach it correctly from the outset. That means laying a great deal of groundwork before you ask sensitive questions. Start with procedural matters or some other non-sensitive topic, and ask the fraud-related questions toward the end of your conversation.

1. *Mr. Assistant, part of my job as an auditor (fraud examiner) is to assess the risk that the company's books are not materially correct as a result of fraud by employees or management. I already have talked about these issues to your boss, and he understands the importance of this, and that in the audit I will be talking to everyone about the subject to some extent. Do you have any problem with that? (Wait for negative response.)*

2. *Do you think fraud is a problem for business in general? (Icebreaker)*

3. *How do you think this company stacks up with others in terms of honesty of its employees and managers?*

4. *Have you ever heard rumors in the company that someone is committing fraud, especially someone high up in the organization?*

5. *Is the company in any kind of financial trouble that would motivate management to misstate the company's profits?*

6. *Do you think your co-workers are essentially honest?*

7. *Has anyone you work with ever asked you to do something you felt was not legal or ethical?*

8. *How would you handle that situation if someone asked you? (Solicit information on fraud reporting program.)*

9. *If someone in a position of authority in the company wanted to commit fraud, what would be the easiest way to do it?*

10. *As your auditor, may I ask you to report any instances in the future if someone asks you to do something to the books and records that you feel is not right? (Solicit future cooperation.)*

THE CHIEF FINANCIAL OFFICER

In the vast majority of cases the CFO is an integral part of any financial statement fraud, as illustrated previously. As a result, the interview with the CFO should concentrate not only on possible motivations to commit fraud, but the opportunity to do so. Since most CFOs are accountants, they should more readily understand your fraud-related mission. This can be both good and bad; good if the CFO is honest, and bad if he isn't. Among all financial personnel, the CFO is in the best position to know how to cook the books and keep it from being uncovered. If that weren't enough, many CFOs are hired directly from the firms who audit the company. Is there any other person more likely to be at the center of the fraud?

- Mr. CFO, you now know that new audit standards require us to actively assess the risk that material fraud could be affecting the financial statements. We have talked to the CEO, and he is fully aware that we will be inquiring of most everyone we speak with about the possibility of fraud or irregularities. You understand that, don't you? (Wait for affirmative response.)

- Of the accounts on the company's books, which do you suspect might be the most vulnerable to manipulation, and why?

- What kind of history does the company have with fraud in general, including defalcations and employee thefts? (Look for signs of a weak corporate culture.)

- We know that fraud usually exists to some extent—even if it is small—in most companies. How does your company compare to others, do you think?

- What is your overall impression of the company's ethics and corporate culture?

- During our assessment of risk of fraud in your company, are there any specific areas you'd like to discuss with us?

- Is there any reason that someone in the company might say that management had a motive to misstate the financials?

- Has anyone you work with ever asked you to do something with the books that you thought was questionable, unethical, or illegal?

- Are you involved in the personal finances of the CEO? If so, is there anything about them that might make you think he is under personal financial pressure?

- Does the CEO's lifestyle or habits give you any reason to think he may be living above his means?

- Has anyone in a position of authority ever asked that you withhold information from the auditors, alter documents, or make fictitious entries in the books and records?

- Is there anything about your own background or finances that would cause someone to suspect that you had the motive for committing fraud?

- Because of your importance as CFO, I must ask you one final question: Have you yourself committed fraud or illegal acts against this company? (Remember—don't apologize.)

THE ACCOUNTING STAFF

If a financial statement fraud has been ordered by the CFO, either he will do the actual dirty work himself, or he will get his staff to do it. In some cases, the staff will understand the big picture, but in most situations, the employee is told only what he or she needs to know. It is uncommon for a CFO to share with a lower staff person the fact that he is cooking the books.

As a result, the examiner generally must complete his audit work before beginning the interviews of the accounting staff. This will allow specific transactions to be discussed with the people who actually entered them in the company's records. For example, all thorough audits will examine the major journal entries. Frequently, these journal entries will be ordered by the CFO but actually entered by a staff member. There generally would be no record of the CFO requesting the entry, so this fact must be established through interviews.

Interviews of the accounting staff will allow sufficient examination of procedures and controls over assets. After these questions are answered, you can generally pursue the line of inquiry suggested above for the CEO's assistant.

It should be noted that there are similarities and differences in the questions asked of the CEO, the CFO, and their staffs. In the case of the CEO and the CFO, both were specifically asked if they had committed fraud against the company, albeit in a nice way. The staffers were not asked that specific question.

The reasoning is this: significant financial statement fraud, as we have stated, generally originates with one or both of these two executives. Staffers have less motivation to engage in financial statement fraud, and are therefore at less risk to do so. They are also less likely to have the financial authority to enter transactions in the books without higher approval.

So absent of any specific information to the contrary, asking the employees point blank if they have committed fraud is less likely to produce information and more likely to offend them. But with the CFO and the CEO, asking the direct question will add measurably to the prevention of fraud. There are few defenses to not asking the question, other than the specter of embarrassing the executives you are auditing. That will, of course, sound pretty weak in a court of law where you are fighting for your professional life.

Prevention of Financial Statement Fraud

Prevention and deterrence of statement fraud consists of those actions taken to discourage the perpetration of fraud and limit the exposure, if fraud does occur. Internal auditing is responsible for helping deter fraud by examining and evaluating the adequacy and the effectiveness of controls, commensurate with the extent of the potential exposure/risk in the various segments of the entity's operations.

Auditors

The internal audit standard states that the principal mechanism for deterring fraud is control. Primary responsibility for establishing and maintaining control rests with management. Treadway addresses this issue by recommending that internal audit departments or staffs have not only the support of top management, but also the necessary resources available to carry out their mission. The internal auditors' stated responsibility is to aid management in the deterrence of fraud. Specifically, the internal auditor should determine if:

- The organizational environment fosters control consciousness.
- Realistic organizational goals and objectives are set.
- Written corporate policies (for example, code of conduct) exist that describe prohibited activities and the action required whenever violations are discovered.
- Appropriate authorization policies for transactions are established and maintained.
- Policies, practices, procedure reports, and other mechanisms are developed to monitor activities and safeguard assets, particularly in high-risk areas.
- Communication channels provide management with adequate and reliable information.
- Recommendations need to be made for the establishment or enhancement of cost-effective controls to help deter fraud.

Management

It is management's responsibility to set the ethical tone of the organization. As with other occupational fraud and abuse, reducing the three factors that produce fraud will greatly help in the prevention of financial statement fraud. Reducing existing pressures to commit fraud, removing the potential opportunities, and relieving possible reasons for rationalizing fraud will greatly aid in the prevention of financial statement fraud.

Reduce the Situational Pressures that Encourage Statement Fraud

- Avoid setting unachievable financial goals.
- Eliminate external pressures that might tempt accounting personnel to prepare fraudulent financial statements.

- Remove operational obstacles blocking effective financial performance such as working capital restraints, excess production volume, or inventory restraints.
- Establish clear and uniform accounting procedures with no exception clauses.

Reduce the Opportunity to Commit

- Maintain accurate and complete internal accounting records.
- Carefully monitor the business transactions and interpersonal relationships of suppliers, buyers, purchasing agents, sales representatives, and others who interface in the transactions between financial units.
- Establish a physical security system to secure company assets, including finished goods, cash, capital equipment, tools, and other valuable items.
- Divide important functions between employees, separating total control of one area.
- Maintain accurate personnel records including background checks on new employees.
- Encourage strong supervisory and leadership relationships within groups to ensure enforcement of accounting procedures.

Reduce Rationalization of Fraud—Strengthen Employee Personal Integrity

- Managers should set an example by promoting honesty in the accounting area. It is important that management practice what they preach. Dishonest acts by management, even if they are directed at someone outside the organization, create a dishonest environment that can spread to other business activities and other employees, internal and external.
- Honest and dishonest behavior should be defined in company policies. Organizational accounting policies should clear up any gray areas in accounting procedures.
- The consequences of violating the rules and the punishment of violators should be clear.

ASSET MISAPPROPRIATION: CASH RECEIPTS

Asset misappropriations are by far the most common of all occupational frauds. There are three major categories of asset misappropriation schemes. Cash receipts schemes will be discussed in this section, fraudulent disbursements of cash will be addressed in the next section, and the following section will cover schemes involving the theft of inventory and other non-cash assets.

Cash is the focal point of most accounting entries. Cash, both on deposit in banks and petty cash, can be misappropriated through many different schemes. These schemes can be either on-book or off-book, depending on where they occur.

Cash receipts schemes fall into two categories, *skimming* and *larceny*. The difference in the two types of fraud depends completely on when the cash is stolen. Cash larceny is the theft of money that has *already appeared* on a victim organization's books, while skimming is the theft of cash that has *not yet been recorded* in the accounting system. The way in which an employee extracts the cash may be exactly the same for a cash larceny or skimming scheme.

Skimming

Skimming is the removal of cash from a victim entity prior to its entry in an accounting system. Employees who skim from their companies steal sales or receivables before they are recorded in the company books. Skimming schemes are known as "off-book" frauds, meaning money is stolen before it is recorded in the victim organization's accounts. This aspect of skimming schemes means they leave no direct audit trail. Because the stolen funds are never recorded, the victim organization may not be aware that the cash was ever received. Consequently, it may be very difficult to detect that the money has been stolen. This is the prime advantage of a skimming scheme to the fraudster.

Skimming is one of the most common forms of occupational fraud. It can occur at any point where cash enters a business, so almost anyone who deals with the process of receiving cash may be in a position to skim money. This includes salespeople, tellers, waitpersons, and others who receive cash directly from customers.

In addition, many skimming schemes are perpetrated by employees whose duties include receiving and logging payments made by customers through the mail. These employees slip checks out of the incoming mail instead of posting those checks to the proper revenue or receivables accounts. Those who deal directly with customers or who handle customer payments are obviously the most likely candidates to skim funds.

Sales Skimming

The most basic skimming scheme occurs when an employee sells goods or services to a customer, collects the customer's payment, but makes no record of the sale. The employee simply pockets the money received from the customer instead of turning it over to his employer. (See "Unrecorded Sales" flowchart)

Consider one of the simplest and most common sales transactions, a sale of goods at the cash register. In a normal transaction, a customer purchases an item and an employee enters the sale on the register. The register tape reflects that the sale has been made and shows that a certain amount of cash (the purchase price of the item) should have been placed in the register. By comparing the register tape to the amount of money on hand, it may be possible to detect thefts. For instance, if there were $500 worth of sales recorded on a particular register on a given day, but only $400 cash in the register, it would be obvious that someone had stolen $100 (assuming no beginning cash balance).

If the employee is skimming money, however, it will be impossible to detect theft simply by comparing the register tape to the cash drawer. Returning to the example in the paragraph above, assume that an employee wants to make off with $100. Through the course of the day, there are $500 worth of sales at his register; one sale is for $100. When the $100 sale is made, the employee does not record the transaction on his register. The customer pays $100 and takes the merchandise home, but instead of placing the money in the cash drawer, the employee pockets it. In order to create the appearance that the sale is being entered in the register, the employee might ring a "no sale" or some other non-cash transaction. Since the employee did not record the sale, at the end of the day the register tape will only reflect $400 in sales. There will be $400 on hand in the register ($500 in total sales minus the $100 that the employee stole) so the register will balance. Thus by not recording the sale the employee is able to steal money without the missing funds appearing on the books. Of course, the

Financial Transactions

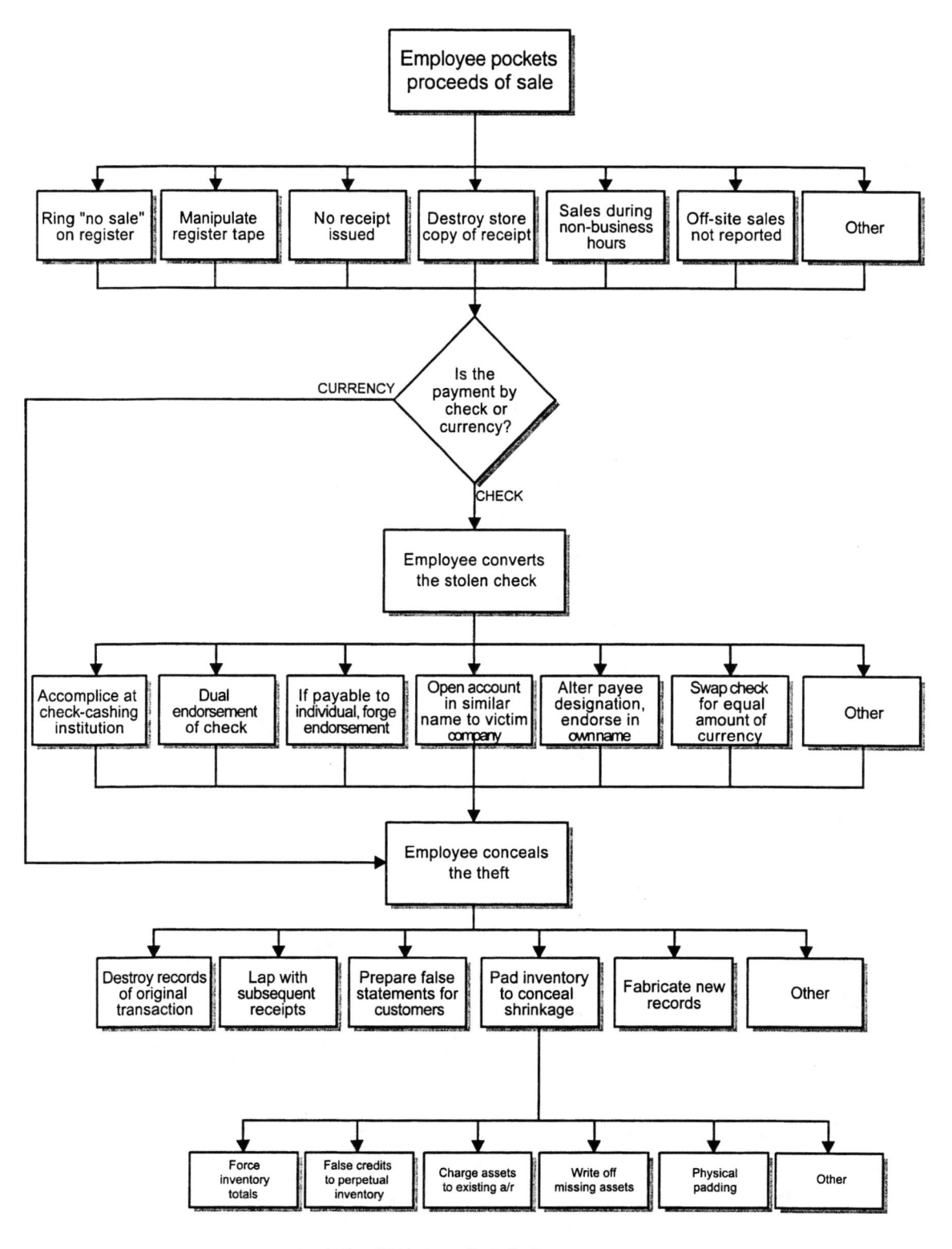

Asset Misappropriation: Cash Receipts

Employee pockets proceeds of sale
- Ring "no sale" on register
- Manipulate register tape
- No receipt issued
- Destroy store copy of receipt
- Sales during non-business hours
- Off-site sales not reported
- Other

Is the payment by check or currency?
- CURRENCY → (to Employee conceals the theft)
- CHECK → Employee converts the stolen check

Employee converts the stolen check
- Accomplice at check-cashing institution
- Dual endorsement of check
- If payable to individual, forge endorsement
- Open account in similar name to victim company
- Alter payee designation, endorse in own name
- Swap check for equal amount of currency
- Other

Employee conceals the theft
- Destroy records of original transaction
- Lap with subsequent receipts
- Prepare false statements for customers
- Pad inventory to conceal shrinkage
- Fabricate new records
- Other

Pad inventory to conceal shrinkage
- Force inventory totals
- False credits to perpetual inventory
- Charge assets to existing a/r
- Write off missing assets
- Physical padding
- Other

Unrecorded Sales

2005 Fraud Examiners Manual

theft will show up indirectly in the company's records as inventory shrinkage. But the books will provide no direct evidence of the theft.

The most difficult part in skimming at the register is that the employee must commit the overt act of taking money. If the employee takes the customer's money and shoves it into his pocket without entering the transaction on the register, the customer will probably suspect that something is wrong and might report the conduct to another employee or a manager. It is also possible that a manager, a fellow employee, or a surveillance camera will spot the illegal conduct. Therefore, it is often desirable for a perpetrator to act as though he is properly recording a transaction while he skims sales.

Register Manipulation

Some employees might ring a "no sale" or other non-cash transaction to mask the theft of sales. The false transaction is entered on the register so that it appears a sale is being rung up. The perpetrator opens the register drawer and pretends to place the cash he has just received in the drawer, but in reality he pockets the cash. To the casual observer it looks as though the sale is being properly recorded.

Some employees may also rig their registers so that a sale can be entered on the register keys, but will not appear on the register tapes. The employee can then safely skim the sale. Anyone observing the employee will see the sale entered, see the cash drawer open, etc., yet the register tape will not reflect the transaction.

> EXAMPLE
>
> *A service station employee hid stolen gasoline sales by simply lifting the ribbon from the printer on his register. He collected and pocketed the sales, which were not recorded on the register tape. The fraudster would then roll back the tape to the point where the next transaction should appear and replace the ribbon. The next transaction would be printed without leaving any blank space on the tape, apparently leaving no trace of the fraud.*

When the ribbon is removed from the register, the result is a blank space on the register tape where the skimmed sale should have been printed. Unusual gaps between transactions on a register tape may mean that someone is skimming sales.

Fraudsters will often manually roll back the tape when they replace the ribbon on their registers so that there is no gap between transactions. However, most register transactions are sequentially numbered. If a transaction has been omitted from the register tape, the result is a break in the sequence. For instance, if an employee skimmed sale #155, then the register tape would only show transactions #153, #154, #156, #157 and so on. The missing transaction numbers, omitted because the ribbon was lifted when they took place, would indicate fraud.

Skimming During Nonbusiness Hours

Another way to skim unrecorded sales is to conduct sales during nonbusiness hours. For instance, some employees will open stores on weekends or after hours without the knowledge of the owners. They can pocket the proceeds of all sales made during these times because the owners have no idea that their stores are even open for business.

> EXAMPLE
>
> *A manager of a retail facility went to work two hours early every day, opening his store at 8:00 a.m. instead of 10:00 a.m., and pocketed all the sales made during these two hours. He rang up sales on the register as if it was business as usual, but then removed the register tape and all the cash he had accumulated. The manager then started from scratch at 10:00 as if the store was just opening. The tape was destroyed so there was no record of the before-hours revenue.*

To this point skimming has been discussed in the context of cash register transactions, but skimming does not have to occur at a register. Some of the most costly skimming schemes are perpetrated by employees who work at remote locations or without close supervision. This can include on-site sales persons who do not deal with registers, independent salesmen who operate off-site, and employees who work at branches or satellite offices. These employees have a high level of autonomy in their jobs, which often translates into poor supervision and in turn to fraud.

Skimming of Off-Site Sales

Several industries rely on remote salespersons to generate revenue. The fact that these employees are largely unsupervised puts them in a good position to skim revenues. For example, consider the apartment rental industry, where apartment managers handle the day-to-day operations without much oversight. A common scheme is for an on-site employee to identify the tenants who pay in currency and remove them from the books. This causes a particular apartment to appear as vacant on the records when, in fact, it is occupied. The manager can skim the rental payments from the "vacant" unit, and the revenue will never be missed. As long as no one physically checks the apartment, the perpetrator can continue skimming indefinitely.

Another rental-skimming scheme occurs when apartments are rented out but no lease is signed. On the books, the apartment will still appear to be vacant, even though there are tenants on the premises. The perpetrator can skim the rental payments from these tenants without fear that they will show up as past due in the company records. Sometimes the employees in these schemes work in conjunction with the renters and give a "special rate" to these people. In return, the renter's payments are made directly to the employee and any complaints or maintenance requests are directed only to that employee so the tenant's presence in the apartment remains hidden.

Instead of skimming rent, some property managers focus on less predictable forms of revenue like application fees and late fees. Ownership may know when rent is due and how many apartments are occupied, but often there is no control in place to track the number of people who fill out rental applications or how many tenants pay their rent a day or two late. Property managers can make thousands of dollars by skimming these "nickel and dime" payments.

Off-site skimming is by no means limited to the apartment rental industry. The schemes described above can easily translate into any arena where those who generate or collect revenues operate in an independent fashion. A prime example is the insurance agent who sells policies to customers, then neglects to file the policies with the carrier. Most customers do not want to file claims on a policy, especially early in the term, for fear that their premiums will rise. Knowing this, the agent keeps all documentation on the policies instead of turning it over to the carrier. The agent is able to skim the customer's payments because the carrier does not know the policy exists. The customer continues to make his payments, thinking that he is insured, when in fact the policy is a ruse.

Poor Collection Procedures

Poor collection and recording procedures can make it easy for an employee to skim sales or receivables.

EXAMPLE

A governmental authority that dealt with public housing was victimized because it failed to itemize daily receipts. This agency received payments from several public housing tenants, *but at the end of the day, "money" received from tenants was listed as a whole. Receipt numbers were not used to itemize the payments made by tenants, so there was no way to pinpoint which tenant had paid how much. Consequently, the employee in charge of collecting money from tenants was able to skim a portion of their payments. She simply did not record the receipt of over $10,000. Her actions caused certain accounts receivable to be overstated where tenant payments were not properly recorded.*

Understated Sales

The discussion above focused on purely off-book sales, those which are never recorded. Understated sales work differently because the transaction in question is posted to the books, but for a lower amount than what the perpetrator actually collected. (See "Understated Sales" flowchart) One way employees commit understated sales schemes is by altering receipts or preparing false receipts that misstate the amount of sales.

EXAMPLE

An employee wrote receipts to customers for their purchases, but she removed the carbon paper backing on the receipts so that they did not produce a company copy. The employee then used a pencil to prepare company copies that showed lower purchase prices. For example, if the customer had paid $100, the company copy might reflect a payment of $80. The employee skimmed the difference between the actual amount of revenue and the amount reflected on the fraudulent receipt.

Understated sales schemes are commonly undertaken by employees who work at the cash register. In a typical scheme an employee enters a sales total which is lower than the amount actually paid by the customer. The employee skims the difference between the actual purchase price of the item and the sales figure recorded on the register. For instance, if an item is sold for $100, the employee could ring up the sale of an $80 item and skim the excess $20.

Rather than reduce the price of an item, an employee might record the sale of fewer items. If 100 units are sold, for instance, an employee might only record the sale of 50 units and skim the excess receipts.

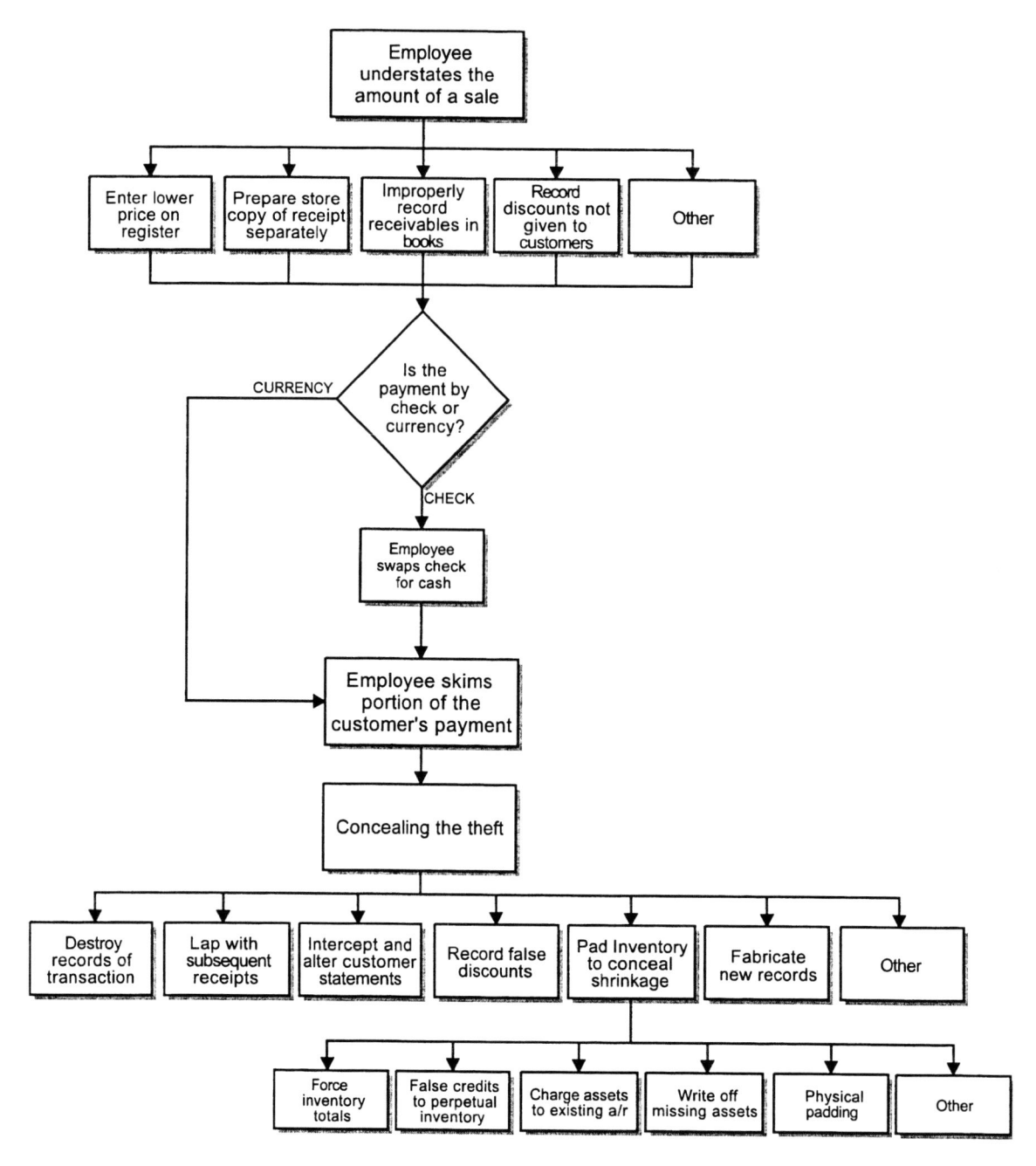

Asset Misappropriation: Cash Receipts — Financial Transactions

```
                    Employee
                  understates the
                  amount of a sale
                         │
   ┌──────────┬──────────┼──────────┬──────────┐
Enter lower  Prepare   Improperly   Record     Other
 price on   store copy   record    discounts
 register   of receipt receivables not given
            separately  in books  to customers
                         │
              CURRENCY  ◇ Is the payment
              ←─────────  by check or
                         currency?
                         │ CHECK
                         ▼
                      Employee
                     swaps check
                      for cash
                         │
                         ▼
                   Employee skims
                   portion of the
                  customer's payment
                         │
                         ▼
                  Concealing the theft
                         │
 ┌────────┬────────┬────────┬────────┬────────┬────────┐
Destroy  Lap with  Intercept  Record   Pad      Fabricate Other
records  subsequent and alter  false  Inventory  new
of       receipts  customer  discounts to conceal records
transaction        statements        shrinkage
                                        │
                  ┌──────┬──────┬──────┼──────┬──────┐
                Force   False   Charge  Write off Physical Other
                inventory credits assets to missing padding
                totals  to perpetual existing a/r assets
                        inventory
```

Understated Sales

A similar method is used when sales are made on account. The bill to the customer reflects the true amount of the sale, but the receivable is understated in the company books. For instance, a company might be owed $1,000, but the receivable is recorded as $800. (Sales are correspondingly understated by $200.) When the customer makes payment on the account, the employee can skim $200 and post the $800 to the account. The account will appear to have been paid in full.

FALSE DISCOUNTS

Those employees with the authority to grant discounts may utilize this authority to skim sales and receivables. In a false discount skimming scheme, an employee accepts full payment for an item, but records the transaction as if the customer had been given a discount. The employee skims the amount of the discount. For example, on a $100 purchase, if an employee granted a false discount of 20%, he could skim $20 and leave the company's books in balance.

Theft of Checks Received through the Mail

Checks received through the mail are a frequent target of employees seeking illicit gains. Theft of incoming checks usually occurs when a single employee is in charge of opening the mail and recording the receipt of payments. This employee simply steals one or more incoming checks instead of posting them to customer accounts. (See "Theft of Incoming Checks" flowchart) When the task of receiving and recording incoming payments is left to a single person, it is all too easy for that employee to make off with an occasional check.

> EXAMPLE
> *A mailroom employee stole over $2 million in government checks arriving through the mail. This employee simply identified and removed envelopes delivered from a government agency known to send checks to the company. Using a group of accomplices acting under the names of fictitious persons and companies, this individual was able to launder the checks and divide the proceeds with his cronies.*

The theft of checks is not usually complicated, but it is sometimes more difficult to conceal a check theft scheme than other forms of skimming. If the stolen checks were payments on the victim company's receivables, then these payments were *expected*. As receivables become past due, the victim company will send notices of nonpayment to its customers. A customer is likely to complain when he receives a second bill for a payment he has already made. In

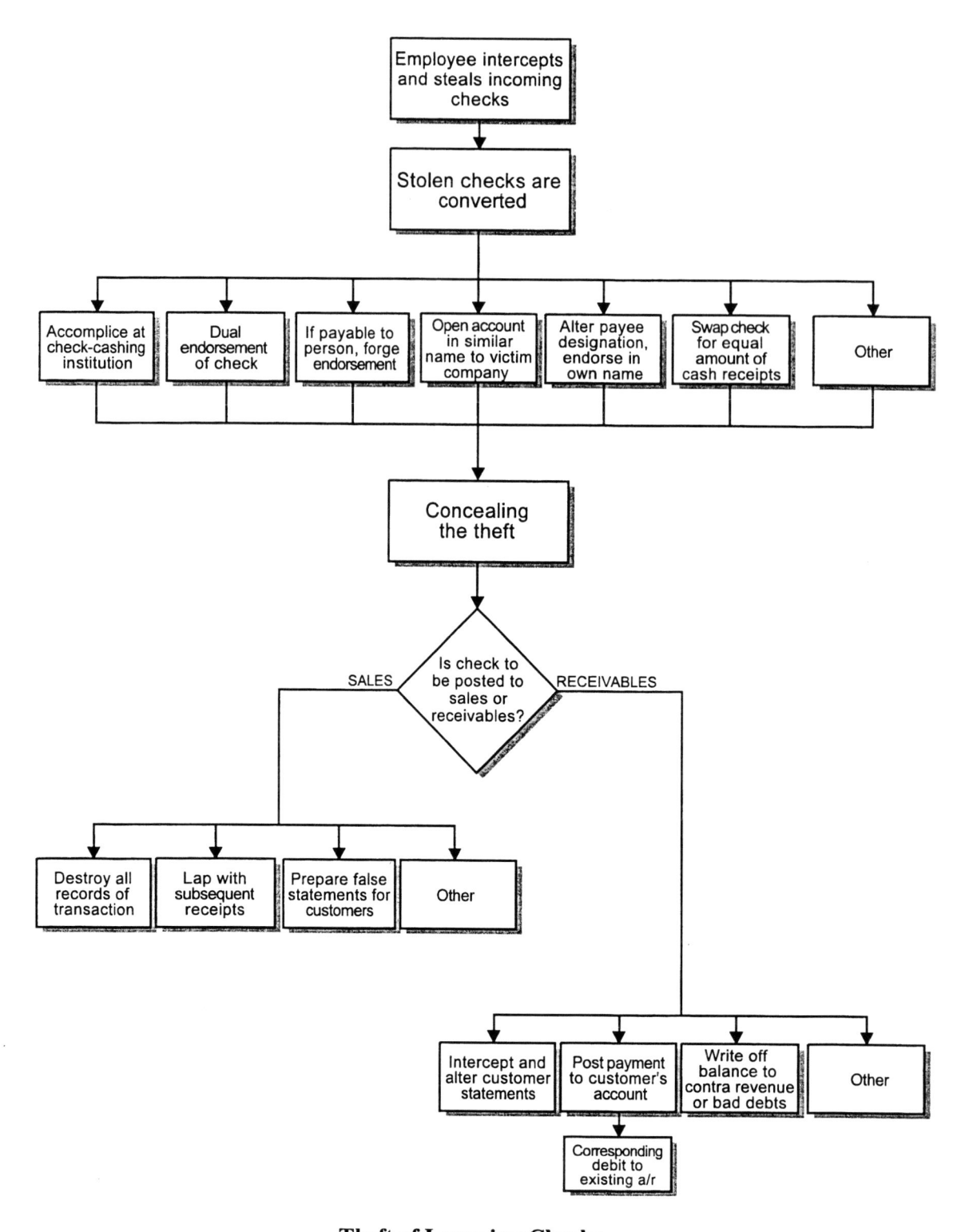

Theft of Incoming Checks

addition, the cashed check will serve as evidence that the customer made his payment. The methods used to conceal check theft schemes will be discussed later in this section.

Check for Currency Substitutions

The intelligent criminal will generally prefer to steal currency rather than checks if given the opportunity. The reasons why are obvious. First, currency is harder to trace than a check. A cashed check eventually returns to the person who wrote it and may provide evidence of who cashed it or where it was spent. Endorsements, bank stamps and so forth may indicate the identity of the thief. Currency, on the other hand, disappears into the economy once it is stolen.

The second reason that currency is preferable to a check is the difficulty in converting the check. When currency is stolen it can be spent immediately. A check, on the other hand, must be endorsed and cashed or deposited before the thief can put his hands on the money it represents. To avoid this problem, employees who steal unrecorded checks will frequently substitute them for receipted currency. If, for example, an employee skims an incoming check worth $500, he can add the check to the day's receipts and remove $500 in currency. The total receipts will match the amount of cash on hand, but payments in currency are replaced by the check.

> EXAMPLE
>
> *An employee responsible for receipting ticket and fine payments on behalf of a municipality abused her position and stole incoming revenues for nearly two years. When payments in currency were received by this individual, she issued receipts, but when checks were received she did not. The check payments were therefore unrecorded revenues—ripe for skimming. These unrecorded checks were placed in the days' receipts and an equal amount of cash was removed. The receipts matched the amount of money on hand except that payments in currency had been replaced with checks.*

The check for currency substitution is very common. While these substitutions make it easier for a crook to convert stolen payments, the problem of concealing the theft still remains. The fact that the stolen checks are not posted means that some customers' accounts are in danger of becoming past due. If this happens, the perpetrator's scheme is in danger because these customers will almost surely complain about the misapplication of their payments. However, the misapplied payments can be concealed on the books by forcing account totals, stealing customers' account statements, lapping, and making other fraudulent accounting entries. These concealment techniques will be discussed in some detail in the Skimming Receivables section.

Check for currency substitutions are especially common when an employee has access to some unexpected source of funds such as a manufacturers refund that arrives outside the regular stream of sales and receivables payments. In these cases the check can be swapped for cash and there is usually no additional step required to conceal the crime. The refund check, an unexpected source of funds, will not be missed by the victim organization, and the party who issued the check expects no goods or services in return.

Skimming Receivables

It is generally more difficult to conceal the skimming of receivables than the skimming of sales because receivables payments are *expected*. The victim organization knows the customer owes money and it is waiting for the payment to arrive. When unrecorded sales are skimmed, it is as though the sale never existed. But when receivables are skimmed, the absence of the payment appears on the books as a delinquent account. In order to conceal a skimmed receivable, a perpetrator must somehow account for the payment that was due to the company but never received. There are a number of common techniques fraudsters use to conceal the skimming of receivables.

Forcing Account Balances or Destroying Transaction Records

Among the most dangerous receivables skimming schemes are those in which the perpetrator is in charge of collecting and posting payments. If a fraudster has a hand in both ends of the receipting process, he or she can falsify records to conceal the theft of receivables payments. For example, the fraudster might post the customer's payments to their receivables accounts, even though the payments will never be deposited. This keeps the receivable from aging, but it creates an imbalance in the cash account. The perpetrator hides the imbalance by forcing the total on the cash account, overstating it to match the total postings to accounts receivable.

EXAMPLE

The chief financial officer of a small corporation stole approximately $100,000 from his company by diverting customer checks. This individual controlled all the books and records for the victim company. He stole checks from customers and deposited them in his personal bank account. The customers' payments were still posted to keep the receivables from aging.

> *The perpetrator stole checks in an amount equal to the victim company's tax liability. To keep the books in balance, he would prepare checks payable to the IRS, but he never mailed them. The checks were recorded in the victim's records and the false disbursements offset the amount of false postings to accounts receivable. The scheme was uncovered when the IRS notified the victim company that its taxes were delinquent.*

Some fraudsters simply destroy all records that might prove that they have been stealing. Destroying records en masse does not prevent the victim organization from realizing that it is being robbed, but it may help conceal the identity of the thief.

Lapping

Lapping customer payments is one of the most common methods of concealing receivables skimming. Lapping is the crediting of one account through the abstraction of money from another account. It is the fraudster's version of "robbing Peter to pay Paul."

Suppose a company has three customers, A, B, and C. When A's payment is received, the fraudster steals it instead of posting it to A's account. Customer A expects that his account will be credited with the payment he has made. If the payment has not been posted by the time A's next statement is mailed, he will see that the payment was not applied to his account and will almost certainly complain. To avoid this, the thief must take some action to make it appear that the payment was posted.

When B's check arrives, the thief posts this money to A's account. Payments now appear to be up-to-date on A's account, but B's account is behind. When C's payment is received, the perpetrator applies it to B's account. This process continues indefinitely until one of three things happens: (1) someone discovers the scheme, (2) restitution is made to the accounts, or (3) some concealing entry is made to adjust the accounts receivable balances.

> EXAMPLE
>
> *A clerk working for a government agency committed a lapping scheme that involved the theft of more than 150 customer payments, causing a total misappropriation of more than $30,000 in government funds. This individual stole taxes, fees and other incoming payments from customers to cover his personal expenses. When a customer's payment was stolen, the documentation on that payment would be hidden until a later payment was received. The later payment would be applied to the earlier customer's records.*

As the rotating schedule of applying and misapplying payments became more and more complicated, the perpetrator insisted on exerting more and more control over the receipting process. He insisted on handling all incoming mail, preparing the deposit and delivering the deposit to the bank so that he could continue to delay the posting of payments. The fraud was detected in large part because several consumers complained that they had not received confirmation of their payments, even though their checks had cleared months earlier.

Because lapping schemes can become very intricate, fraudsters sometimes keep a second set of books on hand detailing the true nature of the payments received. In many skimming cases, a search of the fraudster's work area will reveal a set of records tracking the actual payments and how they have been misapplied to conceal the theft. It may seem odd that people would keep records of their illegal activity on hand, but many lapping schemes become extremely complicated as more and more payments are misapplied. The second set of records helps the perpetrator keep track of the funds that were stolen and which accounts need to be credited to conceal the fraud. Uncovering these records, if they exist, will greatly facilitate the investigation of a lapping scheme.

While lapping is more commonly used to conceal receivables skimming, it can also be used to disguise the skimming of sales. Employees sometimes steal all or part of one day's receipts and replace them with the receipts from the following day. This type of concealment requires the employee to delay making the company deposit until enough money can be collected to recoup the stolen funds. If an organization rigidly adheres to a deposit schedule, it is unlikely that lapping will be effective in concealing this type of fraud.

Stolen Statements

When employees skim receivables, they may let the targeted accounts age instead of attempting to force the balances. In other words, they steal an incoming check intended as payment on a receivable, and they simply act as if the check never arrived. This method keeps the victim organization's cash account in balance, because the stolen payment is never posted.

Of course, if the customer's payment is not posted, the receivable will eventually become past due. The customer will have proof in the form of a canceled check that a payment was made on the account. The question will arise: where did the payment go? The answer, of course, is that it went into the fraudster's pocket. So the goal of the fraudster must be to keep the customer from realizing that his or her account was not credited with the payment.

If this can be accomplished, the customer will not complain about the missing payment, and the victim organization will not realize that skimming has occurred.

One way fraudsters attempt to conceal the fact that they have skimmed a payment from a customer is to intercept the customer's account statement and/or late notices. In some cases, the perpetrator intercepts the account statement by changing the customer's address in the billing system so that statements are sent directly to the perpetrator's home or to an address where he or she can retrieve them. In other instances, the perpetrator physically intercepts the statements before they are mailed.

Once the real statement indicating that the payment was not received has been intercepted, the fraudster usually alters the statement or produces a counterfeit. The false statements indicate that the customer's payment was properly posted. This leads the customer to believe that his account is up-to-date and keeps the customer from complaining about stolen payments.

False Account Entries

Intercepting the customer's statements will keep him in the dark as to the status of his account, but as long as the customer's payments are being skimmed, his account is slipping further and further past due. The perpetrator must bring the account back up-to-date in order to conceal his crime. Lapping is one way to keep accounts current as the employee skims from them. Another way is to make false entries in the victim organization's accounting system.

DEBITS TO EXPENSE ACCOUNTS

An employee might conceal the skimming of funds by making unsupported entries in the victim company's books. If a payment is made on a receivable, for instance, the proper entry is a debit to cash and a credit to the receivable. Instead of debiting cash, the employee might choose to debit an expense account. This transaction still keeps the company's books in balance, but the incoming cash is never recorded. In addition, the customer's receivable account is credited, so it will not become delinquent.

DEBITS TO AGING OR FICTITIOUS RECEIVABLES

The same method discussed above is used when employees debit existing or fictitious accounts receivable in order to conceal skimmed cash. For example, an employee who has skimmed one customer's payments might add the stolen amounts to aging accounts which are soon to be written off as uncollectable, or to very large accounts where a small debit might go unnoticed.

Some perpetrators also set up completely fictitious accounts and debit them for the cost of skimmed receivables. The employees then simply wait for the fictitious receivables to age and be written off as uncollectable. In the meantime, the fictitious receivables carry the cost of a skimming scheme where it will not be detected.

WRITING OFF ACCOUNT BALANCES

Some employees cover their skimming by posting entries to contra revenue accounts such as "discounts and allowances." If, for instance, an employee intercepts a $1,000 payment, he would create a $1,000 "discount" on the account to compensate for the missing money. Another account that might be used in this type of concealment is the bad debts expense account.

EXAMPLE

A billing manager was authorized to write off certain patient balances as hardship allowances. This employee accepted payments from patients, then instructed billing personnel to write off the balance in question. The payments were never posted; they were intercepted by the billing manager. She covered approximately $30,000 in stolen funds by using her authority to write off patients' balances.

Inventory Padding

A problem for fraudsters in some skimming schemes is the victim organization's inventory. Off-book sales of goods will always leave an inventory shortage and a corresponding rise in the cost of goods sold.

When a sale of goods is made, the physical inventory is reduced by the amount of merchandise sold. For instance, when a retailer sells a pair of shoes there is one less pair of shoes in the stock room. However, if this sale is not recorded, the shoes are not removed from the perpetual inventory records. Thus, there is one less pair of shoes on hand than in the perpetual inventory. A reduction in the physical inventory without a corresponding reduction in the perpetual inventory is known as "shrinkage."

When an employee skims sales of services there is no shrinkage (because there is no inventory for services), but when sales of goods are skimmed, shrinkage always occurs. Some amounts of shrinkage are expected due to customer theft, faulty products, and spoilage, but high levels of shrinkage serve as a warning that a company could be a victim of occupational fraud. The general methods used to conceal inventory shrinkage are discussed in detail in the Inventory and Other Assets section.

Detection of Skimming Schemes

The following are some detection methods that may be effective in detecting skimming schemes.

Receipt or Sales Level Detection

Key analytical procedures, such as vertical and horizontal analysis of sales accounts, can be used for skimming detection on a grand scale. These procedures analyze changes in the accounts and can possibly point to skimming problems including understated sales.

Ratio analysis can also provide keys to the detection of skimming schemes. These procedures are discussed in detail in the fraudulent financial statement section.

Detailed inventory control procedures can also be utilized to detect inventory shrinkage due to unrecorded sales. Inventory detection methods include statistical sampling, trend analysis, reviews of receiving reports and inventory records, verification of material requisition and shipping documentation, as well as actual physical inventory counts. These procedures are reviewed in the section on Inventory and Other Assets.

Journal Entry Review

Skimming can sometimes be detected by reviewing and analyzing all journal entries made to the cash and inventory accounts. Journal entries involving the following topics should be examined:

- False credits to inventory to conceal unrecorded or understated sales.
- Other write-offs of inventory for reason of lost, stolen, or obsolete product.
- Write-offs of accounts receivable accounts.
- Irregular entries to cash accounts.

Detecting Lapping of Sales or Receivables

Lapping usually can be detected by comparing the dates of the customer's payments with the dates the customer's accounts are posted. This will require an examination of the source documents, such as the composition of bank deposits. Discrepancies should be investigated.

Confirmation of customers' accounts is another method that might detect lapping. Confirmations are especially effective on large accounts where the time value of money is an issue. However, customers who pay on invoice rather than on balance might not know the exact balance of their account. If this is the case, it might be more effective to confirm by invoice and reconstruct the account balance using the source documents in the files and the results of the confirmation. If fraud is suspected, ask the customer to return a copy of both the front and the back of the check(s) used to pay specific invoices. Match the data on the check copies with the posting dates in the customer's account.

Prevention of Skimming Schemes

Receipt or Sales Level Control

As with most fraud schemes, internal control procedures are a key to prevention of skimming schemes. An essential part of developing control procedures is management's communication to employees. Controlling whether or not an employee will not record a sale, understate a sale, or steal incoming payments is extremely difficult.

General Controls

Sales entries and general ledger access controls should include documented policies and procedures, which are communicated directly from management. The control procedures will generally cover the following subjects:

- Appropriate segregation of duties and access control procedures regarding who makes ledger transactions will be followed.
- Transactions must be properly recorded as to amount, date of occurrence, and ledger account.
- Proper safeguard measures will be adopted to ensure physical access to the account systems. Additional measures should ensure the security of company assets.
- Independent reconciliations as well as internal verification of accounts will be performed on ledger accounts.[*]

Skimming Controls

The discovery of thefts of checks and cash involves proper controls on the receipt process. Deficiencies in the answers to these typical audit-program questions may be red flags.

- Is mail opened by someone independent of cashier, accounts receivable bookkeeper, or other accounting employees who may initiate or post journal entries?

---

[*] George Georgiades, *Audit Procedures* (New York: Harcourt Brace Professional Publishing, 1995).

- Is the delivery of unopened business mail prohibited to employees having access to the accounting records?
- Does the employee who opens the mail:
  - Place restrictive endorsements ("For Deposit Only") on all checks received?
  - Prepare a list of the money, checks, and other receipts?
  - Forward all remittances to the person responsible for preparing and making the daily bank deposit?
  - Forward the total of all remittances to the person responsible for comparing it to the authenticated deposit ticket and amount recorded?
- Is a lock box used?
- Do cash sales occur? If yes:
  - Are cash receipts prenumbered?
  - Is an independent check of prenumbered receipts done daily and reconciled to cash collections?
- Do cash refunds require approval?
- Are cash receipts deposited intact daily?
- Are employees who handle receipts bonded?
- Is the accounts receivable bookkeeper restricted from:
  - Preparing the bank deposit?
  - Obtaining access to the cash receipts book?
  - Having access to collections from customers?
  - Are banks instructed not to cash checks drawn to the order of the company?
- Is the cashier restricted from gaining access to the accounts receivable records and bank and customer statements?
- Are areas where physical handling of cash takes place reasonably safeguarded?
- Is the person who makes postings to the general ledger independent of the cash receipts and accounts receivable functions?
- Does a person independent of the cashier or accounts receivable functions handle customer complaints?

Cash Larceny

In the occupational fraud setting, a cash larceny may be defined as the intentional taking of an employer's cash (the term cash includes both currency and checks) without the consent and against the will of the employer.

A cash larceny scheme can take place in any circumstance in which an employee has access to cash. Every company must deal with the receipt, deposit, and distribution of cash, so every company is potentially vulnerable to a cash larceny scheme. While the circumstances in which an employee might steal cash are nearly limitless, most larceny schemes involve the theft of incoming cash, currency on hand (in a cash register, cash box, etc.), or theft of cash from the victim organization's bank deposits.

Incoming Cash
Theft of Cash from the Register

A large percentage of cash larceny schemes occur at the cash register, and for good reason—the register is usually where the cash is. The register (or similar cash collection points like cash drawers or cash boxes) is usually the most common point of access to cash for employees, so it is understandable that this is where larceny schemes frequently occur. Furthermore, there is often a great deal of activity at the register, numerous transactions that require employees to handle cash. This can serve as a cover for the theft of cash. In a flurry of activity, with money being passed back and forth between customer and employee, an employee can often slip cash out of the register and into his pocket undetected.

The most straightforward cash larceny scheme is to simply open the register and remove currency or checks. (See "Cash Larceny from the Register" flowchart) The theft is often committed as a sale is being conducted so that it appears to be part of the transaction. In other circumstances, the perpetrator waits for a slow moment when no one is around to notice him digging into the cash drawer.

Recall that the difficulty in detecting skimming schemes comes from the fact that the stolen funds are never entered on the victim organization's accounts. In a larceny scheme, on the other hand, the funds that the perpetrator steals have already been reflected on the register tape. As a result, an imbalance will result between the register tape and the cash drawer.

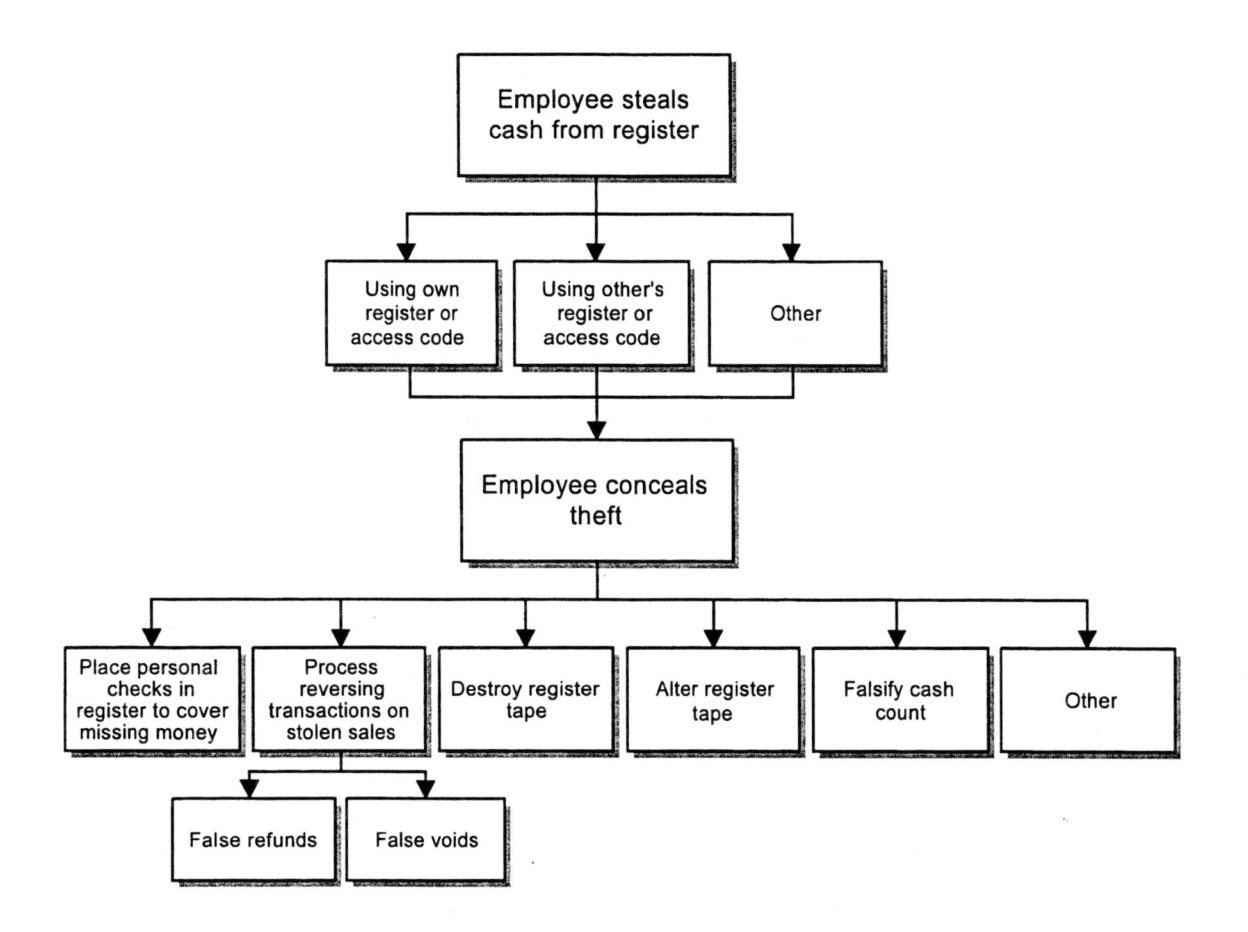

```
                    ┌─────────────────────┐
                    │  Employee steals    │
                    │  cash from register │
                    └─────────────────────┘
                              │
            ┌─────────────────┼─────────────────┐
            ▼                 ▼                 ▼
    ┌──────────────┐  ┌──────────────┐   ┌─────────┐
    │  Using own   │  │ Using other's│   │  Other  │
    │ register or  │  │ register or  │   │         │
    │ access code  │  │ access code  │   │         │
    └──────────────┘  └──────────────┘   └─────────┘
                              │
                              ▼
                    ┌─────────────────┐
                    │Employee conceals│
                    │      theft      │
                    └─────────────────┘
                              │
    ┌──────────┬──────────┬───┴────┬──────────┬──────────┐
    ▼          ▼          ▼        ▼          ▼          ▼
┌────────┐ ┌────────┐ ┌────────┐┌────────┐┌────────┐┌───────┐
│Place   │ │Process │ │Destroy ││ Alter  ││Falsify ││ Other │
│personal│ │reversing│ │register││register││ cash   ││       │
│checks  │ │trans.  │ │  tape  ││  tape  ││ count  ││       │
│...     │ │...     │ │        ││        ││        ││       │
└────────┘ └────────┘ └────────┘└────────┘└────────┘└───────┘
               │
         ┌─────┴─────┐
         ▼           ▼
    ┌─────────┐ ┌─────────┐
    │  False  │ │  False  │
    │ refunds │ │  voids  │
    └─────────┘ └─────────┘
```

Cash Larceny from the Register

A register is balanced by comparing the transactions on the register tape to the amount of cash on hand. Sales, returns, and other register transactions that are recorded on the register tape are added to or subtracted from a known balance to arrive at a total for the period in question. The actual cash is then counted and the two totals are compared. If the register tape shows that there should be more cash in the register than what is present, the discrepancy may be due to larceny.

The actual method for taking money at the register—opening the register and removing currency—rarely varies. It is the methods used by perpetrators to avoid getting caught that distinguish larceny schemes. Oddly, in many instances the perpetrator has no plan for avoiding detection. A large part of fraud is rationalizing; the employee convinces himself that he is somehow entitled to what he is taking, or that what he is doing is not actually a crime. Register larceny schemes frequently begin when the perpetrator convinces himself that he is only "borrowing" the funds to cover a temporary monetary need. These people might carry the missing currency in their registers for several days, deluding themselves in the belief that they will one day repay the funds they have stolen.

The employee who does nothing to camouflage his crimes is easily caught. More dangerous is the person taking active steps to hide his crimes. One basic way for an employee to disguise the fact that he is stealing currency is to take money from someone else's register.

In some retail organizations, employees are assigned to certain registers. Alternatively, one register is used and each employee has an access code. When cash is missing from a certain cashier's register, that cashier is obviously the most likely suspect for the theft. Therefore, by stealing from a co-worker's register, or by using someone else's access code to enter the register, the perpetrator makes sure that another employee will be the prime suspect in the theft.

EXAMPLE

A teller for a retail sales company simply signed onto a register, rang a "no sale" and took currency from the drawer. Over a period of time, the teller took approximately $6,000 through this simple method. In order to get away with the theft, the teller waited until a co-worker was on break, then logged onto that person's register, rang a "no sale" and took the cash. The resulting cash shortage therefore appeared in the register of an honest employee, deflecting attention from the true thief.

A very unsophisticated way to avoid detection is to steal currency in very small amounts over an extended period of time. Because the missing amounts are small, the shortages may be dismissed as accounting errors rather than theft. Typically, the employee becomes dependent on the extra money he is pilfering and his thefts increase in scale or become more frequent, which causes the scheme to be uncovered. Most retail organizations track overages or shortages by employee, making this method largely ineffective.

REVERSING TRANSACTIONS
Some employees conceal cash larceny by processing reversing transactions, which cause the register tape to reconcile to the amount of cash on hand after the theft. By processing false voids or refunds, an employee can reduce the cash balance reflected on the register tape.

EXAMPLE

A cashier received payments from a customer and recorded the transactions on her system. She stole the payments from the customers, then destroyed the company's receipts which reflected the transactions. To complete the cover-up, the cashier went back and voided the transactions that she had entered at the time the payments were received. The reversing entries brought the receipt totals into balance with the cash on hand.

REGISTER MANIPULATION

Instead of using reversing entries, an employee might manually alter the register tape. Again, the purpose of this activity is to force a balance between the cash on hand and the actual cash received. An employee might use white-out to cover up a sale whose proceeds were stolen, or he might simply cross out or alter the numbers on the tape so that the register total and the cash drawer balance. This type of concealment is not common because, in general, the alterations will be noticeable.

ALTERING CASH COUNTS

Another method for concealing cash larceny is to alter the cash counts on registers. When cash from a register is totaled and prepared for deposit, an employee simply records the wrong amount so that the cash on hand appears to balance with the total on the register tape. Obviously, employees who deal with the receipt of cash should not be charged with verifying the amount of cash on hand in their own register, but this control is often overlooked.

DESTROYING REGISTER TAPES

If the fraudster cannot make the cash and the tape balance, the next best thing is to prevent others from computing the totals and discovering the imbalance. Employees who are stealing from the register sometimes destroy detail tapes that would implicate them in a crime. When detail tapes are missing or defaced, it may be because someone is trying to conceal a fraud.

Other Larceny of Sales and Receivables

Not all receipts arrive via the cash register. Employees can just as easily steal money received at other points. One of the more common methods is to take checks received through the mail, post the payments to the accounting system, but steal the checks. (See "Other Cash Larceny" flowchart) Obviously, this type of scheme leaves the cash account out of balance. From a perpetrator's perspective, it would make much more sense to take checks that have not yet been posted to customer accounts. Often, this type of cash larceny scheme is committed by an employee who claims to only be "borrowing" the funds for a short while — one of the classic rationalizations in occupational fraud schemes.

Those employees who have total control of a company's accounting system can overcome the problem of out-of-balance accounts. It is surprisingly common, especially in small businesses, for a single person to control all of a company's deposits and ledgers. These employees can steal incoming cash that has already been posted, then conceal the crime by making unsupported entries in the victim organization's books. Poor separation of duties is very often the weakness that allows cash larceny schemes to go undetected.

EXAMPLE

An employee posted customer payments to the accounts receivable journal but stole the cash received. This resulted in an imbalance in the victim company's cash account. But the perpetrator had control over the company's deposits and all its ledgers. This allowed her to conceal her crime by making unsupported entries in the company's books which produced a fictitious balance between receipts and ledgers.

In circumstances in which payments are stolen but nonetheless posted to the cash receipts journal, reversing entries are sometimes used to balance the victim company's accounts. The incoming payment is initially credited to the customer's account, but the entry is later reversed with an unauthorized adjustment such as a "courtesy discount."

A less elegant way to hide a crime is to simply destroy all records which might prove that the perpetrator has been stealing. This "slash and burn" concealment technique does not prevent the victim company from realizing that it has been robbed, but it may help conceal the identity of the thief.

Cash Larceny from the Deposit

At some point in every revenue-generating business, someone must physically take the company's currency and checks to the bank. This person or persons, left alone literally holding the bag, will have an opportunity to take a portion of the money prior to depositing it into the company's accounts.

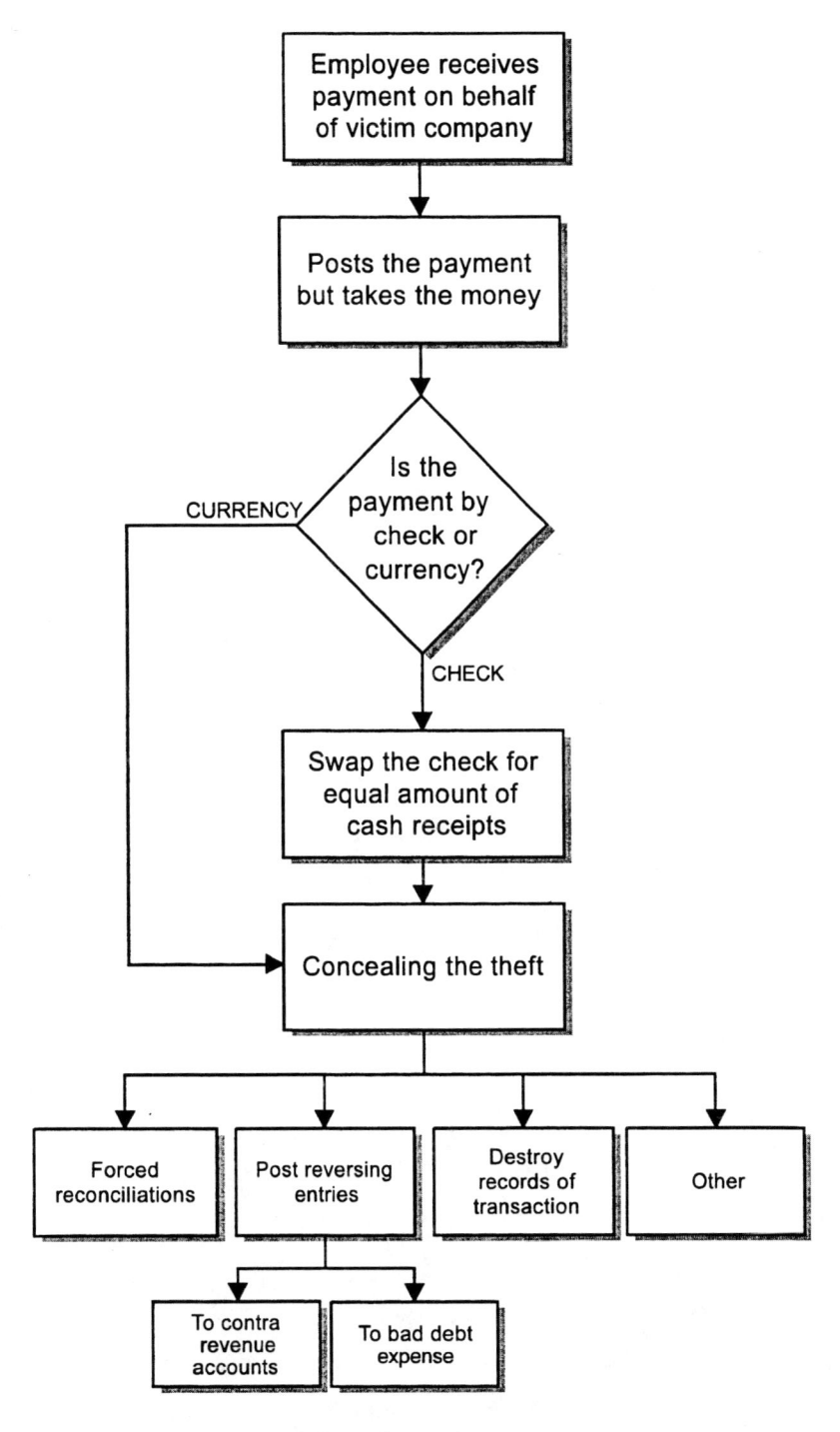

Financial Transactions — Asset Misappropriation: Cash Receipts

```
            ┌─────────────────────┐
            │ Employee receives   │
            │ payment on behalf   │
            │ of victim company   │
            └──────────┬──────────┘
                       ▼
            ┌─────────────────────┐
            │ Posts the payment   │
            │ but takes the money │
            └──────────┬──────────┘
                       ▼
                     ◇ Is the
        CURRENCY  payment by     
         ◄──────   check or
                   currency? ◇
                       │ CHECK
                       ▼
            ┌─────────────────────┐
            │ Swap the check for  │
            │ equal amount of     │
            │ cash receipts       │
            └──────────┬──────────┘
                       ▼
            ┌─────────────────────┐
            │ Concealing the theft│
            └──────────┬──────────┘
        ┌──────────┬───┴──────┬──────────┐
        ▼          ▼          ▼          ▼
     Forced    Post       Destroy     Other
   reconcil-  reversing   records of
   iations    entries     transaction
                 │
           ┌─────┴─────┐
           ▼           ▼
        To contra   To bad debt
        revenue     expense
        accounts
```

Other Cash Larceny

Typically, when a company receives cash, someone is assigned to tabulate the receipts, list the form of payment (currency or check), and prepare a deposit slip for the bank. Then another employee takes the cash and deposits it in the bank. The person who made out the deposit generally retains one copy of the slip. This copy is matched to a receipted copy of the slip which is stamped by the bank when the deposit is made.

This procedure is designed to prevent the theft of funds from the deposit, but thefts still occur, often because the process is not adhered to. (See "Cash Larceny from the Deposit" flowchart) For example, when one person is in charge of preparing the deposit slips, making the deposit, and reconciling the bank statement, that person can pilfer money from the day's receipts and conceal it by falsifying the deposit slips. If the day's receipts are $1,000, the perpetrator might fill out a deposit slip for $500 and steal the other $500. The employee then makes correspondingly false entries in the books, understating the day's receipts. This process creates a false balance in the victim organization's records.

A failure to reconcile the bank copy of the deposit slip with the office copy can result in fraud. When the person making the deposit knows his company does not reconcile the two copies, he can steal cash from the deposit on the way to the bank and alter the deposit slip so that it reflects a lesser amount. In some cases sales records will also be altered to match the diminished deposit.

When cash is stolen from the deposit, the receipted deposit slip will of course be out of balance with the company's copy of the deposit slip (unless the perpetrator also prepared the deposit). To correct this problem, some perpetrators alter the bank copy of the deposit slip after it has been validated. This brings the two copies back into balance.

EXAMPLE

An employee altered 24 deposit slips and validated bank receipts in the course of a year to conceal the theft of over $15,000. These documents were altered with white-out or ball point pen to match the company's cash reports.

One common-sense issue that is sometimes overlooked by organizations is the handling of the deposit on the way to the bank. Once prepared, the deposit should immediately be put in a safe place until it is taken to the bank. Unfortunately, some organizations leave their deposits carelessly unattended. For example, some companies prepare the daily deposit, then

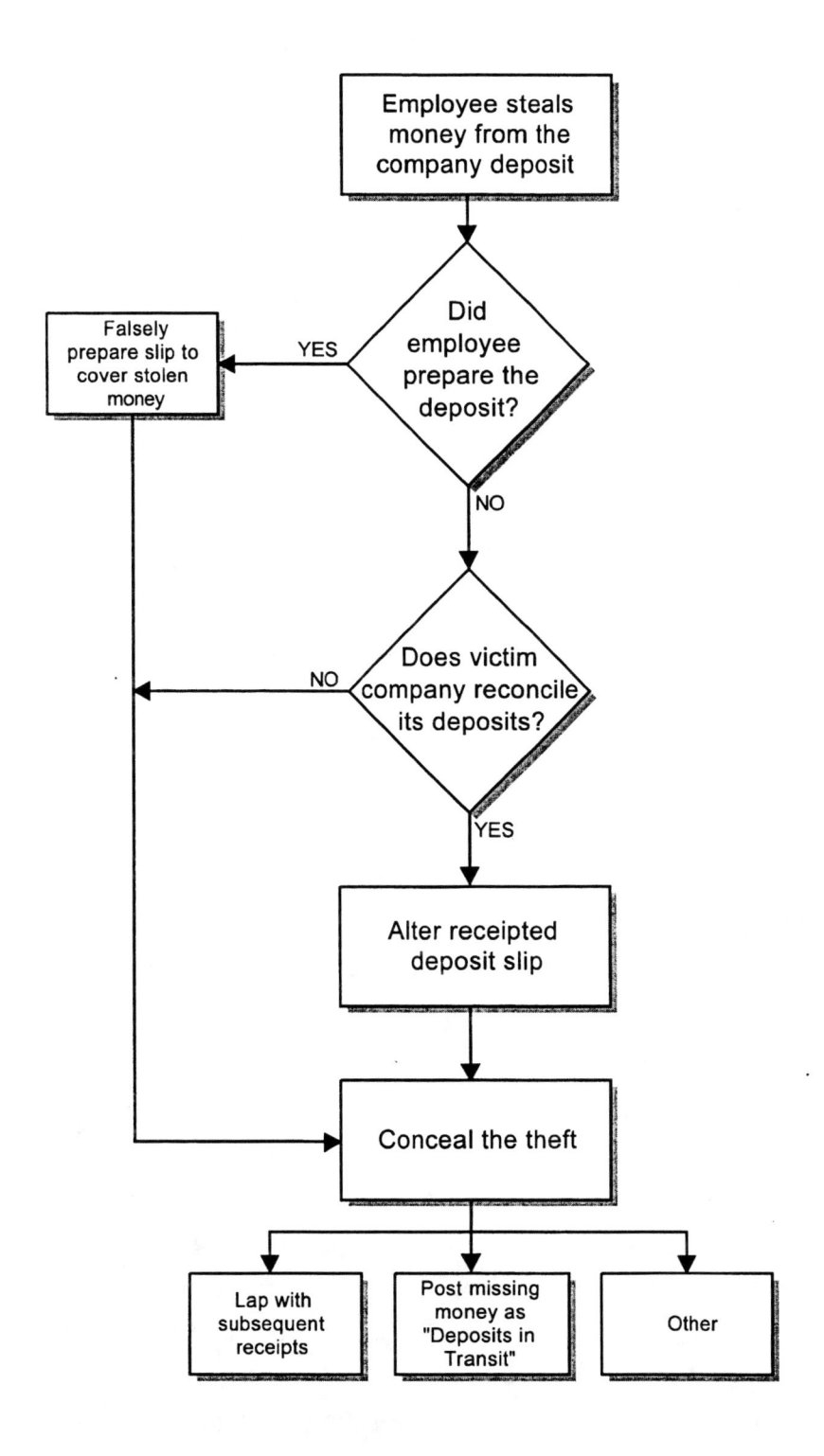

Cash Larceny from the Deposit

```
Employee steals money from the company deposit
        │
        ▼
   Did employee prepare the deposit?
   ├── YES ──► Falsely prepare slip to cover stolen money
   └── NO
        ▼
   Does victim company reconcile its deposits?
   ├── NO ──► (to Conceal the theft)
   └── YES
        ▼
   Alter receipted deposit slip
        ▼
   Conceal the theft
        ├── Lap with subsequent receipts
        ├── Post missing money as "Deposits in Transit"
        └── Other
```

Cash Larceny from the Deposit

leave it in the office overnight to be taken to the bank the next morning. Employees familiar with this routine have little trouble pilfering checks and currency from the deposit after hours.

As with all cash larceny schemes, stealing from the company deposit can be rather difficult to conceal. In most cases these schemes are only successful in the long term when the person who counts the cash also makes the deposit. In any other circumstance the success of the scheme depends primarily on the inattentiveness of those charged with preparing and reconciling the deposit.

Deposit Lapping

One method that fraudsters sometimes use to conceal cash larceny from the deposit is the *lapping method*. Lapping occurs when an employee steals the deposit from day one, then replaces it with day two's deposit. Day two is replaced with day three, and so on. The perpetrator is always one day behind, but as long as no one demands an up-to-the minute reconciliation of the deposits to the bank statement—and if daily receipts do not drop precipitously—he may be able to avoid detection for a period of time. Lapping is discussed in more detail in the Skimming section.

Deposits in Transit

A final strategy used to conceal stolen deposits is to carry the missing money as *deposits in transit*, which are a way of accounting for discrepancies between the company's records and the bank statement.

> EXAMPLE
>
> *An employee was responsible for receiving collections, issuing receipts, posting transactions, reconciling accounts, and making deposits. This employee took over $20,000 in collections from her employer over a five-month period. To hide her theft, the perpetrator carried the missing money as deposits in transit, meaning that the missing money would appear on the next month's bank statement. Of course, it never did. The balance was carried for several months as "d.i.t." until an auditor recognized the discrepancy and put a halt to the fraud.*

Detection of Cash Larceny
Receipt Recording

In-depth analysis of the cash receipts and recording process is the key to detecting a cash larceny scheme. Areas of analysis may include:

- Mail and register receipt points.
- Journalizing and recording of the receipts.
- The security of the cash from receipt to deposit.

Control Objectives

In analyzing the cash receipt process, it is important to meet the following control objectives:

- Cash receipts must be complete. Each day's receipts must be promptly collected and deposited in full.
- It must be assured that each receivable transaction recorded is legitimate and has supporting documentation.
- All information included in the transaction must be correctly verified as to amount, date, account coding, and descriptions.
- The cash must be safeguarded while in the physical possession of the company.
- There must be appropriate personnel responsible for overseeing cash control processes.
- Cash register tape totals should be reconciled to the amount of cash in drawer.
- An independent listing of cash receipts should be prepared before the receipts are submitted to the cashier or accounts receivable bookkeeper.
- An independent person should verify the listing against the deposit slips.
- Authenticated deposit slips should be retained and reconciled to the corresponding amounts in the cash receipts records.
- The bank deposit should be made by someone other than the cashier or the accounts receivable bookkeeper. A person independent of the cash receipts and accounts receivable functions should compare entries to the cash receipts journal with:
  - Authenticated bank deposit slips
  - Deposit per the bank statements
- Areas where physical handling of cash takes place should be reasonably safeguarded.

Analytical Review

Analyzing the relationship between sales, cost of sales, and the returns and allowances can detect inappropriate refunds and discounts.

- If a large cash fraud is suspected, a thorough review of these accounts may enlighten the examiner as to the magnitude of the suspected fraud.
- An analysis of refunds and returns and allowances with the actual flow of inventory may reveal some fraud schemes. The refund should cause an entry to inventory, even if it is

damaged inventory. Likewise, a return will cause a corresponding entry to an inventory account.

- There should be a linear relationship between sales and returns and allowances over a relevant range. Any change in this relationship may point to a fraud scheme unless there is another valid explanation such as a change in the manufacturing process, change in product line, or change in price.

Register Detection

- As cash is received, whether at a register or through the mail, it is important to ensure that the employees responsible for completing these important tasks are informed of their responsibility and properly supervised.
- Access to the register must be closely monitored and access codes must be kept secure.
- An employee other than the register worker should be responsible for preparing register count sheets and agreeing them to register totals.
- Popular concealment methods must be watched for. These methods, discussed earlier, include checks for cash, reversing transactions, register tape destruction or alteration, and sales cash counts.
- Complete register documentation and cash must be delivered to the appropriate personnel in a timely manner.
- Cash thefts sometimes are revealed by customers who have either paid money on an account and have not received credit, or in some cases, when they notice that the credit they have been given does not agree with the payment they have made. Complaints and inquiries also are received frequently from banks.

Cash Account Analysis

Cash larceny can be detected by reviewing and analyzing all journal entries made to the cash accounts. This review and analysis should be performed on a regular basis. If an employee is unable to conceal the fraud through altering the source documents, such as the cash register tape, then he may resort to making a journal entry directly to cash. In general (and except in financial institutions), there are very few instances in everyday business activity where an independent journal entry is necessary for cash. One of these exceptions is the recording of the bank service charge. However, this is an easy journal entry to trace to its source documentation, namely the bank statement. Therefore, all other entries directly to cash are suspect and should be traced to their source documentation or explanation. Suspect entries will generally credit the cash account and correspondingly debit various other accounts such as a sales contra-account or bad debt expenses.

Prevention of Cash Larceny

Segregation of Duties

The primary prevention of cash larceny is segregation of duties. Whenever one individual has control over the entire accounting transaction (e.g., authorization, recording, and custody), the opportunity is present for cash fraud. Each of the following duties and responsibilities should ideally be segregated:

- Cash receipts
- Cash counts
- Bank deposits
- Deposit receipt reconciliation
- Bank reconciliations
- Posting of deposits
- Cash disbursements

If any one person has the authority to collect the cash, deposit the receipts, record that collection, and disburse company funds, the risk that fraud can occur is high.

Assignment Rotation and Mandatory Vacations

Many internal fraud schemes are continuous in nature and require ongoing efforts by the employee to conceal defalcations. Mandatory job rotation is an excellent method of detecting cash fraud. By establishing a mandatory job or assignment rotation, the concealment element is interrupted. If mandatory vacations are within the company's policies, it is important that during the employee's absence, the normal workload of that employee be performed by another individual. The purpose of mandatory vacations is lost if the work is allowed to remain undone during the employee's time off.

Surprise Cash Counts and Procedure Supervision

Surprise cash counts and supervisory observations are a useful fraud prevention method if properly used. It is important that employees know that cash will be counted on a sporadic and unscheduled basis. These surprise counts must be made at all steps of the process from receiving the check to deposit.

Physical Security of Cash

- Ensure proper segregation of duties of key personnel.
- Review the check and cash composition of the daily bank deposit during unannounced cash counts and during substantive audit tests of cash receipts.

- Review the entity's records of the numerical series of printed prenumbered receipts, and verify that these receipts are used sequentially (including voided documents).
- Review the timeliness of deposits from locations to the central treasurer function.
- Observe cash receipting operations of locations.
- Prepare and review a schedule of all cash receipting functions from a review of revenue reports, from cash receipt forms at the central treasurer function, and from discussion with knowledgeable employees.
- Prepare and analyze an inventory of all imprest and change funds by purpose, amount, custodian, date, and location.
- Audit all revenue sources on a cycle.
- Periodically use comparative analytical reviews to determine which functions have unfavorable trends.
- Determine reason(s) why revenue has changed from previous reporting periods.
- Confirm responses obtained from managers by using alternative records or through substantive audit tests.
- Adhere to a communicated policy of unannounced cash counts.

ASSET MISAPPROPRIATION: FRAUDULENT DISBURSEMENTS

In fraudulent disbursement schemes, an employee makes a distribution of company funds for a dishonest purpose. Examples of fraudulent disbursements include forging company checks, the submission of false invoices, doctoring timecards and so forth. On their face, the fraudulent disbursements do not appear any different from valid disbursements of cash. For instance, when an employee runs a bogus invoice through the accounts payable system, the victim organization cuts a check for the bad invoice right along with all the legitimate payments it makes. The perpetrator has taken money from his employer in such a way that it appears to be a normal disbursement of cash. Someone might notice the fraud based on the amount, recipient, or destination of the payment, but the *method* of payment is legitimate.

Register Disbursement Schemes

Fraudulent disbursements at the cash register are different from the other schemes that often take place at the register, such as skimming and cash larceny. When cash is stolen as part of a register disbursement scheme, the removal of the cash is recorded on the register tape. A false transaction is entered so it appears that the disbursement of money was legitimate.

There are two basic register disbursements schemes: *false refunds* and *false voids*. While the schemes are largely similar, there are a few differences between the two that merit discussing them separately.

False Refunds

A refund is processed at the register when a customer returns an item of merchandise that was purchased from the store. The transaction that is entered on the register indicates the merchandise is being replaced in the store's inventory and the purchase price is being returned to the customer. In other words, a refund shows cash being disbursed from the register to the customer. (See "False Refunds" flowchart)

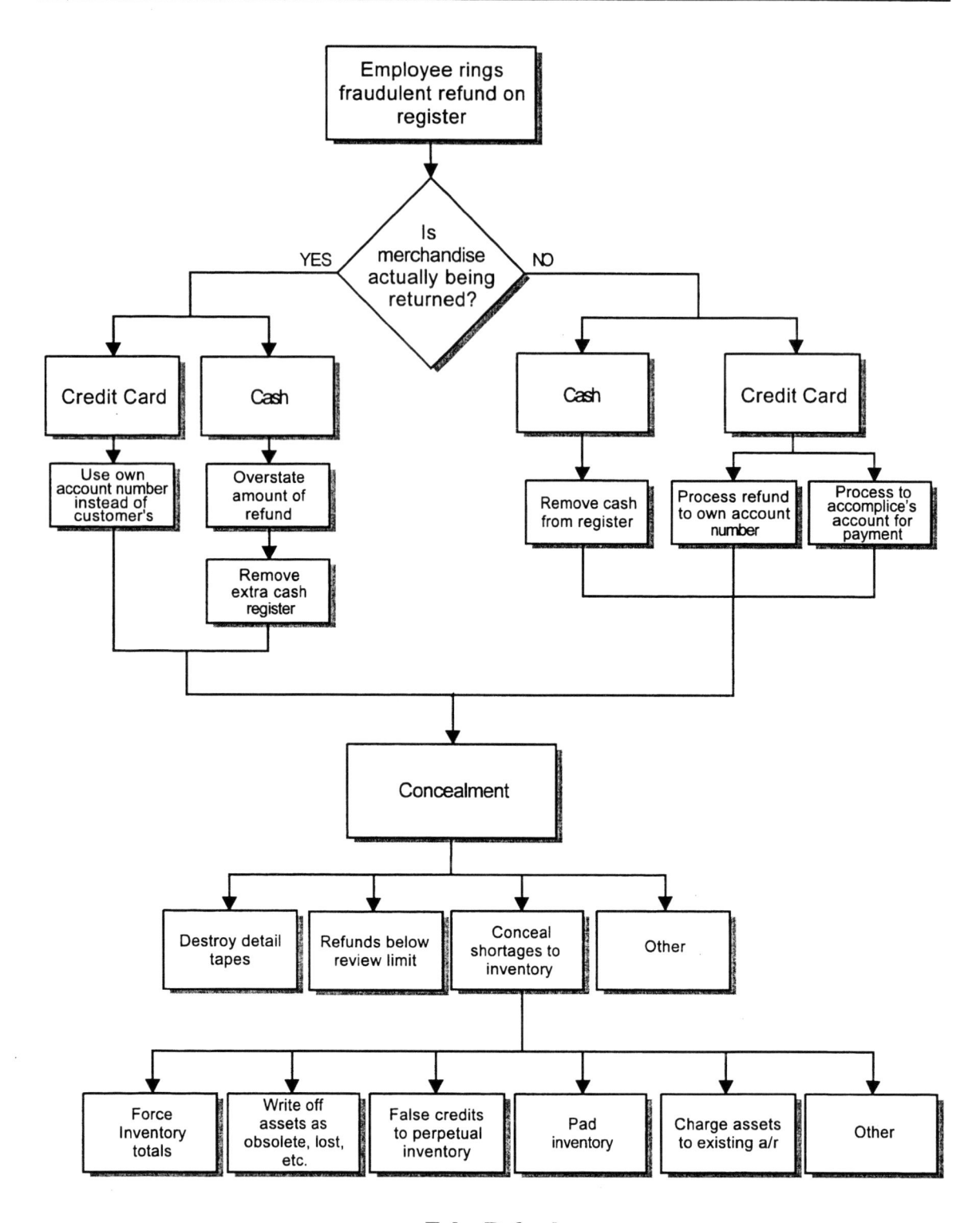

Asset Misappropriation: Fraudulent Disbursements   Financial Transactions

```
                    ┌──────────────────┐
                    │ Employee rings   │
                    │ fraudulent refund│
                    │   on register    │
                    └────────┬─────────┘
                             ▼
                          ╱     ╲
                        ╱    Is   ╲
            YES       ╱ merchandise╲      NO
         ┌──────────╱ actually being ╲──────────┐
         │         ╲   returned?    ╱           │
         │           ╲             ╱            │
         │             ╲         ╱              │
  ┌──────┴──────┐              ┌─────────┴─────────┐
  ▼             ▼              ▼                   ▼
┌──────┐    ┌──────┐        ┌──────┐          ┌──────────┐
│Credit│    │ Cash │        │ Cash │          │Credit Card│
│ Card │    │      │        │      │          │           │
└───┬──┘    └──┬───┘        └──┬───┘          └─────┬─────┘
    ▼          ▼               ▼                ┌───┴────┐
┌────────┐ ┌────────┐      ┌────────┐           ▼        ▼
│Use own │ │Overstate│     │Remove  │       ┌────────┐┌────────┐
│account │ │amount of│     │cash    │       │Process ││Process │
│number  │ │refund   │     │from    │       │refund  ││to      │
│instead │ │         │     │register│       │to own  ││accompl-│
│of      │ └───┬────┘      └────┬───┘       │account ││ice's   │
│customer│     ▼                │           │number  ││account │
└───┬────┘ ┌────────┐           │           └───┬────┘│for pmt │
    │      │Remove  │           │               │     └───┬────┘
    │      │extra   │           │               │         │
    │      │cash    │           │               │         │
    │      │register│           │               │         │
    │      └───┬────┘           │               │         │
    └──────────┴────────────────┴───────────────┴─────────┘
                             ▼
                    ┌──────────────┐
                    │  Concealment │
                    └──────┬───────┘
          ┌──────────┬─────┴─────┬──────────┐
          ▼          ▼           ▼          ▼
      ┌───────┐ ┌────────┐  ┌────────┐ ┌───────┐
      │Destroy│ │Refunds │  │Conceal │ │ Other │
      │detail │ │below   │  │shortag-│ │       │
      │tapes  │ │review  │  │es to   │ │       │
      │       │ │limit   │  │inventry│ │       │
      └───────┘ └────────┘  └───┬────┘ └───────┘
                                │
   ┌──────┬─────────┬──────────┼────────┬──────────┬────────┐
   ▼      ▼         ▼          ▼        ▼          ▼        ▼
┌──────┐┌────────┐┌────────┐┌───────┐┌─────────┐┌───────┐
│Force ││Write   ││False   ││Pad    ││Charge   ││ Other │
│Inven-││off     ││credits ││inven- ││assets   ││       │
│tory  ││assets  ││to      ││tory   ││to exist-││       │
│totals││as obso-││perpetual│       ││ing a/r  ││       │
│      ││lete,   ││inventory│       ││         ││       │
│      ││lost,   ││         │       ││         ││       │
│      ││etc.    ││         │       ││         ││       │
└──────┘└────────┘└────────┘└───────┘└─────────┘└───────┘
```

False Refunds

Fictitious Refunds

In a fictitious refund scheme, an employee processes a transaction as if a customer were returning merchandise, even though there is no actual return. Two things result from this fraudulent transaction. The first is that the employee takes cash from the register in the amount of the false return. For instance, if the employee processes a fictitious return for a $100 pair of shoes, he removes $100 from the register. The register tape will indicate that the shoes were returned, so the disbursement appears to be legitimate. The register tape balances with the amount of cash on hand because the fraudulent refund accounts for the cash that the employee stole.

The second thing that happens in a fictitious refund scheme is that a debit is made to the inventory system showing that the merchandise has been returned to the inventory. Since the transaction is fictitious, no merchandise is actually returned. The result is that the company's inventory is overstated.

EXAMPLE

A manager created $5,500 worth of false returns, resulting in a large shortage in the company's inventory. He was able to carry his scheme on for several months, however, because (1) inventory was not counted regularly, and (2) the perpetrator, a manager, was one of the people who performed inventory counts.

Overstated Refunds

Rather than create an entirely fictitious refund, some employees merely overstate the amount of a legitimate refund and skim the excess money. For example, if a customer returns $100 worth of merchandise, the employee might ring up a $200 return. The employee gives the customer $100 in return for the merchandise, then pockets the remaining $100. This will result in shrinkage of $100 worth of inventory.

Credit Card Refunds

When purchases are made with a credit card rather than cash, refunds appear as credits to the customer's credit card rather than as cash disbursements. Some dishonest employees process false refunds on credit card sales in lieu of processing a normal cash transaction. One benefit of the credit card method is that the perpetrator does not have to physically take cash from the register and carry it out of the store. By processing the refunds to a credit card account, a perpetrator reaps a financial gain and avoids the potential embarrassment of being caught red-handed taking cash.

In a typical credit card refund scheme, the perpetrator rings up a refund on a credit card sale, even though the merchandise is not actually being returned. The employee credits his own credit card number rather than the customer's. The result is that the cost of the item is credited to the perpetrator's credit card account.

A more creative and wide-ranging application of the credit card refund scheme occurs when employees process refunds to the accounts of other people, and in return receive a portion of the refund as a kickback. Suppose a person is $100 short on the rent. That person goes to the retail store where his friend is a teller and has the teller process a credit of $150 to his account. The "customer" then goes to an ATM machine and withdraws $150 in cash. He pays $50 to the teller and keeps $100 for himself.

False Voids

Fictitious voids are similar to refund schemes in that they make fraudulent disbursements from the register appear to be legitimate. When a sale is voided on a register, a copy of the customer's receipt is usually attached to a void slip, along with the signature or initials of a manager indicating that the transaction has been approved. (See "False Voids" flowchart) In order to process a false void, then, the first thing the perpetrator needs is the customer's copy of the sales receipt. Typically, when an employee sets about processing a fictitious void, he simply withholds the customer's receipt at the time of the sale. In many cases customers do not notice that they are not given a receipt.

With the customer's copy of the receipt in hand, the culprit rings a voided sale. Whatever money the customer paid for the item is removed from the register as though it is being returned to a customer. The copy of the customer's receipt is attached to the void slip to verify the authenticity of the transaction.

Before the voided sale will be perceived as valid, a manager generally must approve the transaction. In many instances, the manager in question simply neglects to verify the authenticity of the voided sale. A number of managers will sign most anything presented to them and thus leave themselves vulnerable to voided sales schemes. It is not a coincidence that the perpetrators of these crimes present their void slips to managers who are lackadaisical about authorizing them. These kinds of managers are generally targeted by the fraudsters and are essential to the success of the schemes.

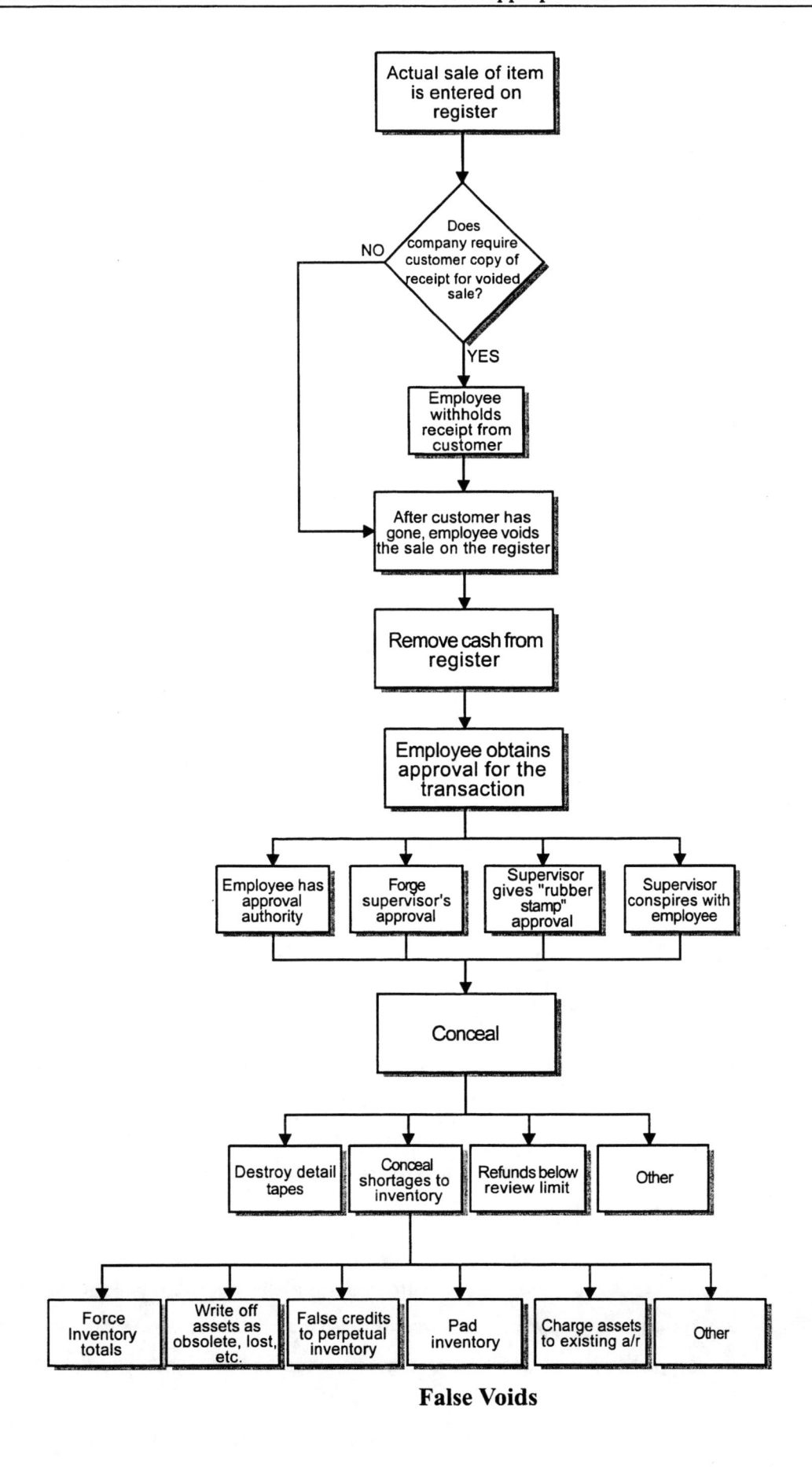

```
                    ┌─────────────────────┐
                    │ Actual sale of item │
                    │    is entered on    │
                    │      register       │
                    └──────────┬──────────┘
                               │
                               ▼
                           ╱ Does  ╲
              NO         ╱ company  ╲
         ◄────────────  ╲ require    ╱
         │               ╲customer  ╱
         │                ╲ copy...╱
         │                   │ YES
         │                   ▼
         │           ┌───────────────┐
         │           │   Employee    │
         │           │   withholds   │
         │           │ receipt from  │
         │           │   customer    │
         │           └───────┬───────┘
         │                   │
         ▼                   ▼
   ┌──────────────────────────────┐
   │ After customer has gone,     │
   │ employee voids the sale      │
   │ on the register              │
   └──────────────┬───────────────┘
                  ▼
        ┌──────────────────┐
        │ Remove cash from │
        │     register     │
        └────────┬─────────┘
                 ▼
       ┌──────────────────┐
       │ Employee obtains │
       │ approval for the │
       │   transaction    │
       └────────┬─────────┘
```

Approval branches: Employee has approval authority | Forge supervisor's approval | Supervisor gives "rubber stamp" approval | Supervisor conspires with employee

→ **Conceal**

Conceal branches: Destroy detail tapes | Conceal shortages to inventory | Refunds below review limit | Other

Conceal shortages to inventory sub-branches: Force Inventory totals | Write off assets as obsolete, lost, etc. | False credits to perpetual inventory | Pad inventory | Charge assets to existing a/r | Other

False Voids

> EXAMPLE
>
> *An employee processed fraudulent voids, kept customer receipts, and presented them to her supervisors for review at the end of her shift, long after the alleged transactions had taken place. Her supervisors approved the voided sales and the accounts receivable department failed to notice the excessive number of voided sales processed by this employee.*

Obviously, not all managers give rubber-stamp approval to voided sales. Some employees must therefore take other routes to get their voided sales "approved." In most of these cases the perpetrator simply forges his supervisor's authorization on the fraudulent void slips. It is also possible that managers will conspire with register employees and approve false voids in return for a share of the proceeds from the scheme.

Concealing Register Disbursements

As has already been discussed, two things happen when a false refund or void is entered into the register. The first is that the employee committing the fraud removes cash from the register, and the second is that the item allegedly being returned is debited back into the perpetual inventory. Of course, there really is no merchandise being returned. This leads to inventory shrinkage, a situation in which there is less inventory actually on hand than the perpetual inventory records reflect. A certain amount of shrinkage is expected in any retail industry, but too much of it raises concerns of fraud. It is therefore in the perpetrator's best interests to conceal the appearance of shrinkage on the books.

Inventory is essentially accounted for by a two-step process. The first part of the process is the perpetual inventory, which is a running tabulation of how much inventory *should be on hand*. When a sale of merchandise is made, the perpetual inventory is credited to remove this merchandise from the records. The amount of merchandise that should be on hand is reduced. (Conversely, when merchandise is returned the perpetual inventory is debited.) Periodically, someone from the company takes a physical count of the inventory, going through the stockroom or warehouse and counting the amount of inventory that *is actually on hand*. The two figures are then compared to see if there is a discrepancy between the perpetual inventory (what should be on hand) and the physical inventory (what is on hand).

In register disbursement schemes, shrinkage is often concealed by overstating inventory during the physical count, especially if taking inventory is one of the perpetrator's duties. The perpetrator simply overstates the amount of inventory on hand so it matches the perpetual inventory. For a more detailed analysis of methods used to conceal inventory shrinkage, please see the Inventory and Other Assets section.

Small Disbursements

Another way for employees to avoid detection in a refund scheme is to keep the sizes of the disbursements low. Many companies set limits below which management review of a refund is not required. Where this is the case, employees simply process copious numbers of refunds that are small enough that they do not have to be reviewed.

> EXAMPLE
>
> *An employee created over 1,000 false refunds, all under the review limit of $15. He was eventually caught because he began processing refunds before store hours and another employee noticed that refunds were appearing on the system before the store opened. Nevertheless, before his scheme was detected the man made off with over $11,000 of his employer's money.*

Destroying Records

One final means of concealing a register scheme, as with many kinds of fraud, is to destroy all records of the transaction. Most concealment methods are concerned with keeping management from realizing that fraud has occurred. When an employee resorts to destroying records, however, he typically has conceded that management will discover his theft. The purpose of destroying records is usually to prevent management from determining *who* the thief is.

Detection of Register Schemes

Fictitious Refunds or Voided Sales

Fictitious refunds or voided sales often can be detected when closely examining the documentation submitted with the cash receipts.

- One detection method is to evaluate the refunds or discounts given by each cashier or salesperson. This analysis may point out that a single employee or group of employees has a higher incidence of refunds or discounts than others. Further examination is then necessary to determine if the refunds are appropriate and properly documented.
- Signs in the register area asking customers to ask for and examine their receipts employ the customer as part of the internal control system. This helps assure that the cashier or salesperson is properly accounting for the sale and prevents employees from using customer receipts as support for false void or refunds.

- Random service calls to customers who have returned merchandise or voided sales can be used to verify the legitimacy of transactions.

Review and Analysis of Decreases in Gross Sales and/or Increases in Returns and Allowances

Analyzing the relationship between sales, cost of sales, and the returns and allowances can detect inappropriate refunds and discounts. If a large cash fraud is suspected, a thorough review of these accounts might enlighten the examiner as to the magnitude of the suspected fraud. An analysis of refunds and returns and allowances with the actual flow of inventory might reveal some fraud schemes. The refund should cause an entry to inventory, even if it is damaged inventory. Likewise, a return will cause a corresponding entry to an inventory account. There should be a linear relationship between sales and returns and allowances over a relevant range. Any change in this relationship might point to a fraud scheme unless there is another valid explanation such as a change in the manufacturing process, change in product line, or change in price.

Register Scheme Red Flags

- Inappropriate employee segregation of duties. For example, register counting and reconciling should not be done by the cashier.
- Cashiers, rather than supervisors, have access to the control keys which are necessary for refunds and voids.
- Register employee has authority to void own transactions.
- Register refunds are not methodically reviewed.
- Multiple cashiers operate from a single cash drawer without separate access codes.
- Personal checks from cashier found in register.
- Voided transactions are not properly documented or not approved by a supervisor.
- Voided cash receipt forms (manual systems) or supporting documents for voided transactions (cash register systems) are not retained on file.
- Missing or obviously altered register tapes.
- Gaps in the sequence of transactions on register tape.
- An inordinate number of refunds, voids, or no-sales on register tape.
- Inventory totals appear forced.
- Multiple refunds or voids for amounts just under the review limit.

Prevention
- Review the segregation of duties of key employees who staff the register as well as the duties of their supervisors.
- As cash is received it is important to ensure that the employees responsible for completing these important tasks are informed of their responsibilities and properly supervised.
- An employee other than the register worker should be responsible for preparing register count sheets and agreeing them to register totals.
- Complete register documentation and cash must be delivered to the appropriate personnel in a timely manner.
- Cash thefts sometimes are revealed by customers who have paid money on an account and have not received credit, or in some cases, who have been credited for an amount that does not agree with the payment they have made. Complaints and inquiries also are received frequently from banks.
- Access to the register must be closely monitored and access codes must be kept secure.
- Quantity of refunds should be analyzed to detect multiple small refunds.
- Communicate and adhere to company policy of performing unannounced cash counts.
- Maintain the presence of a manager or supervisor near the area of the cash register as a deterrent to theft.
- Review supporting documents for voided and refunded transactions for propriety (i.e., legitimacy and approvals).
- Review the numerical sequence and completeness of cash register tapes.

Check Tampering

Check tampering is unique among the fraudulent disbursement schemes because it is the one group in which the perpetrator physically prepares the fraudulent check. In most fraudulent disbursement schemes, the culprit generates a payment to himself by submitting some false document to the victim organization such as an invoice or a timecard. The false document represents a claim for payment and causes the victim organization to issue a check that the perpetrator can convert.

Check tampering schemes are fundamentally different. In these schemes the perpetrator takes physical control of a check and makes it payable to himself through one of several methods. Check tampering frauds depend upon factors such as access to the company checkbook, access to bank statements, and the ability to forge signatures or alter other information on the face of the check. Most check tampering crimes fall into one of four categories: forged maker schemes, forged endorsement schemes, altered payee schemes, and authorized maker schemes.

Forged Maker Schemes

The legal definition of forgery includes not only the *signing of another person's name* to a document (such as a check) with a fraudulent intent, but also the fraudulent *alteration* of a genuine instrument.[*] This definition is so broad that it would encompass all check tampering schemes. For the purposes of this manual, the definition of forgery has been narrowed to fit the fraud examiner's needs. In order to properly distinguish the various methods used by individuals to tamper with checks, the concept of "forgeries" will be limited to those cases in which an individual signs another person's name on a check. The person who signs a check is known as the "maker" of the check. A forged maker scheme, then, may be defined as a check tampering scheme in which an employee misappropriates a check and fraudulently affixes the signature of an authorized maker thereon. (See "Forged Maker Schemes" flowchart) Frauds that involve other types of check tampering, such as the alteration of the payee or the changing of the dollar amount, are classified separately.

In order to forge a check, an employee must have access to a blank check, he must be able to produce a convincing forgery of an authorized signature, and he must be able to conceal his crime. Concealment is a universal problem in check tampering schemes; the methods used are basically the same whether one is dealing with a forged maker scheme, an intercepted check scheme, a concealed check scheme, or an authorized maker scheme. Therefore, concealment issues will be discussed as a group later in this section.

Obtaining the Check
EMPLOYEES WITH ACCESS TO COMPANY CHECKS

One cannot forge a company check unless one first possesses a company check. Most forgery schemes are committed by accounts payable clerks, office managers, bookkeepers, or other employees whose duties typically include the preparation of company checks. These are people who have access to the company checkbook on a regular basis and are therefore in the best position to steal blank checks.

---

[*] Henry Campbell Black, *Black's Law Dictionary, Fifth Edition* (St. Paul: West Publishing Co., 1979) p. 585.

EMPLOYEES LACKING ACCESS TO COMPANY CHECKS

If the perpetrator does not have access to the company checkbook through his work duties, he will have to find other means of misappropriating a check. The way a person steals a check depends largely on how the checkbook is handled within a particular company. In some circumstances the checkbook is poorly guarded, left in unattended areas where anyone can get to it. In other companies where blank checks are kept in a restricted area, the perpetrator might have surreptitiously obtained a key or combination to this area. An accomplice might provide blank checks for the perpetrator in return for a portion of the stolen funds. Perhaps a secretary sees the checkbook left on a manager's desk or a custodian comes across blank checks in an unlocked desk drawer.

In some companies, checks are computer generated. When this is the case, an employee who knows the password for preparing and issuing checks can usually obtain as many unsigned checks as he desires. There are an unlimited number of ways to steal a check, each dependent on the way in which a particular company guards its blank checks. In some instances, employees go so far as to produce counterfeit checks.

EXAMPLE
An employee had an accomplice who worked for a check-printing company. The accomplice was able to print blank checks with the account number of the perpetrator's company. The perpetrator then wrote over $100,000 worth of forgeries on these counterfeit checks.

To Whom is the Check Made Payable?

TO THE PERPETRATOR

Once a blank check has been obtained, the perpetrator must decide to whom it should be made payable. In most instances forged checks are made payable to the perpetrator himself so that they can be easily converted. Canceled checks that are payable to an employee should be closely scrutinized for the possibility of fraud.

If the perpetrator owns his own business or has established a shell company, he will usually write fraudulent checks to these entities rather than himself. These checks are not as obviously fraudulent on their faces as checks made payable to an employee. At the same time, these checks are easy to convert because the perpetrator owns the entity to which the checks are payable.

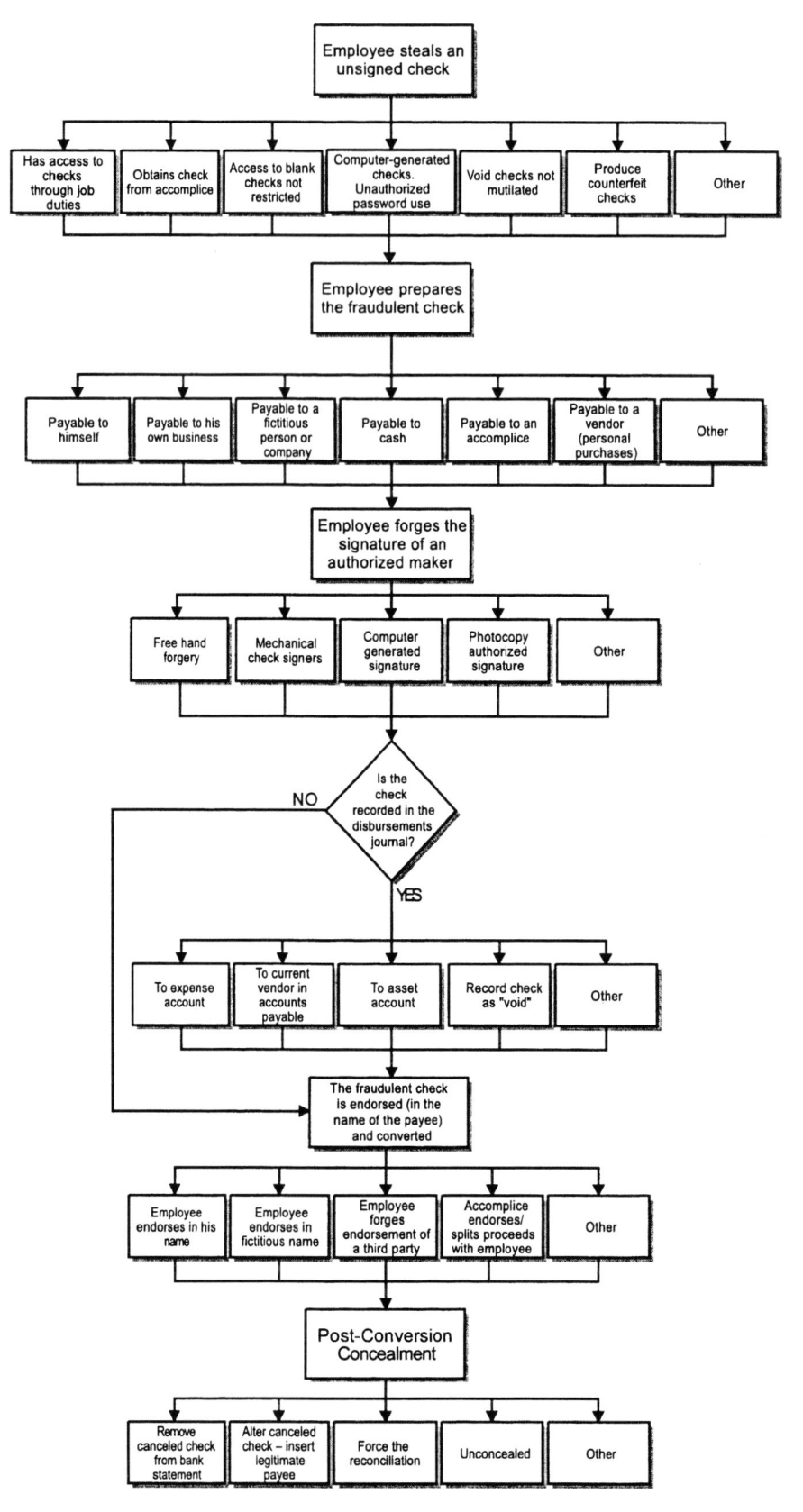

Forged Maker Schemes

Employee steals an unsigned check
- Has access to checks through job duties
- Obtains check from accomplice
- Access to blank checks not restricted
- Computer-generated checks. Unauthorized password use
- Void checks not mutilated
- Produce counterfeit checks
- Other

Employee prepares the fraudulent check
- Payable to himself
- Payable to his own business
- Payable to a fictitious person or company
- Payable to cash
- Payable to an accomplice
- Payable to a vendor (personal purchases)
- Other

Employee forges the signature of an authorized maker
- Free hand forgery
- Mechanical check signers
- Computer generated signature
- Photocopy authorized signature
- Other

Is the check recorded in the disbursements journal?

If YES:
- To expense account
- To current vendor in accounts payable
- To asset account
- Record check as "void"
- Other

The fraudulent check is endorsed (in the name of the payee) and converted
- Employee endorses in his name
- Employee endorses in fictitious name
- Employee forges endorsement of a third party
- Accomplice endorses/splits proceeds with employee
- Other

Post-Conversion Concealment
- Remove canceled check from bank statement
- Alter canceled check – insert legitimate payee
- Force the reconciliation
- Unconcealed
- Other

TO AN ACCOMPLICE

If a fraudster is working with an accomplice, he can make the forged check payable to that person. The accomplice then cashes the check and splits the money with the employee-fraudster. Because the check is payable to the accomplice in his true identity, it is easily converted. An additional benefit to using an accomplice is that a canceled check payable to a third-party accomplice is not as likely to raise suspicion as a canceled check to an employee. The obvious drawback to using an accomplice in a scheme is that the employee-fraudster usually has to share the proceeds of the scheme.

PAYABLE TO "CASH"

The perpetrator may also write checks payable to "cash" in order to avoid listing himself as the payee. Checks made payable to cash, however, must still be endorsed. The perpetrator will have to sign his own name or forge the name of another in order to convert the check. Checks payable to "cash" are usually viewed more skeptically than checks payable to persons or businesses. Some institutions may refuse to cash checks made payable to "cash."

PAYABLE TO VENDORS

Not all fraudsters forge company checks to obtain cash. Some employees use forged maker schemes to purchase goods or services for their own benefit. These fraudulent checks are made payable to third-party vendors who are uninvolved in the fraud. For instance, an employee might forge a company check to buy a computer for his home. The computer vendor is not involved in the fraud at all. Furthermore, if the victim organization regularly does business with this vendor, the person who reconciles the company's accounts may assume that the check was used for a legitimate business expense.

Forging the Signature

After the employee has obtained and prepared a blank check, he must forge an authorized signature in order to convert the check. The most obvious method, and the one that comes to mind when one thinks of the word "forgery," is to simply take pen in hand and sign the name of an authorized maker.

FREE-HAND FORGERY

The difficulty a fraudster encounters when physically signing the authorized maker's name is in creating a reasonable approximation of the true signature. If the forgery appears authentic, the perpetrator will probably have no problem cashing the check. In truth, the forged signature may not have to be particularly accurate. Many fraudsters cash forged checks at liquor stores, grocery stores, or other institutions which are known to be less than diligent in verifying signatures and identification. Nevertheless, a poorly forged signature is a clear red flag of fraud. The maker's signature on canceled checks should be reviewed for forgeries during the reconciliation process.

PHOTOCOPIED FORGERIES

To guarantee an accurate forgery, some employees make photocopies of legitimate signatures. The signature of an authorized signer is copied from some document (such as a business letter) onto a transparency, then the transparency is laid over a blank check so that the signature copies onto the maker line of the check. The result is a check with a perfect signature of an authorized maker.

AUTOMATIC CHECK-SIGNING INSTRUMENTS

Companies that issue a large number of checks sometimes utilize automatic check-signing instruments. Automated signatures are either produced with manual instruments like signature stamps or they are printed by computer. Obviously, an employee who has access to an automatic check-signing instrument will have no trouble forging the signatures of authorized makers. Even the most rudimentary control procedures should severely limit access to these instruments.

> EXAMPLE
> *A fiscal officer maintained a set of manual checks which were unknown to other persons in the company. The company used an automated check signer and the custodian of the signer let the officer have uncontrolled access to it. Using the manual checks and the company's check signer, the fiscal officer was able to write over $90,000 worth of fraudulent checks to himself over a period of approximately four years.*

The same principle applies to computer-generated signatures. Access to the password or program which prints signed checks should be restricted, specifically excluding those who prepare checks and those who reconcile the bank statement.

Converting the Check

In order to convert the forged check, the perpetrator must endorse it. The endorsement is typically made in the name of the payee on the check. Since identification is typically required when one seeks to convert a check, the perpetrator usually needs fake identification if he forges checks to real or fictitious third persons. As discussed earlier, checks payable to "cash" require the endorsement of the person converting them. Without fake I.D. the perpetrator will likely have to endorse these checks in his own name. An employee's endorsement on a canceled check is obviously a red flag.

Forged Endorsement Schemes

Forged endorsements are those check tampering schemes in which an employee intercepts a company check intended to pay a third-party and converts the check by endorsing it in the third-party's name. In some cases the employee also signs his own name as a second endorser. (See "Forged Endorsement Schemes" flowchart.)

A fraudster's main dilemma in a forged endorsement scheme (and in all intercepted check schemes, for that matter) is gaining access to a check after it has been signed. The fraudster must either steal the check between the point where it is signed and the point where it is delivered, or he must re-route the check, causing it to be delivered to a location where he can retrieve it. The manner used to steal a check depends largely upon the way the company handles outgoing disbursements. Anyone who is allowed to handle signed checks may be in a good position to intercept them.

Intercepting Checks Before Delivery
EMPLOYEES INVOLVED IN DELIVERY OF CHECKS

Obviously, the employees in the best position to intercept signed checks are those whose duties include the handling and delivery of signed checks. The most obvious example is a mailroom employee who opens outgoing mail containing signed checks and steals the checks. Other personnel with access to outgoing checks might include accounts payable employees, payroll clerks, secretaries, etc.

POOR CONTROL OF SIGNED CHECKS

Unfortunately, employees are often able to intercept signed checks because of poor internal controls. For instance, many employees simply find signed checks left unattended in the work areas of the persons who signed them or the persons charged with their delivery. In these cases it is easy for the perpetrator to steal the check. Another common breakdown occurs when the person who prepares a check is also involved in the delivery of that check once it has been signed.

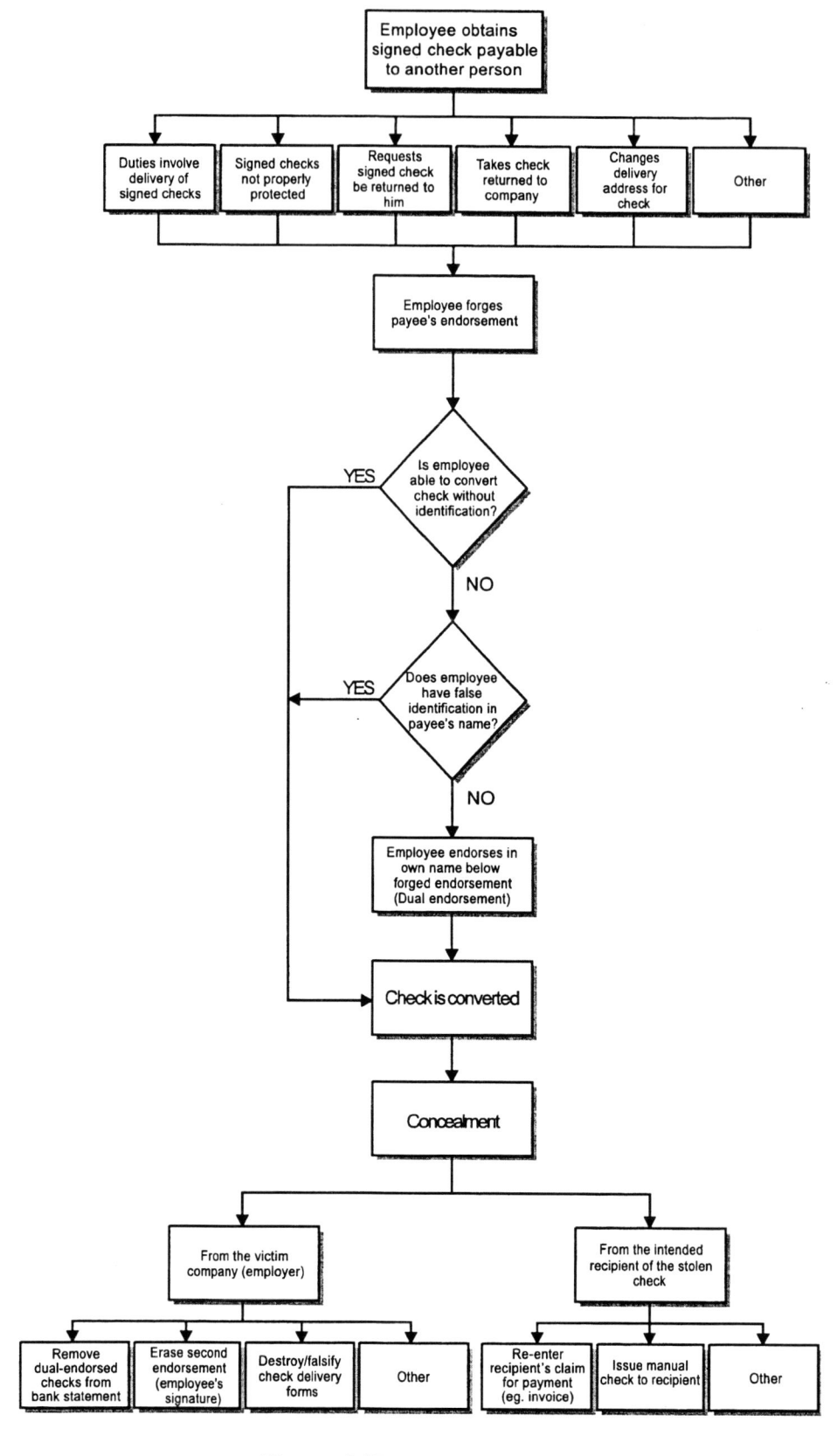

Forged Endorsement Schemes

> EXAMPLE
>
> *A high-level manager with authority to disburse employee benefits instructed accounts payable personnel to return signed benefits checks to him instead of immediately delivering them to their intended recipients. These instructions were not questioned due to the manager's level of authority within the company. The perpetrator simply took the checks that were returned to him and deposited them into his personal bank account, forging the endorsements of the intended payees.*

In addition to the preceding example, secretaries or clerks who prepare checks for their bosses to sign are often responsible for mailing those checks. It is very simple for those employees to make out a fraudulent check and obtain a signature, knowing that the boss will give the signed check right back to them. This scheme is indicative of the key problem with occupational fraud: trust. In order for an office to run efficiently, high-level employees must be able to rely on their subordinates. Yet this reliance is precisely what puts subordinates in a position to defraud their employer.

Theft of Returned Checks

Checks that have been mailed and are later returned to the victim company for some reason, such as an incorrect address, are often targeted for theft by fraudsters. Employees with access to incoming mail are able to intercept these returned checks and convert them by forging the endorsement of the intended payee.

> EXAMPLE
>
> *A manager took and converted approximately $130,000 worth of checks which were returned due to noncurrent addresses. (He also stole outgoing checks, cashed them, and then declared them lost.) The fraudster was well known at his bank and was able to convert the checks by claiming that he was doing it as a favor to the real payees, who were "too busy to come to the bank." The fraudster was able to continue with his scheme because the nature of his company's business was such that the recipients of the misdelivered checks were often not aware that the victim company owed them money. Therefore, they did not complain when their checks failed to arrive. In addition, the perpetrator had complete control over the bank reconciliation, so he could issue new checks to those payees who did complain, then "force" the reconciliation, making it appear that the bank balance and book balance matched when in fact they did not.*

Re-Routing the Delivery of Checks

Employees may also misappropriate signed checks by altering the addresses to which those checks are mailed. These perpetrators usually replace the legitimate address of the payee with an address where the employee can retrieve the check, such as the employee's home or a P.O. box the employee controls. In other instances, the perpetrator might purposely misaddress a check so that it will be returned as undeliverable. The employee steals the check after it is returned to the victim organization.

Obviously, proper separation of duties should preclude anyone who prepares disbursements from being involved in their delivery. Nevertheless, the person who prepares a check is often allowed to address and mail it as well. In some instances where proper controls are in place, employees are still able to cause the misdelivery of checks.

> EXAMPLE
>
> *A clerk in the customer service department of a mortgage company was in charge of changing the mailing addresses of property owners. She was assigned a password which gave her access to make these changes. The clerk was transferred to a new department where one of her duties was the issuance of checks to property owners. Unfortunately, her supervisor forgot to cancel her old password. When the clerk realized this oversight, she would request a check for a certain property owner, then sign onto the system with her old password and change the address of that property owner. The check would be sent to her. The next day the employee would use her old password to re-enter the system and replace the proper address so that there would be no record of where the check had been sent. This fraudster's scheme resulted in a loss of over $250,000 to the victim company.*

Converting the Stolen Check

Once a check has been intercepted, the perpetrator can cash it by forging the payee's signature, hence the term *forged endorsement scheme*. Depending on where he tries to cash the check, the perpetrator may or may not need fake identification at this stage. If a perpetrator is required to produce identification in order to cash his stolen check, and if he does not have a fake I.D. in the payee's name, he may use a dual endorsement to cash or deposit the check. In other words, the perpetrator forges the payee's signature as though the payee had transferred the check to him, then the perpetrator endorses the check in his own name and converts it. When the bank statement is reconciled, dual endorsements on checks should always raise suspicions, particularly when the second signer is an employee of the company.

Altered Payee Schemes

The second type of intercepted check scheme is the altered payee scheme. This is a form of check tampering in which an employee intercepts a company check intended for a third-party and alters the payee designation so that the check can be converted by the employee or an accomplice. (See "Altered Payee Schemes" flowchart) The employee inserts his own name, the name of an accomplice, or the name of a fictitious entity on the payee line of the check. The alteration essentially makes the check payable to the employee (or an accomplice), so there is no need to forge an endorsement and no need to obtain false identification.

Altering Checks Prepared by Others: Inserting a New Payee

The method used to alter the payee designation on a check depends largely on how that check is prepared and intercepted. (Incidentally, the *amount* of the check may also be altered at the same time and by the same method as the payee designation.) Checks prepared by others can be intercepted by any of the methods discussed in the forged endorsements section above. When the perpetrator intercepts a check that has been prepared by someone else, there are basically two methods that may be employed to change the payee. The first is to insert the false payee's name in place of the true payee's. The true name might be scratched out with a pen or covered up with white-out. Another name is then entered on the payee designation line. These kinds of alterations are usually simple to detect.

A more sophisticated method occurs when the perpetrator of the fraud enters the accounts payable system and changes the names of payees before checks are generated. This can be accomplished by anyone with a password that permits access to the accounts payable address file.

> EXAMPLE
>
> *An accounts payable employee was so trusted that her manager allowed her to use his computer password in his absence. The password permitted access to the accounts payable address file. This employee waited until the manager was absent, then selected a legitimate vendor with whom her company did a lot of business. She held up the vendor's invoices for the day, and after work used the manager's log-on code to change the vendor name and address to that of a fictitious company. The new name and address were run through the accounts payable cycle with an old invoice number, causing a fraudulent check to be issued. The victim company had an automated duplicate invoice test, but the perpetrator circumvented it substituting "1" for "I" and "0" (zero) for capital "O." The next day,*

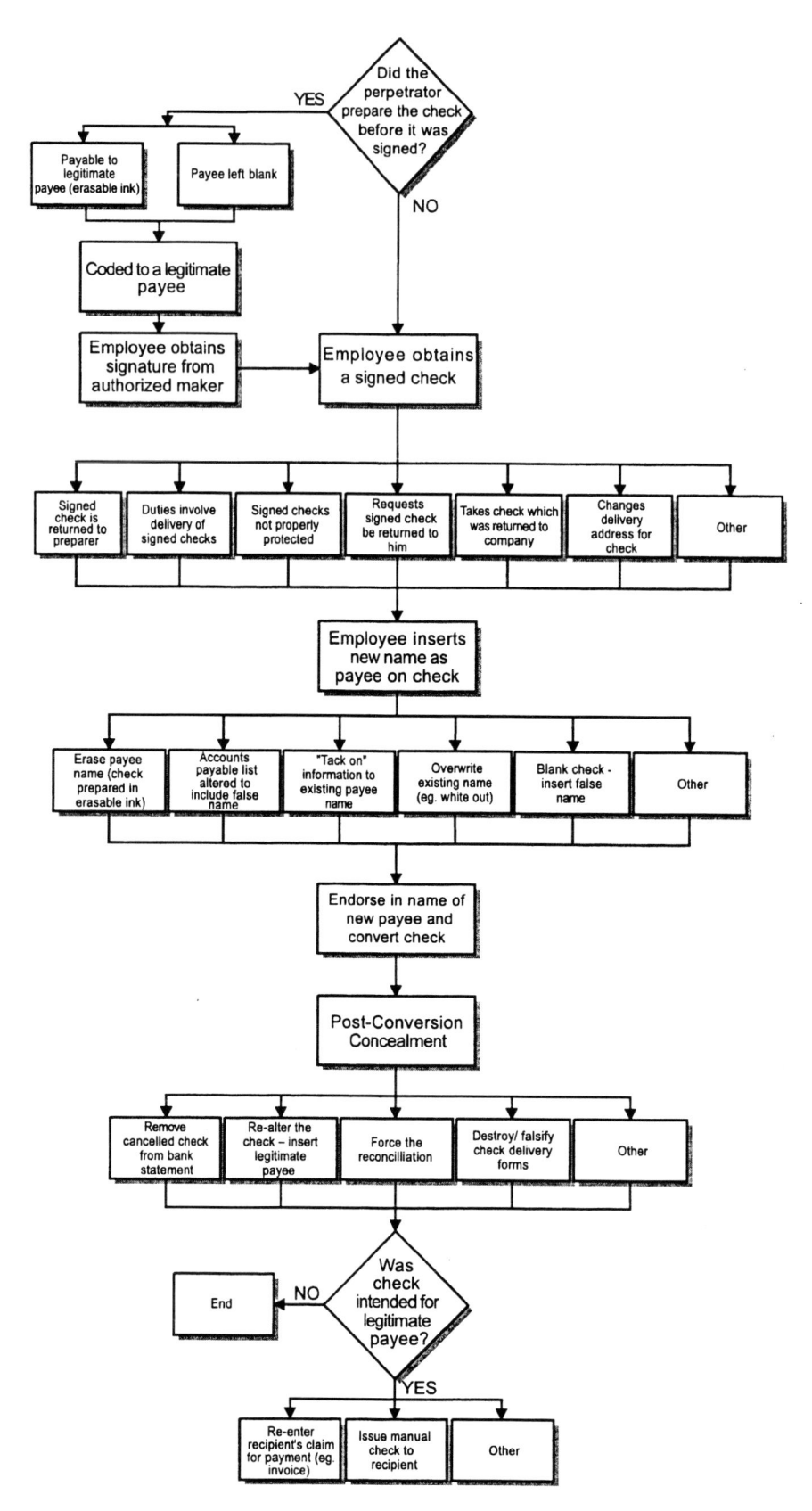

Altered Payee Schemes

Flowchart:

- **Did the perpetrator prepare the check before it was signed?**
  - **YES:**
    - Payable to legitimate payee (erasable ink)
    - Payee left blank
    - → Coded to a legitimate payee
    - → Employee obtains signature from authorized maker
  - **NO:**
    - → Employee obtains a signed check

- **Employee obtains a signed check** (methods):
  - Signed check is returned to preparer
  - Duties involve delivery of signed checks
  - Signed checks not properly protected
  - Requests signed check be returned to him
  - Takes check which was returned to company
  - Changes delivery address for check
  - Other

- **Employee inserts new name as payee on check** (methods):
  - Erase payee name (check prepared in erasable ink)
  - Accounts payable list altered to include false name
  - "Tack on" information to existing payee name
  - Overwrite existing name (eg. white out)
  - Blank check - insert false name
  - Other

- **Endorse in name of new payee and convert check**

- **Post-Conversion Concealment** (methods):
  - Remove cancelled check from bank statement
  - Re-alter the check – insert legitimate payee
  - Force the reconcilliation
  - Destroy/falsify check delivery forms
  - Other

- **Was check intended for legitimate payee?**
  - **NO:** End
  - **YES:**
    - Re-enter recipient's claim for payment (eg. invoice)
    - Issue manual check to recipient
    - Other

the employee would replace the true vendor's name and address, and mutilate the check register so that the check payable to the fictitious vendor was concealed. Approximately $300,000 in false checks was issued using this method.

Altering Checks Prepared by Others: "Tacking On"

The other method that can be used by perpetrators to alter checks prepared by others is "tacking on" additional letters or words to the end of the real payee designation. For instance, checks payable to "ABC" company might be altered to read "A.B. Collins." The employee then cashes the checks in the name of A.B. Collins. It sounds like an odd scheme, but it really happens. In these cases, the simple inclusion of a filler line after the payee designation would prevent the loss.

In addition to altering the payee designation, the amount of the check can be altered by tacking on extra numbers if the person preparing the check is careless and leaves space for extra numbers in the "Amount" portion of the check.

Altering Checks Prepared by the Fraudster: Erasable Ink

When the perpetrator prepares the check that is to be altered, the schemes tend to be a bit more sophisticated. The reason for this is obvious: If the perpetrator is able to prepare the check himself, he can prepare it with the thought of how the payee designation will be changed. One of the most common ways to prepare a check for alteration is to write or type the payee's name (and possibly the amount) in erasable ink. After an authorized maker signs the check, the perpetrator retrieves the check, erases the payee's name, and inserts his own. In some cases employees even obtain signatures on checks written in pencil!

EXAMPLE

A bookkeeper typed out small checks to a local supplier and had the owner of the company sign them. The bookkeeper then used her erasing typewriter to lift the payee designation and amount from the check. She entered her own name as the payee and raised the amount precipitously. For instance, the owner might sign a $10 check that later became a $10,000 check. These checks were entered in the disbursements journal as payments for aggregate inventory to the company's largest supplier, who received several large checks each month. The bookkeeper stole over $300,000 from her employer in this scheme.

Where a proper separation of duties is in place, a person who prepares a check should not be permitted to handle the check after it has been signed. Nevertheless, this is exactly what happens in most altered payee schemes. The person who prepares the check knows that the maker of the check will return it to him after it has been signed.

Altering Checks Prepared by the Fraudster: Blank Checks

The most egregious example of poor controls in the handling of signed checks is one in which the perpetrator prepares a check, *leaves the payee designation blank*, and submits it to an authorized maker who signs the check and returns it to the employee. Obviously, this makes it quite easy for the perpetrator to designate himself or an accomplice as the payee. Common sense should prevent anyone from giving a signed, blank check to another person. Nevertheless, this is a fairly common occurrence, especially when the perpetrator is a trusted long-time employee.

Converting Altered Checks

As with all other types of fraudulent checks, conversion is accomplished by endorsing the checks in the name of the payee. Conversion of fraudulent checks has already been discussed in previous sections and will not be re-examined here.

Authorized Maker Schemes

The final check tampering scheme, the authorized maker scheme, may be the most difficult to defend against. An authorized maker scheme occurs when an employee with signature authority on a company account writes fraudulent checks for his own benefit and signs his own name as the maker. (See "Authorized Maker Schemes" flowchart) The perpetrator in these schemes can write and sign fraudulent checks himself. He does not have to alter a preprepared instrument or forge the maker's signature.

Overriding Controls through Intimidation

When a person is authorized to sign company checks, preparing the checks is easy. The employee simply writes and signs the instruments the same way he would with any legitimate check. In most situations, check signers are owners, officers, or otherwise high-ranking employees, and thus have or can obtain access to all the blank checks they need. Even if company policy prohibits check signers from handling blank checks, the perpetrator can normally use his influence to overcome this impediment. What employee is going to tell the CEO that he can't have a blank check?

The most basic way an employee accomplishes an authorized maker scheme is to override controls designed to prevent fraud. Most authorized signatories have high levels of influence within their companies. The perpetrators use this influence to deflect questions about fraudulent transactions.

A common authorized maker scheme is one in which a majority owner or sole shareholder uses his company as a sort of alter ego, paying personal expenses directly out of company accounts. Instead of paying personal expenses, the perpetrator might cut checks directly to himself, his friends, or family. Using fear of job security as a weapon, the owner can maintain a work environment in which employees are afraid to question these transactions.

High-level managers or officers might also use their authority to override controls in those companies whose ownership is either absent or inattentive. Intimidation can play a large part in the commission and concealment of any type of occupational fraud where powerful individuals are involved.

EXAMPLE

The manager of a sales office stole approximately $150,000 from his employers over a two-year period. This manager had primary check-signing authority and abused this power by writing company checks to pay his personal expenses. The manager's fraudulent activities were well known by certain members of his staff, but these employees' careers were controlled by the perpetrator. Fear of losing their jobs combined with lack of a proper whistleblowing structure prevented the manager's employees from reporting his fraud.

Poor Controls

Although overriding controls is the most blatant way to execute an authorized maker scheme, it is not the most common. Far more of these schemes occur because no one is paying attention to the accounts and few controls are present to prevent fraud. Some employees who write checks to themselves or to purchase items for themselves simply code the checks to expense accounts that they know are not likely to be reviewed.

The failure to closely monitor accounts is supplemented by lack of internal controls, specifically the absence of separation of duties in the cash disbursements process. Employees who commit authorized maker fraud are often in charge of reconciling the bank accounts of the business. This is especially common in small businesses. Employees with total control over the disbursements process are in a perfect position to write fraudulent checks for their own benefit.

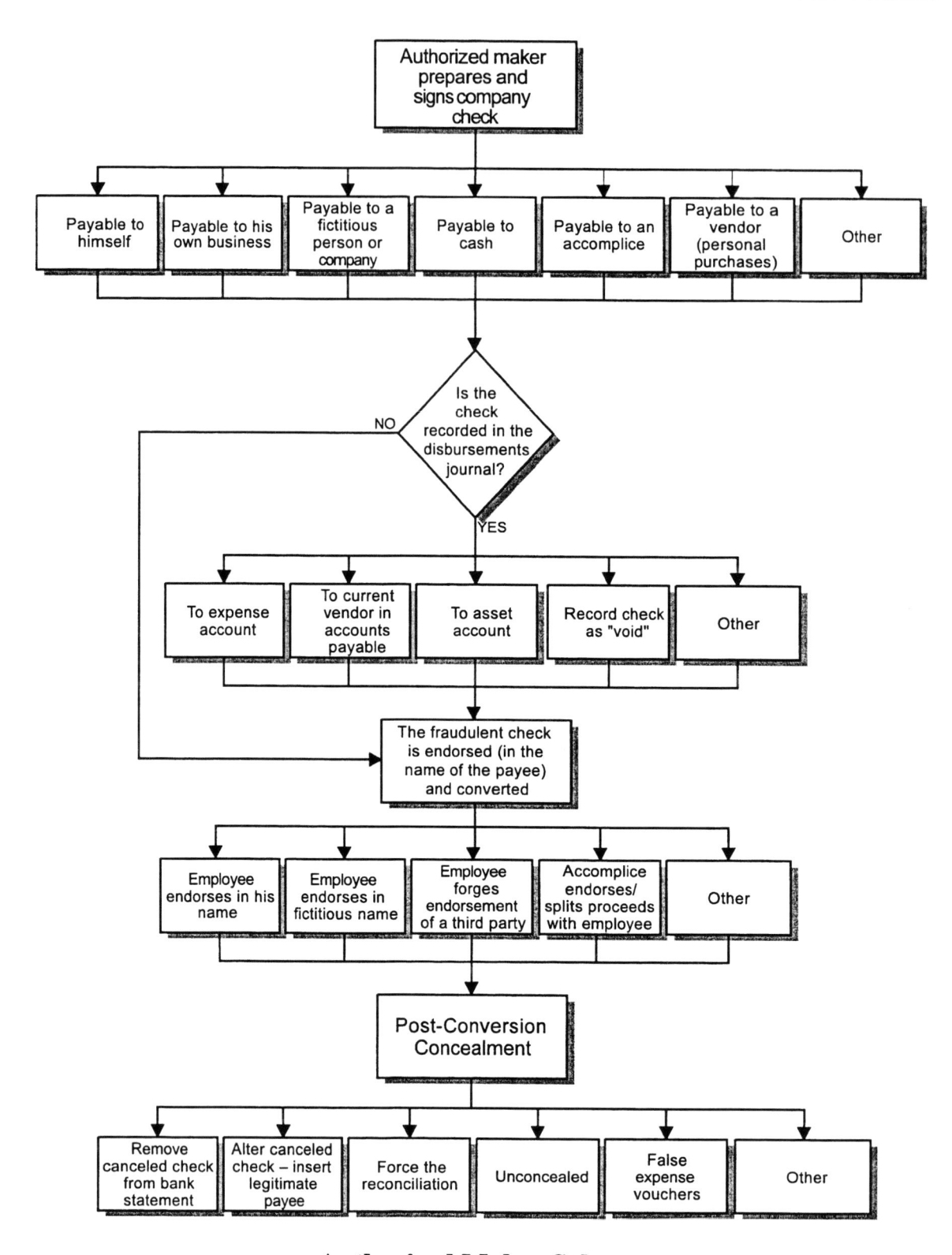

Authorized Maker Schemes

```
Authorized maker prepares and signs company check
├── Payable to himself
├── Payable to his own business
├── Payable to a fictitious person or company
├── Payable to cash
├── Payable to an accomplice
├── Payable to a vendor (personal purchases)
└── Other

Is the check recorded in the disbursements journal?
  NO → (to endorsement step)
  YES →
    ├── To expense account
    ├── To current vendor in accounts payable
    ├── To asset account
    ├── Record check as "void"
    └── Other

The fraudulent check is endorsed (in the name of the payee) and converted
    ├── Employee endorses in his name
    ├── Employee endorses in fictitious name
    ├── Employee forges endorsement of a third party
    ├── Accomplice endorses/splits proceeds with employee
    └── Other

Post-Conversion Concealment
    ├── Remove canceled check from bank statement
    ├── Alter canceled check – insert legitimate payee
    ├── Force the reconciliation
    ├── Unconcealed
    ├── False expense vouchers
    └── Other
```

EXAMPLE

The bookkeeper of a medium-sized company was charged with paying all bills and preparing the company payroll. She had access to an automatic check signer and total control over company bank accounts. The bookkeeper wrote extra checks to herself, coded the expenditures to payroll, and destroyed the canceled checks when they were returned with the bank statement.

Concealment

Most check tampering schemes do not consist of a single occurrence but instead continue over a period of time. Therefore, concealing the fraud is arguably the most important aspect of the scheme. If an employee intended to steal a large sum of money and skip to South America, hiding the fraud might not be so important. But the vast majority of occupational fraudsters remain employees of their companies as they continue to steal from them, which makes concealment the key to the crime.

Concealment of the fraud means not only hiding the identity of the criminal, but in most cases hiding the fact that a fraud has even occurred. The most successful frauds are those in which the victim organization is unaware that it is being robbed. Obviously, once a business learns that it is being victimized it will take steps to staunch its bleeding and the end of the scheme will be at hand.

Check tampering schemes can present especially tricky concealment problems for dishonest employees. In other types of fraudulent disbursements such as invoice or payroll schemes, the fraudulent payment is entered in the books as a legitimate transaction by someone other than the perpetrator. The payments in those schemes are generated by the production of false documents which cause accounts payable personnel to think that money is owed to a particular person or vendor. When accounts payable issues a disbursement for a bogus invoice, it does so because it believes the invoice to be genuine. The payment is then entered in the books as a legitimate payment. In other words, the perpetrator generally does not have to worry about concealing the payment in the books, because someone else unwittingly does it for him. But in forgery and authorized maker schemes the perpetrator is the one writing the check, and he is usually the one coding the check in the disbursements journal. He must "explain" the check on the books.

Forged endorsement schemes and altered payee schemes are different because they involve the alteration of checks which were already prepared and coded by someone else.

Nevertheless, they create a problem for the perpetrator because the intercepted check was intended for a legitimate recipient. Someone is out there waiting for the check which the perpetrator has taken. The culprit in these schemes must worry not only about hiding the fraud from his employer, but also about appeasing the intended payee.

The Fraudster Reconciling the Bank Statement

A large percentage of those who perpetrate check tampering frauds are involved in reconciling the company's bank statement. The bank statement that a company receives normally includes the canceled checks that have been cashed in the preceding period. A person who reconciles the accounts is therefore in a position to hide the existence of any fraudulent checks he has written to himself. He can remove the fraudulent checks or doctor the bank statement or both.

In forged maker and authorized maker schemes, the perpetrator usually has to code the check in the disbursements journal. The most basic way to hide the check is to code it as "void" or to include no listing at all in the journal. Then, when the bank statement arrives, the perpetrator removes the fraudulent check from the stack of returned checks and destroys it. Now there is no record of the payment in the journal and no physical evidence of the check on hand. Of course, the bank will have a copy of the check, but unless someone questions the missing check it is unlikely that the company will discover the problem. And since the perpetrator is the one who reconciles the account, it is unlikely that anyone will even notice that the check is missing.

The problem with simply omitting the fraudulent check from the disbursements journal is that the bank balance will not reconcile to the book balance. For instance, if the perpetrator wrote a $25,000 check to himself and did not record it, then the book balance will be $25,000 higher than the bank balance ($25,000 was taken out of the bank account by the perpetrator, but was not credited out of the company's cash account). Employees usually omit their illicit checks from the disbursement journal only in situations where they personally reconcile the bank statement and no one reviews their work. This allows the perpetrator to "force" the reconciliation. In other words, the perpetrator reports that the bank balance and book balance match, when in fact they do not.

Some victim organizations simply do not regularly reconcile their accounts. This makes it easy for employees to write checks without recording them. In a system where controls are so lax, almost any concealment method will be effective to disguise fraud. In fact, it may not be necessary to make any effort at all to conceal the crime.

Some fraudsters physically alter the bank statement to cause it to match the company's book balance. For instance, a person engaging in a forged maker scheme may decide to steal blank checks from the back of the checkbook. These checks are out of sequence and therefore will be listed last on the bank statement. This employee can delete the clump of fraudulent checks at the end of the statement and alter the balance to match the victim company's books.

Re-Alteration of Checks

In altered payee schemes, remember that it is common for the perpetrator to take a check intended for a legitimate recipient, then doctor the instrument so that the perpetrator becomes the designated payee. But a canceled check payable to an employee will obviously raise suspicions of fraud. Therefore, some employees re-alter their fraudulent checks when the bank statement arrives. It has already been discussed how employees can alter checks by writing the payee's name in erasable ink when the check is prepared. These employees obtain a signature for the check, then erase the true payee's name and insert their own. When the fraudulent checks return with the bank statement, the employee erases his own name and re-enters the name of the proper payee. Thus there will be no appearance of mischief.

Miscoding Fraudulent Checks

Rather than omit a fraudulent check from the disbursements journal or list it as void, the perpetrator might write a check payable to himself but list a different person as the payee on the books. Usually, the fake payee is a regular vendor—a person or business that receives numerous checks from the victim company. Employees tend to pick known vendors for these schemes because one extra disbursement to a regular payee is less likely to be noticed than a check to an unknown person.

The fraudster can also conceal a fraudulent check overstating the amounts of *legitimate* disbursements in the journal in order to absorb the cost of a fraudulent check. For instance, assume that a company owes $10,000 to a particular vendor. The fraudster would write a check to the vendor for $10,000, but enter the check in the disbursements journal as a $15,000 payment. The company's disbursements are now overstated by $5,000. The fraudster can write a $5,000 check to himself and list that check as void in the disbursements journal. The bank balance and the book balance will still match, because the cost of the fraudulent check was absorbed when the amount of the legitimate check was overstated. Of course, the fact that the canceled checks do not match the entries in the journal should indicate potential fraud. This type of concealment is really only effective when the bank accounts are not closely monitored or where the employee is in charge of reconciling the accounts.

If possible, employees will try to code their fraudulent checks to existing accounts that are rarely reviewed or to accounts that are very active. Most of these checks are coded to expense accounts or liability accounts. This particular method can be very effective in concealing fraud, particularly when the victim company is not diligent in reconciling its bank accounts. For instance, some organizations reconcile their accounts by cross-referencing check numbers with the amounts of the checks, but they do not verify that the payee on the actual check matches the payee listed in the disbursements journal. These organizations will be unable to detect checks which have been coded to the wrong payee in the disbursements journal.

Re-Issuing Intercepted Checks

In intercepted check schemes, the employee faces detection not only through his employer's normal control procedures, but also from the intended recipients of the stolen checks. When the real payees do not receive their checks they are likely to complain. These complaints, in turn, could trigger a fraud investigation. One way for an employee to avoid this problem is to issue new checks to the intended payees.

> EXAMPLE
> *An accounts payable troubleshooter was in charge of auditing payments to all suppliers, reviewing supporting documents, and mailing checks. Every once in a while, she would purposely fail to mail a check to a vendor. The vendor, of course, would call accounts payable about the late payment and would be told that his invoice had been paid on a certain date. Since accounts payable did not have a copy of the canceled check (because the fraudster was still holding it), they would call the troubleshooter to research the problem. Unfortunately for the company, the troubleshooter was the one who had stolen the check. She would tell accounts payable to issue another check to the vendor while she stopped payment on the first check. Thus the vendor received his payment. Meanwhile, instead of stopping payment on the first check, the troubleshooter deposited it into her own account.*

Bogus Supporting Documents

While some perpetrators attempt to wipe out all traces of their fraudulent disbursements by destroying the checks, forcing the bank reconciliation and so on, others opt to justify their checks by manufacturing fake support for them. These persons prepare false payment vouchers, including false invoices, purchase orders, and/or receiving reports to create an appearance of authenticity. This concealment strategy is only practical when the employee writes checks payable to someone other than himself (e.g., an accomplice or a shell company). A check made payable to an employee may raise suspicions regardless of any supporting documents that he manufactures.

Detection

Account Analysis through Cut-Off Statements

Bank cut-off statements should be requested for 10 to 15 days after the closing date of the balance sheet. These statements may be used to detect cash fraud during periods between monthly bank statements. Cut-off statements are often used by auditors to ensure that income and expenses are reported in the proper period. If employees know that at any time during the month a cut-off statement may be ordered and reviewed independently, cash fraud will be less likely.

A cut-off statement generally is ordered from the bank, delivered unopened to the auditor (or outsider), and reconciled. It can be ordered at any time during the accounting cycle. If cut-off bank statements are not ordered or received, obtain the following period bank statement and perform account analysis and investigation.[*]

Bank Reconciliations

Copies of the bank reconciliations and account analysis should be obtained along with the complete set of bank statements on all checking and savings accounts, as well as certificates of deposit and other interest bearing and non-interest bearing accounts. From the reconciliations perform the following tests:
- Confirm the mathematical accuracy of the reconciliation.
- Examine the bank statement for possible alterations.
- Trace the balance on the statement back to the bank cut-off and bank confirmation statements.
- Foot the balance to the company's ledger.

---

[*] George Georgiades, *Audit Procedures* (New York: Harcourt Brace Professional Publishing, 1995).

- Trace the deposits in transit to the bank cut-off statement to ensure recording in proper period.
- Examine canceled checks and compare to the list of outstanding checks.
- Sample supporting documentation of checks written for a material amount.
- Verify supporting documentation on outstanding checks written for a material amount.
- Verify accuracy of nonoperational-cash or cash-equivalent accounts (CDs and other investment accounts). Analysis should include the verification of the institution holding the funds, interest rate, maturity date, beginning and ending balances, and current period activity. Book and bank balances should be compared and any accruals of interest analyzed.*

Bank Confirmation

Another method related to the cut-off statement is the bank confirmation request. Unlike the cut-off statement, this detection method is merely a report of the balance in the account as of the date requested. This balance should be requested to confirm the statement balance as well as any other necessary balance date. If fraud is occurring at the bank reconciliation stage, this independent confirmation may prove to be very helpful.

Check-Tampering Red Flags

The following irregularities may indicate fraud:

- Voided checks may indicate employees have embezzled cash and charged the embezzlement to expense accounts. When the expense is paid (from accounts payable), fraudulent checks are marked and entered as void and removed from distribution points. An account-balancing journal entry is then made. The list of voided checks should be verified against physical copies of the checks. Bank statements should be reviewed to ensure that voided checks have not been processed.
- Missing checks may indicate lax control over the physical safekeeping of checks. Stop payments should be issued for all missing checks.
- Checks payable to employees, with the exception of regular payroll checks, should be closely scrutinized. Such an examination may indicate other schemes such as conflicts of interest, fictitious vendors, or duplicate expense reimbursements.
- Altered endorsements or dual endorsements of returned checks may indicate possible tampering.

---

* Id.

- Returned checks with obviously forged or questionable signature endorsements should be verified with original payee.
- Altered payees on returned checks should be verified with intended payee.
- Duplicate or counterfeit checks indicate fraud. These checks may be traceable to depositor through bank check coding.
- Questionable deposit dates should be matched to the corresponding customer accounts.
- An examination of all cash advances may reveal that not all advances are properly documented and, therefore, inappropriate payments have been made to employees.
- Customer complaints regarding payments not being applied to their accounts should be investigated.
- A questionable payee or payee address on a check should trigger review of the corresponding check and support documentation.

Prevention

Check Disbursement Controls

The following list of activities will help tighten controls and possibly deter employees from giving in to the temptation to commit check fraud.
- Check "cutting" and preparation is not done by a signatory on the account.
- Checks are mailed immediately after signing.
- Theft control procedures are adhered to (see below).
- Accounts payable records and addresses are secure from possible tampering. Changes in vendor information should be verified.
- Bank statements should be reviewed diligently ensuring that amounts and signatures have not been altered.
- Bank reconciliations should be completed immediately after monthly statements are received. The Uniform Commercial Code states that discrepancies must be presented within 30 days from the bank statement in order to hold the bank liable.
- Bank reconciliations are not made by signatories on the account.
- Bank statements should be reconciled and reviewed by more than one person.
- Appropriate separation of duties should be documented and adhered to.
- Detailed comparisons are routinely made between check payees and the payees listed in the cash disbursement journal.
- Personnel responsible for handling and coding checks are periodically rotated, keeping total personnel involved to a minimum.

Bank-Assisted Controls

Companies should work in a cooperative effort with banks to prevent check fraud. Consider the following control measures that may be taken in regard to a firm's checking accounts.

- Establish maximum dollar amounts above which the company's bank will not accept checks drawn against the account.
- Use positive pay banking controls. Positive pay allows a company and its bank to work together to detect fraudulent items presented for payment. The company provides the bank with a list of checks and amounts that are written each day. The bank verifies items presented for payment against the company's list. The bank rejects items that are not on the list. Investigations are conducted as to the origin of "nonlist" items.

Physical Tampering Prevention

The following list details check-tampering prevention techniques that are being used today, by some institutions, to secure business's check integrity. These methods can be used individually or in combination.

- Signature Line Void Safety Band—The word VOID appears on the check when photocopied.
- Rainbow Foil Bar—A horizontal, colored bar placed on the check fades and is shaded from one bar to the next. Photocopied foil bars appear solid.
- Holographic Safety Border—Holographic images are created in a way that reflect light to reveal a three dimensional graphic.
- Embossed Pearlescent Numbering—Checks are numbered using a new technique that is revealed by a colored highlighter pen or by a bright light held behind the check.
- Other Chemical Voids—Checks reveal an image or the word VOID when treated with an eradicator chemical.
- Micro Line Printing—Extremely small print is too small to read with the naked eye and becomes distorted when photocopied.
- High Resolution Microprinting—Images are produced on the check in high resolution, 2,400 dots per inch or higher. This technique is very difficult to reproduce.
- Security Inks—Checks contain inks which react with eradication chemicals reducing a forger's ability to modify the check.
- Chrome Coloring—The use of chrome-like coloring deters photocopying even with color copiers. The chrome pattern or numbering develops solid black.
- Watermark Backers—Hidden images can only be seen when the check is held at an angle. This image is very difficult to reproduce.

- Ultraviolet Ink—This ink displays an image or message when held under ultraviolet lighting.

Check Theft Control Procedures

It is very important to provide internal controls which will minimize the possibility of check tampering and theft. Below is a list of items that should be incorporated into company's policies and procedures to help deter check tampering.

- New checks should be purchased from reputable, well-established check producers.
- Unused checks should be stored in a secure area such as a safe, vault, or other locked area. Security to this area should be restricted to authorized personnel only. Routinely change keys and access codes to storage areas.
- Review all hiring procedures. One of the most important means of fighting fraud is to not hire people with questionable backgrounds. Develop a distinct separation of duties in the accounts payable department, including written policies and procedures for all personnel who have the opportunity to handle checks, from mailroom clerks to the CEO.
- Use electronic payment services to handle large vendor and financing payments, eliminating the use of paper checks.
- Report lost or stolen checks immediately.
- Properly and securely store canceled checks.
- Destroy unused checks for accounts that have been closed.
- Printed and signed checks should be mailed immediately after signing.

Billing Schemes

The asset misappropriation schemes discussed up to this point—skimming, larceny, register schemes, and check tampering—all require the perpetrator of the scheme to physically take cash or checks from his employer. The next three sections will cover a different kind of asset misappropriation scheme, one which allows the perpetrator to misappropriate company funds without ever actually handling cash or checks while at work. These succeed by making a false claim for payment upon the victim organization. This group consists of *billing schemes* (which attack the purchasing function of a company), *payroll schemes*, and *expense reimbursement schemes*. The most common of these is the billing scheme.

Billing schemes are a popular form of employee fraud mainly because they offer the prospect of large rewards. Since the majority of most businesses' disbursements are made in the purchasing cycle, larger thefts can be hidden through false-billing schemes than through other kinds of fraudulent disbursements. There are three principal types of billing schemes: false invoicing via shell companies, false invoicing via nonaccomplice vendors, and personal purchases made with company funds.

Invoicing Via Shell Companies
Forming a Shell Company

Shell companies are fictitious entities created for the purpose of committing fraud. They may be nothing more than a fabricated name and a post office box that an employee uses to collect disbursements from false billings. However, since the checks received will be made out in the name of the shell company, the perpetrator will normally also set up a bank account in his new company's name, so he can deposit and cash the fraudulent checks. (See "False Billings from Shell Companies" flowchart)

A person will probably have to present a bank with a certificate of incorporation or an assumed-name certificate in order to open a bank account for a shell company. These are documents that a company must obtain through a state or local government. The documents can be forged, but it is more likely that the perpetrator will simply file the requisite paperwork and obtain legitimate documents from his state or county. This can usually be accomplished for a small fee, the cost of which will be more than offset by a successful fraud scheme.

If it is discovered that a vendor is falsely billing a company, investigators for the victim company may be able to identify the owner of the suspect company by reviewing its business registration filings, which are a matter of public record.

To avoid being detected through a records search, some perpetrators form their shell companies under another name. It is common, for instance, for employees to set up shell companies in the name of a spouse or other close relative. Male fraudsters often establish shell companies under their wives' maiden names. An employee might also form the company under a completely fictitious name.

EXAMPLE

An employee used a co-worker's identification to form a shell vendor. The fraudster then proceeded to bill his employer for approximately $20,000 in false services. The resulting checks were deposited in the account of the shell company and currency was withdrawn from the account through an ATM.

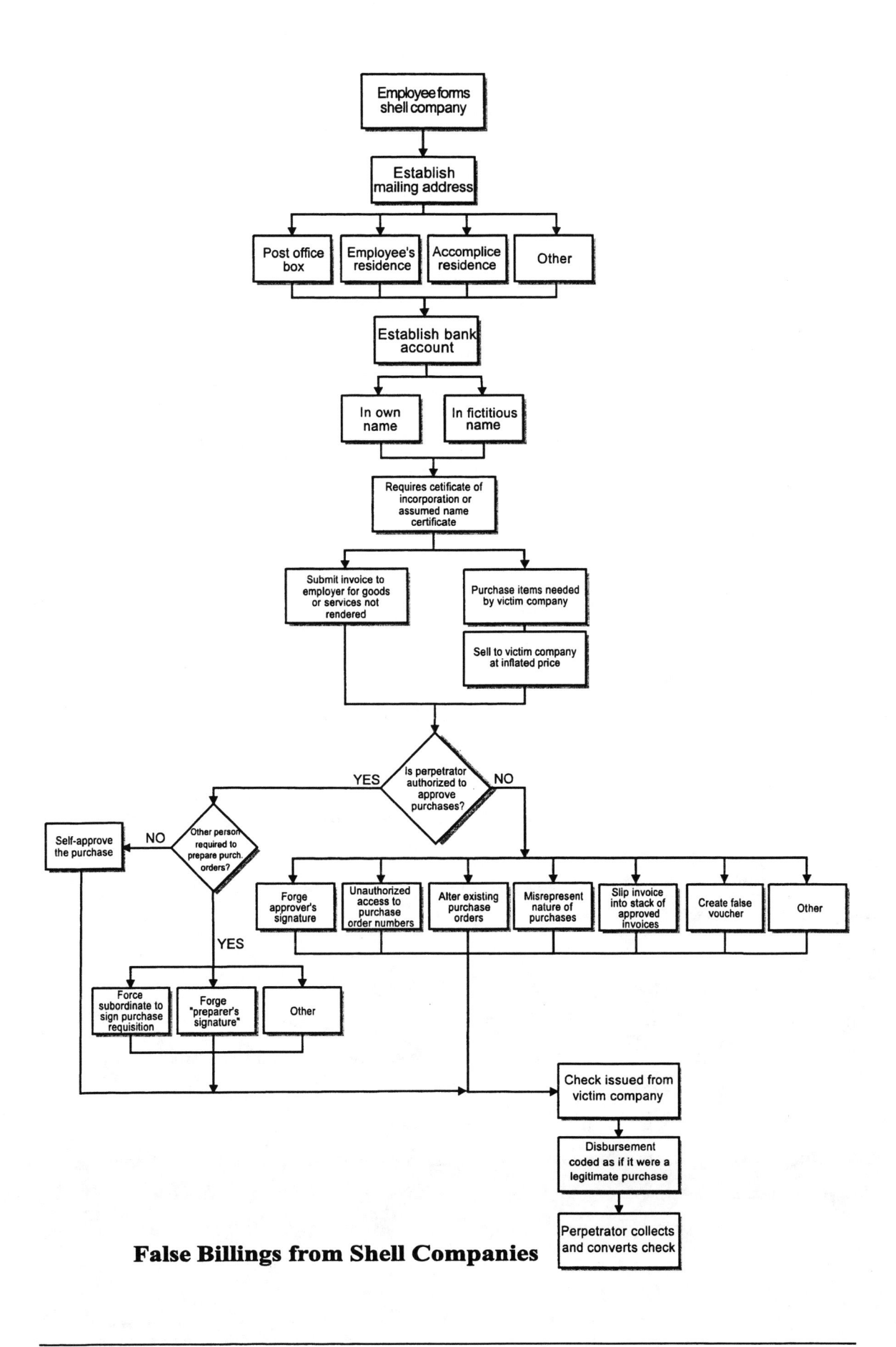

False Billings from Shell Companies

- Employee forms shell company
  - Establish mailing address
    - Post office box
    - Employee's residence
    - Accomplice residence
    - Other
  - Establish bank account
    - In own name
    - In fictitious name
  - Requires certificate of incorporation or assumed name certificate
    - Submit invoice to employer for goods or services not rendered
    - Purchase items needed by victim company
      - Sell to victim company at inflated price

Is perpetrator authorized to approve purchases?

- **YES** → Other person required to prepare purch. orders?
  - **NO** → Self-approve the purchase
  - **YES** →
    - Force subordinate to sign purchase requisition
    - Forge "preparer's signature"
    - Other
- **NO** →
  - Forge approver's signature
  - Unauthorized access to purchase order numbers
  - Alter existing purchase orders
  - Misrepresent nature of purchases
  - Slip invoice into stack of approved invoices
  - Create false voucher
  - Other

- Check issued from victim company
- Disbursement coded as if it were a legitimate purchase
- Perpetrator collects and converts check

Another issue involved in forming a shell company is the entity's address—the place where fraudulent checks will be collected. Often, an employee rents a post office box and lists it as the mailing address of his shell company. Some employees list their home address instead. A comparison of employee addresses to vendor addresses might reveal shell companies in an accounts payable system.

EXAMPLE

A department head set up a dummy company using his residence as the mailing address. Over a two-year period, this man submitted over $250,000 worth of false invoices. Eventually, the scheme was detected by a newly hired clerk. The clerk was processing an invoice when she noticed that the address of the vendor was the same as her boss's address. (By a lucky coincidence, the clerk had typed a personal letter for her boss earlier that day and remembered his address.) Had the department head used a P.O. box instead of his home address on the invoices, his scheme might have continued indefinitely.

Employees often use their home addresses to collect fraudulent disbursements because many businesses are wary of sending checks to vendors that have a post office box for a mailing address. Other common collection sites for shell company schemes are the addresses of relatives, friends, or accomplices.

Submitting False Invoices

Once a shell company has been formed and a bank account has been opened, the corrupt employee begins billing his employer. Invoices can be manufactured by various means such as a professional printer, a personal computer, or a typewriter. False invoices do not always have to be of professional quality to generate fraudulent disbursements. Typewritten invoices are often sufficient to generate checks.

Self-Approval of Fraudulent Invoices

The difficulty in a shell company scheme is not usually in producing the invoices, but in getting the victim organization to pay them. Authorization for the fictitious purchase (and therefore payment of the bill) is the key. In a large percentage of shell-company cases, the perpetrator is in a position to approve payment on the very invoices he is fraudulently submitting. It is obvious the duties of preparing and approving vouchers should be separated to avoid this kind of scheme.

In companies where a proper separation of duties exists, the employee with approval authority sometimes creates fraudulent vouchers or purchase orders and forges the signature of the person who is in charge of preparing these documents. Then the perpetrator approves payment on the fraudulent vouchers he has generated. This makes it appear that two employees have signed off on the voucher as mandated by the victim organization's controls.

Not all companies require the completion of payment vouchers before they will issue checks. In some enterprises, checks are written based on less formal procedures, such as the submission of "check requests." These requests simply list the name of the payee, the amount to be paid, and a brief narrative stating the reason for the check. Obviously, this is not a very sound procedure for preventing fraud. Dishonest employees have little trouble running shell company schemes in organizations that operate this way.

"Rubber Stamp" Supervisors

If an employee cannot authorize payments himself, the next best thing is if the person who has that authority is inattentive or overly trusting. "Rubber stamp" supervisors like this are destined to be targeted by unethical employees. In some cases, supervisors are attentive to the purchase orders they are asked to authorize, but they lack the technical knowledge to spot fraud as it is happening. For instance, a manager or administrator might not completely understand the costs associated with upgrading computer software to modernize a work area. This manager will have to rely on his subordinates who have the necessary technical expertise to determine that costs are being kept in line. The subordinates may be able to take advantage of this situation to cause the company to overpay for the equipment required to upgrade the system.

Reliance on False Documents

When an employee does not have approval authority for purchases and does not have the benefit of a rubber stamp supervisor, he must run his vouchers through the normal accounts payable process. The success of this kind of scheme will depend on the apparent authenticity of the false voucher he creates. If the perpetrator can generate purchase orders and receiving reports that corroborate the information on the fraudulent invoice from his shell company, he can fool accounts payable into issuing a check.

Collusion

Collusion among several employees is sometimes used to overcome well-designed internal controls. For example, in a company with proper separation of duties, the functions of purchasing goods or services, authorizing the purchase, receiving the goods or services, and making the payment to the vendor should all be separated. If this process is strictly adhered to, it will be extremely difficult for any single employee to commit a false-billing scheme. But if several employees work together, they can overcome the internal controls of their employer.

EXAMPLE

A warehouse foreman and a parts ordering clerk conspired to purchase approximately $300,000 of nonexistent supplies. The parts ordering clerk would initiate the false transactions by obtaining approval to place orders for parts he claimed were needed. The orders were then sent to a vendor who, acting in conjunction with the two employee fraudsters, prepared false invoices which were sent to the victim company. Meanwhile, the warehouse foreman verified receipt of the fictitious shipments of incoming supplies. The perpetrators were therefore able to compile complete vouchers for the fraudulent purchases without overstepping their normal duties.

Even if all internal controls are observed, at some point a company must rely on its employees to be honest. One of the purposes of separating duties is to prevent any one person from having too much control over a particular business function. It provides a built-in monitoring mechanism where every person's actions are in some way verified by another person. But if *everyone* is corrupt, even proper controls will not prevent fraud.

Purchases of Services Rather than Goods

Most shell company schemes involve the purchase of services rather than goods. The primary reason for this is that services are not tangible. If an employee sets up a shell company to make fictitious sales of goods to his employer, these goods will obviously never arrive. By comparing its purchases to its inventory levels, the victim organization might detect the fraud. It is much more difficult, on the other hand, for the victim organization to verify that the services were never rendered. For this reason, many employees involved in shell company schemes bill their employers for things like "consulting services."

Pass-Through Schemes

In most shell company schemes, victim organizations are billed for completely fictitious purchases of goods or services. However, there is a subcategory of shell-company schemes in which actual goods or services are sold to the victim company. These are known as *pass-through schemes*.

Pass-through schemes are usually undertaken by employees in charge of purchasing on behalf of the victim company. Instead of buying merchandise directly from a vendor, the employee sets up a shell company and purchases the merchandise through that fictitious entity. He then resells the merchandise to his employer from the shell company at an inflated price.

> EXAMPLE
>
> *A department director was put in charge of purchasing computer equipment. Because of his expertise on the subject and his high standing within the company, he was unsupervised in this task. The director set up a shell company in another state and bought used computers through the shell company, then turned around and sold them to his employer at a greatly exaggerated price. The money from the victim company's first installment on the computers was used to pay the shell company's debts to the real vendors. Subsequent payments were profits for the bogus company. The scheme cost the victim company over $1 million.*

Invoicing Via Nonaccomplice Vendors

Pay-and-Return Schemes

Instead of using shell companies in their overbilling schemes, some employees generate fraudulent disbursements by using the invoices of legitimate, third-party vendors who are not a part of the fraud scheme. In *pay-and-return* schemes, employees intentionally mishandle payments which are owed to legitimate vendors. (See "Pay and Return Schemes" flowchart) One way to do this is to purposely double-pay an invoice. For instance, a clerk might intentionally pay an invoice twice, then call the vendor and request that one of the checks be returned. The clerk then intercepts the returned check.

Another way to accomplish a pay-and-return scheme is to intentionally pay the wrong vendor. In this type of scheme an employee sends Vendor A's check to Vendor B. After the checks are mailed, the employee calls the vendors to explain the "mistake" and requests that they return the checks to his attention. When the checks arrive, the employee converts them and keeps the money. The employee usually runs the vouchers through the accounts payable system a second time so that the vendors eventually get their money.

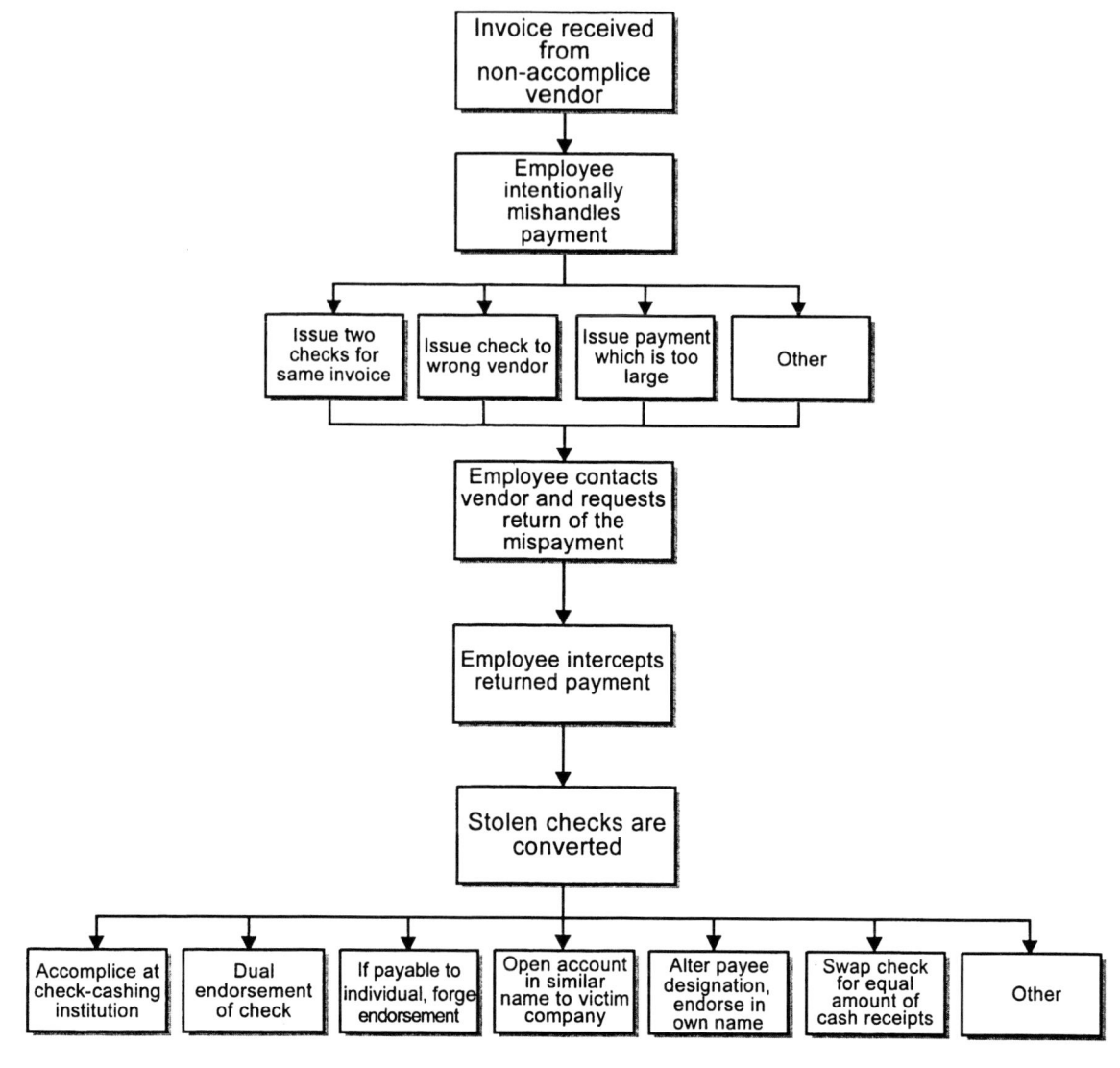

Pay and Return Schemes

An employee might also pay the proper vendor, but intentionally overpay him. Once again, the employee contacts the vendor, this time to request that the excess payment be returned. Finally, an employee might intentionally purchase excess merchandise, return the excess and pocket the refund.

Overbilling with a Nonaccomplice Vendor's Invoices

In most instances where an employee creates fraudulent invoices to overbill his employer, he uses a shell company. It is not as common for an employee to submit the invoice of an existing vendor. Nevertheless, in some instances an employee will undertake such a scheme by altering an existing vendor's invoice or by creating a counterfeit copy of a vendor's invoice form.

Personal Purchases with Company Funds

Instead of undertaking billing schemes to generate cash, many fraudsters simply purchase personal items with their company's money. Company accounts are used to buy items for employees, their businesses, their families, and so on.

Personal Purchases through False Invoicing

Employees who undertake purchases schemes may do so by running unsanctioned invoices through the accounts payable system. The perpetrator in this type of scheme buys an item and submits the bill to his employer as if it represented a legitimate company expense. The victim company ends up unknowingly buying goods or services for a dishonest employee. (See "Invoice Purchasing Schemes" flowchart)

THE FRAUDSTER AS AUTHORIZER OF INVOICES

The person who engages in a purchases scheme is often the very person in the company whose duties include *authorizing* purchases. Obviously, proper controls should preclude anyone from approving his own purchases. Such poorly separated functions leave little other than his conscience to dissuade an employee from fraud. Fraud arises in part because of a perceived opportunity. An employee who sees that no one is reviewing his actions is more likely to turn to fraud than one who knows his company diligently works to detect employee theft.

> EXAMPLE
>
> *A manager of a remote location of a large, publicly traded company was authorized to order supplies and approve vendor invoices for payment. For over a year, the manager routinely added personal items and supplies for his own business to orders made on behalf of his employer. The orders often included a strange mix of items. For instance, technical supplies and home furnishings might be purchased in the same order. Because the manager was in a position to approve his own purchases, he could get away with such blatantly obvious frauds. In addition to ordering personal items, the perpetrator changed the delivery address for certain supplies so that they would be delivered directly to his home or side business. This scheme cost the victim company approximately $300,000 in unnecessary purchases.*

In some situations, the perpetrator is authorized to approve purchases, but controls prevent him from also initiating purchase requests. This procedure is supposed to prevent an employee from purchasing personal items with company funds. Unfortunately, those with authority to approve purchases often have a good deal of control over their subordinates. These persons can use their influence to force subordinates to assist in purchases schemes. In other cases, the manager might simply initiate the purchase order himself by forging the subordinate's signature.

EXAMPLE

Purchases for under $1,000 at a certain utility company could be made with limited value purchase orders (LPOs), which required two signatures —the originator of a purchase request and the approver of the request. An LPO attached to an invoice for less than $1,000 would be paid by the accounts payable department. In this case, a manager bought goods and services on company accounts, and prepared LPOs for the purchases. (In some cases, the LPO would falsely describe the item to conceal the nature of the purchase.) Once the LPO was prepared, the manager forced a clerk in his department to sign the document as the originator of the transaction. The clerk, intimidated by her boss, did not question the authenticity of the LPOs. With two signatures affixed, the LPO appeared to be legitimate and the bills were paid. The scheme cost the victim company at least $25,000.

FALSE PURCHASE REQUISITIONS

If an employee does not have purchasing authority, he or she may get approval for a fraudulent purchase by misrepresenting the nature of the acquisition. In many companies, those with the power to authorize purchases are not always attentive to their duties. If a trusted subordinate says that the company needs to buy a certain item or items, busy supervisors often give rubber stamp approval to the purchase requisition. Additionally, employees sometimes misrepresent the nature of the items they are purchasing in order to pass a cursory review by their superiors.

EXAMPLE

An engineer bought over $30,000 worth of personal items. The engineer dealt directly with vendors and was also in charge of overseeing the receipt of the materials he purchased. He was therefore able to misrepresent the nature of the merchandise he bought, listing it as "maintenance items." Vendor invoices were altered to agree to this description.

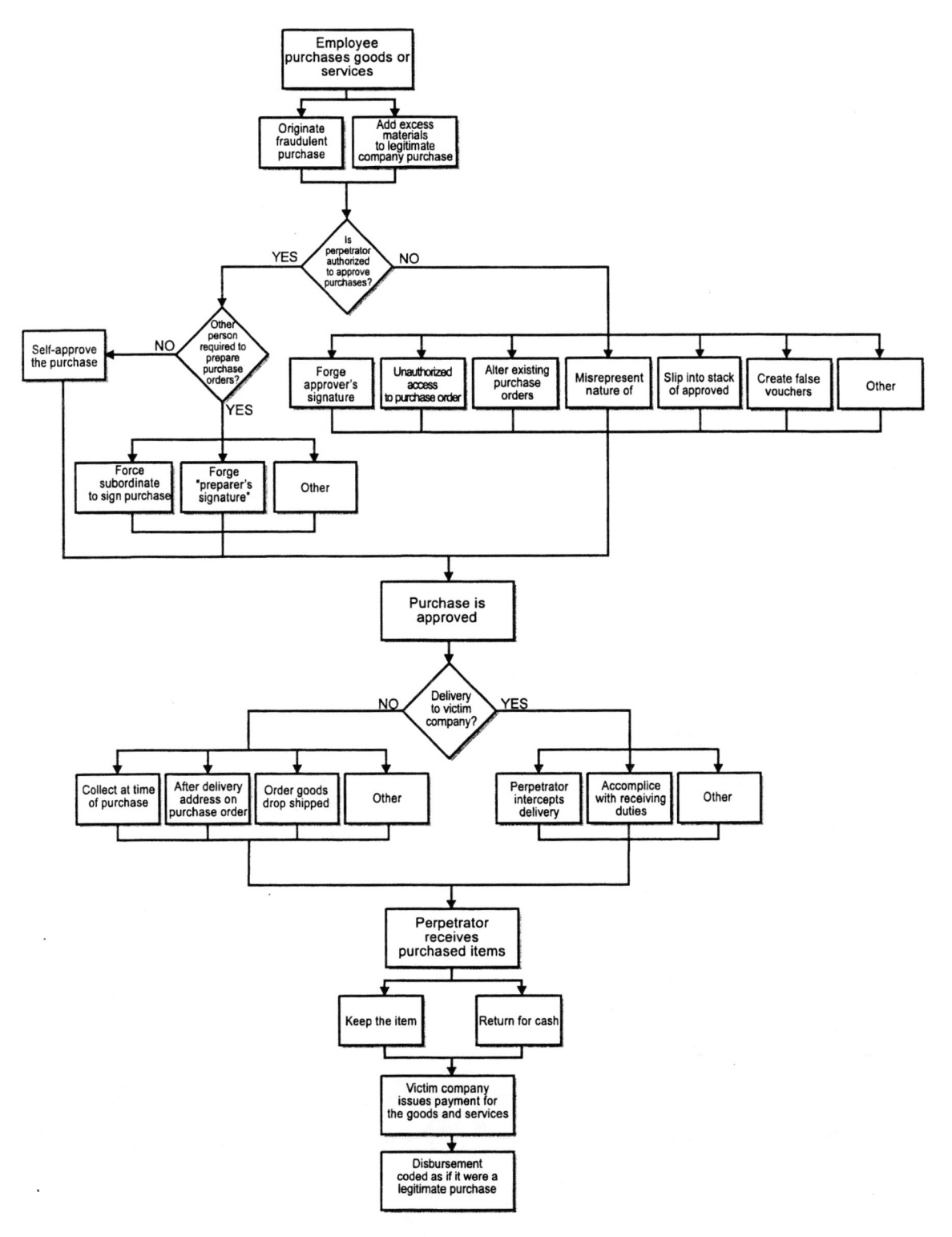

Invoice Purchasing Schemes

If the perpetrator falsifies his purchase requisition in this manner, the fraud should be detected when delivery occurs. For example, if the purchase requisition says "maintenance items" but the vendor delivers home furnishings, it will be obvious that the perpetrator has committed fraud. The problem of delivery can be avoided if the perpetrator is in charge of receiving incoming shipments. He can verify that delivery of "maintenance items" was received. This is a breach of separation of duties, but unfortunately it is fairly common for purchasing agents to verify delivery of their own orders. Even if the victim organization enforces a centralized delivery point, the perpetrator might enlist the aid of an accomplice in the receiving department to falsify the organization's receiving reports.

Another way to avoid detection at the delivery stage is to change the delivery address for purchases. Instead of being shipped to the victim organization, the items that the employee buys are sent directly to his home or business. The perpetrator might also order the goods drop shipped to a remote location.

Personal Purchases on Credit Cards or Other Company Accounts

Instead of running false invoices through accounts payable, some employees make personal purchases on company credit cards or on running accounts with vendors. (See "Purchases on Credit Card or Company Account" flowchart) As with invoicing schemes, the key to getting away with a false credit card purchase is avoiding detection. Unlike invoicing schemes, however, prior approval for these purchases is not required. An employee with a company credit card can buy an item merely by signing his name (or forging someone else's) at the time of purchase. Later review of the credit card statement, however, may detect the fraudulent purchase. Unfortunately, many high-level employees approve their own credit card expenses, making it very easy to carry out a purchasing scheme.

Of course, only certain employees are authorized to use company credit cards. Employees without this privilege can only make fraudulent purchases with a company card if they first manage to get hold of one. To this end, company cards are sometimes stolen or "borrowed" from authorized users.

EXAMPLE

An accountant falsely added her name to a list of employees to whom cards were to be issued. She used her card to make fraudulent purchases, but forged the signatures of authorized cardholders to cover her tracks. Since no one knew she even had a company card, she would not be a prime suspect in the fraud even if someone questioned the purchases. For over five years this employee continued her scheme, racking up a six figure bill on her employer's account. In addition, she had control of the credit card statement and was able to code her purchases to various expense accounts, thereby further delaying detection of her crime.

Another way to conceal a credit card purchasing scheme is to doctor the credit card statement so that fraudulent purchases do not show up. Some employees go so far as to destroy the real credit card statement and produce counterfeit copies on which their fraudulent purchases are omitted.

RETURNING MERCHANDISE FOR CASH

The fraudulent purchases schemes discussed to this point have all involved false purchases of merchandise for the sake of obtaining the merchandise. In some cases, however, an employee buys items and then returns them for cash.

EXAMPLE

An employee made fraudulent gains from a business travel account. The employee's scheme began by purchasing tickets for herself and her family through her company's travel budget. Poor separation of duties allowed the fraudster to order the tickets, receive them, prepare claims for payments, and distribute checks. The only review of her activities was made by a busy and rather uninterested supervisor who approved the employee's claims without requiring support documentation. Eventually, the employee's scheme evolved. She began to purchase airline tickets and return them for their cash value. An employee of the travel agency assisted in the scheme by encoding the tickets as thought the fraudster had paid for them herself. That caused the airlines to pay refunds directly to the fraudster rather than to her employer. In the course of two years, this employee embezzled over $100,000 through her purchases scheme.

Detection

Because there are many variations of purchasing fraud schemes, there also are several detection methods. Detection methods are most effective when used in combinations. Each detection method is likely to point out anomalies that can then be investigated further to determine if a fraud scheme has occurred or is currently underway. Additionally, the detection methods will point out the weaknesses in internal controls and alert the auditor to potential opportunities for future fraud schemes.

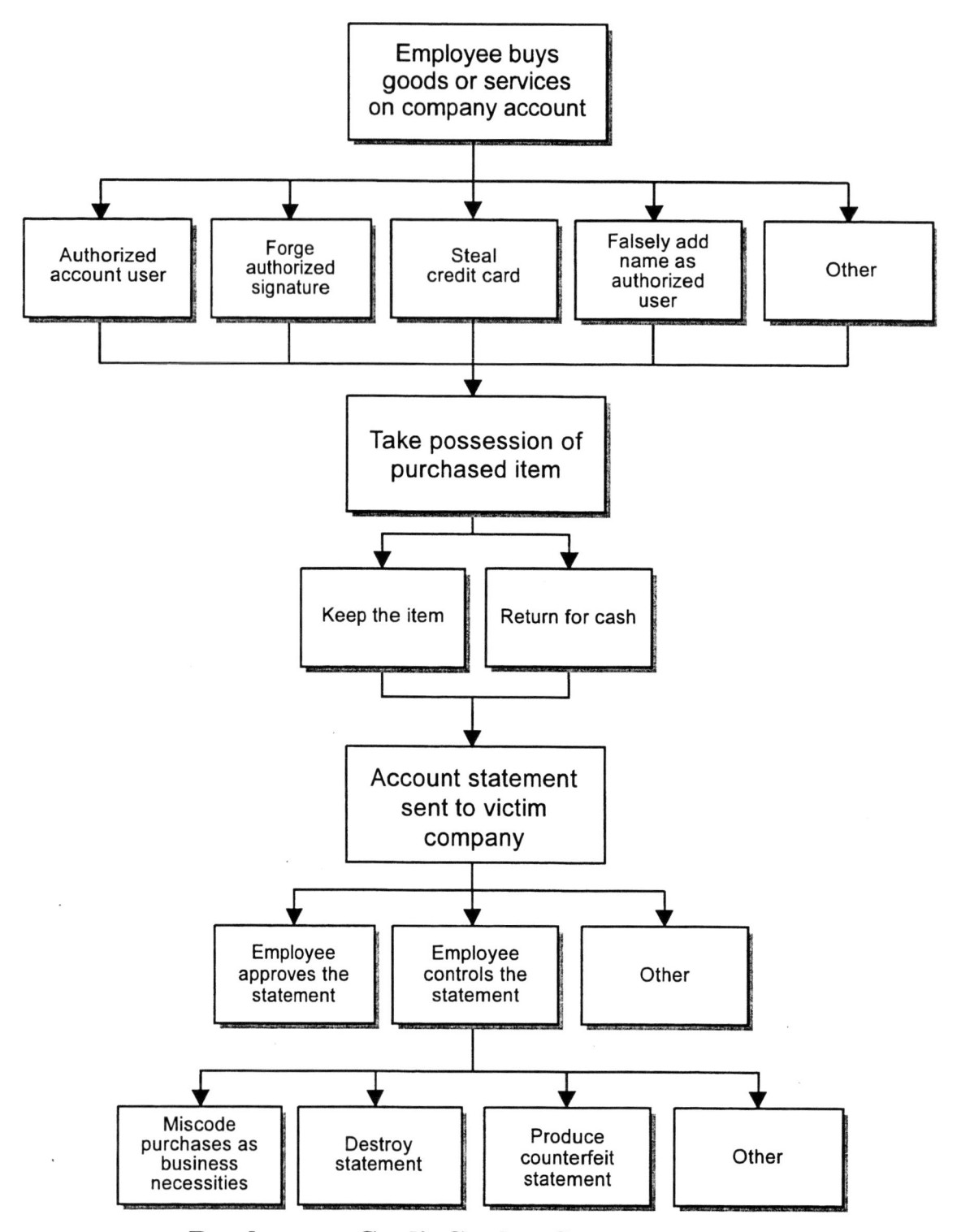

```
                    ┌─────────────────┐
                    │  Employee buys  │
                    │ goods or services│
                    │ on company account│
                    └─────────────────┘
                             │
   ┌─────────┬───────────────┼───────────────┬─────────┐
   ▼         ▼               ▼               ▼         ▼
┌────────┐┌────────┐    ┌────────┐    ┌──────────┐┌───────┐
│Authorized││Forge   │    │Steal   │    │Falsely add││Other  │
│account  ││authorized│   │credit  │    │name as   ││       │
│user     ││signature│    │card    │    │authorized││       │
│         ││         │    │        │    │user      ││       │
└────────┘└────────┘    └────────┘    └──────────┘└───────┘
```

Purchases on Credit Card or Company Account

Flowchart nodes:
- Employee buys goods or services on company account
  - Authorized account user
  - Forge authorized signature
  - Steal credit card
  - Falsely add name as authorized user
  - Other
- Take possession of purchased item
  - Keep the item
  - Return for cash
- Account statement sent to victim company
  - Employee approves the statement
  - Employee controls the statement
    - Miscode purchases as business necessities
    - Destroy statement
    - Produce counterfeit statement
    - Other
  - Other

Analytical Review

A review of the various general ledger accounts might reveal unusual or unexpected events. These events could be undetected purchasing fraud. For example, a comparison of inventory purchases in relationship to net sales might indicate that purchases are too high or too low for that level of sales. This might be a "red flag," indicating excess purchasing schemes or fictitious sales schemes, respectively.

Another analytical method uses a comparison of the inventory purchases of prior years with those of the current year. This comparison might indicate that an overbilling scheme or a duplicate-payment scheme is in progress.

Analyses such as those described above can be performed for any acquisition of goods or services of a company. Analytical reviews are most effective in detecting fraud schemes that are large, such that the anomalies will be apparent. Other detection methods are more effective for fraud schemes that are smaller in relationship to the financial statements taken as a whole. Regardless of fraud size, examination of source documentation will be necessary. When an anomaly is detected, further investigation is required which will demand an examination of source documentation.

Computer-Assisted Analytical Review

The computer can assist the auditor in determining the presence of unusual patterns in the acquisition or purchasing function. The computer can provide the auditor with a matrix of the purchasing activity to determine the presence of unusual patterns. An analysis of the following data might uncover purchasing schemes, such as:

FRAUD SCHEME	DETECTION METHOD
Fictitious vendors	Vendors and employees with matching addresses More than one vendor with the same address Vendors with only post office box addresses
Overbilling	Unusual, or "one-time," extra charges
Conflict of interest	Vendors with employees who are employee family members An unusually high occurrence rate of complaints Complaints about specific vendors Higher prices and/or substandard quality

Statistical Sampling

As with inventory, the source documentation for purchases can be statistically sampled and examined for irregularities. Statistical samples can be drawn to test specific attributes. This detection method is particularly effective if a single attribute is suspected, such as fictitious vendors. A listing of all post office box addresses might reveal fictitious vendors.

Vendor or Outsider Complaints

Fraudulent schemes often will unravel because a vendor or other outsider complains to the employer/company. Complaints from customers, vendors, and others are good detection tools that can lead the fraud examiner to further inquiry.

Site Visits—Observation

A site visit often will reveal much about the internal control, or lack thereof, for any location. The observation of how the accounting transactions actually are transcribed sometimes will alert the fraud examiner to potential problem areas.

Sample Audit Program

The following audit program may be beneficial in detecting red flags to billing schemes:

- Does the company have a purchasing department? If yes, is it independent of (1) the accounting department, (2) the receiving department, or (3) the shipping department?
- Are purchases made only after the respective department heads sign purchase requisitions?
- Are purchases made by means of purchase orders sent to vendors for all purchases or only for purchases over a predetermined dollar limit?
- Do purchase orders specify a description of items, quantity, price, terms, delivery requirements, and dates?
- Is a list of unfilled purchase orders maintained and reviewed periodically?
- Are purchase order forms prenumbered and is the sequence accounted for periodically?
- Does the client maintain an approved vendors list?
- Are items purchased only after competitive bids are obtained? If so, are competitive bids obtained for all purchases or only for purchases over a predetermined dollar limit?
- Is a log maintained of all receipts?
- Does the receiving department prepare receiving reports for all items received? If yes, are receiving reports (1) prepared for all items, (2) prepared only for items that have purchase orders, or (3) renumbered?

- At the time the items are received, does someone independent of the purchasing department check the merchandise before acceptance as to description, quantity, and condition?
- Are copies of receiving reports (1) furnished to the accounting department, (2) furnished to the purchasing department, or (3) filed in the receiving department?
- Are receipts under blanket purchase orders monitored, and are quantities exceeding authorized total returned to the vendor?
- Are procedures adequate for the proper accounting for partial deliveries of purchase orders?
- Are purchasing and receiving functions separate from invoice processing, accounts payable, and general ledger functions?
- Are vendors' invoices, receiving reports, and purchase orders matched before the related liability is recorded?
- Are invoices checked as to prices, extensions, footings, freight charges, allowances, and credit terms?
- Are controls adequate to ensure that all available discounts are taken?
- Are purchases recorded in a purchase register or voucher register before being processed through cash disbursements?
- Does a responsible employee assign the appropriate general ledger account distribution to which the invoices are to be posted?
- Are procedures adequate to ensure that invoices have been processed before payment and to prevent duplicate payment (e.g., a block stamp)?
- Does a responsible official approve invoices for payment?
- Are procedures adequate to ensure that merchandise purchased for direct delivery to customers is promptly billed to the customers and recorded as both a receivable and a payable?
- Are records of goods returned to vendors matched to vendor credit memos?
- Are unmatched receiving reports, purchase orders, and vendors' invoices periodically reviewed and investigated for proper recording?
- Is the accounts payable ledger or voucher register reconciled monthly to the general ledger control accounts?
- Are statements from vendors regularly reviewed and reconciled against recorded liabilities?
- Do adjustments to accounts payable (e.g., writing off of debit balances) require the approval of a designated official?

- Are budgets used? If yes, are budgets approved by responsible officials, and are actual expenditures compared with budgeted amounts and variances analyzed and explained?
- If excess inventory purchasing is suspected, verify that all inventory purchased was received (receiving report) at the proper location. Receiving reports or invoices examination might reveal alternate shipping sites.

Prevention

The preventing of purchasing fraud can be especially difficult. Purchasing personnel are often held to a different standard than other employees of a company. For example, sales people often are given inducements or perquisites in order to persuade potential customers. These same inducements are offered to the purchasing personnel of the company from the company's vendors. And yet, the company expects the purchasing personnel to perform their function without bias and to make decisions that are in the best interest of the company, without regard to the inducements offered by suppliers. Additionally, the personnel involved in the purchasing and payment functions are generally not compensated on a basis commensurate with their performance, as are salespeople. Therefore, there is a reverse incentive to perform in the best interest of the company.

Probably the most effective purchasing fraud prevention measure is education (training) of the purchasing and payable personnel. Second to training, is an objective compensation arrangement with people responsible for purchasing decisions.

Education (Training)

Purchasing personnel should be trained thoroughly in ethical situations. The National Association of Purchasing Management has a code of ethics for its Certified Purchasing Managers. As a deterrent to fraud, companies might consider enrollment and certification.

Compensation

People responsible for the purchasing decisions (buyers) should be paid well enough to reduce the motive and rationalization for fraud. Auditors can examine the compensation of purchasers and determine if any buyers were recently passed over for raises. This might be an indication of discontent which could lead to the formation of a fraudulent scheme against the employer.

Proper Documentation
Proper documentation for purchasing should include prenumbered and controlled purchase requisitions, purchase orders, receiving reports, and checks.

Proper Approvals
Before adding a vendor to the list, there should be an investigation of the "proposed" vendor, performed by someone other than the personnel in purchasing and accounts payable. If a vendor number is required before payment is made and the personnel responsible for the investigation assigns the vendor that identification number, then the buyer cannot place fictitious vendors on the list. Large or unusual purchases should be approved by someone independent of the purchasing department.

Segregation of Duties
For the best results and accountability, each company sufficient in size should have a separate purchasing department. Regardless of the company size, the purchasing function should be separate from the payment function.

Hotlines
Companies should study the feasibility of installing hotlines to provide a forum for complaints by employees and outsiders.

Competitive Bidding
Ensure that bid policies and procedures are thoroughly reviewed. Whenever possible, enforce competitive bidding. After the bidding process has been completed, a questionnaire can be sent to successful and unsuccessful bidders. This questionnaire can reveal areas to not only make the bidding process more effective but it also can provide a forum for bidders to express concerns over questionable or fraudulent activities.

Prevention Checklist
The following is a list of billing-scheme-prevention methods that may be helpful in the deterrence of billing fraud:
- Authorization procedures of purchase orders, invoicing, and payments should be documented and adhered to.
- The accounts payable list of vendors should be periodically reviewed for strange vendors and addresses.
- Payment codings should be reviewed for abnormal descriptions.

- Vendor purchases should be analyzed for abnormal levels on both a monthly and yearly basis.
- Purchases and inventory levels should be compared and analyzed. (see Inventory and Other Assets).
- Control methods to check for duplicate invoices and purchase order numbers should be in place.
- A separation of duties between authorization, purchasing, receiving, shipping, and accounting should be in place.
- Payment of vouchers should be periodically reviewed to ensure integrity of proper documentation.
- Receiving and shipping reports should be reviewed for completeness and accuracy.
- Asset information should include purchasing trails and other information.
- Journal entries to inventory accounts should be strictly scrutinized.
- Appropriate bank reconciliation and review procedures should be periodically performed checking for out-of-place vendors and endorsements.
- Credit card statements should be reviewed often for irregularities.
- The validity of invoices with a post office box address should be verified.
- Proper controls for the receipt and handling of "return to sender" checks should be installed.

Payroll Fraud

Payroll schemes are similar to billing schemes. The perpetrators of these frauds produce false documents which cause the victim company to unknowingly make a fraudulent disbursement. In billing schemes, the false document is usually an invoice (coupled, perhaps, with false receiving reports, purchase orders, and purchase authorizations). In payroll schemes, the perpetrator typically falsifies a timecard or alters information in the payroll records. The major difference between payroll schemes and billing schemes is that payroll frauds involve disbursements to employees rather than to external parties. The most common payroll frauds are ghost employee schemes, falsified hours and salary schemes, and commission schemes.

Ghost Employees

The term *ghost employee* refers to someone on the payroll who does not actually work for the victim company. Through the falsification of personnel or payroll records a fraudster causes paychecks to be generated to a ghost. The fraudster or an accomplice then converts these paychecks. (See "Ghost Employees" flowchart) The ghost employee may be a fictitious person or a real individual who simply does not work for the victim employer. When the ghost is a real person, it is often a friend or relative of the perpetrator.

In order for a ghost employee scheme to work, four things must happen: (1) the ghost must be added to the payroll, (2) timekeeping and wage rate information must be collected, (3) a paycheck must be issued to the ghost, and (4) the check must be delivered to the perpetrator or an accomplice.

Adding the Ghost to the Payroll

The first step in a ghost employee scheme is entering the ghost on the payroll. In some businesses, all hiring is done through a centralized personnel department, while in others the personnel function is spread over the managerial responsibilities of various departments. Regardless of how hiring of new employees is handled within a business, it is the person or persons with authority to add new employees that are in the best position to put ghosts on the payroll.

> EXAMPLE
> *A manager who was responsible for hiring and scheduling janitorial work added over 80 ghost employees to his payroll. The ghosts in this case were actual people who worked at other jobs for different companies. The manager filled out time sheets for the fictitious employees and authorized them, then took the resulting paychecks to the ghost employees, who cashed them and split the proceeds with the manager. It was this manager's authority in the hiring and supervision of employees that enabled him to perpetrate this fraud.*

Employees in payroll accounting also sometimes create ghost employees. In a perfect world, every name listed on the payroll would be verified against personnel records to make sure that those persons receiving paychecks actually work for the company, but in practice this does not always happen. Thus, persons in payroll accounting may be able to create fictitious employees by simply adding a new name to the payroll records. Access to these records is usually restricted, with only high-level employees having the ability to make changes to the payroll. These persons would therefore be among the most likely suspects in a ghost employee scheme. On the other hand, lower level employees sometimes gain access to restricted payroll information and should not be disregarded as possible suspects.

> EXAMPLE
>
> *An employee in the payroll department was given the authority to enter new employees into the payroll system, make corrections to payroll information, and distribute paychecks. This employee's manager gave rubber-stamp approval to the employee's actions because of a trusting relationship between the two. The lack of separation of duties and the absence of review made it simple for the culprit to add a fictitious employee into the payroll system.*

One way perpetrators try to conceal the presence of a ghost on the payroll is to create a ghost with a name very similar to that of a real employee. The name on the fraudulent paycheck, then, will appear to be legitimate to anyone who glances at it. For instance, if a victim organization has an employee named John Doe, the ghost may be named "John Doer."

Instead of adding new names to the payroll, some employees undertake ghost employee schemes when they decline to remove the names of terminated employees. Paychecks to the terminated employee continue to be generated even though the employee no longer works for the victim organization. The perpetrator intercepts these fraudulent paychecks and converts them to his own use.

Collecting Timekeeping Information

The second thing that must occur in order for a paycheck to be issued to a ghost employee, at least in the case of hourly employees, is the collection and computation of timekeeping information. The perpetrator must provide payroll accounting with a timecard or other instrument showing how many hours the fictitious employee worked over the most recent pay period. This information, along with the wage rate information contained in personnel or payroll files, will be used to compute the amount of the fraudulent paycheck.

Timekeeping records can be maintained in a variety of ways. Employees might manually record their hours on timecards or punch timeclocks that record the time at which a person starts and finishes his work. In more sophisticated environments, computer systems can track an employee's hours.

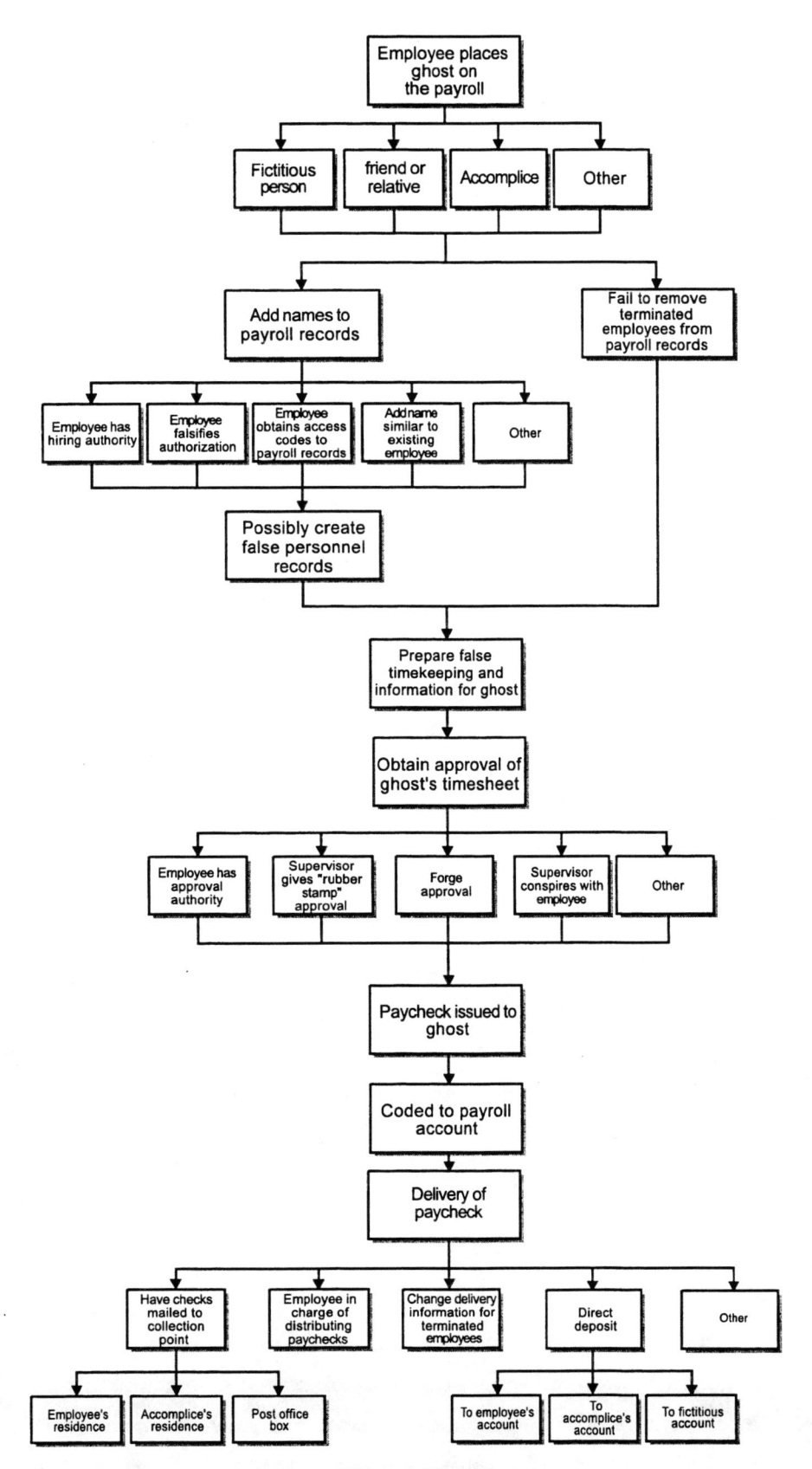

Ghost Employees

```
                    Employee places
                       ghost on
                      the payroll
                           |
        ┌──────────────┬───┴────┬──────────┐
    Fictitious     friend or  Accomplice   Other
     person        relative
        │              │          │
        └──────┬───────┴──────────┘
               │                              │
        Add names to                    Fail to remove
        payroll records                 terminated
                                        employees from
                                        payroll records
               │
  ┌─────────┬──────┬──────────┬──────────┐
Employee  Employee Employee  Add name    Other
has       falsifies obtains  similar to
hiring    authoriz- access   existing
authority ation    codes to  employee
                   payroll
                   records
  └─────────┴──────┬──────────┴──────────┘
               │
        Possibly create
        false personnel
        records
               │
               ├──────────────────────────────┘
               │
        Prepare false
        timekeeping and
        information for ghost
               │
        Obtain approval of
        ghost's timesheet
               │
  ┌──────────┬─────────┬──────────┬──────────┐
Employee   Supervisor  Forge    Supervisor   Other
has        gives       approval conspires
approval   "rubber             with
authority  stamp"              employee
           approval
  └──────────┴─────────┴──────────┴──────────┘
               │
        Paycheck issued to
        ghost
               │
        Coded to payroll
        account
               │
        Delivery of
        paycheck
               │
  ┌──────────┬─────────┬──────────┬──────────┐
Have checks Employee  Change      Direct    Other
mailed to   in charge delivery    deposit
collection  of distri-information
point       buting    for
            paychecks terminated
                      employees
  │                              │
┌─┼──┬──────┐                ┌───┼──────┐
Employee's Accomplice's Post To      To          To
residence  residence    office employee's accomplice's fictitious
                        box   account    account    account
```

When a ghost employee scheme is in place, someone must create documentation for the ghost's hours. This essentially amounts to preparing a fake timecard showing when the ghost was allegedly present at work. Depending upon the normal procedure for recording hours, a fraudster might write up a fake timecard and sign it in the ghost's name, punch the timeclock for the ghost or so on. The preparing of the timecard is not a great obstacle to the perpetrator. The real key is obtaining approval of the timecard.

A supervisor should approve the timecards of hourly employees before paychecks are issued. This verifies to the payroll department that the employee actually worked the hours that are claimed on the card. A ghost employee, by definition, does not work for the victim organization, so approval will have to be fraudulently obtained. Often, the supervisor himself is the one who creates the ghost. When this is the case, the supervisor fills out a timecard in the name of the ghost, then affixes his own approval. The timecard is thereby authenticated and a paycheck will be issued. When a nonsupervisor is committing a ghost employee scheme, he will typically forge the necessary approval, then forward the bogus timecard directly to payroll accounting, bypassing his supervisor.

In computerized systems, a supervisor's signature might not be required. In lieu of this, the supervisor inputs data into the payroll system and the use of his password serves to authorize the entry. If an employee has access to the supervisor's password, he can input data for the ghost which will appear in the payroll system with a seal of approval.
If the perpetrator creates ghosts who are salaried rather than hourly employees, it is not necessary to collect timekeeping information. Salaried employees are paid a certain amount each pay period regardless of how many hours they work. Because the timekeeping function can be avoided, it may be easier for a perpetrator to create a ghost employee who works on salary. However, most businesses have fewer salaried employees and they are more likely to be members of management. The salaried ghost may therefore be more difficult to conceal.

Issuing the Ghost's Paycheck

Once a ghost is entered on the payroll and his timecard has been approved, the third step in the scheme is the actual issuance of the paycheck. The heart of a ghost employee scheme is in the falsification of payroll records and timekeeping information. Once this falsification has occurred, the perpetrator does not generally take an active roll in the issuance of the check. The payroll department prints the check—based on the bogus information provided by the perpetrator—as it would any other paycheck.

Delivery of the Paycheck

The final step in a ghost employee scheme is the distribution of the checks to the perpetrator. Paychecks might be hand delivered to employees while at work, mailed to employees at their home addresses, or direct deposited into the employees' bank accounts. If employees are paid in currency rather than by check, the distribution is almost always conducted in-person and on-site.

Ideally, those in charge of payroll distribution should not have a hand in any of the other functions of the payroll cycle. For instance, the person who enters new employees in the payroll system should not be allowed to distribute paychecks because this person can include a ghost on the payroll, then simply pocket the fraudulent check when paychecks are being disbursed. Obviously, when the perpetrator of a ghost employee scheme is allowed to mail checks to employees or pass them out at work, he is in a perfect position to assure that the ghost's check is delivered to himself.

In most instances the perpetrator does not have the authority to distribute paychecks, and so must make sure that the victim organization sends the checks to a place where he can recover them. When checks are not distributed in the workplace, they are usually mailed to employees or deposited directly into those employees' accounts.

If the fictitious employee was added into the payroll or personnel records by the perpetrator, the problem of distribution is usually minor. When the ghost's employment information is inputted, the perpetrator simply lists an address or bank account to which the payments can be sent. In the case of purely fictitious ghost employees, the address is often the perpetrator's own (the same goes for bank accounts). The fact that two employees (the perpetrator and the ghost) are receiving payments at the same destination may indicate payroll fraud. Some fraudsters avoid this duplication by having payments sent to a post office box or a separate bank account.

Remember that a ghost employee is not always a fictitious person. It may, instead, be a real person who is conspiring with the perpetrator to defraud the company. For example, some employees place their relatives or spouses on the company payroll. When real persons are falsely included on the payroll, the checks are sent to the homes or accounts of these persons.

Distribution is a more difficult problem when the ghost is a former employee who was simply not removed from the payroll. If paychecks are distributed through the mail or by direct deposit, the perpetrator will have to enter the terminated employee's records and change their delivery information. In companies where paychecks are distributed by hand or are held at a central location for employees to collect, the perpetrator can ignore the payroll records and simply pick up the fraudulent paychecks.

Falsified Hours and Salary

The most common method of misappropriating funds from the payroll is the overpayment of wages. For hourly employees, the size of a paycheck is based on two factors, the number of hours worked and the rate of pay. It is therefore obvious that for an hourly employee to fraudulently increase the size of his paycheck, he must either falsify the number of hours he has worked or change his wage rate. (See "Falsified Hours and Salary" flowchart) Since salaried employees do not receive compensation based on their time at work, in most cases these employees generate fraudulent wages by increasing their rates of pay.

When discussing payroll frauds that involve overstated hours, one must first understand how an employee's time at work is recorded. Time is generally kept by one of three methods. Timeclocks may be used to mark the time when an employee begins and finishes work. The employee inserts a card into the clock at the beginning and end of work, and the time is imprinted on that card. In more sophisticated systems, computers may track the time employees spend on the job based on log-in codes or a similar indicator. Finally, timecards showing the number of hours an employee worked on a particular day are often prepared manually by the employee and approved by his manager.

Manually Prepared Timecards

When hours are recorded manually, an employee typically fills out his timecard to reflect the number of hours he has worked, then presents it to his supervisor for approval. The supervisor verifies the accuracy of the timecard, signs the card to indicate his approval, then forwards it to the payroll department so that a paycheck can be issued.

If an employee fills out his own timecard, it is easy to falsify the number of hours worked. He simply writes down false information, showing that he arrived at work earlier or left later than he actually did. The difficulty is not in falsifying the timecard, but in getting the fraudulent card approved by the employee's supervisor. There are basically three ways for the employee to obtain the authorization he needs.

FORGING A SUPERVISOR'S SIGNATURE

When using this method, an employee typically withholds his timecard from those being sent to the supervisor for approval, forges the supervisor's signature or initials, then adds the timecard to the stack of authorized cards which are sent to the payroll department. The fraudulent timecard arrives at the payroll department with what appears to be a supervisor's approval and a paycheck is subsequently issued.

COLLUSION WITH A SUPERVISOR

The second way to obtain approval of a fraudulent timecard is to collude with a supervisor who authorizes timekeeping information. In these schemes, a supervisor knowingly signs false timecards and the employee kicks back a portion of the overpaid wages to the supervisor. In some cases, the supervisor may take the entire amount of the overpayment. It may be particularly difficult to detect payroll fraud when a supervisor colludes with an employee, because managers are often relied upon as a control to assure proper timekeeping.

EXAMPLE

A supervisor assigned employees to better work areas or better jobs, but in return she demanded payment. The payment was arranged by the falsification of the employees' timecards, which the supervisor authorized. The employees were compensated for fictitious overtime, which was kicked back to the supervisor.

"RUBBER STAMP" SUPERVISORS

The third way to obtain approval of fraudulent timecards is to rely on a supervisor to approve them without reviewing their accuracy. The "lazy manager" method seems risky and one would think that it would be uncommon, but the truth is that it occurs quite frequently. A recurring theme in occupational fraud schemes is the reliance of perpetrators on the inattentiveness of others. When an employee sees an opportunity to make a little extra money without getting caught, that employee is more likely to be emboldened to attempt a fraud scheme. The fact that a supervisor is known to "rubber stamp" timecards or even ignore them can be a factor in an employee's decision to begin stealing from his company.

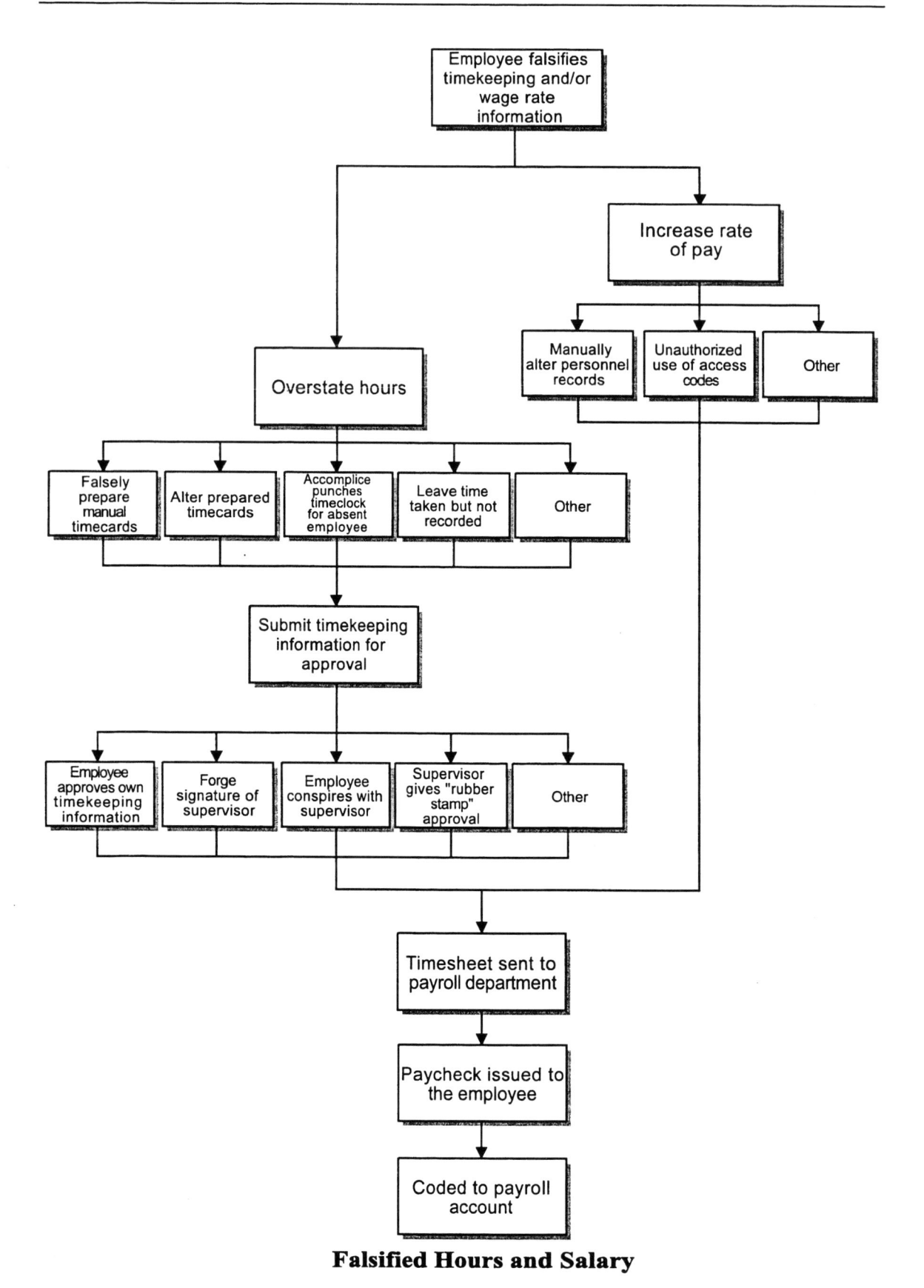

Asset Misappropriation: Fraudulent Disbursements   Financial Transactions

```
                    ┌─────────────────────┐
                    │ Employee falsifies  │
                    │ timekeeping and/or  │
                    │    wage rate        │
                    │   information       │
                    └──────────┬──────────┘
                               │
              ┌────────────────┴──────────────┐
              │                               │
              ▼                               ▼
                                    ┌──────────────────┐
                                    │  Increase rate   │
                                    │     of pay       │
                                    └────────┬─────────┘
                                             │
                              ┌──────────────┼──────────────┐
                              ▼              ▼              ▼
                        ┌──────────┐  ┌──────────┐   ┌──────────┐
                        │ Manually │  │Unauthorized│  │   Other  │
                        │   alter  │  │use of access│ │          │
                        │personnel │  │   codes   │  │          │
                        │ records  │  │          │   │          │
                        └──────────┘  └──────────┘   └──────────┘
        ┌─────────────────┐
        │ Overstate hours │
        └────────┬────────┘
                 │
   ┌──────┬──────┼──────┬──────┐
   ▼      ▼      ▼      ▼      ▼
┌──────┐┌──────┐┌──────┐┌──────┐┌──────┐
│Falsely││Alter ││Accompl││Leave ││Other │
│prepare││prepar││-ice  ││time  ││      │
│manual ││ed    ││punches││taken ││      │
│timecar││timeca││timeclo││but   ││      │
│ds     ││rds   ││ck for ││not   ││      │
│       ││      ││absent ││record││      │
│       ││      ││employ ││-ed   ││      │
└──────┘└──────┘└──────┘└──────┘└──────┘
                 │
        ┌────────▼────────┐
        │Submit timekeeping│
        │information for  │
        │    approval     │
        └────────┬────────┘
                 │
   ┌──────┬──────┼──────┬──────┐
   ▼      ▼      ▼      ▼      ▼
┌──────┐┌──────┐┌──────┐┌──────┐┌──────┐
│Employ││Forge ││Employ││Superv││Other │
│ee    ││signat││ee    ││isor  ││      │
│approv││ure of││conspi││gives ││      │
│es own││superv││res   ││"rubbe││      │
│timeke││isor  ││with  ││r     ││      │
│eping ││      ││superv││stamp"││      │
│info  ││      ││isor  ││approv││      │
│      ││      ││      ││al    ││      │
└──────┘└──────┘└──────┘└──────┘└──────┘
                 │
        ┌────────▼────────┐
        │ Timesheet sent to│
        │ payroll department│
        └────────┬────────┘
                 ▼
        ┌─────────────────┐
        │Paycheck issued to│
        │  the employee   │
        └────────┬────────┘
                 ▼
        ┌─────────────────┐
        │ Coded to payroll │
        │     account     │
        └─────────────────┘
```

Falsified Hours and Salary

EXAMPLE

A temporary employee noticed that his manager did not reconcile the expense journal monthly. Thus, the manager did not know how much was being paid to the temporary agency. The fraudster completed fictitious time reports which were sent to the temporary agency and which caused the victim company to pay over $30,000 in fraudulent wages. Since the fraudster controlled the mail and the manager did not review the expense journal, this extremely simple scheme went undetected for some time.

POOR CUSTODY PROCEDURES

One form of control breakdown that often occurs is the failure to maintain proper control over timecards. In a properly run system, timecards that have been authorized by management should be sent directly to payroll. Those who prepare the timecards should not have access to them after they have been approved. If this separation of duties is not observed, the person who prepared a timecard can alter it after his supervisor has approved the timecard but before it is delivered to payroll. For instance, the employee might fill out his timecard in erasable ink, obtain his supervisor's signature on the timecard, and then change the hours reflected on the timecard so that he will be overcompensated.

Another way hours are falsified is in the misreporting of leave time. This is not as common as timecard falsification, but it does occur with some frequency. Incidentally, this is the one instance in which salaried employees commit payroll fraud by falsifying their hours. A leave time scheme is very simple. An employee takes a certain amount of time off of work as paid leave or vacation, but does not report this leave time. Employees typically receive a certain amount of paid leave per year. If a person takes a leave of absence but does not report it, those days are not deducted from his allotted days off. In other words, he gets more leave time than he is entitled to. The result is that the employee shows up for work less, yet still receives the same pay.

Timeclocks and Other Automated Timekeeping Systems

In companies that use timeclocks to collect timekeeping information, payroll fraud is usually uncomplicated. In the typical scenario, the timeclock is located in an unrestricted area, and a timecard for each employee is kept nearby. The employees insert their timecards into the timeclock at the beginning and end of their shifts and the clock imprints the time. The length of time an employee spends at work is thus recorded. Supervisors should be present at the beginning and end of shifts to assure that employees do not punch the timecards of absent co-workers, but this simple control is often overlooked. Without proper supervision, employees can punch the timecards of absent co-workers so that it appears the absent employee was at work that day. The absent employee is therefore overcompensated on his next paycheck.

Rates of Pay

It should be remembered that an employee can also receive a larger paycheck by changing his pay rate. An employee's personnel or payroll records reflect his rate of pay. If an employee can gain access to these records, or has an accomplice with access to them, he can adjust them so that he receives a larger paycheck.

Commission Schemes

Commission is a form of compensation calculated as a percentage of the amount of transactions a salesperson or other employee generates. It is a unique form of compensation that is not based on hours worked or a set yearly salary, but rather on an employee's revenue output. A commissioned employee's wages are based on two factors, the amount of sales he generates and the percentage of those sales he is paid. In other words, there are two ways an employee on commission can fraudulently increase his pay: (1) falsify the amount of sales made, or (2) increase his rate of commission. (See "Commission Schemes" flowchart)

Fictitious Sales

Establishing unobtainable sales quotas that employees think are arbitrary will increase the pressure to establish fictitious performance levels. If the pressure becomes significant, the employee might resort to adding fictitious sales and accounts receivable to meet the sales quotas.

An employee can falsify the amount of sales he has made in one of two ways, the first being the creation of fictitious sales. The manner in which fictitious sales are created depends on the industry in which the perpetrator operates. Fictitious sales might be constructed by the creation of fraudulent sales orders, purchase orders, credit authorizations, packing slips, invoices and so on. On the other hand, a culprit might simply ring up a false sale on a cash register. The key is that a fictitious sale is created, that it appears to be legitimate, and that the victim organization reacts by issuing a commission check to the perpetrator.

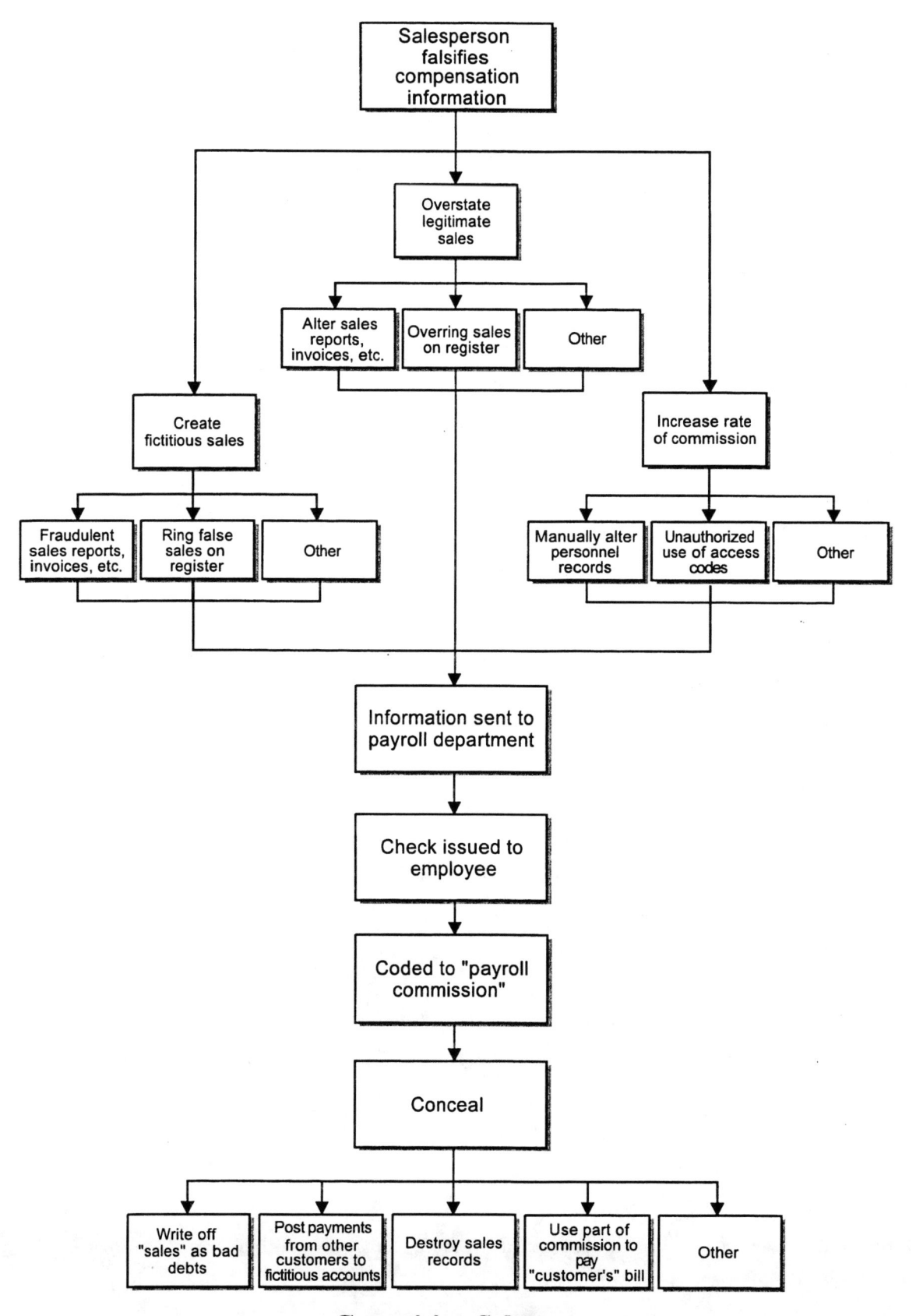

Financial Transactions — Asset Misappropriation: Fraudulent Disbursements

Commission Schemes

- Salesperson falsifies compensation information
  - Overstate legitimate sales
    - Alter sales reports, invoices, etc.
    - Overring sales on register
    - Other
  - Create fictitious sales
    - Fraudulent sales reports, invoices, etc.
    - Ring false sales on register
    - Other
  - Increase rate of commission
    - Manually alter personnel records
    - Unauthorized use of access codes
    - Other
- Information sent to payroll department
- Check issued to employee
- Coded to "payroll commission"
- Conceal
  - Write off "sales" as bad debts
  - Post payments from other customers to fictitious accounts
  - Destroy sales records
  - Use part of commission to pay "customer's" bill
  - Other

2005 Fraud Examiners Manual

EXAMPLE

An unscrupulous insurance agent took advantage of his company's incentive commissions which paid $1.25 for every $1.00 of premiums generated in the first year of a policy. The agent wrote policies to fictitious customers, paid the premiums, and received his commissions, which created an illicit profit on the transaction. For instance, if the fraudster paid $100,000 in premiums, he would receive $125,000 in commissions, a $25,000 profit. No payments were made on the fraudulent policies after the first year.

If a salesperson's primary compensation is based on sales, without regard to collection, then there is an incentive to produce quantity rather than quality sales. It is natural for companies to push for higher sales levels to sustain growth. However, if the salespersons' compensation is based solely on quantity and not on a combination of quantity *and* quality, then the compensation incentive is misplaced. This might create an atmosphere which, if coupled with opportunity, will produce inflated or fictitious sales.

Altered Sales

The second way for a fraudster to overstate the amount of sales he has made is to alter the prices listed on sales documents. In other words, the perpetrator charges one price to a customer, but records a higher price in the company books. This causes the victim company to pay a larger commission than the perpetrator deserves. To make these schemes work, the employee might have to intercept and alter the invoices that are sent to the customer. (The invoices the company sends out will reflect a higher purchase price than the customer agreed to, so if the customer receives these invoices he is likely to complain about the discrepancy.) The employee may also overstate the revenue received from his customers.

Altering Commission Rates

As mentioned above, the other way to manipulate the commission process is to change the employee's rate of commission. This would likely necessitate the alteration of payroll or personnel records, which should be off-limits to the sales staff.

Detection of Payroll Schemes
Independent Payroll Distribution

Ghost employee schemes can be uncovered by having personnel (other than the payroll department) distribute the payroll checks, and by requiring positive identification of the payee.

Analysis of Payee Address or Accounts
If payroll checks are either mailed or deposited automatically, then a list of duplicate addresses or deposit accounts may reveal ghost employees or duplicate payments.

Duplicate Identification Numbers
Because each employee is required to have a government-issued identification number (such as a Social Security or Social Insurance number), a listing of duplicate numbers may reveal ghost employees.

Overtime Authorization
Requiring employees to have overtime authorized by a supervisor, having the supervisor be responsible for the timecards, and having the supervisor refer the timecards directly to payroll will aid in reducing overtime abuses. In addition, the payroll department should scan the time reports and question obvious abuses such as only one employee working overtime in a department or excessive overtime on a timecard. By examining the source documentation, one may detect unauthorized overtime and falsified hours abuses.

Commissions
Commission schemes can often be detected with the following techniques:
- Compare commission expenses to sales figures to verify linear correlation.
- Prepare a comparative analysis of commission earned by salesperson verifying rates and calculation accuracy. Inordinately high earnings by an individual could signal fraud.
- Analyze sales by salesperson for uncollected sales amounts.
- Determine proper segregation of duties in calculation of commission amounts. Commissions should be independently provided by personnel outside the sales department.
- Contact a random sample of customers to confirm sales.

TREND ANALYSIS ON WRITTEN-OFF ACCOUNTS RECEIVABLE
Stratify the written-off accounts receivable data and examine it for possible trends and patterns. For example, do any of the following trends appear?
- Same salesperson
- Same accounting period (unless only an annual review of accounts receivable is performed)
- Same collector
- Collection rates by agency or collector

Any of these trends might indicate fictitious accounts receivable, or that only new or good accounts are being assigned to collectors or collection agencies.

Analysis of Deductions from Payroll Checks

An analysis of the payroll withholdings may reveal either ghost employees or trust account abuses. Ghost employees often will have no withholding taxes, insurance, or other normal deductions. Therefore, a listing of any employee without these items may reveal a ghost employee.

An analysis of withholding-tax deposits may reveal that trust account taxes have been "borrowed," even for a short period, before the taxes are deposited. Comparing the disbursement date with the deposit date should reveal if the trust account taxes have been borrowed. Additionally, any delinquent payroll tax notices from the taxing authorities should serve as a red flag to potential trust account tax "borrowings."

Prevention of Payroll Schemes

There are two basic preventive measures for payroll-related fraud: segregation of duties and periodic payroll review and analysis.

Segregation of Duties

The following duties should be segregated:
- Payroll preparation
- Payroll disbursement (into payroll and withholding tax accounts)
- Payroll distribution
- Payroll bank reconciliations
- Human resource departmental functions

If payroll is prepared by personnel not responsible for its distribution and reconciliation, it will be difficult for anyone to successfully add ghost employees. They also will be prevented from "borrowing" the trust account taxes because they will not have access to the disbursing function. In smaller companies, this function often is handled outside the firm at pennies per employee.

After the payroll checks are prepared, the transfer of funds from the general accounts to the payroll accounts should be handled by accounting. The personnel department should distribute checks and require identification in exchange for the payroll checks. This will curtail the opportunity to add ghost employees to the payroll. A suggested form of identification might be company-issued access passes, if available.

If the bank reconciliation function for the payroll account is assigned to someone other than those in the above-described functions, then all the payroll functions have been segregated. No one is able to add ghost employees or "borrow" the withholding taxes without the opportunity for discovery by someone else.

Periodic Review and Analysis of Payroll

Periodically, an independent review of the payroll might reveal that internal controls are not working as designed. Comparing deposit dates with dates of payroll disbursement or transfer may reveal ghost employees. An occasional independent payroll distribution may reveal ghost employees.

The existence of the following may indicate the presence of ghost employees:
- More than one employee with the same address
- More than one employee with the same government identification number
- More than one employee with the same account number (automatic deposit)
- Employees with no withholding

Indicators of Payroll Fraud

In addition, the following audit program will help spot red flags to payroll distribution fraud and help with installing control procedures:
- Are personnel records maintained independently of payroll and timekeeping functions?
- Is the payroll accounting function independent of the general ledger function?
- Are changes to payroll not made unless the personnel department sends approved notification directly to the payroll department?
- Are references and backgrounds checked for new hires?
- Are all wage rates authorized in writing by a designated official?
- Are signed authorizations on file for employees whose wages are subject to special deductions?
- Are bonuses, commissions, and overtime approved in advance and reviewed for compliance with company policies?
- Are sick leave, vacations, and holidays reviewed for compliance with company policy?
- Are appropriate forms completed and signed by employees to show authorization for payroll deductions and withholding exemptions?

- Is the payroll periodically checked against the personnel records for terminated employees, fictitious employees, etc.?
- Is a time clock used for office employees as well as factory workers?
- If a time clock is used, are timecards (1) punched by employees in the presence of a designated supervisor and (2) signed by a supervisor at the end of the payroll period?
- Are timecards and production reports reviewed and compared with payroll distribution reports and production schedules?
- Are payroll registers reviewed and approved before disbursements are made for (1) names of employees, (2) hours worked, (3) wage rates, (4) deductions, (5) agreement with payroll checks, and (6) unusual items?
- Are all employees paid by check out of a separate bank payroll account?
- Are payroll checks prenumbered and issued in numerical sequence?
- Is access restricted to unissued payroll checks and signature plates?
- Are checks drawn and signed by designated officials who do not (1) prepare payroll, (2) have access to the accounting records, or (3) have custody of cash funds?
- Are payroll checks distributed by someone other than the department head or the person who prepares the payroll?
- Is the distribution of the payroll rotated periodically to different employees without prior notice?
- Is the payroll bank account reconciled by a designated employee who (1) is not involved in the preparing of payroll, (2) does not sign the checks, or (3) does not handle the check distributions?
- Do payroll bank account reconciliations procedures include comparing the paid checks to the payroll, and scrutinizing canceled check endorsements?
- Are the payroll registers reconciled to the general ledger control accounts?
- Is a liability account set up for all wages that have remained unclaimed for a certain period of time? If yes, (1) have these wages been redeposited in a special bank account, and (2) is identification required to be presented at the time of their subsequent distribution?
- Are distributions of hours (direct and indirect) to activity or departments reviewed and approved by supervisory personnel?
- Are actual payroll amounts reviewed and compared to budgeted amounts, and are variances analyzed regularly?
- Do adequate procedures exist for timely and accurate preparation and filing of payroll tax returns and related taxes?

- Are employee benefit plan contributions reconciled to appropriate employee census data?
- Are adequate, detailed records maintained of the entity's liability for vacation pay and sick pay? Are they reconciled to the general ledger control accounts periodically?

Expense Reimbursement Schemes

Employees can manipulate an organization's expense reimbursement procedures to generate fraudulent disbursements. Expense reimbursements are usually paid by the company in the following manner. An employee submits a report detailing an expense incurred for a business purpose, such as a business lunch with a client, airfare, hotel bills associated with business travel or so forth. In preparing an expense report, an employee is usually required to explain the business purpose for the expense, as well as the time, date, and location in which it was incurred. Support documentation for the expense, typically a receipt, should be attached to the report. In some cases canceled checks written by the employee or copies of a personal credit card statement showing the expense are allowed in lieu of receipts. The report usually must be authorized by a supervisor in order for the expense to be reimbursed. The four most common types of expense reimbursement schemes are mischaracterized expenses, overstated expenses, fictitious expenses, and multiple reimbursements.

Mischaracterized Expense Reimbursements

Most companies only reimburse certain expenses of their employees. Which expenses a company will pay for depends to an extent upon policy, but in general, business-related travel, lodging, and meals are reimbursed. One of the most basic expense reimbursement schemes is perpetrated by simply requesting reimbursement for a personal expense by claiming that the expense is business related. (See "Mischaracterized Expenses" flowchart) Examples of mischaracterized expenses include claiming personal travel as a business trip, listing dinner with a friend as "business development," and so on. Employees submit the receipts from their personal expenses along with their expense reports, but concoct business reasons for the incurred costs. The false expense report induces the victim organization to issue a check, reimbursing the perpetrator for his personal expenses.

In cases involving airfare and overnight travel, a mischaracterization can sometimes be detected by simply comparing the employee's expense reports to his work schedule. Often, the dates of the so-called "business trip" coincide with a vacation or day off. Detailed expense reports allow a company to make this kind of comparison and are therefore very

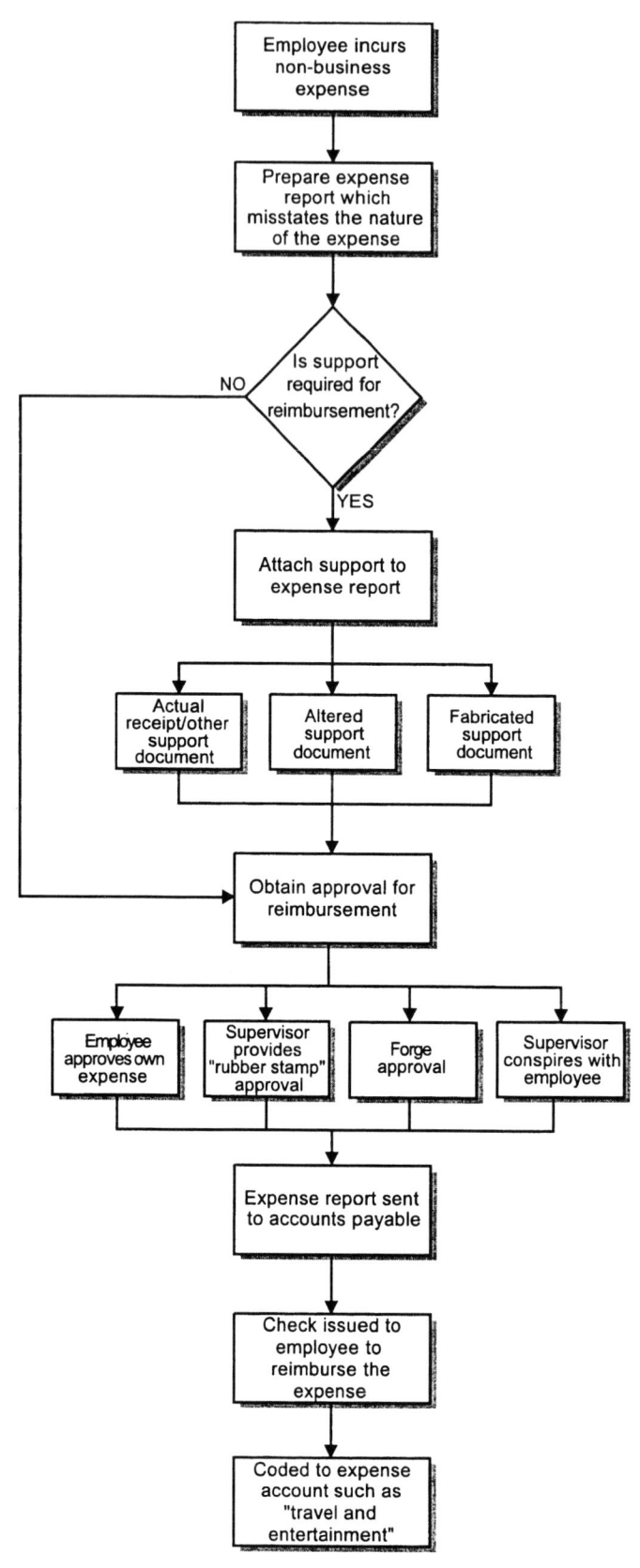

```
┌─────────────────┐
│ Employee incurs │
│  non-business   │
│     expense     │
└────────┬────────┘
         ▼
┌─────────────────┐
│ Prepare expense │
│  report which   │
│misstates nature │
│  of the expense │
└────────┬────────┘
         ▼
      ╱     ╲
     ╱ Is    ╲
NO  ╱ support ╲
◄──╱ required  ╲
    ╲   for    ╱
     ╲reimburs╱
      ╲ement?╱
         │YES
         ▼
┌─────────────────┐
│ Attach support  │
│to expense report│
└────────┬────────┘
         │
    ┌────┼────┐
    ▼    ▼    ▼
 Actual Altered Fabricated
 receipt support support
         │
         ▼
┌─────────────────┐
│Obtain approval  │
│for reimbursement│
└────────┬────────┘
         │
   ┌──┬──┼──┬──┐
   ▼  ▼  ▼  ▼
Employee Supervisor Forge Supervisor
approves "rubber  approval conspires
own      stamp"         with
expense  approval       employee
         │
         ▼
┌─────────────────┐
│Expense report   │
│sent to accounts │
│    payable      │
└────────┬────────┘
         ▼
┌─────────────────┐
│ Check issued to │
│   employee to   │
│  reimburse the  │
│     expense     │
└────────┬────────┘
         ▼
┌─────────────────┐
│Coded to expense │
│account such as  │
│  "travel and    │
│  entertainment" │
└─────────────────┘
```

Mischaracterized Expenses

helpful in preventing expenses schemes. A common element to mischaracterized expense schemes is the failure to submit detailed expense reports, or any expense reports at all. Some companies allow employees to simply turn in receipts, without explaining the business purpose of the expenses reflected in the receipts. This makes it exceedingly easy for an employee to turn in, for example, a receipt from a restaurant and receive a check to reimburse him for a "business dinner." Requiring detailed information means more than just supporting documents; it should mean precise statements of what was purchased, as well as when and where.

EXAMPLE
A fraudster submitted credit card statements as support for expenses, but he only submitted the top portion of the statements, not the portion that describes what was purchased. Over 95% of his expenses which were reimbursed were of a personal rather than a business nature.

Even when detailed expense reports are required, it may be difficult to detect a mischaracterized expense reimbursement scheme. For example, suppose a traveling salesman goes on a trip and runs up a large bar bill one night in his hotel, saves his receipt, and lists this expense as "business entertainment" on an expense report. Nothing about the time, date, or nature of the expense would readily point to fraud, and the receipt would appear to substantiate the expense. Short of contacting the client who was allegedly entertained, there may be little a victim organization can do to identify the expense as fraudulent.

Overstated Expense Reimbursements
Instead of seeking reimbursement for personal expenses, some employees overstate the cost of actual business expenses. (See "Overstated Expenses" flowchart) This can be accomplished in a number of ways.

Altered Receipts
The most fundamental example of an overstated expense reimbursement scheme occurs when an employee doctors a receipt or other supporting documentation to reflect a higher cost than what he actually paid. The employee may use white-out, a ballpoint pen, or some other method to change the price reflected on the receipt before submitting his expense report. If the company does not require original documents as support, the perpetrator

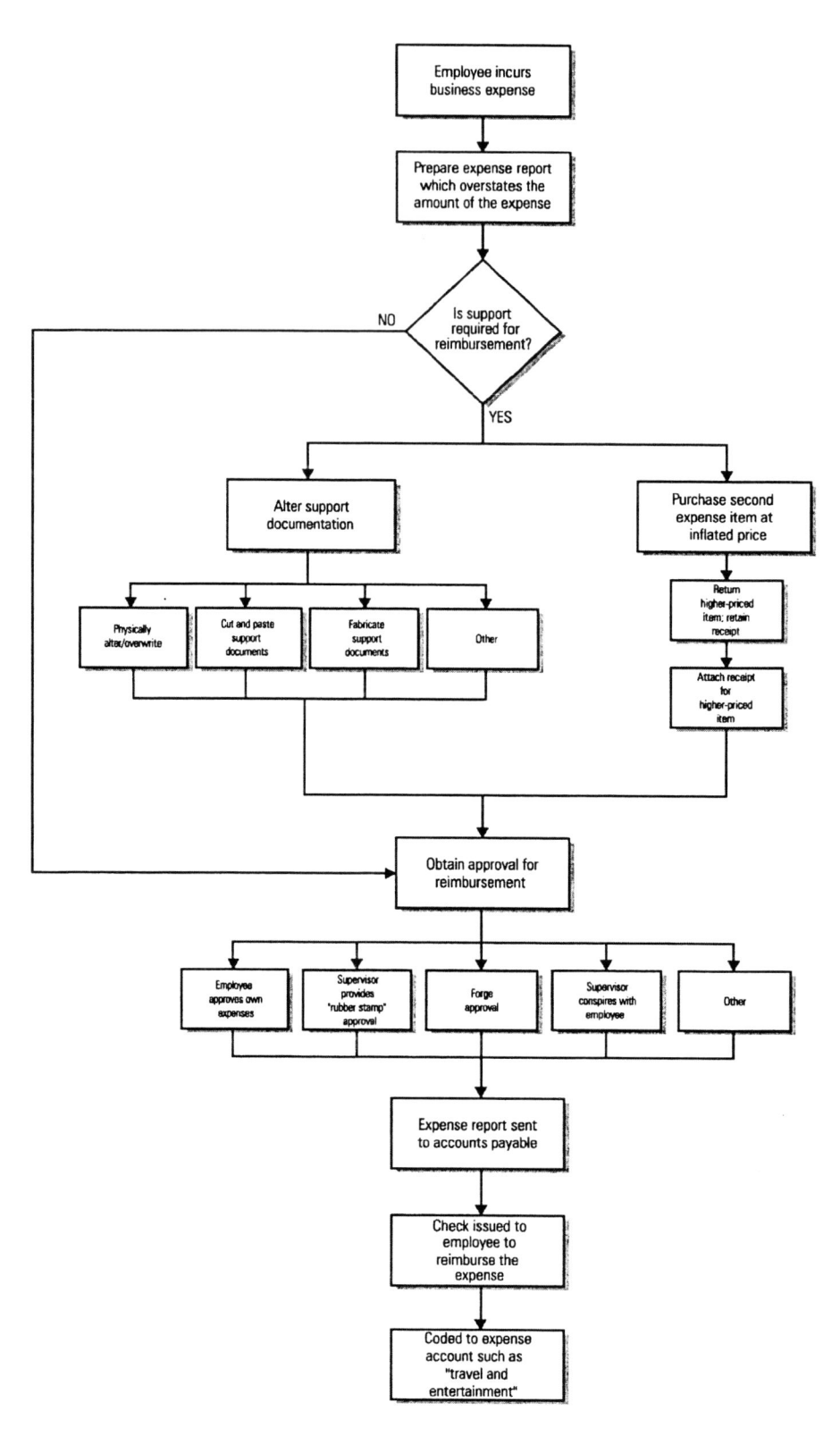

Overstated Expenses

generally attaches a copy of the receipt to his expense report. Alterations are usually less noticeable on a photocopy than on an original document. For precisely this reason, businesses should require original receipts and ink signatures on expense reports.

As with other expense frauds, overstated expense reimbursement schemes often succeed because of poor controls. In companies where supporting documents are not required, for example, fraudsters simply lie about how much they paid for a business expense. With no support available, it may be very difficult to disprove an employee's false expense claims.

Overpurchasing

Another way to overstate a reimbursement form is the "overpurchasing" of business expenses. This method is typically used by employees seeking reimbursement for travel expenses. Assume an employee is scheduled to make a business trip to another city. The employee purchases an airline ticket far in advance of the trip when rates are low. When it is close to the day of the trip, the employee purchases another ticket to the same destination. This ticket will be more expensive than the first one. To further jack up the price, the second ticket might include several stops and layovers on a very circuitous route. The employee removes the passenger receipt coupon from the second ticket then returns it for a full refund. He actually flies on the first (less expensive) ticket he purchased, but attaches the receipt from the more expensive ticket to his expense report.

Overstating Another Employee's Expenses

Overstated expense reimbursement schemes are not only committed by the person who actually incurs the expense. Sometimes, they may be committed by a co-worker who handles or processes expense reports.

EXAMPLE
A petty cashier whited-out other employees' requests for travel advances and inserted larger amounts. The cashier then passed on the legitimate travel advances and pocketed the excess.

This kind of scheme is most likely to occur in a system where expenses are reimbursed in currency rather than by a check, since the perpetrator would be unable to extract his "cut" from a single check made out to another employee.

Orders to Overstate Expenses

Finally, some employees knowingly falsified their own reports, but do so at the direction of their supervisors. The employees may be threatened with loss of their jobs if they do not go along with the scheme. Sometimes the supervisor splits the proceeds of the fraud with his subordinates. In other cases, the excess money goes into a slush fund or is used for some other business purpose that is not in the company budget. The supervisors who engage in these schemes often believe they are really acting in the best interests of their companies.

EXAMPLE

A sales executive instructed his salesmen to inflate their expenses in order to generate cash for a slush fund. This fund was used to pay bribes and to provide improper forms of entertainment for clients and customers.

Fictitious Expense Reimbursements

Employees sometimes seek reimbursement for wholly fictitious expenses. Instead of overstating a real business expense or seeking reimbursement for a personal expense, an employee just invents an expense and requests that it be reimbursed. (See "Fictitious Expenses" flowchart)

Producing Fictitious Receipts

One way to generate a reimbursement for a fictitious expense is to create bogus support documents, such as false receipts. The emergence of personal computers has enabled some employees to create realistic-looking counterfeit receipts at home. These counterfeits are often very sophisticated, even including the logos of the stores where goods or services were allegedly purchased. Computers are not the only means of creating support for a fictitious expense. Some employees use calculator tapes, others cut and paste old receipts from suppliers, and some even use professional printers to generate fictitious receipts.

Unfortunately, not all companies require receipts to be attached to expense reports. Checks written by the employee or copies of his personal credit card bill might be allowed as support in lieu of a receipt. Some employees write personal checks that appear to be for business expenses, then photocopy these checks and attach them to reimbursement requests. In actuality, nothing is purchased with the checks; they are destroyed after the copies are made. The perpetrator ends up receiving a reimbursement from his employer without ever actually incurring a business expense. The same method can be used with credit cards, where

Fictitious Expenses

Flowchart: Fictitious Expenses

- Employee prepares expense report claiming fictitious expenses
  - Is support required for reimbursement?
    - NO → Obtain approval for reimbursement
    - YES → Create fake support documents
      - False receipts
        - Produce on personal computer
        - Calculator tapes
        - Cut and paste legitimate receipts – photocopy
        - Receipts provided by accomplice
        - Receipts from expenses not incurred by employee
        - Other
      - Other support
        - Copy of check → Stop payment on the check
        - Credit card statement → Return the item
        - Other
- Obtain approval for reimbursement
  - Employee approves own expenses
  - Supervisor provides "rubber stamp" approval
  - Forge approval
  - Supervisor conspires with employee
- Expense report sent to accounts payable
- Check issued to employee to reimburse the expense
- Coded to expense account such as "travel and entertainment"

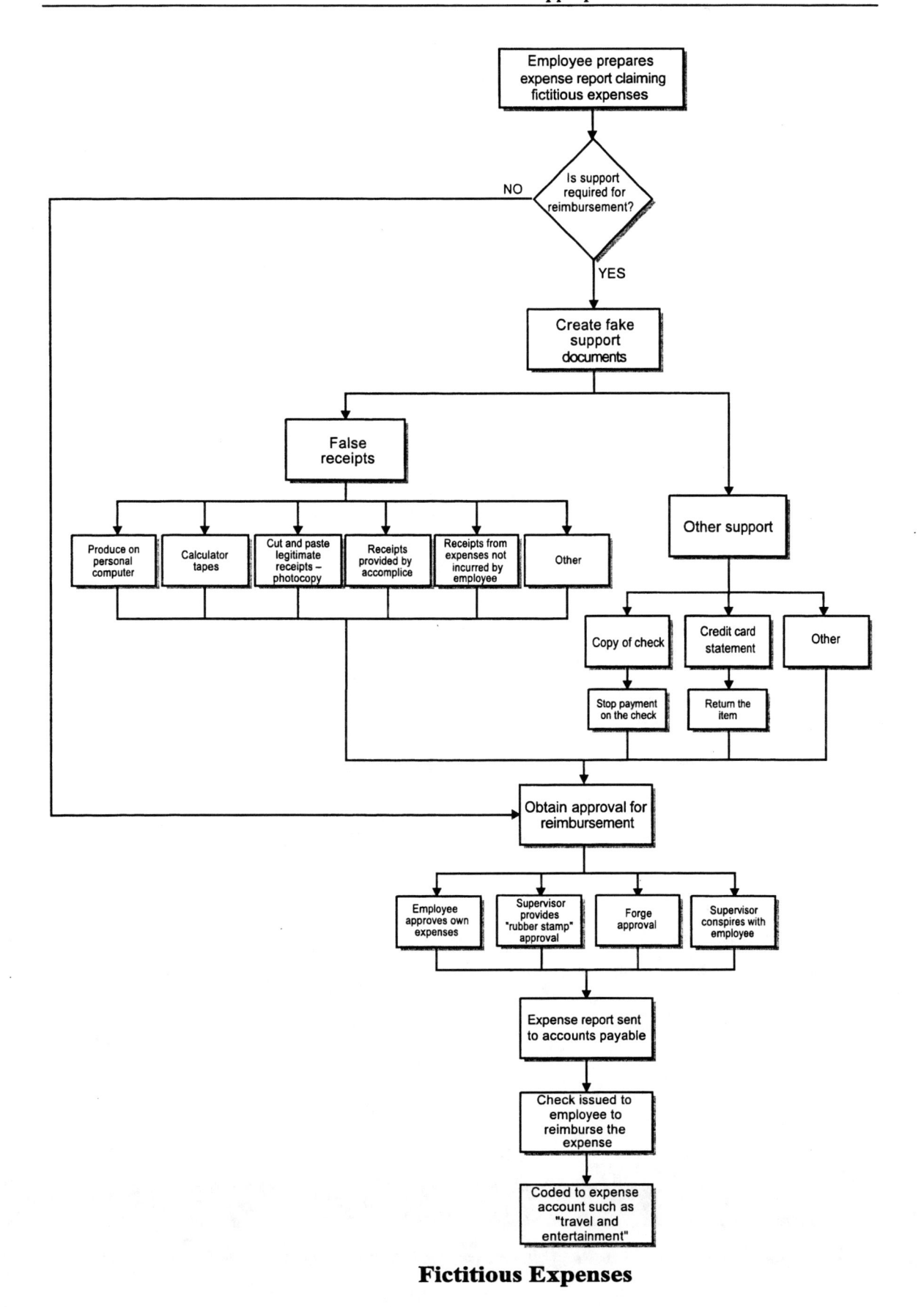

a copy of a statement is used to support a purchase. Once the expense report is filed, the perpetrator returns the item and receives a credit to his account.

Obtaining Blank Receipts from Vendors

If the perpetrator does not create receipts, they can be obtained from legitimate suppliers in a number of ways. Some employees request blank receipts from waiters, bartenders, etc. These persons fill in the blank receipts to "create" business expenses. A fraudster might also have a friend, spouse, relative, etc. who can provide receipts for "business expenses" that never really occur.

> EXAMPLE
>
> *An employee's girlfriend worked at a restaurant near the victim organization. This girlfriend validated credit card receipts and gave them to the fraudster so that he could submit them with his expense reports.*

In some cases a fraudster will steal an entire stack of blank receipts from a hotel, restaurant, etc., then fill them in and, over time, use them to verify fictitious business expenses.

Claiming the Expenses of Others

Another way perpetrators use actual receipts to generate unwarranted reimbursements is by submitting expense reports for expenses that were paid by others. For instance, an employee might save the receipt from a meal that was paid for by another party, then request reimbursement for the meal himself.

Multiple Reimbursements

The least common of the expense reimbursement schemes is the multiple reimbursement. This type of fraud involves the submission of a single expense several times. The most frequent example of a multiple reimbursement scheme is the submission of several types of support for the same expense.

> EXAMPLE
>
> *An employee would use, for example, an airline ticket stub and a travel agency invoice on separate expense reports so that he could be reimbursed twice for the cost of a single flight. The fraudster would have his division president authorize one report and have the vice president approve the other so that neither would see both reports. Additionally, the*

perpetrator allowed a time lag of about a month between the filing of the two reports so that the duplication would be less noticeable.

In cases where a company does not require original documents as support, some employees even use several copies of the same support document to generate multiple reimbursements. Rather than file two expense reports, employees may also charge an item to the company credit card, save the receipt, and attach it to an expense report as if they paid for the item themselves. The victim organization therefore ends up paying twice for the same expense.

Detection of Expense Reimbursement Schemes

Detecting expense reimbursement fraud involves two basic methods. The first of these is a review and analysis of expense accounts. The second detection method is a detailed review of expense reports.

Review and Analysis of Expense Accounts

Generally, expense account review uses one of two methods: historical comparisons or comparisons with budgeted amounts. A historical comparison compares the balance expended this period in relation to the balance spent in prior, similar periods. When performing this review, consider changes to the marketing, servicing, or other company operations.

Budgets are estimates of the money and/or time necessary to complete the task. They are based on past experience with consideration for current and future business conditions. Therefore, when comparing actual and budgeted expenses, determining inordinate expenses or inaccurate budget estimates is important.

Detailed Review of Expense Reports

Overall, the best detection method is a detailed review of employee expense reports. This method requires that the fraud examiner have, at the time of the examination, a calendar and a copy of the employee's schedule for the relevant period. The examiner should be familiar with the travel and entertainment policies of the company. Additionally, the following two steps may help to detect and deter employee expense abuses:
- Require employees to submit their expense reports for a detailed review before payment is reimbursed. If an employee knows that his expense report will be thoroughly reviewed, he will be less likely to include fraudulent expenses on the report.

- Periodically audit travel and entertainment accounts. This is particularly effective shortly before employee performance reviews.

Prevention of Expense Reimbursement Schemes
Detailed Expense Reports: Submission and Review

Detailed expense reports should require the following information:
- Receipts or other support documentation
- Explanation of the expense including specific business purpose
- Time period expense occurred
- Place of expenditure
- Amount

It is not enough to have the detailed reports submitted if they are not reviewed. A policy requiring the periodic review of expense reports, coupled with examining the appropriate detail, will help deter employees from submitting personal expenses for reimbursement.

ASSET MISAPPROPRIATION: INVENTORY AND OTHER ASSETS

Employees target inventory, equipment, supplies, and other non-cash assets for theft in a number of ways. These schemes can range from stealing a box of pens to the theft of millions of dollars worth of company equipment. The term *inventory and other assets* is meant to encompass the misappropriation schemes involving any assets held by a company other than cash.

Misuse of Inventory and Other Assets

There are basically two ways a person can misappropriate a company asset. The asset can be *misused* or it can be *stolen*. Simple misuse is obviously the less egregious of the two. Assets that are misused but not stolen typically include company vehicles, company supplies, computers, and other office equipment.

EXAMPLE
An employee made personal use of a company vehicle while on an out-of-town assignment. The employee provided false information, both written and verbal, regarding the nature of his use of the vehicle. The vehicle was returned unharmed and the cost to the perpetrator's company was only a few hundred dollars. Nevertheless, such unauthorized use of a company asset does amount to fraud when a false statement accompanies the use.

One of the most common examples of the misuse of company assets occurs when an employee uses company equipment to do personal work on company time. For instance, an employee might use his computer at work to write letters, print invoices, or do other work connected with a business he runs on the side. In many instances, these side businesses are of the same nature as the employer's business, so the employee is essentially competing with his employer and using the employer's equipment to do it.

The Costs of Inventory Misuse

The costs of inventory misuse are difficult to quantify. To many individuals this type of fraud is not viewed as a crime, but rather as "borrowing." In truth, the cost to a company from this kind of scheme is often immaterial. When a perpetrator borrows a stapler for the night or takes home some tools to perform a household repair, the cost to his company is negligible, as long as the assets are returned unharmed.

On the other hand, misuse schemes could be very costly. Take, for example, the situation discussed above in which an employee uses company equipment to operate a side business during work hours. Since the employee is not performing his work duties, the employer suffers a loss in productivity. If the low productivity continues, the employer might have to hire additional employees to compensate, which means more capital diverted to wages. If the employee's business competes with the employer's, then lost business could be an additional cost. Unauthorized use of equipment can also mean additional wear and tear, causing the equipment to break down sooner than it would have under normal business conditions. Additionally, when an employee "borrows" company property, there is no guarantee that he will bring it back. This is precisely how some theft schemes begin. Despite some opinions to the contrary, asset misuse is not always a harmless crime.

Theft of Inventory and Other Assets

While the misuse of company property might be a problem, the *theft* of company property is obviously of greater concern. Losses resulting from larceny of company assets can run into the millions of dollars. Most schemes where inventory and other non-cash assets are stolen fall into one of four categories: larceny schemes, asset requisition and transfer schemes, purchasing and receiving schemes, and false shipment schemes.

Larceny Schemes

The textbook definition of *larceny* is: "Felonious stealing, taking and carrying, leading, riding, or driving away another's personal property, with intent to convert it or to deprive owner thereof. The unlawful taking and carrying away of property of another with intent to appropriate it to use inconsistent with latter's rights.*" This definition is so broad, it encompasses every kind of asset theft. In order to gain a more specific understanding of the methods used to steal inventory and other assets, the definition of larceny has been restricted. For the purposes of classifying asset misappropriations, the term *larceny* is meant to refer to the most basic type of inventory theft, the schemes in which an employee simply takes inventory from the company premises without attempting to conceal the theft in the books and records. (See "Non-cash Larceny" flowchart) In other fraud schemes, employees may create false documentation to justify the shipment of merchandise or tamper with inventory records to conceal missing assets. Larceny schemes are more blunt. The culprit in these crimes takes company assets without trying to "justify" their absence.

---

* Blacks, p. 792.

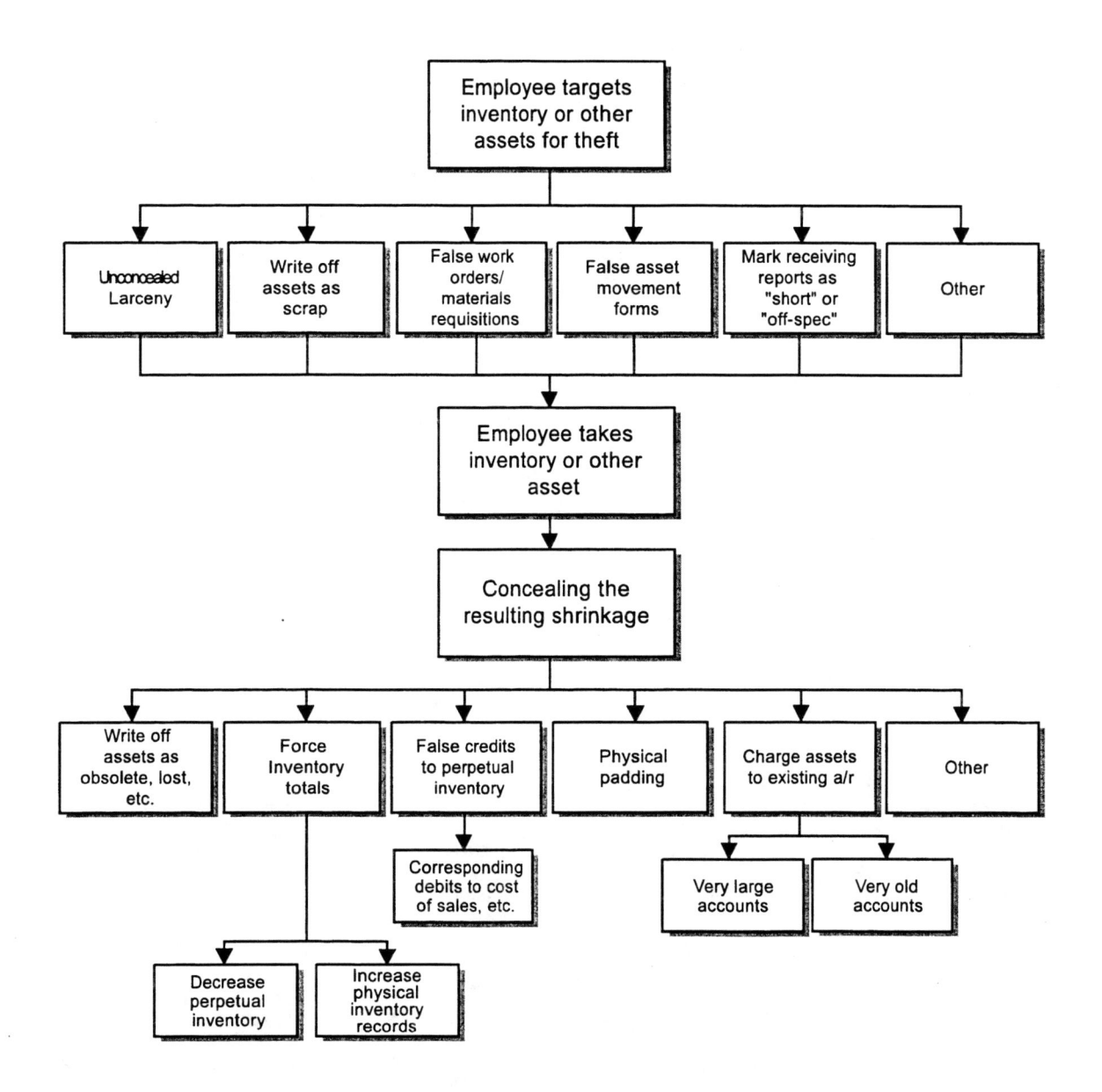

Asset Misappropriation: Inventory and Other Assets

```
                    ┌─────────────────────┐
                    │  Employee targets   │
                    │ inventory or other  │
                    │   assets for theft  │
                    └──────────┬──────────┘
   ┌──────────┬──────────┬─────┼─────┬──────────┬──────────┐
   ▼          ▼          ▼     ▼     ▼          ▼          ▼
```

- Unconcealed Larceny
- Write off assets as scrap
- False work orders/ materials requisitions
- False asset movement forms
- Mark receiving reports as "short" or "off-spec"
- Other

```
                    ┌─────────────────────┐
                    │  Employee takes     │
                    │ inventory or other  │
                    │       asset         │
                    └──────────┬──────────┘
                               ▼
                    ┌─────────────────────┐
                    │   Concealing the    │
                    │  resulting shrinkage│
                    └──────────┬──────────┘
```

- Write off assets as obsolete, lost, etc.
- Force Inventory totals
  - Decrease perpetual inventory
  - Increase physical inventory records
- False credits to perpetual inventory
  - Corresponding debits to cost of sales, etc.
- Physical padding
- Charge assets to existing a/r
  - Very large accounts
  - Very old accounts
- Other

Non-cash Larceny

Most non-cash larceny schemes are not very complicated. They are typically committed by employees (warehouse personnel, inventory clerks, shipping clerks, etc.) with access to inventory or supplies. Many employees simply carry company assets away in open view of other employees. People tend to assume that their friends and acquaintances are acting honestly. When they see a trusted co-worker taking something out of the workplace, most people assume that the culprit has a legitimate reason for doing so.

EXAMPLE

A university faculty member was leaving his offices to take a position at a new school. This person was permitted to take a small number of items to his new job, but certainly exceeded the intentions of the school when he loaded two trucks full of university lab equipment and computers worth several hundred thousand dollars. The perpetrator simply packed up these stolen assets along with his personal items and drove away.

Unfortunately, in all too many cases the co-workers of the perpetrator are fully aware that he is stealing company assets, yet they refrain from reporting the crime. There are several reasons that employees might ignore illegal conduct, such as a sense of duty to their friends, a "management vs. labor" mentality, poor channels of communication for whistleblowers, or intimidation of honest employees by the thief. When high-ranking personnel are stealing from their companies, employees often overlook the crime because they fear they will lose their jobs if they report it. In some cases, the co-workers may be assisting in the theft.

EXAMPLE

A school superintendent was not only pilfering school accounts but was also stealing school assets. A search of his residence revealed a cellar filled with school property. A number of school employees knew or suspected the superintendent was involved in illegal dealings, but he was very powerful and people were afraid to report him for fear of retaliation. As a result, he was able to steal from the school for several years.

Ironically, employees who steal inventory are often highly trusted within their organizations. Because these employees are trusted, they may be given access to restricted areas, safes, supply rooms, or other areas where company assets are kept. This access makes it easy for these employees to steal.

It can be unwise for an employee to physically carry inventory and other assets off the premises of his company. This practice carries with it the inherent risk and potential embarrassment of being caught red-handed with stolen goods on his person. Some employees avoid this problem by mailing company assets from the victim organization to a location where they can retrieve them without fear of being observed.

EXAMPLE

A spare-parts custodian took several thousand dollars worth of computer chips and mailed them to a company that had no business dealings with the custodian's employer. He then reclaimed the merchandise as his own. By taking the step of mailing the stolen inventory, the fraudster allowed the postal service to unwittingly do his dirty work for him.

The False Sale

In many cases, corrupt employees utilize outside accomplices to help steal inventory. The fake sale is one method that depends upon an accomplice. Like most inventory thefts, the fake sale is not complicated. The accomplice of the employee-fraudster pretends to buy merchandise, but the employee does not ring up the sale. The accomplice takes the merchandise without paying for it. To a casual observer, it will appear that the transaction is a normal sale. The employee bags the merchandise, and may act as though a transaction is being entered on the register, but in fact, the "sale" is not recorded. The accomplice may even pass a nominal amount of money to the employee to complete the illusion. A related scheme occurs when an employee sells merchandise to an accomplice at an unauthorized discount.

Employees also sometimes enlist accomplices to return goods that the employee has already stolen. This is an easy way for the employee to convert the stolen inventory into cash.

Asset Requisitions and Transfers

Asset requisitions and other documents that allow non-cash assets to be moved from one location in a company to another can be used to facilitate the theft of those assets. Employees use internal transfer paperwork to gain access to merchandise which they otherwise might not be able to handle without raising suspicion. These documents do not account for missing merchandise the way false sales do, but they allow a person to move the assets from one location to another. In the process of this movement, the thief steals the merchandise.

The most basic scheme occurs when an employee requisitions materials for some work-related project, then makes off with the materials. In some cases the employee simply overstates the amount of supplies or equipment it will take to complete his work and pilfers the excess. In more ambitious schemes the employee might invent a completely fictitious project which necessitates the use of certain assets he intends to steal.

> EXAMPLE
>
> *An employee of a telecommunications company used false project documents to request approximately $100,000 worth of computer chips, allegedly to upgrade company computers. Knowing that this type of requisition required verbal authorization from another source, the employee set up an elaborate phone scheme to get the "project" approved. The fraudster used his knowledge of the company's phone system to forward calls from four different lines to his own desk. When the confirmation call was made, it was the perpetrator who answered the phone and authorized the project.*

Dishonest employees sometimes falsify asset transfer forms so they can remove inventory from a warehouse or stockroom. The false documents allow the employee to remove merchandise from the warehouse, but instead of using it for a work-related purpose, the perpetrator simply takes it home. The obvious problem with this type of scheme is that the person who orders the merchandise will usually be the primary suspect when it turns up missing.

> EXAMPLE
>
> *A manager requested merchandise from the company warehouse to be displayed on a showroom floor. The pieces he requested never made it to the showroom, because he loaded them into a pickup truck and took them home. In some instances he actually took the items in broad daylight and with the help of another employee. This individual thought he was immune from detection because the merchandise was requested via computer using a management level security code. The code was not specific to any one manager, so there would be no way of knowing which manager had ordered the merchandise. Unfortunately for the thief, the company was able to record the computer terminal from which the request originated. The manager had used his own computer to make the request, which led to his undoing.*

Purchasing and Receiving Schemes

Dishonest employees can also manipulate the purchasing and receiving functions of a company to facilitate the theft of inventory and other assets. It might seem that any purchasing scheme should fall under the heading of false billings, which were discussed earlier. There is, however, a distinction between the purchasing schemes that are classified as false billings and those that are classified as non-cash misappropriations.

If an employee causes his company to purchase merchandise that the company does not need, this is a false billing scheme. The harm to the company comes in paying for assets for which it has no use. On the other hand, if the assets were intentionally purchased by the company and later misappropriated by the perpetrator, this is classified as an inventory larceny scheme. Here the company loses both the value of the merchandise and the *use* of the merchandise.

Falsifying Incoming Shipments

One of the most common examples of an employee abusing the purchasing and receiving functions occurs when a person charged with receiving goods on behalf of the victim company—such as a warehouse supervisor or receiving clerk—falsifies the records of incoming shipments. If, for example, 1,000 units of a particular item are received, the perpetrator indicates that only 900 were received. By marking the shipment short, the perpetrator can steal the 100 units that are unaccounted for.

The obvious problem with this kind of scheme is the fact that the receiving report does not match the vendor's invoice, which will likely cause a problem with payment. In the example above, if the vendor bills for 1,000 units but the accounts payable voucher only shows receipt of 900 units of merchandise, then someone will have to explain where the extra 100 units went.

Some employees avoid this problem by altering only one copy of the receiving report. The copy that is sent to accounts payable indicates receipt of a full shipment so the vendor will be paid without any questions. The copy used for inventory records indicates a short shipment so that the assets on hand will equal the assets in the perpetual inventory.

Instead of marking shipments short, the perpetrator might reject portions of a shipment as not being up to quality specifications. The perpetrator then keeps the "substandard" merchandise rather than sending it back to the supplier. The result is the same as if the shipment had been marked short.

False Shipments of Inventory and Other Assets

To conceal thefts of inventory and other assets, employees sometimes create false shipping documents and false sales documents to make it appear that the inventory they take was sold rather than stolen. (See "False Shipments of Inventory and Other Assets" flowchart) The document that tells the shipping department to release inventory for delivery is usually the packing slip. By creating a false packing slip, a corrupt employee can cause inventory to be fraudulently delivered to himself or an accomplice. The "sales" reflected in the packing slips are typically made to a fictitious person, a fictitious company, or an accomplice of the perpetrator.

One benefit of using false shipping documents to misappropriate inventory or other assets is that the product is removed from the warehouse or storeroom by someone other than the perpetrator. The victim organization unknowingly delivers the targeted assets to the perpetrator of the scheme.

False packing slips allow inventory to be shipped from the victim company to the perpetrator, but alone they do not conceal the fact that inventory has been misappropriated. In order to hide the theft, fraudsters may create a false sale on the books so it appears that the missing inventory was shipped to a customer. Depending on how the victim organization operates, the perpetrator may have to create a false purchase order from the "buyer," a false sales order, and a false invoice along with the packing slip to create the illusion of a sale.

The result is that a fake receivable account goes into the books for the price of the misappropriated inventory. Obviously, the "buyer" of the merchandise will never pay for it. How do employees deal with these fake receivables? In some cases, the employee simply lets the receivable age on his company's books until it is eventually written off as uncollectable. In other instances he might take affirmative steps to remove the sale—and the delinquent receivable that results—from the books.

EXAMPLE

An employee generated false invoices and delivered them to the company warehouse for shipping. The invoices were then marked "delivered" and sent to the sales office. The perpetrator removed all copies of the invoices from the files before they were billed to the fictitious customer.

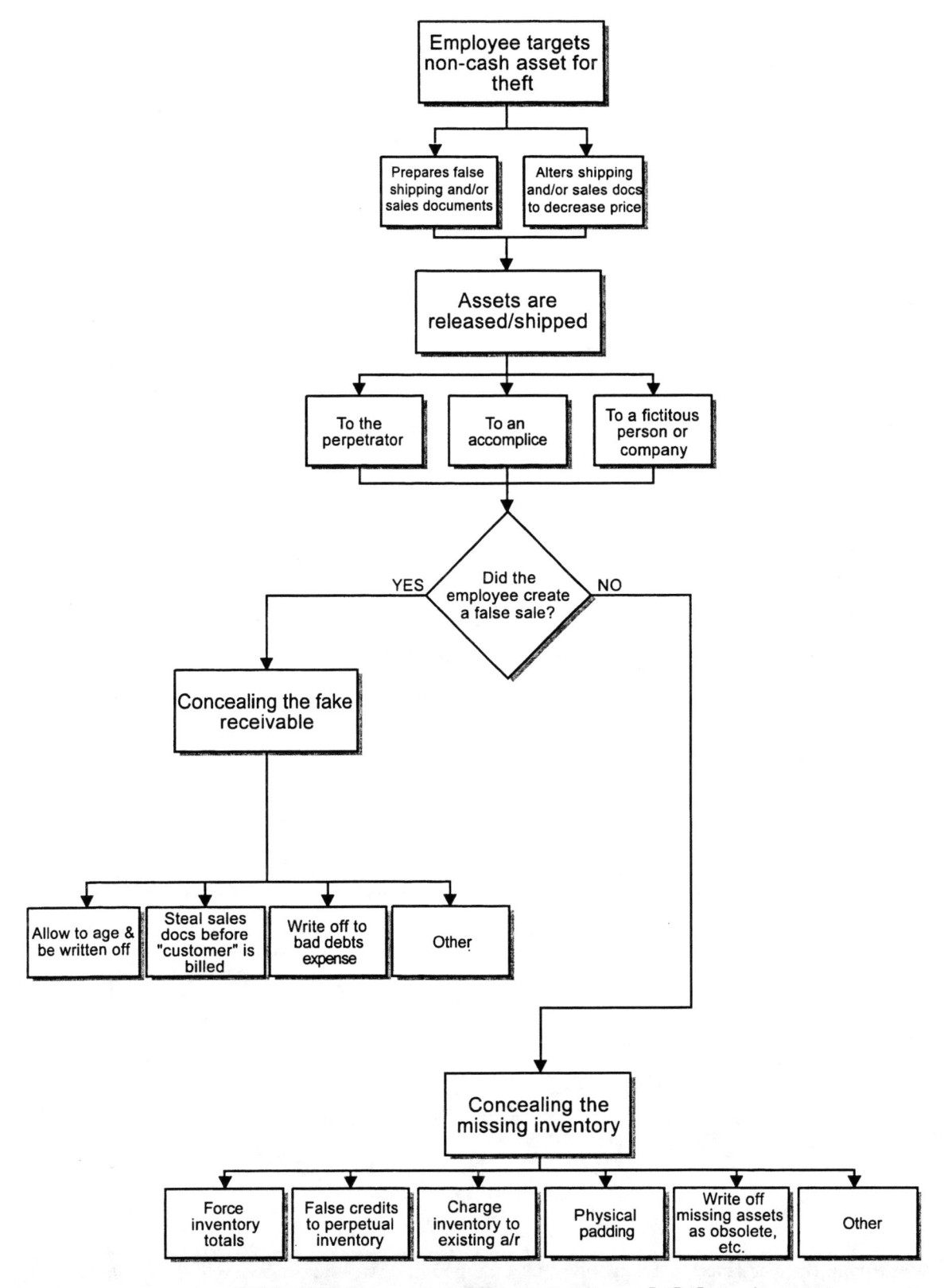

```
                    ┌─────────────────┐
                    │ Employee targets│
                    │non-cash asset for│
                    │      theft      │
                    └────────┬────────┘
              ┌──────────────┴──────────────┐
              ▼                             ▼
    ┌──────────────────┐         ┌──────────────────┐
    │  Prepares false  │         │  Alters shipping │
    │ shipping and/or  │         │ and/or sales docs│
    │ sales documents  │         │ to decrease price│
    └────────┬─────────┘         └────────┬─────────┘
             └────────────┬───────────────┘
                          ▼
                ┌──────────────────┐
                │     Assets are   │
                │  released/shipped│
                └────────┬─────────┘
        ┌────────────────┼────────────────┐
        ▼                ▼                ▼
  ┌───────────┐   ┌───────────┐   ┌───────────────┐
  │   To the  │   │   To an   │   │  To a fictitious│
  │perpetrator│   │ accomplice│   │person or company│
  └─────┬─────┘   └─────┬─────┘   └────────┬──────┘
        └───────────────┼──────────────────┘
                        ▼
                   ╱─────────╲
           YES   ╱  Did the   ╲   NO
        ┌──────╱   employee    ╲──────┐
        │      ╲  create a      ╱      │
        │       ╲ false sale?  ╱       │
        │        ╲────────────╱        │
        ▼                              │
  ┌─────────────────┐                  │
  │Concealing the   │                  │
  │fake receivable  │                  │
  └────────┬────────┘                  │
    ┌──────┼──────┬──────────┐         │
    ▼      ▼      ▼          ▼         │
 ┌──────┐┌──────┐┌────────┐┌──────┐    │
 │Allow ││Steal ││Write   ││Other │    │
 │to age││sales ││off to  │└──────┘    │
 │& be  ││docs  ││bad     │            │
 │writ- ││before││debts   │            │
 │ten   ││"cust-││expense │            │
 │off   ││omer" │└────────┘            │
 └──────┘│is    │                      │
         │billed│                      │
         └──────┘                      │
                        ┌──────────────┘
                        ▼
                ┌──────────────────┐
                │  Concealing the  │
                │ missing inventory│
                └────────┬─────────┘
    ┌──────┬──────┬──────┼──────┬──────┐
    ▼      ▼      ▼      ▼      ▼      ▼
 ┌──────┐┌──────┐┌──────┐┌──────┐┌──────┐┌──────┐
 │Force ││False ││Charge││Physi-││Write ││Other │
 │inven-││cred- ││inven-││cal   ││off   │└──────┘
 │tory  ││its to││tory  ││pad-  ││miss- │
 │totals││perp- ││to    ││ding  ││ing   │
 │      ││etual ││exis- │└──────┘│assets│
 │      ││inven-││ting  │        │as    │
 │      ││tory  ││a/r   │        │obso- │
 └──────┘└──────┘└──────┘        │lete, │
                                 │etc.  │
                                 └──────┘
```

False Shipments of Inventory and Other Assets

Another common way to get rid of delinquent receivables that result from theft schemes is to write off the receivables to accounts such as *discounts and allowances, bad debt expense,* or *lost and stolen assets.*

Instead of creating completely fictitious sales, some employees understate legitimate sales so that an accomplice is billed for less than delivered. The result is that a portion of the merchandise is sold at no cost. In a typical scenario, a salesman fills out shipping tickets which are forwarded to the warehouse. After the merchandise is shipped, the salesman instructs the warehouse employees to return the shipping tickets to him for "extra work" before they are sent to the invoicing department. The salesman then alters the shipping tickets, reducing either the quantity of merchandise sold or the price per unit sold.

Write-offs are often used to conceal the theft of assets after they have been stolen. In some cases, however, assets are written off in order to make them available for theft. For instance, an employee with the authority to declare inventory obsolete can write off this inventory as "scrap." Once assets are designated as scrap, it is often easier to misappropriate them. Fraudsters may be allowed to take the "useless" assets for themselves, buy them or sell them to an accomplice at a greatly reduced price, or simply give the assets away.

Concealing Inventory Shrinkage

When inventory is stolen, the key concealment issue for the perpetrator is shrinkage. *Inventory shrinkage* is the unaccounted-for reduction in the company's inventory that results from theft. For instance, assume a computer retailer has 1,000 computers in stock. After work one day, an employee loads ten computers into a truck and takes them home. Now the company only has 990 computers, but since there is no record that the employee took ten computers, the inventory records still show 1,000 units on hand. The company has experienced inventory shrinkage in the amount of 10 computers.

Shrinkage is one of the red flags that signal fraud. The goal of the perpetrator is to proceed with his scheme undetected, so it is in his best interest to prevent anyone from looking for missing assets. This means concealing the shrinkage that occurs from asset theft.

Inventory and other assets are typically tracked through a two-step process. The first step, the perpetual inventory, is a running count that records how much inventory should be on hand. When new shipments of merchandise are received, for instance, this merchandise is entered into the perpetual inventory. Similarly, when goods are sold they are removed from the perpetual inventory records. In this way a company tracks its inventory on a day-to-day basis.

Periodically, a physical count of assets on hand should be made. In this process, someone actually goes through the storeroom or warehouse and counts everything that the company has in stock. This total is then matched to the amount of assets reflected in the perpetual inventory. A variation between the physical inventory and the perpetual inventory totals is shrinkage. While a certain amount of shrinkage may be expected in any business, large shrinkage totals may indicate fraud.

Altered Inventory Records
One of the simplest methods for concealing shrinkage is to change the perpetual inventory record so that it will match the physical inventory count. This is also known as a forced reconciliation of the account. The perpetrator simply changes the numbers in the perpetual inventory to make them match the amount of inventory on hand. For example, the employee might credit the perpetual inventory and debit the cost of sales account to bring the perpetual inventory numbers into line with the actual inventory count. Instead of using correcting entries to adjust the perpetual inventory, some employees simply delete or cover up the correct totals and enter new numbers.

There are two sides to the inventory equation, the perpetual inventory and the physical inventory. Instead of altering the perpetual inventory, a perpetrator who has access to the records from a physical inventory count can change those records to match the perpetual inventory. Returning to the computer store example, assume the company counts its inventory every month and matches it to the perpetual inventory. The physical count should come to 990 computers, since that is what is actually on hand. If the perpetrator is someone charged with counting inventory, he can simply write down that there are 1,000 units on hand.

Fictitious Sales and Accounts Receivable
When the perpetrator makes an adjusting entry to the perpetual inventory and cost of sales accounts as discussed above, there is no sales transaction on the books that corresponds to these entries. In order to fix this problem, a perpetrator might enter a debit to accounts receivable and a corresponding credit to the sales account so that it appears the missing goods have been sold.

Of course, the problem of payment then arises, because no one is going to pay for the goods which were "sold" in this transaction. There are two routes that a fraudster might take in this circumstance. The first is to charge the sale to an existing account. In some cases, employees charge fake sales to existing receivables which are so large that the addition of the assets that the perpetrator has stolen will not be noticed. Other corrupt employees charge the "sales" to accounts that are already aging and will soon be written off. When these accounts are removed from the books, the perpetrator's stolen inventory effectively disappears. The other adjustment that is typically made is a write-off to *discounts and allowances* or *bad debt expense*.

Write Off of Inventory and Other Assets
Writing off inventory and other assets is a relatively common way for employees to remove assets from the books before or after they are stolen. This eliminates the problem of shrinkage that inherently exists in every case of non-cash asset misappropriation.

Physical Padding
Most methods of concealment deal with altering inventory records, either changing the perpetual inventory or miscounting during the physical inventory. In the alternative, some employees try to make it appear that there are more assets present in the warehouse or stockroom than there actually are. Empty boxes, for example, may be stacked on shelves to create the illusion of extra inventory.

Detection
Statistical Sampling
Companies with inventory accounts typically have enormous populations of source documents. Statistical sampling allows the fraud examiner to inspect key attributes on a smaller portion (or sample) of those documents. For example, the examiner may select a statistically valid, random sample of purchase requisitions to determine that all requisitions in the sample selected were properly approved. Statistical sampling enables the examiner to predict the occurrence rate for the population and, therefore, determine with some accuracy the error rate or the potential for fraud.

Other items which may be sampled on a statistical basis include the following:
- Receiving reports
- Perpetual inventory records
- Raw materials requisitions
- Shipping documents

- Job cost sheets

The attributes tested for on the above-mentioned documents might include a specific date, item, or location.

Perpetual Inventory Records
Unexplained entries in the perpetual records might reveal embezzlement losses.
- Are all the reductions to the perpetual inventory records explained by source documents (such as sales invoices, approvals to remove to scrap inventory, or spoilage)?
- Are all increases in perpetual records explained by source documents such as receiving reports?

Shipping Documents
Inventory theft may be uncovered by answers to questions such as:
- Are all sales properly matched with a shipping document?
- Are any shipping documents not associated with a sale?
- Is inventory disappearing from storage?

Physical Inventory Counts
Physical inventory counts can sometimes give rise to inventory theft detection. However, because other explanations satisfy inventory shortages (such as shrinkage), historical analysis of inventory is usually necessary. Furthermore, if the only method used to detect inventory fraud is the year-end physical count, the perpetrators will have had all year to devise concealment methods to circumvent potential detection.

Analytical Review
By using an analytical review, inventory fraud may be detected because certain trends become immediately clear. For example, if the cost of goods sold increases by a disproportionate amount relative to sales, and no changes occur in the purchase prices, quantities purchased, or quality of products purchased, the cause of the disproportionate increase in cost of goods sold might be one of two things: (1) ending inventory has been depleted by theft, or (2) someone has been embezzling money through a false billing scheme (i.e. submitting invoices and collecting the payments for inventory that was never delivered).

An analytical review of all the component parts of the cost of goods sold should indicate to the examiner where to direct further inquiries. For example, assuming that the type of inventory purchased is the same and there is no change in the manufacturing process or purchase price, if sales and cost of sales change from $5,650,987 and $2,542,944 to $6,166,085 and $2,981,880, respectively, what is the data telling the examiner? To begin, sales have increased by 9.12% whereas cost of sales increased by 17.26%. The profit margin has decreased by 3% (from 55% to 52%). Based on this data, the fraud examiner might want to look further at the components of inventory, such as beginning inventory, purchases, and ending inventory. If beginning inventory was $1,207,898, purchases were $2,606,518, and $2,604,972, respectively, and ending inventory was $894,564, then an inventory matrix would look like the following:

	Year 1	Year 2	Percentage Change
Beginning Inventory	$1,207,898	$1,271,472	5.26%
Purchases	2,606,518	2,604,972	<0.06%>
Goods Available for Sale	$3,814,416	$3,876,444	1.63%
Ending Inventory	<1,271,472>	<894,564>	<29.64%>
Cost of Sales	$2,542,944	$2,981,880	17.26%

Inventory purchases, as a percentage of sales, have declined from 46.13% to 42.25%. From this example, one can hypothesize that: (1) inventory purchases were purposely increased in year one only to be liquidated in year two, (2) the increased sales in year two were unexpected and the purchase of inventory did not keep pace with the sales, or (3) there might be some fraud scheme in inventory. If, by interview, the examiner is unable to ascertain a reasonable explanation such as (1) or (2) above, then further examination of the ending inventory may be warranted.

The fraud examiner may next look at the differences in the physical inventory procedures, to see if that created a more (or less) accurate inventory count at the end of either year one or year two. If there is no other logical explanation, then further investigation into these and other inventory accounts may be necessary to explain the anomalies occurring in inventory.

Computer-Generated Trend Analysis

The computer can be used to facilitate obtaining lists of items with specified attributes. For example, in a lumberyard operation, the computer can be programmed to list all purchases of four by four cedar fence posts eight feet in length. Examine all the source documents that are represented by the listing. By examining the source documents for each of these purchases, the examiner can plot trends to determine the occurrence of the following (or other) patterns:

SEARCHES	SCHEMES
Purchases by vendor	If the same vendor is receiving favorable treatment
Inventory levels by types and dates	If inventory is being purchased at its reorder point or if excess inventory is being ordered
Inventory shipped by address	If the vendor's address matches either an employee address or the address of another vendor
Cost per item	If discounts are properly credited to purchases
Direct labor by item	If there are excess labor hours being added to a particular job or item
Direct materials by item	If materials are properly charged to the job (too much or the wrong materials)
Overhead per inventory item	If overhead is being properly applied, and applied only once
Disposals then reorders	If usable inventory is being prematurely designated as scrap
Shortages by inventory item	If there is inventory theft or the reorder system is not functioning
Returns and Allowances	If there is an unusually high incidence of returns and allowances
Sales Allowances	If sales allowances are not properly credited to promotional allowances
Buyer	If the buyer is not acting within scope of authority

Detailed Audit Program

The following audit program will also be helpful in establishing inventory control:

- Do adequate, detailed, written inventory instructions and procedures exist? Do inventory procedures give appropriate consideration to the location and arrangement of inventories?
- Do inventory procedures give appropriate consideration to identification and description of inventories?
- Is the method of determining inventory quantities specified (e.g., weight, count)?
- Is the method used for recording items counted adequate (e.g. count sheets, prenumbered tags)?
- Are inventory tags used? If yes: (1) Are they prenumbered? (2) Is accounting for inventory tags adequate and does it include control with respect to tags used, unused, and voided?
- Are adequate procedures in place to identify inventory counted, ensure that all items have been counted, and prevent double counting?
- Are obsolete, slow-moving, or damaged inventories properly identified and segregated?
- Is the inventory reasonably identifiable for proper classification in the accounting records (e.g., description, stage of completion)?

- Are inventory counts subject to (1) complete recounts by persons independent of the ones involved in the initial counts, (2) recounts only of merchandise having substantial value, or (3) spot checks by supervisory personnel?
- Are counts performed by employees whose functions are independent of the physical custody of inventories and record-keeping functions?
- Do proper accounting controls and procedures exist for the exclusion from inventory of merchandise on-hand which is not property of the client (e.g., customers' merchandise, consignments in)?
- Do proper accounting controls and procedures exist for the inclusion in inventory of merchandise not on-hand, but the property of the client (e.g., merchandise in warehouses, out on repair, consignments out)?
- Will identical inventory items in various areas be accumulated to allow a tie in total counts to a summary listing subsequent to the observation?
- Is the movement of inventory adequately controlled (e.g., shipping and receiving activities suspended) during the physical count to ensure a proper cut-off?
- Are significant differences between physical counts and detailed inventory records investigated before the accounting and inventory records are adjusted to match the physical counts?
- Will inventory at remote locations be counted?
- Will special counting procedures or volume conversions be necessary (e.g., items weighed on scale)?
- How will work-in-process inventory be identified?
- How will the stage of completion of work-in-process inventory be identified?
- Are there any other matters that should be noted for the inventory count?[*]

Prevention

There are four basic measures which, if properly installed and implemented, may help prevent inventory fraud. They are proper documentation, segregation of duties (including approvals), independent checks, and physical safeguards.

Proper Documentation

The following items should be prenumbered and controlled:
- Requisitions
- Receiving reports

---

[*] George Georgiades, *Audit Procedures*, (New York: Harcourt Brace Professional Publishing, 1995).

- Perpetual records
- Raw materials requisitions
- Shipping documents
- Job cost sheets

However, not all inventory requires the purchasing of raw materials. In these cases, the proper documentation might take the form of prenumbered and controlled tickets and receipts for sales.

Segregation of Duties
The following duties should be handled by different personnel:
- Requisition of inventory
- Receipt of inventory
- Disbursement of inventory
- Conversion of inventory to scrap
- Receipt of proceeds from disposal of scrap

Independent Checks
Someone independent of the purchasing or warehousing functions should conduct physical observation of inventory. The personnel conducting the physical observations also should be knowledgeable about the inventory.

Physical Safeguards
All merchandise should be physically guarded and locked; access should be limited to authorized personnel only. For example, strategic placement of security guards may aide in the detection and deterrence of potential theft schemes. Electronic methods may also be used, such as cameras and surveillance devices. The effectiveness of any device will, however, depend on the employee's knowledge that physical safeguard controls are adhered to and on the type of inventory available for misappropriation.

BRIBERY AND CORRUPTION

Bribery

Generally, bribery and corruption are off-book frauds that occur in the form of kickbacks, gifts, or gratuities to government employees from contractors or to private business employees from vendors. For a detailed discussion of the legal elements of bribery and corruption, please see the Law section.

At its heart, a bribe is a business transaction, albeit an illegal or unethical one. A person "buys" something with the bribes he pays. What he buys is the influence of the recipient. Bribery schemes can be difficult and expensive. Though they are not nearly as common as other forms of occupational fraud such as asset misappropriations, bribery schemes tend to be much more costly.

Bribery may be defined as the offering, giving, receiving, or soliciting any thing of value to influence an official act. The term *official act* means that traditional bribery statutes only proscribe payments made to influence the decisions of government agents or employees.

Many occupational fraud schemes, however, involve *commercial bribery*, which is similar to the traditional definition of bribery except that something of value is offered to influence a business decision rather than an official act of government. Commercial bribery may or may not be a criminal offense. For example, in the United States there is no general federal law prohibiting commercial bribery in all instances. However, there are statutes prohibiting bribery of employees of financial institutions to influence a loan. Therefore, the law of your particular jurisdiction and the facts of the case will determine whether bribery in the private sector may be prosecuted criminally. Commercial bribery can often be pursued in the civil courts as breach of fiduciary duty or conflict of interest. See the Legal section for more information.

Bribery schemes generally fall into two broad categories: *kickbacks* and *bid-rigging schemes*. Kickbacks are undisclosed payments made by vendors to employees of purchasing companies. The purpose of a kickback is usually to enlist the corrupt employee in an overbilling scheme. Sometimes vendors pay kickbacks simply to get extra business from the purchasing company. Bid-rigging schemes occur when an employee fraudulently assists a vendor in winning a contract through the competitive bidding process.

Kickback Schemes

Kickbacks, in the commercial sense, are the giving or receiving anything of value to influence a business decision without the employer's knowledge and consent. Kickback schemes are usually very similar to the billing schemes described in the Asset Misappropriation section. They involve the submission of invoices for goods and services that are either overpriced or completely fictitious. (See "Kickbacks" flowchart)

Kickbacks are classified as corruption schemes rather than asset misappropriations because they involve collusion between employees and vendors. In a common type of kickback scheme, a vendor submits a fraudulent or inflated invoice to the victim organization and an employee of that organization helps make sure that a payment is made on the false invoice. For his assistance, the employee-fraudster receives a payment from the vendor. This payment is the kickback.

Kickback schemes almost always attack the purchasing function of the victim company, so it stands to reason that these frauds are often undertaken by employees with purchasing responsibilities. Purchasing employees often have direct contact with vendors and therefore have an opportunity to establish a collusive relationship.

EXAMPLE

A purchasing agent redirected a number of orders to a company owned by a supplier with whom he was conspiring. In return for the additional business, the supplier paid the purchasing agent over half the profits from the additional orders.

Diverting Business to Vendors

In some instances, an employee-fraudster receives a kickback simply for directing excess business to a vendor. There might be no overbilling involved in these cases; the vendor simply pays the kickbacks to ensure a steady stream of business from the purchasing company.

If no overbilling is involved in a kickback scheme, one might wonder where the harm lies. Assuming the vendor simply wants to get the buyer's business and does not increase his prices or bill for undelivered goods and services, how is the buyer harmed? The problem is that, having bought off an employee of the purchasing company, a vendor is no longer subject to the normal economic pressures of the marketplace. This vendor does not have to compete with other suppliers for the purchasing company's business, and so has no

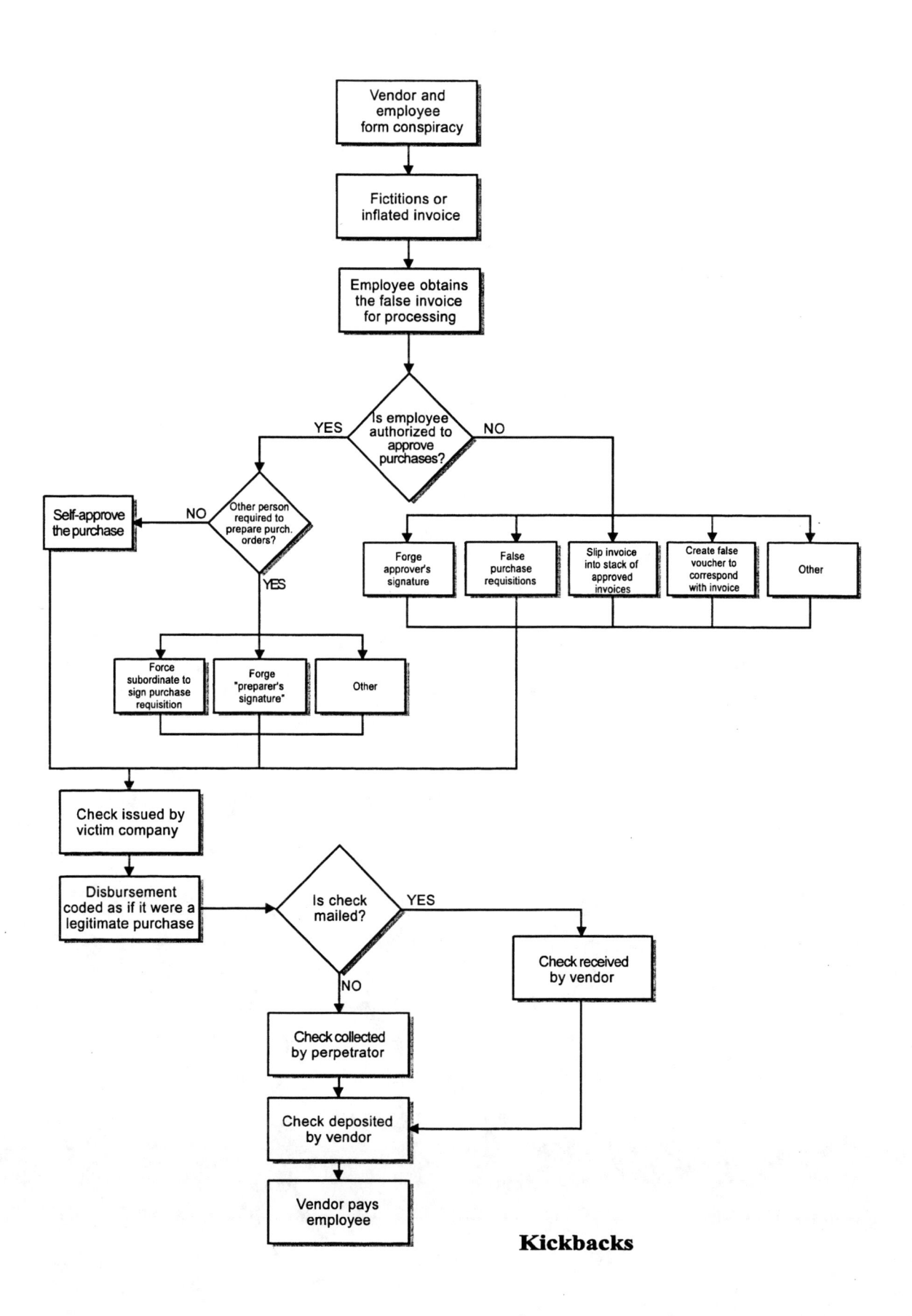

Kickbacks

- Vendor and employee form conspiracy
- Fictitious or inflated invoice
- Employee obtains the false invoice for processing
- Is employee authorized to approve purchases?
  - YES → Other person required to prepare purch. orders?
    - NO → Self-approve the purchase
    - YES →
      - Force subordinate to sign purchase requisition
      - Forge "preparer's signature"
      - Other
  - NO →
    - Forge approver's signature
    - False purchase requisitions
    - Slip invoice into stack of approved invoices
    - Create false voucher to correspond with invoice
    - Other
- Check issued by victim company
- Disbursement coded as if it were a legitimate purchase
- Is check mailed?
  - YES → Check received by vendor
  - NO → Check collected by perpetrator
- Check deposited by vendor
- Vendor pays employee

incentive to provide a low price or quality merchandise. In these circumstances the purchasing company almost always ends up overpaying for goods or services.

> EXAMPLE
>
> *A travel agency provided free travel and entertainment to the purchasing agent of a retail company. In return, the purchasing agent agreed to book all corporate trips through the travel agent. The victim company estimated that it paid $10,000 more for airfare over a two-year period by booking through the corrupt travel agency than if it had used a different company.*

Once a vendor knows it has an exclusive purchasing arrangement, its incentive is to raise prices to cover the cost of the kickback. Most bribery schemes end up as overbilling schemes even if they do not start that way. This is one reason why most business codes of ethics prohibit employees from accepting undisclosed gifts from vendors. In the long run, the employee's company is sure to pay for his unethical conduct.

Overbilling Schemes

EMPLOYEES WITH APPROVAL AUTHORITY

In most instances, kickback schemes begin as overbilling schemes in which a vendor submits inflated invoices to the victim organization. The false invoices either overstate the cost of actual goods and services, or reflect fictitious sales. The vendor in a kickback scheme generally seeks to enlist the help of an employee with the authority to approve payment of the fraudulent invoices. This authority assures payment of the false billings without undue hassles.

> EXAMPLE
>
> *A manager was authorized to purchase fixed assets for his company as part of a leasehold improvement. The materials he ordered were of a cheaper quality and lower price than what was specified, but the contract he negotiated did not reflect this. Therefore, the victim company paid for high-quality materials, but received low-quality materials. The difference in price between the true cost of the low-quality materials and what the company paid was diverted back to the manager as a kickback.*

The ability of the employee to authorize purchases (and thus to authorize *fraudulent* purchases) is usually a key to kickback schemes. If the fraudster can authorize payments himself, he does not have to submit purchase requisitions to an honest superior who might question the validity of the transaction.

FRAUDSTERS LACKING APPROVAL AUTHORITY

While the majority of kickback schemes involve persons with authority to approve purchases, this authority is not an absolute necessity. When an employee cannot approve fraudulent purchases himself, he can still orchestrate a kickback scheme if he can circumvent accounts payable controls. In some cases, all that is required is the filing of a false purchase requisition. If a trusted employee tells his superior that the company needs certain materials or services, this is sometimes sufficient to get a false invoice approved for payment. Such schemes are generally successful when the person with approval authority is inattentive or when he is forced to rely on his subordinate's guidance in purchasing matters.

Corrupt employees might also prepare false vouchers to make it appear that fraudulent invoices are legitimate. Where proper controls are in place, a completed voucher is required before accounts payable will pay an invoice. One key is for the fraudster to create a purchase order that corresponds to the vendor's fraudulent invoice. The fraudster might forge the signature of an authorized party on the purchase order to show that the acquisition has been approved. Where the payables system is computerized, an employee with access to a restricted password can enter the system and authorize payments on fraudulent invoices.

In less sophisticated schemes, a corrupt employee might simply take a fraudulent invoice from a vendor and slip it into a stack of prepared invoices before they are input into the accounts payable system. A more detailed description of how false invoices are processed can be found in the Billing Schemes section.

Kickback schemes can be very difficult to detect. In a sense, the victim company is being attacked from two directions. Externally, a corrupt vendor submits false invoices that induce the victim organization to unknowingly pay for goods or services which it does not receive. Internally, one or more of the victim company's employees waits to corroborate the false information provided by the vendor.

OTHER KICKBACK SCHEMES

Bribes are not always paid to employees to process phony invoices. Some outsiders seek other fraudulent assistance from employees of the victim organization. For instance, inspectors are sometimes paid off to accept substandard materials, or to accept short shipments of goods.

Representatives of companies wishing to purchase goods or services from the victim organization at unauthorized discounts sometimes bribe employees with billing authority. The corrupt employees make sales to their accomplices at greatly reduced rates—sometimes even selling items at a loss—and in return they receive a portion of the discount.

SLUSH FUNDS

It should also be noted that every bribe is a two-sided transaction. In every case where a vendor bribes a purchaser, there is someone on the vendor's side of the transaction who is *making* an illicit payment. It is therefore just as likely that your employees are paying bribes as accepting them.

In order to obtain the funds to make these payments, employees usually divert company money into a slush fund, a noncompany account from which bribes can be made. Assuming that bribes are not authorized by the briber's company, he must find a way to generate the funds necessary to illegally influence someone in another organization. Therefore, the key to the crime from the briber's perspective is the diversion of money into the slush fund. This is a fraudulent disbursement of company funds, which is usually accomplished by the writing of company checks to a fictitious entity or the submitting of false invoices in the name of a false entity. Payments to a slush fund are typically coded as "fees" for consulting or other services.

It is common to charge fraudulent disbursements to nebulous accounts like "consulting fees." The purchase of goods can be verified by a check of inventory, but there is no inventory for these kinds of services. It is therefore more difficult to prove that the payments are fraudulent. The discussion of exactly how fraudulent disbursements are made can be found in the sections on Check Tampering and Invoices.

Bid-Rigging Schemes

As we have said, when one person pays a bribe to another, he does so to gain the benefit of the recipient's influence. The competitive bidding process, in which several suppliers or contractors are vying for contracts in what can be a very cutthroat environment, is tailor-made for bribery. Any advantage one vendor can gain over his competitors in this arena is extremely valuable. The benefit of "inside influence" can ensure that a vendor will win a sought-after contract. Many vendors are willing to pay for this influence.

In the competitive bidding process, all bidders are legally supposed to be placed on the same plane of equality, bidding on the same terms and conditions. Each bidder competes for a contract based on the specifications set forth by the purchasing company. Vendors submit confidential bids stating the price at which they will complete a project in accordance with the purchaser's specifications.

The way competitive bidding is rigged depends largely upon the level of influence of the corrupt employee. The more power a person has over the bidding process, the more likely the person can influence the selection of a supplier. Therefore, employees involved in bid-rigging schemes, like those in kickback schemes, tend to have a good measure of influence or access to the competitive bidding process. Potential targets for accepting bribes include buyers, contracting officials, engineers and technical representatives, quality or product assurance representatives, subcontractor liaison employees, or anyone else with authority over the awarding of contracts.

Bid-rigging schemes can be categorized based on the stage of bidding at which the fraudster exerts his influence. Bid-rigging schemes usually occur in the presolicitation phase, the solicitation phase, or the submission phase of the bidding process. (See "Bid-Rigging" flowchart)

The Presolicitation Phase
In the presolicitation phase of the competitive bidding process—before bids are officially sought for a project—bribery schemes can be broken down into two distinct types. The first is the need recognition scheme, where an employee of a purchasing company is paid to convince his company that a particular project is necessary. The second reason to bribe someone in the presolicitation phase is to have the specifications of the contract tailored to the strengths of a particular supplier.

NEED RECOGNITION SCHEMES
The typical fraud in the need recognition phase of the contract negotiation is a conspiracy between the buyer and contractor where an employee of the buyer receives something of value and in return recognizes a "need" for a particular product or service. The result of

such a scheme is that the victim organization purchases unnecessary goods or services from a supplier at the direction of the corrupt employee.

There are several trends that may indicate a need recognition fraud. Unusually high requirements for stock and inventory levels may reveal a situation in which a corrupt employee is seeking to justify unnecessary purchase activity from a certain supplier. An employee might also justify unnecessary purchases of inventory by writing off large numbers of surplus items to scrap. As these items leave the inventory, they open up spaces to justify additional purchases. Another indicator of a need recognition scheme is the defining of a "need" that can only be met by a certain supplier or contractor. In addition, the failure to develop a satisfactory list of backup suppliers may reveal an unusually strong attachment to a primary supplier—an attachment that is explainable by the acceptance of bribes from that supplier.

SPECIFICATIONS SCHEMES

The other type of presolicitation fraud is a specifications scheme. The specifications of a contract are a list of the elements, materials, dimensions, and other relevant requirements for completion of the project. Specifications are prepared to assist vendors in the bidding process, telling them what they are required to do and providing a firm basis for making and accepting bids.

One corruption scheme that occurs in this process is the fraudulent tailoring of specifications to a particular vendor. In these cases, the vendor pays off an employee of the buyer who is involved in preparing specifications for the contract. In return, the employee tailors the specifications to accommodate that vendor's capabilities so that the contractor is effectively assured of winning the contract.

The methods used to restrict competition in the bidding process may include the use of "prequalification" procedures that are known to eliminate certain competitors. For instance, the bid may require potential contractors to have a certain percentage of female or minority ownership. There is nothing illegal with such a requirement, but if it is placed in the specifications as a result of a bribe rather than as the result of other factors, then the employee has sold his influence to benefit a dishonest vendor, a clear case of corruption.

Bid-Rigging

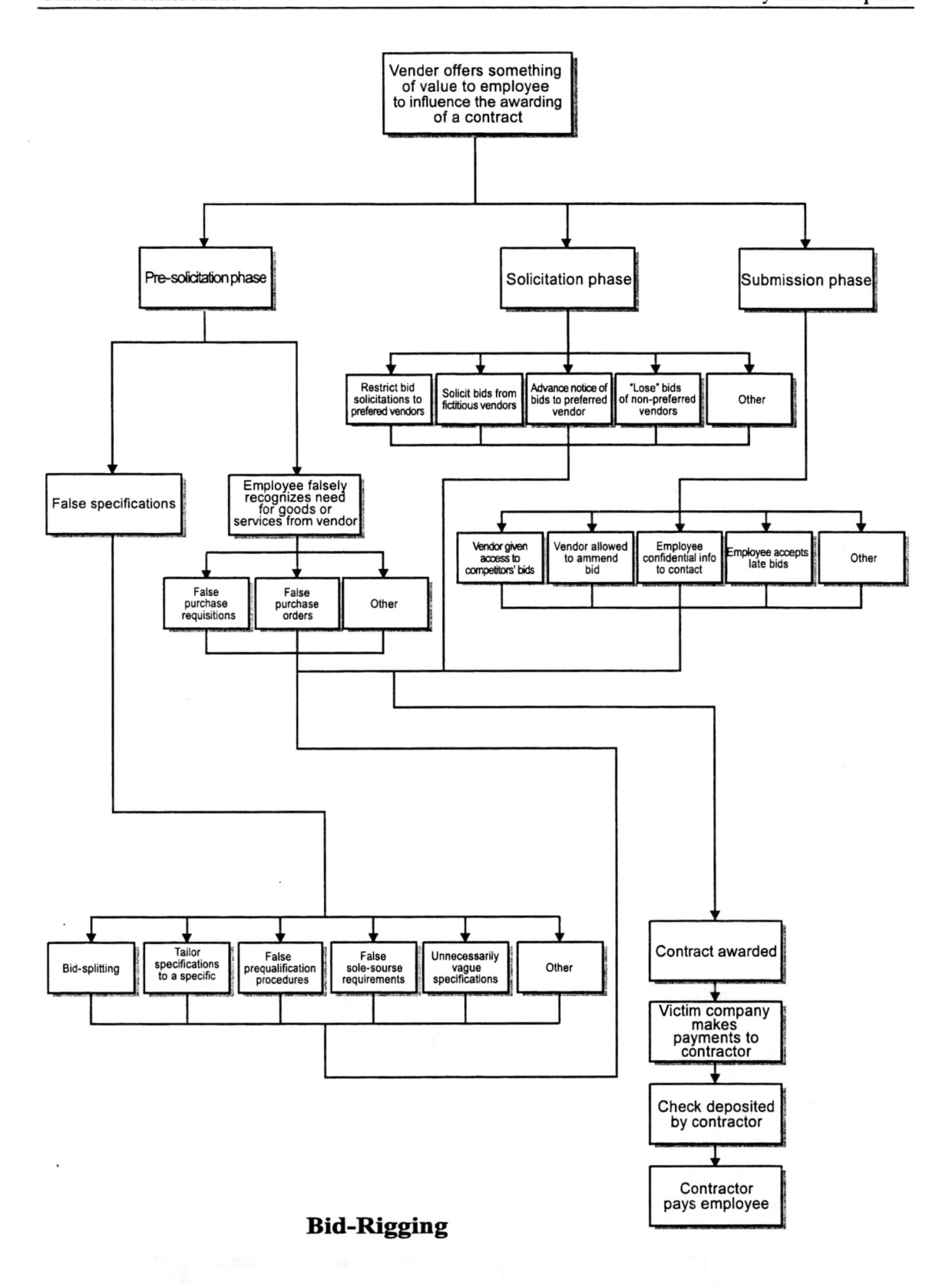

```
                    Vender offers something
                     of value to employee
                      to influence the awarding
                         of a contract
                                │
          ┌─────────────────────┼─────────────────────┐
          ▼                     ▼                     ▼
  Pre-solicitation phase  Solicitation phase   Submission phase
```

Pre-solicitation phase branches to:
- False specifications
- Employee falsely recognizes need for goods or services from vendor
  - False purchase requisitions
  - False purchase orders
  - Other

Solicitation phase branches to:
- Restrict bid solicitations to preferred vendors
- Solicit bids from fictitious vendors
- Advance notice of bids to preferred vendor
- "Lose" bids of non-preferred vendors
- Other

Submission phase branches to:
- Vendor given access to competitors' bids
- Vendor allowed to ammend bid
- Employee confidential info to contact
- Employee accepts late bids
- Other

Pre-solicitation techniques:
- Bid-splitting
- Tailor specifications to a specific
- False prequalification procedures
- False sole-sourse requirements
- Unnecessarily vague specifications
- Other

Final flow:
- Contract awarded
- Victim company makes payments to contractor
- Check deposited by contractor
- Contractor pays employee

Some employees distort the requirements of contracts by claiming the specifications called for a sole-source provider or noncompetitive procurement. This causes competitive bidding to be disregarded and the contract to be awarded to a particular supplier. The supplier typically charges a much higher price than the company could have obtained through bidding. Sole-source or noncompetitive procurement justifications may also be used to eliminate competition and steer contracts to a particular vendor.

EXAMPLE

A requisitioner distorted the requirements of a contract up for bid, claiming the specifications called for a sole-source provider. Based on the requisitioner's information, competitive bidding was disregarded and the contract was awarded to a particular supplier. A review of other bids received at a later date showed that certain materials were available for up to $70,000 less than what the company paid in the sole-source arrangement. The employee had helped divert the job to the contractor in return for a promise of future employment.

Another type of specifications scheme is the deliberate writing of vague specifications. In this type of scheme, a supplier pays an employee of the purchasing company to write specifications that will require amendments at a later date. This will allow the supplier to raise the price of the contract when the amendments are made. As the buyer's needs become more specific or more detailed, the vendor can claim that, had he known what the buyer actually wanted, his bid on the project would have been higher. In order to complete the project as defined by the amended specifications, the supplier will need more money.

Another form of specifications fraud is bid splitting. Government entities are often required to solicit bids on projects over a certain dollar amount. In order to avoid this requirement, employees might break a large project up into several small projects that fall below the mandatory bidding level. Once the contract is split, the employee can award some or all of the component parts to a contractor with whom he is conspiring.

A less egregious but nevertheless unfair form of bid-rigging occurs when a vendor pays an employee of the buyer for the right to see the specifications earlier than his competitors. The employee does not alter the specifications to suit the vendor, but instead simply gives him a head start on planning his bid and preparing for the job.

The Solicitation Phase

In the solicitation phase of the competitive bidding process, fraudsters attempt to influence the selection of a contractor by restricting the pool of competitors from whom bids are sought. In other words, a corrupt vendor pays an employee of the purchasing company to assure that one or more of the vendor's competitors do not get to bid on the contract. In this manner, the corrupt vendor is able to improve his chances of winning the job.

One type of scheme involves the sales representative who deals on behalf of a number of potential bidders. The sales representative bribes a contracting official to rig the solicitation, ensuring that only those companies represented by him get to submit bids. It is not uncommon in some sectors for buyers to "require" bidders to be represented by certain sales or manufacturing representatives. These representatives pay a kickback to the buyer to protect their clients' interests. The result of this transaction is that the purchasing company is deprived of the ability to get the best price on its contract. Typically, the group of "protected" vendors will not actually compete against each other for the purchaser's contracts, but instead engage in "bid pooling."

BID POOLING

Bid pooling is a process by which several bidders conspire to split contracts up and assure that each gets a certain amount of work. Instead of submitting confidential bids, the vendors discuss what their bids will be so they can guarantee that each vendor will win a share of the purchasing company's business. For example, if vendors A, B, and C are up for three separate jobs, they may agree that A's bid will be the lowest on the first contract, B's bid will be the lowest on the second contract, and C's bid will be the lowest on the third contract. None of the vendors gets all three jobs, but on the other hand, they are all guaranteed to get at least one. Furthermore, since they plan their bids ahead of time, the vendors can conspire to raise their prices. Thus the purchasing company suffers as a result of the scheme.

FICTITIOUS SUPPLIERS

Another way to eliminate competition in the solicitation phase of the selection process is to solicit bids from fictitious suppliers. This gives the appearance of a competitive bidding situation, when in fact only one real supplier bids on the job. Furthermore, the real contractor can hike up his prices, since the other bids are fraudulent and sure to be higher than his own. In effect, the bids from fictitious suppliers serve to validate the exaggerated quote from the real contractor.

OTHER METHODS

In some cases, competition for a contract can be limited by severely restricting the time for submitting bids. Certain suppliers are given advanced notice of contracts before bids are solicited. These suppliers are therefore able to begin preparing their bids ahead of time. With the short time frame for developing bid proposals, the supplier with advance knowledge of the contract will have a decided advantage over his competition.

Bribed purchasing officials can also restrict competition for their co-conspirators by soliciting bids in obscure publications where other vendors are unlikely to see them. Again, this is done to eliminate potential rivals and create an advantage for the corrupt suppliers. Some schemes have also involved the publication of bid solicitations during holiday periods when those suppliers not "in the know" are unlikely to be looking for potential contracts. In more blatant cases, the bids of outsiders are accepted but are "lost" or improperly disqualified by the corrupt employee of the purchaser.

Typically, when a vendor bribes an employee of the purchasing company to assist him in any kind of solicitation scheme, the cost of the bribe is included in the corrupt vendor's bid. Therefore, the purchasing company ends up bearing the cost of the illicit payment in the form of a higher contract price.

The Submission Phase

In the actual submission phase of the process, where bids are proffered to the buyer, several schemes may be used to win a contract for a particular supplier. The principal offense tends to be abuse of the sealed bid process. Competitive bids are confidential; they are, of course, supposed to remain sealed until a specified date at which all bids are opened and reviewed by the purchasing company. The person or persons who have access to sealed bids are often the targets of unethical vendors seeking an advantage in the process.

EXAMPLE

Gifts and cash payments were given to a majority owner of a company in exchange for preferential treatment during the bidding process. The supplier who paid the bribes was allowed to submit his bids last, knowing what prices his competitors had quoted, or in the alternative, he was allowed to actually see his competitors' bids and adjust his own accordingly.

Vendors also bribe employees of the purchaser for confidential information that will help them prepare their bid. Other reasons to bribe employees of the purchaser include to ensure receipt of a late bid or falsify the bid log, to extend the bid opening date, and to control bid openings.

Economic Extortion

Economic extortion cases are the "Pay up or else ..." corruption schemes; basically the flip side of bribery schemes. Instead of a vendor offering a payment to influence a decision, an employee demands that a vendor pay him in order to make a decision in that vendor's favor. If the vendor refuses to pay, he faces some harm such as a loss of business with the extorter's company. In any situation where an employee might accept bribes to favor a particular company or person, the situation could be reversed to a point where the employee extorts money from a potential purchaser or supplier.

EXAMPLE

A plant manager for a utility company started his own business on the side. Vendors who wanted to do work for the utility company were forced by the manager to divert some of their business to his own company. Those that did not "play ball" lost their business with the utility.

Illegal Gratuities

Illegal gratuities are similar to bribery schemes except there is not necessarily an intent to influence a particular business decision before the fact. In the typical illegal gratuities scenario, a decision is made which happens to benefit a certain person or company. The party who benefited from the decision then gives a gift to the person who made the decision. The gift could be anything of value. An illegal gratuity does not require proof of an intent to influence.

EXAMPLE

A city commissioner negotiated a land development deal with a group of private investors. After the deal was approved, the commissioner and his wife were rewarded with a free international vacation, all expenses paid.

At first glance, it may seem that illegal gratuities schemes are harmless as long as the business decisions in question are not influenced by the promise of payment. But most company ethics policies forbid employees from accepting unreported gifts from vendors. One reason is that illegal gratuities schemes can (and do) evolve into bribery schemes. Once an employee has been rewarded for an act such as directing business to a particular supplier, an understanding might be reached that future decisions beneficial to the supplier will also be rewarded. Additionally, even though an outright promise of payment has not been made, employees may direct business to certain companies in the hope that they will be rewarded with money or gifts.

Methods of Making Illegal Payments

Certain traditional methods of making illegal payments fall into the hierarchical pattern described below.

Gifts, Travel, and Entertainment

Most bribery (corruption) schemes begin with gifts and favors. Commonly encountered items include:

- Wine and liquor (consumable)
- Clothes and jewelry for the recipient or spouse
- Sexual favors
- Lavish entertainment
- Paid vacations
- Free transportation on corporate jets
- Free use of resort facilities
- Gifts of the briber's inventory or services, such as construction of home improvements by a contractor

Cash Payments

The next step usually involves cash payments. However, cash is not practical when dealing with large sums, because large amounts are difficult to generate, and they draw attention when they are deposited or spent. The use of currency in major transactions might itself be incriminating.

Checks and Other Financial Instruments

As the scheme grows, illicit payments often are made by normal business check, cashier's check, or wire transfer. Disguised payments on the payer's books appear as some sort of legitimate business expense, often as consulting fees. Payments can be made directly or through an intermediary.

Hidden Interests

In the latter stages of sophisticated schemes, the payer might give a hidden interest in a joint venture or other profit-making enterprise. The recipient's interest might be concealed through a straw nominee, hidden in a trust or other business entity, or merely included by an undocumented verbal agreement. Such arrangements are very difficult to detect, and even if identified, proof of corrupt intent might be difficult to demonstrate.

Loans

Three types of "loans" often turn up in fraud cases:
- A prior outright payment falsely described as an innocent loan.
- Payments on a legitimate loan guaranteed or actually made by someone else.
- An actual loan made on favorable terms, such as interest-free.

Payment of Credit Card Bills

The recipient's transportation, vacation, and entertainment expenses might be paid with the payer's credit card, or the recipient might forward his own credit card bills to the payer for payment. In some instances, the payer simply lets the recipient carry and use the payer's card.

Transfers at Other than Fair Market Value

The corrupt payer might sell or lease property to the recipient at far less than its market value, or might agree to buy or rent property at inflated prices. The recipient also might "sell" an asset to the payer, but retain title or the use of the property.

Promises of Favorable Treatment

Promises of favorable treatment commonly take the following forms:
- A payer might promise a governmental official lucrative employment when the recipient leaves government service.
- An executive leaving a private company for a related government position might be given favorable or inflated retirement and separation benefits.
- The spouse or other relative of the intended recipient also might be employed by the payer company at an inflated salary or with little actual responsibility.

Detection

Red Flags of Bribery Schemes

Most bribery schemes are detected through tips from honest and disgruntled co-workers or vendors. These allegations can be evaluated through analysis of the "red flags" associated with the suspect people or transactions.

The Corrupt Recipient

A person taking payoffs or embezzling funds often exhibits the following characteristics:

- *The Big Spender* – This is the most common way to detect corrupt recipients. Some recipients spend their money less conspicuously by paying off debts or paying down mortgages.
- *The Gift Taker* – An official or executive who regularly accepts inappropriate gifts is often one susceptible to larger payments.
- *The "Odd Couple"* – Corrupt payers and recipients often appear to have very friendly social relationships. Frequent outside contacts, particularly between parties who do not appear to have much in common, might be a sign of deeper and more troublesome ties between the parties.
- *The Rule Breaker* – This is often the most significant characteristic. A person taking payoffs often will take action on his own, or direct a subordinate to bend, break, or ignore standard operating procedures or rules to benefit the payer. Particular attention should be directed toward those who insert themselves into areas in which they normally are not involved or attempt to assert authority or make decisions for which they are not responsible.
- *The Complainer* – A corrupt recipient often makes excuses for deficiencies in the payer's services, such as poor quality, late deliveries, or high prices. Look for higher prices, "extra" payments, or commissions approved by the suspect, because these might be the source of kickback fraud.
- *Genuine Need* – Greed, rather than need, seems to be the motivating factor in most cases. Occasionally, however, legitimate pressures, such as illness of family members or drug addiction, can induce participation in an illegal scheme.

The Corrupt Payer

Like the recipients of bribery payments, the payer also will demonstrate certain identifiable characteristics:

- *The Gift Bearer* – The businessperson who routinely offers inappropriate gifts, provides lavish business entertainment, or otherwise tries to ingratiate himself often is the one offering still more valuable inducements.
- *The Sleaze Factor* – The corrupt payer frequently is a person known or suspected in the industry to be involved in payoffs or other fraudulent activities.
- *The Too-Successful Bidder* – A supplier who consistently is awarded work, without any apparent competitive advantage, might be providing under-the-table incentives.
- *Poor Quality, Higher Prices* – Particularly after the corrupt relationship has been sealed, the quality of product and service provided by the payer might deteriorate and prices increase.
- *The One-Person Operation* – In certain industries, small, closely held companies that do not have the reporting and internal control requirements of their larger, publicly held competitors resort to payoffs as a means of marketing advantage. Be alert for independent sales representatives, consultants, or other middlemen, because they are favored conduits for funneling and concealing illegal payments.

General Purchasing

The following practices may indicate that single (sole) source vendors are being favored, or competitive bidding policies are not being followed:

- Materials are not being ordered at the optimal reorder point.
- Orders are consistently made from the same vendor.
- Established bidding policies are not being followed.
- The costs of materials are out of line.

Presolicitation

Restrictions in an organization's solicitation documents that tend to restrict competition are a red flag. Examples of restrictive conditions include:

- Specifications and statements of work which are tailored to fit the products or capabilities of a single contractor.
- "Prequalification" procedures that restrict competition.
- Unnecessary sole-source or noncompetitive procurement justifications:
  – Containing false statements
  – Signed by unauthorized officials
  – Bypassing necessary review procedures

Other red flags in the presolicitation phase include:
- A buyer who provides information or advice to a contractor on a preferential basis.
- New vendors that are added to the "qualified" list for no apparent reason.
- Statements of work, specifications, or sole-source justifications that are developed by, or in consultation with, a contractor who will be permitted to bid.
- Consultants who assisted in the preparation of the statements of work, specifications or design, and are later permitted to work on the contract as subcontractors or consultants.
- Projects that are split into smaller contracts to avoid review.
- Information that is released by firms participating in the design and engineering to contractors competing for the prime contract.
- Requirements that are split up so contractors can each get a "fair share" and can rotate bids.
- Specifications that are not consistent with similar procurements in the past.

Bid Solicitation

The following are examples of suspicious activity that might signal fraud in the bid solicitation phase:
- The time for submitting bids is limited so that only those with advance information have adequate time to prepare bids or proposals.
- One contractor receives confidential information which is not revealed to his competitors.
- The conducting of a bidders' conference which permits improper communications between contractors, who then are in a position to rig bids.
- The failure to ensure that a sufficient number of potential competitors are aware of the solicitation by:
  - Using obscure publications to publish bid solicitations
  - Publishing bid solicitations during holiday periods
- Bid solicitations which are vague as to the time, place, or other requirements for submitting acceptable bids.
- Inadequate internal controls over the number and destination of bid packages sent to interested bidders.
- Improper communication between purchasers and contractors at trade or professional meetings.
- Improper social contact with between purchasers and contractor representatives.
- A purchasing agent who has a financial interest in the business of a contractor.
- A purchaser who discusses possible employment with a contractor.

- The purchaser assisting a contractor in the preparation of his bid.
- A contractor being referred to a specific subcontractor, expert, or source of supply by an employee of the purchasing organization.
- The failure to amend a solicitation to include necessary changes or clarifications in the bid, such as telling one contractor of changes that can be made after the bid.
- The falsification of documents or receipts so that a late bid is accepted.
- Any indications of collusion between bidders.
- The falsification of a contractor's qualifications, work history, facilities, equipment, or personnel.

Bid Submission or Contract Acceptance

Red flags in the submission and post-submission phase of the bidding process include the following:

- Procurement that has been restricted to exclude or hamper any qualified contractor.
- The improper acceptance of a late bid.
- A bidder who always bids last on contracts and consistently wins them.
- The falsification of documents or receipts to get a late bid accepted.
- Bids that are changed after other bidders' prices are known. This is sometimes done by mistakes deliberately "planted" in a bid.
- A low bidder who withdraws to become a subcontractor of a higher bidder who gets the contract.
- Collusion between bidders.
- Bidders who reveal their prices to one another.
- Bids tend to be awarded in a geographic pattern or in a noticeable rotation.
- Bids for a particular type of work are always awarded to a particular company.
- False certifications by a contractor.
- The falsification of information concerning contractor qualifications, financial capability, facilities, ownership of equipment and supplies, qualifications of personnel, and successful performance of previous jobs, etc.

Methods of Proving Corrupt Payments

There are three basic ways to prove illegal payments: identify and trace them by audit steps, turn an inside witness, or secretly infiltrate or record ongoing transactions. An audit might focus on the point of suspected payment or receipt, or both. As a very general proposition, suspected on-book schemes are best approached from the point of payment, and off-book schemes are most easily identified at the suspected point of receipt, or through the use of an inside witness, or surveillance.

The Business Profile—Analysis

The *business profile* begins the examination process. It identifies prospective witnesses and targets, as well as relevant documents and transactions, and should provide leads as to whether an on-book or off-book scheme is being used.

Information of the suspect business should be obtained about the organization, personnel, money flow pattern (source of available funds, related expenditures, etc.), location of bank accounts, financial condition, and recordkeeping system. This information can be obtained through interview of employees, customers, and competitors; business bank account and loan records; financial statements; tax returns; business reporting companies; and business public filings.

HOW IS THE BUSINESS ORGANIZED, LEGALLY AND STRUCTURALLY?

Knowing this information helps determine what records are available (corporate, partnership, etc.) and where to go to get them.

WHO ARE THE KEY PERSONNEL ASSOCIATED WITH THE ENTERPRISE?

This helps to identify potential witnesses and informants, as well as possible subjects. Key positions include the owners of the business; the people directly involved in the suspect transactions, including secretarial and clerical staff, present and former employees; the "number crunchers"; the bookkeeper, outside accountants, and tax preparers; outside consultants, sales representatives, and independent contractors (a popular conduit for payoffs); and competitors (often eager witnesses who can identify leads to sources of off-book funds such as customers and rebate practices).

WHAT IS THE MONEY FLOW PATTERN INVOLVED IN THE SUSPECT TRANSACTION?

Tracing the flow of funds in the suspect transactions is important. Where does the money come from and where does it go? Information about the source of funds can provide leads as to whether an on-book or off-book scheme is being employed, and the location of off-book accounts. Expenditures related to the suspect transactions might cover on-book payments.

Determine all sources of funds with the following questions:
- What goods or services does the business provide?
- Who are its customers or clients?
- What mode of payment is used: cash or check?
- What other sources of funds are available, such as rebates from suppliers and shippers, or proceeds of insurance claims, liquidation sales, sale of assets, and loans?

Identify all expenditures associated with the suspect transactions with the following:
- What disbursements are made to third parties, such as commissioned sales agents, consultants, subcontractors, suppliers, and shippers?
- Did the business have any extraordinary expenses during the suspect time period, such as extra commissions, advertising allowances (payments made by a manufacturer to the retail customer to assist the customer in meeting its advertising expenses), or inventory losses?
- How are the expenses and disbursements paid: by cash, or by check? From which accounts?
- Does the business maintain an account or fund used to pay miscellaneous expenses? If so, where is it located, who keeps the records, and who signs the checks or authorizes payments?
- How are travel and entertainment expenses reimbursed? From which account?
- What is the company's policy toward business gifts? What gifts were given to the suspect and/or recipients? How were they paid for? Which records are maintained regarding them?

WHERE ARE THE COMPANY'S BANK ACCOUNTS?
Find out where the business deposits its receipts. This is quickly determined from the bank stamp on checks deposited from customers. Identify all company accounts by bank, account number, and authorized signature.

WHAT IS THE FINANCIAL CONDITION OF THE BUSINESS?
This data might provide evidence of a motive for the fraud, or the fruits thereof.

WHAT IS THE COMPANY'S RECORD-KEEPING SYSTEM?
What kind of records does the company keep? For how long, and where are they kept? Who maintains them?

Sources of Information for the Business Profile

PRINCIPALS, EMPLOYEES, AND RECORDS OF SUSPECT BUSINESS

People suspected of making illegal payments might submit to an interview, particularly if they are confident that the payments are well hidden. Interviews also should include other key employees (including the financial personnel) involved in the suspect transactions, particularly those who have since left the company. Use the Business Profile as a guide to questioning.

CUSTOMERS AND COMPETITORS

In a kickback case, the "customer" (agency) is the employer of the person taking payoffs, and is also the victim of the crime. Customers and competitors can provide valuable information about the payer's business operation, particularly concerning the payer's regular bank account, which can be identified through canceled checks. The customer also might have invoices and shipping documents that might lead to off-book funds.

BANKS AND LENDING INSTITUTIONS

The business' banker might have credit applications, financial statements, loan files, and bank account information that might help the examiner.

BUSINESS REPORTING COMPANIES

Dun & Bradstreet and other commercial reporting companies disseminate basic information about the size, structure, sales, and employees of the business. Information about larger companies is found in Standard & Poors and other business directories. See also other public record information in the Investigation section.

Proving On-Book Payments

There are three basic methods for concealing on-book payments of bribes and/or kickbacks. They are fictitious payables, ghost employees, and overbilling. The following are the examination steps for identifying and tracing these payments.

Fictitious Disbursement Schemes

In order to examine on-book payments, obtain the following records from the entity suspected of making the illegal payments:

BANK ACCOUNT INFORMATION
- All records of payments, canceled checks, wire transfer receipts, receipts for the purchase of cashier's checks and money orders, and withdrawal slips
- Check registers
- Account statements

SALES BACKUP DOCUMENTATION
- Purchase orders
- Invoices
- Documents showing receipt of goods ordered

ACCOUNTING BOOKS AND RECORDS

Examine the cash disbursement journals and ledgers. The most important of the above information (and often the only information needed) is the bank account information. Begin by examining the checks, check register, and/or the cash disbursement journal and paying particular attention to the following:

- *Payables and Expenses Charged to the Account (Customer) on which the Illicit Payments were Made* — If the examiner suspects that kickbacks were paid on sales to the ABC Corporation, for example, look at the payables and expenses charged to that account/customer.
- *Payments for Services* — Check payments for services such as sales commissions or consulting fees, which do not require the delivery of goods and need relatively little documentation to obtain payment.
- *Anomalous Charges* — For the business, an example of anomalous payments can be those for design fees paid by a company that is engaged in business that normally would not require such services.
- *The Endorsement on the Check* — This might be by signature, or more commonly, by a stamp in the name of the business payee. Note the identity of the endorser. (Some corrupt recipients have been known to endorse such checks in their own name.)
- *The Location where the Check was Negotiated* — If not obvious from the endorsement, identify the bank where the deposit was made by checking the depository bank's stamp on the back of the check. The geographical location of the depository bank is an important lead that can connect the check to the suspected recipient. Determining the depository bank's identity is critical to obtaining the recipient's bank account information.
- *Checks with a Second Endorsement* — A typical indication of a phony payable check is one paid to, and endorsed by, a business, which is then endorsed by an individual, thereby

permitting it to be cashed or deposited in a personal account. In similar fashion, a check payable to a third-party can be signed over to the issuer of the check.

- *Cashed (not deposited) Checks Payable to a Business* — Generally, a "For Deposit Only" stamp appears on the back of deposited checks, although this is not always the case. Most banks have a code stamp which indicates whether the check was cashed or not. These codes vary, and can be obtained from the bank where the check was negotiated.
- *Checks which Fall into an Unexplained Pattern* — An example of a suspicious payable scheme is one where checks are drawn once a month in an amount equal to some percentage of the sales against which they are charged, and are not otherwise explained. Such a pattern might indicate a kickback scheme. If an examination of the checks themselves does not yield any clear leads, compare the various records of payment with the backup documentation. Note particularly the following circumstances:
- *The Absence of Documentation* — The absence of documentation to support a particular payment can include:
  - No invoice appearing in the files for a payment to a supplier or contractor
  - No receipt to indicate that materials paid for were delivered
  - No consultant's work product to substantiate consulting fees paid
- *Discrepancies* — Discrepancies between payment information and backup documentation can include:
  - A check payable to a supplier in an amount different than his invoice
  - A check payable to a person or entity different than that identified on the invoice
- *Anomalies in Support Documents* — Anomalies in the backup documentation can include invoices from several suppliers in different names that:
  - Have the same business address
  - Are signed by the same person
  - Returned to a post office box
- *Unnumbered or Sequentially Numbered Invoices* — An example of invoice scam uses invoices numbered "101," "102," and "103," which are dated 30 days apart. Of course, it is highly unlikely that a legitimate business would refrain from issuing invoices in the interim.
- *Alterations* — Copies of originals can be made for concealing alterations of original documents. Examples can include alterations or photocopies of backup papers.
- *Location and Other Information on the Invoices that Tie it to the Suspected Recipient* — If the above steps still do not yield any suspect payments, return to the check registers and cash disbursement journals to look for discrepancies between the entries and the checks or backup documentation, or their absence. The register and journals also might indicate the purpose of payments made by wire, cashier's check, or cash.

TRACING PROCEDURES

When a suspect payment has been isolated, begin the tracing process. Remember that the phony payable might go directly to the recipient (deposited in a shell account), or through an intermediary account, person, or entity. It might even be converted to cash by the payer, and the cash given to the recipient.

In instances where the identity of the individual recipient is not clear from the face of the check (as in checks payable to a business entity), do the following:

- Examine the back of the check. Note where the check was deposited, and the account number, if available. If the check is not endorsed, the bank still will be able to locate the account to which it was deposited through its own internal records.
- Obtain the records of the account where the check was deposited. The signature card and the monthly account statement will show the nominal account holder. In the case of business accounts, the bank also should have a copy of the corporate resolution or partnership agreement authorizing the account.
- If the identity of the individual recipient still is not clear, check the public filings required of business entities to determine ownership. Corporate documents (articles of incorporation, annual reports, and some other basic documents) and limited partnerships also might be filed in some jurisdictions at the county level. The fictitious name index, business license files, telephone billing records, and even utility billing records also can lead to the identity of the principals.
- If the original check is missing or has been destroyed, a microfilm copy can be obtained from the bank on which the check was drawn. (The bank where the check was deposited will also have a microfilm copy of the check. Unless the exact date of deposit and the identity of the depository bank are known, it will be very difficult to locate it.)
- Payments by wire transfer or cashier's check can be traced to the recipient. A wire transfer from an account appears on that account statement as a *debit memo* (often abbreviated as *DM*). The *Wire Transfer Request* should show the name of the purchaser, the payee, and the bank and account number to which the funds were transferred. The sender receives a copy of this request, and the bank also maintains a copy, which usually is filed by date.
- The bank's retained copy of a cashier's check will identify the payee. The bank also keeps the negotiated check when it is returned for payment. It will contain the endorsement and show where it was negotiated. Banks usually file cashier's checks by number, making it necessary to know the approximate date they were issued to link them to the purchasers. Look for a cashier's check or wire transfer on the dates of suspect cash

withdrawals, checks to cash, or checks to the issuing bank. Remember that such instruments can be purchased for cash from any bank, not only from the bank where the payer's account is located.
- If the trail described above leads to an intermediary, the entire process must be repeated.

Ghost Employee Schemes

Illicit funds can be generated by funneling phony salary payments to fictitious or former employees, or by making extra payments to presently salaried employees who then either return them to the payer or pass them on to the recipient. This is in addition to ghost employee schemes used for embezzlement, described previously. To trace such payments, payroll and employee lists, personnel files, employment applications, tax withholding forms, and payroll checks should be obtained from the suspect payer company.

Attempt to identify the ghost through the following steps:
- Compare a list of all current and former employees from the personnel office to the payroll list. Note discrepancies. Determine whether any employees have failed to execute tax withholding forms, or have not elected to receive any health benefits or other optional withdrawals, such as enforced savings plans. The absence of such elections is often an indication that the employee does not exist.
- A regular employee's normal salary also might be inflated, or, more commonly, travel and expense reimbursements might be padded to generate illicit funds. Look for unusual disbursements from the accounts in which such checks are deposited.

Once a suspect paycheck has been identified, determine whether the check was cashed or deposited. Note the endorsement, the bank, and account where the check was deposited. Determine whether there are any second endorsements which might transfer the check to the ultimate recipient.

Overbilling Schemes

As described above, illicit funds might be added to legitimate payments for goods or services provided by actual suppliers, subcontractors, engineers, and agents, with the additional amounts being passed on by the supplier or returned to the payer (usually in cash) for distribution.

Obtain the same records required for tracing phony payables—bank account information, backup documentation, and accounting records—from both the original payer and the intermediary. Note the following indicators of suspect payments to the intermediary:

- Notations on invoices or other billing documents breaking out "extra" or "special" charges, particularly those which require no delivery of goods for payment.
- Discrepancies between the purchase order or invoice amounts and the amount of payment. Particularly note invoices which appear to have been altered or copied.
- Unusually large amounts appearing on particular bills, or bills which break a consistent pattern of amounts, schedule, or purpose.

Disbursements from the intermediary might be covered in the same ways as in other on-book schemes, such as by means of phony payables, direct cash withdrawals or disbursements charged to miscellaneous accounts, such as travel or entertainment. The tracing process is the same as in any on-book scheme. Remember that the overbilling entity usually will add its own fee for providing such services. Therefore, the disbursements coming from its account might not be in the same amount as the additional payments made to it.

Proving Off-Book Payments

Identifying and tracing off-book payments usually is more difficult than locating on-book schemes. Success generally depends upon identifying the source of the funds or accounts (from which payments can be traced out), using an inside witness, and focusing on the point of receipt. The source of off-book funds might be located by the following:

Indirect Evidence of Unrecorded Sales on the Suspect Company's Books and Records

The suspect company's books and records might reflect unusual costs and expenses not associated with the business' known sales, such as rental payments for an undisclosed warehouse, shipping documents reflecting deliveries to an unlisted customer, and commissions paid to sales agents in a region where sales are not reported. These indicate possible unrecorded sales.

Unbalanced Ratios of Costs to Sales

The cost of producing and selling a particular item usually bears some fixed relationship to the revenue it generates. A significant imbalance in such a ratio, such as in a situation where twice the supplies are ordered than are needed to produce the reported sales (and the extra is not located in inventory), indicates possible unrecorded transactions. This technique is used to identify unreported sales by bars and restaurants.

Investigation in the Marketplace

Customers of the suspect business whose payments might have been diverted to off-book accounts might have records, including canceled checks, which would reflect such sales, and the bank and account to which the funds were deposited. Customers also might reveal cash payments which could be used to create a slush fund. Additionally, competitors might be aware of other customers and transactions which could lead to evidence of off-book sales.

Proving Payments in Cash

The following techniques can be used to prove cash payments circumstantially, or to corroborate testimony of such payments by an inside witness:

- Match evidence of cash withdrawals or disbursements by the payer with corresponding deposits, expenditures, or visits to a safe deposit box by the recipient.
- Look for the purchase of cashier's checks, traveler's checks, or wire transfers payable to the recipient at, or shortly after, cash withdrawals or disbursements. Also look for a correlation between cash-generating transactions and money wires or courier services, which sometimes are used to send cash.
- If the scheme is ongoing, consider the use of visual or electronic surveillance (if you're a member of law enforcement), or try to introduce an undercover agent or implement a sting operation.
- Unexplained or unusual cash disbursements or withdrawals, particularly from a business which does not normally deal in cash, might itself indicate illicit transactions, or corroborate such testimony. To be effective, the examiner must identify and rebut all legitimate explanations, which usually requires interviewing the payer.
- Focus the investigation on the suspected recipient, as discussed below.

EXAMINATION FROM THE POINT OF RECEIPT

Often, the only practical approach to identifying and tracing illegal payments is to focus on the suspected recipient, particularly if the person making the payments is unknown, one person is suspected of taking from many, the payments are in cash or from off-book funds, and so on.

THE FINANCIAL/BEHAVIORAL PROFILE

The Financial/Behavioral Profile is outlined in the "Tracing Illicit Transactions" chapter in the Investigation section. The Financial Profile will identify most illicit funds deposited to accounts or expended in significant amounts. It will not reveal relatively small currency transactions, particularly if they were for concealed activities, consumables, or unusual one-time expenses, such as medical bills. The Financial Profile might give inaccurate or false negative readings unless such activities are identified. This is done through preparation of the Behavioral Profile. During the interview be alert and review documents for signs that the target has:

- A drug and/or alcohol addiction
- A gambling habit
- Loan shark or other private debts
- A girlfriend (or boyfriend) supported by the target
- Extraordinary medical expenses
- Significant, regular cash expenses for entertainment and/or travel

The Behavioral Profile also might provide evidence of a possible motive of the crime, such as large debts, as well as additional evidence of illicit funds. For example, if the suspect spent significant amounts of cash, and had no corresponding cash withdrawals from disclosed bank accounts or no admitted sources of cash income, *there must be* other, undisclosed sources of income.

THE SUSPECT RECIPIENT

An interview should almost always be requested with the target. Use the Financial/Behavioral Profile as a guide. Pin down the target's income, assets, and accounts. If the witness claims to have legitimate sources of large sums of currency, determine the following:

- What was the source of the cash?
- What was the amount of cash on hand at the starting point of the investigation, at the end of each year thereafter, and on the date of the interview?
- Where was the cash kept?
- Why was the cash not deposited in a financial institution or invested?
- Who knew about the cash?
- What records of the cash exist?
- What were the denominations?
- When and for what was any of the cash spent?

- Will the subject consent to an inventory of the remaining cash during the interview? If not, why not? If so, the cash should be counted at least twice in the presence of another examiner. A list of serial and series numbers also should be made.

If the witness testifies that suspect funds were legitimate loan proceeds, ask:
- Who was the lender?
- When was the loan made?
- What was the amount of the loan?
- What was the purpose of the loan?
- Was the loan repaid?
- How was the loan documented?

Also attempt to interview the subject's spouse separately. Although one spouse generally will not be required to testify against the other, spouses can be an important source of lead information—if handled carefully.

THIRD-PARTY WITNESSES

Potential third-party sources include business colleagues, personal associates, bankers, brokers, real estate agents, accountants and tax preparers, ex-spouses, and romantic interests (particularly former romantic interests). Subjects often boast to their close associates of their new wealth, or entertain them with the fruits thereof. Casual remarks by a subject to a colleague (and repeated to an examiner) have undone the suspect, even when intensive audits have failed. Follow the Financial/Behavioral Profile format to the extent feasible. Of course, no single third-party witness is likely to possess all this information, but a complete picture can be assembled from bits and pieces provided by a number of such sources.

TRACING ILLICIT TRANSACTIONS

Other techniques for tracing illicit payments can be found in the Investigation Section in the chapter on "Tracing Illicit Transactions."

Conflicts of Interest

Conflict of interest schemes generally constitute violations of the legal principal that a fiduciary, agent, or employee must act in good faith, with full disclosure, and in the best interest of the principal or employer. A conflict of interest occurs when an employee, manager, or executive has an undisclosed economic or personal interest in a transaction that adversely affects that person's employer. As with other corruption frauds, conflict schemes involve the exertion of an employee's influence to the detriment of his company. In bribery schemes, fraudsters are paid to exercise their influence on behalf of a third-party. Conflict cases instead involve self-dealing by an employee.

If an employee engages in a transaction that involves a conflict of interest, then the employee might also have breached his *fiduciary duty* to his employer. An agent (employee) owes a fiduciary duty (*duty of loyalty*) to the principal (employer). The agent must act solely in the best interest of the principal and cannot seek to advance personal interest to the detriment of the principal.

Breach of fiduciary duty is a civil action that can be used to redress a wide variety of conduct that might also constitute fraud, commercial bribery, and conflicts of interest. The elements of proof of breach of fiduciary duty are considerably simpler than fraud, and do not require proof of wrongful intent. As in conflicts of interest, the wrongdoer must reimburse the principal for any losses and pay over profits earned, even if the principal suffered no loss.

The vast majority of conflicts cases occur because the fraudster has an undisclosed economic interest in a transaction. But the fraudster's hidden interest is not *necessarily* economic. In some scenarios an employee acts in a manner detrimental to his company in order to provide a benefit to a friend or relative, even though the fraudster receives no financial benefit from the transaction himself.

In order to be classified as a conflict of interest scheme, the employee's interest in the transaction must be undisclosed. The crux of a conflict case is that the fraudster takes advantage of his employer; the victim organization is unaware that its employee has divided loyalties. If an employer knows of the employee's interest in a business deal or negotiation, there can be no conflict of interest, no matter how favorable the arrangement is for the employee.

Any bribery scheme we discussed in the previous section could occur as a conflict of interest. The only difference is the fraudster's motive. For instance, if an employee approves payment on a fraudulent invoice submitted by a vendor in return for a kickback, this is bribery. If, on the other hand, an employee approves payment on invoices submitted by his own company (and if his ownership is undisclosed), this is a conflict of interest.

The distinction between the two schemes is obvious. In the bribery case the fraudster approves the invoice in return for a kickback, while in a conflict case he approves the invoice because of his own hidden interest in the vendor. Aside from the employee's motive for committing the crime, the mechanics of the two transactions are practically identical. The same duality can be found in bid-rigging cases, where an employee influences the selection of a company in which he has a hidden interest instead of influencing the selection of a vendor who has bribed him.

Conflict schemes do not always simply mirror bribery schemes, though. There are a numbers of ways in which an employee can use his influence to benefit a company in which he has a hidden interest. This section will discuss some of the more common conflict schemes.

Purchase Schemes

Purchase schemes are very similar to the billing schemes discussed in the Asset Misappropriation section, so it will be helpful at this point to discuss the distinction we have drawn between traditional billing schemes and purchasing schemes that are conflicts of interest.

While it is true that any time an employee assists in the overbilling of his company there is probably some conflict of interest (the employee causes harm to his employer because of a hidden financial interest in the transaction), this does not necessarily mean that every false billing will be categorized as a conflict scheme. In order for the scheme to be classified as a conflict of interest, the employee (or a friend or relative of the employee) must have some kind of ownership or employment interest in the vendor that submits the invoice.

This distinction is easy to understand if we look at the nature of the fraud. Why does the fraudster overbill his employer? If he engages in the scheme only for the cash, the scheme is a fraudulent disbursement billing scheme. If, on the other hand, he seeks to better the financial condition of his business at the expense of his employer, this is a conflict of interest. In other words, the fraudster's *interests* lie with a company other than his employer. When an employee falsifies the invoices of a third-party vendor to whom he has no relation, this is not a conflict of interest scheme because the employee has no interest in that vendor. The sole purpose of the scheme is to generate a fraudulent disbursement.

One might wonder, then, why shell company schemes are classified as fraudulent disbursements rather than conflicts of interest. After all, the fraudster in a shell company scheme owns the fictitious company and therefore must have an interest in it. Remember, though, that shell companies are created for the sole purpose of defrauding the employer. The company is not so much an entity in the mind of the fraudster as it is a tool. In fact, a shell company is usually little more than a post office box and a bank account. The fraudster has no interest in the shell company which would cause a division of loyalty; he simply uses the shell company to bilk his employer. Shell company schemes are therefore classified as false billing schemes.

A short rule of thumb can be used to distinguish between overbilling schemes that are classified as asset misappropriations and those that are conflicts of interest: if the bill originates from a *real company* in which the fraudster has an economic or personal interest, and if the fraudster's interest in the company is undisclosed to the victim company, then the scheme is a conflict of interest.

Now that we know what kinds of billing schemes are classified as conflicts of interest, the question is, how do these schemes work? After our lengthy discussion about distinguishing between conflicts and fraudulent disbursements, the answer is somewhat anticlimactic. The schemes work the same either way. The mechanics of a billing scheme, whether conflicts or fraudulent disbursement, do not change. (See "Conflicts of Interest" flowchart)

> EXAMPLE
> *A purchasing superintendent defrauded his employer by purchasing items from a certain vendor at inflated prices. The vendor in this case was owned by the purchasing superintendent but established in his wife's name and run by his brother. The perpetrator's interest in the company was undisclosed. The vendor would buy items on the open market, then inflate the prices and resell the items to the victim company. The purchasing superintendent used his influence to assure that his employer continued doing business with the vendor and paying the exorbitant prices.*

Fraudsters also engage in bid-rigging on behalf of their own companies. The methods used to rig bids are discussed in detail in the Bribery section and will not be dealt with in depth here. Briefly stated, an employee of the purchasing company is in a perfect position to rig bids if he has access to the bids of his competitors. Since he can find out what prices other vendors have bid, the fraudster can easily tailor his own company's bid to win the contract. Fraudsters also sometimes use bid waivers to avoid competitive bidding outright.

EXAMPLE

A manager processed several unsubstantiated bid waivers in order to direct purchases to a vendor in which one of his employees had an interest. The conflict was undisclosed and the scheme cost the victim company over $150,000.

In other cases a fraudster might ignore his employer's purchasing rotation and direct an inordinate number of purchases or contracts to his own company. Any way in which a fraudster exerts his influence to divert business to a company in which he has a hidden interest is a conflict of interest.

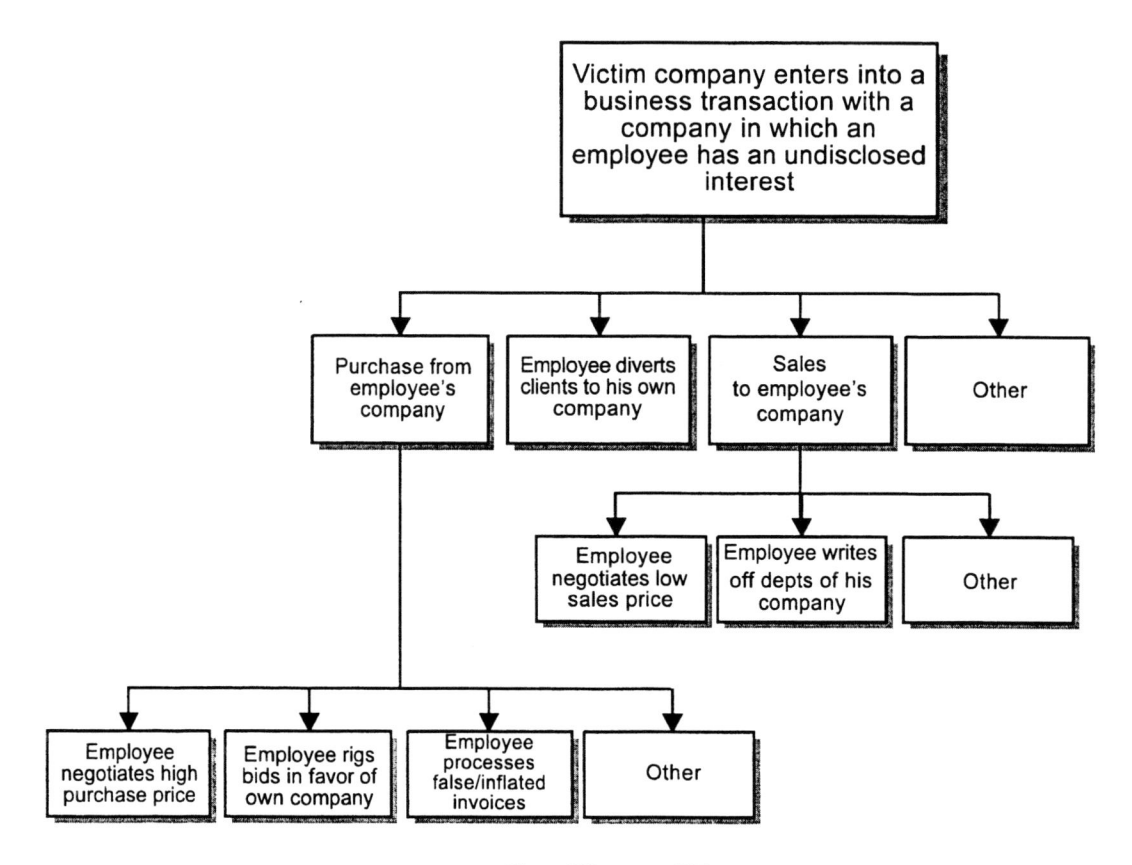

```
                    ┌─────────────────────────┐
                    │ Victim company enters   │
                    │ into a business         │
                    │ transaction with a      │
                    │ company in which an     │
                    │ employee has an         │
                    │ undisclosed interest    │
                    └─────────────────────────┘
    ┌──────────┬──────────────┬──────────────┬──────────┐
    ▼          ▼              ▼              ▼
 Purchase   Employee       Sales to        Other
 from       diverts        employee's
 employee's clients to     company
 company    his own
            company
                                  │
                    ┌─────────────┼─────────────┐
                    ▼             ▼             ▼
                 Employee      Employee       Other
                 negotiates    writes off
                 low sales     depts of his
                 price         company
    │
    ┌───────────┬───────────┬───────────┐
    ▼           ▼           ▼           ▼
 Employee   Employee    Employee     Other
 negotiates rigs bids   processes
 high       in favor    false/
 purchase   of own      inflated
 price      company     invoices
```

Conflicts of Interest

Unique Assets

Not all conflict schemes occur in the traditional vendor-buyer relationship. Sometimes schemes involve employees negotiating for the purchase of some unique, typically large asset such as land or a building in which the employee had an undisclosed interest. It is in the process of these negotiations that the fraudster violates his duty of loyalty to his employer. Because he stands to profit from the sale of the asset, the employee does not negotiate in good faith to his employer; he does not attempt to get the best price possible. The fraudster will reap a greater financial benefit if the purchase price is high.

For example, an employee in charge of negotiating mineral leases on land that he secretly owns is obviously in a position of compromise. There will be no financial motive for this employee to negotiate a favorable lease on behalf of his employer.

Turnaround Sales

A special kind of purchasing scheme sometimes used by fraudsters is called the *turnaround sale* or the *flip*. In this type of scheme an employee knows his employer is seeking to purchase a certain asset and takes advantage of the situation by purchasing the asset himself (usually in the name of an accomplice or shell company). The fraudster then turns around and resells the item to his employer at an inflated price.

> **EXAMPLE**
>
> *A chief executive officer, conspiring with a former employee, sold an office building to the CEO's company. What made the transaction suspicious was that the building had been purchased by the former employee on the same day that it was resold to the victim company, and for $1.2 million less than the price charged to the CEO's company.*

Sales Schemes

There are two principal types of conflict schemes associated with sales of goods or services by the victim company. The first and most harmful is the underselling of goods or services. Just as a corrupt employee can cause his employer to *overpay* for goods or services sold by a company in which he has a hidden interest, so too can he cause the employer to *undersell* to a company in which he maintains a hidden interest.

Underbillings

Many employees who have hidden interests in outside companies sell goods or services to these companies at below-market prices. This results in a diminished profit margin or even a loss for the victim organization, depending upon the size of the discount.

> **EXAMPLE**
>
> *An employee disposed of his employer's real estate by selling it below fair market value to a company in which he had a hidden interest, causing a loss of approximately $500,000.*

Writing Off Sales

The other type of sales scheme involves tampering with the books of the victim company to decrease or write off the amount owed by the company in which the employee has a hidden interest. For instance, after an employee's company purchases goods or services from the victim organization, credit memos may be issued against the sale, causing it to be written off to contra accounts such as Discounts and Allowances. A large number of reversing entries to sales may be a sign that fraud is occurring in an organization.

EXAMPLE

A plant manager assisted favored clients by delaying billing on their purchases for up to 60 days. When the receivable on these clients' accounts became delinquent, the perpetrator issued credit memos against the sales to delete them. The plant manager issued new invoices on the sales after the "old" receivables were taken off the books. In this way, the receivables could be carried indefinitely on the books without ever becoming past due.

Other Schemes

In other cases, the perpetrator might not write off the scheme, but simply delay billing. This is sometimes done as a "favor" to a friendly client and is not an outright avoidance of the bill but rather a dilatory tactic. The victim organization eventually gets paid, but loses time value on the payment which arrives later than it should.

Business Diversions

A number of employees end up starting their own businesses which compete directly with their employers. While still employed by the victim organization, these employees might begin siphoning off clients for their own business. This activity clearly violates the employee's duty of loyalty to the employer. There is nothing unscrupulous about free competition, but while a person acts as a representative of his employer it is certainly improper to try to undercut the employer and take his clients. Normal standards of business ethics require employees to act in the best interests of their employers.

Resource Diversions

Some employees divert the funds and other resources of their employers to the development of their own business. This kind of scheme involves elements of both conflicts of interest and fraudulent disbursements.

EXAMPLE
A vice president of a company authorized large expenditures to develop a unique type of new equipment used by a certain contractor. Another firm subsequently took over the contractor, as well as the new equipment. Shortly after that, the vice president retired and went to work for the firm that had bought out the contractor. The fraudster had managed to use his employer's money to fund a company in which he eventually developed an interest.

While these schemes are clearly corruption schemes, the funds are diverted through the use of a fraudulent disbursement. The money could be drained from the victim organization through a check tampering scheme, a billing scheme, a payroll scheme, or an expense reimbursement scheme. For a discussion of the methods used to generate fraudulent disbursements, please refer to the Asset Misappropriation section.

Financial Interest in Companies Under Perpetrator's Supervision
Sometimes an employee will have a direct or indirect financial interest in a company under his supervision. For example, accountants sometimes hold stock in a company they audit. These problems often occur in government.

Financial Disclosure
Management has an obligation to disclose to the shareholders significant fraud committed by officers, executives, and others in positions of trust. Management does not have the responsibility of disclosing uncharged criminal conduct of its officers and executives. However, if and when officers, executives, or other persons in trusted positions become subjects of a criminal indictment, disclosure is required.

The inadequate disclosure of conflicts of interests is among the most serious of frauds. Inadequate disclosure of related-party transactions is not limited to any specific industry; it transcends all business types and relationships.

Appearance of Conflict of Interest
A final type of conflict of interest is the *appearance* of such. For example, ownership in a blind trust, in which the employee has no authority to make investment decisions, or an external auditor owning a minority interest in a company that is audited by the auditor's firm. Such matters are rarely prosecuted as criminal offenses.

Detection

Conflicts of interest are probably one of the most difficult schemes to uncover. Therefore, no fast and easy detection methods exist for this type of fraud. Some of the more common methods that can be used are tips and complaints, comparisons of vendor addresses with employee addresses, review of vendor ownership files, review of exit interviews, comparisons of vendor addresses to addresses of subsequent employers, and interviews with purchasing personnel for favorable treatment of one or more vendors.

Tips and Complaints

If a particular vendor is being favored, then competing vendors may file complaints. Additionally, employee complaints about the service of a favored vendor may lead to the discovery of a conflict of interest.

Comparison of Vendor Addresses with Employee Addresses

If nominee or related parties are used as owners of vendors, then the business address of the vendor may match that of the employee. Also, look for post office box addresses for vendors. This detection method is similar to that used for locating phony vendors.

Review of Vendor Ownership Files

When a vendor is selected, a complete file of the ownership of that vendor should be kept. This is particularly important for closely held businesses. If the vendor is required to update the file annually then changes in ownership also will be disclosed. A computer comparison of the vendor ownership and the employee file may reveal conflicts of interest.

Review of Exit Interviews and Comparisons of Vendor Addresses to Addresses of Subsequent Employers

If a review of an employee's exit interview yields the name and address of the subsequent employer, then a simple comparison of that name and address with the vendor file may reveal conflicts of interest wherein the employee has obtained employment from a contractor.

Interviews of Purchasing Personnel for Favorable Treatment of One or More Vendors

Employees are generally the first to observe that a vendor is receiving favorable treatment. Therefore, by asking employees if any vendor is receiving favorable treatment, the examiner may discover conflicts of interest that would otherwise have gone unnoticed. Another question which may be asked of employees is whether any vendor's service (or product) has recently become substandard.

Prevention

Organizations should establish policies clearly defining what constitutes a conflict of interest, and prohibiting any such entanglements by officers, directors, employees, or other agents of the organization. A policy requiring employees to complete an annual disclosure statement is an excellent proactive approach to dealing with potential conflicts. Comparing the disclosed names and addresses with vendor and customer lists may reveal real conflicts of interest or the appearance of such. Furthermore, these statements will reinforce in employees the idea that engaging in conflicts of interests is unacceptable and will result in severe consequences.

THEFT OF INTELLECTUAL PROPERTY

Futurist Alvin Toffler identified *information* as the highest value commodity for the new Millennium. He speculated that multinational corporate security departments might evolve into private armies to protect their company's assets where host countries cannot.

The world has indeed become a more complex and competitive place. Individual corporate organizations have become more powerful than some entire nations and the balance of economic power has shifted to the corporation, within which ideas and information have become the most highly prized assets — indeed, with more value than a company's products or physical assets.

To a considerable degree, businesses, administrations and society as a whole have come to depend on the efficiency and security of information technology, resulting in information acquiring a new and distinct value that cannot be protected in the same way as tangible objects.

Information exists in many forms, and its security is achieved by implementing a process of risk assessment and commensurate controls to ensure the preservation of:
- *Confidentiality*: ensuring that information is accessible only to those authorized to have access, and that they can only use it for specified purposes;
- *Integrity*: safeguarding the accuracy and completeness of information and processing methods; and
- *Availability*: ensuring that authorized users have access to information and associated assets when required.

Intellectual property is a catch-all phrase. It is used here to denote knowledge-based assets and capital, including information but extending to ideas, designs, and innovations howsoever expressed or recorded.

This chapter addresses the broad issues relating to the vulnerability and criticality of information and other intangible property. It advocates a mix of procedural, logical, and physical protective measurers to combat threats posed by opponents who make it their business to try to obtain an advantage by illegally or unethically abusing intellectual property belonging to another.

Competitive Intelligence (CI) Versus Espionage

History is used to the practice of intelligence, or what the Duke of Wellington described as "knowing what was over the other side of the hill." Intelligence and espionage transferred from the military to a civilian setting with the return of service personnel from World War II and integrated itself into the economic environment through management education, which was focused on strategy and external influences.

This approach to intelligence was formalized by one of the early proponents of business intelligence, Dr Gerald Albaum, who realized that companies had a need for a "more organized and systematic method for gathering, processing, analyzing, and reporting information about competitors."

CI has been defined as the analytical process that transforms disaggregated competitor data into relevant, accurate and usable knowledge about competitors' positions, performance, capabilities and intentions. Yet in today's market this is not enough. Companies are faced with three influencing factors: customers, competitors, and change. These forces are modifying the face of corporate strategy, driving the company of today deeper into unfamiliar and frightening territory. To address these fears companies are now adopting organized business intelligence systems to monitor the environment in which they do business.

CI is a legitimate business function that sits comfortably alongside Marketing, Research & Development, as well as general business strategy and the newer discipline of "knowledge management." It helps businesses to anticipate a competitor's R & D strategy, determine their operating costs, pricing policies and financial strength, as well as their capacity. Knowledge about their competitors is one of the advantages that can enable companies to succeed and lead the field in their respective market place.

CI has become a growth industry that is practiced by professionals trained to use information in the public domain or to otherwise utilize legally available resources to compile information. This information is then collated, processed, and disseminated into intelligence that is usable and has strategic value. Gathering intelligence is not espionage, if the collection effort is done without recourse to criminal methods or intent. CI practitioners mostly work within a code of ethics drawn up by the Society for Competitive Intelligence Professionals (SCIP). This strict code includes the requirement that members identify themselves during an inquiry and do not use deception in their quest for such information.

To the detriment of the reputation of fraud examiners and CI professionals, certain private investigators and information brokers access financial and criminal information and other protected data, and generally disregard the laws governing data protection. Conversely there are firms that will use quite aggressive techniques to investigate a client organization's opponent. Whilst not conforming to the SCIP's code of ethics, these techniques are not illegal and firms using these methods appear to be prepared to stand by their techniques in a court of law. They provide a valuable service to their top-tier clients, many of whom do not believe that all evidence of malpractice is reflected solely in books and records.

There is, therefore, a world of difference between competitive intelligence and espionage. Espionage may be defined as *"intelligence activity directed towards the acquisition of information through clandestine means and proscribed by the laws of the country against which it is committed."* It does not cover legitimate intelligence collection and analysis using legal means.

Espionage can be further sub-divided into industrial espionage: referring to the clandestine collection of information by companies and individuals, such as information brokers, about competitors; and economic espionage, referring to state sponsored or sanctioned collection which is often associated with a nation's Foreign Intelligence Service.

Open Sources of Information

Open source information is public domain information, data that is legally available to anyone. Spies do not have to penetrate corporate security measures to obtain this type of information; it is available to anyone who wants to collect it. The term "public," however, does not necessarily mean free. Many sources have access charges that may be simple low-cost copying fees or rather substantial database expenses.

The dividing line between open source information and other targets of corporate intelligence (such as trade secrets) is the right to access. A member of the public can obtain open source data openly, without fear of legal consequences, and the provider of the data desires or has no objection to its release into the marketplace. Trade secrets are the exact opposite: no one but the owner has the right of access, and the owner has no desire to cast the trade secret freely upon the marketplace's waters. The taking of trade secrets, without the owner's permission, violates both state and federal law. Known as economic, industrial, or corporate espionage, theft of trade secrets is a form of business intelligence that goes far beyond open source research.

Most of the information sought on any topic, according to intelligence professionals, is publicly available. Estimates go as high as ninety-five percent (95%) as to what is discoverable in the public sector.

There is only so much that a security professional can do to limit the open source information that is available on an organization. Some forms of information, such as financial statements of publicly traded companies, are legally required to be published. Other pieces of information such as product descriptions or job listings are posted out of business necessity. Corporate security professionals do not operate in a vacuum; the need to protect an organization's secrets must always be balanced against the need or duty to publish information. One of the first things a security professional must do is realize that they cannot protect everything.

With a thorough understanding of how CI practitioners use open source information, however, a security officer can limit their company's vulnerability to the disclosure of secrets through accident or negligence. The knowledgeable security professional will identify key information assets, then review the open source information that is available on the company from a spy's perspective to see if the safety of those assets could be endangered. The security professional will also be able to work with other departments to limit or edit the information that is available on the organization so that no inadvertent gifts are made to potential intruders. Finally, if a theft of information should occur, understanding how open sources are used may help a security officer track down the perpetrator.

Why do Companies Resort to Corporate Espionage?
If so much lies "out there," why do people pay for industrial and corporate spies? Why do they bother with illegal methods? Why do companies not stick to standard research to learn what they need about their competitors, and why do they use intelligence agents and analysts instead of routine researchers? The answer to these questions is twofold.

First, even if the intelligence gatherer adheres strictly to using only open sources, mere facts do not constitute intelligence or knowledge. Collecting raw data brings one only to the threshold of the process. Data must then undergo analysis to be turned into a useful product. Analysis involves summarizing, comparing, and explaining the data. The craft of intelligence lies in the ability of the provider to distill mountains of "facts" from diverse sources into a concise product that is actionable by its consumer.

The term "actionable" means the product must have the depth, character, and quality on which an executive may base sound decisions. Merely knowing what one's competitors are "up to" falls short of the mark. Good intelligence identifies the actions an executive should take to seize an opportunity or to diminish or eliminate a threat. It is good to know what the problem is, but far better to know how the problem can be solved. Even though open sources are available to the general public, organizations still utilize intelligence professionals' skills to create actionable intelligence from the mass of public information.

The second reason organizations utilize intelligence professionals is that the remaining five percent (5%) of needed information is proprietary. This last segment often becomes critical to competitive survival, and organizations or individuals are sometimes willing to sidestep the law to obtain it. Intelligence professionals know the "tricks of the trade" for gathering sensitive, proprietary information that can give their clients a competitive edge.

While legal protections exist for trade secrets and other proprietary information, smart organizations do not passively rely on the threat of civil actions or criminal penalties to protect their information assets. Rather, they take affirmative steps to erect their own security barriers around their critical, proprietary information. Such barriers dramatically increase the costs, never mind the legal liabilities, of obtaining protected information.

If a company or foreign intelligence service must have the trade secrets of a target to complete the information picture they are formulating, they must be willing to invest. In many cases, this means employing the services of intelligence professionals. Utilizing experience and training, the intelligence professional conducts a campaign or mission using secure methods to protect the collection effort, preventing legal repercussions for the client.

There is a cost factor involved in intelligence gathering, which tends to keep companies and corporate spies from rushing into covert proprietary intelligence activity. A wise intelligence campaign will utilize open sources, at least initially, as much as possible. Only when the effort can go no further, and business needs dictate acquiring additional information, does intelligence gathering enter the proprietary realm.

The Bootstrap Effect

With an understanding of the intelligence process, it becomes clear that open sources play two important roles. They may in some cases provide all the basic intelligence a company needs. A skilled intelligence analyst uses logic and the principles of inference to summarize, compare, and explain any missing pieces. In other words, the company never has to venture on the high seas of espionage, it satisfies itself in the safe harbor of open sources. It learns what it needs to know at low cost and by legal means.

But if penetrating the proprietary realm becomes necessary, open source information provides a bootstrap for the covert effort. The more one knows about a subject, the easier it is to discover additional information on that subject. Open sources serve as the homework a corporate spy does prior to conducting covert operations in hostile territory.

As any filmmaker knows, the more time spent in preproduction (which is relatively inexpensive), the less time and money will have to be dedicated to production (which is very expensive). The professional filmmaker does his homework before shooting a foot of film. Likewise, the professional corporate spy does not just show up at the target's factory at 3 a.m., armed with a crowbar, clumsily trying to break into the facility.

Instead, the effective spy obtains plans on the layout of the targeted plant in advance, notes what type of alarm system is in place, learns about any security patrols, and then devises an appropriate penetration plan. But unlike a common thief, the effective spy sets that plan aside and first considers other options—less blatant means that may exist to ferret out the sought-after information. He understands that information is a unique commodity, and the theft of information can be accomplished in a number of unique ways. Often, information can be "stolen" without the target realizing it; copies or photographs can provide access to sensitive facts without requiring the source documents or files to ever be removed from their owner's control. Burglary, something the police understand and take great interest in, is not always the best way to steal information.

The Intelligence Pyramid

Leonard Fuld, in his landmark book, *Competitor Intelligence*, argues that open sources exist at three levels, forming an Intelligence Pyramid. At the base of the pyramid are Fundamental Intelligence Techniques, the second level is composed of Basic Sources of Information, and the final level is Creative Sources.

```
        Creative
        Sources
    ─────────────
    Basic Sources of
      Information
  ─────────────────────
  Fundamental Intelligence Techniques
```

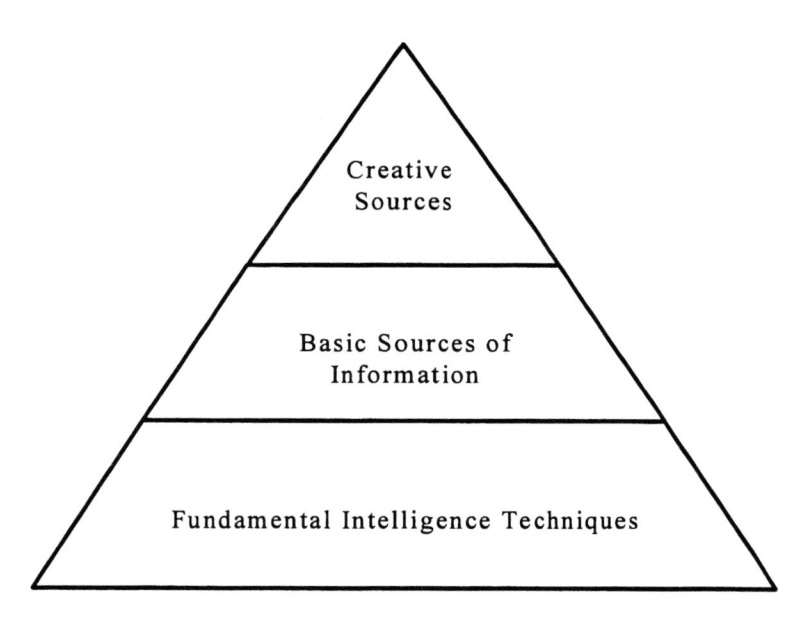

Figure 1: The Intelligence Pyramid

Fundamental Research Techniques

The initial level of the Intelligence Pyramid is composed of Fundamental Research Techniques, which include researching articles in magazines, journals or newspapers, and consulting industry guidebooks. These fundamental sources of information allow the spy to build a partial picture of the target, and equally important, to develop checklists of the information needed to fill in the blank spaces. These checklists are very important, because no intelligence effort should proceed without precise goals. For a spy to be effective, he or she must know exactly what is sought. Vague expeditions for information will produce vague results, so a shopping list becomes an absolute must. A competitive intelligence (CI) professional may spend many hours meeting with a client discussing in exacting detail the specifics of the mission. If the client is not clear on the objective, clarifying that issue becomes the first order of business.

Basic Sources

After establishing clearly defined goals, the CI professional crafts a collection plan. In a well-organized intelligence-gathering plan, the CI professional moves up the pyramid, collecting additional information while they continue to narrow the focus of their search. After exercising fundamental techniques, the second level of the pyramid involves accessing basic sources. These sources include some that are already familiar:

- Government sources
    - SEC (from the EDGAR database, www.sec.gov/edgarhp.htm)
        * 10-K annual report

- * 10-Q quarterly report
  - * Proxy statements
  - * 13-D major stock acquisitions
  - * 14-D tender offers
  - State corporate filings
    - * Corporate registrations
    - * UCC filings
    - * Regulatory filings, professional licensing, etc.)
    - * Officer/Director database
- Industrial reports and studies
- Industry analyst reports
- State industrial directories
- Trade and business magazines
- Statistical sources (example: Standard Rate and Data Service [advertising])
- Trade associations (from the Encyclopedia of Associations and Directories in Print provided by Gale Industries)
- Databases with stories
  - Thomson Research (http://research.thomsonib.com)
  - DataTimes — Fulltext newspapers

Government Sources

SEC FILINGS

Publicly traded companies are required to make certain filings with the SEC. These documents can be extremely helpful to the spy seeking to build a financial profile on the target. Information such as annual and quarterly reports on publicly traded companies can be accessed for free through the SEC's EDGAR database at www.sec.gov/edgar.shtml.

Through this avenue, the spy can obtain the target's Form 10-K, which contains the company's income statement and balance sheet, information on its debt structure, foreign ownership, properties owned, subsidiaries, industry descriptions, depreciation, dilution, and other key business information. If the target company has filed for bankruptcy, been the target of a shareholder lawsuit, or been sued for patent infringement, this may also show up in the 10-K. Most publicly traded companies must also file 10-Qs, which are statements of quarterly income, earnings per share, etc. Other forms that are available from the SEC include proxy statements, which provide information on stockholder votes taken on key issues; and 13-D and 14-D forms, which indicate major movements in stock ownership that are pending.

STATE CORPORATE FILINGS

States require that companies that do business within their jurisdictions register each year with the state government, usually through the Secretary of State's office. This requirement extends to all companies operating in the state, not just those that are publicly traded.

Many Secretarys of State websites have enhanced search capabilities for business organizations including searching by entity name, and by name of the person listed as a registered agent, officer, or director of a corporation. This search capability allows an intelligence analyst to find all the companies within a state in which a person serves as an officer or as a director. A search can help the CI professional develop a family tree of the officer's business interests. It becomes a useful tool for uncovering lesser-known or hidden connections between businesses. The financial strength of a targeted business often lies in its affiliates or subsidiaries, which rise to the surface in an officer/director search.

INDUSTRIAL REPORTS AND STUDIES

State and federal governments periodically issue industrial reports and studies on various industries ranging from appliance manufacturers to high technology companies. These studies provide statistical benchmarks useful to establish where a company stands in its industry. In addition, they help delineate the standards for evaluating successful companies in that industry. State industrial directories, special industry issues in magazines like *Fortune* and *Forbes*, and directories from trade associations serve the same function.

Industry Analyst Reports

There are a number of industry analyst reports that CI gatherers use to estimate unknown figures in a target's balance sheet. The Standard Rate and Data Service, for instance, provides information on advertising rates that may help a spy benchmark the target's expenditures on advertising, an indicator of the organization's financial health. For practically any industry, a statistical source exists which serves as a powerful estimating tool for CI analysts.

Industry analyst reports from investment firms, when properly researched and written, are akin to having a personal intelligence briefing about the target. Striving for a balanced presentation, they aim to tell both the good and the bad about a company. They often contrast sharply with the company's annual report.

Electronic Sources

Electronic sources of data are some of the most powerful research tools in the intelligence analyst's arsenal. These resources, which include CD-ROMs and on-line databases, contain compilations of data on bankruptcies, new business filings, telephone directories, UCC filings, criminal records, corporate data, and many other types of information. If one includes the many local, regional, and national newspapers available electronically, the research capabilities of one intelligence analyst sitting at their computer are truly staggering.

Large public or university libraries frequently provide free network access to newspaper, magazine, and other journalistic sources. More information about electronic sources is contained in the chapter on "Accessing Information On-Line" in the Investigation Section of the *Manual*.

MULTIPLIER EFFECT

CD-ROMs and other analytical software produce a multiplier effect when processing case information. They generate output greater than the individual inputs of information. Facts A, B, C, and D standing by themselves may offer minimal insight, but when combined and organized those facts can generate an understanding of what is really going on in an organization. The Analyst's Notebook by i2, for example, is popular among police intelligence analysts, because it can track patterns and linkages from large databases. (Further information about these types of products is contained in the chapter on "Data Analysis and Reporting Tools" in the Investigation Section of the *Manual*.)

The functions performed by analytical software programs can easily be translated to business intelligence needs, uncovering patterns related to corporate filings, O/D searches, patent and trademark applications, and other diverse compilations of data that, when pieced together, can indicate the potential direction in which a competitor is headed. For example, some software programs can be designed to crosscheck patent authors extracted from a patent database against an Officer/Director search to show the companies for which key scientists serve as directors. The software also generates visual displays of the relationships between the companies. All of this makes the corporate spy's task of unearthing hidden relationships and confidential facts easier.

Creative Sources

The final step in the open source intelligence pyramid is the use of creative sources. Leonard Fuld lists the following types of information as examples of creative sources: classified ads, environmental impact statements, close examination of UCC filings, proxies, and the building of financial statements.

Classified Ads

Employment advertisements, in particular, can provide valuable information about the job skills that a target company needs and the number of employees it is seeking to hire. This can help a spy infer what kinds of new projects are being developed within a company or where personnel resources are being devoted. Large scale hiring could indicate that a competitor has signed or expects to sign a large contract. In some cases, employment ads also point out defections of key personnel.

Employment ads also give a spy an indication of what the target company pays its employees. This could be valuable for the spy's employer in recruiting battles for coveted personnel. It could also help the spy identify employees who may be susceptible to recruitment tactics because of low pay or a high rate of employee dissatisfaction (as evidenced by a high rate of turnover in a particular department).

Environmental Impact Statements

Environmental impact statements contain large amounts of historical, financial, and operational information. The company filing the statement not only has to supply this background data on itself, but it also has to explain its proposed project in detail. Those details on emissions, hazardous materials used, and possible accidents stemming from operations provide a wealth of facts for analysis by an expert. From such analysis a CI professional can develop an excellent picture on the size and operational capability of a plant or company. Very often, this kind of information can allow one's competitors to establish the date operations will begin at a targeted plant.

UCC Filings

UCC filings, in addition to financial data previously discussed, provide operational details by describing equipment and materials that have been purchased or pledged for a loan. Sometimes previously unknown assets and ties to other businesses will be listed in the filings. UCC filings are made at the county level or with the Secretary of State, depending on the nature of the collateral provided as security in a financing agreement. Savvy intelligence professionals review these documents with a fine-toothed comb for tidbits of information that can help them gain an understanding of a target's business transactions.

Proxies

Developing "proxies"—people who work with the target on a day-to-day basis—helps CI professionals color in many necessary details. Suppliers in particular can be a rich source of inside information about a targeted business. Suppliers spend significant time and resources to learn about their customers. They know what a customer orders, when they place orders, how much they spend, how long they take to pay their bills, and what the business cycle of the customer's industry is. Interviews with these persons can be an invaluable source of information for a corporate spy.

Posing as a Customer

If a spy cannot cultivate or bribe key employees of a supplier, he may pose as a customer himself. He can exploit the two fundamental axioms of corporate espionage: (1) all salespeople want to make a sale, and (2) all salespeople will do almost anything to make a sale, *including* talking their heads off about what they've done for other customers.

In a prospective sales meeting, the spy, armed with business cards and even a brochure about his "company," conveys that he works for a prosperous business. (He can even pick a legitimate business with a good Dun & Bradstreet rating and pose as their employee.) During the course of the meeting, he can ask what the supplier has done for other customers. He will casually mention that he has a friend who works for the target company. How well has the supplier served that business? As an additional enticement, the spy can place on the table impressive looking spreadsheets showing financial data and production run-levels and ask if the target's level of business matches these figures. The spy tells the salesperson that he just wants to see if the supplier has the experience necessary to handle his business.

Building Financial Statements

The one piece of information desired universally by consumers of intelligence is the financial statement. At times, the balance sheet becomes the "Holy Grail," a magic key, which opens all sorts of doors to understanding a business. Spies can, of course, steal balance sheets and other financial documents. But, often the theft is not worth the risk. Large publicly owned companies are required by law to publish their financial statements. This information is freely available on the SEC's EDGAR database. Even large privately owned companies frequently leave enough of a paper trail in the public sector that figuring out their financial posture is not terribly difficult. More difficulty generally arises when the CI professional seeks to build a financial profile of private small- and medium-sized companies. The finances in these companies are usually held close to the vest. Getting in proximity to key financial documents may be risky given that a limited number of people in these companies have access.

A much safer approach lies in estimating the balance sheet with research methods. Every good CI specialist knows how to perform this procedure. The technique forms a central tool in the intelligence professional's arsenal. The process by which balance sheets are estimated affords an inside look at the open source process used by CI professionals.

It is important to remember that the financial statements that the CI professional "builds" are nothing more than estimates of a target's financial status. Confirming that estimate by further intelligence gathering is an option, but the process begins as a refined, educated guess. While only a guess, a well-calculated estimate may provide all the information needed by the client, and this method involves a considerably lower degree of risk than outright theft of the sought-after information.

The CI specialist must always be aware that financial statements only tell part of the story about a company. He knows to evaluate them in the light of other information such as the history of the business, the condition of its market, technological developments, and the condition of its suppliers. Quite frankly, estimating works best when done on manufacturing companies. The "inputs" and "outputs" of a manufacturing firm are easier to spot, track, and measure than with service companies. Service companies, however, can be compared to other similar businesses by size, location, and number of employees. If the financials of the similar company are known, then an educated inference can be made about the target's financial statements. For the purposes of the discussion in this section, and in order to best illustrate the methods used by intelligence professionals, the hypothetical target will be a manufacturing company.

How Income Statements are Calculated

To build the financials of a manufacturing firm, spies first calculate the *income statement*. They break down an income statement into three components: (1) revenue, (2) cost of goods sold, and (3) overhead.

Revenue Estimates

Revenue estimates can come from state air pollution control permit applications, hazardous materials permit applications, articles in the local press about sales volumes, state industrial directories, or by indirect methods. One of the most common indirect methods for estimating revenue is to count truck activity at a site, both receiving and shipping, over a given period of time. Knowing the shipping dimensions and retail costs of the company's products, a spy can estimate what each truck holds. The same goes for railcars and ships or barges. Talking to truck drivers, railroad personnel, and longshoremen can also fill in details on the size of outgoing loads and their frequency. In the service industry, revenue estimates are frequently made by conducting interviews with suppliers, customers, or employees of the target. Pretext calls and social engineering might also be used to trick employees into divulging key financial information.

Costs of Goods Sold

Labor costs can be derived by a spy from wages listed in newspaper classified ads and from wage surveys at the local chamber of commerce. The state workforce commission will also have wage surveys for certain occupations. The number of employees for the target can be gathered from OSHA (Occupational Safety and Health Administration) records and by counting cars in the parking lot for each shift.

Determining indirect labor costs can be accomplished in several ways. The best method is to consult statistical manuals for the target's industry, which give the respective percentages of direct and indirect labor costs. In addition, estimating the numbers of managerial and professional workers entering the plant will supply a guideline. Spies look for clues such as the types of cars that employees drive (a Saab or a pickup truck?), the clothing they wear (a suit or overalls?), and the items they carry to work (briefcases and laptops or lunchboxes?) The chamber of commerce may also be able to supply the numbers of salaried personnel at a plant.

The types and amount of raw materials used at a plant may be available from the state air pollution control board or the local fire department's hazardous materials unit. Surveillance of truck deliveries to the site is another source. The cost of materials is available from suppliers or their catalogues.

Overhead

Overhead costs such as advertising derive from manuals discussed earlier such as the Standard Rate and Data Service. Calculating utility costs is as simple as calling the local electric, gas, or water company. While a utility company may not reveal what the target consumes directly, they will disclose what the average company of that size in that industry purchases annually. Newspaper ads and real estate brokers serve as sources on the costs of leased plant facilities. The local tax assessor can supply the value of property owned by the target. Mortgage information will be available from real estate records at the county clerk's office.

Debts of the targeted business emerge from researching UCC filings, bond rating manuals, state economic commission records (if the target is big enough), and from the state securities board file of privately placed prospectuses.

How Balance Sheets are Calculated

From these various sources, a competitive intelligence analyst can compile a preliminary income statement. The elements of a balance sheet derive from the income statement with the help of a financial ratio manual like Dun & Bradstreet's Industry Norms and Key Business Ratios. The process of deriving the balance sheet begins by taking a known figure (for instance, Sales) and looking up the ratio, for the target's industry, between Sales and Net Worth. The intelligence professional simply needs to do some simple algebra (divide the Sales figure by the ratio) to derive the unknown, which is the Net Worth.

A similar procedure works for other standard ratios. The rule of thumb is that if a person knows the annual sales, the line of business (LOB), the number of employees, and how long a company has been in business, then that person will be able to create a reasonable balance sheet estimate. An analyst will compare the estimate against known or published balance sheets of similar size companies in the same LOB to check accuracy. Consulting experts on the industry (bank loan officers, investment analysts) provides further confirmation.

Nontraditional Sources

A spy or intelligence analyst bolsters data developed from public records and estimated financial statements by accessing lesser-known sources. Historical archive centers like the Center for American History at the University of Texas at Austin have large collections of old telephone directories, industrial and corporate directories, and business reference works. These materials enable a researcher to trace the history of a business or a person's association with that business. They also serve to track the growth of a business over time. Changes in Yellow Pages listings, in telephone numbers, and in statistics in state manufacturing directories can be charted to show long-term trends for the business. These archives also document where a person served as an officer, as a key employee, or ran their own business.

Gale Research, a publisher of many fine reference books, has two works of primary interest to CI specialists. *Directories in Print* (25th edition) has over 15,000 entries for every kind of directory imaginable. Any good CI specialist knows that a good trade directory saves valuable research time. In addition, most directories generally run ads from suppliers to the industry, so the industry directory serves as an informal reference book for locating suppliers. These directories are also a strong way to do background research on an industry, to learn the buzzwords and key concepts governing that business. After reviewing the directory, a spy will be able to talk like an insider.

Gale also produces the *Encyclopedia of Associations* in regional, national, and international editions. From these works a CI specialist can locate experts and resources in almost any business field or manufacturing line. Contacting experts for interviews by telephone is a fast, inexpensive way to confirm estimates and research findings from open sources. The *Encyclopedia* also lists annual meetings of organizations and their key officers. It serves as a source to identify experts, their trade shows, and related seminars. Savvy CI professionals will touch base with professionals prior to an annual meeting or seminar. They strike up a professional relationship in advance so when they meet at the convention, they are in a position to comfortably chat with targeted professionals and draw out key information. Virtually every text on competitive intelligence mentions attending trade shows, but few mention doing the necessary homework before attending. Good spies do their homework on whom to contact by using Gale Research or similar sources as a starting point.

InfoTrac

Spies also do their homework by using InfoTrac, a large family of databases from Gale Research. One thing about these databases that makes them especially attractive to spies is that most libraries have them available in-house (usually on a CD-ROM network) for use at no charge. Since they index, abstract, and provide fulltext on hundreds of publications, the competitive intelligence researcher essentially has a multitude of field agents working for them. Keeping in mind the estimate that ninety-five percent (95%) of needed information lies in the public domain, InfoTrac's databases form a good middle tier source. The information that InfoTrac commonly provides includes:

- Number of employees
- Manufacturing capacity
- Product lines
- Levels of expertise within the company
- Markets
- Market position
- Key products
- Internet participation
- Product details
- Competitive advantages

A Closer Look at Databases

There are three tiers of electronic databases: (1) The Internet and the Web, (2) InfoTrac databases and reference works like the Million Dollar Directory on CD-ROM, and (3) Commercial databases such as Dialog, Profound, Lexis/Nexis, and Dun & Bradstreet.

Electronic Databases		
First Tier		
Examples: • Internet • World Wide Web	Advantages: Quick, easy to use, usually free.	Disadvantages: Chaotically organized, information not always current or reliable.
Second Tier		
Examples: • InfoTrac • Million Dollar Directory • Investext	Advantages: Fairly easy to use, available at large public libraries, usually free access, information reasonably reliable.	Disadvantages: Expensive subscription rates, so not always practical as an in-house source for security units.
Third Tier		
Examples: • Dialog • Lexis/Nexis • Investigative Works • Dun & Bradstreet • Profound	Advantages: Most use powerful search engines or have vast databases. Capable of highly refined conceptual searches.	Disadvantages: Can be very expensive for intelligence and security units. However, these databases represent an emerging tool for the future.

First Tier Databases

Competitive intelligence involves more than just "surfing the Net." Of course any CI specialist will be well acquainted with Web search engines like Alta Vista, Yahoo, Lycos, Google, MetaCrawler, and Northern Light. These engines are useful for locating the highlights on the Internet. However, with URLs constantly changing, and the quality and depth of data on the Internet being highly variable, the Internet is just a first step for CI work.

Second Tier Databases

As indicated above, more in-depth, cleaner, and better organized data lies in middle tier databases such as Infotrac. While hypertext linking on the Web affords the user the ability to establish his own pathways through information, this mode of searching often leads to haphazard, lengthy, and even chaotic journeys. Middle tier databases provide well-organized, carefully indexed data that takes less time to search and carries a greater informational punch. Because intelligence frequently has a short half-life, time can be a very critical factor for intelligence specialists. The more quickly a search is completed, the more valuable is the information obtained.

Third Tier Databases

Competitive intelligence campaigns frequently operate under a short time frame; finding out if a competitor is about to expand production, for instance, may only be valuable if the spy learns in time for his employer to beat that rival to the punch. Because time is frequently a critical factor in an intelligence campaign, analysts tend to use the third tier of databases as a central tool. Those employing the most sophisticated search technologies include Dialog, Profound, Dun & Bradstreet, and Lexis/Nexis. These databases are generally able to provide more useful information in less time than lower tier alternatives.

Newsgroups

Spies also utilize search engines specifically geared to scanning newsgroups on the Internet. These sites can contain immense amounts of intelligence information. When people start chatting on the Internet, they frequently reveal a great deal about what they are working on. Examples of this type of search engine include Google (www.google.com) and Supernews (www.supernews.com).

Dun & Bradstreet and Lexis/Nexis

Dun & Bradstreet's business and marketing databases and Lexis/Nexis' employ conventional search technologies both fall in the upper tier due to their vastness. A starting point for researching almost any business is a D&B report. If the report is lacking, there is probably not much out there on that company. With millions of records, these databases are useful in developing histories and backgrounds on companies and officers. Lexis/Nexis has so many periodicals and transcripts on its database that it is one of the best commercial intelligence databases in the world.

i2

As previously mentioned, i2 also figures into the database equation. It can perform pattern development functions similar to other top-level databases. The trend of doing more with open sources and squeezing additional information out of them is growing rapidly in the CI community. The multiplier effect, discussed earlier, is clearly at work. Information organized and cross-referenced internally generates knowledge that can help a client make a decision or that can support and enhance further intelligence efforts.

Competitive Intelligence Websites

In addition to the tools discussed above, CI professionals can utilize a number of websites that provide free information about how to conduct business intelligence operations. Many of these sites will take a visitor step-by-step through intelligence techniques and strategies.

A Corporate Spy Uses Open Sources: What of It?

A corporate spy uses some or all of the following open sources of information:

1. Public records (regulatory, civil, criminal)
2. Annual reports
3. Telephone directories (internal and external)
4. Analyst reports
5. News accounts
6. Magazine articles
7. Constructed balance sheets
8. Reference books
9. Biographical sources
10. Visual sightings and surveillance
11. Electronic databases and CD-ROMs
12. Internet/Web

All of these materials blend together to develop actual, actionable intelligence. In the alternative, they act as a springboard for gaining additional data. The question is, if all this data is out there by default, what can a company do about it?

Certainly a company can educate its employees to be careful about what they say in public, put into print, or place on the Internet. Security training may also teach them to recognize pretext telephone calls designed to obtain inside information. It may also be beneficial to train employees on how spies use open sources to gather competitive intelligence on a business. Employees can be taught not to divulge proprietary data, to think before they speak.

The reality, however, is that companies must operate in an open society, not a police state. The free exchange of ideas and information will be absolutely essential to 21st century commerce. The first step in protecting sensitive corporate information is to realize that a security manager, a security investigator, or an internal auditor cannot protect everything. In the words of John Keegan, the noted military historian, "to defend everything is to defend nothing."

A security professional must identify the key pieces of intellectual property belonging to the company. Those items whose compromise could cause grave harm to the business require utmost protection. Knowing the tools and paths in the open source sector a spy could use to cut a swath to this critical data will be essential if the security professional is to effectively protect it. From a security perspective, an investigator should try to exploit the available open sources herself to see if an avenue of attack can be completed. If so, the security professional can institute countermeasures before a loss occurs.

If an information loss does occur, a security investigator or auditor can attempt to reconstruct a trail back to a possible spy with a sound knowledge of open source techniques.

Favorite Targets

Some of the favorite targets of intelligence gatherers include research and development, marketing, manufacturing and production, and human resources.

Research and Development

One would think that R&D would be the most heavily guarded department in a company, but access to R&D information is surprisingly easy. R&D personnel are almost always in the flow of information. The open exchange of information is part of the nature of their job. They participate in conferences, attend trade shows, and work with academic institutions; however, at each of these functions, they leave themselves open for intelligence spies to listen, mingle, and ask questions.

Researchers who publish their findings in industry journals may inadvertently include details of a project on which they may be working. This is particularly true in the case of academic professionals who may be hired by a company to perform research or conduct a study. More than one company has been surprised to learn that the results of a supposedly confidential study were published in an academic journal. If an academician is hired to conduct research, make sure that he or she understands that the results are to be kept confidential. Also make sure that the use of teaching assistants or graduate students is kept to a minimum and that those individuals understand the confidentiality requirements.

Marketing

Insight into a company's marketing plan is a valuable gift to a competitor. Being careless with vital information such as test marketing results, promotional strategies, and planned introduction dates can be disastrous.

Manufacturing and Production
Production managers are often good sources of information. Also, almost anyone answering the phone on the plant floor can unwittingly provide valuable information to a crafty caller from a competitor.

Human Resources
Intelligence professionals often pay close attention to help wanted ads, job postings, and job announcements. More ominously, they may use this information to arrange a job interview to get information about the firm and what the job will entail.

Although the departments listed above are some of the favored targets of information thieves, other personnel in an organization can provide enormous amounts of useful information. For instance, salespeople like to talk and are an excellent source of information on pricing, product innovations, and market programs. Purchasing agents are helpful in divulging suppliers, information about what is selling, and the costs of raw materials and services.

How Information is Lost
Information thieves utilize a wide variety of methods—some legal, some not—to gain access to an organization's business secrets. There are seven common ways for information to fall into the wrong hands. They are:
- Accident
- Poor information security procedures
- Recruited spies
- Deception techniques
- Physical penetration of the company
- Surveillance
- Computer system penetrations

Accident
Accidental losses of information are fairly common and occur in a number of ways. Publications such as newsletters or reports to shareholders that are printed by a company can inadvertently provide valuable information to its competitors. Also, speeches or papers that are presented at conferences are a danger point. Organizations should implement a system of review whereby technical and/or security staff review in advance all works up for

publication or presentation. Another common source of accidental leaks is the press. Executives eager to brag about their companies often reveal more than they should about research, new products, sales levels, and so on.

A company's website may also be a source of accidental leaks. Corporate spies frequently visit the websites of their targets to gather information that these companies have unknowingly assembled for them. Information such as employee telephone and e-mail directories, financial information, biographical data on key employees, product features and release dates, details on research and development, and job postings can all be found on many corporate websites. In some cases this information gives an information thief direct access to company secrets; in other instances it helps the spy build a profile of his target that will be the basis of an intelligence campaign. Businesses should pay attention to the information that is placed on their websites and in other marketing materials. As a general rule of thumb, anything that does not forward the marketing mission of an organization should be removed.

Poor Information Security Procedures

Companies that do not have a system in place for protecting and disposing of confidential information leave themselves wide open to attack by corporate spies. An information thief will generally attack one or more of the following areas: manual systems (hardcopy documents), computer-based systems (electronic files), or personnel (people employed by a company or associates of the business). Below are a number of techniques that companies should implement to protect manual and electronic information.

On-site Materials that are Targeted

Spies attempt to gather manual systems information by gaining surreptitious access to a target's premises. Common methods include posing as a temporary employee, as a vendor, or as a visitor on a plant tour. Materials that these spies generally target include the following:

- Archives (financial, sales data, marketing)
  - In print form
  - Stored on computer media
- Draft documents, formal documents, and internal correspondence lying on desks
- Scrap paper in wastepaper baskets and by copying machines
- Minutes of meetings
- Legal and regulatory filings

- Computer printouts
- Travel documents and receipts
- Patent documents
- Pending lawsuits
- Papers pertaining to mergers and acquisitions
- Licensing and franchise agreements
- Special management reports
- Audits of Internet access
- Billings for database access

ARCHIVES

Archives provide a view of the target's performance over time. They offer an excellent source for trend analysis. Even if a visitor on a plant tour is not able to handle documents, he can note their location and availability for a later penetration.

DRAFT DOCUMENTS

Draft documents, internal correspondence, and resulting formal documents may reveal the evolution of products, designs, and marketing plans within a company.

SCRAP PAPER

Paper thrown away often contains valuable information in preliminary plans and reports. Hackers "dumpster dive" for this sort of information all the time. Often in the form of manuals, technical specifications, and instructions, these discards can provide a road map to penetrate computer systems. They can also provide insight into evolving products or business plans of a target.

MINUTES OF MEETINGS

Records of high-level meetings can provide key insight on corporate strategies, investment policies, product development plans, marketing plans, and other crucial information about a business' direction. They can also help the spy identify key employees; possibly even those who are unhappy with the current direction of their own company or careers and who, therefore, might be potential recruits as spies.

LEGAL DOCUMENTS AND REGULATORY FILINGS

Legal documents range from trade secrets to pending litigation to summaries of regulatory problems the company faces. Pending lawsuits often detail problems with the company's products, services, or operations.

Papers pertaining to mergers and acquisitions have obvious commercial value. The same goes for licensing and franchise agreements. Special management reports document a myriad of challenges the target faces. For example, a report may examine what is wrong with the company's inventory control system or that the base of parts suppliers is inadequate.

AUDITS OF INTERNET ACCESS AND BILLINGS FOR DATABASE ACCESS

Audit reports on Internet access, usually from a proxy server log, can tell a spy what topics and sites a company researches and which employees are doing it. Billings for database access of services like Dun & Bradstreet, Dialog, or Lexis/Nexis reveal companies the target is checking out and doing business with, plus topics they're investigating.

In addition, these audit reports often reveal if employees are stealing computer resources for their own personal ends. Undetected activity over a period of time indicates a lack of security oversight. These employees may be candidates for recruitment as inside spies.

Guarding Manual Systems

Manual systems are all human-readable files and documents. These include commonly overlooked items like rolodexes and calendars. Attacks on these systems range from pilfering trash to infiltrating a company in the guise of a cleaning crew or vendors to outright theft or burglary. Reasonable measures to protect documents include the following:

1. **Place sensitive documents in high-grade locked filing cabinets.** It might also be advisable to lock sensitive documents in a safe when not in use and at the end of the day. Locks or safes should be able to withstand a physical attack of at least one to two hours.
2. **Use a shredder for sensitive documentary waste.** In the alternative, organizations may opt to have sensitive trash disposed of by a bonded waste-disposal company. If so, the trash should be securely stored until it is collected by that company.
3. **Receive and send mail at a secure site.** Options include mail drops, post office boxes, or locked mailboxes. The key is that the site remains secure.
4. **Provide reasonable perimeter security for offices.** Use an alarm system, add secure locks to doors and windows, or employ both.
5. **Pay attention to securing auxiliary materials such as:**
    - Calendars (they may note key events in a sensitive matter.)
    - Specialized internal telephone directories.
    - Notebooks and expense logs from sensitive cases.
    - Works in progress such as reports, notes, and graphics on sensitive cases.

- Mailing lists. All such lists which have proprietary value should have "trapped names" placed on them as a safeguard. A "trapped name" is a fictitious one with an address that the organization controls. If mail is ever delivered to the trapped name, it will be apparent that the list has been compromised. Furthermore, the nature of the mailing will probably indicate who bought the list, and may help the victim determine where the security breach occurred.
- Index cards and Rolodexes (if they contain sensitive information.)
- Blackboards, as well as diagrams and charts on easel pads (If they cannot be easily locked up, take a Polaroid photo of them and then erase the original. Secure these photographs.)
- Computer-paper carbons and writing tablets which have impressions from notes on sensitive topics. (Shred them every day.)
- Computer printouts of sensitive data (keep locked up and use a shredder to dispose of them.)

Organizations concerned about the possibility of corporate espionage should establish procedures for classifying and marking sensitive items and should have provisions for their short-term and long-term storage, as well as their disposal or destruction. Large offices should have a structured log-out procedure for sensitive files so it is always possible to determine who had what document, as well as where and when they had it.

Guarding Information Stored in Electronic Format

Electronic data presents a number of security problems that do not exist with manual documents. A small, high-density 1.2 MB computer disk can hold the equivalent of more than two regular size novels. CDs, zip cartridges, and USB storage devices can hold hundreds of times more. With a computer disk, a spy can walk out of a building with hundreds of sensitive files tucked into his shirt pocket. Furthermore, it is fairly quick and simple to copy even large files from a hard disk to a floppy. Employees seeking to remove sensitive data can even e-mail it to an external address so that they never have to physically carry secret information out of the premises.

Since floppy disks, CDs, zip drives, USB storage devices, and 8mm magnetic tape backups have extreme portability, organizations must take rigid measures to protect them and prevent unauthorized copying of sensitive files onto them. The following guidelines will help organizations maintain control over data stored on electronic media:

- **Write sensitive data files to portable disks.** Back them up with another disk. Lock up originals on-site and securely store backups off-site. Furthermore, secured storage areas should blend into their surroundings as much as possible in order to make the information thief's job that much more difficult.
- **Label sensitive magnetic media.** This should include both an external label and an internal, electronic label designating the file's classification. (The Label command in the Properties Section of Windows can do this.)
- **Guard against accidental erasure.** Files should be set so that accidental erasures cannot occur. This will also prohibit a technique used by some corporate spies whereby a sensitive disk is deleted, then the disk, which appears to be blank, is taken off-site. Once off-site, the targeted files are undeleted.
- **Employ password security on sensitive files.** Many word processors can place password protection on files. Combined with other security measures, this provides a fairly good perimeter of security for files. Software that encrypts entire files can also be purchased.
- **Have a consistent backup procedure for all files.** Backup sensitive files onto disks designated and labeled for that purpose.
- **Do not leave disks containing sensitive files unattended or unsecured.** In large offices, require authorized users of classified disks to sign them in and out from a designated librarian.
- **Scan outgoing disks to ensure they have no deleted but recoverable sensitive files.** If a disk does contain such files, reformat the disk, and then write the non-sensitive files onto the disk.
- **Before disposing of disks, cut them up.** For damaged disks containing highly sensitive files, it may be advisable to use a degausser on the disks first. A degausser removes all data from the disk so its contents cannot be retrieved, even by "undelete" programs.

Organizations should also make sure that sensitive files are not kept on hard drives. In addition, employees should be trained not to leave computers unattended if they have sensitive information on them. Before employees go to lunch or on break, they should be required to place their computers in a secure state.

To prevent spies from finding valuable information in the organization's trash, sensitive computer printouts should be shredded and mixed with non-sensitive shredded documents before disposal.

Access to sensitive information must be limited on a need-to-know basis. Organizations should maintain a system such as a supervised access log that enables security to track the information that each person has handled. If sensitive information is to be transmitted over a modem, the files should be encrypted, not just password-protected. Although employees might appreciate the convenience, they should not be allowed to dial into company computers that contain sensitive information from their homes. Any system containing sensitive information should be isolated.

Basic Principles of Spying

Recruited Spies

In order to obtain inside information on a targeted company, a spy will frequently try to recruit an existing employee of that company to act as her agent on the inside. An employee recruited to spy against his employer is known as a "mole." The mole agrees to betray the trust of his employer by handing over confidential information that belongs to his organization. The three most common recruiting methods are false flag recruitment, recruiting by justification, and trapping.

False Flag Recruitment

"False flag" recruitment is among the most common recruiting ploys. If a spy discovers that a subject has strong social or political feelings, he attempts to twist those feelings into an appeal to help the "cause." The spy convinces the recruit that providing information will help save the environmental conditions in the Amazon, will further the interests of the recruit's native country, or will provide some other worthwhile benefit. Of course, the actual intelligence product is used for corporate espionage, not to help the cause, but the recruit does not learn that until it's too late.

Another method that can be used to gain information from a recruit is romantic or sexual seduction. This is not as common as the use of social or political causes as a justification for misappropriating company secrets, but it does happen. The spy or an operative does not necessarily trade sexual favors for company secrets. Often all that is needed is for an operative of the opposite sex to show some interest in the subject.

Recruiting by Justification

If a spy understands basic psychology, she may be able to convince a recruit that spying is not amoral or immoral *in his circumstance*. When recruiting by justification, the spy looks for a person who thinks of himself as a victim. An employee who is bitter at having been passed over for a promotion, for example, provides an excellent prospect for a recruit. Other typical targets include employees who feel they have been underpaid or unrecognized by their employer, and who harbor a great deal of resentment because of it. Under the right conditions, these employees may agree with a spy that the time is ripe for them to "look after number one."

Trapping Recruits
In order to trap an employee of the target so that she is essentially forced to spy on her company, the recruiting spy will look for some sort of weakness in the potential recruit. Common examples include excessive gambling, drug or alcohol abuse, socially unacceptable sexual proclivities, past criminal convictions, and wild spending habits.

Once a weakness has been identified in one of the target's employees, the recruiting spy will do one of two things. If the recruit has some sort of chemical dependency or serious financial problem, the recruiting spy will typically finance the recruit's weakness to the extent that the recruit becomes dependent on the spy's favor. If the recruit has something embarrassing in her past such as a criminal record, the spy will more likely blackmail the recruit to force her to cooperate. In most situations, the recruiter starts as a "friend," helping the target meet his or her needs, but later turns to blackmail to keep the recruit in line.

Regardless of the method by which an employee is recruited, once that recruit has stolen or divulged a secret piece of information, the spy can easily keep that person in line and force them to continue spying. If the recruit tries to back out, the spy simply threatens to turn him in to his employer or the police. The threat of losing his job or possible criminal prosecution is usually sufficient to keep an otherwise hesitant recruit on a tight leash.

Counter-Recruitment Training
Compromising a person's credibility and integrity requires a series of moves that are generally played out over a fairly extended period of time. The methods spies use to "turn" an employee can be very complex and can occur in a multitude of situations; no security officer can see far enough ahead to forestall every potential compromise. It is therefore imperative to train employees to report any suspected recruitment effort made against them as early as possible. The importance of this statement cannot be overestimated. Key employees should be made aware of the most common recruitment techniques, which were described above. In particular, they should be trained to be wary of people who:

- Encourage and finance some vice of the employee.
- Express a great deal of sympathy for a cause that is important to the employee.
- Offer to help with a serious financial problem.
- Attempt to seduce the employee.
- Attempt to blackmail the employee.

Obviously, some of these techniques involve very personal matters that the typical employee will not feel comfortable discussing with their company. That is precisely why spies use these avenues to attack recruits. No amount of training will convince every employee to bring their dark secrets out into the light, but by making employees aware of the ways in which spies operate, an organization may be able to help its employees resist their initial overtures. This sort of training prepares employees to recognize a recruitment campaign before it has advanced to the stage at which the employee can no longer back out.

After Recruitment

Once on board, the mole receives training on gathering intelligence safely and productively. This is not merely an afterthought; the success of the mission depends upon it. Recruits are taught what information they should target, how to collect data safely, how to follow security procedures, how to plant "bugs," and other techniques that will help them effectively extract information from the target.

Targeted Information

Recruits are typically instructed to provide a specific piece or category of information, rather than being allowed to indiscriminately retrieve whatever secret information they happen to come in contact with. The reason is that most recruits lack the technical expertise to identify truly important intelligence data. Furthermore, most recruits are not sophisticated intelligence-gatherers, so the more information they attempt to retrieve, the more likely it is that they will be detected. Therefore, the control (the spy who recruited the mole and directs her activities) typically assigns the recruit a narrowly defined information goal. If the mole successfully completes this task, her objective might be expanded to include other items.

Methods for Safely Collecting Data

In order to reduce the likelihood of an intelligence campaign being compromised, a spy will generally provide the recruit with some training or instruction on how to safely collect information. For instance, when a spy targets sensitive documents, she generally does not steal those documents outright. It is more effective to copy the documents, if possible. The spy still gets the information she needs, and the victim does not know that its secrets have been compromised. If classified documents were to go missing, this could alert the victim to the presence of a spy and cause it to tighten its security controls.

Most spies do not try to remove computer media with sensitive security labels from the site. Instead, they copy files from labeled media onto plain unmarked disks that will not attract attention from security personnel. Rather than carry sensitive information off the premises, they might opt to e-mail the files out to a neutral, relatively anonymous e-mail address. One of a spy's main goals is to keep a low profile. There are a number of red flags that corporate security might look for if espionage is suspected, and an effective spy will try to avoid exhibiting any of these characteristics. For example, a person who consistently shows up at work early or stays late may make people suspicious, particularly if that individual has not, in the past, worked long hours. While it may seem like the best times to steal sensitive information are before or after hours, this activity might actually tip off the victim.

In general, recruits are told not to stand out, and to avoid being labeled as a "problem" employee. If an investigation commences as a result of any security leaks, the recruit wants to be far down the list of potential suspects. Recruits are also instructed to keep their mouths shut. Obviously, they should not to discuss their covert activities with anyone else. Finally, recruits are told to spend their extra income from spying gradually and in a low-key manner. The goal is to avoid attracting attention.

Communications between the Employee and the Control
One of the major rules for an employee-spy is that she should not make direct contact with her control. Instead, the spy and control will typically communicate via a system of signals: a chalk mark in a public place, an innocuous e-mail to a secure address, an innocent note left on a bulletin board, graffiti on a wall, or a mundane newspaper ad. When e-mail is used to transfer documents, it is usually sent to untraceable addresses or employs intermediaries known as "cutouts."

When spies must make direct deliveries to their controls, they leave documents, computer media, or film and tapes at secure spy drops. These drop sites can be in parks, abandoned buildings, behind vending machines, or in other similar locations. The only requirements are accessibility, cover, security, and the imagination of the spy and his contact. Prearranged signals such as those described above are used to let the control know that an item has been left at the site. The control may leave the spy's compensation at the same site.

Security Measures for the Recruit

Spies are instructed not to leave incriminating evidence at their home or at their company workspace. The goal is to eliminate any evidence trail that could lead back to them. Furthermore, they do not want to give the target any indication that it is actually being infiltrated.

Computer security measures for a spy can be of particular importance. Recruits are generally instructed not to save any documents—even for a short time—on a hard drive or floppy drive without encryption. For added security, many corporate spies double-encrypt everything they steal with two different systems. The overriding goal is to leave no incriminating evidence of the intelligence campaign and to avoid detection at all costs. The longer the spy can continue his activities undetected, the more damage he can do.

Planting Bugs

Recruits are taught where listening devices should be planted in order to gather needed information and, at the same time, avoid detection. Bugs are usually placed in meeting rooms, offices of key employees, or other areas conducive to the discussion of secret information. Equally important is the decision of where to deploy taping equipment. The spy needs to place the equipment in a remote location where tapes can be safely retrieved. If taping is done on-site, the spy risks losing the tapes if the listening device is discovered. Finally, the spy must know when and how to service hidden listening devices, and how to safely remove them when the surveillance is finished.

Deception Techniques

In many cases, spies are able to gather information from employees of a target without recruiting those employees in the surveillance campaign. Instead, the spy tricks the employee into revealing confidential information. Typical scams include using fake employment interviews, posing as a corporate headhunter, conducting bogus "market research," soliciting contract bids on fictitious projects, and social engineering. Each of these scams is designed to get the employee to reveal sensitive information about her company's business.

Employment Advertisements

Employment want ads are a great way for intelligence thieves to get existing employees from a target company to turn over sensitive information. The bogus ads offer great job opportunities to people with qualifications that match those of a target's key personnel. The employees who answer the ads think they are applying for a real job; they expect a "technical interview" on what they do. During the bogus interview, the spy will seek to obtain as much information as possible about what the employees do, the projects they work on, the equipment they utilize, etc. This is a very low cost collection method. If the spy meets with the employee in a restaurant, for example, he is only out the cost of a meal and the cost of placing the advertisement. In a highly competitive job market, fake interviews serve as a powerful tool in corporate espionage.

Headhunter Scams

In a variation on the fake employment ad scheme, a spy calls a key employee of the target while posing as a headhunter with a client who is interested in that employee. The "headhunter" asks for a résumé and information about projects on which the employee is currently working. An in-depth interview by the "client" can provide additional details. This method allows the spy to target key employees more directly than simply running fake employment ads.

Market Research Scams

In a market research scam, the spy contacts companies by telephone posing as a representative of a well-known market research company. The spy uses a phony questionnaire designed to obtain background data to assist in further penetration of the company. The spy might, in some cases, attempt to obtain direct intelligence data during the telephone interview. The spy frequently offers the employee a bogus reward of some kind in return for responding to the questionnaire. These calls tend to aim at lower level workers who have operational knowledge of the business, but who are not likely to be as defensive as higher level managers.

Phony Contract Bids

Another indirect method for obtaining intelligence from human sources is the call for phony bids. For instance, a spy might send out an impressive-looking "Request for Proposals" (RFP) package on a construction or manufacturing project. The RFP states that certain operational and financial data must be submitted as part of the bid. This ruse works very well when assessing the ability of a company to manufacture a certain product. The bigger the bait, the more information the target company is likely to reveal. The return address on the RFP is a mail drop, which insulates the spy from detection. The deadline set forth in the phony bid requirements helps ensure that the spy gets the information he needs by the date he needs it.

One advantage of the scams discussed above is that the victims remain unaware that they have turned over sensitive information to a spy, even after the leak has sprung. If there is no follow-up over a job interview, for example, the applicant simply thinks he did not get the job. If there is no feedback on a bid proposal, the victim thinks it failed to get the bid. In general, no feedback is expected on marketing research other than receipt of the promised gift.

Infilitration Techniques

A corporate spy may choose to collect intelligence information himself rather than recruit an employee of the target. Factors that weigh in this decision include a tight time schedule, the lack of available recruits, or expense constraints. The spy might simply have specialized knowledge that makes him the best one to do the job.

Posing as an Employee or Contract Laborer

Penetrating a company can be very simple. As indicated earlier, one common technique is to obtain work as a security officer or a member of the janitorial crew for the victim organization. Anyone who saw the movie *Wall Street* might remember Charlie Sheen's character putting on a janitor's overalls to gain access to sensitive information at a rival company. Even if the hiring company does a background check on all potential employees (usually nothing more than a cursory criminal history search) a good corporate spy will rarely have a serious criminal record. It is not likely that a spy will be screened out during a routine hiring process.

Security professionals often comment that the best spies are people who have advanced technical knowledge: for example, Ph.Ds in electrical engineering or biotechnology. If a spy needs highly technical information on a competitor, he may have to use a person with an advanced technical background who knows how to identify and/or access the sought after materials.

Individuals with high level technical skills and high security privileges generally have to be recruited from within a targeted organization. However, in some intelligence campaigns a spy will plant a person with advanced technical credentials in a targeted company in a professional capacity. That person gains access to the target's proprietary information and funnels it out to the spy. A person who penetrates a company in this manner is known as a "sleeper," an infiltrator who works on a long-term basis with an acceptable cover. Sleepers will be discussed in more detail later in this section.

Stealing Badges

Stealing or counterfeiting employee badges is one fairly common infiltration method utilized by corporate spies. If badges are in use at the target's site, the spy can generally fake a copy using a desktop publishing program. Contractor badge patterns can be viewed on workers eating lunch at local restaurants. Even if the badges have magnetic strips, the spy may still be able to enter the plant at a highly traveled entry point where a guard only makes a quick visual inspection of security badges as people enter the site, allowing anyone displaying a badge to enter. Even if the only method of entry is by an electronic badge scan, a spy can still piggyback in on another person's badge. If the spy displays a badge, an employee of the target can be talked into letting him into the facility.

Stealing badges is also an option. At bars and nightclubs, women might leave their purses and handbags lying about with security badges protruding in open view. Men do the same thing with jackets hung over barstools. A badge purloined on Friday night will probably not be missed until Monday. Once a spy has the badge, he just pastes his picture on the front and he's ready to go. More sophisticated techniques include having someone "lift" a badge from an employee's purse or jacket. The card is passed on to a colleague who runs it through a magnetic card reader. This can be done quickly, in the car in a parking lot, for example. The badge is then returned to the employee before anyone notices it is missing. Later, the magnetic image that was scanned from the stolen card is transfused on to blank ID card stock containing a magnetic strip. With the addition of an appropriate picture and printing, the spy now has a badge that will get him into the facility, and no one knows that security has been compromised.

Moles and Sleepers

If a client has a very long-range interest in monitoring a company, he or she may place a spy in that company as a permanent employee. This employee, known as a sleeper, keeps a low profile and reports to his control on a regular basis about the operations of the company. This kind of spy, especially if well schooled in tradecraft, will be extremely difficult to detect. With all the electronic spydrops available through e-mail, the sleeper never even has to risk exposure by meeting directly with his control.

One way to help prevent the introduction of sleepers is to perform thorough background checks on all applicants. This may help detect operatives who have padded their résumés to make sure they get hired. Of course, a clever spy will make sure that there is a convincing reference for every piece of information on an operative's résumé.

A mole functions in the same manner as a sleeper. The difference between the two is that a sleeper is a person who is deliberately planted as an employee in a company to extract information. A mole, by contrast, is usually an existing employee of the targeted organization who is somehow compromised, agreeing to turn over her company's secrets to the business intelligence professional. When recruiting moles, intelligence specialists look for employees who are stable enough in their professional and personal life to function as a spy on a long-term basis. As discussed earlier, there are a number of ways to recruit a mole, but the prime motivation is usually greed.

Places Where Spies Snoop

When spies do infiltrate a company's premises, they rarely have to break into file cabinets or desk drawers to get the information they need. Due to laziness, ignorance, or just poor organizational skills, employees often fail to lock up sensitive documents each night. Messy desks are the rule, not the exception. Messy desks are easier for a spy to rifle through than neatly organized workstations. If documents are removed from a sloppy desktop, they may not be missed for quite some time.

Messiness is not confined to documents. Computers often have mounds of disks, zip cartridges, and other media lying unprotected around them. Notes on the sides of terminals and screens or in unlocked desk drawers frequently broadcast passwords and userIDs to anyone who cares to look. User manuals lying about often have similar information scribbled inside. All this clutter is created by employees who place convenience before security. Companies that do not enforce clean desk policies and do not require sensitive materials to be locked up are asking for trouble. Employees should be trained to report signs that their offices have been searched (for example, papers have been moved, disks seem to have been shuffled, files are out of order), even when no information is actually missing.

Mailroom

The mailroom is one of the corporate spy's favorite places to snoop. A great deal of information can be obtained from the mailroom by making a simple phone call. The spy can learn where to ship and receive packages, how the target's internal billing system works, where to locate employees of the target company, and even the company's Federal Express account number. A spy can also walk into most mailrooms and, simply by acting like he is supposed to be there, walk away with cost center account numbers, telephone directories, copies of internal communications, and in some cases even correspondence and packages.

Loading Docks

Despite the fact that many companies maintain video cameras and security guard patrols at their loading docks, these can still be great places to gather intelligence and to slip sensitive information out the door. The security personnel at the loading docks are frequently contract workers with minimal training on how to spot a sophisticated infiltrator. Furthermore, contract security personnel may not be familiar with managers and employees from other departments. A spy can sometimes don a badge and a clipboard and move about the loading docks with impunity, unquestioned by the security officers who assume he is supposed to be there. Meanwhile, the spy is copying down purchase order numbers, address label data, and types of merchandise being shipped and received.

Security guards may be trained to prevent the removal of manuals, documents, or software that are labeled or color-coded as "confidential." However, spies can easily change labels and covers to a different color. Security officers generally do not have the training to look for other indicators of sensitive materials that are being removed.

Storage Areas

Spies frequently target storage areas for information because they are generally low traffic areas, thus the risk of being detected is minimal. If someone does come into the area while the spy is there, he will have a cover story handy; he is doing research, an audit, etc. A prop like a clipboard will usually make the story convincing.

For manual documents, the spy will check:
- Unlocked file cabinets
- Unlocked closets and storage rooms
- Areas containing archived microfiche records and computer printouts
- Off-site, rented storage lockers

For computer media, he will be on the lookout for:
- Unlocked storage areas for computer media (disks, tapes, opticals)
- Unsecured media libraries

For the open storage of critical equipment, parts, or raw materials, the spy will note amount, type, and transit information found on the merchandise. If the materials are kept in a secure area, the spy will try to obtain the access code by observing an employee as he or she enters the area. It is also possible to spray entry keypads with an ultraviolet solution that remains invisible to the naked eye. The user unknowingly wipes the solution off the keys that he or she presses when entering the code. The spy can determine the keys the user punched by viewing the keypad with a portable ultraviolet lamp.

Hotels

Hotel rooms are remarkably easy to bug and to search. Whenever a key corporate player travels, there is a chance that spies will be at her heels listening. By using transactional intelligence, spies determine which hotels an executive frequents. Once that piece of information is determined, the spy can set up surveillance of the target's room. For example, spies frequently bribe hotel staff to allow them to enter hotel rooms and plant eavesdropping devices.

Knowing where an executive is staying also makes it easier to set up fixed surveillance of the comings and goings of visitors to the hotel rooms or meeting rooms. For example, the spy can spot the target's vehicle and rig it with satellite tracking to determine follow her movement during a business trip.

Electronic and visual surveillance are not the only spy activities conducive to the hotel environment. If a spy can gain access to an executive's room, whether by bribery or simply by finding the door left open by a maid, he can copy sensitive files from a laptop left in the room. There also may be sensitive documents in the room that the spy can photograph, and trash in the room's waste paper baskets is also a potential source of information.

If sensitive documents are being delivered by a service such as UPS or Federal Express, they can be intercepted after they are delivered to the hotel but before the target has received them. The spy opens the envelope and copies or photographs the contents. The documents are then resealed in a new delivery envelope. The invoice is removed from the plastic holder on the original envelope and placed in the new envelope. The spy affixes a shipping label, which is easy to generate on a desktop program, and no one suspects that the message has been intercepted.

Spies can view materials delivered in a conventional paper envelope without even opening it. There are special solvents called "Mail Inspectors" that can be sprayed on the outside of an envelope that allow the spy to see through the envelope and view the contents inside. After a few minutes, the solution dries and the envelope becomes opaque again. With considerably less sophistication, the spy can simply resort to steaming open envelopes and then resealing them after she has read their contents. It is not generally difficult for a spy to bribe hotel employees in order to gain to access the target's correspondence. The same is true of employees of message and delivery services.

Warning Signs of Infiltrations

If a spy does his or her job properly, it will be very difficult to detect an infiltration. Generally, organizations have a better chance of preventing infiltrations by establishing appropriate security measures such as accompanying all vendors while on-site, requiring security badges for access to sensitive areas, etc. Detection can be difficult, but there are some signs that organizations can look for that might indicate there is a spy in their midst:

- Employees who are most likely to be recruited as spies are those who exhibit some sort of bitterness or resentment toward their employer. Be alert for abnormal activities by employees who seem to feel that they are under-appreciated, under-utilized, or are treated unfairly.

- Employees who express some sort of political or moral opposition to an organization's operations may be susceptible to a false flag recruitment.

- Employees who are undergoing a personal financial problem (frequently associated with drug addiction, gambling addiction, high medical expenses, or some other personal crisis) may also be vulnerable to recruitment.

- Employees who suddenly undergo a major lifestyle change, buying luxury items, taking exotic vacations, etc., with no apparent increase in income should be watched. This is a common red flag of fraud schemes, but may also indicate an employee who is being paid for divulging trade secrets.

- Employees who frequently work late or come to work early may be trying to get access to confidential materials. This behavior is particularly suspicious when the employee in question works unusual hours as compared to others in his or her department.

- In some cases, "moles" will actually discuss their covert activity with their co-workers. Employees should be trained to report this, as well as other suspicious behavior.

- Employees who seem to spend a lot of time in areas not necessary to their work functions, particularly areas where sensitive materials are stored, may be attempting to misappropriate company secrets. This should be investigated, particularly if the employee is found in these areas after hours.

- Similarly, employees who attempt to access sensitive computer files that are either above their authorization level or outside the scope of their work duties might warrant investigation. Organizations should maintain an automated journal that records events such as attempted access of restricted files.

- If employees have sensitive files saved on their hard drives or disks, this may be a sign that they are misdirecting that information. This is especially true when the employee in question is not working on or should not have access to the file in question. If records

reveal that this employee has e-mailed the proprietary information to an off-site location, this is another indicator of information theft.
- Vendors should be escorted at all times when on the organization's premises. Any time a vendor is seen loitering unescorted around file rooms, offices, mail rooms, shipping docks, computer media storage areas or other sensitive zones, the incident should be reported as a security violation and potential intrusion attempt. The same is true for janitorial personnel, security guards, trash collectors, and other non-employees.
- Spies may come disguised as repairpersons, janitors, deliverymen, etc. Incidents in which service technicians show up without having been called may indicate an attempted infiltration.
- Employee reports of lost security badges, access cards, passwords, etc. could be a sign that a spy has stolen these items in order to infiltrate a site.
- Obviously, if files or computer disks that contain sensitive information are missing, this is a clear sign of a theft or misappropriation of information. In general, spies will copy—rather than steal—proprietary information, but sometimes sensitive documents are actually pilfered.
- Employee desks or offices that have been tampered with are a common sign of intrusion. Reports of stolen materials clearly point to an infiltration, but more frequently intruders will only rifle through files, desks, computer disks, etc, choosing to copy sensitive information rather than steal it. Employees should be trained to report incidents where their offices or desks appear to have been "messed up," even when no materials have been stolen.
- Security personnel should log reports of persons who try to enter a facility without proper identification or authorization. Similarly, attempts to "piggyback" into a facility by following a person with authorization could be a sign of an attempted intrusion.
- Reports of trespassing or other criminal activity near a secure facility may also indicate a surveillance campaign. In particular, instances where strangers are seen loitering around the outside of the facility or digging through trash bins could be signs of corporate spying.

Countermeasures

While security officers cannot turn their organizations into impenetrable fortresses, they can implement specific countermeasures to thwart a spy's attempts at infiltrating their company:
- Materials bearing proprietary data should not be stored in areas visible to the public. If no other option exists, the organization should use only unlettered, color-coded

containers as opposed to labeling a particular file drawer "Confidential." This will make it more difficult for spies to tell where sensitive information can be found.

- Organizations should ask their bank about its confidentiality policy and make sure that their bank does not permit tellers to access information on any major account without a manager's permission. If the company has sensitive financial accounts, it should find a bank with computer systems that use mandatory access controls. Such controls prevent employees of the bank, without proper level of privilege, from accessing large accounts. Information on large commercial accounts should be maintained on a need-to-know basis.
- Security should establish a procedure for tracking and locking up sensitive data.
- Cleaning personnel should be properly bonded and identified, and their access to the facility needs to be controlled.
- Vendors should have verified credentials and must be escorted by a company representative during their visit.
- Any proprietary lists must be password protected and trapped.
- Other general countermeasures include educating employees to properly store sensitive data and to question the credentials of anyone visiting the site. Employees should also be instructed as to what information they may disclose over the telephone.
- Employees should sign nondisclosure agreements. In addition, the legal department should be consulted about integrating vendor and supplier nondisclosure agreements into standard contracts.

Transactional Intelligence

Just about any mundane business transaction can offer a potential information payoff to a spy. Frequent flyer miles document where an executive has traveled. Credit card receipts record a trip's itinerary and goods or services purchased. Even videos purchased or rented at a video store are useful for documenting a targeted employee's tastes and proclivities. Any one piece of information by itself has minimal value. Properly compiled, however, this information can provide an extensive dossier on a target.

Informants

The serious corporate spy will develop a network of paid informants who can get this monitoring intelligence for him. These informants come from a wide range of businesses:

- Travel agents
- Airline reservation personnel

- Major credit card companies
- Staff at major Internet providers
- Employees at video, music, and other entertainment outlets
- Staff of adult entertainment providers that the target frequents
- Telephone company employees with access to telephone records
- Employees of commercial database providers such as Dialog and Dun & Bradstreet who have access to transaction records

While the purpose of these informants is not to act as regular spies, they will, for a fee, provide transactional intelligence on a subject. That transactional information can have a critical impact. It can tell a corporate spy about:

- A person's vices
- Details of business travel
- Hotels where the target stayed and where she is likely to stay again in the future (Useful for setting up surveillance)
- Whom the target has called
- Interests and hobbies (another way to edge into the target's confidence)
- Companies or subjects the target has researched

This type of intelligence is really a hybrid of documentary source intelligence (combining purely open sources and gray sources) and HUMINT. An inside contact is needed to obtain the information, but once the contact sells it to a corporate spy, the spy can analyze it without need of additional assistance.

Monitoring intelligence is very helpful in the collection of human intelligence. If a spy knows a subject's hobbies, she can see to it that she "meets" the target at a restaurant, convention, etc., striking up a conversation or possibly a friendship. A targeted employee in this scenario becomes an unwitting source of information.

The spy does not necessarily have to direct these efforts at an employee of the targeted organization. For instance, if the organization uses a contractor to microfilm its records, the spy might attempt to compromise an employee of the contractor or penetrate its security rather than attacking the target organization directly.

A spy can also become his or her own inside source of transactional intelligence. For example, if a spy wants to develop a telephone history on a subject, he can send the subject a free phone card for 60 minutes of calling time. There are companies that will mail the phone cards to the subject and then track all their calls for a small fee (less than $50.00). This kind of service can be a powerful intelligence-gathering device. Employees should be trained to be wary of this kind of scam.

Decoy Websites

The Internet offers additional avenues for collecting information. One tactic used by spies is to set up a website to collect résumés for particular technical specialties. Included on the website is a questionnaire that visitors are instructed to fill out "to aid in placing you." The site can also require visitors to register for "free" research services. The information that the applicants provide makes it possible to keep a log of the links that they access.

It is not difficult to create a site that targets will visit; it is simply a matter of doing some research on hot topics in a particular field. The spy creates a site that has the necessary metatags for search engines to pick up the title. She fills the site with relevant links and builds logging software into the site to track the links that users access. This can create a profile of the user and help the spy determine what he is interested in. The spy can even call users as a follow-up. The user is impressed because someone from the site took an interest in him, and this gives the spy a natural lead-in to pump the subject for information.

A decoy website might also enable the spy to gain access to the target's computer system. For instance, people frequently use the same userID and password for a number of different applications because it is easier to remember than having several different passwords. The spy's website might require visitors to enter a userID and password for the "research services" or to view bogus job postings. This information is stored by the website and later used to try to gain access to the target's computer system. Decoy websites can also be set up so that visitors unwittingly download viruses or other malicious software. This may not necessarily help a spy gain information, but it can help sabotage a company's computer system.

Telling Good Lies

Rather than infiltrate a company to extract needed information, a spy might mislead employees of the target so that they are induced to divulge sensitive information. Given the nature of the data required, it may be simpler and safer to develop a cover story and simply coax the target's employees into revealing information, rather than using an operative to steal the necessary data. This approach can be a powerful one, especially when the spy has a specialized knowledge or background. For example, if the spy has training as an electronic engineer, approaching people in the circuit design department of a high-tech company would have a natural flow or quality. The key to this type of attack is for the spy to be able to mislead the target about her intentions; in other words, the spy has to be able to tell good lies.

Regardless of the spy's background, the lie that she tells must contain a large measure of truth. Lies not built on a foundation of truth falter quickly under skeptical questioning. She must be familiar with the background of her story. Hence, she has to do her homework in advance. If she does not have a firm knowledge of electronic engineering, she has to learn enough about it to carry on a conversation well enough to convince others she knows what she is talking about. This does not mean the spy has to be able to solve complex electrical engineering equations. She just needs to know enough about the subject to keep a conversation going and to steer clear of areas of which she is obviously ignorant.

Suppose the spy is after specifics on the design of a microprocessor. She poses as a sales engineer in a field office. In this position, she would not be expected to know all the details of microprocessor design. Nevertheless, she has a good pretext for contacting someone who is familiar with the design. She could claim, for example, that she is under a time constraint from a customer and she needs some details to help close a sale. To give the call a greater air of authenticity, she can have the "salesman" she's supporting on the line too. She can also tie in the call to current events, dropping the name of a customer who has been written up in the trade press. In other words she creates an internally consistent lie that the employee in the design department can accept and believe.

If the spy has to meet with the employee in person, rather than over the phone, she would bring the necessary props. These include:
- Fake ID
- Bogus business cards
- Product displays
- Associates she can call on the telephone during the meeting to back up her story

The important factor is to make the target comfortable. In advance of the conversation, she prepares by studying technical details about the product and personal details about other people in the company or the industry. These facts are peppered into the conversation with the target, the goal being to get the target to let his guard down and divulge the sought after information.

Visual Surveillance Against People

Pre-Recruitment Surveillance

In developing human sources, spies know that they should never underestimate the importance of doing pre-recruitment surveillance on targets. There are a number of goals for this kind of surveillance. They include:

- To discover:
  - Who they are
  - Where they live
  - What they do in their spare time
  - What they want to keep secret
  - Who their friends are
  - Who their enemies are
- To look for:
  - Cars
  - Homes
  - Recreational activities
  - Levels of income and debts
  - The subject's importance to the organization
- To uncover what they throw in the trash. For example:
  - Financial papers
  - Medical problems
  - Family problems
- To learn about their enemies, such as:
  - Ex-lovers
  - Fired employees
  - Political opponents
  - Competitors
  - People owed money
- To make contact with the target:
  - By finding out what he thinks about his job, family, or life in general
  - By determining the degree to which the target will confide in others

Briefing Files on the Subject

Beyond the fundamentals of doing pre-recruitment surveillance, the corporate spy also must master regular techniques to monitor ongoing operations. These techniques begin with a

briefing file on the intended subject. If a spy were to follow a key executive for the company, the following would be essential starting details:
- Name of the subject
- Photos of the subject
- Detailed description
- Known associates
- Frequent hangouts
- Routine activities and schedule
- Vehicles used (with tag numbers)
- Type of neighborhood where subject lives
- Street or location layout

Moving Surveillance
The spy has to be flexible and imaginative in conducting a moving surveillance. For example, placing a reflectorized stripe on the back of the subject's car makes it more distinctive at night. Laying a cheap wristwatch under the rear tire of the subject's car will establish when he or she leaves; the broken face will stop the watch at the time they depart. If a subject goes into a bar or restaurant, the spy knows to order food or drink and pay for it immediately so that he can blend in and to be ready to leave at a moment's notice.

Fixed Surveillance
Fixed surveillance, while it has many advantages over moving surveillance, has one great vulnerability. The base from which the surveillance is conducted (for example, a van parked across the street from the subject) might be spotted by the target, as well as neighbors and curious passersby. In order to camouflage a fixed surveillance campaign, the spy must be familiar with the surroundings and choose a cover that will blend in.

E-Mail
E-mail is frequently dense with data on company problems, personnel issues, status on projects, travel plans, and merger activity. It is also the most vulnerable form of computer information. The vulnerability arises from the fact that almost anyone in the company has access to the service. Literally, everybody from "temps" to the CEO has an e-mail address. This wide-open access creates an immense exposure that is compounded by the desire for convenience. Employees in many companies are able to check their e-mail from home. Direct access from off-site via modem can permit compromises of the e-mail server.

Once a penetration of an e-mail server occurs, whether by hacking through search engines or by using a legitimate account, a spy is in position to do great harm. She can forge an e-mail address for her account and send messages about the company requesting information. People will respond thinking she is from auditing, for example, when she may be just a "temp" working in customer service.

An internal spy can arrange to intercept sensitive e-mail by inserting e-mail addresses into internal mailing lists. When proprietary or sensitive information is distributed (for example, to the "management" mailing list) the spy receives a copy at either an internal or an external e-mail site. With an external e-mail address embedded into a sensitive mailing list, it is quite possible that an internal spy can monitor electronic mail long after ceasing to work for the targeted company.

E-mail security programs can detect unauthorized addresses planted into lists, so long-term implants are not always an effective strategy. However, when a spy knows intensive activity is afoot, (for example, on a merger or acquisition) short-term "taps" into e-mail lists can be very productive.

Social Engineering

In a social engineering scheme, the information thief manipulates people into handing over secret information through use of trickery, persuasion, threats, or cajolery. The social engineer usually, though not always, operates by phone or e-mail. In some cases, the social engineer obtains direct information from her victim about a company's business operations, contracts, customer lists, or so on. In other cases, a hacker uses social engineering to obtain passwords or otherwise gain access to a computer system. Social engineering is thought to play at least some part in most computer system penetrations.

There are a wide variety of social engineering techniques; the only common denominator being that the spy attempts to extract confidential information from an employee of the target company through some form of trickery or deceit. Some of the more common schemes are described in the following sections.

The Neophyte

In one of the most common social engineering schemes, the spy calls the help desk of a target company and claims to be a new employee on her first day at work. The spy complains that she has not yet been given a password and so she has been unable to start her computer and begin working. The help desk employee gives the spy a password, thereby enabling her to enter the company's system. Typically, the spy does not call the help desk directly in this type of scheme. Instead, she calls another department and asks to be transferred to the help desk so the call appears to be internal.

The Power Broker

In another common scheme, the attacker contacts the help desk and claims to be a high-ranking company official, an influential client, or some other imposing figure. Background searches of securities filings, government filings, company websites, or annual reports are used to choose the fake identity the spy will use. The spy uses his false credentials to bully the help desk into handing out passwords, remote-access software, or even some key piece of business information.

The Systems Administrator

In this scheme, an information thief contacts a computer user in an organization and claims to be an IT employee of the company. She tells the user that a "network problem" has been identified with the user's computer. The spy asks for the password the user logged on with so she can fix the problem. Most employees are willing to give their password out to a systems administrator when requested, making this technique very effective. In a similar scheme, the spy will pass out a memo on customer letterhead asking users to verify their log-on information for "security reasons."

Fraudulent Surveys

Fake surveys are another common social engineering scheme. Posing as survey takers, either in person or over the Internet, spies gather information from people about their names, nicknames, ages, birth dates, names and birthdays of spouses or children, pets, favorite hobbies, favorite song, favorite movie, and dozens of other personal preferences and attributes. The theory is that most people choose a password that has some level of personal importance. The spies take the responses from their "surveys" and try them as passwords when they attempt to break into a system.

Fake Prizes

Finally, fake gift certificates or sweepstakes can be used to get access to a person's password. For instance, an employee of a target company is sent an e-mail gift certificate from a fake vendor the spy has set up. The employee might be told the gift certificate is a prize, or that it was purchased for them by a "secret admirer." In any event, the employee only has to access the "vendor's" website in order to select the merchandise she wants to buy with her gift certificate. Of course, in order to make the purchase she has to log onto a special area of the website, which requires a userID and password. The spy in this scheme is betting that the employee will use the same userID and password that she uses at work.

Reverse Social Engineering

Reverse social engineering creates the impression in the target's mind that the spy is someone who can help them. It is actually a form of false flag recruitment. The scam can be perpetrated by telephone, e-mail, or regular mail. In a typical scheme, the spy poses as a representative of some software company. He sends a message to the target indicating that a software product (Product X) that the target owns has a possible defect. The target is instructed to call the software company (the spy) with her userID and password in order to receive the fix. When the target calls, the spy obtains her access codes and then pronounces that her edition of the product is okay. Now the spy has access to that software product (for instance, a sensitive database) to use at will.

Countering Social Engineering

There are a number of security measures organizations can adopt to counteract social engineering schemes. While a few technical solutions may help, the majority of controls for this type of attack involve training employees to be aware of how social engineering works, the data that spies will seek, and the information that employees are allowed to disseminate.

Help desk employees should be trained to ask specific, identifying questions before giving out any information over the phone. The organization should clearly explain the minimum identification requirements that callers must meet before information can be distributed. A two-factor authentication rule should be mandatory. If a caller fails to identify himself according to the authentication rule, the person taking the call should report this incident to the security group as an unauthorized intrusion attempt.

When information is given out, it should be harmless, boilerplate information. Passwords or personal identification numbers should never be distributed over the phone without concrete proof of the caller's identity. References to key administrative, technical, and billing contacts for the corporate Internet domain should also be as anonymous as possible. If a company does not list its domain administrator by title, then a spy may not know exactly whom to impersonate when he or she calls the help desk. Techniques already discussed such as properly disposing of confidential trash will also help prevent dumpster divers from coming up with contact information that they can use to trick employees.

Employee awareness is another key to fighting social engineering. Employees may be told what information to give out and what authentication factors to require, but it is another thing to get them to follow these procedures. One of the most effective ways to promote compliance with security policies is to make people aware of threats and actual instances of social engineering attacks. Some organizations maintain internal websites or distribute employee newsletters with stories about security breaches, along with prevention tips and information.

An even more effective awareness method is to selectively test employees' security readiness. For instance, security personnel should call their own organization's help desk to see what information they can obtain without identifying themselves. It is also a good idea to run the "systems administrator" scam on employees six months after they have started, to see if they remember not to give out their passwords to random MIS calls. If employees give up information without following procedures, they should get a stern warning about their security responsibilities. This type of reminder will be remembered far longer than a training session.

Cloaking and Misdirection

While honesty is essential in business dealings with associates and investors, it cannot always be a security team's primary strategy. In some circumstances, misdirecting the opponent is essential. Rather than remaining passively behind the static defenses of security officers, perimeter fences, locks, and access controls, a security manager may need to create an active counterattack program. Such a program ensures that information thieves are as misinformed as possible. A misinformed opponent is a defeated one.

Intelligence Needs

Good intelligence gathering is a prelude to any successful counteroffensive against industrial espionage agents. If a manager does not know the opponents and their methods of attack, effective cloaking and misdirection will not be possible.

An effective intelligence-gathering network need not employ an army of spies. Basic intelligence can be gathered from a variety of sources, which include print media, commercial databases, networking with other security managers, existing staff within the company, and regular security surveys of the business. This type of ongoing, low-level intelligence program helps identify potential and emerging security problems. Increasing the activity during periods of heightened threat to the business is not difficult. Because a preliminary intelligence system will already be in place, bringing on additional personnel and resources will not be overwhelming.

Print Media

Print sources should not consist of an unread mountain of journals on the manager's desk. It is far more productive to subscribe to just a few professional publications that are read and indexed. *Security Management,* the National Association of Legal Investigators' *The Legal Investigator,* and the *Journal of Security Administration* offer insight on the latest security and investigative trends.

Local newspapers can provide an overview of general criminal activity relevant to the business, and area business journals are good sources for accounts of industrial espionage. The security team should also read employment ads for phony job interview schemes.

Database Searches

Computer databases are an excellent intelligence resource. Most security managers do not have the time to regularly read all the major national newspapers and business or technical magazines relevant to their client company. However, a security professional can go to the public library for a few hours once a month and scan magazine databases like InfoTrac for company references. A more efficient method is to subscribe to a clipping service, which will scan hundreds of articles from a variety of sources each month and provide articles containing any keywords (such as a company or employee name) that have been specified.

Managers may want to explore the cost/benefit trade-off of buying a modem and PC for their office that provides immediate access to the growing number of online resources, including ASISNET from the American Society for Industrial Security (www.asisonline.org) and a host of news databases. In scanning such databases, the security manager can run searches on any references to the company's name, officers, or products, as well as on the following key case topics:

- Industrial espionage
- Business intelligence
- Competitor intelligence

The researcher should read all online abstracts and save any articles if further details are required. A picture will emerge of what is available in the public domain about the company. The security team should then evaluate how this information could work to an information thief's advantage.

More and more local newspapers are becoming electronically available via the Internet or through libraries. The astute security manager should use this resource to check for local criminal trends, locate mentions of the company and its officers, and perform background investigations on security risks.

Networking

Networking with other security professionals should not be difficult. Local chapters of ASIS, fellow CFEs, investigative organizations, and former law enforcement officers' societies deserve full participation. Meetings of technical societies that are relevant to the business may also be worthwhile. Even though these meetings may not directly address security issues, they provide useful intelligence about the business. For example, if a company manufactures chemicals, the security manager could attend the state chemical society meeting to learn what is being publicly discussed about her company and the industry in general.

Existing Staffing

An organization's employees are often its most neglected intelligence tool. Proper training of all company employees fosters the passage of vital intelligence to the security manager or investigator. For example, security officers can report patrol observations such as attempts by outsiders to search the company's trash bins by outsiders. Sales staff can identify incidents when strangers have tried to pump them for information at a trade show. Technical personnel might report overly friendly members of the opposite sex who ask too many business-related questions at the local watering hole.

Communication with senior management is also essential. If the development of a new product line creates new security risks or problems, the security manager, investigator, or internal monitor needs to know. Efforts to protect a product prior to market release require the coordination of various company departments.

Security Surveys

Frequent security surveys help reveal potential weaknesses and new threats to any organization. They offer insight on where and how attacks might happen, and if a company suspects that it has already been infiltrated by a spy, a security survey can help determine how that infiltration could have occurred and help focus the investigation on the most probable techniques. These surveys provide the security professional with a chance to see the business through the eyes of an information thief. A perceptive security manager analyzes the company's business in a creative way, looking through a spy's eyes for pathways to information that might otherwise have been overlooked. If a manager wishes to deceive potential information thieves, security surveys can tell where the pickings for a thief are best and where to leave the bait.

TESTING THE PERIMETER

A security survey should begin at the perimeter of the organization. The security professional needs to visualize themselves as a determined attacker. Do the alarm and video camera systems deter from entering the premises without authorization? How easy is it to bypass the access control systems? Can badges be obtained without much trouble through deception or theft? Are basic defenses (fences, locks, barriers, and security patrols) in place and in good repair?

PENETRATION TECHNIQUES

The person performing the security survey should use penetration techniques at various times of the day to determine when the company has the greatest degree of vulnerability. Are they able to easily walk into the plant on the third shift? Are vendors allowed to wander about the facility unescorted? Can a visitor or employee walk unchallenged out of the facility past guard stations carrying sensitive documents, computer disks, or a portable computer? Are cleaning personnel properly supervised when on-site?

CHECKING FOR UNSECURED WORK AREAS

Security personnel should also study the way employees' work areas are maintained. Are sensitive documents locked up at night? Are the copy machines electronically locked down so a special access card is needed to use them? Do sensitive areas such as research labs and computer media libraries have their own separate alarm systems and access controls? Are filing cabinets locked at night? Does security do random patrols of the office areas and the plant at night? Are all persons in sensitive areas challenged for proper credentials?

PRETEXT CALLS

Security officers can determine their organizations' vulnerabilities to certain external threats by calling their own employees at work. It is important to determine what an outsider could learn by making pretext calls. Do employees accept what they are told over the phone at face value, or do they verify to whom they are talking before giving out sensitive information?

TESTING PROPRIETARY LISTS AND DIRECTORIES

It is important to make sure that proprietary lists are trapped. Audits of e-mail lists should be periodically conducted to ensure that no one plants unauthorized addresses. Are internal directories and telephone lists distributed in a secure manner? Is sensitive waste (paper and computer media) shredded and disposed of securely?

SECURITY STAFF AWARENESS AND LINES OF COMMUNICATION

The organization's security force should have training in protecting proprietary information. If something out of the ordinary happens, do they have a means of communicating those incidents to management? Is an intelligence collection strategy in place? Will patrol officers lock up sensitive documents they find unsecured and make out a report detailing the security oversight? Do they know how to check for spy drops? Are they taught to observe suspicious activity such as an employee who always works late?

EMPLOYEE SECURITY TRAINING

It should be the goal of every corporate security office to make sure that employees are aware of the importance of security and are trained how to protect sensitive information. What kind of proprietary information safeguards do employees learn? How regularly do they receive training? Are they encouraged to report suspicious activity?

MULTIPLE LAYERS OF SECURITY

There should be multiple layers of security protecting the most sensitive information. It should get progressively harder to breach security controls as one gets closer to the "inner sanctum." Does the organization have more than one layer of protection for its information, and is each layer effective? Or is perimeter security the only real impediment? If multiple layers exist, do they offer real impediments to spies, or are they minor hurdles?

Cloaking Operations

With good intelligence to identify probable channels for information thieves, a security manager can commence the cloaking of sensitive operations. Fluctuations in traffic offer industrial spies the best indirect insight into a business. Changes in the rates, deliveries, shipments, emissions, and the types and amounts of trash can reveal a great deal.

The cost to mask these fluctuations may be significant at times. Appropriate guidance from senior management must be a factor in computing the cost-benefit trade-off. If the risks to a product line outweigh the security costs, the security staff should begin a cloaking program.

Trash and Waste Disposal

Trash and waste disposal are excellent places to start. Adding a consistent amount of shredded, non-sensitive paper to sensitive document waste greatly diminishes the chance of traffic analysis. Non-documentary waste should be secured in a locked holding area. From there, it can be sorted into uniform shipment modules before release to the waste disposal vendor. When the contents of waste shipments are fairly uniform, deciphering plant operations from them becomes much more difficult.

Deliveries and Shipments

Deliveries and shipments should be made on as uniform a schedule as possible. Ideally, organizations should avoid scheduling major deliveries just before a product manufacturing run. This is just the sort of tip-off corporate spies are looking for. Maintaining adequate inventory levels can go a long way toward eliminating this problem.

If the manufacturing process dictates tight parts delivery schedules, the use of a common carrier will at least mask the identity of the supplier to external surveillance. Utilizing a mix of common carriers and company trucks helps cloak shipments. Company drivers should be trained to vary their schedules and delivery routes. They should also be instructed to report any suspicions of intelligence gathering operations.

Hours of Operation and Power Consumption

During highly sensitive manufacturing, testing, or research operations, the hours of operation and levels of power consumption should be kept as uniform as possible. Lights can be left on continuously, and some kind of around-the-clock activity can be maintained to mask sensitive operations.

Emissions

If the heightened activity during a crisis period will result in additional smoke or steam emissions, the change should be made as gradually as possible. The key is to avoid creating an unusual pattern of activity. Management should ease the company into any critical period of operations to avoid drawing the attention of the outside world. Similarly, it should ease out of the critical period when it is over.

Food Deliveries

If significant numbers of employees need to work unusual hours in a crisis period, the company should provide food service for them from the company's cafeteria. Increased food deliveries to the site can indicate that something out of the ordinary is going on.

Computer Emanations

If increased computer use creates unusual traffic in emanations, the company can start masking it early with a buildup of non-sensitive processing. In addition, appropriate shielding will cut down on emanations whenever feasible.

Travel Plans

Travel by key executives and technical staff offers useful intelligence information to a spy. During periods of intense financial activity such as a possible acquisition or merger, meetings can be scheduled at neutral locations with short notice to any outside parties, such as hotels, travel agents, and rental car agencies.

Use the names of low-profile employees or businesses when booking rooms and travel arrangements. Group travel by key executives should be minimized, and the company should be sure to stagger the arrival and departure of senior managers at the neutral site. Executives should be briefed not to discuss sensitive matters in their hotel rooms or on the telephones in those rooms. When feasible, security should be present in the executive's room when the executive is out. If not feasible, the executives should be trained not to leave sensitive information unattended in their rooms.

Technical staff members traveling to research centers or facilities for fact-finding purposes should mix in some non-sensitive stops on their itinerary. The additional destinations will confuse onlookers in case of possible surveillance. Stops at technical or research libraries to do some non-sensitive personal research can leave a spy unsure about which facility on the trip was actually important.

Misdirection

Attempts to compromise employees or information controls demand an immediate response. The question is whether to simply shore up security or use the situation to misdirect the opposition. Misdirection involves feeding information thieves false facts in order to neutralize their intelligence efforts.

Careful guidance from senior management will be necessary. If misdirection is determined to be the best way to protect the organization, the false facts that are released must not come back to hurt the company, its officers, its stockholders, or its investors.

Assuming that a misdirection policy is approved and carefully crafted, it might work as follows. Suppose security has detected an employment advertisement that appears designed to lure technical staff to phony interviews so they can be pumped for information. Security can go on the offensive to counter this threat by sending technical staff members with business intelligence training as decoys. Their goal is to give an impressive technical interview that sends the opponent following dead end leads. At the same time, the decoy is able to gather intelligence on what the industrial spies are after. This type of information strengthens defenses at the target company.

At trade fairs, conventions, and technical meetings, employees should have a prepared story to tell industrial spies. When confronted with camouflaged questioning about an industrial process, employees can relate information that sounds convincing but that actually leads the opposition astray. Again, such misinformation must be sufficiently technical in nature so its general release to the public would not damage the company.

Spotting False Suitors

A tactic sometimes utilized by business intelligence professionals is to initiate false negotiations for the purchase of services, product lines, or portions of the target company. During the course of the negotiations, the spy attempts to gain valuable information about the target, its cost structure, production schedule, manufacturing processes, etc. Other similar tactics that have already been discussed include spies posing as headhunters, conducting false employment interviews to gather information, and posing as a potential customer through the use of bogus RFPs.

Management and employees should be trained to spot these schemes. False inquiries by purchasers can be terminated quickly if organizations require interested parties to demonstrate financial qualifications before commencing with any high-level negotiations. Financial statements of the suitor should be verified. Similarly, before replying to any RFP, it goes without saying that an organization should verify the existence and interest of the company seeking proposals. This can be easily accomplished by simply looking up the company in the phone book or traveling to its physical address to verify that the company exists. A search of state and county records can also be conducted to determine if the company is legally registered. Another simple technique is to contact others in the relevant industry to see if they have heard of the suitor company. In cases where a spy is posing as a representative of an existing company, a phone call to this company to verify the information in the RFP will help ensure that the request is legitimate. If evidence suggests that the party or company is a false front, security can again take the opportunity to provide misleading information to the potential information thieves.

If employees are approached by companies interested in hiring them, similar steps should be taken to ensure that these suitors are not actually corporate spies fishing for information. Employees should be trained to report suspicious offers by outsiders. Of course, it is unrealistic to expect employees to report every job offer they receive or every employment interview they take. What organizations can do is train their employees—particularly those in possession of key information—to be wary of the deception tactics spies use. It is a good idea to explain to key personnel how these schemes are generally initiated, and what information the spy will be trying to obtain. Hopefully, this will help employees spot phony suitors and report them before any meetings or bogus interviews are conducted. In the alternative, employees may at least be wary of suspicious questions during bogus interviews and know enough not to divulge sensitive information.

In addition to training key employees to spot deception techniques, it may be advantageous to train these employees in some of the simple methods they can use to determine if a suitor is legitimate, such as verifying its phone number or address, contacting others in the industry, or simply calling the company's number in the phone book (if one is listed) to verify the time of an interview. These are steps that employees can take without having to tell their employer about outside job offers, and which might uncover a corporate espionage campaign.

Vendors and Suppliers

Secondary interviewing of suppliers and vendors by corporate spies poses a problem. A company rarely has direct control over what its suppliers and vendors tell third parties. So suppliers and vendors should be given information on a need-to-know basis only.

Proper training of purchasing agents is also helpful. Suppliers of highly critical components or services need to be signatories to nondisclosure agreements. If intelligence reveals a supplier to be a major leak, the short-term answer may be sending misinformation through that supplier. The long-term solution would be termination, legal action, or both.

Technical Articles and Publications

Articles published by technical staff can create cavernous holes in an information security program. Staff may unintentionally leak sensitive information as part of an innocent academic exchange. The same is true for public speaking engagements. A policy of pre-publication review by security personnel and technical management is an absolute must.

While pre-publication reviews of articles and speeches are certainly appropriate, organizations should not use technical articles and speeches as a method for disseminating misinformation. There are other means for conducting a counterespionage campaign that trammel less on issues such as freedom of expression, the right to academic inquiry, and the right to be fairly informed.

Consultants

Consultants can be a source of leaks, and their access to confidential or sensitive information should therefore be kept on a need-to-know status. Their activities should be compartmentalized as much as possible. As with vendors and suppliers, consultants can be fed misinformation if they are suspected of leaking data to a competitor.

If highly sensitive information must be discussed with a consultant, it may be advisable to place the discussions in a context that limits the consultant's knowledge of inside information. For example, an expert can tell you what the melting point of a semiconductor material is, but they do not necessarily need to know why you need to know that information. Obviously, the need to protect information must be weighed against the business need of consultants to have access to information and a free flow of ideas in order to be able to perform their work effectively.

Dealing with Employees who are Leaving

Technical employees who give notice that they are leaving their jobs while working on highly sensitive projects should be transferred to non-sensitive projects until their termination date. All employees (as well as vendors, contractors, consultants, temporary help, etc.) should be required to sign nondisclosure agreements at the time of their hiring. When employees are leaving an organization, they should be reminded of their obligation to protect the organization's secrets, even after their employment ends. It is a good idea to have employees sign a statement at their exit interviews in which they affirm that they understand and will comply with the terms of the nondisclosure agreements they have signed.

If reliable intelligence reveals that an employee intends to sell the organization's proprietary information, placing misleading information in his hands may dilute some of the impact. Planting technical gossip in the company lunchroom, for example, may be an effective method for misinforming an employee.

Hackers

If hackers or information thieves penetrate the computer system, security should give them something to munch on. The idea is to place worthless, highly technical sounding files on the company's system. If someone signs on from an off-site location and starts to download one of these files, security is notified and an investigation begins.

The same tactic applies to PCs. Sensitive data should be placed on disks and locked in a safe when not in use. Bogus files containing misinformation can be left on the hard drive for prying eyes. If a security manager really wants spies to take the bait, she can add password protection to the system to protect the bogus files. The fact that the files are protected helps convince potential thieves that they contain valuable information. The same idea works for a computer sent out for repair. Placing bogus data on the hard drive prevents service technicians from stealing and selling actual company trade secrets.

Another twist on the same theme is to place documents and computer auxiliary items containing bogus data in the trash. Auxiliary items include spent computer ribbons, old floppy disks, old magnetic tapes, used computer paper, and other media. This technique is an excellent method for managing information thieves who like to go dumpster diving.

If an employee is suspected of stealing computer files, that individual should be assigned a computer with a honey pot of bogus technical information. If the information shows up in the public sector, security will know who is leaking the information.

Technical Surveillance

The popular image of the spy, at least as portrayed on television and in the movies, is very often associated with all sorts of high-tech gadgets; everything from miniature cameras to exotic listening devices to radio wristwatches and telephones hidden in shoes. Obviously, many of these devices are fanciful and, while they may provide interesting entertainment, they are far removed from the real world of corporate espionage.

Corporate spies do, however, employ various forms of technological surveillance equipment, the tools varying according to the needs of the job at hand. In general, corporate spies only resort to using high-tech equipment when simpler means are not available to accomplish the task. In some cases a miniature camera might be called for to copy sensitive documents, but not when a nearby copy machine can be used to achieve the same result. In other instances a wiretap may be needed, but only when there is no other means to monitor a subject's communications. Sometimes satellite tracking of motor vehicles becomes necessary, but not when simple visual surveillance will tell the spy where the subject has traveled. In other words, corporate spies that know what they are doing do not employ technology for the sake of using fancy gadgets.

When spies do resort to the use of technical surveillance equipment, it is usually to gather nondocumentary evidence; information that cannot be found through open sources or in the target's files. The methods that spies employ to gather nondocumentary information include: (1) taking photographs, (2) conducting surveillance and visual sightings, (3) listening to conversations, (4) monitoring computers and computer communications, (5) analyzing traffic at a plant, and (6) monitoring emanations from computers and telecommunications equipment.

Nondocumentary information has certain advantages. It captures changes over time (photographs taken at different times) or processes as they occur (videotaping). Electronic surveillance can provide the spy with information that would take many hours of documentary analysis to acquire. Aerial photography provides a broad perspective on the manufacturing physical plant that is not ordinarily possible with documents alone. Intercepting computer communications and emanations can provide an inside look at the supply, purchasing, manufacturing, and marketing channels of a target that cannot be replicated by another source.

The fact that a technical activity is possible does not mean that it is advisable. Most types of electronic surveillance carry potentially serious repercussions. In many cases they are clearly illegal. Any prudent spy will employ technical intelligence methods with restraint. Only amateurs will rush into a surveillance operation by "bugging" this line and that junction box. These novices ignore the fact that the more one bugs, the greater the chances of having the surveillance campaign discovered. In addition, a corporate spy with any seasoning will realize that indiscriminate bugging produces too much signal traffic to analyze.

Experienced corporate spies know what they are looking for and devise carefully protected collection plans before initiating their surveillance campaigns. They know that the more time spent planning, the more likely it is that their electronic surveillance will go undetected and the greater the intelligence yield will be. The rules most BI professionals use for protected electronic surveillance include the following:

1. If devices (such as microphones or video cameras) are to be left on-site, those devices must not be traceable back to the spy or the client. The markings on the equipment must

not establish a paper trail on which to build an investigation. Experienced spies use generic equipment available from multiple sources.

2. Wire taps and their associated devices must blend into their surroundings so nothing appears out of the ordinary to the layperson. Smart spies do not use contraptions that can easily be identified as "bugs."

3. Radio transmitters must not send signals in those parts of the electromagnetic spectrum that are in common commercial use. Professionals avoid using cellular telephone bands, CB channels, or AM or FM radio channels for covert transmissions. They also find out if the target site uses commercial two-way radio frequencies and avoid using those bands.

4. A competent spy does not leave a hard wire connection between the wiretap and the place where he or she conducts listening. If someone located the tap, all that person would have to do is trace the hard wire line to locate the spy.

5. If the spy conducts off-site reception of computer emanations and signals, the reception vehicle or site should have sufficient camouflage or should be adequately disguised to avoid any notice or detection.

6. A good spy never reveals anything about an intelligence campaign to anyone except her client, even after the job is finished.

7. Once a job is finished, a report has been written and delivered to the client, a spy destroys all documentary evidence of the campaign.

Aerial Photography

Though its origins lie in the military sector, aerial photography has emerged as a valuable tool in business intelligence. There are private aerial photography firms that have fairly complete negatives for land in their service area. These firms also accept special assignments to photograph specific ground areas on a schedule specified by the client. Aerial photography is used by spies to gather information on a competitor's construction or expansion products, to measure the size of its shipments, or to determine the number of employees that the company has working, among other things.

Bugging and Wiretapping

Hidden microphones, wiretaps, and other forms of electronic surveillance equipment have become extremely common ways for intelligence professionals to keep tabs on their competition. The spy has two primary considerations in a wiretapping campaign: where to insert the surveillance equipment and which of the various technologies to employ.

The Insertion Point

In identifying the insertion point, the spy not only has to choose an area where proprietary information is likely to be discussed or displayed on computer screens, but also where background noise and electronic interference remain minimal. Spies frequently choose areas with proximity to computers and telecommunications equipment carrying proprietary data as an insertion point.

Spies may also target areas conducive to employee conversations. This can include any place, inside or outside the targeted company, where key personnel gather and chat. Examples include smoking areas, recreational areas such as bars, lounges, and coffeehouses, employee cafeterias, relaxation areas, exercise rooms, and meeting rooms. To target particular operations such as information services, spies might wire the offices of key managers, which are likely to provide access to a large portion of human information flow.

The Technology

In determining which technologies to employ, the spy must factor in environmental conditions such as lighting (if video surveillance is employed), noise levels, and distance from the source. Other factors include the risk of the sensing device being discovered, power supply problems, and access to the device for servicing after installation.

Common electronic eavesdropping devices include:
- "Drop-in" telephone bugs
- Carbon microphones
- Magnetic or dynamic microphones
- Electret microphone
- Spike microphones
- Cavity microphones
- Low power consumption transmitters
- Infinity transmitters
- Shotgun or parabolic microphones
- Cellular telephone receivers

- Video cameras and transmitters
- Satellite tracking of vehicles

It is not difficult at all for spies to purchase electronic listening equipment. The Internet, for example, has a number of sites that advertise vast inventories of equipment ranging from audio devices to miniature video cameras to satellite tracking systems. Most of these sites urge their customers to use their merchandise only in a "legally appropriate" manner and advertise the equipment for purposes like checking for intruders or ensuring one's own privacy. In truth, however, these devices can and are used by corporate spies to pilfer the proprietary secrets of their targets.

Some of the more common forms of surveillance equipment are discussed in the following sections.

SATELLITE TRACKING SYSTEMS

In most satellite tracking systems, a small transmitter is surreptitiously attached to the subject's vehicle. Common hiding areas include the trunk, inside fenders, or under the rear bumper. The transmitter communicates with Global Positioning Satellites (GPS) and converts the coordinates of the vehicle onto a map. The spy only needs access to the Internet and a password to enter a special, private home page where he can view maps that show the vehicle's location and path. These systems are capable of generating event lists and plain-text histories of where the vehicle has traveled. A variation on this tracking design is that in some satellite tracking software the system creates a trail of electronic breadcrumbs on the map display. The map can be a powerful tool in tracking the movements of executives and key company employees.

DROP-IN TELEPHONE BUGS

Spies frequently use drop-in telephone bugs, which have the advantage of blending in with everyday existing telephone equipment. Drop-in bugs are simply inserted into the handset device on a normal telephone. The target's conversations are transmitted to a remote receiver where they are recorded.

Drop-in bugs are rarely detected because most people never bother to unscrew the plastic covers on the handset and perform a detailed check of the internal components. Thus, a drop-in telephone bug offers minimal risk of exposure to the spy. When a spy has access to the physical premises of a target and wants to be able to listen to conversations on a particular telephone line, this device is usually the chosen method of surveillance.

CARBON MICROPHONES

Carbon microphones, while larger than most spy audio devices, provide good pick-up if properly hidden and located. They offer excellent coverage of fixed locations: smoke rooms, employee lounges, and other gathering spots. As with other forms of listening equipment, these microphones are usually equipped with a transmitter that relays intercepted conversations off-site to a recorder. This is much safer, from the spy's perspective, than maintaining a recorder on-site. With a remote transmitter, even if the microphone is detected, the recorded material cannot be located or recovered by the target.

MAGNETIC AND ELECTRET MICROPHONES

Magnetic or dynamic microphones can be very small. They are useful when a microphone needs to be close to the speakers and hidden inside something small. Electret microphones also provide good close range coverage. Both types of microphones are smaller than the standard carbon microphone, though they tend to offer a lower range of coverage.

SPIKE AND CAVITY MICROPHONES

Spike and cavity microphones work best when the spy has access to an adjoining area and needs to penetrate his surveillance into the next room. For example, if a spy has free range in a utility room next door or in an adjacent hotel or motel room, a spike microphone can be inserted through the adjoining wall to monitor conversations in the target's room. This type of microphone is so small at its insertion point that it is virtually undetectable to the casual observer.

INFINITY TRANSMITTERS

Infinity transmitters are a special kind of device that can be activated from a remote location. Once an infinity transmitter has been inserted in a phone, a spy can call that telephone from anywhere in the world and turn it into a listening device. Unknown to the parties present, the telephone becomes a hidden microphone.

SHOTGUN OR PARABOLIC MICROPHONES

For listening to conversations at a long distance, shotgun microphones, parabolic mike devices, and laser audio detection equipment can overhear even quiet discussions, provided background noise is not too high. The spy has to be mindful of having adequate cover to protect the listening post.

WIRETAPS

Wiretapping involves splicing a listening or recording device into a wire (such as a telephone wire, a PBX cable, an alarm system, or a local area network cable) that is used for communication by the target. Standard phone systems, in particular, are very vulnerable to wiretapping. Taps are usually placed at the telephone box in the basements of buildings, on lines outside buildings, or on telephone pole junction boxes near the target's offices.

Warning Signs of Bugging

Covert eavesdropping may be difficult to detect, particularly because most people do not know what signs to look for. James M. Atkinson of the Granite Island Group, one of the leading technical surveillance countermeasures firms in the U.S., has compiled a list of 23 warning signs which might indicate that an organization is the target of an electronic eavesdropping campaign.[*] Those red flags are listed below:

1. Others seem to know your confidential business or trade secrets. This is the most common indicator of a bugging campaign.
2. Information discussed in secret meetings or contained in secret bids does not remain secret. Confidential meetings are among the most popular targets of corporate spies.
3. People seem to know about your organization's activities when they should not.
4. Strange sounds or volume changes are detected on your phone lines. This is a common byproduct of wiretaps.
5. You notice unusual static, popping, or scratching on phone lines. Another common sign of a wiretap or bug.
6. You can hear sounds coming from your phone handset when it is hung up. This is typically caused by a device called a "hook switch bypass," which turns a telephone receiver into a microphone and allows a spy to monitor conversations near the phone.
7. Your phone rings and nobody is on the other end of the line, but you hear a very faint tone, or a high-pitched squeal and beep.
8. An office radio suddenly develops strange interference. This could be caused by eavesdropping devices that use frequencies within the FM radio band. These signals tend to "quiet" FM radios in the vicinity of the bug. To check for bugs, look for transmissions at the far ends of the FM radio band, and at any quiet area along the FM band. If the radio begins to squeal, slowly move it around the room until the sound becomes very high pitched. The radio should be set to the "mono" function rather than "stereo," as this will increase its level of sensitivity.

---

[*] This list is provided courtesy of James M. Atkinson and The Granite Island Group, 127 Eastern Avenue, #291, Gloucester, MA 01930, (978) 546-3803. (www.tscm.com). e-mail: jmatk@tscm.com

9. An office television suddenly develops interference. Eavesdropping devices can tend to interfere with television reception.
10. Your office appears to have been burglarized, but nothing was taken. Someone could have entered the premises in order to plant a listening device.
11. Electrical wall plates (covering outlets, switches, and lighting fixtures) appear to have been moved slightly. These are among the most popular locations for hiding listening devices, which requires that the plates be removed.
12. A dime-sized discoloration appears on an office wall. This is a sign that a pinhole microphone or video camera has been installed.
13. One of your vendors gives you an electronic device such as a desk radio, alarm clock, CD player, small television, and so on. These gifts frequently contain secret eavesdropping devices.
14. A smoke detector, clock, lamp or exit sign in your office or home looks slightly crooked, has a small hole in the surface, or otherwise appears to have been tampered with. These items are also common places for concealing bugs.
15. Certain items such as clocks, radios, lamps, and sprinkler heads just appear in your office without anyone knowing how they got there. They may contain listening equipment and could have been placed in your offices by a spy.
16. Drywall dust or debris is found on the floor next to a wall. This could be a sign that a pinhole microphone or video camera has been installed nearby.
17. Small pieces of ceiling tile or "grit" are found on the floor or on a desk. This indicates that a ceiling tile has been moved, possibly because someone has installed a technical surveillance device above your ceiling.
18. Phone company trucks and utilities workers seem to be spending a lot of time near your home or office. These workers could actually be corporate spies in disguise.
19. Telephone, cable, plumbing, or air conditioning repair people show up to work when no one called them. This is a very common method for an eavesdropper to plant a bug.
20. Service or delivery trucks are often parked nearby with nobody in them. These vehicles may be listening posts for spies. In particular, look for vehicles that have ladders or pipe racks on the roof, have tinted windows, and are large enough to conceal a person in the back.
21. Your door locks suddenly do not "feel right," they become "sticky," or they fail altogether. This is evidence that the lock has been picked or manipulated by an intruder.
22. Furniture appears to have been moved slightly and no one knows why. Eavesdropping devices are commonly hidden behind or inside furniture.
23. Things seem to have been rummaged through, but nothing is missing. This could be a sign that someone has been looking through your papers, perhaps even copying them before returning them to your work area.

Preliminary Search Procedures

If an organization suspects that wiretapping has occurred, there are a number of preliminary search procedures that the layperson can perform. This section is not designed to make the reader an expert at counter-surveillance techniques; professionals who offer those services can easily be located. However, it is quite feasible for an ordinary person to conduct a basic search for wiretapping equipment. When conducting an inspection for electronic surveillance equipment, be mindful of safety concerns. Never reach into electrical boxes or outlets unless you are sure the power is off, and do not grasp bare wires unless you know they are not live.

KNOW YOUR DEVICES

Wiretapping devices, for the most part, look like hobbyist electronic circuit boards[*]. The major difference is that they are much smaller than the circuit boards of the past. Satellite tracking equipment is usually housed in small metal boxes about the size of a paperback book. They require small antennae that have to face toward the sky.

INSPECTING TELEPHONES

If the mouthpieces or earpieces on telephone handsets have screw-off plastic covers, remove them and make sure no transmitters or unusual looking components are attached to the microphone condensers. Also examine the markings on the condenser unit. Do they match a condenser from a similar telephone kept in a secure area? If the markings are significantly different, have them checked by a representative from the telephone manufacturer.

If the cover on the handset is one solid piece of plastic, look at the two screws that hold the plastic plate on. If the screws have scratches on them (e.g., from a screwdriver) remove the screws and take the plate off. Examine the condensers for signs of tampering or for miniature transmitters.

Examine the back or underside of the telephones. Look for unusual components taped or held by a magnet to the back metal plate. Also look for unusual wires protruding from the phone. (This means any wires other than the regular plastic sheathed cord that is found on all telephones.) If these examinations are negative, then the telephone is probably secure.

If you still suspect the presence of a listening device, do not attempt to disassemble the main part of the telephone. You may damage the unit. Instead, look at the screws holding down

---

[*] The Granite Island Group, a technical surveillance countermeasures firm, provides photographs of some electronic surveillance equipment on its website. (www.tscm.com/whatistscm.html)

the main body of the phone to the metal plate. If those screws show signs of tampering, have someone from the manufacturer examine the unit (or units).

It is also a good idea to inspect the wall box where the telephone attaches to the wall. Carefully remove the cover and check for any electronic components inside. In a normal wall box, you should only see wires and screw points where the wires are tied together. Extraneous components could be electronic listening devices. If you are not sure whether the item you have identified is actually a transmitter or microphone, contact a qualified countermeasures expert, the phone company, or a representative from the phone manufacturer.

INTERFACE BOX

The interface box is a gray box typically located on the side of the building. If a business operates in a multiple occupancy structure, the interface box may be located in a utility closet close to the company's offices. In order to examine the interface box, unscrew the side of the box that is designed for customer access. Look inside with a flashlight. All wiring in the box should look the same, using colors red, blue, green, yellow, and black. You might see some striped colors, but that is fine. There should also be a line coming into the side of the box from the telephone company. What you should be looking for is a transmitter or some form of unusual wiring that does not appear to come from the telephone company and does not lead into your building or office. This could indicate a wiretap.

ABOVE THE CEILING

If an open space exists above the ceiling in your offices, access that area and look around with a flashlight. Be on the lookout for everything from sophisticated transmitters to tape recorders that are crudely hooked into telephone lines. If listening devices have been placed in an attic or in a crawlspace above the ceiling, they probably have not been elaborately camouflaged. It should not be exceedingly difficult to spot surveillance equipment in these areas.

It is a good idea to have the lights turned on in the room below while you search overhead. If someone has drilled holes in the ceiling to insert a microphone, the light should shine through the ceiling and you will be able to detect the holes. Surveillance personnel frequently drill multiple holes before selecting just one as a listening spot or inserting a miniature video camera.

OTHER PLACES TO SEARCH

Use a flashlight to look through the grill panels covering all air conditioning ducts for transmitters or listening devices. Carefully inspect all electrical outlets by removing the cover plates and looking inside with a flashlight. Examine any central utility closets for unusual wiring and electronic devices. Look for signs of debris on the floor under outlets or light switches; this might indicate that someone has removed the wall plates to insert a listening device. Anytime ducts, outlet plates, light fixtures, or similar items have been searched and replaced, their orientation and screw-head positions can be designated with ultra-violet markers. By shining an ultra-violet light on the screws, it is easy to tell if the panels have been removed. This technique makes it much easier to determine if someone has tampered with those items since the last search.

Look under desks and tables in all office spaces for electronic devices or wires that seem out of place. Do not try to tear your office apart while conducting your search; feel your way around and explore with your hands. Look under and behind couches and sofas. It is especially important to closely examine furniture in areas where people are likely to sit and chat. The tables and credenzas in meeting rooms should be checked on a regular basis.

Check any television sets, radios, lamps, telephones, computers, clocks, smoke detectors, or sprinkler heads in the room. If any areas are served by cable TV, be sure to check out the cable lines, converter box, line splitters, and connectors for anything that seems out of place. Any electronic items and wiring that are not essential should be removed, as unused wiring can be used for eavesdropping.

COMPUTERS

Always check the back of computers for monitoring devices taped to the back panel. Examine all connections between the computer and the outside world: lines to printers, network cables, lines to peripheral devices, or lines to monitors. Pay attention to any connectors that have been placed between the computer and its external lines. These connectors may look like they perform a legitimate function, but if the external line could have been plugged directly into the computer, find out why the interface was inserted and who put it there.

The area immediately around the computer should be checked for unusual wiring, electronic boxes, or devices. Any closets or rooms dedicated to housing network equipment such as hubs, routers, cabling rigs, or network monitoring gear needs close examination by a qualified network technician to make sure no alien electronic devices are present.

Video Surveillance

The role that video cameras play in the corporate espionage campaigns has several dimensions. Microcameras placed in a room of computer screens can focus on individual screens and result in the taping of: passwords, logins, user manuals, text specifics, error messages, contents of documents, and keyboard overlays during many hours of transactions. Cameras can be used to monitor activity on receiving and shipping docks. Planted microcameras can track activity on production lines or presentations in meeting rooms. They can also capture executives or key employees at embarrassing moments. Such documentation can later be used for blackmail.

Video cameras with a time and date stamp on the footage offer a means of determining the security activity in the company. Times of security patrols, access to special areas like labs, the emptying of security wastebaskets, and other activities can all be tracked. This information can aid a spy in penetrating restricted or sensitive areas.

Photographic Cameras

Almost as ubiquitous as the "bug," the miniature camera plays a lead role in the canon of spycraft. Many a motion picture has shown the spy, whether after military or industrial secrets, bent over documents quickly snapping the shutter. With the tiny cameras available today, industrial spies can sneak out of a company's premises with numerous secrets tucked away in a purse or shirt pocket.

Minicameras

With the advent of copy machines in almost every American business, the need to employ the minicamera to capture information from documents dramatically declined. Because many sensitive documents stored are in electronic format, computer media such as floppy disks, CDs, zip cartridges, USB storage devices, and the like have also eroded the need for film cameras. Some applications do, however, still exist for the minicamera. Documents such as maps, schematics, diagrams, and engineering drawings frequently cannot be easily copied due to their size. The minicamera is a viable option for capturing the information on these items.

Concealed, stationary cameras with large rolls of film have largely been replaced by video cameras. Film is difficult to replace at hidden, sensitive sites. It is also expensive to process. Videotape is cheap, needs no processing, and can be recorded off-site, far from the video camera/transmitter. Thus, even if the target company discovers the hidden video camera, the footage will remain safely in the spy's control.

Digital Cameras

As digital cameras become smaller in both cost and size, they may become a more formidable tool in the corporate spy's arsenal. Digital images are captured on a small disk whose contents can be loaded into a computer. The image can be enhanced and manipulated using various photo shop programs, thereby offering excellent resolution. The disk carrying the stolen image can be carried off and on premises with little chance of detection.

Infrared Film

Infrared film has value when surveillance is done under very low light or when the spy needs to examine damaged or erased documents. Even the contents of burned documents can be detected under the right conditions with infrared film.

35mm Cameras

For any good spy, a 35mm film camera remains the mainstay in his surveillance arsenal. Even if extensive aerial photographs are taken, observation of the target site at ground level is essential. From the ground view many features like signs, lettering on the side of vehicles, the configuration of buildings and streets, license plates, and other important details become visible. Photographs of key employees of the target can also be valuable information in many intelligence campaigns.

To avoid attracting attention, the intelligence specialist generally uses telescopic or reflective lenses to zoom in on details from a safe distance. In building a visual file on a plant site, a spy will take ground level photographs from around the entire circumference of the targeted area. He will even photograph CRT and computer screens that are visible through windows.

To aid in analyzing photographs at a later date, the specialist will catalogue all photographs as to:

- Subject matter
- Date/Time of day
- Direction of shot
- Number in a sequence of shots
- Important features in shot

This data can be stored in a database like Microsoft Access®. Photographs themselves can be incorporated into the database by scanning them into the computer from a flat glass scanner or by loading them from a digital camera. Photographic images, excerpts from videotape surveillance, aerial photographs, and relevant diagrams, document images, or drawings, can be also integrated into one database for extensive analysis. Analytical investigative databases like i2 allow for the organization of visual data. A database generates various narrative reports, charts, diagrams, and chronologies. The opportunities for an information multiplier effect are tremendous.

Cellular Telephones

Anyone who conducts a sensitive or confidential conversation on a cellular telephone is either highly naive or plain foolish. These transmissions are transparent to the secret services of all governments. Any amateur with a receiver can also pick up cellular communications. Most corporate spies will, as a matter of course, scan cellular frequencies around a targeted plant. They will also focus in on cellular telephone calls by executives and key employees. By simple physical surveillance, a spy can observe an executive pull out his cellular telephone in the car, in a restaurant, or in the grocery store. This will alert the spy to begin monitoring the target's cellular frequency. Employees should always keep in mind that someone could be listening to their conversations. Sensitive information should not be conveyed by cellular phone. As with other surveillance equipment, the tools necessary to monitor cellular telephone conversations are easy to come by.

Monitoring Computer Emanations

Digital computers process information with a series of 0s and 1s. These two digits do not translate to "on" and "off" states, but rather to high and low currents. These currents cause pixels on a computer screen to fire, producing high voltage pulses that emanate into the surrounding environment. Computer emanations form a detectable and decodable pattern. A detector or receiver, known as a Van Eck unit, can reproduce keyboard entries on a computer screen even from a considerable distance.

A Van Eck unit consists of a directional antenna, logic circuits, and two adjustable oscillators (one for the vertical and one for the horizontal). With proper adjustments, a van parked across the street, equipped with a Van Eck receiver, can decode the emanations from a keyboard operator inside a neighboring building. Devices like CPUs, taped drives, disk drives, and communications devices all generate electromagnetic radiation which Van Eck receivers can detect.

To prevent competitors from monitoring computer emanations, organizations can shield their computer equipment and transmission lines: a process known as *Tempesting*. While this process is used extensively in the military and by certain defense contractors, the costs involved prevent many private sector businesses from employing *Tempest* procedures.

Tape Recorders

The best place for a spy to place a tape recorder is off-site, far away from the microphone. A transmitter located with the microphone sends a signal to an off-site receiver that is connected to the tape recorder. This precaution assures that a compromise of the microphone will not result in capture of the tape. Recorders can also be hooked up directly to telephones in order to record tapped phone conversations.

All that is necessary to create a crude wireless phone tap is a capacitor (to block the DC voltage from the telephone line) wired in series with a small AM or FM transmitter across the telephone wire pair. An AM or FM radio plugged into a tape recorder picks up the signal by taking the output from the radio's audio jack. A professional would not use this kind of tap, but a security investigator has to be on the lookout for the amateur spy too. Some employees want to get inside information to gain an advantage over their co-workers. "Bugging" the boss' telephone is a good way to do it.

Computer System Penetrations

In some cases, information thieves will attempt to extract information by penetrating a company's computer defenses. This can be part of an organized intelligence campaign, or in some cases it is simply a random attack by a hacker bent on mischief. For more information on how outsiders attempt to penetrate computer systems, see the chapter on Computer and Internet fraud.

Investigating an Information Theft Case

Most corporate espionage cases begin with the discovery of the offense. Something is missing, or information is out in the public sector. The critical first step is finding out how the sensitive information was compromised. Knowing how the data went out the door often reveals who stole the secret. For example, if a trapped list becomes compromised, the organization will know the list has been compromised because it receives a mailing. From the mailing envelope and its contents, the organization will be able to determine who bought the list. By checking the company's internal records, it will be possible to determine who had access to the list within the company. So simply by knowing how the leak occurred and that someone bought the list, two avenues of inquiry are already established. The company that mailed the list should be contacted, and an internal investigation of people who had an opportunity to compromise the list should be commenced.

The first step in any corporate espionage investigation is to determine the means of the compromise. Investigators should attempt to rule out accidental and procedural causes first. In response to a compromise, the security investigator or auditor will need to do a survey to see if inadequate measures are the causative factor. Once the company's negligence is ruled out, the investigation can focus on potential suspects.

Most investigations should begin with the persons closest to the sensitive information and then work outwards. For example, if a marketing list were stolen, it would make the most sense to first look for suspects among the group that manages the list. Background investigations on these employees should be run. Check to see if any of those employees have risk factors that would make them likely recruits for corporate spies. Risk factors include recent financial or lifestyle changes that appear out of the ordinary. Red flags that particularly stand out are employees who suddenly seem to spend a lot more money and/or work a lot of extra hours that do not seem particularly necessary, given the employee's job.

If the members of the closest circle pass muster, the investigation moves outward to consider other employees, vendors, customers, and visitors. For example, a security officer might examine visitor logs to see who has visited the marketing group recently. General service personnel like the cleaning crew, the copier or computer repairperson, or a delivery person who has regular access to the area should also be considered a suspect. It is a good idea to look for records or observations of suspicious activity: people coming in at unusual hours, being in places not necessary to their work, pumping employees for information, or accessing computer files.

If the investigation fails to develop any leads on employees, vendors, or visitors, look to deception techniques. Re-interview employees in the affected areas to find out if they received any suspicious telephone calls, e-mails or redirecting mail processes at or near the time of the loss. Also, be sure to ask employees if anyone has approached them for information at trade shows or in social situations.

If deception does not appear to have been the avenue of attack, the next consideration should be physical penetration of the site. Review surveillance videotapes of recent traffic in and out of the affected area for intruders pretending to be employees. Again, interviewing employees may uncover memories of persons who appeared suspicious.

Obviously, an investigator would also check internal records for any incidents of criminal activity onsite at or near the time of the loss. Such activity could include a burglary or theft that appeared unrelated to information security at the time. It could be a trespassing charge or disorderly conduct on company property. Do not overlook intelligence or incident reports of security personnel on activities such as people trying to get into the trash dumpster and loitering about the parking lot. Conducting a security survey at this stage is also a good idea. It will help the investigator detect weaknesses in the organization's physical security and may help point out how an intruder could have entered the site.

After exhausting all other options, consider the possibility of surveillance against the site. If sensitive details are going out the door, electronic eavesdropping, Van Eck monitoring, or computer system penetrations could be to blame. The response to electronic eavesdropping should be a physical inspection of the affected areas and perhaps the engagement of a TSCM sweep as outlined later in this section. At the same time, research all records regarding work orders or vendor access to the affected areas. This documentation may help identify who planted the devices.

Program for Safeguarding Proprietary Information (SPI)

Companies should develop a program for *safeguarding proprietary information* (SPI). Businesses should seek out a corporate information officer (CIO) to develop and manage an SPI program. An alternative is to hire a security management consultant to develop a program and then maintain it on a yearly basis. In either case, the CIO should have information management skills and be knowledgeable about trade secret protection.

Task Force

To coordinate a companywide SPI program, a task force should be assembled. The task force should include managers and staff from departments that deal with proprietary information such as research and development, and production. The team should also include representatives from corporate security, human resources, records management, data processing, and legal.

The process should begin by determining what information should be protected. The task force should identify those areas that give the company its competitive edge, such as quality of the product, service, price, manufacturing technology, marketing, and distribution. One way of accomplishing this is to ask the team, "If you were our competitor, what information would you like to know?"

Once these sensitive areas have been identified, the primary focus should be on the information security procedures for each department. They should identify where proprietary information is kept and survey the risk if such information is lost to a competitor.

Employee Awareness

An effective program must educate employees about security awareness. Employees should understand that their professional growth and well-being depends on the success of the company. It should be made clear that the success of the company is directly tied to the protection of information and data. Employees should be taught how to respond to telephone information requests. A procedure should be set out whereby information requests are sent to public relations or some other department.

Nondocumentary communications should also be protected. Employees need to know that they are accountable for what they say, whether it be over the phone or at a social gathering. Employees should never discuss confidential business information at airports, restaurants, or any place they could be overheard. They should also be instructed about using a laptop computer wherever there may be a chance it could be read in public by someone "shoulder surfing."

Regular reminders of the importance of information security should be published regularly in company newsletters, on bulletin boards, or in memos.

Nondisclosure Agreements

All employees should sign a nondisclosure agreement. Everyone involved with the company should sign such an agreement including subcontractors and their employees, clerical staff, consultants, and temporaries. Besides the legal value, a comprehensive nondisclosure agreement sends a signal to employees that the company has a tough attitude toward preventing leaks. It might also be necessary to have suppliers and distributors sign nondisclosure agreements. Although suppliers and distributors have to receive information about certain aspects of a business, employees dealing with them should be made aware of the potential for the misuse of the information and should be instructed to provide them with only the information that is essential for them to do their job.

Document Classification

Document classification is also an important area in a protection plan. Working closely with each department, proprietary documents should be classified according to the level of security that best meets the company's needs. For instance, documents may be labeled "private" for personnel matters and move up to "restricted" for pricing or marketing information. Trade secrets or highly sensitive information might be labeled "authorized access only." Notes and drafts of documents should also be safeguarded or destroyed when the final document is completed.

Visitors

Visitor access should be closely monitored. Visitors should be required to sign in and out in a logbook, and they must be escorted by their host at all times and should not be allowed into areas where there might be sensitive information.

Offices

Engineering and executive offices should always be locked to discourage browsing, theft, or the planting of an eavesdropping device. Keys to office doors should be kept secure. Keeping proprietary information and computer disks in locked cabinets greatly reduces the risk of theft.

Maintenance Workers

Management should designate security personnel or someone to monitor maintenance work done in areas in which there might be sensitive information. We have all seen scenes in movies where the hero, or villain, gains access to confidential information by walking into a building or office posing as a maintenance worker.

Meeting Rooms

Paging systems, background music speakers, and unused wiring can be used for eavesdropping. Any electronic items and wiring that are not essential should be removed. A mirror and a light affixed to a flexible handle can be used to search for recording and transmitting devices in air ducts. After the search, when the duct grills are replaced, their orientation and screw-head positions can be designated with ultra-violet markers. By shining an ultra-violet light on the screws, it is easy to tell if the panels have been removed. Meeting rooms should be locked when not in use. If blackboards or flip charts are used, they should not face the windows, or the blinds should be closed to prevent observation from telescopes or binoculars.

Quiet Rooms

A "quiet room" may cost anywhere from $15,000 to $200,000, but it may be justified based on the risk involved. A quiet room is acoustically shielded and radio-frequency shielded. The room can also be equipped with intrusion monitoring sensors and CCTV cameras.

Communications Equipment

Cellular or cordless telephones must not be used to discuss sensitive business matters. These devices are radio transmitters and are frequently monitored by both hobbyists and professional information brokers.

Electronic Mail and Voice Mail

For knowledgeable hackers, e-mail and voice mail systems are easy targets.

Confidential information should not be left on a voice mail system. Likewise, it should never be left on a home answering machine. Hotels often offer voice mail messages for their guests. These systems require no passwords to gain access and should never be used for sensitive information. Author Michael Stedman reports that when he wanted to interview Robert Gates, the former director of the U.S. Central Intelligence Agency (CIA), he called the hotel where Gates was staying and was given a room number. Stedman said he was astonished when he punched the room number into the phone and suddenly found himself listening to Gate's messages that had been left on the hotel's voice mail service.

To prevent this kind of espionage, instruct staff, family, and friends never to leave anything but routine messages on voice mail. Tell them only to leave return numbers, or better yet, use a beeper or pager. Make sure voice mail is cleaned out daily.

Computer Systems

Passwords are the most common defense against computer intrusion, but to be effective, there must be good control procedures. Passwords should be as complex as the user can memorize, but never less than six random alphanumeric characters. The company must change passwords regularly and close them out as soon as an employee leaves the organization. Management should train employees to log off terminals before leaving them unattended. The company can also install an automatic log off program whereby a terminal that is not in use for a certain number of minutes will be automatically logged off.

A secure encryption device can be employed to protect confidential files, especially when transmitting them by modem. Encryption techniques found in popular software packages available at the local computer store are probably not secure enough. These programs are in wide use and are usually no match for a sophisticated hacker. If files are not encrypted, they may be vulnerable to anyone with access to your computer.

A company should also consider the use of virus scanning software. One of the best safeguards against viruses or any other kind of data loss is to have a secure backup procedure.

Many companies have not yet figured out what to do with the electronic data stored in their systems. While some form of paperwork filing or shredding system may be in place, often electronic information is organized according to each user's personal system and deleted only when the individual chooses to do so. Even when files are deleted, savvy computer experts can often re-create the erased material. This means that everything sent through the computer from a birthday greeting to a "smoking gun" document is being preserved.

This is potentially crippling in the event of a lawsuit. Lawyers are becoming aware of the storage of data and are requesting electronic evidence in many cases. Lawyers, pouring through backups of documents long ago thought deleted, find incriminating memos such as "I know this may be illegal, but do it anyway," or "Please destroy this evidence." Often such documents result in the case being settled for more than it may really be worth because the company does not want to run the risk that such documents will inflame the jury into awarding large punitive damages.

Companies should institute procedures for deciding what should be kept and what shouldn't. Also, backup files should be kept under lock and key. One 8mm tape can hold as much as 1,500 boxes of information. Anyone can grab such a tape and easily sneak it out of the building.

Faxing Documents

Sensitive documents should not be sent through the fax machine unless both machines are equipped with a high-level encryption device. Some fax machines are equipped with a storage and retrieval system similar to that of voice mail systems. From a remote number, you enter a PIN number and stored faxes can be sent to another machine. This allows a competitor to be able to retrieve those faxes as well.

Video Encryption

Teleconferencing is growing in popularity. Unfortunately, satellite teleconferencing signals can be received by millions of home satellite dish owners, some of whom have deliberately tuned in to find out things they shouldn't. Teleconferencing should only be used when there is an encryption system in place that will fully scramble both the video and audio signals.

Corporate Telephone Exchanges

Private branch exchanges (PBXs) are located in a company's telephone closet where wires, mounted neatly and predictably upon row after row, lead to corporate executives' offices and other areas of interest to competitors. These rooms should be, but seldom are, locked and physically secured. People with tool belts go in and out with little notice from anyone. Keeping the eavesdropper out is easier than trying to detect his handiwork.

> EXAMPLE
>
> *In one case, a surveillance team found that an executive's phone line had been tampered with. They installed a motion detector in the telephone closet. The alarm sent report-only signals to an alarm central station. After two weeks, the central station's records revealed a pattern of early morning visits to the closet on Mondays and Thursdays. Surveillance was set up and the eavesdropper was caught.*

Another good idea is to have an escort for anyone entering the area. The identity of the worker should also be verified.

Computer-driven PBXs or switches present numerous opportunities for eavesdropping. Using an on-site or off-site control terminal, the information thief can hide invisible wiretaps among millions of software instruction codes. The hidden codes, for example, could cause a second phone line to connect to a target phone line and terminate into a hidden tape recorder.

An appropriately trained investigator should regularly print out the user configuration instructions. Paying particular attention to those extensions which are likely to be of interest to eavesdroppers, the investigator can look for modified instruction codes.

Trade Shows and Public Events

Sales materials, trade show exhibits, and the text of speeches should be carefully reviewed for information that a competitor might find useful. Employees should be instructed not to say anything to anyone that they would not say directly to a competitor. During shows, employees should not leave demonstration materials or sensitive documents unattended. New design models have been stolen during their transportation in or out of a show.

Foreign Travel

Corporate executives traveling out of the country should be especially cautious. Many foreign governments are unleashing huge and sophisticated intelligence gathering operations. The executive should use encryption systems on all voice, fax, or modem transmissions. He or she should also assume that their room is bugged and act accordingly.

Technical Surveillance Countermeasures (TSCM) Survey

If an organization has a reasonable suspicion that it has been bugged, it may be advisable to engage an expert to conduct a Technical Surveillance Countermeasures (TSCM) Survey. Commonly referred to as "debugging," TSCM is designed to help the organization achieve two goals: (1) to detect the presence and location of technical surveillance equipment, and (2) to identify existing and potential security weaknesses.

TSCM professionals should never be contacted from the area where suspected bugging has taken place, as this could alert the spy to the fact that his operation has been discovered. Instead, it is recommended that organizations contact TSCM professionals from a secure phone, fax or computer that is located far away from the targeted area. Heavily used public telephones are probably the most secure method for making contact. Messages should not be sent from the home phones or computers of company employees, because they might also be under surveillance. In no event should an organization discuss suspicions of wiretapping or technical surveillance on a cellular phone.

In choosing TSCM professionals, a company should make sure that the professionals are competent in electronics, and have extensive knowledge of design, engineering, and maintenance. They must also be trained in eavesdropping techniques, practiced in RF (radio frequency) allocation and propagation, and knowledgeable about all techniques of modulation, electrical wiring, and installation principles.

Before conducting an actual TSCM survey, experts start with a pre-inspection survey and vulnerability sweep of the targeted premises. The TSCM team usually requires a full set of facility blueprints as well as a visual inspection of the premises so that they can obtain a complete understanding of the information that spies might target, where the organization is vulnerable, and how spies might attempt to penetrate the information security system. This phase of the project can take several days, as the TSCM specialists test for weaknesses in the facility's perimeter security, network and communications systems, alarm systems, video surveillance systems and other security components.

Once a vulnerability analysis has been completed and the organization's risks have been assessed, the TSCM search can proceed. A TSCM survey or sweep is a comprehensive examination of a facility, designed to make sure that the facility is free of any form of technical surveillance equipment. This includes electronic, visual and physical examination of the site. Typically, the sweep begins with an RF examination, in which all radio emanations are analyzed to determine their source. An electronically enhanced search will then be conducted to locate items or devices that were not detected from the RF search. A physical examination will be performed to locate clandestine devices such as recorders, microphones, and transmitters. The team will also examine the phones and the phone lines to detect bugs. TSCM searches are not only conducted on business premises, but also may include the vehicles, cellular phones, computer equipment, and residences of key employees.

TSCM sweeps are sensitive operations that should be conducted with as much secrecy as possible. It is best to limit the number of persons within the organization that are notified of the operation, because it is always possible that there is a mole within the company. Once again, the company does not want to tip off the spy to the operation. TSCM operatives normally operate under a cover story to explain their presence at the facility. When possible, sweeps are scheduled after hours to limit the number of personnel who encounter the team. As with other contractors, TSCM experts should be accompanied at all times during their sweep.

Although TSCM surveys can be expensive, if a company believes that it is the victim of corporate espionage, it may be the only way to help track down the source of the leak of information.

Preventing Employee Theft of Proprietary Information

A company can spend years developing a competitive advantage over its competitors. That advantage can be eliminated in an instant by an employee walking out the door.

When an employee leaves a company, there is usually little if any attention paid to where he goes afterwards. However, if a company begins to notice that a rival is suddenly taking away its business, it should sit up and take notice. Often employees leave one company for another, and take with them the knowledge of how that particular company operates, its pricing policies, its manufacturing methods, its customers, and so on. When an employee shares what he has learned with a competitor, the competitive edge is lost.

Today's work force is extremely mobile. Employees rarely start with one company and stay until retirement. On top of that, companies are continually downsizing and laying off employees. In most cases, experienced employees have little choice but to go to work for a competitor or begin consulting in their field. Cutbacks and firings do little to foster an attitude of loyalty among employees.

Employee Awareness

Employees must be educated as to what information is proprietary. It is hard to protect something if no one knows what needs protecting. A secret formula may be easy to identify, but employees often are not aware that subjects they may be discussing over lunch in a crowded restaurant are also trade secrets that would prove invaluable to a competitor. It does not help that the courts and legal scholars cannot decide on what constitutes proprietary information. Definitions of what is a trade secret depend on the organization and the industry. Examples of trade secrets include everything from notes in the margin of an employee manual to a procedure for tying a fishing lure. In addition, different jurisdictions have different laws defining what can or cannot potentially be a trade secret.

Generally, to establish a trade secret, a company has to show that the information is not known in the industry, that the company has made efforts to keep it confidential, and that the information gives the company some sort of competitive edge. Just because information is confidential, does not make it a trade secret under the law. However, even though information may not be a "trade secret" as that term is defined under the statutes, it should be protected by employees. Again, the best test for deciding what is *confidential* information is to ask yourself, would this information provide an advantage to the competition.

Nondisclosure and Noncompetition Agreements

A nondisclosure agreement is a written agreement which the employee should sign as soon as he or she starts work. It usually provides that all proprietary, confidential, or trade secret information the employee learns must be kept confidential and must not be disclosed to anyone. A noncompetition agreement is an agreement whereby the employee agrees not to work for competing companies within a certain period of time after leaving.

General Motors Corporation began requiring its senior-level executives to sign these agreements shortly after a well-publicized case against one of the company's former purchasing executives. GM accused the executive of taking millions of dollars worth of proprietary information to his new employer, Volkswagen. GM accused him of pushing up strategy meetings before he left so that he could gather even more data. The employee denied the charges. GM concluded after this happened that the use of noncompetition agreements could help prevent a similar occurrence.

However, the use of nondisclosure and noncompetition agreements is not an overall solution. There are several legal problems with using these agreements. As mentioned earlier, there is no clear definition of what constitutes a trade secret. In some instances it can be extremely difficult to determine what belongs to the company and what belongs to the employee.

Noncompetition agreements also have a variety of problems. First, courts in some jurisdictions have held that such agreements are against "public policy" because they limit the future employment of a person; therefore, in these jurisdictions noncompetition agreements are unenforceable. Other uphold the agreements, but only if they are part of an otherwise valid employment agreement. In these cases, the employment agreement and the noncompetition agreement must be signed at the same time or the noncompetition agreement is unenforceable. In addition, if the employee is an "at will" employee who is not covered by an employment agreement, any noncompetition signed by such an employee would be unenforceable.

Although nondisclosure and noncompetition agreements can be excellent tools for preventing the loss of confidential information to competitors, their use is limited, and legal counsel familiar with employment laws for the specific jurisdiction should be consulted.

However, many professionals say that the real value of such agreements is not their legal power, but their ability to create the right image. This includes making certain that employees and outsiders clearly understand that the company is serious about preventing the loss of proprietary information and will do everything they can to pursue those individuals who are stealing information.

Make Sure Employees Know When Not to Speak

Often, employees are willing to abide by nondisclosure agreements, but they do not understand that the information they are communicating may be confidential. For instance, a software company employee who worked on product updates attended a trade association meeting and entertained the other attendees with war stories about the development process and what things worked and what didn't. The employee was later reprimanded, and seemed genuinely unaware that the information he had provided was proprietary information of great value to the company's competitors.

Exit Interviews

One of the most effective ways to protect a company's trade secrets and confidential business information is to conduct an exit interview. During the exit interview, the departing employee should be specifically advised about the company's trade secrets and confidential business information and the obligation not to disclose or use such information for her own benefit or the benefit of others without the express written consent of the company. The employee should be given a form to sign stating that during the exit interview the employee was once again informed that any proprietary information should not be disclosed and that the employee agrees not to disclose any such information without the consent of the company.

Protecting the Trade Secrets of Others

In the rush to protect its trade secrets from competitors, many companies forget the other half of the equation—preventing their employees from appropriating the proprietary information of competitors.

If a company hires an employee from a competitor, it should realize that it may be opening itself up to a lawsuit for theft of proprietary information. Such claims are expensive to defend, and the losses can be substantial even before the jury verdict.

> EXAMPLE
>
> *Diametrics Medical, Inc., a U.S.-based medical equipment provider, was forced to abort a $30 million initial public offering after PPG Industries, Inc. filed a lawsuit alleging theft of trade secrets and patent infringement. Diametrics denied the charges, but the accusations were enough to prevent the public offering from going through.*

A company does not have to be actually aware that the employee is using proprietary information. There may be liability for "willful blindness," that is, company executives had reason to suspect that an employee could be using confidential information, but did nothing to investigate or prevent it.

> EXAMPLE
>
> *Novopharm, Inc. was found guilty by a court in Vancouver, British Columbia, of stealing trade secrets from its rival Apotex, Inc. Court documents state that a biochemist left Apotex and "secretly joined" Novopharm bringing with him valuable trade secrets. Under the verdict, Novopharm must pay damages of more than $3.7 million. The judge found that the chief executive officer, Leslie Dan, "closed his eyes to what was going on around him." Dan denied the judge's characterization.*

Human resources personnel should ask potential employees whether they are subject to any agreements which bar them from competing with any current or former employer. If the employee is subject to any such agreement, a copy of the agreement should be forwarded to the legal department before any hiring decision is made.

If companies seek to use confidential information from former employees of competitors, then it may run a greater risk of losing its information to competitors in the long run. As discussed above, the most important element of any confidential information protection program is the cooperation of the employees. If the employees of a company see that management has a policy of pumping new hires for knowledge about competitors, it is unlikely that the employees will take pride or interest in protecting the company's trade secrets.

Legal Issues Related to Theft of Intellectual Property

The Economic Espionage Act of 1996 (Title 18, U.S. Code §§1831-1839) makes the theft of trade secrets a federal criminal offense. Under this statute, the Department of Justice has sweeping authority to prosecute trade secret theft whether it is in the United States, via the Internet, or outside the United States. This statute is discussed in more detail in the Law section in the chapter on "Law Related to Fraud."

Bibliography

Calhoun, James. "Clean the Air with TSCM." *Security Management.* September, 1992.

Flanagan, William G. and Toddi Gutner. "The Perils of Voice Mail (Information Theft)" *Forbes.* January 17, 1994.

Hansen, Michael. "Counterespionage Techniques That Work." *Security Management* September, 1992.

Himelstein, Linda. "Computers, The Snitch in the System." *Business Week.* April 17, 1995.

Murray, Kathleen. "HR Takes Steps to Protect Trade Secrets." *Personnel Journal.* June, 1994.

Tanzer, Marc. "Foiling the New Corporate Spy." *Security Management.* September, 1992.

External fraud schemes are those committed by outside organizations, typically by individuals or groups of individuals against organizations. Fraud schemes committed by outsiders usually occur in industry. Therefore, the rest of this section is organized by type of industry, starting with financial institution frauds. Because some schemes are committed by collusion between an organizational insider and an outsider, some frauds can be classified as both internal and external schemes.

FINANCIAL INSTITUTION FRAUD

Financial institutions include banks, savings and loans, credit unions, and other federally insured repositories. Financial institution fraud is also known by the more generic term of *bank fraud*. Check fraud and credit card fraud as it applies to both merchants and financial institutions is discussed in a separate chapter.

A *bank* is defined as an organization engaged in any or all of many financial functions, such as receiving, collecting, transferring, paying, lending, investing, dealing, exchanging and servicing (safe deposit, custodianship, agency, trusteeship) money and claims to money, both domestically and internationally. This broad concept applies to institutions such as central banks for cooperatives, export-import banks, federal intermediate credit banks, federal land banks, investment banks, and mortgage lenders.

Embezzlement Schemes

Embezzlement is defined as the wrongful taking or conversion of the property of another for the wrongdoer's benefit. *Misapplication* often accompanies embezzlement, but is a separate and distinct offense. Misapplication is the wrongful taking or conversion of another's property for the benefit of someone else.

Types of Embezzlement Schemes

There are various embezzlement schemes which have been utilized over time. The following examples are not an exhaustive list, but are rather a summary of the more commonly employed schemes.

False Accounting Entries

Employees debit the general ledger to credit their own accounts or cover up customer account thefts.

Unauthorized Withdrawals

Employees make unauthorized withdrawals from customer accounts.

Unauthorized Disbursement of Funds to Outsiders

Employees cash stolen/counterfeit items for outside accomplices.

Paying Personal Expenses from Bank Funds

An officer or employee causes bank to pay personal bills, then causes amounts to be charged to bank expense accounts.

Theft of Physical Property

Employees or contractors remove office equipment, building materials, and furnishings from bank premises.

Moving Money from Customers' Dormant or Inactive Accounts

Persons with apparent authority create journal entries or transfer orders not initiated by customers to move money among accounts. *Dormant* accounts are defined by the *Encyclopedia of Banking and Finance* as "bank or brokerage accounts showing little or no activity, presumably with small and without increasing balances." Contact with the account holder by confirmation, letter, or telephone contact is not possible. Such accounts are to be transferred to dual control and recorded in an inactive accounts ledger. State statutes usually provide for escheat or forfeiture to the state after a period of years.

An *inactive* account is defined as "an account with a bank which shows a stationary or declining balance and against which both deposits and withdrawals are infrequent; or an account with a broker which shows few transactions, either purchases or sales." If the bank cannot establish contact with the account holder, then the account would qualify as a dormant account as defined above. However, if there is a risk of misuse of the account, such as an account holder who is quite elderly or incapacitated, then the account should be classified as an inactive account.

Unauthorized, Unrecorded Cash Payments
A director, officer, or employee causes cash to be disbursed directly to self or accomplices and does not record the disbursements.

Theft and Other Unauthorized Use of Collateral
Custodians steal, sell, or use collateral or repossessed property for themselves or accomplices.

Detection Methods
There are several methods by which embezzlement can be detected. Generally, if the dollar amount of the embezzlement scheme is small enough such that the financial statements will not be materially affected, embezzlement fraud can be most effectively detected through the review of source documents.

If the scheme is so large that the financial statements of the institution are affected, then a review of the source documents will serve to confirm or refute an allegation that an embezzlement scheme has occurred, or is occurring. Generally, for large embezzlements, the most efficient method of detection is an analysis of the financial statements (which is also a review of documents).

Loan Fraud
Loan fraud is a multifaceted activity that includes several types of criminal activities. Larger loan fraud schemes often involve real estate lending and collusion between insiders and outsiders. Loan fraud represents the highest risk area for financial institutions. Although the number of occurrences might be small, the dollar amount per occurrence tends to be large.

Financial Institution Failures as a Result of Real Estate Loan Fraud
Losses reported by financial institutions across the globe are in the billions. Most financial institutions invest heavily in real estate transactions; a substantial portion of these losses relate to real estate loans.

Common Loan Fraud Schemes
Loans to Nonexistent Borrowers
False applications, perhaps with inaccurate financial statements, are knowingly or unknowingly accepted by loan officers as the basis for loans. These types of loan fraud can

be perpetrated by people either external to the lending institution ("external fraud") or by officers, directors, or employees of the victim institution ("internal fraud").

Sham Loans with Kickbacks and Diversion

Loan officers sometimes will make loans to accomplices who then share all or part of the proceeds with the lending officer. In some instances, the loans are charged off as bad debts; in other instances, the bogus loans are paid off with the proceeds of new fraudulent loans.

Double-Pledging Collateral

Borrowers pledge the same collateral with different lenders before liens are recorded and without telling the lenders.

Reciprocal Loan Arrangements

Insiders in different banks cause their banks to lend funds to the others, or sell loans to other banks with agreements to buy their loans—all for the purpose of concealing loans and sales.

Swapping Bad Loans—Daisy Chains

In a daisy chain, a bank buys, sells, and swaps its bad loans for the bad loans of another bank, creating new documentation in the process. Its purpose is to mask or hide bad loans by making them look like they are recent and good.

Linked Financing

Large deposits are offered to a bank (usually brokered deposits) on the condition that loans are made to particular persons affiliated with the deposit broker. High returns are promised, but the loans are longer term than the deposits (hot money). Sometimes kickbacks are paid to the broker or banker.

False Applications with False Credit Information

Sometimes loan applicants provide false information about their credit situation, and/or overstate their assets.

Single-Family Housing Loan Fraud

In this scheme, unqualified borrowers misrepresent personal creditworthiness, overstate ability to pay, and misrepresent characteristics of the housing unit.

Construction Loans

Construction lending has different vulnerabilities than other permanent or interim lending. More risks are associated with construction projects than with already-built projects. Construction fraud schemes are numerous; the more common are related to estimates of costs to complete, developer overhead, draw requests, and retainage schemes.

ESTIMATES OF COSTS TO COMPLETE

When borrowers approach a lending institution for construction financing they typically have a development plan, complete with an engineering report, appraisal, and budget for construction costs. The construction cost budget is, by definition, an estimate. As the project is built out, the budget will be revised to reflect actual expenses. Budgets are delineated by specific line item, e.g., slab, exterior glass, grading, landscaping, and tenant improvements. As the project proceeds, certain over- and underbudget costs are incurred. These costs should be represented by a change order.

If the loan agreement has been properly documented and enforced, no material differentiation from the budget should occur without the lender's knowledge and consent. However, the developer/borrower might misrepresent the true nature of the under- or overbudget amount to mislead the lender. The architect/engineer and the lender's inspector should examine all budget changes. The impact of change orders might result in the loan becoming out of balance (cost to complete exceeds available loan and equity funds). Generally, developers hide or conceal their overbudget construction costs in two common places. The first place is contingency and the second is to remove allocations from tenant improvements and apply them to shell construction.

Most budgets contain a contingency line item in the event actual costs exceed the budgeted amounts. Unfortunately, many developers and lenders do not monitor the total impact on removing allocations from the contingency budget. In addition, savings are not allocated to the contingency line item when underbudget costs are realized. It also is common to rob one account to make up for a shortfall in another account. Generally, tenant finish is estimated at a particular dollar amount per square foot. This allows the developer considerable latitude in negotiating with tenants.

However, before the entire space has been leased, and the construction costs have been incurred, the amount allocated to tenant improvements remains budgetary. If the developer is allowed to reallocate amounts from this budget line to shell construction, then when it comes time to negotiate leases and finish out the space, the developer might be short of available funds. If the tenant finish is treated as a hold-back and not to be reallocated or disbursed except for its intended purpose, then there is a greater chance of the loan not becoming overdisbursed (cost to complete exceeding the available financing).

DEVELOPER OVERHEAD

It is not uncommon in construction financing to have a budget line item for developer overhead. This is a ripe area for abuse. The purpose of developer overhead is to supply the developer with operating capital while the project is under construction. This overhead allocation should not include a profit percentage, as the developer realizes profit upon completion.

In essence, the overhead budget is as if the lender is making two types of loans: a real estate loan and a working capital loan for the overhead. Unfortunately, there is seldom, if ever, any separate underwriting for the overhead portion. The overhead is merely added as a construction cost, whose ultimate collateral is the property and not some other short-term collateral. Historically, troubled construction loans or foreclosures due to fraud have been totally disbursed in the developer overhead category.

DRAW REQUESTS

Construction loan advances generally are supported by draw requests. A draw request is the documentation substantiating that a developer has incurred the appropriate construction expenses and is now seeking reimbursement or direct payment. A typical fraud scheme in this area involves requesting advances on the loan for inappropriate costs, such as personal expenses and/or construction costs for an unrelated project. Draw requests provide the greatest opportunity for a developer to commit fraud against the lender because the lender relies upon the developer's documentation.

Generally, a draw request is made once a month and is submitted on a standard form such as the one promulgated by the American Institute of Architects (AIA). The request should be accompanied by the following documents:
- Paid invoices for raw materials
- Lien releases from each subcontractor
- Inspection reports
- Canceled checks from previous draw requests
- Bank reconciliation for construction draw account for previous month

- Loan balancing form—demonstrating that the loan remains in balance
- Change orders, if applicable
- Wiring instructions, if applicable
- Proof of developer contribution, if applicable

The documentation required as support for each draw request will vary depending on the payment method (direct, dual payment, disbursing agent, wire transfer, reimbursement). Any missing or altered documentation is a red flag that something is amiss with the draw request. All advances on the loan should be adequately documented.

Some or all of the following steps should be performed before advancing funds on a construction loan. These steps are not represented as being all-inclusive, but rather the preliminary disbursement questions that the disbursing party should address.

- Examine the draw and determine if sufficient supporting documentation has been submitted.
- Reconcile the amounts requested with the approved budget. Account for any differences.
- Determine that the amounts requested have been properly inspected and approved.
- Determine if the proper lien releases have been submitted for work performed.
- Reconcile any change orders with the approved budget. Determine if the change orders have been approved.
- Prove the clerical accuracy of the documentation submitted.
- Ensure that work completed has been inspected by the lender's architect/engineer.
- Determine if there are any requests for soft (nonconstruction) costs and whether they are appropriate.
- Determine if there are any budget changes. If so, what are they for? Have they been approved?
- Prepare a cost to complete estimate to determine that the loan remains in balance.
- If tenant improvement funds have been requested, establish that there is a signed lease on file. Is the request appropriate for the terms and conditions of the lease? Has the lease been approved?
- If homeowner option funds have been requested, establish that there is a signed purchase contract on file. Is the request appropriate for the terms and conditions of the contract? Has the contract/ purchaser been approved?
- Examine payment requests and determine if there are new or previously undisclosed subcontractors. If so, determine why.

- Ensure that the title update has been received.

RETAINAGE

The final area of major concern in construction lending is retainage. Retainage is the amount withheld from each draw request until such time as the construction is complete and the lien period has expired. There are at least two reasons why construction loans contain a retainage provision. The first reason is to keep the contractor's interest in the project until all the work has been completed and accepted by the owner. The amount of the retainage represents part, if not all, of the contractor's profit. Therefore, if the profit is not paid until the project has been completed, then presumably the contractor will complete the assignment on time and on budget.

The second reason for the retainage is to assure that the work of subcontractors is completed and that the general contractor pays the subcontractor so that no liens are filed. If the general contractor fails to pay the subcontractor then the subcontractor will probably file a lien on the project. If the retainage will not be released until such time as the lien period has expired, then there are at least some funds available to defray the cost of fighting the lien or making a duplicate payment because the general contractor might have embezzled the first payment without paying the subcontractor.

Red Flags of Loan Fraud

There are several red flags of loan fraud. Many times the schemes are perpetrated in tandem with other schemes, so what appears to be a red flag for one scheme, might in fact lead the fraud examiner to one or more schemes.

Nonperforming Loans

Although this information might not be available to all, a nonperforming loan is not performing for some reason. One of those reasons might be that a fraud scheme has or is occurring.

Fraud schemes resulting in a nonperforming loan include:
- *Fraudulent Appraisals*—The cash flow cannot support an inflated loan and, therefore, debt amount.
- *False Statements*—The loan was made on false or fraudulently presented assumptions.
- *Equity Skimming*—There was never any intention to make the underlying loan payments.

- *Construction Overbudget Items*—The overbudget amount might be a concealment method for other schemes such as embezzlement, misappropriation, or false statements.
- *Bribery*—The loan was made because the lender received a bribe or a kickback from the borrower.
- *Land Flips*—The purpose of the loan was to finance the seller out of a property which has an artificially inflated value.
- *Disguised Transactions*—Transactions that are sham transactions, without substance, made to conceal other ills.

High Turnover in Developer's Personnel

One of the first signs to look for, particularly in construction lending, is whether or not the real estate developer is experiencing a higher-than-normal employee turnover. Typically, when a developer experiences a high degree of turnover, something is wrong with the internal operation. This is often a preamble for other problems to come.

High Turnover in Tenant Mix

If the tenant mix in a commercial project (such as a retail center or an office building) is suddenly undergoing a major change, there might be some problem with the management of the project or with the method of allocating the pass-through expenses, such as utilities, maintenance, etc. In addition, a decline in the tenant mix might be an indication that the deferred maintenance for the project is not being properly attended to.

Increased Change Orders

An increase in the number of change orders or amounts on change orders might be an indication that construction changes have taken place that would alter the originally planned project to such an extent as to render the underwriting inappropriate. Change orders can have the same impact on a project as altering the original documents. As with anything that is contracted for on a bid basis, change orders also could be an indication of collusive bidding. Change orders might be an indication that the original project was not feasible and short cuts are shoring up other problem areas. Change orders should be approved by the architect and engineer on the project in addition to the lender's inspector.

Missing Documentation

Missing or altered documentation is a red flag for any type of fraud scheme. Because concealment is a key fraud element, missing documents are a definite giveaway. Missing documents are of particular concern in construction lending. Experience has shown that seldom is a complete draw request submitted without some missing document.

LOAN FILE

Missing documents in the loan file are another indication that things might be amiss. It is important to determine if missing documents have been misplaced or were never received. A waiver of certain documents is one common way for lenders to conceal fraud schemes. Documentation for real estate loans is fairly standard. Listed below are some of the more important documents which should be present in the loan files.

- Appraisal
- Architect and engineers' report
- Assignment of leases and rents
- Assignment of limited partnership notes
- Assignment of take-out Commitment
- Attorney opinion Letter
- Availability of utilities (water, sewer, gas, and electric)
- Budget
- Completion schedule
- Copies of leases (existing or if project is preleased, commitment letters)
- Disburser's notice, if required
- Easements
- Environmental impact study
- Ingress and egress
- Inspection report (lender's inspector)
- Insurance binder (lender should be loss payee)
- Letters of credit, if applicable
- List of general and subcontractors
- Loan agreement
- Plans and specifications
- Promissory notes from limited partners to partnership, if applicable
- Road dedications
- Soils report
- Subscription agreements, similar to limited partnership notes, if applicable
- Survey
- Take-out commitment, if applicable
- Title policy, including instruction letter from closing

- Zoning

DISBURSEMENT FILE
- Copies of all checks issued at closing
- Lien releases issued at closing (architect, engineers, etc.)
- Loan closing statement

DRAW REQUESTS
- Draw request form (AIA Form or its equivalent)
- Bank reconciliation (general contractor disbursement account)
- Canceled checks (if general contractor pays subcontractors, copies of the canceled checks should be included in the following draw)
- Inspection report (lender's inspector)
- Lien releases for each subcontractor for the previous draw
- Loan balancing form (The lender should prepare some form of reconciliation to ensure that with each draw the loan remains in balance. Items of particular concern are interest, tenant finish, and retainage.)
- Receipts (for all items submitted on the draw request form)
- Title updates from the title company
- Wire transfer instructions (from the lender to the general contractor's disbursement account

In addition to the normal loan files, the lender should require a continuing report from the borrower. For example, the borrower could be required to report annual financial condition coupled with a tax return. Missing documents in these follow-up files might indicate that the project or the borrower is having difficulty that might be the result of a fraud scheme.

Loan Increases or Extensions, Replacement Loans
A loan being continually extended and loan increases being made simultaneously might indicate that the real estate project cannot support the debt service. Typically, the loan increases are to pay for the interest and extension fee. This red flag also might indicate that the loan was made to a related-party or made as a loan to hasten a sale or other transaction. In other words, the loan was not properly underwritten.

If the loan is increased and extended several times, it might indicate that higher appraisals are being obtained on a "made-as-instructed" basis. Loan increases and extensions might be the method used by the lender to conceal a nonperforming loan.

However, according to William T. Thornhill, CFE, a consultant in the field of financial institution fraud, fraud perpetrators tend to write a new loan or credit facility to *replace* an existing or old loan because they are aware of the fact that a rewrite may attract loan review, loan administration, or internal audit attention. Accordingly, replacement loans are now increasingly used rather than a simple rewrite of a loan.

Cash Flow Deficiencies

The actual cash flow of a commercial project is a very telling red flag. If the project is experiencing an unexplained cash flow deficiency, then an internal fraud scheme might be the cause. The project cash flow might reflect any of the above schemes.

Change in Ownership Makeup

A change in the ownership makeup, commonly referred to as business divorce, might indicate fraudulent activity. It is not uncommon to have a working partner and an equity (money) partner. When the two partners become disenchanted with their relationship and seek a "separation," it might suggest things have gone sour.

Disguised Transactions

Transactions disguised to conceal their true nature often involve the lender and either an existing customer or new customer. Banking personnel sometimes will engage in fraudulent schemes to forego the requirement to record additional loan loss reserves. One method employed is to "sell" OREO (Other Real Estate Owned) property to an existing customer or a new customer in exchange for making a new loan on an other unrelated project. In other words, the bank is tying one transaction to another, quid pro quo.

Another method of concealing the true nature of a transaction is to conduct the transaction through nominees. For example, the bank might be required to recognize an additional loan loss reserve due to the lack of performance on a particular loan. The borrower might or might not be a good customer of the bank. Regardless of the status of the customer, the bank might request that the project (underlying collateral) be sold to another party, the financing to be arranged by the bank. The borrower can form a new entity (nominee or shell company) to purchase the property; a new (generally higher) appraisal is obtained and the property is sold. In this illustration, the avoidance of loss required the participation of the bank personnel, the borrower, and the appraiser.

Real Estate Fraud

In addition to the real estate loan fraud schemes discussed previously, there are several other external real estate fraud schemes. Some of these schemes are:

- Appraisal fraud
- Mortgage-backed security fraud
- Equity skimming
- Land flips

Most real estate transactions require more money than any single individual or entity can internally finance. Therefore, most of these transactions are financed to some extent. Because these transactions require borrowed money, experts are needed. These experts include appraisers, lenders, and auditors.

Appraisal Fraud

The Role of the Appraiser

The appraiser performs an independent property valuation for the new (or old) owner. Appraisers should be licensed. They should also be certified by an independent professional association. There are several professional associations for real estate appraisers. A list of these organizations can be found at the end of this section. It is important, particularly in regard to complex commercial property, that the appraisers' experience and credentials be carefully scrutinized.

Fundamentals of Real Estate Appraisals

Real estate transactions assume a willing buyer and willing seller. Fraud can occur when the transaction breaks down or the expert assistance is not at arms-length. Many fraud schemes have a false appraisal report as a condition precedent. Several different kinds of reports are used by appraisers. They are summarized below.

LETTER FORM REPORT

The letter form report is used when a client is familiar with the area, and supporting data, therefore, is not necessary. The report consists of a brief description of the property, the type of value sought, the purpose served by the appraisal, the date of value, the value conclusion, and the signature of the appraiser. This form generally is not used by financial institutions for credit decisions.

SHORT FORM REPORT

The short form report is used by financial institutions, usually for residential real estate loans (sometimes referred to as consumer loans). The report varies from one to four pages and consists of check sheets or spaces to be filled in by the appraiser about pertinent property data.

NARRATIVE REPORT

The narrative form includes all pertinent information about the area and the subject property as well as the rationale for the estimated value. It includes maps, photographs, charts, and plot plans. Financial institutions use narrative reports to support real estate lending and investment decisions on large commercial real estate transactions. Any other type of appraisal report (i.e., letter form or short form) on these complex transactions would likely be considered inadequate.

Determining "Value"

Value is comprised of four elements: utility, scarcity, demand, and transferability. Real estate appraisals assign three types of values to property. They are:

FAIR MARKET VALUE

This is the price the property would bring if freely offered on the open market with both a willing seller and a willing buyer. (Estimated)

SALES PRICE

Sales price is the price paid for the property. It might be higher or lower than fair market value. (Actual)

LOAN VALUE

Loan value is the percentage of a property's value (fair market value or sales price) a lender can or might loan a borrower.

Valuation Methods
SALES COMPARISON APPROACH

The sales comparison approach lends itself to the appraisal of land, residences, and other types of improvements that exhibit a high degree of similarity, and where a ready market exists. Compared to the other approaches, this method has great influence on residential portfolio valuations. This method is the least complicated to understand and apply.

Subject property is compared with similar property that is either offered for sale or has recently sold. Items evaluated include time of sale, location of sale (or offer for sale), physical characteristics, and improvements. Adjustments are made to the value of comparable properties (either plus or minus) on the basis of differences between them and the subject property. Relevant items might be an oversized lot, a view, a busy street, or access.

THE COST APPROACH

The cost approach generally does not exert much influence on the appraiser's final value estimate. It serves as a "benchmark" against which the sales comparison and income approaches are measured. The cost approach is more accurate for new properties. It views the value of a parcel as the combination of the land value if vacant and the cost to construct a new building on the given date, less the accrued depreciation the existing building would suffer in comparison with the new building.

The cost approach has five steps:
- Estimate the land value as though vacant and available for development to its highest and best use. (Use the sales comparison approach.)
- Estimate the replacement or reproduction cost of the existing improvements as of the appraisal date.
- Estimate the accrued depreciation amount suffered by the improvements from all causes (physical deterioration and/or functional or external obsolescence).
- Deduct the accrued depreciation from the replacement cost to find the estimate of value of the depreciated improvements.
- Add the improvements' depreciated value to the land value to arrive at the value of the property.

The above is the most frequently used cost approach method. It involves the cost associated with rebuilding with modern methods, design, and materials that would most exactly replace the existing building. Reproduction cost is a cost-approach used to estimate the cost to reconstruct a replica of the building. It generally is used only when dealing with unique construction or for testimony in court.

THE INCOME CAPITALIZATION APPROACH

Under this approach, the property value is based on its capacity to continue producing income. This method is particularly valuable for the valuation of complex commercial properties. The net income the property produces is an important consideration. Net income is the amount of money over the remaining life of the property and its improvements that a fully informed person, using good management, is warranted in receiving.

Income capitalization is the mathematical process of estimating the present value of income property based on the anticipated annual net income it will produce. Key to the application of this approach is the capitalization rate that is used. There are three types of capitalization rates: *interest rate, recapture rate,* and *overall capitalization rate.* Interest rate is the rate of return earned on investment capital. Recapture rate is the rate of return originally invested funds provided the owner. Overall capitalization rate is a combination of the interest and recapture rates.

Fraudulent Appraisals

Fraudulent appraisals result from any number of situations, some of which are:
- Intentional use of an incompetent appraiser
- "Stacking the deck" by giving the appraiser improper or false assumptions to use in arriving at the value such as:
- Assume zoning will be changed for a higher and better use when in fact zoning will not be changed
- Assume unrealistically high vacancy and low expense rates
- Assume unrealistically high income, selling prices, or absorption—the rate at which vacant space will become rented
- Otherwise influencing the appraiser, e.g., paying above-market fee or promising future business
- Direct collusion with the appraiser to commit fraud

Uses for Fraudulent Appraisals

- To obtain approval on marginal or substandard loans to attain or exceed goals in order to be promoted or receive commission, bonus, or raises

- To justify extending or renewing a "bad" loan to avoid recognition of a loss that might defer commission, promotion, bonus, or raises
- To avoid adverse publicity and regulatory, management, and shareholder disapproval because of excessive losses
- To avoid recognition of a loss on real estate owned, and to permit additional capital infusions
- To criminally gain money

Red Flags of "Made-as-Instructed" Appraisals

- The appraiser used never has been used before, is not on an approved list, has no professional credentials, or those offered are of questionable credibility
- Appraisal fee is unusually high
- Invalid comparables are used
- Supporting information is missing, insufficient, or contradictory
- Market data does not support the price and absorption figures used to arrive at value

Detecting Fraudulent Appraisals

To detect unrealistic or bogus appraisals, the fraud examiner should address the following:

(1) Read the appraisal, does it match the documents in the file?
   - Leases
   - Comparables
   - Absorption rates
   - Residual values
   - Capitalization rate
   - Legal description

(2) Is there sufficient demand for the project to assure absorption of the property into the marketplace?

(3) Are there unique characteristics of the project which will assure a competitive advantage over other projects?

(4) Is the project sensitive to changes in local economic conditions?

Mortgage-Backed Securities

A mortgage-backed security is one issued by a financial intermediary, usually a mortgage banker, commercial bank, or savings and loan association, and collateralized by mortgage pools. The collateral pools typically are composed of government-guaranteed mortgages or mortgages guaranteed by the issuing intermediary. The issuer is responsible for acquiring and servicing the mortgages and marketing the securities. Security holders receive a "pass-through" of the principal and interest payments on the entire pool, less amounts to cover the cost of servicing and fees. The most common fraud schemes are those involving mortgage pools.

Equity Skimming

Equity skimming is a scheme whereby an individual, entity, or group of individuals purchase one or several single-family homes. Typically, the financing is for a percentage of the purchase price (e.g., 80% – 90%) and the owner invests the balance of the purchase price as equity. The home(s) is/are then rented.

The owners collect the rent from the tenants but fail to make the mortgage payment(s). When the owner has withheld mortgage payments that equal the amount of the invested equity, he can then either resume payments or allow the mortgage to be foreclosed. Although the mortgage eventually might be foreclosed, the owners have recouped their original investment plus any rental payments not applied to the mortgage. In addition, the owners received state and federal tax benefits during the holding period. This scheme is most successful with non-recourse mortgages.

Although equity skimming eventually collapses and the purchasers risk being sued for deficiencies (if the loans were recourse), the scheme continues to be practiced. It has become an increasing problem as many residential homes are auctioned and bulk purchases are encouraged.

Land Flips

A *land flip* is the practice of buying and selling real estate very quickly, often several times a day or at least within a few months. With each sale the price is increased. The sales often are transacted between related parties or with shell corporations. Their sole purpose is to increase the selling price. Ultimately, it becomes insupportable.

Land flips are either a scheme by themselves or are used to support higher comparable prices for other appraisals. Almost every land flip involves collusion between the customer and the appraiser, with the lender or investor the victim. The lender or investor is led to place a false sense of comfort in the value of the collateral because of the heavy activity and price increase. This scheme also has been perpetrated between lending institutions to avoid loan loss reserve increases. This is referred to as a "Daisy Chain."

Nominee or Strawman Loans
Loans made in the name of a straw borrower or agent having no substance, while the identity of the real borrower is undisclosed to the lender.

Mortgage-Pulling
For the purpose of disguising loans exceeding a bank's legal limits, loans are made to a partnership's members who by prearrangement then invest in a single risky venture in a total amount exceeding the lending limit. In reality, the single borrower is the partnership, and the collateral is the partnership's property. Mortgage-pulling might involve fraudulent loan applications and payoffs to the individual partners for participating.

New Account Fraud Schemes

Fraud is much more likely to occur in new accounts than in established accounts. Special efforts must be taken to properly identify the potential new customer, without offending them. Screening criteria should be established and enforced by everyone handling new accounts. Prompt, decisive action is necessary to manage and/or close apparent problem accounts.

False Identification
New account criminals are actors. They use false identification to open new accounts and steal money before funds are collected by the bank. False identification is easily purchased.

Business Accounts Using Stolen Checks
Some bank customers defraud business institutions by opening a new business account using checks stolen from another business. The fraudsters then withdraw the funds and close the account.

Personal Accounts Using Fraudulent Checks

A similar scheme is to open a new personal account with two checks drawn by other people. The checks are either forged or stolen. The fraudster then deposits one, and takes cash for the other. Shortly thereafter, the fraudster writes checks to overdraw the deposited amount.

Prevention

A relationship with a financial institution should never be established until the identity of a potential customer is satisfactorily established. If the identity cannot be established, the relationship should not be established.

Personal Accounts

No account should be opened without satisfactory identification, such as:
- A locally issued driver's license with a photograph
- A passport or alien registration card, together with:
  - A college photo identification card
  - A major credit card (verify the current status)
  - An employer identification card
  - An out-of-area driver's license
  - A current utility bill from the customer's place of residence (e.g., gas, electricity, telephone)

Consider the customer's residence or place of business. If it is not in the area served by the bank or branch, ask why the customer is opening an account at that location.

Follow up with calls to the customer's residence or place of employment, thanking the customer for opening the account. Disconnected phone service or no record of employment warrant further investigation.

Consider the source of funds used to open the account. Large cash deposits should be questioned.

For large accounts, ask the customer for a prior bank reference and write a letter to the bank asking about the customer.

Check with service bureaus for indications that the customer has been involved in questionable activities such as kiting incidents and NSF situations.

The identity of a customer can be established through an existing relationship with the institution, such as some type of loan or other account relationship. A customer might be a referral from a bank employee or one of the bank's accepted customers. In this instance, a referral alone is not sufficient to identify the customer; but in most instances, it should warrant less vigilance than is otherwise required.

Business Accounts

Business principals should provide evidence of legal status (e.g., sole proprietorship, partnership, or incorporation or association) when opening a business account.

Check the name of a commercial enterprise with a reporting agency and check prior bank references.

Follow up with calls to the customer's business thanking the customer for opening the account. Disconnected phone service warrants further investigation.

When circumstances allow, perform a visual check of the business to verify the actual existence of the business and that the business has the capability of providing the services described.

Consider the source of funds used to open the account. Large cash deposits should be questioned.

Since tellers are oftentimes the front-line defense in preventing check fraud, it is important that they receive training which will allow them to identify fraudulent checks.

Tellers should:
- Be aware of magnetic routing numbers
- Look for checks with a check number less than 200
- Be aware of the date that the account was opened
- Have easy access to the signature card
- Look for perforated edges on the checks
- Be aware of what is acceptable identification
- Recognize forged/altered identification
- Recognize forged negotiable instruments
- Be familiar with patterns of behavior related to potential culprits:

- Overly polite
- Nervous
- Aggressive and hurried

Detection

Some of the more common red flags of potential new account schemes are:

- Customer residence outside the bank's trade area
- Dress and/or actions inconsistent or inappropriate for the customer's stated age, occupation, or income level
- New account requesting immediate cash withdrawal upon deposit
- Request for large quantity of temporary checks
- No order for printed checks

Money Transfer (Wire) Fraud Schemes[1]

Wire transfers of funds are nothing new—they began in the 1940s. However, with today's growing emphasis on a cashless society, the number of wire transfers increases each year.

Typically, fraudsters who commit this type of crime are knowledgeable about wire transfer activity, have at least one contact within the target company, and are aggressive in carrying out the theft.

Instantaneous Transfer

Wire transfer services electronically move funds worldwide from a financial institution to a beneficiary account at any banking point according to a customer's instructions. (A banking point is any institution or business capable of receiving electronic transactions such as banks, savings and loans, credit unions, brokerage firms, and insurance companies.) On any day, $1 trillion to $2 trillion moves among financial institutions. The transactions primarily are for completing interbank purchases and sales of federal funds; purchasing, selling, and financing securities transactions; disbursing loan proceeds or repaying loans; and for conducting real estate business.

---

[1] The Editors wish to thank James Incaprera, CFSSP, CPP, and Joyce C. Lambert, Ph.D., CIA, CPA, for their assistance in preparing this section. Mr. Incaprera is the Louisiana investigations manager for Bank One in New Orleans, LA, and Dr. Lambert is a professor of accounting at the University of New Orleans.

Although these technologies enhance operations and increase the efficiency of the financial institutions, they also provide a tremendous opportunity for criminals who learn to manipulate the electronic environment for their personal gain. Wire transfer fraud is a particularly dangerous risk to a business's solvency—one major wire fraud can destroy any firm. Single losses average $100,000 or more.

Common Schemes
Dishonest Bank Employees
People who have access to correct account identification information can transfer money improperly—insiders wire funds to themselves and/or related parties.

Misrepresentation of Identity
People pose as customers, having used pretext calls to obtain correct account information from the bank. People posing as wire room employees in another bank or a branch office order transfers to dummy accounts in another bank.

System Password Security Compromised
People having legitimate access to sensitive account and daily code information for a limited time (for example, computer consultants) effect improper transfers through unauthorized access.

Forged Authorizations
Bank officers' and customers' authorization, oral or written, is improperly obtained or forged. People forge orders to transfer money to their own accounts when the recipient account is actually in the name of someone else.

Unauthorized Entry and Interception
Unauthorized personnel gain access to the wire room and its equipment, or the actual transmission is intercepted and altered.

Preventing and Detecting Wire Transfer Fraud
Fraud examiners and auditors need to advise management on ways to prevent and detect wire transfer fraud.

Business Audits

Every firm, of course, must have written policies and procedures for wire transactions. In addition, fraud examiners or auditors should conduct unannounced audits of those transactions. Following are other examples of wire transfer controls.

- Make sure the person authorizing the wire transfer isn't the individual who orders the wire transfer.
- Require those ordering transfers to have secure passwords.
- Maintain and keep a current list of those ordering wire transfers, and a log of all transfers.
- Require vacations of persons who handle wire transfers.
- Require that reconciliations of accounts affected by wire transfers be performed by persons not involved with the wire transfer process.
- Keep all confidential information about firms' accounts and wire transfers in safe rooms secured with locks. Give computer key cards to these rooms to authorized personnel only. Shred trash.

Businesses frequently perform vendor audits, but often neglect to audit their bank's wire transfer controls. A fraud examiner should evaluate these areas.

- Pick a sample of transactions and review the log of the calls made back to the banking points to verify their authenticity (You may listen to the tape recording of the actual authorization to assure compliance with call-back rules.)
- Review documentation of past wire transfer activity from bank statements or bank online transaction history for a daily debit and credit match of each transaction.
- Obtain written confirmations of transactions from the wire transfer provider to determine the timeliness of their receipt by your firm.
- Promptly reconcile problems caused by the usual custom of ending all wire transfers for a day in the mid-afternoon. (Some customers believe they should receive credit and interest on funds received at the end of a day. However, wire transfers made after the afternoon closing time aren't credited until the next business day.)

Bank Audits

Financial institutions should ensure the following safeguards when transferring funds:

- Provide customers with unique codes that are required to authorize or order wire transfers.
- Maintain and update lists of employees authorized to perform wire transfer transactions.

- Compile audit trails of incoming and outgoing wire transactions, as well as the employee responsible for each portion of the transaction.
- Review all wire transfer transactions at the end of each day to ensure that the original transfer instructions were executed correctly.
- Make sure the businesses to which the funds are transferred are contacted to ensure authenticity of fund transfer requests. If the businesses are contacted by phone, the phone numbers used should be the original numbers given by the customers when the accounts were opened and not the phone numbers provided by the callers who requested the transfers.
- Don't execute wire transfers solely from faxed instructions. Again, verify authenticity by phoning the original numbers given by the customers when the accounts were opened and not the numbers provided by the callers who requested the transfers.
- Require that all accounts affected by wire transfers be reconciled by bank employees not involved with the wire process.
- Ensure the in-house wire operations manual is available only to authorized personnel and secured when not in use—especially after hours. Cleaning crew employees could help themselves to client pass codes and other confidential information.
- Record all incoming and outgoing calls for wire transfer instructions.
- Carefully screen wire transfer personnel applicants.
- Reassign to other departments wire transfer employees who have given notice that they are resigning but still have some time left with the company.
- Require all employees involved in the transfer of funds to take at least five consecutive days of vacation each year; assign their duties only to other transfer department staff members during their absence.
- Make sure bank employees never disclose sensitive information over the telephone until the caller's identity and authorization have been verified to the customer information file.
- Separate duties among wire employees who transmit or receive requests for funds. These employees shouldn't also verify the accuracy of the transactions.
- Train employees on proper internal controls, fraud awareness, and the importance of protecting information. Share alerts issued by government agencies and professional groups.

Automated Teller Machine (ATM) Fraud

An ATM is a dispensing facility from which the holder of a debit card can draw cash. The facility can also perform other services such as depositing funds and checking account balances, but the most popular use has been to dispense funds. Fraud schemes have been perpetrated involving the unauthorized use of ATM facilities. Schemes include:

- Theft of card and/or unauthorized access to PIN numbers and account codes for ATM transactions by unauthorized persons
- Employee manipulation
- Counterfeit ATM cards
- Counterfeit ATM machines

EXAMPLE

A former Citibank employee was sentenced to 41 months in prison for masterminding a scheme to steal $200,000 in cash from several of the bank's ATMs. The computer expert was the No. 2 official in Citibank's ATM security department, and programmed the bank's money machines to issue money and not leave any record of the transactions. This was done by remotely accessing the company's mainframe computer and instructing it to put particular machines in "test mode."

Detection

When investigating ATM schemes, look for a lack of segregation of duties between the card issuing function and the personal identification (PIN) issuance

Advanced Fee Fraud

Banks find deals that seem "too good to be true" to gain access to large amounts of money (deposits) at below-market interest rates. The catch is that the bank must pay an up-front finder's fee to a person claiming to have access to the money. In some cases, desperate institutions are offered access to illegal money, and they typically do not report the loss of the advance fee when the deal falls through. More information on advance fee swindles can be found in the Consumer Fraud chapter.

EXAMPLE

The bank is contacted by an agent (broker, advisor, consultant, promoter, lawyer, bank customer) offering to provide money at a below-market interest rate for a long period of time (e.g., 10–20 years). The agent asks for a large fee to close the deal. The agent takes the fee

and disappears. The deposits might or might not exist; and if they do, they seldom equate to the agent's representations.

Red Flags
- Agent requests documents on bank stationery, signatures of officers
- Bank is asked to give nondisclosure agreements to protect agents or other parties
- There are several complex layers of agents, brokers, and other middlemen

Brokered Loans

A variation of the advanced fee scheme is the brokered loan. *Loan brokering* applies to either packages of individual residential (consumer) loans or single commercial loans. A variation of a brokered loan is the loan participation, where the purchaser participates in the loan but does not purchase the entire loan. The fraud schemes associated with brokered or participated loans generally involve selling phony loans (packages) or selling participations in loans that have not been properly underwritten. Generally, a large fee is charged for these brokered loans.

With residential loan packages, the broker sells the package, takes the money and disappears. Brokered loans generally are not sold with any recourse to the broker. Therefore, the purchaser must look to the borrower and the underlying collateral for debt satisfaction. With loan participations, the lead bank generally performs the underwriting. However, this does not relieve the participating bank from its obligation to perform its own due diligence. If the participating bank does not independently examine the documentation and perform its own due diligence, then fraud schemes on the part of the selling institution are possible.

Letter-of-Credit Fraud

Most letter-of-credit fraud arises from foreign trade and contracting. Letter-of-credit fraud can be perpetrated by beneficiaries using forged or fraudulent documents presented to the issuing bank with a demand for payment. The documents, however, must conform to the terms of the letter-of-credit agreement.

EXAMPLE
An American exporter might offer to sell goods to an overseas importer. When terms are arranged, a letter of credit is obtained in the exporter's favor, confirmed by a bank near the exporter's location. (The actual export never occurs, and the request for payment is bogus.)

Inside/Outside Frauds

Outside/inside frauds is an area where fraud is increasing, in which the employee (insider) might be co-opted through a bribe or a threat of violence against the insider or a family member. Sometimes the insider is a bank teller who agrees to cash certain items as long as the items look reasonable and are below a cashing limit. Other times the insider is a proof operator or sorter operator who inserts documents directly into the computer system to affect fraudulent deposits. Or, the insider is selling copies of documents to individuals who use new computer techniques to make fraudulent items.

Account Information Frauds

Information is sold to organized rings or insiders who use the information themselves. As financial institutions make more services available to customers and strive to make them more usable, information about customer account relationships reside in many forms, such as 24-hour customer operators, online systems, printed documents which are innocently put in the trash only to be retrieved, credit card information on high line cards, etc.

Trading Activities

Trading activities can be compromised to defraud banks. Usually perpetrated with the assistance of an internal employee or by an employee acting alone, trading can include foreign exchange, securities trading, loan sales, and securitization. Often when this type of problem is suspected, the investigator must turn to traders themselves as the only source to gather information.

Prevention

Financial institutions, like other organizations, should have standard internal control measures to assist in the detection and deterrence of fraud. In addition to normal procedures, such as segregation of duties and budget and actual comparisons, listed below are some specific control measures which might enhance the detection and deterrence of fraud.

Loan Origination, Underwriting, Closing, Disbursement, and Servicing Segregation

By separating all of the functions relating to loans, a lending institution reduces the opportunity for an individual (insider) to perpetrate loan fraud. Additionally, the segregation provides for at least one, if not several, levels of independent review to reduce its external loan fraud exposure.

Committee Approval of all Large or Unusual Transactions

If a loan committee or a board-of-directors committee is responsible for approving loans and other large or unusual transactions, then insiders will have a more difficult time perpetrating large fraud and the transactions submitted by external fraudsters will be subject to another layer of independent review.

Transfer Journal Entries and Orders Review

Regularly review all transfer journal entries and orders. As with an expense review, if a routine but unscheduled review occurs from time to time, then the fraudster loses the vehicle for concealment.

Independent Review of Loans

An independent review of loans provides a nonpartisan approach to all loan transactions. Either the internal or external auditors (or other consultants) can perform this independent review which allows for a "second opinion" on loan transactions. The reviews should be consistent and performed on a regular basis to help establish loan loss reserves. Typically, this loan review is established for loans for more than a certain dollar amount, such as $25,000 or $100,000.

Management Review of Write-Offs

Excessive write-offs are a form of concealment for phantom loans, conflicts of interest, and embezzlement. Therefore, if all write-offs are subject to management review *before they are written off*, then management reduces the potential environment for fraud.

Routine Examination of Officers' Accounts

Routine examination of officers' accounts might prevent fraud schemes such as wire transfer fraud, embezzlement, withdrawals from dormant accounts, conflicts of interest, and so on. This review can be performed when the officer is on mandatory vacation.

Proper Lending Policies

Employees should be trained in the proper (and regulated) lending policies of the institution. Any deviations from the policies will be red flags and will help to prevent loan fraud from both internal and external perpetrators.

Document Requirements for Standard Transactions

Deviations from normal or proscribed documentation should be an automatic red flag. Who better to recognize a potential fraud than the employees routinely handling the documentation? Therefore, employees should be well-schooled in proper documentation for the transactions they are handling.

Information Verification (for example, Loan Applications)

Fraud potential could be eliminated or at the very least detected before companies suffer damages if the employee knows how to verify information. For example, if the loan officer advises a potential borrower that the information submitted on financial statements will be verified, the borrower will be less likely to submit false or fraudulent financial statements. Additionally, if a teller advises a depositor that the deposit will be verified before cash is paid out, then the incidence of split deposits can be reduced.

Employee Training

Fellow employees are generally the first people to recognize unusual transactions or behavior changes of other employees. These might be early indicators that a fraud has or will soon begin. Employees and managers should be properly trained to recognize these symptoms. For example, bank tellers should be adequately schooled in split deposit schemes; new account officers in new account schemes and so on.

Standardized Procedures

An institution can provide a low fraud environment by standardizing procedures in sensitive areas, as detailed below:
- Loan application processing
- Information required for loan approval
- Credit report requests
- Appraisals accepted from pre-approved list of vendors
- Inspection reports on construction draw loans
- Conflict of interest disclosure statements
- Routine confirmation calls for
  - Wire transfers
  - Construction vendors
- Confirmation of registered securities with registrar or transfer agent
- Periodic physical inventory of securities

Suspicious Activity Reports

Effective April 1, 1996, the Office of the Comptroller of the Currency (OCC) requires national banks to submit a Suspicious Activity Report (SAR) under certain circumstances (12 C.F.R. §21.11, as amended). Reports are required if there is a known or suspected criminal violation committed against the bank or involving a transaction conducted through the bank and

- The bank has a substantial basis for identifying responsible bank personnel; or
- The amount involved is $5,000 or more and the bank has a substantial basis for identifying a possible suspect; or
- The amount involved is $25,000 or more (if the amount involved is $25,000 or more, the bank is required to report even if the bank does not have a substantial basis for identifying a suspect); or
- The amount involved is $5,000 or more and the potential for money laundering; or
- The amount involved is $5,000 or more and the violation of the Bank Secrecy Act exists; or
- The amount involved is $5,000 or more and the transaction has no business or apparent lawful purpose or is not the sort in which the particular customer would normally be expected to engage, and the institution knows of no reasonable explanation for the transaction after examining the available facts, including the background and possible purpose of the transaction.

In most cases, the SAR must be filed within 30 days of the date of detection. Other financial institutions have similar reporting requirements, including:

- Federal Deposit Insurance Corporation (FDIC) - 12 C.F.R. § 353
- Office of Thrift Supervision (OTS) - 12 C.F.R. § 563.180
- National Credit Union Administration (NCUA) - 12 C.F.R. § 748
- Federal Reserve Board (FRB) - Form 2230

More information about the Bank Secrecy Act and other reporting requirements can be found in the "Money Laundering" section.

Applicable Federal Statutes

There are many federal statutes related to fraud and false statements involving financial institutions. The following are some common federal statutes employed in the prosecution of bank fraud.

Bank Fraud, Title 18, U.S. Code, § 1344

Section 1344 is the broadest of all bank fraud statutes. It punishes those obtaining assets owned or controlled by a bank by false or fraudulent pretenses, representations, or promises. It covers both insiders and all other persons, even if not affiliated with the bank It also applies to check kiting and to off-shore frauds (extraterritorial reach). Bank fraud is a predicate offense under RICO (Racketeer Influenced Corrupt Organization Statute). Penalties for bank fraud include a fine up to $1 million and/or imprisonment of up to 30 years.

Financial Institutions Reform, Recovery and Enforcement Act (FIRREA) Title 12, U.S. Code, § 1811, et seq.

This legislation greatly strengthens the prosecutorial arm against insiders and outsiders. The law's provisions are applicable to any institution-affiliated party, which includes (but is not limited to) directors, officers, employees, and controlling shareholders. Institution-affiliated parties can include attorneys, accountants, and appraisers.

FIRREA provides for enhanced civil and criminal penalties for convictions of several bank-related statutes. The civil penalties can be $1 million per day, or a total of $5 million for continuing violations, or the amount of wrongful gain or loss. The maximum criminal penalty is either a fine of $1 million or 30 years imprisonment, or both.

Crime Control Act of 1990 Title 12, U.S. Code, § 1821(d)(17)-(19)

This Act defines a host of new crimes and increases the maximum penalties on other offenses. For example, the maximum prison term for financial crimes was increased from 5 years to 20 years. These penalties, however, do not become effective for offenses committed prior to the effective date of this law. Thus far, no court decisions have been made regarding these increased penalties. This statute amended the Racketeer Influenced Corrupt Organization law (RICO), making bank fraud a predicate offense under RICO.

Financial Institution Anti-Fraud Enforcement Act of 1990 *Title 12, U.S. Code, § 4201, et seq.*

This statute sets out procedures for rewarding private parties for reporting violations and providing information concerning the recovery of assets. The statute also allows for the hiring of private counsel to investigate and prosecute civil claims.

Continuing Financial Crime Enterprise Statute
Title 18, U.S. Code, § 225

Also known as the "S&L Kingpin" statute, the law provides for fines of up to $20 million for organizational defendants and fines of up to $10 million and up to life imprisonment for individual defendants receiving $5 million or more during a 24-month period from a criminal enterprise. A *criminal enterprise* is defined as a series of enumerated crimes related to financial institutions.

Embezzlement, Misapplication, and False Entries
TITLE 18, U.S. CODE, §§ 656 AND 657

These sections cover theft, embezzlement, or misapplication by a bank officer or employee. Violations are punishable by up to 30 years in prison and/or fined up to $1 million.

TITLE 18, U.S. CODE, §§ 1001, 1005, 1006, 1007, 1008, 1014

These statutes include all provisions which punish false or fraudulent statements orally or in writing to various federal agencies and federally insured financial institutions. Usually these result from efforts to conceal embezzlements and misapplications.

TITLE 18, U.S. CODE, § 1032, CONCEALMENT OF ASSETS

This statute prohibits any person from corruptly attempting to conceal assets or impede their recovery. Violations are punishable by up to five years in prison plus fines.

Participation in the Affairs of a Financial Institution by a Convicted Felon
Title 12, U.S. Code, § 1829

This statute bars people with banking crime convictions from participating in the conduct of the affairs of a financial institution, with certain exceptions. A knowing violation might result in fines of up to $1million per day and imprisonment of up to five years.

Offer of Loan or Gratuity to a Bank Examiner, Title 18, U.S. Code, § 212

Bank officers, directors, and employees are prohibited from giving a loan or gratuity to a bank examiner or assistant. Section 213 forbids an examiner or assistant from accepting a loan or gratuity. Both offenses are punishable by a fine of up to $5,000 or the amount loaned or given and up to a year's imprisonment.

Receipt of Commissions or Gifts for Procuring Loans, Title 18, U.S. Code, § 215

The corrupt giving or receiving of any thing of value to influence an officer, director, employee, agent, or attorney of a financial institution is punishable by fines of the greater of three times the value of the thing given or no more than $1 million and/or up to 30 years imprisonment.

Other Federal Statutes

The following statutes can also be used in connection with the prosecution of fraud involving financial institutions. Each of these statutes is covered in more detail in the Law section.

- Bribery of Public Officials and Witnesses, Title 18, U.S. Code, § 201
- Disqualification of Former Officers and Employees, Title 18, U.S. Code, § 207
- Fraudulent Use of Credit Cards, Title 15, U.S. Code, § 1644
- Fraud and Related Activity in Connection with Access Devices, Title 18, U.S. Code, § 1029
- Computer Fraud, Title 18, U.S. Code, § 1030
- Mail Fraud, Title 18, U.S. Code, § 1341
- Wire Fraud, Title 18, U.S. Code, § 1343
- Racketeer Influenced and Corrupt Organizations (RICO), Title 18, U.S. Code, § 1961, et. seq.
- The Foreign Corrupt Practices Act (FCPA), Title 15, U.S. Code, §§ 78m, 78a(b), 78dd-1, 78ff
- Tax Evasion, Title 26, U.S. Code, § 7201
- Filing False Tax Return, Title 26, U.S. Code, § 7206(1)
- False Claims Act, Title 31, U.S. Code, § 3729 et seq.
- Anti-Kickback Act of 1986, Title 41, U.S. Code, §§ 51-58

CHECK AND CREDIT CARD FRAUD

Check Fraud

Check fraud is one of the fastest-growing problems affecting the nation's financial system, producing estimated yearly losses of up to $50 billion. Experts estimate that about 2 million worthless checks are introduced in to the banking system daily. Not only is the dollar amount involved in check fraud increasing yearly, the complexity of fraud tools is growing as well. With increased sophistication in laser printers, more accurate color copiers and desktop publishing capabilities, duplicating and forging checks has become more accurate and thus more difficult to detect. Another factor in the rising fraud rate is greater participation in crimes by employees and other insiders. Since 1987, bank frauds committed by insiders have risen dramatically and now account for more than 60% of all financial institution fraud. Most of these frauds involve the counterfeiting of stolen checks. Banks and other financial institutions absorb about one-tenth of check fraud losses; therefore, customers make up the difference through higher fees and charges.

For the period of April 1, 1996 through September 30, 2003, the FBI received 268,536 Suspicious Activity Reports (SARs) of criminal activity related to check fraud, counterfeit negotiable instruments, and related schemes. These schemes accounted for 47% or the 569,924 SARs filed by United States financial institutions (excluding Bank Secrecy Act violations), and equaled approximately $8 billion in losses. The FBI says in the United States "today's biggest fraud problem is large-scale check fraud and counterfeiting operations."

Due to demands of law enforcement, prosecutors fail to pursue 75% of bank check fraud cases. According to the U.S. General Accounting Office, in large cities where a majority of resources are used to prosecute violent crime the percentage rises to 90%. Law enforcement officials may neglect reports of check fraud, feeling that businesses ought to be more vigilant in detecting bad checks. Many merchants have tried to use the police and prosecutors as check collection agencies; therefore, law enforcement and prosecutors are often not eager to pursue these cases. Many bad-check-passers are constantly on the move, as well, making prosecution even more difficult.

The best solution for financial institutions and merchants, then, is to educate employees to recognize forged and fraudulent checks and the schemes behind them. Merchants and financial institutions should have a strict check acceptance policy with which all employees are familiar. When accepting checks, employees should always ask for identification and make sure it is valid. Many check passers mollify store personnel by showing them a small laminated rectangular document with a picture. After looking at several hundred of these, most employees tend not to scrutinize them. Check passers count on this. It is important for employees to examine each piece of identification closely every time they are presented with one.

Employers must also watch for behavior among employees which could be red flags of inside check fraud. Dissatisfaction with job, pay rate, or home life; a lack of recognition, lavish lifestyle; and a problem with gambling, alcohol, or drugs are indications that an employee may be committing internal fraud.

Counterfeiting Checks

An effective check counterfeiting operation can turn a simple $5,000 investment into a $1,000,000 windfall within a 30-day timeframe. This can be done without high levels of computer expertise or programming. Simple check printing software can be purchased in almost any office supply store along with blank paper stock and magnetic ink cartridges. The overall initial investment consists of a quality computer, color inkjet printer, check format and MICR font software, magnetic ink cartridges, and paper stock. After making the initial investment, the printers only have to concern themselves with purchasing additional ink and paper.

Signs of Counterfeit and Forged Checks

A counterfeiter will go to great lengths to make his check appear to be the genuine article. However, there are a few giveaways that a check is counterfeit. If the printing on the check does not seem uniform in texture and color, or slants up or down, the check is not good. Also, the transit number in the top right corner must match the electronically encoded number at the bottom of the check. These numbers normally do not coincide on altered checks. The first three of the electronically encoded numbers indicate the state and district office of the issuer. Again, on forged checks, these numbers do not always match properly. The check number itself should be found in the encoded serial number at the bottom.

Knowing that many merchants regard checks with low check numbers as suspect, forgers often attempt to add a digit. Here again, they may have difficulty matching the ink used to produce the check. A simple and effective method of detecting bad checks is to fan a group of checks. Counterfeit checks will sometimes stand out as a slightly different color.

Check Fraud Vulnerabilities

A particular institution may be targeted for check frauds because of its location, inadequate internal controls, or marketing strategies that present opportunities to savvy check fraud artists. Some mutual funds companies, for example, regularly allow customers to open accounts by mail, a form of communication with many security vulnerabilities. A significant number of check fraud complaints from a particular geographic area may indicate the presence of an active, organized group that warrants law enforcement attention.

Investigators assigned to a region or institution should keep regular contact with businesses and regulators. Specific inquiries aim to identify weaknesses, develop controls, and prevent future losses. Analyzing the complaints filed by other victims of check fraud—including retail operations, check cashing establishments, and food stores—may reveal common elements of schemes that might not otherwise seem related.

Check Theft

Three types of check theft are: using stolen canceled checks to obtain new checks, check washing, and stealing blank check stock.

- *Stolen Canceled Checks and Statements.* Although a stolen canceled check can't be negotiated, a stolen canceled check does have fraud implications. Using a stolen canceled check; a check thief can order checks from a mail-order check printer and have them sent to a mail drop address. Checks can then be written on the new stock and cashed once false identifications are acquired.
- *Check Washing.* Check washing takes place to the tune of $815 million every year in the U.S., and it is increasing at an alarming rate. Checks are stolen from mailrooms and mailboxes, and then the check is inserted into a solution of chemicals that can be purchased at a hardware store. Once dried the fraudster can write in any amount and the checks are usually cashed without question. Most check washers alter the check for relatively small amounts.
- *Stolen Check Stock.* Professional thieves using sophisticated methods steal blank check stock already encoded with customer account information, which makes passing the check even easier. Corporate checks are the most likely target since they are easily cashed and deposited.

Check Fraud Schemes

"Paperhangers"

Paperhangers are the experts of phony check passing. They frequently pick a particular establishment or store and observe its security methods. Any store, which actually appears to scrutinize check writers' identification, is not a good target for a paperhanger. However, they will observe and select the least experienced or most lackadaisical of store employees to whom to pass the check. The paperhanger will then ask the clerk if he or she may have cash back from the transaction and make the check out for an amount greater than the price of the purchase. In some cases, the checks being written are counterfeit; however, in other cases the checks are purposefully being written on a closed account. A variation of this scam is making a fraudulent deposit at a bank and asking for cash back.

These experts will go to great lengths to blend in with the clientele. Standing out in a crowd is not to their advantage. Women are often quite good as paperhangers. A mother with crying children paying with a check is usually not the profile one expects for a bad-check-passer.

Stop Payment Orders

This scheme is quite simple. A "customer" purchases an expensive item with a check, and then notifies his bank to stop payment. Savvy check passers may even contact the merchant, saying the item was defective, and that they should expect to hear from the customer's attorney. Meanwhile, the check passer sells the item for a tidy profit.

Another scenario is that, after purchasing the item and notifying the bank to stop payment, the fraudster goes back to the store, wishing to return the item and receive a full refund. The merchant refunds the amount in cash and the scheme is successful.

Check Kiting

Check kiting is one of the original white-collar crimes. It continues to survive even with a financial institution's ability to detect kiting. In a kiting scheme, multiple bank accounts are opened and money is "deposited" from account to account, although the money never exists.

Floating makes check kiting possible. Floating is the additional value of funds generated in the process of collection and arises because the current holder of funds has been given credit for the funds before it clears the financial institution upon which it is drawn. Businesses are most susceptible to check kiting, if they have employees who are authorized to write checks or make deposits in more than one bank account. Today, check kiting is more difficult because electronic technologies are making the float smaller all the time. In some cases, electronic debiting to an account occurs simultaneously with the transaction. Unless detected, this process can continue indefinitely, covering one check written against insuffienct funds with another check.

Demand Drafts

Demand drafts can also be used to commit check fraud. This practice involves the misuse of account information to obtain funds from a person's bank account without that person's signature on a negotiable instrument. Other terms for demand drafts are "preauthorized drafts" and "telephone drafts." While there are many legitimate business uses for demand drafts, such as quick-turnaround telephone transactions initiated by airlines and car rental companies, demand drafts have been used by deceptive telemarketers who obtain bank account information and withdraw unauthorized funds from consumers' bank accounts, without their realizing that such withdrawals are occurring.

Third-Party Bill Paying Services

The checks produced by these third-party bill paying service providers do not include the payor signature. Instead, the signature line relects something such as "signature on file." Unauthorized checks produced by third-party payment services are not usually detected until the customer reviews the monthly bank statement. By the time the customer identifies the unauthorized check, it is often too late to recover the funds, since the "24-hour window" (actually until midnight of the next banking day) for the timely return of checks has long since passed. These checks usually sail right through the check sorting operation, since they include good account information and sometimes even include good serial numbers. Too often, both business and individual account holders seem unaware of how their account information, given too freely to a requesting party, can be used for fraudulent purposes.

Travelers' Checks

Anyone familiar with travelers' checks knows that $100 checks are quite common. Some check rings specialize in the production and distribution of this type of check. Commonly, check passers of this type make small purchases using a fake $100 travelers' check, and receive the bulk of the amount back in cash. Naturally, this scheme works well in areas which have a lot of tourist business. Rings often pull this scam several times in one area in rapid succession.

Travelers' checks have several distinguishing features. Watermarks and holograms are common, as well as microprinting and ultraviolet ink. There are basically two methods of counterfeiting travelers' checks: color copying and offset lithography/printing. Color copied checks lack the raised ink texture which the intaglio printing press gives most travelers' checks. Instead of a textured feel, a phony check will appear slick and flat. Offset lithographic reproductions of actual checks are of higher quality than color-copied checks. However, neither will have the texture, watermarks, microprinting, or holograms which the genuine articles have.

Payroll Check Fraud

Check procurers employed by payroll check processing companies print duplicate payroll checks which are sold to third parties or are cashed by members of the procurer's organization. To avoid the security employed by financial institutions, the checks are cashed at grocery stores and check-cashing operations with loose controls. The checks are usually written for amounts of $300 or less to avoid suspicion. Of course, check procurers have access to personal information on the legitimate recipients of the payroll checks and make use of it in the future.

Dumpster Diving

Often, check fraud can be as simple as retrieving bank materials from a trash receptacle.

> EXAMPLE
>
> *Thirty people were charged in a $10 million fraud scheme that involved counterfeiting checks, bank statements, and credit card receipts pulled out of the trash. The defendants, who defrauded people in 17 states, used checks, bank statements, credit card receipts, and other documents from garbage bins to create counterfeit checks, false driver's licenses, and false credit reports, officials said. Counterfeit blank checks, printed on high-quality color printers, allegedly were used to defraud banks of $2 million.*

Obviously, this type of fraud is easily preventable through proper disposal by banks, merchants, and individuals of sensitive and confidential materials.

Scanning

Scanning requires a scanner and a legitimate check. Scanners can be purchased for less than $200 and checks are readily available without having to actually steal the check. Checks can then be manufactured by scanning a corporate logo from a business card onto a simple business size check.

System Password Security Compromised

People having legitimate access to sensitive account and daily code information for a limited time (for example, computer consultants) effect improper transfers through unauthorized access.

Check Fraud Rings

Since the late 1980s, foreign crime rings have been the cause of the majority of check fraud in the U.S. Most major financial institutions attribute more than 50% of all check fraud to organized crime rings. The perpetrators are often based in Nigeria, Russia, Vietnam, and Mexico. Most of the Vietnamese and Mexican rings operate in California, notably San Francisco, Orange County, and Sacramento. The Russian and Nigerian rings, centered in the Northeast, spread their criminal activities over a wide area and can be found passing through any part of the U.S. at any time. While most of these gangs are involved in drug trafficking and violent crimes, check and credit card fraud are considered "safe" crimes. The chances of being arrested and prosecuted are relatively low and the penalties are not very harsh.

The equipment essential to a check fraud ring are a laser scanner, laser printer, and a personal computer, easily obtainable items, the total cost of which is about $1,500. These rings use digital scanners and offset printing to counterfeit checks. The checks are cashed by members of the ring or sold to third parties.

Most rings specialize in payroll or other institutional checks, written for amounts less than $300. But some groups infiltrate financial institutions, collecting corporate payroll checks, money orders and master original bank checks, cashing the duplicates for between $2,000 and $5,000.

In recent years, members of Nigerian and Vietnamese rings have infiltrated or obtained accomplices in financial institutions. There they gather personal information on customers, passing the information to counterfeiters who produce falsified identification (driver's licenses, credit cards, etc.), which is used to open accounts, establish lines of credit, and secure loans. An organized group may include a counterfeiter or printer, a distributor, one or more providers of false identification, and several "smurfs," who open false bank accounts or visit check-cashing establishments to negotiate fraudulent checks.

Foreign crime rings which practice check fraud are ethnically homogenous and usually not rigidly structured. It is common for only the leaders of these rings to know the extent of the participation of their subordinates. The leaders of such groups are usually quite intelligent and educated. Often, they have an extensive criminal or business background and direct the group's activities. Gangs have been known to share members and cooperate with one another in the past.

Check Fraud Detection

FBI Profile of Check Fraud Activity

According to an analysis by FBI investigators in the New York City area, fraudulent check passers use the following common techniques:

- Customer attempts to open an account with a corporate check or other third-party check.
- Customer tries to flatter, hurry, or confuse the teller to draw attention away from the transaction.
- Customer delays endorsing a check or producing identification during peak hours to frustrate the teller and hurry the transaction.
- Customer presents for cash a low-numbered check drawn on a new account.
- Customer offers foreign documentation (birth certificate, passport, visa) or non-photo identification (Social Security card, credit card) in lieu of photo identification to open an account or cash a check.
- Customer offers altered or damaged identification to open an account or cash a check.
- Customer attempts to cash or convert several small checks into wire transfer, gold, or other tender.
- Customer requests an exception to established rules to force the transaction.

Detection Techniques

The cashier or teller is the front-line defense in preventing check fraud. It is important that they receive the training necessary to identify fraudulent checks. They should:

- Be aware of magnetic routing numbers.

- Look for checks with a check number less than 400 on personal checks or below 1,500 on business checks (90% of bad checks are written on accounts less than one-year old).
- Be aware of fonts used to print the customer's name that are visibly different from the font used to print the address.
- Be aware that the magnetic ink (MICR) used for routing codes should appear non-reflective and dull.
- Look for MICR coding that does not match the bank district and the routing symbol in the upper right-hand corner of the check.
- Be aware of date that the account was opened.
- Be aware of stains or discolorations on the check possibly caused by erasures or alterations.
- Have easy access to the signature card.
- Look for perforated edges of the checks.
- Be aware that a color copy might reflect odd colors at times due to a failure of the toner to mix satisfactorily.
- Notice absence of any design in the background of the check paper.
- Notice absence of bank logo and the printing of the bank name in the regular lettering.
- Notice absence of the address of the bank on the check.
- Be cautious of information that is typed or stamped.
- Be aware of what is acceptable identification.
- Recognize forged/altered information.
- Recognize forged negotiable instruments.
- Tellers should telephone the business or account officer for approval on suspicious requests.
- Be familiar with patterns of behavior related to potential culprits:
  - Overly polite
  - Nervous
  - Aggressive and hurried

Check Fraud Prevention and Investigation

Since the Federal Reserve's Regulation CC was implemented, mandating accelerated availability of customers' funds, check fraud at banks has increased. Most bank customers' funds are available for withdrawal a day after deposit, leaving the bank little time to verify the validity of the transaction. Regulation CC, however, allows banks two days to make funds available. Most banks provide next-day withdrawal in order to stay competitive.

Special security printing techniques have been developed to make counterfeiting blank checks more difficult. One of the features is to use pastel blue ink or "prismatic lithography," a pattern in colors which are difficult to separate even with special cameras, filters, and film. Another technique used is scrambled indicia printing which is a seemingly random pattern of tiny colored dots printed on the paper. Using a colored filter to view the check will make a word or pattern develop.

Still another technique, which is also used by credit card issuers, is to print a "micro-line" on the check which appears as a solid line when viewed normally. But using a magnifying glass will show that the line is actually very small words or letters, which are very difficult to recreate with the normal printing process. Other security measures include using a three dimensional hologram which is easily identifiable by the human eye, but is impossible to reproduce via ordinary copying or printing. Some checks have a security seal on the back of the check that is visible when held up to a light. Reproductions, even good ones, will not have a seal.

Check Fraud Investigations

During a check fraud investigation, look for the following:
- Frequent deposits and checks:
    - In the same amounts
    - In round numbers
    - With checks written on the same (other) bank
- Frequent ATM account balance inquiries.
- Many large deposits made on Thursday or Friday to take advantage of the weekend.
- Large periodic balances in individual accounts with no apparent business.
- Low average balance compared to high level of deposits.
- Many checks made payable to other banks.
- Bank willingness to pay against uncollected funds.
- Deposits not made daily or intact.
- Entity uses receipts which do not indicate mode of payment.
- One or more personal checks in the cash drawer by the fund custodian.
- Deposit timing lags.
- Irregular check endorsements.
- Amount of deposit does not agree with daily activity report.
- Inappropriate access to signature plate.

- Check numbers, payee name, date, and amount don't agree with entries in the check register.
- Voided checks are not retained.
- Checks are issued to individuals for large, even dollar amounts.
- Supporting documentation for checks is not available or has been prematurely destroyed.
- Cash withdrawal with deposit checks drawn on another bank.

There are several tips for businesses to use when cashing business and payroll checks:
- Examine all checks. Insist that the check by signed in front of the clerk. Compare the signature written on the check with the signature on the driver's license or state identification.
- Be particularly careful with large-dollar checks presented by noncustomers.
- Examine all checks for signs of counterfeiting, such as a glossy, "crayonish" appearance and any lack of detail and sharpness.
- Look for signs of alterations or erasures, especially in the signature or numerical and written amounts.
- Compare the bank identification and routing numbers for a match.
- The texture of the check should appear smooth; a rough document might signal erasures.
- Be cautious of information that is typed or stamped.
- All checks, except government issue, should have at least one perforated edge.
- The magnetic ink used for routing codes should appear nonreflective and dull.
- Look for faded colored paper which can indicate that the check has been chemically bleached.
- A color copy might reflect odd colors at times due to a failure of the toner to mix satisfactorily.
- Black lettering might have a slightly greenish cast when examined under a magnifying glass.
- A light colored or delicate background might fade out when copied.
- Absence of any design in background of check paper.
- Absence of bank logo and the printing of the bank name in regular lettering.
- Absence of the address of the bank on the check.
- Overall appearance of poor quality of printing and paper.
- A payroll check usually will be for an odd amount and will appear neat, clean, and usually unfolded.

- Tellers should telephone the business or account officer for approval on suspicious requests.

Check Fraud Prevention Tools

Fingerprint Identifiers

A *biometric fingerprint identifier* requires the check writer to match fingerprints with the account holder's, which are on file. Banks reported reductions in check fraud of 40% after the machine was introduced in the mid-1990s.

Non-account holders who want checks cashed at banks which have implemented this system are required to put an inkless fingerprint on their check. If the check does prove false, law enforcement will already have evidence regarding the fraudster's identity. The cost to a bank of implementing the inkless fingerprint system could be redeemed by preventing a single instance of check fraud. Banks throughout the nation now use this technique to cut fraud losses.

Forensic Document Examination

Through handwriting, an individual can be positively identified, as is the case with DNA or fingerprinting. When investigating check fraud, a forensic document examiner focuses on the signature and the handwriting itself.

Signature

If the examiner were investigating a forged signature, he would compare the suspicious signature to a sample of the actual one, noting discrepancies between the two. While one's signature may change over time, it would be close to impossible for a forger to duplicate a signature with one hundred percent accuracy; minute identifying characteristics mark people's writing and are unreproducible.

The eBank ™ Discovery System, developed by ASV Technologies, employs signature verification software. Using "multiple feature set extraction" technology drawn from forensic science, the state and quality of a signature's two-dimensional characteristics are analyzed and verified against samples. The program identifies flourishes, arcs, distances between letters, and up to 100 other features. Rejected signatures, along with the reason for rejection and signature samples, are forwarded to a human for visual verification. ASV Technologies claim its results match those of the most highly trained and accurate signature verifier.

Handwriting

Like fingerprints, handwriting is unique to an individual. When examining a forged check, it is to be hoped the narrative portion of the check is handwritten. This naturally offers a document examiner greater opportunity to identify a forgery.

Video Spectral Comparator

Forensic examiners use this tool to test questionable documents. The document is examined for photocopying and liquid paper under a controlled light source. Lettering added to a document can be detected with this device.

Electrostatic Detection Apparatus

This tool allows examiners to detect indented writing from the top page of a pad of paper up to five pages below the original. The Electrostatic Detection Apparatus uses photocopier toner to develop the areas of indentation after a document has been covered with an electrically charged plastic film. In the best of cases, when the document is processed with the electrostatic device and the toner image is developed, the writing impressions are clearly defined and highly contrasted. If the developed writing is to be used in an investigation or to demonstrate results for the courts, the examiner must turn to electronic image processing technology for further enhancement.

Credit Card Fraud

Credit card fraud is the misuse of a credit card to make purchases without authorization, or counterfeiting a credit card. Eighty-one percent of U.S. households have at least one credit card, and 80% of teenagers between the ages 18 and 20 have a credit card. The average household with at least one credit card has 6.0 bank credit cards, 8.3 retail credit cards, and 2.4 debit cards for a total of 16.7 cards. As the industry continues to expand and offer credit to more and more consumers, fraud will also grow.

Credit card fraud in the U.S. has reached the $1 billion mark and is expected to reach $3 billion by 2007. Surveys show that 90% of Internet-based purchases are paid online with a credit card, and that fraud represents about 5% of all online shopping. Seventy percent of credit card fraud occurs during the holiday season, because time is short and sales associates are hurried.

As over 70% of all credit cards are issued in the U.S., most credit card fraud also occurs there. However, the perpetrators frequently are not Americans. The same ethnically homogenous foreign fraud rings involved in check fraud also perpetrate a substantial amount of credit card fraud.

Credit card fraud is successful because the chances of being caught are small and prosecution is not assured. Retail stores have identified credit card thieves and contacted law enforcement only to be turned down for action.

Online Credit Card Fraud

In 2001, total annual online sales were $61.8 billion; this number rocketed to $114 billion in 2003, representing 5.4 percent of all retail sales. Total online sales are expected to grow 27 percent to $144 billion in 2004, representing 6.6 percent of total retail value. More than $700 million in online sales were lost to fraud in 2001; this number had increased to $2.4 billion by 2003. The lack of face-to-face or voice interaction on the Internet makes fraudsters more daring by providing them with anonymity, which makes the detection and prevention of online frauds more difficult. Lists of stolen credit card numbers are also being posted on the Internet or sold in newsgroups and can be used by a variety of individuals to purchase goods online without the authorization of the credit card's owner.

Credit Card Schemes

There are many different types of credit card schemes including selling the cards to thieves, family members using the credit cards without authorization, and fraudulently obtaining a card. Statutes relating to the misuse of credit cards generally prohibit the obtaining of property or services through the use of a credit card if the use of the card is for any reason unauthorized. The federal statute prohibiting the use of fraudulent credit cards is found at 15 U.S.C. 1664. This statute provides penalties for the use of counterfeit, fictitious, altered, forged, lost, stolen, or fraudulently obtained credit cards. A violator may be fined up to $10,000 and/or imprisoned for up to ten years.

Unauthorized Use of a Lost or Stolen Card

Fraudulent activity normally occurs within hours of the loss or theft, before most victims have called to report the loss. Increasingly, victims aren't even aware that their credit cards are being fraudulently used until they receive their monthly statement. It is extremely important that victims report the loss or theft of their card within 3 days, as they will not be held responsible for any charges that occur during that time frame. If the credit card company is not notified of the theft and the card is used, the customer will be liable.

Organized Crime Rings
Nigerian rings are especially notorious for stealing credit card and bank information from the mail. These articles are used to generate false identification documents, such as driver's licenses and Social Security cards. The credit cards themselves are duplicated and distributed to members of the rings. The false IDs are then displayed during purchases made with the stolen cards. Members of the ring go on spending sprees, ending only when the credit has dried up or the legitimate owner reports their card as stolen. Often, counterfeit and stolen cards are express-mailed to members of the ring in other parts of the country.

Advance Payments
Consumer regulations require credit card issuers to credit customers' accounts immediately upon receipt of payment. This means deducting from the balance of the account before the check or other payment instrument has actually cleared the bank. A loophole such as this is easily exploited by experienced fraud rings.

Using a forged or counterfeit check, an advance or overpayment is made on a stolen credit card. Since the issuer must credit the payment at the time it is made, there is no time to verify the authenticity of the check. Consequently, cash advances and purchases can be made immediately. This scheme can be extremely lucrative to the perpetrators.

Shave and Paste
Any number of alpha or numeric characters are sliced from the card surface and other characters are attached to the card surface, utilizing fast drying epoxy-type glues. This might be done to put an entirely different but valid account number on the card or to change the name.

De-Emboss/Re-Emboss
In this scheme, the credit card is exposed to heat, usually from a household iron, a candle, or hot water in the microwave. Plastic cards, comprised primarily of polyvinylchloride, become more elastic when heated, and the embossed alpha/numeric characters are removed. An embosser puts new numbers and names on the cards. This process will generally create a "ghost image."

Counterfeit Cards

The fastest growing type of bankcard fraud involves the illegal counterfeiting of credit cards. Known as "white plastic" cards, this scheme utilizes credit card sized plastic with account numbers and names embossed on the card. This scheme works in conjunction with a corrupt and collusive merchant or a merchant's employee. Other counterfeit cards are manufactured from scratch using high speed printing facilities and used in association with organized crime groups. Manufacturing facilities have been traced to the Far East.

Counterfeiting operations are centered in Taiwan, China, and Hong Kong, where the specialty is producing the holograms and magnetic strips which appear on many cards. Forged holograms are smuggled into the U.S. and Canada by ring members from Asia and distributed throughout both countries. A substantial amount of them end up in California, where most of the Asian counterfeiting operations in the U.S. are located. Not surprisingly, California, notably Orange County, experiences more credit card fraud than any area in the country.

The actual counterfeiting process has been immeasurably eased by new technology which allows more accurate duplication. Duplicating legitimate cards is still an intricate operation, however. Magnetic strips, numbers, holograms, and logos must all appear authentic. Desktop computers, embossers, tipping foil, and laminators are common tools in the reproduction process. Perhaps most difficult of all to accurately reproduce, however, is the hologram. Most phony holograms can be sold for between $5 and $15. True holograms use a "lenticular refraction" process; counterfeits are generally only reflected materials, usually a foil with an image stamped on it. These decals are attached to the surface of the card, rather than fixed into the plastic, as is the case with legitimate cards. Some holograms do not change colors, as legitimate ones do, when viewed from various angles. Counterfeit credit cards are the most damaging scheme of the ones mentioned here.

Telephone/Mail Order Fraud

The fraudster might offer a free trip or other nice prize, with the only catch being that the winner must have a credit card. Once the thief has the number, he can order merchandise or have money wired to himself.

A great deal of credit card fraud is childishly simple to complete. Many crooks have great success by simply selecting a name from the phone book, calling, and pretending to be a Visa/MasterCard representative. The victim is told that his or her card number may have been obtained and used illegally by criminals. Or, a representative of a travel agency may call, claiming the victim has won a discount travel package. In any case, the victim is asked to read the card number off for verification or inclusion in the discount deal. A surprisingly large amount of people fall for this scheme and give out their credit card information. Purchases through catalogues and mail orders are then often made using the victim's card number. They may select an unoccupied address to which their merchandise can be delivered, perhaps leaving a note asking the delivery service to simply put the package by the back door.

False Applications

Perpetrators might apply for a new card using information stolen from a wallet, purse, or the trash; or stealing a pre-approved credit card application out of the mail or trash. Also "take-one" applications that are prominent in stores offering credit cards to the public, are ripe for fraud.

Credit "Doctors"

Credit doctor is the term used for fraudsters who sell stolen credit card account numbers via newspaper ads to people unable to get credit cards.

True Name Fraud

New credit card accounts can be opened by individuals possessing a victim's true name identification such as a driver's license or Social Security number. The true identification was either obtained as a secondary objective in the commission of a more aggressive offense such as robbery or as the primary target of a lesser crime such as pickpocketing.

Non-Receipt Fraud

A form of credit card fraud in which the perpetrator intercepts credit cards that are in transit between the credit issuer and the authorized account holder. Losses attributable to mail theft have declined significantly as a result of "card activation" programs, where the cardholder must call their financial institution and confirm their identity before the card is activated.

Key-Enter Counterfeiting

When banks began using the CVV (for Visa) and CVC (for MasterCard) security system, fraudsters came up with this clever ruse in response. The CVV system uses a three-digit number embedded in the magnetic strip of a credit card, identifying it as a legitimately issued credit instrument. Credit card counterfeiters figured out a way to beat the system, however. By leaving the magnetic strip uncoded or making it unreadable, fraudsters force merchants handling the transaction to enter the credit card number manually. This means the transaction never falls under the scope of the CVV system.

Clever bank and credit card officials have already found a patch for this scheme though. The CVV2 and CVC2 systems use a three-digit security code that is printed on the backs of cards. It is designed to validate that a genuine card is being used during a transaction. When a point-of-sale (POS) terminal reads a card's magnetic stripe, Visa's card Verification Value (CVV) or MasterCard's Card Validation Code (CVC) can be verified during the authorization. Merchants using CVV2/CVC2 can expect to reduce their chargebacks by as much as 26%. Most companies' cards, both credit and debit, were required to contain CVC2 by 2001. The number appears in reverse italic at the top of the signature panel at the end. The CVV2 and CVC2 programs can also be used to reduce fraud in card-not-present transactions.

Creditmaster

This software program, downloadable from the Internet, allows the user to produce valid credit card numbers. Counterfeiters can then put these numbers to use in phony cards.

Probing

The fraudster sets up a computer program that lets him run stolen numbers through various financial institutions in the hopes that one of them will still honor the number. Numbers that clear are often sold en masse to counterfeiters.

Skimming

This scheme requires a device known as a *wedge*, which stores up to 200 credit card numbers. Credit card skimming is more frequent in businesses where an employee must leave the customer's presence in order to run the transaction. A restaurant patron, for example, hands his credit card to a waiter who swipes the card into a wedge while conducting the legitimate transaction. Once the waiter has collected enough numbers, he can either sell them to a counterfeiter or simply produce his own fake cards using the stolen information. It may be months before the customer notices phony transactions on his statement, making the point of loss very difficult to determine. It follows that the guilty waiter is, therefore, unlikely to get caught. Skimming can also occur by tapping into a line used to transport credit card data.

Information on how to commit credit card fraud is readily available to anyone willing to make the effort to look. Postings on the Internet give step-by-step instructions on how obtain carbon paper receipts and call credit-reporting agencies using merchant numbers. The latter is done in order to verify that the card is valid and to obtain the amount of credit available. The fraudster usually watches a store employee dial the number of the agency, noting the numbers as they are dialed. They then listen to the employee give the merchant number. This number can often be found next to registers and can be copied down if in plain sight. The fraudster now has an excellent avenue to test stolen cards.

Merchant Scams

Collusion occurs between the sales people and the credit card fraudster to process valid credit card numbers on white plastic cards. They might also make several imprints on sales tickets and fill them in later on.

Magnetic Stripe Diagram

Track 1

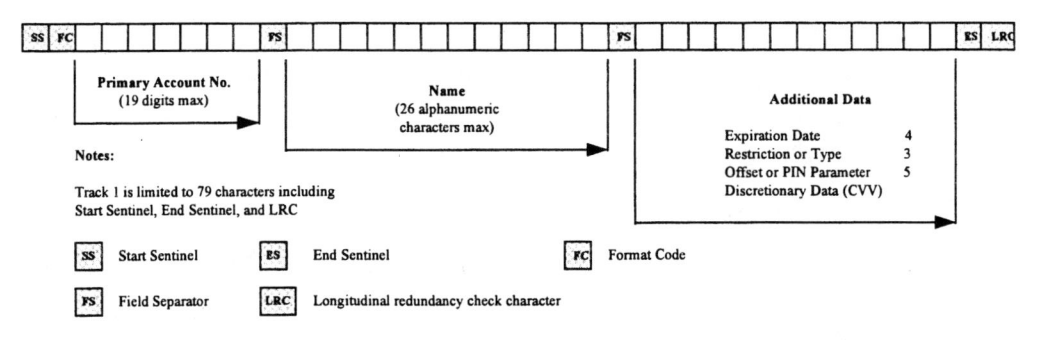

| SS | FC | | | | | FS | | | | | | | | FS | | | | | | | | | ES | LRC |

Primary Account No. (19 digits max)

Name (26 alphanumeric characters max)

Additional Data
- Expiration Date   4
- Restriction or Type   3
- Offset or PIN Parameter   5
- Discretionary Data (CVV)

Notes:
Track 1 is limited to 79 characters including Start Sentinel, End Sentinel, and LRC

| SS | Start Sentinel | ES | End Sentinel | FC | Format Code |
| FS | Field Separator | LRC | Longitudinal redundancy check character |

Track 2

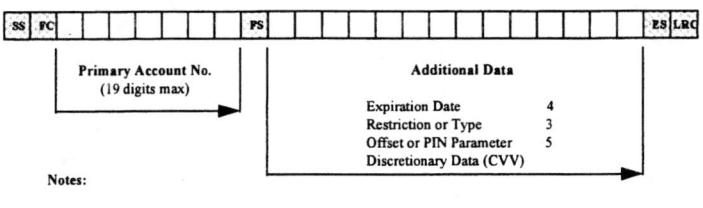

| SS | FC | | | | | FS | | | | | | | | | | ES | LRC |

Primary Account No. (19 digits max)

Additional Data
- Expiration Date   4
- Restriction or Type   3
- Offset or PIN Parameter   5
- Discretionary Data (CVV)

Notes:
Track 2 is limited to 40 characters including Start Sentinel, End Sentinel, and LRC

As shown in the above Magnetic Stripe Diagram above, two tracks appear on the credit card's magnetic stripe. Track two is the most widely read. It is 40 characters in length, is strictly numeric containing the account number, expiration date, a security code, and discretionary bank data. Track one is 79 characters in length, is alpha numeric, and contains the above information plus the cardholder's name.

Magnetic stripe compromise is a more sophisticated method of obtaining account information for fraudulent purposes. It requires the transfer, or encoding, of legitimate account information, along with a security code, from the legitimate magnetic stripe to a counterfeited card with a magnetic stripe. The full, unaltered, legitimate magnetic stripe must be obtained to accomplish fraud by this method.

Skimmers are becoming prevalent in credit card frauds. A skimmer is a card-reading device similar to the swipe machine used by cashiers to validate credit cards. It can be purchased at electronic stores and used by credit card thieves to read data imprinted on information tracks within the magnetic strip located on the card. In addition, criminals are using the device to swipe credit information from one credit card and put it on another.

Company Credit Cards

Company credit cards are provided to employees for convenience in conduction of company business. No personal expenses may be charged on the company credit card except as specifically authorized by company procedures. The employee must pay any charged personal expenses promptly. Company credit cards should not be used to avoid preparing documentation for direct payment to vendors. Where allowed by local law, charges on company credit cards for which a properly approved expense report has not been received at the time of an employee's termination of employment may be deducted from the employee's last paycheck. The company will pursue repayment by the employee of any amounts it has to pay on the employee's behalf.

Prevention and Detection of Credit Card Fraud

The essential part of any detection program is the education of the tellers and merchants who are responsible for handling the transactions. In a study by *Money Magazine*, it was found that 95% of store clerks and cashiers did not check credit card signatures.

While any of the following can occur in a perfectly legitimate transaction, these characteristics frequently are present during fraudulent transactions. Tellers and merchants should be advised to be alert for the customer who:
- Takes a card from a pocket instead of a wallet or purse.

- Purchases an unusual number of expensive items.
- Makes random purchases, selecting items with little regard to size, quality, or value.
- Makes several small purchases to stay under the floor limit, or asks what the floor limit is.
- Signs the sales draft slowly or awkwardly.
- Charges expensive items on a newly valid credit card.
- Cannot provide a photo identification when asked.
- Rushes the merchant or teller.
- Purchases a large item, such as a television console, and insists on taking it at the time, even when delivery is included in the price.
- Becomes argumentative with the teller or merchant while waiting for the transaction to be completed.

Tellers and merchants should be aware of the common signs of forged credit cards:
- Holograms crudely stamped or badly faked with tiny bits of aluminum foil.
- Misspelled words on the card.
- Altered signature panel.
- Discolored.
- Glued.
- Painted.
- Covered with white tape.
- Cards which appear to have been flattened and restamped.

At the consumer level, the credit card user should remember the following:
- Know where your card is at all times.
- Never leave your card unattended at work—There are more credit card thefts in the workplace than in any other single situation.
- Don't leave the store or ATM without all of the copies and carbons.
- Don't leave your card in plain sight where others can get the number.
- Don't leave receipts in a public trash can, hotel, or shopping bag.
- Review monthly statements for accuracy and any items that you might not have charged.
- Sign the back of a new card as soon as you get it and destroy old cards that are outdated or no longer used.
- Make a list of all of your cards and their numbers. This key information is helpful when reporting lost or stolen cards. Store this list in a secured area.
- Be wary of offers that come through the mail.

- Never reveal your number over the phone to anyone who has offered you a prize
- Report missing cards immediately.
- Don't reveal personal information such as your address and telephone number.
- Don't allow the salesperson to record your credit card number on your check.
- Keep your card out of the view of others in a store or at public telephone so they cannot read the name and account number.
- Use a tiered, see-through container in your wallet for credit cards, so it will be easier to notice missing cards.
- Always check your card when returned to you after a purchase. Make sure it is your card.

If you become suspicious of a telephone call offer or mail solicitations, call the National Consumer's League fraud hotline at (800) 876-7060.

Prevention

Prevention is the key to reducing credit card losses. Several programs can and are in place to reduce losses. Some of them are:

Education Programs

Tellers and merchants should be trained to be familiar with the security features of the credit card. Although the majority of counterfeit cards contain some of the security features, they usually are not complete and offer indicators that the card is not legitimate. Credit card issuers should take measures to inform their customers about credit card fraud, what the financial institution is doing about fraud, and how the consumer can help.

Liaison with Law Enforcement

Companies should develop strong liaison with law enforcement. When a company receives intelligence of hot frauds, law enforcement should be notified immediately.

Physical Security Features

In response to the counterfeiting problems, VISA and MasterCard are mastering the possibilities of making credit card fraud more difficult. Some of their programs are:

VISA AND MASTERCARD CARD FEATURES
- The first four digits of the Visa Account number (the bank identification number [BIN]) must be pre-printed above the embossed number. If these numbers do not match exactly, the card has been altered or is counterfeit.

- Visa's embossed account numbers begin with a 4 and contain either 13 or 16 digits. A unique embossed **V** appears in **CV**, **BV**, or **PV** on Visa Classic, Business, or Gold cards.
- The embossed characters should be in alignment and of the same size, height, and style.
- If there are "ghost images" of the numbers behind the embossing on either the front or back of the card, it has been re-embossed. If the card has been re-embossed the hologram might be damaged.
- Check the valid dates for evidence of tampering. Do not accept an expired card.
- The hologram is distinct and three-dimensional.
- MasterCard's embossed account numbers begin with a 5 and contain 16 digits.
- If the unique security character "MC" appears next to the expiration date of a MasterCard, make sure the card account number is indent-printed in reverse italics on the signature panel (this feature did not appear on all cards until 1997).
- A repetitive, color design of either the Visa or MasterCard name should appear on all signature panels.
- Microprinting appears around the VISA logo.
- A large "MC" is visible under ultraviolet light for MasterCard and a large dove is visible under ultraviolet light for VISA.
- Numbers printed on the signature panel slant to the left and match the number on the front of the card.
- The gold or silver holograms should show clear, three-dimensional images that appear to move when the card is tilted. Imitations can often be easily damaged by scratching.

AMERICAN EXPRESS FEATURES

- Ultraviolet inks are used such that when a genuine card is examined with a black light, the letters AMEX as well as phosphorescence in the portrait of the Centurion are visible.
- The card member account number is 15 digits beginning with "37"; the prefix "34" is also reserved for use by American Express, with limited use beginning in 1988.
- A duplicate account number is on the reverse of the card to ensure the card number appearing on the front of the card has not been altered.

HOLOGRAMS

Holograms have been used by issuers as security devices since the early 1980s. Not long after implementation of this new feature, however, it was found that a very accurate counterfeiting industry was emerging in Asia. If one assesses the average credit limit of fraudulent cards at a conservative $2,000, it takes few in circulation to add up to considerable losses to the issuer. In 1994, Visa/MasterCard suffered losses estimated at over $700 million caused by one Chinese hologram-producing syndicate alone.

SIGNATURE PANEL

Signature panels usually contain images of the issuer's logo. Blank or damaged signature panels are red flags of forged credit cards. Signatures on the panel and the sales receipt should always be compared for consistency. While it may be most merchants' policy that employees compare these signatures, it is often ignored.

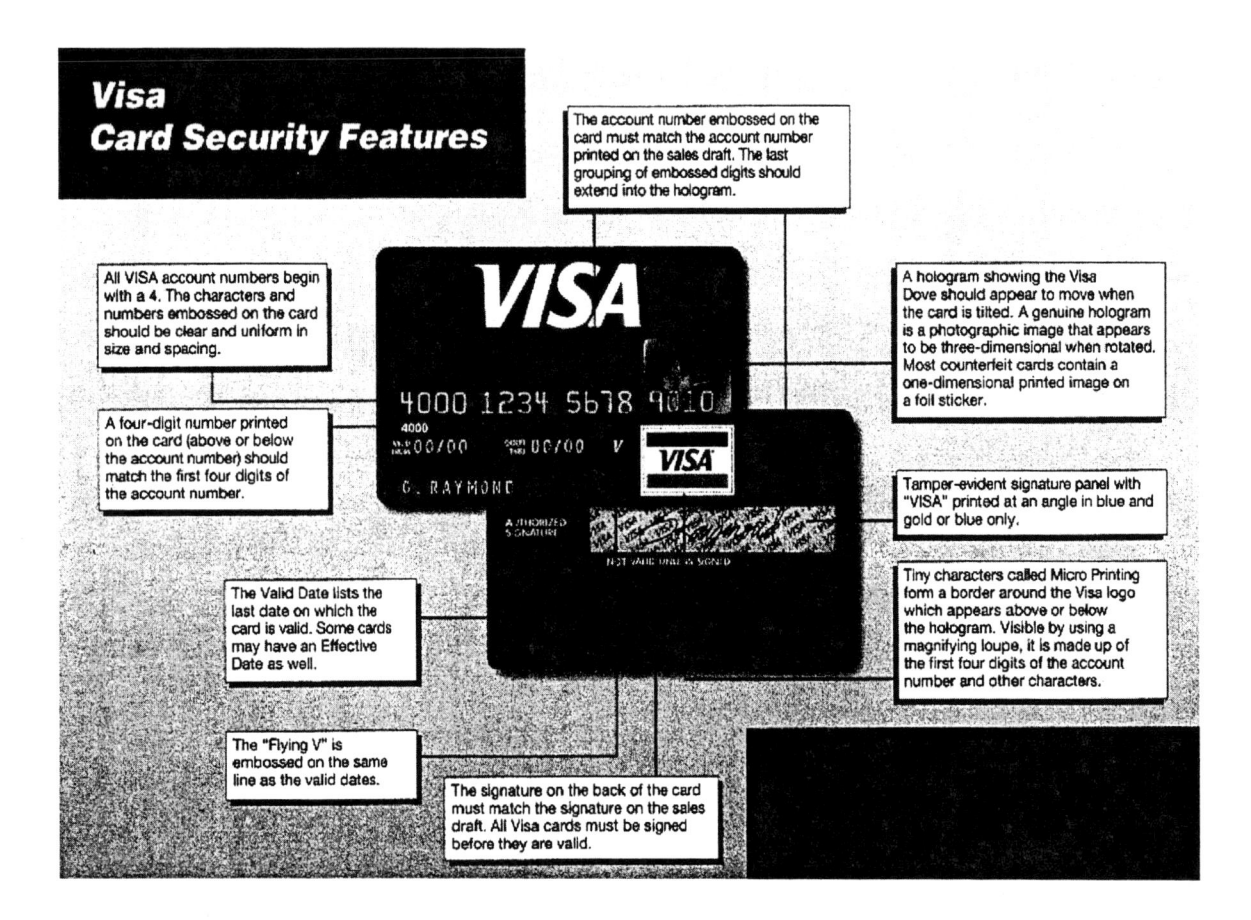

AMERICAN EXPRESS Card Security Features

- American Express cards are not transferable. Only the person whose name is embossed on the card is entitled to use it.
- All American Express account numbers begin with 37. The characters and numbers embossed on the card should be clear and uniform in size and spacing.
- The card may not be accepted for use prior to the valid date or after the expiration date.
- The portrait of The Centurion is printed with a high degree of clarity and detail such as the portraits on US Currency.
- When examined under an ultraviolet light, the letters AMEX and a phosphorescence in the portrait of The Centurion becomes visible.
- The Card Identification Number is an inventory control number that, together with the Cardmember account number, can be associated internally to assure the validity of the Card.
- With this statement on the card, American Express sets forth the right to "pick-up" the card at any time.
- Erasure or tampering with the signature panel will cause the waved print background to appear white or smudged.
- A duplicate account number is etched into the back of the card to ensure the card number appearing on the front of the card has not been altered.

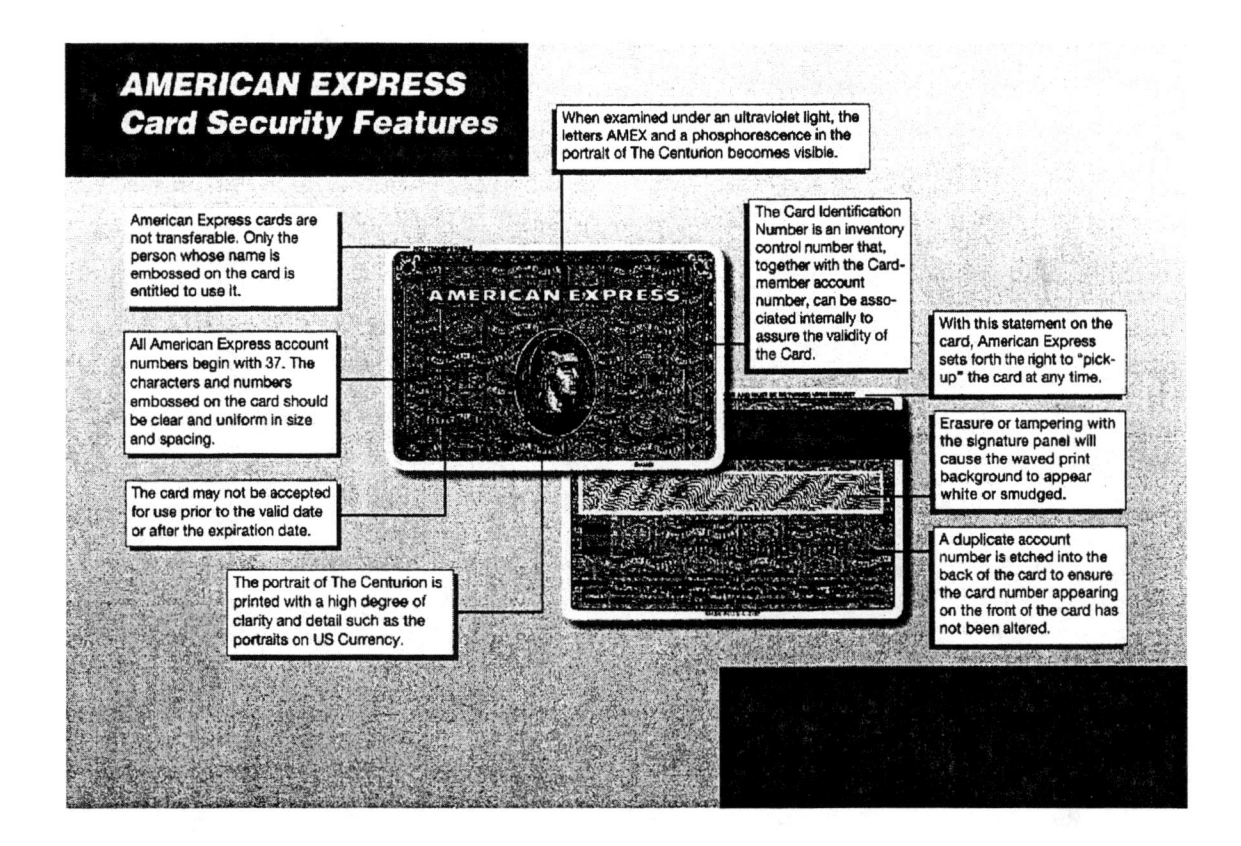

Source: National Check Fraud Center (www.ckfraud.org)

Activation of Cards

In an effort to curb credit card fraud perpetrated using the mail, companies sending new cards in the mail do not activate them until the customer contacts the credit card company. Upon contact, the credit card issuer then asks the caller for personal information such as their mother's maiden name and birth date, or other information that the ordinary thief probably would not have. Once the information has been satisfactorily answered, the card is activated for use.

Computer Edits

Computer edits are built-in to some credit cards such that if the card is usually used five times per month, and it is used 25 times in one day, the system will prohibit authorization of further purchases.

Card Scrutiny at Point of Sale

How often do merchants scrutinize your card? In many stores, they never get the chance. Consumers use the credit/debit card machines at the sales counter and the cards never leave their possession. While this makes things more convenient for the consumer, it often means that the merchant is left holding the bag when a transaction is returned. If one of the key authorization components is missing (signature, expiration date, authorization number, card imprint) the merchant has to swallow the loss.

Internet/Telephone Orders

With these transactions, vendors never have the opportunity to see the customer's credit card. The only fail-safe, self-protective measure open to them is to postpone delivery until the transaction has cleared the customer's account. In our next-day-delivery society, however, this is may be detrimental to business for some vendors. There are a couple other options open to merchants:

- Beware of orders with different "bill to" and "ship to" addresses unless the item is intended as a gift.
- Setting up free e-mail accounts with companies like *Hotmail* or *Yahoo* is very simple and allows the user anonymity. Orders received from free e-mail accounts should be treated with extra scrutiny.

Financial Institution Measures

Banks and other financial institutions have great resources at their disposal to prevent fraudulent transactions. Many of them need merely to enforce their existing policies.

- New account screening—educate personnel to thoroughly check applicants' information, comparing ID information, addresses, and credit reports for accuracy.
- PIN activation—bank customers are often required to provide personal identification numbers in order to activate their cards over the phone. Callers who are not able to provide the PIN number may have manufactured or stolen the card in question.
- Caller ID—most people calling to activate their card will do so from home. If the number on Caller ID does not match any of the telephone numbers listed in the customer's account information bank personnel should ask some identifying questions.
- CVV2/CVC2—implement these systems as soon as possible. They are the best new defense financial institutions have against credit card fraud.

Smart Cards

Smart Cards contain a microprocessor memory chip instead of holograms. These cards are able to identify the user through encrypted information on the chip, and must be inserted into a "card reader" attached to the computer. That means the card cannot be used unless the purchaser is currently holding it. A pin number is also required for the card so the thief needs to physically have the card and the security code in order to use it. This allows cardholders more purchasing options as well as increased security.

Judging from the past, credit opportunities for consumers will increase over time and, consequently, more will fall victim to fraud. In the future, the trend will be one card for all types of financial transactions. Prototypes are currently being developed and tested by the major credit card issuers. Fraud rings will adjust accordingly and new counterfeiting methods will emerge. Law enforcement and investigators must maintain a global outlook when facing this type of fraud, as much of it originates outside the U.S.

INSURANCE FRAUD

The insurance business, by its very nature, is susceptible to fraud. Insurance is a risk distribution system that requires the accumulation of liquid assets in the form of reserve funds which are in turn available to pay loss claims. Insurance companies generate a large steady flow of cash through insurance premiums. Steady cash flow is an important economic resource which is very attractive and easily diverted. Large accumulations of liquid assets make insurance companies attractive for *take over* and *loot* schemes. Insurance companies are under great pressure to maximize the return on investing the reserve funds, thus making them vulnerable to high yielding investment schemes.

Types of Insurance Policies

Property insurance indemnifies against pecuniary loss to the insured's property (and, in some policies, to the property of others) for specific losses, for example, from fire, theft, or auto collision. *Casualty insurance* indemnifies against legal liability to others for injury or damage to people, property, or other defined legal interests because of specified risks or conduct. Casualty insurance is of several types, such as health, disability, life, fidelity, and bonds. *Health insurance* indemnifies against medical care costs under specified circumstances.

Disability insurance indemnifies against income loss under defined circumstances. *Life insurance* indemnifies for the death of the insured. *Fidelity insurance* indemnifies against economic loss to the insured because of employee dishonesty. *Bonds* indemnify against loss to third-party beneficiaries when the insured fails to fulfill a specific undertaking for the third-party's benefit.

Insurance policies can be marketed in combinations. Homeowners insurance and auto insurance policies usually include features of both property and casualty insurance. Some health insurance plans, for example, also might include disability benefit provisions. There are a multitude of insurance fraud schemes. Likewise, there are fraud schemes that are prevalent only in specific insurance areas. The largest amount of fraud is in health care. Like all other industries, insurance is susceptible to both internal and external fraud schemes.

External health care fraud is perpetrated by outsiders against the company. The two main types of external fraud schemes are those committed by providers (such as doctors, institutions, and home health agencies) and claim fraud by the insured. Health care frauds—a specific variation of insurance fraud—will be discussed in the next chapter.

Agent/Broker Fraud

Cash, Loan, and Dividend Checks

A company employee without the knowledge of an insured or contract holder requests cash, a loan, or a dividend check, and either deposits the check into his bank account or into a fictitious account. The employee, in order to minimize his chances of being detected committing a fraudulent act, might change the company policyholder's address of record to either his address or a fictitious address. Once the check is issued, the address is then changed back to the previous address.

Settlement Checks

Company employees can misdirect settlement checks such as Matured Endowment, Paid Up, etc., to the branch office, to their homes, or to a fictitious address. The employee can easily create a check defalcation by changing the address of record prior to the settlement check issue date, thus misdirecting the check in question. Also, periodically an orphan contract holder might be transferred to his agency affording the opportunity to improperly request the issuance of a settlement check.

An *orphan contract holder* is a policyholder or contract holder who has not been assigned to a servicing agent or the whereabouts of this individual is unknown. The servicing agent attempts to locate this family group and possibly can influence them to purchase additional insurance.

A clerical support employee might receive notification that the orphan contract holder does not reside at the given address. This will give the support staffer an opportunity to change the address to either his or her home or a fictitious address and possibly create a fraud.

Premium Fraud

Agent collects the premium, but doesn't remit the check to the insurance company. The insured has no coverage.

Fictitious Payees

An agent or a clerk can change the beneficiary of record to a fictitious person and subsequently submit the necessary papers to authorize the issuance of a check.

Fictitious Death Claims

An agent or employee obtains a fictitious death certificate and requests that a death claim check be issued. The agent receives the check and cashes it.

The sales representative can also write a fictitious application and, after the contestable period (two years), submit a phony death claim form and obtain the proceeds. The agent, by investing a couple of thousand dollars, could receive $50,000 or more in misappropriated claims.

A company is particularly vulnerable to this scheme if the perpetrator has knowledge of the underwriting procedures such as the limits under which insurance can be written without a medical exam and what should be submitted on a death claim.

Underwriting Irregularities

Equity Funding

Equity funding is the process of using existing premium/policy values to finance new businesses. So long as the insured is aware of what is being done by the agent and fully understands the long range method of payment on the new contract, there is no apparent underwriting irregularity.

Equity funding techniques, also known as *piggybacking*, usually do not produce quality business. Furthermore, the company increases the amount of life insurance on the books but receives little or no new funds while incurring increased sales and administrative expenses associated with the issue of that new business.

Each jurisdiction has its own requirements on piggybacking as it relates to replacement insurance. Companies must comply with these regulations to prevent being fined or the possibility that the company's insurance license can be suspended or taken away for noncompliance.

Equity funding irregularities might involve improper financial benefits to field personnel as well as annual incentive compensation bonuses paid to management if applicable. The fraud examiner should determine what financial benefit will occur from an improper equity transaction.

Misrepresentation

Misrepresentation might occur if a sales representative makes a false statement with the intent to deceive the prospective insureds in order to knowingly obtain an unlawful gain.

False Information

A company employee might submit the following false information to obtain unlawful financial gain:

- Improper medical information to obtain a better insurable rate for the prospective policyholder, i.e., standard to preferred rate.
- Improper date of birth to obtain a cheaper premium on the new policy.
- Improper home address to obtain a cheaper premium for home or automobile insurance.
- Improper driving history prior to purchasing automobile insurance to reduce the annual premium or obtain insurance where normally the individual would have to apply through the risk pool.

Fictitious Policies

A salesman, in order to keep his position, submits fictitious policies to improve his writing record. Also prior to an individual leaving the company he writes fictitious policies called *tombstone cases* to improve his commission pool so that his compensation will be greater. *Tombstone* means an agent literally takes names from tombstones in a cemetery and writes new policies.

Surety and Performance Bond Schemes

Surety and performance bonds guarantee that certain events will or will not occur. An agent issues worthless bonds to the insured for high-risk coverage in hopes that a claim is never made. If a claim is made, the agent might pay it off from agency funds, delay the payment, or skip town.

Sliding

Sliding is the term used for including additional coverages in the insurance policy without the knowledge of the insured. The extra charges are hidden in the total premium and since the insured is unaware of the coverage, few claims are ever filed. For example, motor club memberships, accidental death, and travel accident coverages can usually be slipped into the policy without the knowledge of the insured.

Twisting

Twisting is the replacement, usually by high pressure sales techniques, of existing policies for new ones. The primary reason, of course, is for the agent to profit since first year sales commissions are much higher than commissions for existing policies.

Churning

Churning occurs when agents falsely tell customers that they can buy additional insurance for nothing by using built-up value in their current policies. In reality, the cost of the new policies frequently exceeds the value of the old ones.

Vehicle Insurance Schemes

Ditching

Ditching, also known as owner give-ups, is getting rid of a vehicle to cash in on an insurance policy or to settle an outstanding loan. The vehicle is normally expensive and purchased with a small down payment. The vehicle is reported stolen, although in some cases, the owner just abandons the vehicle hoping that it is stolen, stripped for parts, or taken to a pound and destroyed. The scheme sometimes involves homeowner's insurance for the property that was "stolen" in the vehicle.

Past Posting

Past posting is a scheme in which a person becomes involved in an automobile accident, but doesn't have insurance. The person gets insurance, waits a little bit of time, and then reports the vehicle as being in an accident, thus collecting for the damages.

Vehicle Repair

This scheme involves the billing of new parts on a vehicle when used parts were actually replaced in the vehicle. Sometimes this involves collusion between the adjuster and the body repair shop.

Vehicle Smuggling

This is a scheme which involves the purchase of a new vehicle with maximum financing. A counterfeit certificate of the vehicle's title is made showing that it is free and clear. The vehicle is insured to the maximum, with minimum deductible theft coverage. It is then shipped to a foreign port and reported stolen. The car is sold at its new location and insurance is also collected for the "theft."

Phantom Vehicles

The certificate of title is a document that shows the legal ownership of a vehicle. Even though it is not absolute proof that a vehicle exists, it is the basis for the issuance of insurance policies. Collecting on a phantom vehicle has been shown to be easy to do.

Staged Accidents

Staged accidents are schemes in which an accident is predetermined to occur on a vehicle. The schemes are organized by rings and the culprits move from one area to another. They often use the same vehicle over and over which sometimes causes their scheme to be uncovered.

Two Vehicle Accident

Perpetrators cause an accident and then lead the innocent driver to believe it's his fault.

Three or More Vehicle Accident

Perpetrators set up an accident in which all the drivers are involved.

Other Staged Accidents

Two drivers purposely collide where they will not be observed. Additional damage may be added to the vehicles after impact. The cars are then driven to a road or highway and arranged so that the accident appears to have occurred there. The police are then notified.

SWOOP AND SQUAT

A victim of this scheme will find himself passed by two cars while driving. The car in the lead will cut in front of the second, forcing it to stop abruptly. The victim rear-ends the second car while the other driver speeds away. Victims usually accept responsibility for the accident, thinking it their fault for not paying attention. The rear-ended vehicle usually contains the maximum amount of passengers possible, all with injuries.

Inflated Damages

The business environment and competition for work in the automobile repair industry have motivated a scheme where some establishments inflate the estimated cost to cover the deductible. The insured is advised by the repair shop that the shop will accept whatever the company authorizes.

Vehicle Identification Number (VIN)-Switch

VIN-switch fraud schemes are the work of professionals in which a wrecked vehicle is sold and reported as being repaired. The vehicle is not repaired, but the VIN plate is switched with a stolen vehicle of the same make and model.

Rental Car Fraud

A person doesn't need to own a vehicle to incur automobile fraud. There are several schemes that can be perpetrated using rental cars. The most prevalent involve property damage, bodily injury, and export fraud.

Property Schemes

Property schemes usually involve the filing of insurance claims for property that never existed or for inflated loss amounts.

Inflated Inventory

Property that is lost through fire is claimed on an insurance form. However, property that doesn't exist also finds its way onto an inventory of the property claimed. Property claimed might have been previously sold or never owned by the claimant.

Phony or Inflated Thefts

A home or car that has been burglarized is the basis for filing a claim for recoveries of monies lost. However, as with items "destroyed" by fire above, the items never existed or were previously sold.

Paper Boats

A claim is filed for a boat that sank, but actually never existed. It is not difficult to register a boat which is based on a bill of sale. After a period of time, a loss is claimed for the sinking of the boat. It is difficult to prove that the boat didn't exist or wasn't sunk intentionally.

Life Insurance Schemes

Fraudulent Death Claims

To obtain reimbursement for life insurance, a death certificate is required. However, phony death certificates are not that difficult to obtain. The person might be very much alive and missing or the person might be dead, and the death is past posted. With small settlements, death claims aren't closely scrutinized and paid relatively easily.

Murder for Profit

This scheme involves the killing (or arranging for the killing) of a person in order to collect the insurance. The death might be made to look like it was an accident or a random killing.

Liability Schemes

In a liability scheme the claimant has claimed an injury that did not occur. The slip and fall scam is the most common, where a person claims to fall as the result of negligence on behalf of the insured.

"Red Flags" of Insurance Fraud

Red flags of insurance fraud may include any of the following:

- The claim is made a short time after inception of the policy, or after an increase or change in the coverage under which the claim is made. This could include the purchase of a scheduled property or jewelry floater policy, or more than one during the time before the loss.
- The insured has a history of many insurance claims and losses.
- The insured earlier asked his insurance agent hypothetical questions about coverage in the event of a loss similar to the actual claim.

- The insured is very pushy and insistent about a fast settlement, and exhibits more than the usual amount of knowledge about insurance coverage and claims procedures, particularly if the claim is not well documented.
- In a burglary loss, the claim includes large, bulky property which is unusual for a burglary.
- In a theft or fire loss claim, the claim includes a lot of recently purchased, expensive property, or the insured insists that everything was the best or the most expensive model, especially if the insured cannot provide receipts, owner's manuals, or other documentary proof of purchase.
- In a fire loss claim, property which would be personal or sentimental to the insured and which you would expect to see among the lost property—photographs, family heirlooms, or pets—is conspicuous by its absence.
- A large amount of the property was purchased at garage and yard sales and flea markets, or otherwise for cash, and there are no receipts (the insured usually will be unable to recall exactly where these sales took place or by whom).
- The insured cannot remember, or does not know, where he or she acquired the claimed property, especially unusual items, and/or he cannot provide adequate descriptions.
- On the other hand, the insured already has receipts and other documentation, witnesses, and duplicate photographs for everything; the claim is too perfect.
- Documentation provided by the insured is irregular or questionable, such as:
  - Numbered receipts are from the same store and dated differently or sequentially.
  - Documents show signs of alteration such as dates, descriptions, or amounts.
  - Photocopies of documents are provided and the insured cannot produce the originals.
  - Similar handwriting or signatures—or the insured's apparent handwriting—on different receipts, invoices, gift verifications, appraisals, etc.
  - The amount of tax is wrong, either for the price of the property or for the date appearing on the receipt.
  - Receipts, invoices, or shipping documents do not have "paid," "received," or other shipping stamps.
  - In a theft or loss away from home, the insured waits an unusually long time before reporting the theft to the police.
  - The insured is able to give the police a complete list of lost property on the day of the burglary or shortly after.
  - The amount of the claim differs from the value given by the insured to the police.

- In a business inventory or income loss claim, the insured does not keep complete books, or the books do not follow accepted accounting principles.
- The physical evidence is inconsistent with the loss claimed by the insured.
- In a burglary loss, there is no physical evidence of breaking and entering, or a burglary could not have occurred unnoticed under the circumstances.
- In a fire loss:
  * The apparent cause and origin of the fire is inconsistent with an accidental cause and origin, or there is evidence of the use of an accelerant.
  * The remains of the property do not match the claimed property.
- The premises do not show signs of having contained the claimed property, or the amount of property will not fit into the space where the insured says it was.
- Physical damage to the insured's car is inconsistent with its having been in a collision with an uninsured car.
- The insured has discarded the claimed damaged property before the adjuster can examine it.
- The cost of the claimed property, over the period of time it allegedly was acquired, seems to exceed the insured's financial ability to purchase it.
- The insured refuses or is unable to answer routine questions.
- The insured provides supporting evidence and documentation which cannot be corroborated.

- Information on a life application is very vague or ambiguous as to the details of health history: dates, places of treatment, names of physicians or hospitals, or specific diagnosis.
- Applicant fails to sign and date the application.
- Pertinent questions on the application are not answered, such as income, other insurance carried, hazardous duties, or aviation or flying activity, etc.
- The insured has "excess insurance," either shown at the time of application or developed through an underwriting report of database information.
- Earned income does not warrant amount of insurance being applied for.
- The applicant's date of birth as shown on the application is much earlier than shown with other carriers or in previous applications or policies.
- The agent is putting on a great deal of pressure to have the policy issued because of the large amount applied for, but is going over the underwriter's head in order to do so (working out of the system).
- The physician's report is very vague on details of past medical history and does not coincide with the information shown on the application.
- A death claim is presented in which the death has taken place outside of the country.

- The signature on the application for insurance does not appear to be the same signature as shown on an authorization at the time of claim.
- A claimant or claimant's attorney attempts to limit the type of information to be related by a signed authorization which is a standard authorization used by the company.
- An attorney is immediately brought into a contestable death claim, attempting to interfere with the investigation and to withhold information required by the company.
- The contestable death claim which is reported as an accidental death could possibly be a suicide (fatal accident involving only one vehicle, a hunting accident, an accidental shooting while cleaning a weapon or repairing same, etc.).
- An autopsy report discloses a different height and weight than what is shown on the recent application (auto or house fire death). Dental records do not coincide with those dental findings as shown by an autopsy report.
- Records are missing on a patient who was confined to a hospital, or records are missing on a patient from a physicians's office.
- The death claim package sent to the insurance company is too well packaged and complete in every detail with supportive documents. Documentation which was not initially asked for or required by the insurance company was voluntarily sent, such as newspaper reports, burial certificates, shipment of the body from one country to the home country.
- The routine audit of a designated insured group shows a significant increase of added employees whose names do not show up on the payroll.
- Gunshot wounds or stabbings were inflicted by the insured as the aggressor or were self-inflicted.
- Police accident reports were submitted by the claimant.
- Pressure for speed of handling—claimant wants to stop by the office to pick up his check "as we're leaving for vacation in the morning."
- Series of prescription numbers from the same drug store don't coincide chronologically with the dates of the prescriptions.
- Automobile fire in a very remote rural area with no witness, but the driver claims an electrical shortage in the engine compartment caused the entire car to be gutted by flames.
- Preliminary information for a business fire loss or home fire loss indicates considerable financial difficulties and financial pressures being brought upon the owner and the fire is suspicious in nature and/or origin.

- An employee within the claims operations of an insurance company is known to be having a drinking problem, drug problem, financial pressures, or is having serious marital difficulties or having a known affair with another and irregularities start to appear.
- On burglary losses from a business or especially a home, the investigator observes that the remaining contents at the scene are of much inferior quality than that which is being reported stolen. There is no indication of indentation in the piling of the carpet where heavy items of furniture or equipment were to have been placed. There are no hooks or nails on the walls where valuable pictures might have been hung. Entrances or exits are too small to take a large item through without laboriously disassembling it.
- Any information on a claim that has been filed if it is determined that there is deliberate cover-up or false statements contained therein.
- A disability income protection claim is filed and it is determined that the claimant had recently purchased numerous expensive items on credit and had them all covered by credit A&H insurance coverage.
- Public transportation accidents in which there are more passenger claims filed than there were passengers at the time of the accident.
- A witness to an accident or incident deliberately tries to hide from investigators rather than come forth and tell the truth.
- An official document of findings is in complete conflict with the facts in the case and there is no explanation for this conflict of facts. Photographs or other documents do not substantiate the reported findings.

Computer-Generated Detection Reports

Computers can be used to generate detection reports that provide the fraud examiner with good leads to possible fraud.

Address Similarity Report

Address similarity reports electronically compare multiple checks going to the same address. They are extremely useful because they might show a check defalcation or funds going to another insurance company, broker, or fictitious payee.

Downloading of Files

Comparison of issue files to disbursement files can determine if funds are being used to place new policies by using the equity of old policies. For example, Computer Assisted Auditing Tools and Techniques (CAATT) is used to download electronic files and compare another file, i.e., comparing administrative file on group business to Social Security file to determine if the company is paying out monthly payments on people who have passed away.

Electronic Confirmations

Mailed disbursements in force or lapsed premiums, change of address, etc., to verify that company records agree with policyholder records.

Exception or Manual Override Reports

Computerized reports that list all exceptions to normal electronic processing. All human intervention can appear on a periodic management information report and be test-checked by management. It is imperative that management review on an ongoing basis all exception reports for possible frauds.

Workers Compensation Fraud

Workers compensation laws require employers or their insurance plan to reimburse an employee (or on his behalf) for injuries that occurred on the job regardless of who is at fault and without delay of legal proceedings to determine fault. The injury may be physical, such as a broken limb, or mental, such as stress.

Common Schemes

Schemes are generally broken into four categories: premium fraud, agent fraud, claimant fraud, and organized fraud schemes.

Premium Fraud

Misrepresenting information to the insurer by employers to lower the cost of workers compensation premiums.

EMPLOYEE CLASSIFICATION

Workers compensation rates vary depending on the job classification of an employee. Employees that have a higher risk for injury on the job will have a higher premium rate. Clerical employees have a lower probability for an injury than, for example, truck drivers or construction workers, and accordingly their premiums should be lower. Therefore to lower their premium rate, an employer might intentionally misclassify employees.

UNDERSTATEMENT OF PAYROLL

The premium for a specific job classification is based upon the total payroll for that classification. The employer may understate the amount of the payroll for higher risk classifications.

EXAMPLE

Two men in Massachusetts pleaded guilty to charges of conspiracy and mail fraud in connection with a fraudulent scheme to reduce workers compensation claims for a construction company. The men falsely reported that workers in high-risk trades were engaged in less dangerous occupations in order to lower premiums. They also concealed millions of dollars on the company payroll from the insurance company, thereby avoiding workers compensation payments on those dollars.

EXAMPLE

A Boise couple found themselves responsible for a $71,049 judgment after being accused of misreporting payroll in their drywall business. Two former employees tipped off investigators that they were being paid with checks bearing different company names.

Half of their payroll money was paid by an insured drywall company, and the other half came from one that was not insured. Workers compensation claims came from the company that was paying premiums.

GEOGRAPHIC LOCATION OF THE INSUREDS OPERATION

Premium rates differ significantly based upon geographic location from state to state. An employer might have a storefront location or a P.O. box in a state that has lower rates. A multistate employer may list all of its employees as operating in the state which has the lowest rates.

HISTORY OF PAST LOSSES

The modification or "mod" factor is a multiplier that is used to determine premium rates. The multiplier is derived by comparing the employer's claims history with other employers' claims histories in the same industry. The higher the claims loss, the higher the mod, and thus the higher the premium. A new business will start with a neutral "mod" for that type of business. Employers that have a high mod factor may become a "new" business that does not have a "mod" established and thus have lower premiums than it should.

CORPORATE GERRYMANDERING

The risk pool assigned to an employer will accept any business no matter what the claim experience is. However it does not have to accept any employer that owes premiums. Some employers will create a new corporate entity in order to obtain coverage or to avoid higher premiums due to past heavy losses.

> EXAMPLE
>
> *Fireman's Fund Insurance was awarded a $15 million judgment against a Hollywood entertainment company in a suit involving a workers compensation fraud scheme. The entertainment company set up a shell corporation to pose as a start-up production company needing insurance. The ruse allowed the company to get workers compensation at much lower rates than if Fireman's Fund had known who they were actually insuring. The entertainment company then manipulated the coverage to other films in which it had an interest, again at significantly lower rates.*

FORGED DOCUMENTS

Some employers will forge or alter prior certificates showing coverages in order to collect payment for work done or as proof of coverages to authorities.

Agent Fraud

POCKETING PREMIUMS

Agents issue certificates of coverage indicating the customer is insured, but never forward the premium to the insurance company.

CONSPIRING TO REDUCE PREMIUMS

Agents may alter the application for coverage completed by the employer in order to be able to offer a lower premium to his client.

The agent may also improperly advise the employer as to how to complete the application.

The agent may also advise the employer to transfer a group of employees into a lower risk classification to avoid the experience modifier.

While the employer may not be aware that the schemes are a violation of law, since the employer signs the application, he can be charged for his part in the scheme however unknowing.

Claimant Fraud

Misrepresenting the circumstances of any injury or fabricating that an injury occurred.

INJURY FRAUD

In this type of fraud, false information about the injured worker is submitted to the workers compensation carrier. The report describes the injury and states the employee is either totally or partially disabled and either unable to work or only able to work part-time. In many of these schemes the fraud is helped along by a doctor who, for a fee, will provide a false diagnosis and false medical records for phony treatments.

The employee may stage an accident and fabricate an injury, or actually have an accident, and then exaggerate the injury.

> EXAMPLE
>
> *A former personnel supervisor for the city of Los Angeles was charged with embezzling funds from the city's workers compensation system. It was charged that she provided information to a doctor which enabled him to submit almost $500,000 in fake claims for medical services which were supposedly provided to city employees. The supervisor was also alleged to have, working on her own, altered the computerized personnel records and then authorized payment of $300,000 in bogus disability claims to her friends and relatives.*

> EXAMPLE
>
> *A firefighter in Washington was arrested for insurance fraud related to workers compensation payments he had received. The man claimed he fell off a ladder and injured his knee while working as a meatcutter in a grocery store. He collected temporary disability benefits and received medical treatment for six months, complaining of pain and telling doctors that he could barely walk. At the same time, the man was training with his city fire department as a reserve firefighter. The training consisted of strenuous exercise such as heavy lifting and an hour of physical training each day.*

SECONDARY EMPLOYMENT

Employees who are collecting workers compensation benefits may also secure a job with another employer—either part-time or full-time. The employee may fake his or her identity or assume someone else's identity to receive compensation.

Organized Fraud

Organized fraud schemes are composed of the united efforts of a lawyer, a capper, a doctor, and the claimant. This scheme is used not only in workers compensation cases, but also in other medical frauds such as in automobile injuries.

THE LAWYER

The lawyer is usually the organizer of the scheme and the one who will profit the most. The majority of workers compensation cases are accepted on a contingency fee basis. If no settlement is awarded, then the lawyer will not be paid. This is a high volume business, and the lawyers do not want the cases to be litigated. They are relying on the insurance company's desire to settle as quickly as possible.

The lawyer will entice the claimant into securing his services by promising a large settlement from the insurance company. The claimant may or may not have to undergo the medical tests, since the only requirement of the claimant is that he be insured. The lawyer will then refer the injured party to a doctor for "treatment."

THE CAPPER

A capper, also known as a runner, is used to recruit patients for the scheme. He may be employed by either the attorney or doctor and is paid, either on a percentage of the total take or on a per person basis, for bringing in patients. A capper may make as little as $150 per patient up to $1,500 per patient depending on the area of the country. The capper may approach the patient at unemployment compensation lines, the work site, the scene of the accident, or at any other type of organized gathering. With promises of enrichment, the patient is brought into the scheme.

THE DOCTOR

The doctor may be one of the organizers or a player in the scheme, but must be a part of it in order for it to work properly. The doctor is used to lend authenticity to the scheme, and he is well compensated for his efforts. The doctor bills for services that he may or may not render as well as for unnecessary services. In addition, if the patient has regular health insurance, the doctor may double bill for the services. If the injury incurred as the result of an automobile accident while the patient was on the job, the doctor may bill all three insurance companies: the workers compensation carrier, the employee's health insurance, and the automobile carrier.

Because of coordination of benefit clauses in most insurance contracts, the insurance companies will coordinate the benefits to the extent that the maximum amount paid will be 100% of the injuries. However, the doctors will not let the patient's health insurance company know that the injury is work-related or accident-related and thus the claim may be overpaid, since both claims are paid at their full liability.

Most of the treatment rendered will be office visits, x-rays, vascular studies, physical therapy, and spinal manipulations. In some cases hospital employees will be part of the scheme and allow the use of the facility fraudulently.

Red Flags
- Documents that have obviously been altered; white-out or erasure is evident.
- Documents that are improperly filled out with entries in the wrong place or information that doesn't make sense.
- Claims filed where the carrier indicated no record of coverage.
- Poor quality photocopies of documents which should be original documents.
- Small payrolls for large contractors or employee leasing operations.
- Payroll figures reported to insurers which disagree with payroll reported for other purposes.
- Claims for employee injuries inconsistent with that employee's classification.
- Industrial or construction enterprises with a work force reported to be in low-rate categories.
- "New" corporations on ongoing jobs.
- Most of the employees from an employer with a high experience suddenly become employees in a new business.
- Agency employs large numbers of support staff and only has one licensed agent.
- The agent only accepts cash or money orders for premiums.
- No policy is received after an extended time.
- No bill is received for premiums.
- Employer review of the application indicates that it is inaccurate.
- The reclassification of the individual employees into a lower classification.
- The employer begins to declare a smaller payroll.
- Claimants that have or are:
    - Disgruntled, soon-to-retire, or facing disciplinary action or layoffs.
    - Involved in seasonal work that is about to end.
    - Taken unexplained or excessive time off prior to claimed injury.

- Taken more time off than the claimed injury seems to warrant.
- No witnesses to the accident.
- Accidents which occurred in an area where the employee normally would not be working (especially if it's a high-risk area).
- Delayed the reporting of an accident.
- New on the job or have a history of short-term employment.
- A history of injuries.
- Inappropriate or lack of medical treatment for injuries.
- Experiencing financial difficulties.
- Changed physicians when a work release has been issued.
- Frequently changed medical providers.
- Demands for quick or early settlement.
- Never at home after a "serious" injury or can only be reached by return telephone calls.
- Unusually familiar with workers compensation procedures.
- Consistently uncooperative.
- Received mail at a post office box or at an address different from employment or Department of Motor Vehicles.
- Soft tissue injuries that are hard to prove.
- Incapacitated, but seen in activities that require full mobility.
- Independent medical exams which reveal conflicting medical information.
- A history of self or family employment; have a trade or work in a cash business.
- Injuries that occur in an area where the employee would normally not be working.
- Injuries that would not normally be the type the employee should have.
- Injuries that occur on a late Friday afternoon or are reported on a Monday morning (if injuries are reported Monday morning, the injury could have resulted over the weekend).
- Actively involved in contact sports or physically demanding hobbies.
- Dates of disability or absences from work that does not coincide with the physician's date of disability or dates of treatment.
- Unprofessional diagnostic terminology.
- Misspelled medical terminology throughout the medical report or hospital record.
- A pattern of accident claims by an individual or family members.
- Claimant that repeatedly doesn't show up for his requested independent physical examinations or is not home when the regularly scheduled nurse stops by for therapy.
- The claimant's attorney is known for handling suspicious claims.

- Attorney reports his representation began on the day of the reported incident.
- Same doctor and attorney are known to handle these types of cases.
- Claimant complains to the insurance company's CEO in order to press for payment.
- The attorney threatens further legal action unless a quick settlement can be made.
- The attorney inquires about a settlement early into the life of the claim.
- Wholesale claim handling by law firms and multiple class action suits.
- Dates of the accident are vague or contradictory.
- Treatment for the injury follows previous first-time visits to a provider.
- Same provider always bills for extra time or extra consideration on a claim.
- Provider is working through an attorney.
- Provider is reluctant to communicate with the insurance company.
- Provider shares the same patients with the same colleagues.
- Provider refers patients to specific other providers.
- Provider prescribes unnecessary supplies and/or care by a specific provider.
- Medical records are "canned."
- Medical records are out of sequence and missing dates of service.
- Different handwriting with same dates of service.
- Lost, burned, or stolen records when requested.
- Progress notes consistently reflect that the patient has a high degree of pain, yet his condition is improving or progressing as planned.
- Inconsistent diagnosis for the treatment rendered.
- Provider bills on a holiday or Sundays.
- Conflicting medical reports.
- Claims are photocopied.
- Claims for other patients are identical.
- Billing or harassing the insurance company for payment.
- Claimants address is different on the claim form than it is on the enrollment file.

Investigation Tips

Premium Fraud

- Review the application for coverage for completeness and accuracy.
- If the business is claiming to be new, then it should be verified that it is indeed new and no mod factors have been established.
- Review the underwriting of the application for suspicious activity. If the company is a large company and has a small payroll, verify the number of employees, as well as their classification.

- Review claims to determine if they are consistent with the type of employment reported and the number of employees claimed.
- Conduct an on-site audit of their payroll and related records for the policy period as well as to determine where their principal place of employment is located.
- Observe if there are too many clerical employees or other low risk occupations that make up the calculation leading you to believe that the records are misstated.
- Analyze the financial statements, when available, to determine what payroll expenses actually are compared to what is reported.
- Review accident and injury reports for suspicious activities.
- Conduct surveillance as needed to observe and document various activities.
- Document findings and report the results of the activity as required.

Claimant Fraud
- In spite of the possible indicators of fraud, medical treatment must be secured immediately, but an investigation should be opened immediately if there is a suspicion of fraud.
- The manager who is responsible for the area where the injury occurred should initiate an investigation on each reportable accident.
- As soon as possible the accident should be discussed with the employee.
- Obtain a signed statement from the employee as soon as the employee is able to do so.
- In obtaining a signed statement, the following questions should be answered as applicable:
    - What was the employee doing just prior to the accident, and after the accident?
    - Was he carrying out his regular duties and in the manner they should normally be conducted?
    - Had the employee been properly instructed as to how to safely perform the duties? When, and by whom?
    - Did they work in accordance with these instructions?
    - Did another employee cause the injury?
    - Was the equipment or machinery properly guarded and in good condition?
    - Was the equipment suited for the purpose it was being used?
    - Was the workplace properly lighted?
    - What were the housekeeping conditions in the area?
    - Does the work being done by the injured employee differ in any way from that being performed by other employees?
    - Is there a safer way that his operation can be performed?

- Was the injured employee in good health when he reported to work on the date of the accident?

Have an independent medical examination performed to document the illness. The person performing the exam should photograph the patient, obtain a copy of the patient's photo identification such as a driver's license, and obtain the patient's signature.

The following questions should be asked:
- Are you disabled from working?
- Are you now working part-time, full-time, or not at all?
- What are your daily activities?
- What is your activity level with regards to your ability to walk, jog, run, drive, swim, or participate in sports activities or hobbies?

HEALTH CARE FRAUD

In 1997, $969 billion was spent for health care; an excess of $1.4 trillion was spent on healthcare in 2001; and in 2002, $1.6 trillion was spent on health care. The Centers for Medicare and Medicaid Services estimates health care costs will reach $2 trillion by 2006, and by the year 2012, $3.1 trillion. These runaway costs are impacting the economy, making front page news. According to the U.S. General Accounting Office, the most common estimate of health insurance fraud is 10% of our total health care spending. However, because no one knows exactly what the figure is, the figure has also been estimated to be from 3–10% per year. This translates to a minimum loss of $60 billion and perhaps as much as $200 billion by 2006. Health care providers perpetrate the majority of this fraud.

Laws Relating to Health Care Fraud

Numerous criminal and civil federal and state laws are available in the prosecution of health care fraud. In addition, regulatory agencies are also available for licensure action.

HIPAA

As part of the Health Insurance Portability and Accountability Act (HIPAA) of 1996, Congress made a number of changes to the federal criminal code.

The Act established several new criminal statutes related specifically to health care fraud. The new statutes are:
- Health Care Fraud
- Theft or Embezzlement in connection with health care
- False Statements Relating to Health Care Matters
- Obstruction of Criminal Investigations of Health Care Offenses

The term *health care benefit program* as used in these statutes is defined to mean "any public or private plan or contract, affecting commerce, under which any medical benefit, item, or service is provided to any individual, and includes any individual or entity who is providing a medical benefit, item, or service for which payment may be made under the plan or contract."

The Act also provides that a judge order a person convicted of a federal health care offense to forfeit any property that can be traced from the proceeds received from the offense. The text of these statutes is set out in the Law section.

Other Federal Statutes

The following federal laws are also commonly used in the prosecution of health care fraud cases. More detail on each of these statutes can be found in the Law section of the *Manual*.

- Mail Fraud, Title 18, U.S.C. § 1341
- Conspiracy, Title 18, U.S.C. § 371, Title 18 U.S.C. § 286
- Obstruction of Federal Audit, Title 18, U.S.C. § 1516
- Racketeer Influenced and Corrupt Organizations (RICO) Statute, Title 18, U.S.C., § 1961–1968
- Electronic Funds Transfer Act, Title 15, U.S.C. § 1693n

False Claims and Statements

Although there is a statute specifically regarding false claims in connection with health care benefits programs, there may be instances when the original false claims statutes may also be needed. The full text of these statutes is contained in the Law section.

- Title 18, U.S.C., § 287
- Title 18, U.S.C., § 1001
- Title 18, U.S.C., § 1031

Some examples of false claims and statements include:
- Falsified contractor qualifications
- False certifications or assurances
- False records or invoices
- Invoices from nonexistent companies
- Claims made in duplicate or altered invoices
- Billing for fictitious employees
- Billing for goods and services not provided
- Inflated costs or substitution of cheaper goods

Computer Fraud

Any scheme that uses a computer as the instrument or vehicle by which funds could be illegally transferred or the use of the computer to obtain confidential information may be prosecuted as computer fraud. The federal computer fraud statute is contained in Title 18, U.S.C., § 1030.

EXAMPLE

An insurance company employee generates a false claim in the company computer making a fraudulent payment to a friend who then shares the bounty with the employee.

Money Laundering

Using money laundering statutes can be effective in the deterrence and punishment of individuals who have committed health care fraud.

Under the provisions of the Health Insurance Portability and Accountability Act of 1996, Congress amended the money laundering statute to include "any act or activity constituting an offense involving a Federal health care offense" to the definition of "specified unlawful activity." Accordingly, the money laundering statute can now be easily applied in those health care fraud cases to which it applies.

Using money laundering statutes allows the government to claim by forfeiture property purchased with the illegal proceeds. The text of these statutes can be found in the Law section:

- Laundering of Money (Title 18, U.S.C., § 1956)
- Engaging in Monetary Transactions in Property Derived from Specified Unlawful Activity (Title 18, U.S.C., § 1957)

Civil Remedies

The False Claims Act and RICO both provide for civil remedies in addition to criminal penalties. One of the most effective civil remedies is the Civil Monetary Penalty Law (42, U.S.C. § 1320a-7a) which was passed to impose administrative sanctions against providers who defraud any federally funded program by filing false claims or other improper billing practices. Any person (including an organization, agency, or other entity, but excluding a beneficiary) that presents or causes to be presented a claim for a medical or other item or service that the person knows or should know is false or fraudulent is subject to a civil monetary penalty.

The recent health care amendments revised the law to include higher penalties. Now, the penalty is not more than $10,000 (formerly $2,000) per line item or service and an assessment of not more than three times (formerly twice) the amount claimed. In addition, the person may be excluded from participation in government programs.

State Statutes

Although fraud is illegal in every state, not all states have specific legislation against insurance fraud. Laws such as "grand theft," "scheme to defraud," or "fraud by deception" must be used to charge offenders. Nineteen states have passed legislation which specifically prohibits insurance fraud although the effectiveness varies according to the provisions in each statute. For example, in some states, health insurance fraud is illegal, but there is no immunity to the insurance company for reporting fraud.

The National Association of Insurance Commissioners (NAIC) adopted the Insurance Fraud Prevention Model Act. The key provisions include:
- Mandatory reporting of fraud
- Immunity from prosecution for reporting fraud
- Making insurance fraud a felony under state law
- Requiring a fraud warning on claim forms
- Requiring anti-fraud initiatives including mandatory special investigation units
- Restitution to the victim

Regulatory Boards

Since most medical practitioners are required to be licensed by their state in order to practice, the regulatory boards have jurisdiction over the licensees and can take action when appropriate. The regulatory boards will take action when the patient's health is in jeopardy, fraud has been committed, continuing education requirements are not met, or other similar circumstances. In most instances, when a licensee is convicted of fraud, it is **not** automatic that his or her license is suspended or revoked. A separate action and investigation must be completed in order for that to happen. However, in many cases, when there is not enough evidence to sustain a criminal conviction, the licensing boards may be able to take action and offer relief.

"Running" and "Capping" Legislation

Many states are instituting legislation to prevent the problem of attorneys using runners or cappers to solicit business. Although state disciplinary rules generally prohibit this practice, very few attorneys have received any substantial sanctions. Some states, such as California, have taken the initiative to criminalize running and capping.

Under a California law passed in July 1993, insurance companies now have the right to bring a lawsuit on their own against any person who hires runners or cappers to procure clients or patients to obtain workers compensation benefits (Ins. Code 1971.7). This action need not be brought in the insurance company's name. Instead the insurance company can act on behalf of the "People of the State of California." Each violation of the law subjects the violator to a fine from $5,000 - $10,000 plus treble damages for the amount of the claim. At a minimum, an insurance company gets to keep 15% of the total recovery, plus its reasonable attorneys' fees. At a maximum, the insurer can receive 30% of the recovery plus attorneys' fees. The rest goes to the state.

Fraud by the Insurance Company

Frauds committed by insurance companies include some of the following:
- Submission of false documentation and improper billing
- Mishandling claims
- Failure to pay legitimate claims
- Charging unapproved rates
- Requesting rate increases based on fraudulent data
- Using illegal or deceptive tactics to sell insurance
- Failure to give "fee breaks"
- Patient screening

Submission of False Documents

If the insurance company acts as an intermediary for the payer, such as Medicare, then the insurance company commits fraud when it improperly bills the government or submits false cost reports or audits.

Mishandling Claims

Mishandling claims also arises primarily in the area of an insurance company acting as an intermediary administering the insurance program of the payer. The insurance company is under a duty to try to detect false claims. Although it is impossible to detect every fraudulent claim, if a company bypasses its own claims verification procedures, it can be guilty of fraud.

Failure to Pay Legitimate Claims

The insurance company or carrier is required to pay any claim that is properly submitted, contains all the required the information, absent of fraud, and has benefits available. An insurance company might commit fraud when claims are consistently rejected even though the required information has been submitted. Many states have regulations regarding the amount of time an insurance company has to pay a "clean" claim, one which has all the needed information. Even if an insured has committed fraud in the past, and for some reason or another is still an insured, the insurance company must still adjudicate a valid claim.

Charging Unapproved Rates

Some states require insurance companies to obtain approval on their premium rates. Until the approval is received, the rates cannot be charged to the insured. An insurance company may improperly begin charging the unapproved rate before it is allowed to.

Requesting Rate Increases Based on Fraudulent Data

Similar to the above, insurance companies or carriers needing regulatory approval for rate increases use cost data to justify their increases. In order to get their rate hike, they may use fraudulent cost data.

Deceptive or Illegal Sales Practices

Insurance companies may promote or condone deceptive or illegal sales practices in order to increase sales. The most common example is to disguise an insurance policy as a savings plan or investment.

Failure to Give "Fee Breaks"

An insurance company may be guilty of fraud if it fails to pass on fee breaks it negotiates with its providers. The alleged overcharging occurs when an insurance company negotiates a discount on a medical bill. If the company does not pass along the discount, the consumer's co-payment is made on the full price rather than the discounted price, and the consumer ends up paying a higher percentage of their bill than they should. For example, if a bill is $1,000 and a 50% discount is negotiated, the consumer's 20% portion should equal $100. If the company does not pass along the discount, the consumer pays 20% of the full $1,000, or $200.

Patient Screening

In the managed care environment, because so much emphasis is placed on preventive care, some insurance companies may be reducing their risk by limiting their insured to only healthy patients.

Detection

Detection of fraud committed by an insurance company may include the following:
- Review complaints by insureds
- Compare financial statement data to data used to request rates
- Compare rates charged with rates approved
- Compare discounts negotiated with providers with the amounts allowed on the claims and co-insurance charged
- Review rejected members to determine if underwriting guidelines were abused

Employee Claims Fraud

Employees of insurers, especially claims examiners and customer service representatives, can present additional problems to the fraud examiner. Due to their ability to access claims and subscriber files, the frauds perpetrated can be almost limitless.
- Claims fraud using the employee's contract
- Claims fraud using another insured's contract number
- Claims payment using a relative's contract
- Claims adjustment system
- Payment for canceled contracts or deceased insureds
- Improper payee

Claims Fraud Using the Employee's Contract

Claims employees generally have access to claims data and claim forms. They can sometimes adjust claims or pull someone's claim, change the claimant's contract number, and have the claim processed.

Claims Fraud Using Another Insured's Contract Number

Employees who have access to insureds enrollment file can locate an insured with a similar name as the employee. From there, the employee only has to complete a claim form and submit the claims through the regular processing system. The employee only has to put his or her own address in order to receive the payment.

Claims Payment Using a Relative's Contract

Employees can fabricate claims and submit them under a relative's contract number.

Claims Adjustment System

Claims that are legitimately paid incorrectly need to be adjusted. An adjustment examiner can adjust a claim for fraudulent purposes also.

Payment for Canceled Contracts or Deceased Insureds

If an adjuster has access to the enrollment files, he/she may run across a deceased insured. By submitting or processing a claim before cancellation, an examiner can manipulate the claims system and divert payment to himself.

Improper Payee

A claim approver overrides a claim payment system and pays out claims to improper payees. The claim approver inserts her son and daughter-in-law as payee. Checks are submitted to other than the insured's address.

Detection

The following steps can be used to determine if a company is dealing with an employee who is defrauding the system:

- Pull high-dollar claim payments for insureds. Investigate all unusual patterns by verifying services.
- Review printouts for special payee codes to search for employees.
- Review printouts for a high number of adjusted claims per insured.
- Review printouts of recently canceled contracts for unusual claims activity just prior to cancellation.
- Once unusual activity has been identified, follow normal investigative procedures.
- Review address change lists for employee names or unusual activity.

Agent Fraud

Nearly all insurance companies use the services of a broker or agent external to the firm. Unfortunately, the best interests of the insurance company are not always served. Several schemes have been identified which can be classified as fraudulent.

Phony Groups

Agents will set up bogus companies in order to sell health insurance to individuals at group rates.

Phony or Nonexistent Policies

Rather than going to the trouble of setting up a bogus company, many agents will sell a phony policy, and take the money and run.

Medical Underwriting Fraud

The broker will write a policy knowing that the client has pre-existing conditions that would prevent acceptance for coverage.

Eligibility Fraud

A broker may seek to add ineligible family members, girlfriends, or associates to a group policy by representing them as employees.

Another eligibility fraud is where a broker may sell a low-cost group policy to an organization that employs a small percentage of people with serious health problems. A better rate can be obtained by separating healthy people from sick people. The broker splits off the unhealthy people in their own group, placing the coverage with an insurer of last resort such as a carrier that is given favorable tax status in exchange for issuing coverage to anyone.

ERISA Fraud

The Employee Retirement Income Security Act regulates all trust accounts held by an employer for the purpose of paying benefits such as retirement annuities or health and life policies. Under the Act, if an insurance company believes that a plan administrator is engaging in violations of the Act, it is required to report the matter to the U.S. Department of Labor. As an example, a corporation may use funds collected from employees through payroll deduction to finance daily operations of the company.

Payment Inducements

These schemes involve brokers furnishing group coverage to individuals who would not otherwise qualify for such policies by adding them to legitimate groups or establishing a fictitious group for the purpose of obtaining waivers and/or cheaper rates. The broker profits not only from the normal sales commission, but also from a "surcharge" or billing fee that is added to the published premium that is collected from the policy holder by the broker. In another scenario, a broker may charge a markup for adding employees to a legitimate group.

Switching Policies

This scheme involves the agent telling the customer that he is obtaining one policy, taking the premium for that policy, and then buying instead a cheaper policy with less coverage. The agent then pockets the difference.

Provider Fraud

Provider fraud is a fraud perpetrated by a medical practitioner, medical supplier, or medical facility on patients or customers in order to increase their income by illicit means.

A greater potential for fraud exists with providers since they have the availability of more sophisticated equipment, such as computers, to use in generating bills. Providers possess greater knowledge of medical/dental techniques, medical procedures, terminology, etc., that would not be questioned by claim-handling personnel. More insurance companies are contracting with providers for direct billing, leaving the patient out of the loop. In addition, patients are usually reluctant to accuse physicians of wrongdoing since they rely on the provider's continued services, and when providers submit to fraudulent practices, they forgive any out-of-pocket expenses the patient should incur.

Rolling Labs

A *rolling lab* is a mobile laboratory which solicits insureds to participate in health screening tests at no cost to the insured. These labs are usually located in semi-trailers parked at health clubs, spas, shopping centers, or on vacant property.

Patients are contacted by telephone for a free physical exam. Subsequent to exam, the insurance company is billed for 8–10 claims totaling $8,000–$10,000 for a single date of testing using multiple providers.

Additional claims are billed for later service dates even though no more testing is done. The lab moves to another location prior to the patient receiving the test results to avoid detection.

The providers market their services in many ways. One way is to rent office space in a doctor's office for one day and then test all of that doctor's patients. The testing equipment itself might arrive in a truck or van and moves from one office to another.

Another method would be to set up a temporary operation in a shopping center. Health spas have been set up to have all members tested at no charge. By far the most common method was to simply set up a small office for a temporary period and use telephone solicitations.

Clinical Labs

Clinical labs have devised fraudulent billing practices to encourage physicians to order tests unnecessarily. The schemes caused specific blood tests to be included in a panel of frequently ordered tests. The ordering physician paid nothing or a nominal fee for the extra tests. The tests were then unbundled and billed separately by the lab to government payers and insurance companies. Over $475 million has been repaid to government programs to date, and the private payers are also settling claims.

Suppliers

Ambulance Transportation

Bills for more mileage than incurred, for trips never taken, or noncovered trips.

Infusion Care

Services billed at abnormally high fees in comparison to cost, bills for noncovered patients, bills in excess of physician's prescription, bills for unnecessary treatment, and kickbacks to the prescribing physician.

Durable Medical Equipment Suppliers

- Falsified prescriptions
- Excessive supplies
- Equipment not delivered or billed before delivery
- Billing for equipment rental after equipment was returned
- Noncovered supplies, i.e. incontinent care kits
- Milk supplement scam

- Lymphedema pumps
- Scooter scam

Home Health Companies

Fraud involving home health care companies gained national exposure after the federal government's investigation of ABC Home Health Care was released. ABC is the largest privately held home health care provider in the United States. In 1994, ABC made some 7.8 million visits and billed Medicare $615.9 million. Among the types of fraud identified were the following:

- Medical records were altered to make it appear that patients continued to need home health visits.
- Managers directed employees to continue visiting patients who, in the employee's opinion, did not qualify for home health care because they were not "homebound."
- A manager directed a nurse to record visits which were never made.
- One manager forged physicians' signatures on plans of care.
- If a care plan was signed by a physician, employees would alter the number of visits.
- ABC reportedly charged Medicare for the cost of acquiring other home health agencies by paying owners a small sum up front and the balance in salary under the form of employment agreements.
- Managers directed employees to market ABC and its services with the intent of charging Medicare for costs which are not reimbursable.

Pharmacy

- Merchandising—substituting something of value for a prescription drug.
- Billing for brand name drugs but dispensing generic drugs.
- Billing beyond amount prescribed.
- Billing for drugs not prescribed.
- Billing for a high-priced generic drug, but dispensing a lower-priced generic drug
- Package size differential—billing third-party payers for the price of drugs purchased in small package sizes when they were purchased at less cost in larger quantities.
- Black market purchasing—purchasing drugs at significantly reduced rates then dispensing at regular prices.

Chiropractors

- Billing for services never rendered or unnecessary services.
- Billing for multiple family members.

- Hiring foreign doctors speaking little English to perform physical exams only.
- Purchasing individual contracts for their patients.
- Billing by MDs associated with chiropractors, for physical therapy when contract does not cover chiropractors.
- Billing for excessive services.

> EXAMPLE
>
> *While certain treatments by chiropractors are usually not covered by insurance, similar treatments by physicians may be covered. To correct this perceived inequity, some chiropractors have set up medical corporations and then hired medical doctors as employees. The chiropractor is CEO of the corporation and has total discretion of how the funds are disbursed. The net result of this set-up is that a medical doctor gives the stamp of approval to charges that might not otherwise be paid, and the chiropractor reaps the profits.*

Chiro-Shenanigans

Patients for Life

Charging annual fees that exceed $5,000, practice management firms teach chiropractors how to build a million-dollar practice in two years. The literature advises the chiropractors not to tell patients the results of their initial exam or how long they will need treatment until they've been indoctrinated into the benefits of lifelong chiropractic care.

Further, they promote care of infants that will continue for the lifetime of the patient. Patients who question the continuation of treatment are given the guilty treatment: "It's a choice you have to make depending on how important your health is to you."

Patients don't seem to be cured until the insurance benefits run out. When benefits are renewed in the next calendar year, the symptoms return, and a new series of treatment begins until benefits run out.

Patient Recruiting

- Coupons for free meals where the benefits of chiropractic are explained
- Advertising for free initial care
- Booths at health fairs, malls, spas offering free screening
- Patient referrals

Treatment for Nonspinal Conditions

Whereas at one time chiropractors only treated spinal problems, many chiropractors believe that they can treat any medical condition, such as cancer, hernias, pneumonia, anemia, and heart conditions. In one pamphlet, it states "If you are suffering from kidney disease, the logical course is to visit your chiropractor. He will examine your spine to see where your trouble is."

Other

Other types of questionable chiropractic treatment include:
- Surrogate testing where the leg of a mother is flexed to diagnose her child's illness
- Spinal manipulation of newborn babies to get over the trauma of birth
- Spinal manipulation to treat epilepsy, asthma, bedwetting, and learning disabilities
- Applied kenesiology whereby diseases can be diagnosed by testing muscles with the help of particular food or nutrients
- Analysis of x-rays to identify homicidal tendencies
- Treatment plan prior to examination
- Spinal manipulations begun at an early age to prevent colon cancer
- Iridology or the examination of patients' eyes for markings which will indicate what diseases the patient has
- A magnetic device over the thymus gland to diagnose nutrient deficiencies

Red Flags

- Takes full spine or repeated x-rays
- Prescribes treatment before a history and physical are taken
- Offers of vitamin cures, nutritional remedies, and homeopathic remedies
- Solicits family members
- Advises not to have your children immunized
- Promises to prevent disease through regular check-ups
- No out-of-pocket expense
- Treatment ends when insurance benefits are exhausted, but patients are recontacted when benefits renew for maintenance treatment

Podiatrists

- Bills for services never rendered
- Bills for noncovered services
- Kickbacks to suppliers

Ophthalmologists
- Billing for services never rendered and noncovered services
- Billing for unnecessary services

Psychiatrists and Psychiatric Clinics
- Billing for services never rendered and noncovered services such as weight loss services, biofeedback
- Billing for services under psychiatrist's name when service actually performed by a noncovered but licensed provider, i.e., drug counselor, minister
- Billing for services performed by an unlicensed employee
- Admitting patients with false diagnoses

Anesthesiologists
Bills for more time than was rendered.

Dental Fraud
Bills for x-rays that have not been taken; crowns not cemented; amalgams for teeth that were not filled; teeth not extracted, fillings for teeth that have been extracted; and more fillings than a person can possibly have.

Allergists
Bills for allergy testing not performed, unnecessary services, or allergy shots not given.

Infertility Treatment
Infertility treatment is generally not a covered service. However, in order for this to be paid, it is billed as hormonal replacement therapy.

Impostor Provider
A provider who does not exist, but bills fraudulent claims. Another scam is to assume the identify of a deceased provider and practice, or to put together a group of licensed providers and fraudulently bill under the group's provider identification code.

Investigation Tips
If it is suspected that a company is dealing with a fabricated provider:
- Call the telephone number on the bill to determine if the provider exists (a fictitious provider may actually have rented a location and established a telephone number).

- Contact the Licensing Board or Province to determine if the alleged provider is licensed to practice in the area at the time the service was allegedly provided.
- Check the Social Security number or Tax Identification number listed on the provider bill with the Licensing Board.
- Visit the alleged provider's address to determine if it's a valid address (speak to the superintendent to determine who lives at that address).
- Contact a Postal Inspector to verify what mail is being dropped at that address.

False Diagnoses

When a provider knows that a service is not covered, using false diagnoses and procedure code manipulation will generally get the claim paid. In addition, before ordering expensive laboratory x-rays or other similar services, physicians justify the ordering of such procedures by determining that a need exists to make such diagnostic inquiries. The services are rendered, but because it is false information on a claim and is used to deceive the insurance company, the claim is considered a false claim. Examples of common services not covered are:

- Annual physical examination
- School physicals
- Weight loss programs
- Stop smoking programs
- Investigational or experimental procedures
- Cosmetic surgery

Red Flags of Provider Fraud
- Pressure for rapid adjudication of claims.
- Threats of legal action for delay in making payments.
- Frequent telephone inquiries on claim status.
- Assertive providers who demand same-day claim payment and special handling.
- Charges submitted for payment with no supporting documentation available (x-rays, lab results).
- Individual provider using P.O. box as return addresses.
- Insured's address on claim form is the same as provider.
- Routine (not specialized) treatment for patients living more than 150 miles from the provider.
- Referring physician and provider of service in same professional corporation
- Medical records that have been altered.

- Medical records that have additional information attached that would make an apparent noncovered service now covered.
- Missing pages of medical records that would cover the period of time you are reviewing.

Fraud by the Medical Staff

In addition, employees of providers also have an opportunity to steal and cover up theft of cash. They can submit fraudulent claims for their patients and divert the payments to themselves. If they are covered under insurance, they can also use their own contract to submit fraudulent claims. For many employees, care rendered by their employer (doctor) to them or their family is free, but claims may be filed and assignment not accepted.

Another scheme involves the provider's office calling in prescription drugs for their "patients" to pharmacies. Once the drugs are picked up they can be sold. For example, in a case involving collusion between a medical staff employee and an elderly lady in a retirement community, the elderly lady had developed a business selling the drugs purchased from the employee to her friends and neighbors in her community. If the employee is in collusion with an insured, the fraudsters can collect not only from the sale of the drugs, but also from the proceeds of insurance claims.

Kickbacks in the Health Care Industry

Kickbacks relating to the health care industry can come from several sources. The medical community is facing competition that it has not faced in the past, and monetary offers to prospective patients have been difficult to refuse. For example, in a South Florida community, incentives such as free transportation to medical facilities, shopping centers, refreshments, and the like are common.

Examples of kickbacks are:
- Payment for referrals of patients
- Waiver of deductible and co-payments
- Payment for insurance contracts
- Payment for vendor contracts

Payment for Referral of Patients

Providers in an area of high competition will pay from $50 up to about $500 to cappers or runners for new patients. In addition, patients may receive $50 if they refer a patient to a provider. The provider makes up for the kickback in the unnecessary billing of medical expenses or false claims. In addition, providers will pay kickbacks to other physicians for patient referrals.

Waiver of Deductibles and Co-payments

Most insurance contracts require patients to pay a deductible and co-payment for services rendered. One of the reasons for having co-payments is to make insureds take an active part in the financial responsibility for their care. To attract patients however, providers will forgive the patient's out-of-pocket expense, but will make up for it in additional services.

Payment for Insurance Contracts

Physicians with patients who are facing long-term care or lifetime treatment, such as dialysis for kidney failure, may purchase contracts for their patients. This ensures that the provider will be paid, and the patient has no out-of-pocket expense.

Payment for Vendor Contracts

Companies doing business with medical practitioners will pay a "consulting" fee for referring business to them or using their supplies.

Payments to Adjusters

In order to get a claim settled quickly, an insured, or someone operating on his behalf, may bribe adjusters or other claims-handling personnel to approve or speed up payment of a claim.

Inflated Billings

Health care billings can be inflated by providers as well as insureds. The following are some of the most common fraud schemes encountered by investigators and claims approvers:

- Alterations
- Adding services
- Code gaming

Alterations

Altering valid claims can be accomplished using a pen or a photocopier. Common alterations are:

- Altered claim forms/super bills
- Amounts changed
- Date of service changed
- Name of patient changed
- Altered financial ledgers

For example, a prescription/medical bill can be altered by placing an additional number in front of the amount charged. The date of service can be altered so that it becomes a covered expense rather than one which was incurred prior to being eligible for coverage. The individual submitting a claim changes the name on the bill from a noncovered family member to one that is covered under the contract.

Detection

- Computer programs can be developed which identify excessive charges for prescription or medical services above an acceptable level.
- There is a machine that can identify any alterations, erasures, change of ink, or white-outs on the original bill prior to paying the claim. This is important in today's environment in which original bills, checks, etc., are destroyed as soon as they are microfilmed to minimize storage space for record keeping. This machine is produced in England and costs approximately $70,000.
- Train the adjusters to look for obvious alterations when processing claims.

Adding Services

This scheme involves adding on services never rendered to dates of actual services. In these cases, the verification process is the same as the procedures listed under the alteration process.

Code Gaming

Code manipulation is a problem that is faced by all health insurers. Each service is identified using the American Medical Association's uniformly accepted coding system, called the Physicians' Current Procedural Terminology (CPT). Medicare and most private insurers have developed fee schedules that use CPT codes and their accompanying narrative descriptions as the basis for paying providers.

However, because the coding system is complicated, providers and insurers often have difficulty identifying the codes that most accurately describe the services provided. The coding system is difficult to use because it attempts to identify codes for all accepted medical procedures, including codes to describe minor procedures that are components of more comprehensive procedures. Payment policies add to the difficulty. For example, the fee for surgery often includes the cost of related services for the global service period, that is, for a set number of days before and after the surgery.

To prevent overpayment in these cases, insurers need to identify when claims for surgery include codes that represent related services and reduce the payment accordingly. It is also difficult for providers and insurers to maintain proficiency in proper coding practices because a substantial number of the codes are changed each year. These complexities can inadvertently lead providers to submit improperly coded claims. They also make insurers vulnerable to abuse from providers or billing services that attempt to maximize reimbursements by intentionally submitting claims containing inappropriate combinations of codes.

Unbundling Charges/Fragmentation

Simple unbundling occurs when a provider charges a comprehensive code as well as one or more component codes. For instance, in the examples illustrated below, the provider would be overpaid because the fee for the total procedure already includes the value of its component parts.

Procedure Code	Service Billed	Correctly Billed Procedure
58150 58720 49000 44955 58740	Total Hysterectomy ($1300) Removal of ovaries & tubes ($950) Exploration of abdomen ($671) Appendectomy ($250) Lysis of Adhesions ($550) **Total Charge $3721**	Total Hysterectomy 58150 **Total Payment $1300**
29877 29870	Knee arthroscopy with debridement ($1650) Diagnostic knee arthroscopy ($1625) **Total Charge $3275**	Knee arthroscopy with debridement 29877 **Total Payment $1650**
47610 47600	Cholecystectomy with common bile duct exploration ($1997) Cholecystectomy ($705) **Total Charge $2702**	Cholecystectomy with common bile duct exploration 47610 **Total Payment $1997**

Unbundling can be detected through the use of a computer program that determines whether each code submitted is a component of one or more comprehensive codes.

Mutually Exclusive Procedures
Another form of unbundling. It encompasses procedures that are either impossible to perform together or, by accepted standards, should not be performed together.

Global Service Period Violations
Billing for a major procedure — such as a surgery — as well as related procedures, when the fee for the major procedure already includes the fee for related procedures during the predefined time period (the global service period). This type of fraud is possible because most surgery includes all related services for a set number of days before and after the surgery. Detecting these abuses can be difficult because you must determine which services are related to the surgery and which are not. This difficulty is compounded by the fact that such services may be rendered by more than one provider.

Upcoding

Billing a higher level of service than was rendered. One common form of upcoding is in the form of generic substitution — filling a prescription with a less expensive drug, while billing for the more expensive form of the drug.

Misuse of "New Patient" Codes

Billing established patients with new patient codes.

Insured Fraud

Insureds may attempt to perpetrate a fraud by submitting fictitious claims forms:
- Multiple surgeries
- Multiple office visits
- Foreign claims—patient supposedly goes out of the country and falls ill
- Noncovered dependents

Doctor/ER Shopping

Excessive drug claims for controlled substance drugs. Patient "shops" for controlled substance drugs. One physician doesn't know that the other has prescribed the drug. In addition, the patient may shop for drugs in emergency rooms complaining of soft tissue injuries, sprains, and strains.

Misrepresentation on Application

Failure by insured to list all prior medical conditions or group to list medical conditions of employees.

Third-Party Fraud

This category involves an unauthorized use of an insured's identification card by another known person or unknown person. The insurance company is usually notified by the insured once they receive a benefit statement work sheet for services rendered.

Death of Insured

The primary insured passes away; however, the beneficiary does not notify the insurance carrier and continues to submit fictitious claims on medical expenses after the death of the insured.

Investigation Tips

- Determine how the insured lost his/her card. If stolen, the police should be contacted to determine if the crime was reported. A copy of the police report should be obtained.
- Obtain an actual description of the cardholder so that identification can be made of the impostor who used the card improperly.
- Visit the providers or medical doctors to obtain any information to identify the perpetrator.

Criminal Rings

Individual criminals infiltrate mailrooms and are able to obtain copies of legitimate bills submitted to providers. They subsequently establish a mail drop point or rent an office and begin submitting false claims to insurance companies by creating fictitious tax identification numbers. Since the claimants are genuine, insurance companies will normally pay these bills.

Collusion

Collusion is the most difficult insurance fraud to detect since several people are involved in committing the fraud. Usually cases of this nature are disclosed by accident or by a tip received from someone who may have been involved and has had a falling-out.

Any time a fraud is committed by an insured, there is no question on the part of the perpetrator as to the intent to obtain funds to which he or she is not entitled. However, it is also extremely difficult to detect this type of fraud.

Detection

- Excessive billings report may show that a provider is submitting large amounts of expenses. In addition, the claimant requests substantial payments to be made to him/her rather than the provider.
- Explanation of benefits if submitted to the provider will probably generate some reaction from the provider. If substantial, at the time that Form 1099 is submitted to the provider, there may also be comments by the provider.
- Periodically management should compare the membership/enrollment file to the Social Security file to determine if the insurance company is paying claims on deceased insureds. The membership file also may be compared to the file from the vital statistics department to search for divorced policyholders.

Divorce

An insured and a covered spouse file for divorce, but neither party notifies the insurance company. The spouse, who remains at the address of record, continues to submit claims.

Foreign Insured

A foreign insured submits phony information that the primary insured passed away. For the last month he/she was hospitalized in a foreign hospital and a sizable bill was mailed to the carrier for payment.

Investigation Tips

- The claim file should be reviewed to determine if the charges are legitimate.
- Determine if the medical language appears to be proper by comparing samples of bona fide claims.
- It may be necessary to submit a letter to the attending physician to determine if the charges are correct.
- Through law enforcement contacts, it may be necessary to obtain information regarding the legitimacy of the claim.
- Check the style of the date. In many foreign countries, dates are listed with the day first, then the month and year, e.g., 07/01/04 would be 7 January 2004. If the U.S. style of dating is used (month/day/year), it may indicate a fraudulent claim.

Detection of External Fraud

- Misspelled medical/dental terminology.
- Unusual charges for a given service.
- Similar handwriting by the claimant and the provider of service.
- Typed, not printed bill heads.
- Bills with irregular columns.
- Unassigned bills that are normally assigned, such as large hospital or surgical bills.
- Typed or handwritten hospital bills.
- Drug receipts from the same pharmacy but on different color paper.
- Erasures or alterations.
- Lack of any provider's signature on a claim form.
- Absence of the provider's medical degree, i.e., "Dr. John Doe" instead of "John Doe, M.D."

- An illegible provider signature on the bill submitted or the signature does not match the one on file.
- Surgeries that don't have other related services such as hospital charges.
- Physician's specialty does not agree with diagnosis.
- Services billed do not agree with diagnosis.
- Impossible or unlikely services.
- Photocopied bills.
- Other indicators that a claim approver or investigator should be aware of that could result in identifying a possible fraud:
- Pressure by a claimant to pay a claim quickly.
- Individuals who hand deliver their claim insist on picking up their claim check.
- Threats of legal action if a claim is not paid quickly.
- Anonymous telephone call inquiries regarding the status of a pending claim.
- Identical claims for same patient in different months or different years.
- Dates of service just prior to termination of enrollment or just after enrollment.
- Services billed that do not appear to agree with the medical records.
- Billing for services or equipment which are clearly unsuitable for the patient's needs.
- Foreign claims listing charges in U.S. dollars when that isn't the currency of that country.
- Foreign claims giving documentation in English when English is not the primary language spoken.
- Multiple foreign claims for same subscriber.
- Multiple foreign claims from same physician/ hospital.

Fraud by Medical Institutions

Fraud schemes perpetrated by institutions and their employees include those commonly used by doctors and other providers. However, the more common schemes in which hospitals are primarily involved include:

- Filing of false cost reports
- DRG creep
- Billing for experimental procedures
- Improper contractual and other relationships with physicians
- Revenue recovery firms to (knowingly or unknowingly) bill extra charges

False Cost Reports

Cost reports sometimes include noncovered items such as golf outings, parties, and exotic trips disguised as covered items. For example, an investigation disclosed that a hospital recovered silver from the processing of x-ray film, sold it, gave it to the candy stripers, only to have it "donated" back to the hospital. Since Medicare doesn't consider donations as revenue, the hospital was able to claim higher expenses, thus more money from Medicare.

Inclusion of Unallowable Items
- Expenses for tax penalties, late charges, and promotional advertising
- Costs incurred from a related-party transaction with a mark-up over the costs incurred by the related-party
- Expenses which are reimbursed under other programs (i.e., billable medical supplies and therapies)
- Excessive expenses such as hotel, food, travel expenses for recreational events
- Luxury items (i.e., lavish furnishings, corporate planes, swimming pools, spas)

DRG Creep

Diagnostic Related Groupings (DRG) is a reimbursement methodology for the payment of institutional claims. It is a patient classification scheme that categorizes patients who are medically related with respect to primary and secondary diagnosis, age, and complications. Reimbursements are determined by the DRG. For example, a heart bypass operation is worth a certain amount of reimbursement and a hernia repair is worth a different amount. DRG creep occurs when a hospitalization is coded as a more complex admission than occurred. When it becomes a pattern and intent is established, it becomes fraud.

Another type of fraud using DRG codes involves billing for the DRG code and then billing again for services which were included in the DRG payment.

Billing for Experimental Procedures

It is reported that one form of medical fraud that is little known, but apparently widespread, is the third-party billing for experiments with new medical devices which have not yet been approved by the Food and Drug Administration. Some hospitals are deliberately misleading third-party payers by getting them to pay for the manufacturer's research. Many of the doctors involved are alleged to have stock in the manufacturing companies.

Improper Relationships with Physicians

Certain relationships between hospitals and physicians result in fraud to the insurer. For instance, a hospital provides no or token reimbursement to pathologists for Medicare Part A services in return for the opportunity to perform and bill Part B services at that hospital.

The following transactions are generally regarded as suspect:
- Payment of any sort of incentive by the hospital each time a physician refers a patient to the hospital.
- Provision of free or significantly discounted billing, nursing, or other staff services.
- Free training for a physician's office staff in areas such as management techniques, CPT coding, and laboratory techniques.
- Guarantees which provide that, if the physician's income fails to reach a predetermined level, the hospital will supplement the remainder up to a certain amount.
- Low-interest or interest-free loans, or loans which may be forgiven if a physician refers patients to the hospital.
- Payment of the cost of a physician's travel and expenses for conferences.
- Payment for a physician's continuing education courses.
- Coverage on the hospital's group health insurance plan at an inappropriate or very low cost.
- Payment for services (which may include consultation at the hospital) which require few, if any, substantive duties by the physician, or payment for services in excess of the fair market value of services rendered.

Revenue Recovery Firms

Another form of health care fraud involves so-called revenue recovery firms padding medical bills. These billing consultants review patients' bills (months or even years after treatment) looking for charges that were missed. Critics have charged that too often these firms pad medical bills by adding on fictitious charges. The more charges that are added onto the bill, the more the revenue recovery firm gets paid. In addition, their employees may be paid bonuses for piling on extra charges and pressured to meet monthly quotas.

Changing Codes

One of the most common methods used by revenue recovery firms is to change every hospital's or nursing home's billing codes. For instance, changing each code for an ordinary five-cent bandage so that the provider is charged for a $5 surgical dressing.

Adding Items

Extra charges are added onto hospital bills by assuming that hospitals used certain items, even though there was no evidence of the procedure or service. For instance, if the hospital had certain procedures for which they sometimes use a piece of x-ray equipment, the auditor reviewing the bill would always assume that the hospital had used the equipment, and they would put it on the bill.

Kickbacks

Often hospitals are unaware (sometimes intentionally) of the extent of the fraud committed by revenue recovery firms. However, in other cases, revenue firms report that they will contact a hospital or nursing home directly and tell them that if the institution will give them their bills, they will split the profit produced by the added charges.

Billing for Expensive Treatments

Numerous charges for the use of expensive treatments such as laser are added to patients' bills. Charges may be added after the patient had already been billed for the use of the laser.

Altering Records

In some instances, firms may actually alter medical records. For example, in one case a firm added more than $1,300 to a patient's bill for video equipment that was supposedly used during surgery. In order to justify the fraudulent billing, the firm checked a box on the surgical record to indicate that the equipment had been used. After the original document was obtained, it showed that the box was not checked on the original form completed by the surgical staff.

Donating Organs

One hospital, which has ceased using a particular firm, reported that the firm regularly double billed for services and treatments, and in another instance, outside auditors found that the firm had tried to charge for dead patients donating their organs.

Additional Anesthesia Time

Another common scheme is the charging of additional hours of anesthesia. Patients should be billed from when they enter the surgery room to when they leave the surgery room. The revenue firm pads the bill by increasing the time billed to include time spent in a recovery room, or before the patient went into the operating room.

Nursing Homes

Nursing homes have become a multibillion dollar business in the last few years. As such, they have become a common target of fraud. A wide array of providers — including durable medical equipment suppliers, laboratories, physicians, optometrists, and psychiatrists — have been involved in fraudulent or abusive billing for services and supplies furnished to nursing facility patients. Most fraudulent activity involves billing for unnecessary or undelivered services, or misrepresenting a service to obtain reimbursement.

There are several features unique to nursing homes which make them particularly vulnerable to fraud:

- Unscrupulous billers of services can operate their schemes in volume because the patients are all located together under one roof.
- In some instances, nursing homes make patient records available to outside providers who are not responsible for the direct care of the patient (contrary to federal regulations).
- Under the Health Care Financing Administration's reimbursement procedures, providers can bill Medicare directly without the nursing facility or attending physician affirming whether the items were necessary or provided as claimed.
- Scrutiny of the claims at the processor level is inadequate because the automated claims systems used do not accumulate data that would timely flag indications of improbably high charges or levels of service.
- Even when abusive practices are detected and prosecuted, repayment is rarely received from wrongdoers because they usually go out of business or deplete their resources so that they lack any resources to repay the funds.
- Patient personal funds are controlled by nursing home administration and are an inviting target for embezzlement. Individually, patients generally maintain a relatively small balance in their personal funds accounts. Collectively, however, these funds generate a considerable source of income for an unscrupulous nursing home operator or employee.

Failure of the Nursing Facility to Monitor Outside Providers

Although nursing homes are required to perform numerous tasks to monitor patients and meet their needs, there are no requirements that nursing homes monitor the services or supplies provided to their patients. These providers are allowed to bill directly without adequate confirmation that the care or items were necessary or were delivered as claimed.

Most nursing facilities do not have the in-house capability to provide all the services and supplies their patients need. Accordingly, outside providers market their services and supplies to nursing homes to meet the needs of their patients. Typically, provider representatives enter the home and offer to handle the entire transaction — from reviewing medical records to identify those patients who need their services, to billing —with no involvement by the nursing facility. Some homes allow providers or their representatives to review patient medical records contrary to federal regulations. By doing so, these providers can obtain all the information necessary to order, bill, and be reimbursed for services and supplies that are, in many instances, not necessary or even provided.

Excessive Reimbursements

Although carriers do employ automated controls to prevent fraud, often questionable claims and providers are not flagged before excessive reimbursements are paid. In other instances, providers bill for quantities of services or supplies that could not possibly have been furnished or necessary.

Psychiatric Hospital Fraud

Psychiatric hospitals are susceptible to fraud because of the very nature of mental health problems and the manner in which they are diagnosed and treated. Unlike the acute care field, it is often difficult to determine whether a person is in need of hospitalization for psychiatric treatment.

Abuse in the Admissions Process

Some psychiatric treatment facilities have developed programs for patients who exhibit symptoms of both psychiatric illness and substance abuse problems. Fraud occurs when a patient is admitted on the basis of a diagnosis which reflects the patient's insurance coverage rather than the patient's illness. Psychiatric hospitals have been accused of finding something wrong with a patient when it is discovered that he or she has insurance coverage. Such patients may often be admitted without examination by a physician.

Fraud in the Treatment Process

The following types of abuses can occur with regard to psychiatric treatment:
- Extending the length of treatment programs or delaying discharges because patients have additional insurance benefits remaining.

- Illegitimate treatment programs and forms of therapy: "fat farms," biorhthym, art therapy, music therapy, group therapy at ballparks or shopping malls.
- Engaging in excessive treatment of psychiatric patients such as thyroid testing, drug tests, or psychiatric evaluation tests.

Abusive Marketing Practices

Many hospitals rely on marketing as a means of encouraging treatment and generating referrals. Overly aggressive marketing methods include:
- Paying bonuses to employees to persuade or pressure prospective patients to undergo a psychiatric evaluation and to admit themselves for treatment.
- Encouraging patients to admit themselves by offering financial incentives such as payment of plane fare, child care, COBRA payments, and waivers of patient co-payments or deductibles.

Financial Rewards for Referrals

Many facilities are dependent on outside sources of patient referrals such as physicians or other clinicians. This dependence has led some hospitals to develop economic relationships in order to obtain referrals:
- Rewarding clinicians who refer patients by referring patients who need outpatient treatment to those clinicians.
- Allowing allied health professionals who refer patients to provide therapy for their own patients at the hospital; while nonreferring allied professionals are not allowed to use the hospital.
- Paying medical directors or other physicians an incentive bonus linked to the overall profitability of the hospital.
- Paying a physician who is under contract to the hospital but who provides no services.

Red Flags for Psychiatric and Substance Abuse Claims
- Treatment takes place far from patient's home.
- Diagnosis becomes alcoholism when state mandate reimburses alcoholism like any other illness.
- Patient is on disability.
- Provider's credentials are questionable.
- Documentation of treatment is lacking.
- Ancillary services are not treatment oriented.

Other Frauds in the Institutional Setting

Write-Off of Patient Accounts

When a patient account or other type of receivable has been determined to be uncollectible, the account is written-off to bad debts. It becomes a fraudulent transaction when the account has been written-off prematurely and the balance subsequently collected with the proceeds going to the employee. In this scheme, the employee has the opportunity to collect the receivable and divert the funds to himself, because companies typically do not keep track of old, written-off accounts receivable.

Often old accounts receivable are assigned to a collection agency. These agencies typically are paid on a percentage of the collected amounts. Fraud schemes can be perpetrated by these agencies if the company does not monitor the method by which the agency receives old accounts and the collection process itself.

The assignor company needs to assure itself that the collection agency is being assigned truly old accounts only and not good accounts which can reasonably be expected to pay within the normal course of business.

Additionally, the company needs to be sure that the collection agency cannot compromise the indebtedness so that collections are not reported. This would allow the collection agency to compromise indebtedness for its own collection and not remit amounts owed the company.

Credit Balances

When patients have more than one payer responsible for payment of an admission, institutions have been known to collect more than the original amount billed. This may occur when the patient has more than one health insurance company, is in a vehicle accident where multiple insurance carriers are involved, or where workers compensation is applicable. In addition, the facility may also collect the deductible and co-payment from the patient. If the hospital has a credit balance, the amount paid above the charges should be refunded to the applicable parties. However, this does not always occur. Generally the refund will be made upon request, but only upon request.

Theft of Pharmaceuticals and Supplies

Because of the ready market for selling pharmaceuticals and supplies, they have a propensity for being stolen. Narcotic drugs, although they are usually tightly controlled, still may be stolen and sold on the street. Supplies such as canes, sunglasses after cataract surgery, and admission kits are popular items for theft or employee abuse.

Managed Care

The United States' health care system is moving toward more and different types of "managed" care. As the country moves to a different type of health care delivery system, so may the types of fraud.

Traditionally, health care has been provided and paid for on a "fee-for-service" basis where payments were made either directly to the health care provider as payment for services rendered to the insured party, or to the insured as reimbursement for medical expenses incurred. The premise behind managed care is that the medical practitioner is responsible for managing the total needs of the patient. The primary purpose of managed care is to reduce cost by promoting the most appropriate and efficient use of medical services.

The most common managed care arrangements are:
- Modified traditional coverage
- HMOs
- PPOs

Modified Traditional Coverage

Under this type of coverage, the medical practitioner is reimbursed through a fee-for-service arrangement. The patient is free to choose a provider and a claim is submitted for reimbursement by either the insured or the provider. It is a managed care model in that cost-cutting measures are in the form of utilization review, prior authorization, second surgical opinions, and hospital pre-authorizations.

HMOs

HMOs, or Health Maintenance Organizations, have several variations. The HMO may employ all of the providers as in a staff-model HMO, or the managed care organization may contract with individual physicians or physician groups. The insured selects a primary care physician (PCP) who is the gatekeeper. Generally all medical care is initiated through the

PCP. Payment is made by capitation, that is, the PCP receives a flat fee per month from the managed care organization, although some fees still may be paid on a fee-per-service basis usually at a reduced rate. Care which cannot be performed by the PCP is done by a specialty care physician who is also a member of the HMO network. The patient is severely penalized for going outside the HMO network.

PPOs

PPO, or Preferred Provider Organization, is a managed care arrangement in which the patient chooses a provider from a list of participating providers in the PPO network. Their care is not managed by one provider as in the HMO, and they may see any provider in the network. The patient is penalized for going outside the network, although not as severely as in an HMO network. Providers usually must bill the third-party payer and claims are assigned.

How Managed Care Alters the Potential for Fraud

In a managed care environment, fraud is not eliminated. Insured fraud may be reduced substantially, but provider fraud is still alive and well. In addition to billing fraudulent services, managed care has an additional incentive for fraud. Because the providers share in the financial risk of a patient, there is the potential to provide *less* services to a patient since a fixed capitation rate allows the patients unlimited visits to a provider.

Types of Managed Care Frauds

- Inadequate treatment of patients.
- Referring patients automatically to providers outside the network (perhaps in exchange for kickbacks from outside providers).
- Establishment of inconvenient appointment hours, service locations, etc. to suppress the number of patients.
- Inflating reports of patient traffic and treatment costs to induce payers to increase future per patient capitation fees.
- False claims for services not covered by fixed capitation payments.
- Falsification of quality of care and/or treatment-outcome data.
- Providers misrepresenting their credentials or qualifications for admission to a given payer's network of managed care providers.
- Out-of-network overbilling for substandard services.
- Employees' creating claim checks during periods when the plan no longer is doing business with the HMO, but treatment of members continues due to existing problems.

- Providing kickbacks to employees of managed care organizations for putting patients in their panel.

Managed care systems also create the opportunity for fraud by the insureds. Some of the examples of fraud which may be found in the managed care environment include the following:
- Patients (members) loaning or selling use of card to nonmembers.
- Enrolling noneligible persons as members for obtaining treatment.
- Failing to disenroll ex-spouse of family members.
- Out-of-network falsified emergency treatment in collusion with providers.

Red Flags

Some of the red flags for managed care frauds are:
- Identifying providers who regularly waive co-payments or deductibles.
- Unusual referral patterns—either too high or too low.
- Unusually high pattern of referrals to pharmacies, laboratories, or specialty care physicians.
- High number of emergency room referrals.
- Patient complaints about the treatment.
- A pattern of high number of services which fall outside of the captitated services.

Electronic Claims Fraud

Auditing electronic claims may use the same techniques as auditing any other type of health care if the original source documents are used. The difference may be that the audit may use the information electronically transmitted rather than the original information. If reliance could be placed on the information being submitted, then there wouldn't be any difference. However, history has proved that electronic claims can be a fertile source for fraud.

Electronic Data Interchange (EDI) is the exchange of electronic data between computers in which there is no human interaction. This technology has advanced companies' ability to conduct business by light-years, but it has also provided would-be fraudsters an increased opportunity to commit white-collar crimes.

EDI's origins arise in the 1960s, when many industry groups began to develop EDI standards in areas such as purchasing, transportation, and financial transactions. The next major step forward came when the Transportation Data Coordinating Committee and the National Association of Credit Management's Credit Research Foundation developed the first standards of electronic data interchange. At this time, they have developed over 200 different standards for individual industries concerning the transmission of EDI and there are another 100 standards in development. These standards are published by the Data Interchange Standards Association.

Although these standards have been adopted and used worldwide by a multitude of different industries, the health care industry has been notoriously slow in adopting the new technology. Only now have a handful of large health care providers such as Blue Cross Blue Shield announced their endorsements of the health care industry conducting business electronically. The reasoning behind the reluctance to convert is that the health care system is so complicated that a switch in operation procedure of this magnitude would cause considerable headache in the early phases.

EDI can be used internally within a business as a way of communication and data transfer and it can also be used for the same purposes between different businesses. In the case of the health care industry, EDI enables the different companies to send claims, invoices, and other vital data which once was shipped in a paper format via airmail. The fact that EDI allows for an immediate exchange of data makes the process of submitting and approving health care claims much more efficient for the health care industry.

The health care transactions which will be affected by the emerging of EDI technologies include:
- Claims payment
- Enrollments
- Claims submission
- Eligibility
- Claim status
- Crossover COB
- Healthcare service review
- Patient information record
- Managed care encounter
- Capitated payment
- Interactive claim
- HMO reporting

- Provider information

During 2003, Medicare intermediaries received 98% of hospital claims and 75% of physician claims electronically, and more and more private insurance companies and providers are switching to electronic claims.

In the current health care system, there are over 1,500 insurance companies that process over four billion medical claims every year. Because the health care system uses over 450 different types of forms, it is estimated that in the past, the health care industry spent as much as $100 billion per year to process its paperwork. Thus, EDI has the potential to save the health care industry from $8 billion to $20 billion every year. It is very simply a more efficient way for the health care industry to do business. However, fraud examiners fear that a more efficient system also paves the way for more efficient ways to defraud the health care industry.

Solid controls must be established to deal with the health care industry's conversion to EDI or the savings that the more efficient system will produce may be gobbled up by bigger fraud losses. The electronic conversion of information completely removes paper-based controls.

EDI eliminates the abilities that fraud examiners have to detect fraud in the health care industry in three ways:
- The automation of claims has erased claims professionals' ability to detect suspicious-looking claims. Because they are used to handling the paperwork of claims, EDI hampers the claims professional from getting a good picture of the overall nature of an account, instead reducing each transaction to individual claims.
- Because of the impersonal nature of electronic transactions, EDI raises the temptation of would-be fraudsters to commit white-collar crime.
- EDI leaves no paper trail, making the process of fraud detection difficult for the fraud examiner.

The reasons the health care industry is concerned about EDI's potential to stimulate fraudulent activity include:
- The lack of tools to detect EDI fraud.
- The variation of health care services precipitates the potential from a plethora of dissimilar frauds.
- The efficiency of EDI allows for more vendors and thus more claims to account for.

- The swiftness in which transactions take place allow less time to uncover fraud.

In the past, the health care industry has developed sophisticated methods of detecting fraud within the paper-based system. Now that the conversion to EDI is taking place, the health care industry must find a way to convert those methods to uncovering fraud in the electronic format. These methods will only be as sophisticated as the health care industry chooses to make them; the less concern that the industry shows for creating fraud indicators, the more opportunity they will be giving fraudsters to "beat the system."

Fraud examiners should not fear that the conversion to EDI will eliminate any fraud-related job opportunities. In fact, that conversion will actually open up many fraud examination jobs, as the safeguards and red flag system against fraud has not been effectively established at this time. Therefore, fraud examiners need to be aware not only that their jobs are to investigate fraud, but also to create systems which will effectively deter fraud.

Many new and complicated legal issues are raised as a result of the health care industry's conversion to EDI. Some of the difficult questions that have been pressed include:
- How does the insurance company prove that all electronic claims are authentic?
- Who is responsible for errors in electronic health care claims?
- How does the fraud examiner prove that the contents of an electronic health care claim are false?
- How does the health care industry ensure that all electronic transmissions are received exactly as they are sent?
- What terms and conditions govern electronic claims?
- How will fraud examiners determine the actual origin of any electronic submission?

Because automated claims are quite easily altered, the health care industry must ensure that claims are authentic. Fraud examiners must document that claims have been received in the same condition in which they were processed if they are to be admissible as evidence.

Some examples of ways to ensure claims' authenticity include:
- Data encryption
- Digital signatures
- Message authentication codes
- Prior claims' history checkups
- A variety of field checks

The Effects of Prosecution in an Electronic Environment

EDI creates a new type of legal evidence, but the basic legal principles regarding that evidence should remain intact. Therefore, the burden falls on the companies of the health care industry to demonstrate that its electronic system has proven safeguards that counteract fraud. If the system is proven to be reliable, the company can then show that it has created a reliable record of transactions.

The greatest weakness within an EDI system is that in the prosecution, a defendant may claim that he/she did not enter the claim or that the claim was mishandled by the health care company. Thus, a health care company must maintain the integrity of its electronic records. The health care company must have in place several ways to uncover fraud, from automatic red flags to intricate fraud analyzation programs which pick up on familiar patterns which may ultimately lead to fraud.

A health care company must prove the origin of all electronic communication and the original content of the transaction. They must also reduce the possibility that the original claim's content can be intentionally or unintentionally compromised. By doing these things, the health care industry can effectively use EDI without substantially raising the possibility of fraudulent activity.

Health Care Compliance Programs

Recently the government discovered a widespread "upcoding" scheme, in which numerous hospitals across the country routinely and fraudulently coded pneumonia cases in their billing systems under a diagnostic related group (DRG) that caused Medicare to overcompensate the providers by about 28 percent. These "optimization" programs crossed the line of legitimate billing and subsequent criminal and civil investigations followed. In dealing with such a large number of hospitals, the government utilized compliance programs, also known as corporate integrity agreements, to help minimize future instances of fraud without significantly damaging a community's healthcare needs by sanctioning or dismissing medical providers.

The U.S. Department of Health and Human Services, Office of the Inspector General (OIG), is increasingly using corporate compliance programs in lieu of sanctions to control medical providers and related entities who have defrauded federal healthcare programs.

The OIG has devised model compliance guidelines for hospitals, clinical laboratories, durable medical equipment companies, and home health companies. The entire contents of those model plans can be located on the United States Department of Health and Human Service's website at www.hhs.gov.

Compliance programs are simply a set of effective internal controls designed to ensure that company operations adhere to the guidelines, regulations, and laws affecting the organization. Ideally, these internal controls should complement controls that already are in place within the accounting system. This is imperative because many problems OIG investigates center around the financial operations of the company, such as billing and collections. Compliance efforts are meant to encourage a culture that fosters prevention, detection, and resolution of conduct that is outside established company policies. The Federal Sentencing Guidelines also encourage compliance programs in order to reduce criminal fines and penalties.

The sentencing guidelines and the Department of Health and Human Services model plans have some basic characteristics to which a compliance program should adhere. The seven basic elements include:

- Develop and distribute policies that define standards and procedures to be followed by the organization's agents and employees. Specifically, the organization should establish standards of conduct which emphasize the organization's commitment to compliancy in areas such as Health Care Financing Administration (HCFA) regulations; fraud and abuse laws; federal, state, and local laws; and corporate ethical policies, mission, and goals. Annually circulate to every employee a standards of conduct statement that requires the signatures of all directors, officers, managers, employees, and contractors certifying that they have read, understand, and agree to comply with its terms;
- Designate or hire a high-level employee who has ultimate responsibility to operate and monitor the compliance program and to report directly to the CEO or governing body. This employee would be much like the company's own internal inspector general;
- Use reasonable care to identify sanctioned providers and remove those individuals from any activity that would violate a law or regulation. This can be done by dismissing the provider or reassigning him to an area of the company that does not have direct contact with patients covered by government insurance, or to an area that is neither directly nor indirectly reimbursed by a government program. If a sanctioned party works in the supply division, and part of the costs of that division are allocated on the Medicare cost report, then this could constitute a violation;

- Require regular training programs for all employees and contractors. Each entity should have some policy for educating managers, executives, and employees about fraud. This can be conducted during employee orientation and/or through ongoing training programs and other company communication methods. Initial and annual training for all staff, especially for those in the marketing, sales, and billing departments, is essential. Training should focus on billing policies and procedures, application of federal rules and regulations, disciplinary actions for non-compliance, personal responsibility of every employee to comply, HCFA policies and procedures, and fraud and abuse laws;
- Use various kinds of monitoring and proactive auditing systems to detect fraud and unusual trends to ensure compliance. There are many statistical aberrations that an experienced fraud examiner can monitor in a proactive manner to identify potential problem areas, such as noticeable variations in billing patterns. For instance, if suddenly there is a 200 percent increase in billing for physician consultations, the fraud examiner may wish to review those services to determine if simple office visits are being characterized fraudulently as more complex—and thus, more lucrative—consultations;
- Establish and publicize a reporting system in which employees can report criminal conduct without fear of retribution (hot line or ombudsman program). Each employee in the company should know where to report suspicious, unethical, or illegal behavior. Steps should include establishing a self-disclosure policy, which outlines procedures for reporting law violations to the appropriate authorities, and a records retention policy, which sets standards on how long records should be stored and in what format (electronic media, original paper document, etc.). The Office of Inspector General also has a Provider Self-disclosure Program (discussed in detail in the Federal Register dated Oct. 30, 1998) that offers a cooperative effort in reporting problems;
- Develop a system to respond to allegations, investigate those allegations, and, if needed, carry out the appropriate disciplinary measures. Be consistent and also discipline individuals who fail to detect the offense due to negligence. The compliance program should outline specifically who will investigate suspected irregularities, and to whom these irregularities will be reported (i.e., management, internal investigators, law enforcement, and/or legal counsel); and
- Regularly review for systemic weaknesses in company operations and/or policies and make changes as needed.

Essentially, what a compliance program is designed to do is provide insurance for the provider. By taking every reasonable and prudent step possible, a provider will have demonstrated to a prosecutor, judge, or jury that he has taken steps to prevent fraudulent activity from pervading his operations. Consequently, the damage to a provider's reputation, pocketbook, and freedom can be controlled and minimized to the fullest extent possible.

BANKRUPTCY (INSOLVENCY) FRAUD

Introduction

Bankruptcy Court

All bankruptcy cases are filed in the local district of the United States Bankruptcy Court. Bankruptcy judges hear all cases involving debtors' and creditors' rights, approve plans of reorganization, award fees to professionals, and conduct hearings and trials when necessary to resolve disputes.

Bankruptcy judges are not Article III (United States Constitution) judges. Article III states that judicial power of the United States rests with the Supreme Court and in inferior courts established by Congress. Bankruptcy courts are not contemplated within this scheme as "inferior" courts, but they are considered as an adjunct to "inferior" U.S. District Courts.

Office of the United States Trustee

The *Office of the Trustee* is a Department of Justice agency which is responsible for administering bankruptcy cases; appointing trustees, examiners, and Chapter 11 committees; overseeing and monitoring trustees; reviewing employment and fee applications; and appearing in court on matters of interest to the estate and creditors.

There are 21 regions in the Office of the U.S. Trustee comprising one or more federal districts. Each region consists of a U.S. Trustee (or an Assistant Trustee in several regions). The Office of the UST in each region principally is comprised of staff attorneys, bankruptcy analysts (including accountants) and, in some instances, special investigative units.

Staff attorneys review pleadings (e.g., fee applications and motions to appoint trustees and examiners) and represent the UST on these matters. *Bankruptcy analysts* analyze and review operating reports and other relevant financial information and, in general, oversee the debtor's case to assure compliance with the Bankruptcy Code and to protect the assets of the estate. *Special investigative units* investigate criminal referrals (complaints) in bankruptcy cases. In some cases they work with criminal investigative agencies, such as the Federal Bureau of Investigation and the Internal Revenue Service Criminal Investigative Division.

Panel trustees are independent professionals (usually attorneys) who serve in Chapter 7 cases in each federal district in the country. Trustees also might serve in Chapter 11 cases where operation of the debtor's business is considered appropriate. Trustees or others might develop a plan of reorganization to conclude the Chapter 11 proceedings. If the business cannot be reorganized, the trustee might petition the court to convert the case to Chapter 7 or develop a plan of liquidation under Chapter 11. The duties of a trustee are specifically enumerated in Title 11, U.S.C., Section 704 (in Chapter 7 cases) and Title 11, U.S.C., Section 1106 (in Chapter 11 cases). The duties of a trustee are as follows: administer assets, liquidate assets, pay creditors, litigate matters where necessary, have the right to sue and be sued, conduct hearings, conduct investigations of financial affairs of the debtor, file reports as required by the Office of the UST and, where appropriate, file criminal referrals with the United States Attorney's Office. A trustee's compensation is statutorily defined under the bankruptcy code.

Examiners

An *examiner* is normally appointed in a Chapter 11 bankruptcy proceeding to investigate certain allegations of fraud and misconduct on the part of the debtor (or principals of the debtor). In a typical motion for the appointment of a trustee or examiner, allegations of fraud or misconduct are raised by creditors, the Office of the UST, or other interested parties. A bankruptcy judge hears evidence submitted by all parties (creditors, et al), as well as the debtor's response to the allegations. After hearing the evidence, the judge has the option either to appoint a trustee or an examiner, or leave the debtor in possession of the business. If an examiner is appointed, the sole responsibility is to "investigate and report" the results of the investigation to the court and other parties in interest as quickly as possible. Examiners have the power to subpoena records and depose witnesses. They do not have the power to run businesses, make business decisions, or propose plans of reorganizations (generally speaking). Courts might expand the examiner's powers to perform certain duties of trustees or debtors-in-possession.

Debtors

A *debtor* is defined in Title 11, U.S.C., Section 101(13) as a "person" or "municipality" who is the subject of a filing under Title 11. "Person" is defined as an individual, partnership, or corporation. "Municipality" is defined as a political subdivision, public agency, or instrumentality of a state. An individual debtor's objective in a Chapter 7 case is to be relieved of all dischargeable debts and to obtain a fresh start. This is accomplished by the court granting the individual debtor a discharge. The debtor's primary objective in a Chapter 11 should be to have a plan of reorganization confirmed by the court and preserve the business operations.

Creditors

A *creditor* is defined by the code as one who holds a claim. Creditors can be either secured or unsecured.

Secured Creditors

A s*ecured creditor* holds a claim for which there is a properly perfected security interest. It will be considered a secured claim to the extent of the value of the property. When the debt is undersecured (amount of note is greater than the value of the security interest), the debt will be considered both unsecured and secured. For example, if a note for $500 is secured by property having a value of $400, there will be a secured claim for $400 and an unsecured claim for $100. If the debtor and the creditor cannot agree on the value of the collateral, there will be a hearing under Section 506 of the Bankruptcy Code and the court will determine the value of the collateral. The bankruptcy court will rely on state law where the property is located to determine if a secured claim exists. A security interest generally is obtained in personal property by a UCC filing and in real property by filing a lien with the county clerk in the county where the property is located.

At the time of the filing of the bankruptcy petition, an automatic stay precludes the creditor from taking any action to repossess the property, unless relief from the stay is granted. In a Chapter 11 case, the court generally will grant relief only if it can be shown that there is no equity in the property and that the property is not needed for reorganizing the business. The stay also might be removed if the property is declining in value and the debtor fails to compensate the creditor for this decline (referred to as "adequate protection payments"). If the stay is removed, the creditor then can proceed under state law to obtain possession of the property (often through a foreclosure) to satisfy the claim.

Holders of secured claims have priority over unsecured creditors and normally get paid first in the distributions to creditors made by the trustee or debtor-in-possession. In the development of a Chapter 11 plan, the rights of holders of secured claims normally are provided for before the unsecured claim holders will receive material consideration.

Unsecured Creditors

Unsecured creditors are those that have a claim against the debtor that arose before the bankruptcy petition was filed and do not have a perfected security interest. Title 11, U.S.C., Section 507 gives some of the holders of unsecured claims priority over other unsecured claim holders. Among those claims that have priority are administrative expenses (costs associated with the operation of the business and professional fees while the business or individual is in bankruptcy), selected prepetition unpaid wages, prepetition contributions required but not made to employees benefit plans, prepetition unpaid alimony and support payments, and selected prepetition tax claims.

Adjusters

Adjusters, or operations agents as they are frequently called, are the "right hand" to trustees and debtors. An adjuster or operations agent is an individual who handles the peripheral duties of a trustee. Such duties include securing the business location, changing locks, locating assets of the estate, locating business records, opening new bank accounts, investigating thefts of assets in conjunction with the trustee, storing assets of the estate, and arranging sales of assets. Adjusters also can assist debtors and trustees in operating the debtor's business and in helping to prepare bankruptcy schedules, as well as interim statements and operating reports.

The Bankruptcy Code (Title 11, United States Code)

The Bankruptcy Code is broken down into eight chapters (1, 3, 5, 7, 9, 11, 12, and 13) under Title 11 of the United States Code. These chapters are "odd" numbered, except for Chapter 12. In addition, there are two other sources of information dealing with bankruptcy issues which are found in the United States Code. They can be found at Title 18, U.S.C., Chapter 9 (which deals with crimes and criminal procedure) and Title 28, (which deals with the judiciary and judicial procedure). Some of the provisions of the Bankruptcy Code, as amended by the Bankruptcy Reform Act of 1994, are outlined below:

Chapter 1 — General Provisions

Chapter 1 contains definitions, rules of construction, powers of the court, who can be a debtor, and other miscellaneous information. Chapter 1 has been amended to reflect issues dealing with persons who negligently or fraudulently prepare bankruptcy petitions. Section 101 of this chapter is particularly important as it deals with definitions of terms used in bankruptcy proceedings. Section 110 deals with the penalty for persons who negligently or fraudulently prepare bankruptcy petitions (see later section on criminal conduct).

Chapter 3 — Case Administration

Part 1 of Chapter 3 deals with the commencement of cases, filing requirements, and court appearances. Part 2 deals with officers, the qualifications of the trustee, the role of the trustee, and the compensation of trustees and other officers. Part 3 deals with administration, involving meetings of creditors, noticing requirements, property of the estate, and other administrative requirements. Part 4 deals with administrative powers, including the power of the trustee to protect property of the estate; use, lease or sell the property and obtaining credit on behalf of the estate.

Chapter 5 — Creditors, Debtors, and the Estate

Part 1 deals with creditors' claims, their priority, and their allowance. This section contains the prioritization of claims and the distribution of estate assets. Part 2 deals with specific duties of the debtor, the exemptions debtors can claim, and dischargeability of debts. Part 3 deals with property of the estate, recovery of voidable transfers, and contractual rights of the estate.

Chapter 7 — Liquidation of Debtor's Assets

Part 1 of Chapter 7 deals with officers and the administration of Chapter 7 cases and spells out duties of the trustee. Part 2 deals with the collection, liquidation, and distribution of the estate's assets. Part 3 deals with stockbroker liquidations. Part 4 deals with commodity broker liquidations.

Chapter 11 — Reorganization

Chapter 11 deals with debtors in reorganization. The code allows for debtors to restructure their debt, pay their creditors, and emerge from bankruptcy. Part 1 of the chapter deals with officers and administration. Part 2 deals with the plan of reorganization. Part 3 deals with postconfirmation matters. Part 4 deals with railroad reorganization.

The purpose of the Chapter 11 filing is to allow the debtor breathing room from the creditors so that the debtor can reorganize its financial affairs and continue as a going concern. If the court is provided with sufficient probable cause regarding the financial affairs of the debtor, a trustee or examiner can be appointed by the court.

Trustees

Grounds for the Appointment of a Trustee

Title 11, U.S.C., Section 1104 states in part:

(a) At any time after the commencement of the case but before confirmation of a plan, on request of a party in interest or the United States trustee, and after a notice and a hearing, the court shall order the appointment of a trustee:

(1) for cause, including fraud, dishonesty, incompetence, or gross mismanagement of the affairs of the debtor by current management, either before or after the commencement of the case ...

(2) if such appointment is in the interest of creditors, any equity security holders, and other interests of the estate ...

(b) Except as provided in Section 1163 of this title, on the request of a party in interest made not later than 30 days after the court orders the appointment of a trustee under subsection (a), the United States trustee shall convene a meeting of creditors for the purpose of electing one disinterested person to serve as trustee in the case...

(c) If the court does not order the appointment of a trustee under this Section, then at any time before the confirmation of a plan, on request of a party in interest or the United States trustee, and after notice and a hearing, the court shall order the appointment of an examiner to conduct such an investigation of the debtor as is appropriate, including an investigation of any allegations of fraud, dishonesty, incompetence, misconduct, mismanagement, or irregularity in the management of the affairs of the debtor of or by current or former management of the debtor....

The Role of the Trustee in Bankruptcy Fraud Matters

The trustee in bankruptcy matters is often confronted with allegations of fraud and misconduct on the part of the debtor and its principals. In Chapter 11 cases, it is often the primary reason the court appointed a trustee. Creditors, representatives of the creditors' committee, or private investigators might be interacting with a bankruptcy trustee. For this reason, it is important to know how the trustee operates, what the role of the trustee is, and how to make the most of the opportunity to work with the trustee. The trustee's authority to investigate fraud is found in the Bankruptcy Code. The following is a brief outline of the Chapter 7 and Chapter 11 trustee's authority to investigate fraud.

Statutory Authority

In Chapter 7 cases, Section 704 of the code spells out all duties of the trustee, which include reducing the property of the estate to cash, investigating claims filed by creditors, filing reports, paying creditors, and investigating the financial affairs of the debtor. The code also provides that the trustee "shall ... investigate the financial affairs of the debtor ... ."

Chapter 11 follows the duties previously described in Section 704 with the major exception of operating the debtor's business. Pursuant to Sections 1106 and 1108, Chapter 11 trustees can take control of the debtor's business, make decisions regarding the operations of the business, hire and fire employees, and attempt to retain or enhance the value of the business until it can be sold or reorganized. Sections 1106(a)(3) and (a)(4) state:

> *A trustee shall ... except to the extent that the court orders otherwise, investigate the acts, conduct, assets, liabilities, and financial condition of the debtor, the operation of the debtor's business and the desirability of the continuance of such business and ... as soon as practicable ... file a statement of any investigation conducted ... including any fact ascertained pertaining to fraud, dishonesty, incompetence, misconduct, mismanagement, or irregularity in the management of the affairs of the debtor, or to a cause of action available to the estate ....*

Investigation by the Trustee

The trustee's powers enable him to gather financial information from various sources including the debtor's attorneys and accountants. A trustee steps into the shoes of the debtor which allows him the opportunity to break the attorney-client privilege. Attorneys might attempt to raise the attorney-client privilege as a defense to providing information, but they are usually unsuccessful in this regard. Since the trustee is now the client, he must be able to understand what legal actions need to be taken. Therefore, it is imperative that the debtor's attorney cooperate with the trustee. The trustee also should have access to the accountant's work papers, tax returns, and client documents in their possession which might provide the trustee and creditors with the opportunity to locate and recover hidden assets. Another useful tool in the trustee's arsenal is the power to have access to debtor's records that are in the possession of the criminal authorities. Since the trustee steps into the shoes of the debtor, he has the right to inspect and use these records to conduct the business affairs of the debtor.

After the trustee concludes an investigation and sufficient evidence of fraud exists, a report detailing the results of the investigation should be filed with the United States Attorney. This duty is spelled out in Title 18, United States Code, Section 3057 as follows:

(a) Any judge, receiver, or trustee having reasonable grounds for believing that any violation under chapter 9 of this Title or other laws of the United States relating to insolvent debtors ... or that an investigation should be had in connection therewith, shall report to the appropriate United States attorney all the facts and circumstances of the case, the names of the witnesses, and the offense or offenses believed to have been committed ....

(b) The United States attorney thereupon shall inquire into the facts and report thereon to the judge, and if it appears probable that any such offense has been committed, shall without delay, present the matter to the grand jury, unless upon inquiry and examination he decides that the ends of public justice do not require investigation or prosecution, in which case he shall report the facts to the Attorney General for his direction.

Sources of Information

The trustee should obtain the various documents and/or information listed below in the course of an investigation. If any of this information is unavailable, the trustee can subpoena these documents. The subpoenaed documents could either be the original documents, certified copies of these documents, or other information which could be used to reconstruct the missing documents.

Type of Information	Location
Debtor's petition, schedules, statement of financial affairs	Bankruptcy Court's Office and UST
Interim and operating statements	Bankruptcy Court and UST
Adversary proceedings, claims registers, transcripts of hearings, 2004 examinations	Bankruptcy Court
Fee applications	Bankruptcy Court and UST
Real property records	County Clerk, County Assessor
Personal property records	County Clerk
UCC filings	Secretary of State
Financial statements	Lending institutions, debtor's counsel, accountants, Chapter 7 or Chapter 11 filings
Forwarding address	Post Office
DBAs	County recorder; Secretary of State
Partnerships	Secretary of State
Officers of corporations	Secretary of State
Addresses of individuals	Voting records

Insurance policies	Insurance company providing coverage
Current or prior business activities	Interviews conducted of creditors, former employees, former spouses, former business activities
Criminal history, current or prior litigation	Police records, local court records
Tapes and transcripts of sworn testimony [341(a) and 2004 examinations]	UST - 341(a) exams Bankruptcy Court - 2004 exams

Investigative Procedures

In order to fulfill their fiduciary investigative responsibilities, trustees need to gather financial information. If debtor's books and records are missing, incomplete or unreliable, they should be obtained from third parties such as banks, customers, related parties, etc. If the third-party resists the trustee's request, the trustee can subpoena records or testimony under Bankruptcy Rule 2004. After receiving third-party records and testimony, the trustee might then:

- Reconstruct cash receipts and cash disbursements journals, and general ledgers.
- Identify new bank accounts, related-party transactions, and hidden or concealed assets.
- Take 2004 exams (depositions) of uncooperative witnesses.
- Take 2004 exams of third-party witnesses and others who can authenticate documents, records, etc.
- Obtain declaration testimony from cooperative witnesses.
- Interview witnesses—determine direct versus indirect knowledge of facts. Bookkeepers are good sources of information who can provide information regarding cash receipts and disbursements, related-parties transactions, and evidence regarding destruction of records.
- After documentary and other evidence has been gathered and analyzed, the trustee should prepare an investigative report.
- If allegations of fraud are present, file a separate report pursuant to Title 18, Section 3057 (filed with United States Attorney's Office).

Creditors' Rights and Remedies

Normally when businesses or individuals are not paid, they attempt to collect amounts owed to them. When normal collection efforts fail, they resort to legal action. When legal action is met with the filing of a bankruptcy petition by the debtor, what steps can the creditor take?

- Investigate the reasons why payment has not been made.
  - Check with other creditors to see if they have not been paid.

- Check with credit bureaus for credit history.
- File a motion for the appointment of a trustee; other creditors and the office of the UST might join in with the petitioning creditor.
- To succeed, the moving party must demonstrate that fraud is suspected, and, therefore, a trustee should be appointed to oversee the operations of the debtor.
- The creditor should have sufficient documentary and other evidence of fraudulent conduct, including declarations provided by knowledgeable witnesses.
- A hearing is held where the judge hears evidence supporting and refuting the fraud allegations. Thereafter, the judge issues a ruling regarding the appointment of a trustee.
- In some cases, the judge might appoint an examiner instead of a trustee because it is less intrusive. An examiner's role is only to investigate and report back to the judge whether the allegations of fraud are supported by the independent examiner's own evidence.
- If the debtor does not file bankruptcy, the creditor might join other creditors and file an involuntary petition against the debtor.

Creditors' Committees

After filing a Chapter 11 bankruptcy petition, the UST normally appoints a committee of creditors holding unsecured claims. This committee is referred to as a creditors' committee. Title 11, U.S.C., Section 1102 provides guidance in the formation of creditors' committees.

Title 11, U.S.C., Section 1103 details the powers of creditors' committees. They can employ attorneys, accountants, or other agents to assist them in the performance of their duties under the code. In carrying out their duties, creditors' committees are authorized to consult with the trustee or debtor-in-possession concerning the administration of the case; to investigate the acts, conduct, assets, liabilities, and financial condition of the debtor and the operation of the debtor's business; to participate in the formation of a plan of reorganization; to request the appointment of a trustee or examiner; and to perform such other services as are in the interest of those represented.

Involuntary Petitions (Title 11, U.S.C., Section 303)

Most bankruptcy cases are of the voluntary nature. As we have described above, debtors have specific reasons for filing bankruptcy. Individuals, partnerships, and corporations have the statutory right to file bankruptcy as a protection from their creditors. In exchange for exercising their privilege of filing bankruptcy, debtors give up their right to financial privacy and must do other things required under the code.

Most creditors do not want the debtor to file bankruptcy because it might make the recovery on their claim more difficult. It also might diminish the amount they receive on their claim. Prior to a bankruptcy filing, aggressive creditors might sue the debtor in state court in an attempt to collect amounts owed to them or to obtain a judgment against the debtor. Numerous collection actions can be brought against the debtor which might lead to competition to seize the debtor's remaining assets. When this occurs, the debtor normally files bankruptcy to prevent these creditors from seizing its assets. In some rare instances, the filing of an involuntary petition is an extraordinary remedy which is available to creditors. It runs contrary to their normal inclination to do everything they can to keep debtors out of bankruptcy.

That being said, involuntary petitions serve a very important purpose; they can be used to stop the financial hemorrhaging that usually takes place in fraudulently operated businesses. Involuntary petitions also allow the creditors to control the debtor and protect the value of the business while investigating the financial affairs of the debtor.

An involuntary petition can only be filed under Chapters 7 and 11. Creditors who have not been paid by the debtor can file a petition forcing the company into bankruptcy. Generally, the creditors must be able to demonstrate in court that the debtor is not paying debts as they mature.

In order to commence the filing of an involuntary proceeding, creditors must satisfy the following criteria:
- The debts must not be subject to a bona fide dispute and must be noncontingent.
- The creditor(s) must be owed at least $12,300 more than the value of the lien or collateral.
- If there are 12 or more creditors, then three creditors are needed to file.
- If there are fewer than 12 creditors, only one creditor is needed to file.

A court hearing is held following the filing of the involuntary petition. After this hearing, the court might dismiss the petition or enter an order for relief. However, if the court deems it necessary, an interim trustee might be appointed to preserve the property of the estate. At the hearing on the involuntary petition, the creditors are required to demonstrate, through direct testimony, that the alleged debtor is not paying debts as they come due.

Creditors must be careful regarding the filing of an involuntary petition. If the creditors are not successful in court and the judge dismisses the petition, they might be sued by the debtor. Damages for lost profits and goodwill could be assessed against the creditors who filed the involuntary petition. Occasionally, in egregious circumstances, courts have awarded punitive damages against creditors who filed an involuntary petition.

Investigations by Creditors

Individual creditors might conduct their own investigations and also assist Chapter 7 and Chapter 11 trustees in performing their investigations. Trustees are normally very appreciative of creditors who can provide information regarding the financial affairs of the debtor. Creditors also can attend the 341(a) examination of the debtor and ask pertinent questions. Creditors who bring copies of documents, such as prior loan applications or pictures of particular assets, to the 341(a) examination are of great interest to trustees. Creditors can ask the debtor what happened to the various assets listed on the loan applications or assets shown in photographs.

Bankruptcy Crime Statutes

Bankruptcy crimes which are committed during the course of a bankruptcy proceeding, or in contemplation of a bankruptcy proceeding, are contained in federal statutes. They are carried out through the filing of a bankruptcy petition either to accomplish the purpose of the crime or to cover up another crime that has already been perpetrated.

Although the Bankruptcy code is contained within Title 11, U.S. Code, bankruptcy crimes appear within Title 18, U.S. Code, Sections 151 through 155. Section 152 is the most comprehensive of the individual bankruptcy crime statutes. To constitute and be proved as a federal crime, bankruptcy crimes must have been committed *during the pendency of a bankruptcy proceeding, with the defendant's knowledge*, and *with a fraudulent intent* to defeat the bankruptcy laws. The FBI investigates bankruptcy crimes and the U.S. Attorney's office prosecutes them. The Law section provides more information.

Defendants cannot use as a defense to charges the fact that creditors have actual knowledge of concealed assets or that the concealment was not from all creditors. They also cannot use as a defense the fact that they returned the estate's assets, though this might mitigate damages.

Generally, the penalty for each bankruptcy offense is a fine (of up to $500,000 in the case of bankruptcy fraud committed by an organization) or imprisonment for not more than five years, or both. The statute of limitations does not run until the fraud is detected or the debtor receives a discharge or is denied a discharge pursuant to the Bankruptcy Code.

This procedure is spelled out in Title 18, U.S.C., Section 3284, which states:

> *The concealment of assets of a debtor in a case under Title 11 shall be deemed to be a continuing offense until the debtor shall have been finally discharged or a discharge denied, and the period of limitations shall not begin to run until such final discharge or denial of discharge.*

The following sections set out the bankruptcy crime statutes as well as related criminal statutes that frequently arise in bankruptcy cases.

Title 18, U.S. Code, Section 151

This section contains the definition of the term *debtor*, a party who has filed a petition under Title 11 of the U.S. Code.

Title 18, U.S. Code, Section 152

This is the most comprehensive criminal bankruptcy fraud statute. Nine paragraphs define various offenses against the bankruptcy laws. The following is a brief overview of each offense.

Paragraph 1 — Concealment of Property

> *A person who knowingly and fraudulently conceals from a custodian, trustee, marshal, or other officer of the court charged with the control or custody of property, or, in connection with a case under Title 11, from creditors or the United States Trustee, any property belonging to the estate of a debtor;*

For purposes of this paragraph, estate property consists of assets, records, and anything of value.

Paragraph 2 — False Oath or Account

False oaths apply to oral testimony that might be given in 341(a) examinations, 2004 examinations (depositions), and testimony provided at hearings and trials.

> *A person who knowingly and fraudulently makes a false oath or account in or in relation to any case under Title 11.*

Paragraph 3 — False Declarations

> *A person who knowingly and fraudulently makes a false declaration, certificate, verification or statement under penalty of perjury as permitted under section 1746 of Title 28, in or in relation to any case under Title 11.*

Written documents filed with the court under penalty of perjury consist of the debtor's petition, schedules and statements of financial affairs, interim statements and operating reports, as well as declarations filed with the court. Declarations are made in petitions, schedules and in other court filings (motions). This section gives the same weight to unsworn declarations as to those sworn under penalty of perjury.

Paragraph 4 — False Claims

> *A person who knowingly and fraudulently presents any false claim for proof against the estate of a debtor, or uses any such claim in any case under Title 11, in a personal capacity or as or through an agent, proxy, or attorney.*

The purpose of this paragraph is to prevent fictitious or inflated claims from being filed by creditors or others in a bankruptcy case.

Paragraph 5 — Fraudulent Receipt of Property

> *A person who knowingly and fraudulently receives any material amount of property from a debtor after the filing of a case under Title 11 with intent to defeat the provisions of Title 11 ....*

This paragraph relates back to paragraph 1, above, and it implicates those who work in concert with the debtor. This could be a creditor or any other interested party.

Paragraph 6 — Extortion and Bribery

> *A person who knowingly and fraudulently gives, offers, receives or attempts to obtain any money or property, remuneration, compensation, reward, advantage, or promise thereof, for acting or forbearing to act in any case under Title 11 ....*

This paragraph covers bribery, which also is spelled out in Title 18, principally Sections 210 and 1503. Both Sections discuss the attempt to bribe judicial officers and to unlawfully corrupt or influence any officer of the court. Section 1503 also covers threats intended to influence, intimidate, or impede an officer in the performance of his duties.

Paragraph 7 — Fraudulent Transfer or Concealment

> *A person who in a personal capacity or as agent or officer of any person or corporation, in contemplation of a case under Title 11 by or against him or any other person or corporation, or with intent to defeat the provisions of Title 11, knowingly and fraudulently transfers or conceals any of his property or the property of such other person or corporation ....*

This paragraph is the only paragraph under Section 152 which deals with pre-bankruptcy conduct. The Section addresses situations where a bankruptcy petition filing is imminent. It is intended to cover actions by individuals who transfer property rightfully belonging to the creditors of the prospective bankruptcy estate.

Paragraph 8 — Fraudulent Destruction or Alteration of Documents

> *A person who, after the filing of a case under Title 11 or in contemplation thereof, knowingly and fraudulently conceals, destroys, mutilates, falsifies, or makes a false entry in any recorded information (including books, documents, records, and papers) relating to the property or financial affairs of a debtor ....*

Paragraph 9 — Fraudulent Withholding of Documents

> *A person who, after the filing of a case under Title 11, knowingly and fraudulently withholds from a custodian, trustee, marshal, or other officer of the court or a United States Trustee entitled to its possession, any recorded information (including books, documents, records, and papers) relating to the property or financial affairs of a debtor ....*

This Section is particularly useful in cases where the debtor does not turn over estate records after being compelled to do so by the court, and the records are later discovered by federal authorities during the execution of search warrants.

Embezzlement Against the Estate, Title 18, U.S. Code, Section 153

(a) Offense. A person described in subsection (b) who knowingly and fraudulently appropriates to the person's own use, embezzles, spends, or transfers any property or secretes or destroys any document belonging to the estate of a debtor ....

(b) Person to Whom Section Applies. A person described in this subsection is one who has access to property or documents belonging to an estate by virtue of the person's participation in the administration of the estate as a trustee, custodian, marshal, attorney, or other officer of the court or as an agent, employee, or other person engaged by such an officer to perform a service with respect to the estate.

This statute deals with all property and the records or documents that the court officer receives during the tenure of the trustee or officer.

Adverse Interest and Conduct of Officers, Title 18, U.S. Code, Section 154

A person who, being a custodian, trustee, marshal, or other officer of the court—
(1) knowingly purchases, directly or indirectly, any property of the estate of which the person is such an officer in a case under Title 11; (2) knowingly refuses to permit a reasonable opportunity for the inspection by parties in interest of the documents and accounts relating to the affairs of estates in the person's charge by parties when directed by the court to do so; or (3) knowingly refuses to permit a reasonable opportunity for the inspection by the United States Trustee of the documents and accounts relating to the affairs of any estate in the person's charge ... .

Bankruptcy trustees are in a position of trust and, therefore, should be held to a higher standard of conduct than other interested parties. But one critical aspect is the sale of estate property. Trustees can influence the sale of property and can make significant profits if they directly or indirectly purchase assets of the estate. It would be similar to insider trading by individuals in the securities industry. This statute is unlike the others listed above in that a violation of this statute is only a misdemeanor, whereas all of the above are felonies. Conviction under this Section carries a fine, as well as forfeiture of the person's office.

Knowing Disregard of Bankruptcy Law or Rule, Title 18, U.S. Code, Section 156

(a) Definitions. In this section "bankruptcy petition preparer" means a person, other than the debtor's attorney or an employee of such an attorney, who prepares for compensation a document for filing.

"document for filing" means a petition or any other document prepared for filing by a debtor in a United States bankruptcy court or a United States district court in connection with a case under this Title.

(b) Offense. If a bankruptcy case or related proceeding is dismissed because of a knowing attempt by a bankruptcy petition preparer in any manner to disregard the requirements of Title 11, United States Code, or the Federal Rules of Bankruptcy Procedure... .

This Section is the criminal version of the Title 11, U.S.C., Section 110, which deals with "petition mills" and petition preparers who deliberately disregard the Bankruptcy Code or any of its rules and procedures. Petition mills and preparers who fall under this Section might file false documents for debtors with deliberately wrong Social Security numbers or other incorrect information. In some cases, debtors might not even be aware they are filing bankruptcy or the effect of a bankruptcy on their credit rating.

Bankruptcy Fraud, Title 18, U.S. Code, Section 157

A person who, having devised or intending to devise a scheme or artifice to defraud and for the purpose of executing or concealing such a scheme or artifice or attempting to do so — (1) files a petition under Title 11; (2) files a document in a proceeding under Title 11; or (3) makes a false or fraudulent representation, claim, or promise concerning or in relation to a proceeding under Title 11, at any time before or after the filing of the petition, or in relation to a proceeding falsely asserted to be pending under such Title ... .

This Section is very similar to mail and wire fraud statutes both in wording and in concept. This Section applies to insiders who perpetrate bustout schemes, as well as those who attempt to obtain credit immediately prior to filing bankruptcy.

Bankruptcy-Related Violations

Although bankruptcy crimes are the focus of this section, there are other crimes that are usually perpetrated prior to the filing of a bankruptcy petition. In some cases, the bankruptcy process is the culmination of a pattern of prior criminal activity. There are many other crimes frequently associated with bankruptcy including mail fraud, wire fraud, bank fraud, interstate transportation of stolen goods or property, aiding or abetting, false statements, conspiracy, tax evasion, and money laundering. Bankruptcy fraud is also a predicate offense under RICO. For more information on these offenses, see the Law section.

Although the criminal aspects of bankruptcy crimes are heard in District Court, the underlying facts dealing with a debtor's misconduct also are heard in the form of civil proceedings before the United States Bankruptcy Court. Parallel proceedings occur in cases where bankruptcy fraud allegations have been made. Several examples of civil proceedings that ensue as a result of fraud allegations against the debtor are motions for the appointment of trustees and examiners, lawsuits for recovery of fraudulently transferred property, and objections to the debtor's discharge.

Bankruptcy Schemes

Concealed Assets

The most common crime is the concealment of assets rightfully belonging to the debtor estate. Assets might consist of cash, consumer property, houses, and interests in partnerships and corporations, as well as lawsuits in which the debtor is a plaintiff. Assets also include books and records of the debtor. Concealments vary from little or no monetary value to tens of millions of dollars. The various concealment offenses are described in more detail under the bankruptcy crime statutes.

The Planned "Bustout"

A *bustout* is a planned bankruptcy. It can take many different forms. The basic approach is for an apparently legitimate business to order large quantities of goods on credit, then dispose of those goods through legitimate or illegitimate channels. The perpetrators then close shop, absconding with the proceeds, and leaving the suppliers unpaid.

Bustout schemes are planned and perpetrated by individuals both prior to and subsequent to the formation of the new business entity. Other characteristics of bustout schemes follow:
- They are planned from the beginning.
- Sometimes organized crime is involved.

- Credit is established with numerous vendors; prompt payments are made to all vendors; vendors feel comfortable in dealings, thereby extending existing credit lines.
- Perpetrators build inventory by ordering everything they can from vendors; they promise to pay soon and order more merchandise.
- Sell out inventory at deep discount or move it before vendors can take possession of it.
- Business fails or closes up, files bankruptcy, or creditors beat them to it with involuntary bankruptcy.

Detection
Some red flags that signal that a bustout scheme might be in process include:
- A business relationship based principally on trust. Creditors are willing to offer extended terms for payment, hold checks, or take post-dated checks. This makes them vulnerable.
- Buyers with a history of purchasing goods for an unreasonable discount.
- A large number of bank accounts, indicating a possible kiting scheme. The perpetrator occasionally pays some of his creditors with funds generated by floating checks between bank accounts.

Prevention
Lenders and suppliers should evaluate potential customers carefully prior to extending credit by performing due diligence and obtaining detailed background information. Lenders and suppliers should at times visit their customers' locations to verify the legitimacy of the businesses.

Multiple Filings
This scheme involves repeated bankruptcy filings by the same debtor in order to obtain the benefit of the automatic stay. Usually each petition is dismissed for failure to file the required statements or to appear for examination. False statements on petitions are common, including a denial that the debtor has filed any previous petition.

Credit Card Bustout
The debtor intentionally runs up a number of credit cards to their limit and files bankruptcy with no intent to repay. Credit card debts might include purchases for jewelry, luxury items, or other personal property which are not disclosed on the schedules. Credit card debt also might include large cash advances taken prior to filing bankruptcy.

Forged Filings

Bankruptcy petitions sometimes are filed in another (uninvolved) person's name, usually as part of a larger scheme using an assumed identity. It can take years to correct the credit records of the person whose identity has been stolen. Sometimes the debtor's name is obtained from obituary notices.

"Typing Services" or "Petition Mills"

This scheme involves companies which file bankruptcy petitions typically on behalf of low-income, and often, unsuspecting clients. The petitions often contain numerous false statements. The debtor often has no idea a bankruptcy has been filed, as the service has held itself out to be a renter's rights group and has not told the client how it will accomplish what it has promised.

TAX FRAUD

Introduction

The most important distinction in determining whether an individual or company has committed tax fraud is whether the tax-filing party intentionally filed an improper tax return with the federal government. The intent of the party to wrongly file a return will determine the difference between tax *avoidance* and tax *evasion*. The U.S. courts have determined evasion to be unlawful, while avoidance has been deemed lawful.

The definition of tax fraud is

> *... the actual intentional wrongdoing, and the intent required ... to evade a tax believed to be owing. Fraud implies bad faith, intentional wrongdoing, and a sinister motive. It is never imputed or presumed and the courts will not sustain findings of fraud upon circumstances which at most create only suspicion.*[*]

This definition tells us that a false tax return is considered fraudulent if the responsible party has knowingly attempted to defraud the government of owed tax dollars. In, *U.S. v. Pomponio*,[†] the courts further refined the scope of tax fraud by stating that willfulness is "... a voluntary, intentional violation of a known legal duty, (that) does not require proof of an evil motive." It can thus be accepted that accidental false tax returns do not qualify as fraudulent returns.

Fraudulent Intent

An example of *fraudulent intent* is the filing of a tax return in the wrong district, when the taxpayer (a CPA) knew or had reason to know the proper district (*Spencer D. Lorton v. Commissioner*, TC Memo 1954 – 872).

Objectively Reasonable "Good Faith" Misunderstanding of the Law

Good faith or a legitimate misunderstanding of the requirements of the law negates willfulness, [*U.S. v. Cheek*, 91-1 USTC ¶ 50,012 (7th Cir 1991), aff'd. 111 U.S. 604 (1991)]. The case held, however, that the belief that taxes are in violation of the Constitution was not "objectively reasonable" so as to negate willfulness.

---

[*] 14 Mertens, Law of Federal Income Taxation, sec. 55.21, page 64, (1991 Rev); Ross Glove Co. v. Commissioner, 60 TC 569 (1973).

[†] U.S. v. Pomponio, 429 U.S. 10 (1976); 76-2 USTC 9695.

Willfulness can be inferred from conduct, such as:
- Keeping a double set of books (not to be confused with GAAP and tax records)
- Making false entries or alterations or creating false invoices or documents
- Destruction of books or records
- Concealment of assets (illicit income)
- Covering up sources of income
- Avoiding making records usual in transactions of the kind
- Conduct that misleads or conceals [*Spies v. U.S.*, 317 U.S. 492 (1943); 43-1 USTC ¶ 9243.]

Hallmarks (Badges) of Fraud

The courts recognize certain hallmarks or badges of tax fraud. Some of these are:
- Misrepresentation of facts
- Artifice
- Device to hide income or assets
- Double set of books
- Secret bank accounts under false names
- Overstatement of deductions
- Fictitious transactions

Fraud is More Than a Mistake in Judgment

The failure to know and understand the rules of "first in, first out" (FIFO) is not sufficient to sustain a fraud charge, *Smith v. Commissioner*, 40 BTA 387, supplemental opinion 42 BTA 505. There was no indication in this case that the taxpayer misrepresented any fact, withheld any information, or resisted or prevented the discovery by the commissioner of any pertinent data.

False vs. Fraudulent

Definitions of False

- When "false" appears by itself, and not coupled with a penalty or the creation of an offense, then false means incorrect [*Eliot National Bank v. Gill*, 218 F. 600 (1st Cir 1914)].
- False means it is incorrect, but made in good faith [*National Bank of Commerce in St. Louis v. Allen*, 223 F. 472 (8th Cir 1915)].
- *Statements of opinion*, as distinguished from those of material fact, are not fraud [*Ohio Brass Co. v. Commissioner*, 17 BTA 1199 (1929)].

Corporate Fraud

Corporate fraud depends on the intent of the corporate officers [*Auerbach Shoe Co. v. Commissioner*, 21 TC 191; aff'd. 216 F.2d 693; 54-2 USTC ¶ 9673 (1st Cir. 1953)].

EXAMPLE

Charging airline tickets to "air freight" (a false representation) coupled with the failure to credit refunds for redeemed tickets to the corporation was sufficient to render the corporate returns fraudulent [Kreps v. Commissioner, *42 TC 660 (1964)* aff'd*, 351 F.2d 1; 65-2 USTC ¶ 9652 (2nd Cir 1965)].*

EXAMPLE

A 40 percent shareholder/officer of a corporation embezzled corporate funds for her personal use, then falsified corporate records. The corporation incorrectly claimed deductions based on the false records. The fraud claim was not sustained against the corporation [Botwinik Bros. of Mass., Inc. v. Commissioner, *39 TC 988 (1963)].*

Burden of Proof

In July of 1998, President Clinton signed into law the IRS Restructuring and Reform Act. This Act made sweeping changes in the structure and procedures of the IRS. One of the most important changes involves the shift of the burden of proof in civil cases. The general rule prior to the Act was that the taxpayer bears the burden of proof at trial in civil proceedings. The Statutory Notice of Deficiency (90-day letter) enjoyed the presumption of correctness. The presumption of correctness in favor of the IRS required the taxpayer to go forward with prima facie evidence to disprove the IRS's determination. After successfully rebutting the presumption of correctness, taxpayers had the burden of proving their case by at least a preponderance of the evidence.

However the new rule established under the Reform Act is that IRS has the burden of proof in civil court proceedings on income, gift, estate, or generation-skipping tax liability with respect to factual issues that are relevant to determining the taxpayer's tax liability, provided the taxpayer: (i) provides credible evidence on the factual issue; (ii) keeps records and backs up items as presently required under the Code and regulations; and (iii) cooperates with IRS in regard to reasonable requests for meetings, interviews, witnesses, information, and documents. Corporations, trusts, and partnerships with a net worth in excess of $7 million continue to bear the burden of proof. The Senate Finance Committee Report states that if the taxpayer's evidence and the IRS's evidence are equally balanced, the court should find that the IRS has not sustained its burden of proof.

The new provisions shift the burden of proof to the IRS in court proceedings arising out of tax audits beginning after July 22, 1998. In court proceedings involving a matter where there was no tax examination, the new burden of proof provisions apply in court proceedings relating to tax periods beginning (or events occurring) after July 22, 1998.

Fraud

Even under the old IRS Code, there was no presumption of correctness afforded the IRS when fraud was involved. Therefore, the Service had the burden of proving fraud, [*Armstrong v. U.S.*, 354 F.2d 274; 173 Ct.Cl. 944 (1965)]. If the fraud claim is for more than one year, the Service must show that some part of the underpayment was due to fraud for each year that the penalty is added [*Professional Services v. Commissioner*, 79 TC 888 (1982)]. First, there must be a *deficiency* and second, the deficiency must be substantial [*U.S. v. Morse*, 491 F.2d 149; 74-1 USTC ¶ 9228 (1st Cir 1974)]. *Substantiality* is a question of fact [*U.S. v. Marks*, 282 F. Supp. 546 (D Or 1966), aff'd 391 F.2d 210; 68-1 USTC ¶ 9260 (9th Cir 1968); cert denied 393 U.S. 839 (1968)]. There is controversy about whether substantiality applies to the unpaid tax or to unreported income.

Civil vs. Criminal

Although the burden of proving fraud is on the Service, the primary determinant of whether the Service pursues a civil rather than a criminal fraud charge is what it believes it can prove. There also might be budgetary and staffing constraints that might dictate whether a suit is pursued civilly or criminally.

The difference between civil and criminal in the view of the IRS is that a civil case never ripens into a crime, and criminal offenses involve behavior too insidious to be disposed of on a civil basis. Failure to cooperate might raise a civil case to a crime because it might demonstrate willful intent.

Taxpayer Penalties

Civil

Negligence, Title 26, U.S.C., § 6662

Negligence is strongly indicated where information is omitted on tax returns or deductions are "too good to be true."

A penalty based on a percentage of the underpayment will be imposed on any of the following: (1) negligence or disregard of rules and regulations, (2) any substantial understatement of income tax, (3) any substantial valuation misstatement, (4) any substantial overstatement of pension liabilities, or (5) any substantial understatement of estate or gift tax valuations.

Frivolous Return, Title 26, U.S.C., § 6702

A penalty of $500 shall be assessed in addition to other penalties for a frivolous return. An example of a frivolous return is one in Roman numerals rather than the commonly used Arabic numbers.

Fraud, Title 26, U.S.C., § 6663

A penalty of 75 percent of the underpayment is imposed if *any* part of the underpayment is due to fraud. If the taxpayer is successful in proving that a portion of the underpayment is not the result of fraud, then that portion might still be subject to the negligence penalty.

Criminal

Tax Evasion, Title 26, U.S.C., § 7201

A penalty shall be imposed, if convicted of tax fraud, of not more than $100,000 ($500,000 in the case of a corporation) and/or imprisonment for not more than five years.

There are three elements to the crime:

WILLFULNESS

A willful and positive attempt to evade or defeat the tax in any manner lifts a misdemeanor to a felony [*Spies v. United States*, 317 U.S. 492 (1943); 43-1 USTC ¶9243]. A consistent pattern of not reporting or underreporting income is sufficient to infer willfulness [*United States v. Stone*, 770 F.2d 842; 85-2 USTC ¶ 9652 (9th Cir 1985)].

EXISTENCE OF A SUBSTANTIAL DEFICIENCY

There must be a deficiency and that deficiency must be substantial [*Lawn v. United States*, 355 U.S. 339; 58-1 USTC ¶ 9189. *Morse*, supra]. Therefore, there must also be a tax liability [§ 7202. But see *Marks*, supra].

AFFIRMATIVE ACT

An affirmative act constituting an evasion or attempted evasion of tax [*United States v. Goodyear*, 649 F.2d 226; 81-1 USTC ¶ 9423 (4th Cir 1981)].

In order to be found guilty of this felony, one needs only to *attempt* to evade the tax.

Making a False Return (Tax Perjury), Title 26, U.S.C., § 7206(1)

Under this statute and its interpretation by the Supreme Court in *United States v. Bishop*, 412 U.S. 346 (1973), the elements of the crime of tax perjury are:

- The defendant made and subscribed a return, statement, or other document that was false with regard to a material matter;
- The return, statement, or other document contained a written declaration that it was made under the penalties of perjury;
- The defendant did not believe the return, statement, or other document was true and correct as to every material matter; and
- The defendant falsely subscribed to the return, statement, or other document willfully, with the specific intent to violate the law.

Failure to File and Pay, Title 26, U.S.C., § 7203

This statute makes it a crime to willfully do one of the following: (1) fail to pay any tax or estimated tax, (2) fail to file a return, (3) fail to keep required records, or (4) fail to supply any required information. A person convicted under this statute can be fined up to $100,000 or sentenced to up to one year in prison in addition to any other penalties.

Conspiracy to Commit Offense Against the United States or to Impair and Impede the Department of Treasury, Title 18, U.S.C., § 371

The criminal tax statutes of the Internal Revenue Code do not include a statute for the crime of conspiracy. However, tax conspiracies can be prosecuted under the general conspiracy statute, 18, U.S. Code, Section 371, which prohibits two or more persons conspiring to commit an offense against the United States, or to defraud any federal agency. Conspiracy in tax cases usually involves a conspiracy to commit tax evasion or to file false tax returns.

Tax Preparer Penalties

Negligence, Title 26, U.S.C., § 6701

Any person who does the following shall, in addition to other penalties, pay a penalty of $1,000 ($10,000 in the case of a corporation) for each period during which he:

- Aids or assists in, procures, or advises with respect to the preparation of any portion of a false return, affidavit, claim, or other document.
- Knows, or has reason to believe, that the information will be used in connection with any material matter arising under internal revenue laws.
- Knows the portion (if so used) would result in an understatement of tax liability for another person.

Understatement of Taxpayer's Liability, Title 26, U.S.C., § 6694

- Unless there is a reasonable cause for an understatement *and* the preparer acted in good faith, a penalty of $250 will be assessed against any person who is a preparer, who knew or reasonably should have known that a position taken on a return was:
  - Not realistically possible of being sustained on its merits
  - Not disclosed under U.S.C., § 6662(d)(2)(B)(ii)
  - A frivolous position

A penalty of $1,000 (reduced by the amounts previously assessed) will be levied against any preparer, who displays willful or reckless conduct as follows:

- Willful attempt to understate liability
- Reckless or intentional disregard of the rules or regulations
- Understatement means any understatement of the net amount payable or any overstatement of the net amount refundable

Criminal Fraud, Title 26, U.S.C., § 7206(2)

Fraud and False Statements

A person is guilty of a felony and may be subject to a fine of up to $100,000 (or $500,000 in the case of a corporation) and/or imprisonment of up to three years if he or she does any of the following:

- Willfully makes a return, statement, or other document and declares in writing that the document is true under penalty of perjury when the person does not believe the document is true and correct as to every material matter.

- Willfully aids or assists in, or procures, counsels, or advises the preparation of a return, affidavit, claim, or other document under the Internal Revenue laws which is fraudulent or is false as to any material matter.
- Simulates or falsely or fraudulently executes any bond, permit, entry, or other document required by the Internal Revenue Code or IRS regulations, or procures any such document to be falsely or fraudulently executed, or advises, aids in, or connives at the execution of such a document.
- Removes, deposits, or conceals any goods or commodities upon which any tax is or shall be imposed, or any property upon which a levy is authorized, with intent to evade or defeat the assessment or collection of any tax under Title 26.
- In connection with a compromise, or closing agreement or offer of either: (1) willfully conceals any property belonging to the estate of a taxpayer from any officer or employee of the United States; or (2) willfully makes a false statement relating to the estate or financial condition of a taxpayer or receives, withholds, destroys, mutilates, or falsifies any book, document, or record relating to same.

This felony is without regard to the knowledge or consent of the person(s) authorized or required to present the return, affidavit, claim, or other document.

EXAMPLE

Rudolf deSouza, president and owner of defense contractor R.D. International, was indicted on 86 counts of conspiracy, conversion of government property, money laundering, filing false income tax returns, and submitting false claims and false statements. The indictment is the result of a three-and-half-year investigation by the Naval Investigative Service and the Criminal Investigative Division of the IRS.

According to the indictment, deSouza conspired to inflate the expenses of RDI—and his own income—in an effort to impede the IRS. As part of the conspiracy, he allegedly filed false corporate income tax returns for RDI that claimed deductions for salaries that were never paid. The indictment says that RDI used an accrual method of accounting, and deducted as a business expense salaries which accrued to deSouza. During a five-year period, the contractor claimed $490,000 in such deductions. The accrued salaries not paid were entered on RDI's books as loans from an officer.

In addition, the indictment alleges that RDI employees purchased computer equipment from a vendor, and then leased it at deSouza's direction to BKS Trading at an inflated price.

Consequently, RDI billed the government for the cost of the fictitious lease, and did not give the computers to the government even though it had been reimbursed for them. Moreover, the indictment accuses deSouza of claiming thousands of dollars worth of personal expenses as business expenses. Specifically, he is alleged to have charged the government for trips to Disneyland, Disney World, and Canada.

The money laundering charges involve allegations that deSouza used several bank accounts to conduct approximately $900,000 in financial transactions designed to hide corporate assets from the bankruptcy court. Specifically, deSouza is accused of having caused numerous transfers of money from RDI accounts to those of GM Technologies. These transfers had the effect of reducing the balance of funds in RDI accounts. Further, deSouza did not disclose to the bankruptcy court the existence of GM Technologies, his family's controlling interest, or the money transfers from RDI. The indictment also alleges that deSouza transferred money from RDI to another family-owned company while the bankruptcy petition was pending.

Defenses for Tax Fraud

No Deficiency
In order to prove innocence of tax fraud matters, establish that there is no deficiency. If there is no deficiency, there is no tax liability. A lack of willfulness reduces the fraud, no matter how great, to negligence.

Avoidance not Evasion
Establish that the taxpayer was engaging in tax avoidance and not evasion [*Wodenhouse*, supra; *Ross Glove Co.*, supra].

Objectively Reasonable Position
A third defense might be that an "objectively reasonable" position was taken with respect to the tax return. [*Cheek*, supra].

Claim of Right Doctrine
It can be claimed that the receipt of funds was not income as the taxpayer did not have an unrestricted right to such money [*North American Oil v. Commissioner*, 286 U.S. 417 (1931); 3

USTC ¶ 943. But, see *Liberty Asphalt v. Commissioner*, T.C. Memo 1985-145 and *Liddy v. Commissioner*, TC Memo 1985-107].

Other Defenses

Mental Illness

[*Klein v. Commissioner*, TC Memo 1984-392.] This defense is applicable in regard to the time the return was prepared.

Incompetent Bookkeeper

[*Josey v. Commissioner*, TC Memo 1956-153.] In one case a bookkeeper "filed" the tax return by putting it in a file cabinet rather than sending it to the Internal Revenue Service.

Ignorance of the Law

[*Rutana v. Commissioner*, TC Memo 1986-336.] A court has held that consideration must be given to the intelligence and expertise of the taxpayer.

Innocent Spouse

As part of the IRS Restructuring and Reform Act of 1998, several changes were made with regard to innocent spouses relief. Innocent spouse relief permits a spouse to avoid the payment of tax associated with the filing of a joint income tax return where the spouse can show that the underpayment of tax is due to unreported income and/or disallowed deductions which are attributable to the other spouse and that the innocent spouse "did not know and did not have reason to know" of the facts surrounding the underpayment of tax.

Obtaining innocent spouse relief should now be easier to obtain due to the Act's elimination of understatement thresholds (previously a minimum of $500.00 of tax and certain AGI limitations) and providing relief for simply "erroneous," not only "grossly erroneous," income items. The former "grossly erroneous" standard required that, in the case of a deduction, that the deduction have no basis in law or fact (i.e., is frivolous).

Reliance on an Attorney or Accountant

One can assert a defense of reliance on an attorney or accountant if all of the following conditions are met:
- Reliance must be specific
- The qualifications of the expert is a facts and circumstances test
- Full disclosure to the expert is required

(*Preston v. Commissioner*, TC Memo 1983-705; *Turner v. Commissioner*, TC Memo 1985-159; *Bobbitt v. Commissioner*, TC Memo 1987-328.)

Inappropriate Defenses

Some defenses are inappropriate. They include:

Amended or Delinquent Return

There is no mitigation of the fraud penalties from filing an amended or delinquent return. [*Badaracco v. Commissioner*, 464 U.S. 386 (1984); 84-1 USTC ¶ 9150.]

Statute of Limitations

The three-year Statute of Limitations does not apply to fraud. [U.S.C., § 6501(c).]

Death of Taxpayer

Fraud penalties survive the death of the taxpayer. [*Helvering v. Mitchell*, 303 U.S. 391 (1938); Rev. Rule 73-293, 1973-2 C.B. 413.]

Bankruptcy

Taxes owed as a result of filing fraudulent federal income tax returns are not dischargeable in bankruptcy. [11, U.S.C., Sec. 523(a)(1)(c). In Re: Harris, 86-1 USTC ¶ 9315, 59 BR 545 (BC-DC Va. 1986); Rev. Rule 87-99, 1987-2 C.B. 291.]

Evidence of Tax Fraud

Direct Evidence

Certain circumstances constitute reasonable evidence of fraud, including:

Unexplained Bank Deposits

[*Visceglia v. U.S.*, TC Memo 1961-276, aff'd. 311 F.2d 946; 63-1 USTC ¶ 9232 (3rd Cir 1963).] Use of bank accounts in others' or fictitious names. [*Willits v. Commissioner*, 36 BTA 294 (1937); *Hughes v. Commissioner*, TC Memo 1956-150.]

False Documents

Submission of false documents to the IRS. [*Robinson v. Commissioner*, TC Memo 1984-188.] In this case the taxpayer claimed medical deductions but could not substantiate he had seen or paid the bills.

False Explanations for Prior Conduct

In one case, the taxpayer maintained an unexplained cash hoard and destroyed the company's records. In another case, the taxpayer destroyed the cash register tapes which were the only records for the company's sales. (*Phillips v. Commissioner*, TC Memo 1984-133; *Catalnotto v. Commissioner*, TC Memo 1984-215.)

Participation in Illegal Business

Mengarelli was involved in the bookmaking business and Anderson had an illegal lottery. They both substantially underreported income over several years. (*Mengarelli v. Commissioner*, TC Memo 1984-177; *Anderson v. Commissioner*, TC Memo 1983-654.)

False Claims of Extra Withholding Exemptions

Ellis claimed 50 withholding exemptions, but could not substantiate that he was entitled to claim them. (*Ellis v. Commissioner*, TC Memo 1986-386.)

Circumstantial Evidence

Illicit Income

Any illicit income can be considered circumstantial evidence of fraud.

Income in Excess of Deposits

Recent audits of service industry people in Texas led to assessments of several thousand dollars in back taxes and penalties.

Other Legal Elements of Tax Fraud

In *Stephens v. Commissioner*, 905 F2d 667; 90-2 USTC ¶ $50,366 (7th Cir. 1990), a taxpayer embezzled about $530,000 from his employer (Raytheon) and recorded it on his tax return as "consulting income." The taxpayer was ordered to pay restitution to Raytheon plus interest. He was allowed deductions under IRS Code § 165 (c) (2), relating to ordinary and necessary business expense for the restitution amount in the year paid. No deduction for interest was allowed.

SECURITIES FRAUD

Introduction

In order to effectively conduct investigations or examinations of fraudulent securities transactions, fraud examiners and investigators need a general understanding of both federal and state laws and the philosophy behind regulation. Many financial products and opportunities can be deemed to be securities, but that is often far from obvious to an untrained observer. This section helps provide fraud examiners with the tools necessary to recognize a security and conduct a successful investigation.

The primary purpose of securities regulation is to balance the legitimate needs of business to raise capital against the need to protect investors. The worth of a security comes from the value of the interest it represents—it has no inherent value. Securities are not a commodity to be consumed, but resemble more a currency being traded.

Although there is some commonality between federal and state laws regarding the regulation of the securities industry, there exists a complex web of laws from 50 states in addition to federal regulation. Each state has its own securities laws and even where the law is similar, interpretation and rules may differ markedly. Regulation of securities transactions covers not only their sale, but also the offer of securities to the public.

Federal Regulation

Securities Act of 1933

Concern over the 1929 stock market crash and over the manipulation of the securities markets precipitated the need for federal intervention. In 1933, the Securities Act was enacted to regulate the public offering of securities and protect investors. The 1933 Act, sometimes known as the "Truth in Securities Act," defines securities to include:

> *"...any note, stock, treasury stock, bond, debenture, ... investment contract, fractional undivided interest in any oil, gas or other mineral rights, any put, call, straddle, option ... any interest or instrument commonly known as a security..."* [Title 15, U.S.C., § 77b(a)(1)].

Of course, both federal and state laws provide for exemptions. Exemptions basically fall under two categories, *exempt securities* and *exempt transactions*. For example, certain obligations issued or guaranteed by the United States government or by state or local governments are exempted securities.

This Act also requires that investors be given full and fair disclosure of material information concerning their investment or prospective investment. In this way the sale of securities differs from many other commercial transactions where *caveat emptor* is the rule. Here, the investor is entitled to all information necessary for an informed investment decision to be made.

Securities Exchange Act of 1934

Unlike the 1933 Act, the Securities Exchange Act of 1934 mainly deals with post-issuance trading. This Act, which gave birth to the Securities and Exchange Commission (SEC), requires the registration of securities brokers and dealers. Simply put the 1933 Act can be thought of as regulating the issuance of the securities themselves, while the 1934 Act covers subsequent trading. This secondary market trading represents by far the greatest volume of securities transactions. Trading generally takes place on markets with actual trading floors, called "exchanges," or on so-called "over-the-counter" markets such as Nasdaq.

The 1934 Act contains comprehensive anti-fraud provisions. Rule 10b, for example, states that:

> *"It shall be unlawful for any person, directly or indirectly, by the use of any means or instrumentality of interstate commerce, or of the mails, or of any facility of any national securities exchange,*
>
> *(1) to employ any device, scheme or artifice to defraud,*
>
> *(2) to make any untrue statement of a material fact or to omit to state a material fact necessary in order to make the statements made, in the light of the circumstances under which they were made, not misleading, or*
>
> *(3) to engage in any act, practice, or course of business which operates or would operate as a fraud or deceit upon any person,*
>
> *in connection with the purchase or sale of any security."*

Investment Advisor Act of 1940

Registered securities dealers are required to adhere to the Rules of Fair Practice issued by the National Association of Securities Dealers and the Investment Advisers Act of 1940. This Act mandates registration and regulation of investment advisers. It applies to anyone who advises others as part of a regular business and for compensation on the investment, purchase, or sale of securities. This does not apply to those who do not receive compensation or who publish financial advice in a newspaper or magazine.

Investment Company Act of 1940

Under the Investment Company Act of 1940, investment companies are required to register with the SEC, which also regulates their activities. This Act dictates qualifications for officers and directors, requires that certain matters are submitted for stockholder approval, and mandates SEC permission for certain transactions such as those between insiders and affiliates. It divides investment companies into three categories:

- Face-Amount Certificate Companies — any company engaged in issuing fixed income debenture type securities.
- Unit Investment Trusts — companies organized under a trust indenture, contract of agency, or those similar in nature, which do not have a board of directors and issue only redeemable securities.
- Management Companies — firms that do not fit the criteria of the first two categories fall into this one. This includes open and closed-end companies, whether listed on securities exchanges or not. "Open-end" companies are commonly referred to as mutual funds and the net asset value of a share is calculated based on the market value of the fund's portfolio divided by the number of shares outstanding. The shares of "closed-end" companies trade in a similar manner to regular stocks, i.e., the value is determined by the market forces of supply and demand.

Although there are criminal penalties attached to violations of the federal securities laws, the Securities and Exchange Commission does not have the power to take criminal action. SEC investigations that disclose potentially criminal violations are usually referred to the Federal Bureau of Investigation.

Less serious violations may be addressed using the Commission's administrative powers. The SEC has the power to issue "cease and desist" orders, levy fines, and order disgorgement of profits.

The Sarbanes-Oxley Act

The Sarbanes-Oxley Act of 2002 is one of the most significant changes in the securities field since the 1934 Act was passed. It was designed to restore investor confidence in capital markets and help eliminate financial statement fraud in publicly traded companies while at the same time significantly increasing the penalties for corporate accounting fraud.

The most significant changes brought on by the Act include:
- The creation of the Public Company Accounting Oversight Board
- Requirements for senior financial officers to certify SEC filings
- New standards for audit committee independence
- New standards for auditor independence
- Enhanced financial disclosure requirements
- New protections for corporate whistleblowers
- Enhanced penalties for white-collar crime

The Act is discussed in detail in the section on "The Law Related to Fraud" in the Legal section of this Manual. However, some of the more important provisions as they relate to corporate governance are reproduced here.

Certification Obligations for CEOs and CFOs

One of the most significant changes effected by the Sarbanes-Oxley Act is the requirement that the Chief Executive Officer and the Chief Financial Officer of public companies personally certify annual and quarterly SEC filings. These certifications essentially require CEOs and CFOs to take responsibility for their companies' financial statements and prevent them from delegating this responsibility to their subordinates and then claiming ignorance when fraud is uncovered in the financial statements.

There are two types of officer certifications mandated by Sarbanes-Oxley: criminal certifications, which are set forth in Section 906 of the Act and codified at 18, U.S.C., § 1350, and civil certifications, which are set forth in Section 302.

CRIMINAL CERTIFICATIONS (§ 906)

Effective immediately, periodic filings with the SEC must now be accompanied by a statement, signed by the CEO and CFO, which certifies that the report fully complies with the SEC's periodic reporting requirements and that the information in the report fairly presents, in all material respects, the financial condition and results of operation of the company.

These certifications are known as "criminal certifications" because the Act imposes criminal penalties on officers who violate the certification requirements.
- Corporate officers who *knowingly* violate the certification requirements are subject to fines of up to $1,000,000 and up to 10 years imprisonment, or both.
- Corporate officers who *willfully* violate the certification requirements are subject to fines of up to $5,000,000 and up to 20 years imprisonment, or both.

CIVIL CERTIFICATIONS (§ 302)

Section 302 of the Act requires the CEO and CFO to personally certify the following in their reports:
- They have personally reviewed the report;
- Based on their knowledge, the report does not contain any material misstatement that would render the financials misleading;
- Based on their knowledge the financial information in the report fairly presents in all material respects the financial condition, results of operations, and cash flow of the company;
- They are responsible for designing, maintaining, and evaluating the company's internal controls, they have evaluated the controls within 90 days prior to the report, and they have presented their conclusions about the effectiveness of those controls in the report;
- They have disclosed to the auditors and the audit committee any material weaknesses in the controls and any fraud, whether material or not, that involves management or other employees who have a significant role in the company's internal controls; and
- They have indicated in their report whether there have been significant changes in the company's internal controls since the filing of the last report.

Note that in items 2 and 3 the CEO and CFO are not required to certify that the financials are accurate or that there is no misstatement. They are simply required to certify that *to their knowledge* the financials are accurate and not misleading. However, this does not mean that senior financial officers can simply plead ignorance about their companies' SEC filings in order to avoid liability. The term "fairly presents" in item 3 is a broader standard than what is required by GAAP. In certifying that their SEC filings meet this standard, the CEO and CFO essentially must certify that the company: (1) has selected appropriate accounting policies to ensure the material accuracy of the reports; (2) has properly applied those accounting standards; and (3) has disclosed financial information that reflects the underlying transactions and events of the company. Furthermore, the other new certification rules (see 1, and 4-6 above) mandate that CEOs and CFOs take an active role in their companies' public reporting, and in the design and maintenance of internal controls.

It is significant that in item 4, the CEO and CFO not only have to certify that they are responsible for their companies' internal controls, but also that they have evaluated the controls *within 90 days prior to their quarterly or annual report*. Essentially, this new certification requirement mandates that companies actively and continually re-evaluate their control structures to prevent fraud.

In conjunction with the § 302 certification requirements on the responsibility of the CEO and CFO for internal controls, § 404 of the Act requires all annual reports to contain an internal control report that: (1) states management's responsibility for establishing and maintaining an adequate internal control structure and procedures for financial reporting; and (2) contains an assessment of the effectiveness of the internal control structure and procedures of the company for financial reporting.

Item 5 requires the CEO and CFO to certify that they have disclosed to their auditors and their audit committee any material weaknesses in the company's internal controls, and also any fraud, *whether material or not,* that involves management or other key employees. Obviously, this is a very broad reporting standard that goes beyond the "material" standard contemplated in SAS 99 (see the discussion of SAS 99 in the chapter on "Management's and Auditors' Responsibilities" in the Financial Transaction section of the Manual). The CEO and CFO now must report to their auditors and audit committee *any fraud* committed by a manager. This places a greater burden on the CEO and CFO to take part in anti-fraud efforts and to be aware of fraudulent activity within their companies in order to meet this certification requirement.

Item 6 is significant because periodic SEC filings must now include statements detailing significant changes to the internal controls of publicly traded companies.

New Standards for Audit Committee Independence
AUDIT COMMITTEE RESPONSIBILITIES

Section 301 of the Act requires that the audit committee for each publicly traded company shall be directly responsible for appointing, compensating, and overseeing the work of the company's outside auditors. The Act also mandates that the auditors must report directly to the audit committee—not management—and makes it the responsibility of the audit committee to resolve disputes between management and the auditors. Section 301 also requires that the audit committee must have the authority and funding to hire independent counsel and any other advisors it deems necessary to carry out its duties.

COMPOSITION OF THE AUDIT COMMITTEE

The Sarbanes-Oxley Act mandates that each member of a company's audit committee must be a member of its board of directors, and must otherwise be "independent." The term "independent" means that the audit committee member can only receive compensation from the company for his or her service on the board of directors, the audit committee, or another committee of the board of directors. They cannot be paid by the company for any other consulting or advisory work.

FINANCIAL EXPERT

Section 407 of the Act requires every public company to disclose in its periodic reports to the SEC whether or not the audit committee has at least one member who is a "financial expert," and if not to explain the reasons why. The Act defines a "financial expert" as a person who, through education and experience as a public accountant or auditor, or a CFO, comptroller, chief financial officer or a similar position: (1) has an understanding of generally accepted accounting principles and financial statements; (2) has experience in preparing or auditing financial statements of comparable companies and the application of such principles in accounting for estimates, accruals, and reserves; (3) has experience with internal controls; and (4) has an understanding of audit committee functions.

ESTABLISHING A WHISTLEBLOWING STRUCTURE

The Act makes it the responsibility of the audit committee to establish procedures (e.g., a hotline) for receiving and dealing with complaints and anonymous employee tips regarding irregularities in the company's accounting methods, internal controls, or auditing matters.

Enhanced Financial Disclosure Requirements
OFF-BALANCE SHEET TRANSACTIONS

The Sarbanes-Oxley Act directed the SEC to issue rules which require the disclosure of all material off-balance sheet transactions by publicly traded companies. The rules require disclosure of "all material off-balance sheet transactions, arrangements, obligations (including contingent obligations), and other relationships the company may have with unconsolidated entities or persons that may have a material current or future effect on the company's financial condition, changes in financial condition, liquidity, capital expenditures, capital resources, or significant components of revenues or expenses." These disclosures are required in all annual and quarterly SEC reports.

PRO FORMA FINANCIAL INFORMATION

Section 401 also directed the SEC to issue new rules on pro forma financial statements. These rules require that pro forma financials must not contain any untrue statements or omissions that would make them misleading and require that the pro forma financials be reconciled to GAAP. These rules apply to all pro forma financial statements that are filed with the SEC or that are included in any public disclosure or press release.

PROHIBITIONS ON PERSONAL LOANS TO EXECUTIVES

Section 402 makes it illegal for public companies to make personal loans or otherwise extend credit, either directly or indirectly, to or for any director or executive officer. There is an exception that applies to consumer lenders if the loans are consumer loans of the type the company normally makes to the public, and on the same terms.

RESTRICTIONS ON INSIDER TRADING

Section 403 establishes new disclosure requirements for stock transactions by directors and officers of public companies, or by persons who own more than 10 percent of a publicly traded company's stock. Reports of changes in beneficial ownership by these persons must now be filed with the SEC by the end of the second business day following the transaction.

Under § 306, directors and officers are also prohibited from trading in the company's securities during any pension fund blackout periods. This restriction only applies to securities that were acquired as a result of their employment or service to the company. A blackout period is defined as any period of more than three consecutive business days in which at least 50% of the participants in the company's retirement plan are restricted from trading in the company's securities. If a director or officer violates this provision, he or she can be forced to disgorge to the company all profits received from the sale of securities during the blackout period.

CODES OF ETHICS FOR SENIOR FINANCIAL OFFICERS

Pursuant to § 406 of the Act, the SEC must establish rules that require public companies to disclose whether they have adopted a code of ethics for their senior financial officers, and if not, to explain the reasons why. The new rules require immediate public disclosure any time there is a change of the code of ethics or a waiver of the code of ethics for a senior financial officer.

ENHANCED REVIEW OF PERIODIC FILINGS

Section 408 of the Act now requires the SEC to make regular and systematic reviews of disclosures made by public companies in their periodic reports to the SEC. Reviews of a company's disclosures, including its financial statements, must be made at least once every three years. Prior to this enactment, reviews were typically minimal and tended to coincide with registered offerings.

REAL TIME DISCLOSURES

Under § 409, public companies must publicly disclose information concerning material changes in their financial condition or operations. These disclosures must be "in plain English" and must be made "on a rapid and current basis."

Protections for Corporate Whistleblowers under Sarbanes-Oxley

The Sarbanes-Oxley Act establishes broad new protections for corporate whistleblowers. There are two sections of the Act that address whistleblower protections: Section 806 deals with civil protections and Section 1107 establishes criminal liability for those who retaliate against whistleblowers.

CIVIL LIABILITY WHISTLEBLOWER PROTECTION

Section 806 of the Act, which is codified at Title18, U.S.C., § 1514A, creates civil liability for companies that retaliate against whistleblowers. It should be noted that this provision does not provide universal whistleblower protection; it only protects employees of publicly traded companies. Section 806 makes it unlawful to fire, demote, suspend, threaten, harass, or in any other manner discriminate against an employee for providing information or aiding in an investigation of securities fraud. In order to trigger § 806 protections, the employee must report the suspected misconduct to a federal regulatory or law enforcement agency, a member of Congress or a committee of Congress, or a supervisor. Employees are also protected against retaliation for filing, testifying in, participating in, or otherwise assisting in a proceeding filed or about to be filed relating to an alleged violation of securities laws or SEC rules.

The whistleblower protections apply even if the company is ultimately found not to have committed securities fraud. As long as the employee reasonably believes she is reporting conduct that constitutes a violation of various federal securities laws, then she is protected. The protections cover retaliatory acts not only by the company, but also by any officer, employee, contractor, subcontractor, or agent of the company.

If a public company is found to have violated § 806, the Act provides for an award of compensatory damages sufficient to "make the employee whole." Penalties include reinstatement; back pay with interest; and compensation for special damages including litigation costs, expert witness fees, and attorneys' fees.

CRIMINAL SANCTION WHISTLEBLOWER PROTECTION

Section 1107 of Sarbanes-Oxley —codified at Title 18, U.S.C., § 1513—makes it a crime to knowingly, with the intent to retaliate, take any harmful action against a person for providing truthful information relating to the commission or possible commission of any Federal offense. This protection is only triggered when information is provided to a law enforcement officer, it does not apply to reports made to supervisors or to members of Congress, as is the case under § 806.

Additionally, the Act codified three new criminal offenses to Title 18 of the Code. First, it is a criminal offense to alter, destroy, mutilate, conceal, cover-up, or falsify any record or document "with the intent to impede, obstruct, or influence" a federal investigation or bankruptcy proceeding, carrying a maximum sentence of 20 years imprisonment. (18 U.S.C. § 1519). Secondly, all auditing accountants of securities issuers must "maintain all audit or review workpapers for a period of 5 years." Where there is a knowing and willful violation of this offense, a sentence of up to 10 years may be imposed. (18 U.S.C. § 1520). Finally, the Act made codified an additional securities fraud offence that can carry a maximum sentence of 25 years' imprisonment. (18 U.S.C. § 1348).

In general, the coverage of § 1107 is much broader than the civil liability whistleblower protections of § 806. While the § 806 protections apply only to employees of publicly traded companies, § 1107's criminal whistleblower protections cover all individuals (and organizations) regardless of where they work. Also, § 806 only applies to violations of securities laws or SEC rules and regulations. Section 1107, on the other hand, protects individuals who provide truthful information about the commission or possible commission of *any Federal offense.*

Violations of § 1107 can be punished by fines of up to $250,000 and up to 10 years in prison for individuals. Corporations that violate the act can be fined up to $500,000.

Other Criminal Penalties
SECURITIES FRAUD

Section 807 of the Act makes securities fraud a crime under 18, U.S.C., § 1348, providing for fines up to $250,000 and up to 25 years in prison.

SECURITIES FRAUD (TITLE 18, U.S. CODE, § 1348)

Whoever knowingly executes, or attempts to execute, a scheme or artifice—

(1) to defraud any person in connection with any security of an issuer with a class of securities registered under section 12 of the Securities Exchange Act of 1934 (15, U.S.C., 78l) or that is required to file reports under section 15(d) of the Securities Exchange Act of 1934 (15, U.S.C., 78o(d)); or

(2) to obtain, by means of false or fraudulent pretenses, representations, or promises, any money or property in connection with the purchase or sale of any security of an issuer with a class of securities registered under section 12 of the Securities Exchange Act of 1934 (15, U.S.C., 78l) or that is required to file reports under section 15(d) of the Securities Exchange Act of 1934 (15, U.S.C., 78o(d));

shall be fined under this title, or imprisoned not more than 25 years, or both.

DOCUMENT DESTRUCTION

Section 802 of the Act makes destroying evidence to obstruct an investigation or any other matter within the jurisdiction of any U.S. department illegal and punishable by a fine of up to $250,000 and up to 20 years in prison.

The final rules adopted by the SEC under Section 802 specifically require that accountants who perform audits on publicly traded companies must maintain all audit or review work papers for a period of seven years. Although the original provisions of Section 802 only required a retention period of five years, the SEC extended the requirement to be consistent with the seven-year retention period required under the new Auditing Standards promulgated by the Public Company Accounting Oversight Board (PCAOB) per Section

103 of the Act. Violations of the final SEC rules may be punished by fines up to $250,000 and up to 10 years in jail for individuals, or fines up to $500,000 for corporations.

Section 1102 of the Act amends § 1512 of the U.S. Code to make it a criminal offense to corruptly alter, destroy, mutilate or conceal a record or document with the intent to impair its integrity or use in an official proceeding, or to otherwise obstruct, influence, or impede any official proceeding or attempt to do so. Violations of this section are punishable by fines up to $250,000 and imprisonment for up to 20 years.

FREEZING OF ASSETS

During an investigation of possible securities violations by a publicly traded company or any of its officers, directors, partners, agents, controlling persons, or employees, the SEC can petition a federal court to issue a 45-day freeze on "extraordinary payments" to any of the foregoing persons. If granted, the payments will be placed in an interest-bearing escrow account while the investigation commences. This provision was enacted to prevent corporate assets from being improperly distributed while an investigation is underway.

BANKRUPTCY LOOPHOLES

Section 803 amends the bankruptcy code so that judgments, settlements, damages, fines, penalties, restitution payments, disgorgement payments, etc., resulting from violations of Federal securities laws are non-dischargeable. This was intended to prevent corporate wrongdoers from sheltering their assets under bankruptcy protection.

DISGORGEMENT OF BONUSES

One of the most unique aspects of the Sarbanes-Oxley Act is § 304, which states that if a publicly traded company is required to prepare an accounting restatement due to the company's material noncompliance, as a result of "misconduct," with any financial reporting requirement under securities laws, then the CEO and CFO must reimburse the company for:

- Any bonus or other incentive-based or equity-based compensation received during the 12 months after the initial filing of the report that requires restating; and
- Any profits realized from the sale of the company's securities during the same 12-month period.

While the Act requires the CEO and CFO to disgorge their bonuses if the company's financial statements have to be restated because of "misconduct," it makes no mention of *whose* misconduct triggers this provision. There is certainly nothing in the text of § 304 that limits the disgorgement provision to instances of misconduct by the CEO and CFO. Presumably, then, the CEO and CFO could be required to disgorge their bonuses and profits from the sale of company stock even if they had no knowledge of and took no part in the misconduct that made the restatement necessary.

The NASD and Other Regulatory Organizations

SEC delegates significant regulatory authority to "self-regulatory organizations" (SROs). The SROs oversee the markets they operate and police the member firms participating in that market. SROs create and enforce rules dealing with such areas as listing of securities, exchange and settlement procedures, and member qualifications.

The Maloney Act of 1938 amended the Securities Exchange Act of 1934 to allow the National Association of Securities Dealers (NASD) to regulate the business of members subject to Securities and Exchange Commission oversight. With over 5,000 member firms and over 500,000 individual members, there is no doubt that the NASD is the most prominent SRO. Virtually all registered representatives and broker-dealers in the United States that do business with the public are required to be members of the NASD.

NASD is comprised of two subsidiaries. The first is the Nasdaq/Amex Market Group which covers the American Stock Exchange (Amex) and the National Association of Securities Dealers Automated Quotation System, the electronic over-the-counter market commonly known as Nasdaq. In June 2004, the average daily trading volume on Nasdaq was over 2.7 billion shares valued at over $49 billion. The second subsidiary is NASD Regulation (NASDR).

The main functions of NASD are:
- Policing the Nasdaq and Amex markets.
- Testing and licensing. Securities professionals such as salespersons, managers, etc., must obtain various licenses depending on the type of business they wish to conduct and whether they perform supervisory functions. Many of these exams are administered by the NASD, although other SROs also do this. The most common form of license is the Series 7 - General Securities Representative.
- Registration of firms, individuals, and securities offerings (includes branch offices).
- Review of offering literature. Preliminary review of a prospectus to ensure proper disclosure and compliance with rules.

- Establishing financial requirements for firms including minimum net capital requirements to help ensure safety and soundness.
- Conducting market surveillance to detect illegal trading activity using computer systems to track the Nasdaq market for unusual trading patterns and improper activity. The NASD is in the process of introducing a system called Order Audit Trail System (OATS) to speed up detection of trading abuses. Eventually the NASD will probably move toward artificial intelligence to alert surveillance personnel to potential violations.
- Conducting investigations that can lead to enforcement actions against members; it also can make referrals to SEC, Justice Department, and other federal and state agencies.
- Arbitrating disputes. NASD also conducts arbitration proceedings to resolve consumer complaints.

Securities broker-dealers must register with the SEC *and* in those states where they plan to do business. If they plan to do business with the public they must also become NASD members. Typical registration requirements for the SEC, states, and NASD include business, financial, disciplinary information, and disclosure of criminal convictions.

Municipal Securities Rule Making Board (MSRMB)

Established in 1975, the MSRMB regulates securities firms and banks involved in underwriting, trading, and selling municipal securities.

National Futures Association (NFA)

The NFA is the industry wide SRO for the futures industry and performs a similar, though more limited role, than the NASD. The NFA currently has more than 4,000 member firms and more than 51,000 associate members.

Membership is mandatory for firms and individuals that conduct futures-related business with the public.

Regional Exchanges

In addition to the well-known New York Stock Exchange (NYSE) there are also regional stock exchanges including the Pacific Exchange, Philadelphia Stock Exchange, Boston Stock Exchange, Chicago Stock Exchange, Chicago Board of Trade, Chicago Board of Options, Chicago Mercantile Exchange, etc. These bodies police the activities of their members.

Commodities Futures Trading Commission (CFTC)

Trading of commodities (wheat, oil, pork bellies, etc.) and futures is regulated under the Commodity Exchange Act. The Commodity Futures Trading Commission regulates the futures and options markets as well as traders. Essentially, all futures must be traded on markets designated by CFTC.

The main futures markets are:
- Chicago Board of Trade
- Chicago Mercantile Exchange
- New York Mercantile Exchange

CFTC has civil power to take action against violators, and of course can make criminal referrals to the Department of Justice.

State Regulation

The first state securities laws of any substance were enacted in Kansas around 1911. State securities laws are often referred to as "blue sky laws." The term "blue sky" came into use in 1917 after a judge issued an opinion describing their purpose as preventing "speculative schemes, which have no more basis than so many feet of blue sky."

The initial steps taken in Kansas to regulate the securities industry and protect consumers were quickly imitated by other states. In 1956, the National Conference of Commissioners on Uniform State Laws and the American Bar Association promulgated a new Uniform Securities Act. More than 30 states have adopted most or all of the Uniform Securities Act which was revised in 1985 and amended in 1988.

The revised Uniform Act has four parts:
- Regulation of Broker-Dealers — most states require broker-dealers to register with the state securities regulator. "Broker-dealer" means "a person engaged in the business of effecting transactions in securities for the account of others or for the person's own account" and does not include an issuer selling his own securities.
- Registration of Securities — most states require that an issuer proposing to offer securities for sale file some type of registration application.

- Anti-fraud Provisions — fraud is usually defined in language similar to Rule 10b of the Securities and Exchange Act of 1934. Criminal, civil, and administrative penalties are usually attached to violations of state anti-fraud provisions.
- Definitions, Exemptions, Administrative Provisions — the definition of "security" is basically the same as that under the Securities Act of 1933. Provides powers for state regulators to examine books and records and take disciplinary action.

To simplify to a general rule of thumb, unless certain exemptions apply, before a security is sold or offered for sale:
- There must be a registration in place to cover the security.
- The broker-dealer must be registered.
- There must be full and fair disclosure of all material information.

As long as there is no conflict with federal laws, each state can supplement or duplicate federal requirements. However, in 1996, Congress passed the National Securities Markets Improvement Act preempting state regulation in several significant areas.

National Securities Markets Improvement Act of 1996

The most significant federal legislative development in securities regulation in recent years is the National Securities Markets Improvement Act of 1996. Often referred to as NSMIA (pronounced "nismia"), it is an attempt to standardize securities regulation in the United States and use federal law to preempt some of the state requirements. Essentially, the authority of a state to require registration of certain securities or control certain transactions has been removed.

Three main changes that are of particular importance:
- So called "covered securities" are no longer regulated by the states. A state cannot require registration of securities that are deemed covered. Essentially these are securities listed on the major exchanges, mutual funds, and certain private placements.
- Previously all individuals and companies offering investment advice came under state jurisdiction. Now only those with assets of less than $25 million fall under state regulation.
- Although NSMIA significantly reduces the enforcement powers of states in several areas, a state can still take action in cases involving fraud.

What Constitutes a Security?

The definition of securities in both state and federal law includes instruments that can easily be identified as securities. These more traditional securities are usually easy to spot.

"Traditional" Securities

Type of investments most commonly recognized as securities include:

Stocks

A stock is an equity that represents a right of ownership in a corporation. There are many different classes including "common," "preferred," "non-voting," and "restricted."

Bonds

A bond is a debt instrument, for example treasury bills, corporate bonds, municipal bonds, and "junk bonds." Although the term "junk bonds" has a very negative connotation all they really are is high-risk, below investment grade, commercial bonds.

Certificates of Deposit

A certificate of deposit (or CD) is acknowledgement by a bank of the receipt of money with a promise to repay it with interest.

Less obvious, but still clearly securities are:

Futures

A *future* is a contract agreeing to buy or sell a specified quantity of something (e.g., foreign currency, commodities, etc.) at some future time at a price agreed upon now. In futures contracts, the delivery or sale of the product is assumed, and the investor has an obligation to fulfill the contract. Note that in reality, few futures contracts actually result in delivery. Usually, the investor will enter into offsetting futures contracts prior to the delivery date. As futures contracts are freely transferable, the two transactions can offset each other.

Options

An investor can purchase an *option* to buy (known as a "call") or sell (known as a "put") an asset (such as stocks, bonds, commodities, or real estate) on or before a future date at a price agreed upon now. With an option, the investor buys the right, but not the obligation, to perform the contract. The price paid for the option is known as the "option premium."

The price at which the option may be exercised is known as the "strike price." Of course, once an option has expired it ceases to have any value whatsoever.

Futures and options are essentially methods of managing price risk, often called "hedging." They can be used, for example, by farmers or international manufacturing companies as a form of insurance against adverse price or currency exchange rate changes. They are examples of "derivatives." Many esoteric types of investment vehicles have been created, often using complex mathematical models. These derivative products allow trading to take place in various indices (for example the Dow Jones Industrial Index or the Standard and Poor's 500) and also in securities known as "strips," "collateralized mortgage obligations," and "leaps."

Futures and options are discussed in more detail below.

Investment Contracts

Other transactions are less obviously securities, but fall under the catch-all category of an "investment contract." Unfortunately, the term "investment contract" is not usually defined by statute, and it is, therefore, necessary to look to case law to determine whether a particular transaction may constitute an investment contract. Many fraudulent schemes involving exotic investments can be argued to constitute the offer or sale of investment contracts.

The Howey Test

In the case *SEC v. Howey Co.,* 328 U.S. 293, 299 (1946), a company was selling subdivided sections of a Florida orange orchard which were to be managed by a subsidiary company. In its opinion in the case, the U.S. Supreme Court outlined a four-element test to determine if an investment contract was present. In essence, the Supreme Court stated that there must be:

- An *investment* of money or other asset.
- *A common enterprise.* In very general terms, the common enterprise requirement means the success of the investor is dependent on the efforts and success of those seeking the investment of third parties (typically the promoter). The third-party, who provides the entrepreneurial skill, shares in the profits (or losses) with the investor. Usually, the common enterprise requirement will be met where "the fortunes of the investor are interwoven with and dependent upon the efforts and success of those seeking the investment or a third-party." *See, SEC v. Glenn W. Turner Enterprises, Inc., 474 F.2nd 476, 482 n.7 (9th Circuit, 1973).*

- *An expectation of profits.* Profit is generally defined to be either money received for the use of capital or capital appreciation. In *United Housing Foundation, Inc. v. Forman*, 421 U.S. 837 (1975), stock sold to potential apartment renters, which would be applied to their security deposit, was not held to be an investment contract because the individuals were attracted solely by the prospect of somewhere to live, not financial return on their money.
- *Profit must be generated solely from the efforts of others.* The essential managerial efforts, which effect the success or failure of the enterprise, come from the third-party (the promoter) not the investor. In *Howey*, the subsidiary company was to plant, cultivate, and harvest the oranges. As a general rule, the more actively involved an investor is in the enterprise, the *less* likely it is that an investment contract will be held to exist. Subsequent case law has diluted "solely" to "primarily" or "substantially" from the efforts of others. Nevertheless, if the investor's efforts *are* significant in the success of the enterprise, an investment contract will *not* be found to exist. For example, in the *Forman* case mentioned above, the court stated "an investment contract is the presence of an investment in a common venture premised on a reasonable expectation of profits to be derived from the entrepreneurial or managerial efforts of others."

Risk Capital Test

As an alternative to the Howey Test many state and federal courts are using the so-called "Risk Capital Test." This "test" allows the investor to play a more active role if the funds he contributes are part of the "risk capital" of the business. A person entrusts money or other capital to another with the expectation of deriving a profit. The failure or success of the venture is dependent upon the managerial efforts of the other person. Several states have formally adopted this test, sometimes known as the Hawaii Market Test, as an alternative definition of investment contract. However, the Supreme Court has expressly declined to decide if this test should be used.

Examples of Investment Contracts

Following are types of investments that frequently qualify as "investment contracts" and are, therefore, considered securities. Several types of related frauds are also listed to demonstrate the broad and expansive nature of investment contract schemes. More information about these schemes can also be found the "Consumer Fraud" section.

PONZI SCHEMES

A "Ponzi" scheme is named after Charles Ponzi who, in the early 1920s, persuaded tens of thousands of Bostonians to invest over $10 million. He created an entity, aptly named the Securities and Exchange Company, and issued investors a promissory note guaranteeing a 50% return in 90 days on every $1,000 invested.

The scheme involved the alleged buying of international postal reply coupons in Europe using foreign currencies, which had depreciated substantially against the dollar in the years after World War I. Ponzi claimed that these coupons, bought at a discount, could then be redeemed at full face value, yielding a substantial profit.

There were two main problems. First, although Ponzi claimed to be trading over $10 million worth of postal reply coupons, only a few hundred thousand dollars worth actually existed. A more fatal flaw was the fact that the scheme relied on new investor funds to pay returns to earlier investors. In August 1920, after the inevitable collapse of his scheme, Ponzi was arrested for mail fraud and larceny. Ponzi served jail time and was later deported to his native Italy.

A more recent example of a spectacular Ponzi scheme involves a company named Foundation for New Era Philanthropy. In the early 1990's, New Era promised charities and other non-profit institutions that it would double their investment by matching gifts from anonymous donors. Prosecutors alleged that the founder, John Bennett, defrauded museums, universities, and others of $100 million in a modern Ponzi scheme. In reality, there was no "foundation," nor were there any anonymous donors. Bennett pled no contest to 82 counts of fraud and money laundering and was sentenced to 12 years imprisonment. As Will Rodgers allegedly said, "The quickest way to double your money is to fold it over and put it back in your pocket."

PYRAMID SCHEMES

These typically involve a scheme whereby fees or dues paid by a member to join an organization are to be paid to another member and there is a provision for increasing membership through a chain process of new members bringing in other new members. The members make money not by commission on the bona fide retail sale of a legitimate product, but by signing up new people. An organizational structure that, like the Ponzi scheme, relies on bringing in new people must eventually collapse. Although all pyramid schemes are fraudulent, and in many states specifically deemed illegal, not all pyramid schemes necessarily meet the Howey Test.

WORM, RABBIT, AND OSTRICH FARMS

Although sometimes amusing when viewed objectively by the investigator, many investors have been defrauded by being persuaded to invest in exactly these types of opportunities. Fraud examiners can practice applying the Howey Test to these types of cases in an attempt to determine whether an investment contract exists. What, if anything, does the investor need to do in order to get the promised return? If, for example, the investor's involvement is purely passive, then an investment contract will be held to exist. However, where the investor is involved in feeding the ostriches and marketing the meat, then the last element of the Howey Test fails.

"PRIME BANK" FRAUD

These schemes involve the issuance and purported trading of so-called "prime bank" notes or other high yield investment opportunities. Investors are often told that they can obtain returns exceeding several hundred percent per year when their funds are placed in an offshore trading program. Excessive complexity and secrecy generally characterize these fraudulent programs. Investors are usually told that this opportunity is only available to a select few and the signing of non-disclosure agreements is mandatory. Typically the explanation of how the program actually works is full of obscure terminology and makes reference to legitimate banks or organizations such as the International Monetary Fund (IMF) to lend credibility. Often, investors are told that there is little or no risk of losing their principal. Despite warnings published by the state regulators, the SEC, the IMF, the International Chamber of Commerce, and the World Bank, this type of fraud continues to fleece millions of dollars from investors worldwide.

PRECIOUS METAL SCHEMES

Typically these involve the purchase of interests in gold or silver coins, bullion, diamonds, and other precious or semi-precious stones.

VIATICALS

A viatical settlement involves the sale by a terminally ill person, at a discount, of the right to death benefits from the proceeds of their life insurance policy. In and of itself, this does not constitute the offer or sale of a security. However, an industry has evolved to buy these rights and then sell fractional interests in them to investors. Frequently, these policy rights are pooled and the investors are sold an interest in the pool. Investor returns increase according to how deeply the policy is discounted and are inversely related to how long the beneficiary survives. Whether such investments constitute securities is a matter of considerable debate. In July 1996, the Circuit Court of Appeals for the District of Columbia held that viatical settlements sold by Life Partners were not securities because the profits do not predominantly derive from the efforts of a party other than the investor. *See, SEC v. Life Partners, Inc.* 87 F. 3d 536 (D.C. Cir 1996). The appellate court ruled, in essence, that the ministerial functions performed by Life Partners did not have an impact on the profits of the investor and therefore that the last part of the Howey Test was not met.

PARTNERSHIPS

Interests in limited partnerships are generally held to be securities because this type of structure conforms closely to Howey. General partnerships will not usually be held to be securities. This is normally because in a true general partnership the partners take an active role in the operation of the business. However, be warned that some promoters will try to disguise an investment contract as a general partnership. It is important to look beyond the surface wrapping and determine if the partners really take an active role in operating the entity. Some investment opportunities involving wireless cable and pay telephone leasing are good examples of use of this tactic.

JOINT VENTURES

Interests in a joint venture will often be found to be securities. The Howey Test should be applied and, as with partnership interests, careful attention should be paid to the extent to which the investor actively participates in the management or operation of the business.

OIL, GAS, AND MINERAL INTERESTS

Usually the sale of fractional ownership of oil and gas wells, or mineral rights constitutes the sale of a security. The misrepresentations and omissions found in oil and gas scams are often repeated in other mineral mining schemes, such as gold or coal. Investors have a right to be advised of the risks inherent in a securities investment and oil/gas opportunities are traditionally very high risk. If investors have been assured or guaranteed of success in striking oil, fraud examiners should consider that a red flag. Naturally, as in all cases of securities fraud, one should look for discrepancies in promoters' credentials, business history, and commission. The following types of misrepresentations and omissions are often encountered:

- Drilling and Completion Costs: Costs are often hugely inflated to bilk the investor.

- Lease: Promoters frequently do not have a valid mineral rights lease.
- Discovery and Production Potential: The investor may be misled regarding the likelihood of striking oil and the amount produced. This information is usually contained in the geologist's report.
- Wells: The promoter may exaggerate the number and depth of wells, thus inflating the operating costs paid by investors.
- Self-dealing: The promoter may declare a good well dry in order to reap the benefits of a productive well later when the investors have given up.
- Dry Holes: Often these are completed by the promoter solely to improve his completion record and collect completion funds from investors.
- Royalties: Insiders may be assigned the majority of royalties while investors receive only a small portion.
- Number of Partners: Promoters are likely to oversell the well, i.e. 99/64ths.

Occasionally, the investment may be a complete fabrication. This is even more likely in overseas mineral investments. Geologists' reports may be falsified or promoters may rely on investors' reluctance to travel to remote spots in order to see their well or mine for themselves.

EXAMPLE

A good example of this is the Bre-X gold scandal that occurred in the spring of 1997. The Canadian mining company claimed to have found the largest gold deposit discovered in the twentieth century in Busang, on the island of Borneo. Share prices of the before unheard of, penny-stock company skyrocketed as rumors of the tremendous discovery circulated. Optimistic investors largely ignored the red flags that began to emerge. The initial concern which most had was that the mine was located in Indonesia, creating potential difficulties due to poor U.S. relations with that country.

Not to be deterred by proximity or diplomatic difficulties, investors continued to avidly acquire stock in the former junior mining company. Bre-X geological reports of as many as 5.68 grams of gold per ton continued the trend. Then, however, a multitude of problems seemed to arise.

The accuracy of the sampling began to come into question. Instead of preserving parts of the core samples for verification, Bre-X allowed them to be crushed. And soon after, a fire destroyed the geologists' records, further casting the veracity of the discovery into doubt.

> *Insiders began surreptitiously selling off large amounts of their shares. News that the Indonesian government had withheld key permits was concealed from investors. After the exploration manager's mysterious death (he supposedly committed suicide by jumping out of a helicopter), share prices plunged from approximately C$100 to around C$2. Bre-X's market value declined by 90%. The Ontario Municipal Employees Retirement System lost C$45 million and Canada's Caisse de dépôt et placement du Québec recorded a loss of C$70 million. The core samples, it was later revealed, had been "salted."*
>
> *The most disturbing aspect of this case is the severe handicap investigators faced caused by jurisdictional questions. "This could be a monumental scam that will be nearly impossible to prosecute," according to a private investigator on the case. He explains some of the difficulties: "No one really has jurisdiction. The salting [of the gold samples] took place in Indonesia, but what laws were really broken in that country? The law against salting? There is none. The law against deceiving shareholders? That happened in Canada and the U.S. Most of the main suspects probably disappeared in the Philippines. But what law did they break in the Philippines? Are they fugitives? No. Can a prosecutor in Canada get a warrant for those guys in the Philippines for what they did in Indonesia? Very tricky."*
>
> *In Indonesia, no extradition or law-enforcement cooperation agreements exist with Canada or the U.S., which means the criminal investigation is being handled by the Indonesians themselves. Likewise, though the U.S. Embassy in Jakarta has been asked by Washington to look into the Busang fraud, the U.S. and Indonesia have a poor track record of cooperating in criminal matters.*

Investors in such ventures can easily find themselves with no legal recourse if things go wrong. Obviously, different countries have varying laws regarding investor rights. Naturally, this makes investigating a case such as this quite difficult. The principals of Bre-X claimed not to have known about sample salting. They portrayed themselves as victims and blamed the geologists for the fraudulent samples. The geologists, however, are Philippine nationals and have retreated to their homeland, further complicating the investigation. The Philippine government suspects foul play in the death of the head geologist, Michael de Guzman, and is more concerned with the Indonesian inquiry into the matter than with turning over their countrymen for questioning.

When examining the case from a "follow the money" standpoint, the trail seems to lead to Bre-X insiders, however. Even as they concealed news of permits being withheld by the

Indonesian government, insiders secretly sold off huge amounts of stock at great profit. According to the Wall Street Journal, Bre-X Chairman David Walsh, Vice Chairman and Chief Geologist John Felderhof, and two other executives sold nearly C$38 million of stock.

PROMISSORY NOTES

A note is defined as a security, but in practice, the law is more complicated than that. Under certain circumstances, promissory notes are not held to be securities. A note is presumed to be a security unless it bears a strong resemblance to a category of instruments which are not securities. Generally, longer-term commercial paper is similar in many respects to a bond and may be held to be a security unless it relates to such transactions as consumer finance or residential mortgages. For example, in the case of a residential mortgage, the note you sign is simply a promise to repay, not a method to raise capital for some business venture.

With notes and other potential securities it is often helpful to apply the family resemblance test and look at three things:

MOTIVE AND EXPECTATION

What is the issuer's primary motive? If it is to raise money for the general use of a business enterprise then a security may be held to exist. What is the buyer's primary motive? Is it really a loan or an investment-type transaction? What is a reasonable investor thinking, what are his expectations?

PLAN OF DISTRIBUTION

Is there some form of common trading? If so, a security probably exists.

REGULATION

Is there some other regulatory system which significantly reduces the risk of the transaction thereby rendering the application of the securities laws unnecessary? If the transaction is deemed appropriately regulated in ways other than through the application of the securities laws, then it is less likely that securities laws will be brought to bear.

Commodity Futures, Exchange-Traded Options, and OTC Options

There have been numerous frauds involving commodity futures, exchange-traded options and OTC options. In December 1994, Orange County California became the largest municipality ever to file for bankruptcy. This was largely caused by risky investment strategies utilizing OTC options that resulted in trading losses of about $10 billion. In more recent news, the catastrophic failure of Enron was partially caused by a fraudulent hedge transaction utilizing an OTC option. Through a company he controlled, Andrew S. Fastow sold worthless options to Enron making it appear that the value of Enron's investment in Avici Systems, Inc. was hedged. Fastow pocketed the premium for the bogus options while Enron appeared to have established a hedge position protecting the value their investment. Other notable failures related to exchange-traded derivatives include Barings PLC, the 223-year-old London merchant bank that helped finance the Louisiana Purchase, and the Canadian Pacific Railway, which collapsed as a result of hidden derivatives losses.

Derivatives trading is risky business. But a lack of adequate internal controls led to many of the losses mentioned above. Internal controls must be airtight in a firm that engages in hedging or trading activities using exchange-traded or OTC derivatives. Insufficient market and product knowledge was also a major factor in these financial debacles.

Commodity Futures Primer

As mentioned previously, commodity futures contracts are agreements between buyers and sellers to make or take delivery of a commodity at a future date, at an agreed upon price. Commodity futures contracts are standardized. Contract specifications such as the contract size, delivery months, commodity grade, location of delivery and other details for each futures contract are preset in the contract terms. Price and quantity are the only things negotiated by the counterparties to a trade. In the United States, agricultural, industrial and financial futures are traded on organized exchanges known as contract markets.

The possibility of delivery keeps futures contracts in line with their underlying cash markets. If a contract rises too high in price relative to the cash market, traders might sell futures with the intent of making delivery. This forces the futures price down and is the reason futures markets reflect the price of their underlying cash market. Some futures contracts are "cash settled." The value of these contracts is derived from an underlying index value. When a futures contract is cash settled, traders will often use a calculated "fair value" to determine if the futures are high or low compared to the underlying index. If fair value indicates that futures are too high, a trader might sell futures expecting the difference to narrow.

Futures contracts do not have any intrinsic value in and of themselves; their value is derived from the underlying commodity, index or security. Because futures contracts "derive" their price from their underlying cash market they are called derivatives. There are other derivative markets, such as exchange-traded options on futures, options on securities, and over-the-counter (OTC) options, which will be discussed later in this section. The contracts traded on these markets also derive their values from an underlying commodity, security, or index.

The Principle of Offset

One of the features of commodity futures markets that make them so liquid and cost effective is the principle of offset. The obligation of the buyer (to accept future delivery) and the obligation seller (to make future delivery) is not with each other but with the central clearing function of the exchange (exchanges may have a separate clearing corporation or clearing may be a part of the exchange itself). Clearing matches futures transactions and becomes counterparty to both sides of the trade, eliminating counterparty credit risk by guarantying both sides of the transaction. As a result, traders can liquidate their positions (obligations) by merely executing an equal and opposite offsetting transaction (selling out a long position or buying back a short). Clearing also transfers funds between firms when futures trades are marked to market at the end of each day.

Trading on Margin

Commodity futures are traded on margin. Only a small percentage, usually about 5% of the contract's notional value, is required to establish a position (long or short) in a futures market (notional value is the contract size in units multiplied by the price per unit). Margins are set by the exchange for each commodity and are raised or lowered from time to time to reflect changing market volatility and notional contract values. Brokerage firms may require greater margin of their customers but may not require less than what the exchange has set. Each exchange will have a margin committee comprised of exchange members and support personnel that monitors and evaluates the markets and makes margin changes as appropriate.

There are two types of margin: initial margin, the amount of money per contract that must be present in the account when the position is initiated, and maintenance (variation) margin, the minimum amount of money per contract that must be maintained in the account while the position is open. For example, a December corn contract had a closing price of $2.84 1/4 per bushel. The notional value of this contract is $14,212 (5,000 bushels x $2.84 1/4). The Initial margin requirement set by the Chicago Board of Trade (CBOT) is $810 per contract which is 5.69% of the notional contract value while maintenance margin is set at $625 per contract which is 4.39% of the notional contract value. Positions can be liquidated without customer authorization in accounts that violate margin requirements.

Trading Basics

A trader who buys futures contracts (assuming this is not an offsetting transaction) is long the market and will profit if prices rise. (i.e. if you bought a December corn contract at $2.70 per bushel and the price rose to $2.80 per bushel, you would have an unrealized profit of $500 (.10 cents x 5,000 bushels)). Because open commodity positions (transactions that are not offset) are marked to market at the end of the trading day, this $500 profit will be credited to your trading account and is available as margin for additional contract purchases. This transfer of funds occurs through the clearing corporation of the exchange.

The transaction counterpart of the long buyer is the short seller. Using the above example, if you sold a December corn contract at $2.70 per bushel and the price rose to $2.80 per bushel you would have an unrealized loss of $500 (.10 cents x 5,000 bushels). Again, open commodity positions are marked to market at the end of the trading day meaning that this $500 loss will be debited from your trading account.

Options Primer

Like commodity futures contracts, options contracts are agreements between counterparties. The main difference between these markets is that commodity futures impose obligations on both the buyer and the seller to either make or take physical delivery of the commodity or to agree to cash settlement at contract expiration. Options contracts confer rights, not obligations, to the option buyer and impose obligations on the option seller. Importantly, if an option is not exercised, it just expires (over 90% of exchange-traded options expire worthless). In contrast, if a commodity contract is held to expiration, the long gets delivery and the short must make delivery. Options can be exchange-traded, over-the-counter (OTC), between individual business entities, or between individual persons. Businesses and individuals commonly use options in real estate, personal property and interest rate transactions.

Standardized exchange-traded options contracts are known as plain-vanilla options. That is, there are no embedded features that would affect the basic option contract.
(Off-exchange or OTC options often have embedded features that can make them complex or exotic.) Standardized equity options are traded at several exchanges in the United States. The most successful is the Chicago Board Options Exchange (CBOE).

Exchange-Traded Options

Like commodities futures, exchange-traded options are contract markets with central clearing that eliminates individual counterparty credit risk and allows offsetting transactions.

Option contracts are standardized, expire at a future date, are marked to market, call for physical delivery and are derivatives. This is where the similarities to commodity futures markets end.

The buyer of an option contract purchases the right, not the obligation, to buy or sell something at a specified price (exercise or strike price) by the expiration date of the option contract. The object of the option contract (what the option is written on) is called the underlying. The value of the underlying is the main (but not only) factor from which the option contract derives its value.

There are two kinds of options: Calls and Puts. A Call Option is the right but not the obligation to purchase the underlying security at the strike (exercise) price by the option's expiration date. A Put Option is the right but not the obligation to sell the underlying security at the strike (exercise) price by the option's expiration date. In options transactions, the seller of a Call option is the Call Writer while the seller of Put option is the Put Writer. Option buyers pay a premium to option writers for the options they buy. Option writers (sellers) collect this premium for the options they write and are obligated to deliver the underlying security if the option is exercised.

Exchange-traded equity options are standardized, plain-vanilla, American Style options. American Style options can be exercised at any time by the buyer (European Style options can only be exercised on the expiration day). For example, IBM Call Options traded at the CBOE are for 100 shares of IBM common stock. The option writer is obligated to deliver 100 shares of IBM common stock at the strike price if the option buyer chooses to exercise the option.

Relationship of the Underlying to an Option

The value of options is primarily derived from the value of the underlying. For example, IBM common stock closed today at $88.29 per share and the strike prices of the October 2004 IBM Calls ranged from $65 per share to $135 per share. The more that the share price of IBM is above a particular strike price the greater the value of that option. The stock price of $88 per share is about $23 over the strike price of the IBM $65 Calls. The current premium for IBM $65 Calls is $22.90 per share. A trader who had previously bought this call option could sell it back into the market for about $2,290 ($22.90 x 100 shares) or could exercise the option and buy the stock at $65 with the market at $88.

Options can be in the money, out of the money, or at the money. A Call Option is in the money when the price of the underlying exceeds its strike price. Likewise, a Put option is in the money when the price of the underlying is less than its strike price. Options are at the money when the price of the underlying is about the same as the strike price. All other options are out of the money.

Option Values and Premiums

There are two values that make up option premiums: intrinsic value and time value. To have any intrinsic value an option must be in the money. Out of the money options have only time value. From the above example, the IBM $85 Call closed today at a premium of $5.70 per share. This Call option is $3 in the money because the underlying IBM stock closed above the strike price at $88 per share. The premium has $3 intrinsic value while the remaining $2.70 is time value.

While the concept of intrinsic value is rather straightforward the concept of time value is complex and beyond the scope of this writing. It is worth noting, however, that the mathematical formula for pricing option time value was first introduced by Fischer Black and Myron S. Scholes in 1973. The formula takes six factors into account: underlying price, strike price, time to expiration, volatility of the underlying, dividends and interest rates. For further information on this and other topics on options, visit the Learning Center on the CBOE Web page (www.cboe.com).

Over-the-Counter (OTC) Options

OTC options are agreements made between private parties. Banks, large brokerage firms, insurance companies and many other businesses are active in the OTC options markets. Trillions of dollars in notional value are at stake in the OTC market on a daily basis.

OTC options are not centrally cleared or standardized. These options are usually customized by the option writer to fit the needs of the option buyer. Because OTC options are not centrally cleared counterparty, credit risk can be a major concern and risk factor. The option is worthless if the option writer cannot perform.

OTC options can be plain vanilla, complex or exotic. The complex and exotic forms can be particularly problematic for market participants, accountants, and auditors and are beyond the scope of this writing.

Securities Fraud Schemes

Securities Fraud by Registered Persons and Entities

Frequent allegations of misconduct by registered individuals or firms fall into one or more of the following areas:

Churning

Churning is the excessive trading of a customer account for the purpose of generating commissions. For securities and options there is a commission charged when the trade is entered into and when the trade is liquidated. Commodity futures have a round turn commission scheme meaning that the commission covers both the purchase and sale. Commissions on commodity futures are not charged until the trade is closed out.

DEFINITION OF EXCESSIVE TRADING ACTIVITY

The Commodity Futures Trading Commission (CFTC) states that to establish churning, a complainant must prove that (1) the broker controlled the trading in an account; (2) the volume of trading was excessive in light of the complainant's trading objectives; and (3) the broker acted with intent to defraud or with reckless disregard for the customer's interests. Hinch v. Commonwealth Financial Group, Inc., [1996-1998 Transfer Binder] Comm. Fut. L. Rep. ¶ 27,056 at 45,020 (CFTC May 13, 1997); Johnson v. Don Charles & Company, [1990-1992 Transfer Binder] Comm. Fut. L. Rep. (CCH) ¶ 24,986 (CFTC Jan. 16, 1991).

Two questions arise in churning cases: who had trading authorization over the account and when did the account activity and commissions become excessive. If a customer is making his own trades he cannot possibly accuse the broker of churning his account. But if the broker or some other person has trading authority (discretion) over the account and participates in the commissions, a conflict of interest exists and there may be predication for a charge of churning.

The NASD and CFTC definitions of churning are inherently vague and offer little practical guidance. Customer trading objectives are simple: make profits and avoid losses. The best test to detect churning is to calculate the amount of monthly gross commissions generated from the account as a percentage of the average account balance. For example, an active trading account with an average daily balance of $10,000 might reasonably generate (on the high side) about $500 dollars (5%) in gross commissions in an average month. Gross commissions would probably increase in months when the markets are experiencing greater price volatility and trading has been successful. The CFE should look for the following indicators:

- Did the broker have trading authority (discretion) over the account?
- Have gross commissions increased during periods of decreasing market volatility?
- Are the gross commissions for the month in question substantially higher than the average monthly gross commissions for this account?
- Are gross commissions greater than 5% of the average account balance?
- Did commissions consume realized profits and/or aggravate losses?
- Were numerous trades entered into and exited over short time periods for small gains or losses?
- Was the trading unit (number of contracts per trade) too large for this account (overtrading)?
- Were the trades made for this account recommended by the research department of the brokerage and disseminated to other customers?
- Did unauthorized trading take place?

If the broker had discretionary authority to trade the account and any of the above factors are true, further investigation for churning is warranted. Finally, brokerage supervisors are required to perform due diligence to assure that churning and other trading abuses do not occur.

Unsuitable Recommendations

Securities representatives are required to "know their customer." They must take into account the financial profile and level of sophistication of the individual investor. Placing clients into unsuitable securities, for example recommending high-risk options to a senior citizen with limited assets, is prohibited.

EXAMPLE

UNITED STATES SECURITIES AND EXCHANGE COMMISSION
Litigation Release No. 17818 / October 30, 2002
U.S. Securities and Exchange Commission v. Southmark Advisory, Inc., Southmark, Inc., and Wendell D. Belden, Civil Action No. 02-CV-830-E (N.D. Okla. 2002)

SEC charged Southmark Advisory, Inc., Southmark, Inc., and Wendell D. Belden with securities fraud, based on deceptive sales practices that enriched Belden at his clients' expense.

The Securities and Exchange Commission announced that it filed a securities fraud action in the United States District Court for the Northern District of Oklahoma, against Southmark Advisory, Inc., an SEC-registered investment adviser, Southmark, Inc., an SEC-registered broker-dealer, and Wendell D. Belden, the owner of both firms, all located in Tulsa, Oklahoma. According to the SEC's complaint, from 1996 and through 2002, Belden used Southmark Advisory and Southmark, Inc. to defraud his predominantly elderly clients, by misleading them about their investment options and the security of their invested principal, and by investing their money in a manner calculated to enrich himself at their expense.

The SEC alleged that Belden attracted seniors who wanted safe investments by advertising certificates of deposit ("CDs") in local periodicals and the yellow pages, and then, in a classic "bait and switch" maneuver, aggressively pitched to the prospective investors, in lieu of CDs, a purportedly personalized, managed mutual fund investment program. The SEC alleged that Belden defrauded his clients by lying about the safety of the managed mutual fund program; by failing to tell the clients about other investment options that were more advantageous; by failing to tell the clients that his brokerage firm, Southmark, Inc., would earn a 4% sales commission if the clients invested in the managed mutual fund program; and by failing to tell the clients about disciplinary sanctions that the State of Oklahoma and the NASD had imposed against Belden. According to the SEC, since 1996, Belden and his Southmark entities have, by way of this fraudulent scheme, sold mutual fund shares worth at least $82,801,550, victimized at least 400 predominantly elderly or retired investors, and fraudulently earned at least $5,000,000, including $3,312,062 in brokerage commissions. Contrary to Belden's fraudulent assurances that the managed mutual fund investments were "as safe as" or "safer than" CDs, many investors have seen the value of their investment in the mutual fund program diminish significantly during the recent bear market.

Failure to Supervise

Broker-dealer firms are responsible for oversight of their representatives to ensure adherence to Rules of Fair Practice and state and federal laws.

Failure to Report Client Complaints

Investment and advisory firms are required to report client complaints to the SEC, yet may neglect to do so, fearing an investigation.

Parking

Parking is the practice of selling a security to one party with the understanding that the seller will repurchase the security later at an agreed-upon price. This scheme allows circumvention of ownership reporting requirements and net capital rules.

Front Running - Dual Trading

Front running an order is a type of insider trading. Although it usually will not cause a direct loss to the customer it could and is a violation of exchange rules. Front running involves the privileged knowledge of an order, placed by a customer, to buy or sell a large amount of a commodity, options, or security that, because of its size, is likely to move the market. Back office personnel could have knowledge of such an order and buy or sell for their own account ahead of the customer. Because order fillers on the exchange floor are allowed to trade for their own account and fill orders for customers (dual trading) they also have an opportunity.

Consider the following scenario: an order is received from a hedger to sell 500 December cattle futures contracts at the market. If the order filler knows that current market conditions are such that this order will move the market significantly lower, it would be very tempting to sell a few contracts for himself and profit from the market decline when he executes the customer order. Order fillers are required to operate in the best interest of the customer and "work" the order to get the best price. However, once the trader has established his short position, it is really in his own interest to drive the market as far down as possible when executing the 500 contract sell order. In this situation, the order filler may not give his best efforts and could hurt the customer.

The vast majority of exchange members would never put themselves ahead of a customer, but it has happened in the past. In today's markets with sophisticated surveillance, exchange investigative personnel actively guard against this type of activity. The time stamps on the customer order, Time and Sales reports from the exchange, and the account activity of the trader would have to be obtained and examined to substantiate any front running allegation. This information is easily obtainable. Brokerage compliance personnel should easily detect front running by back office personnel by periodically checking their account activity or not allowing them to open trading accounts at all.

Bucket Shops

Bucket shops are fraudulent enterprises that masquerade as licensed brokerage operations. A true retail futures brokerage would be required to be registered and meet certain financial thresholds. Salespeople would be required to pass the Series Three National Commodity Futures Examination and all other personnel would need to be registered as Associated Persons. There may also be other registration or licensing requirements depending on the type of business that the brokerage engages in.
(See www.nfa.futures.org/registration/who_has_to_register.asp). Bucket shops bypass all these requirements and operate like legitimate businesses.

The solution to finding whether or not an individual or firm is legitimate is easy. Go to:
www.nfa.futures.org/basicnet for commodity futures brokers and firms
www.nasdbrokercheck.com for stock, options and futures brokers and firms
www.sec.gov/investor/brokers.htm for securities brokers and firms

You will be able to search files for any firm or individual authorized to do securities, options or futures business, their license status and any complaints brought against them. If a firm or professional does not appear on one of these pages they are not legitimate.

Excessive Markups

Excessive markups involve selling at marked up price or buying at marked down price not reasonably related to the prevailing market price.

Misuse or Misappropriation of Customer's Securities

This scheme may involve outright theft or using the securities in improper ways, e.g., as collateral for loans or to conduct other securities transactions (e.g., margin trading).

Unauthorized Trading

Unless otherwise agreed to in writing, only the customer named on the trading account can authorize trades. Any losses accruing to the customer account because of an unauthorized trade, whether made by mistake or intentionally, are the responsibility of the brokerage firm and must be reimbursed to the customer. Gains from unauthorized trades also belong to the customer. This prevents brokers from executing unauthorized trades, claiming error, and taking any profits that may occur. The only entries to the brokerage company error account should be losses; profits in an error account should be investigated. Customers must report unauthorized trades to the management of the brokerage firm as soon as detected. Silence would imply ratification of the transaction.

Systematically Trading Accounts Against Each Other

Systematically trading accounts against each other usually occurs between investment pools. The scheme involves someone with trading authority simultaneously establishing opposite market positions in two separate investment pools that he controls. A person who has trading authority and other controls over the pool may receive a monthly management fee of about 1.5% of the pool balance, a percentage of any of the pool's gains, perhaps 10% per quarter, and a portion or all of the commissions on trades. The conflicts of interest in such a business arrangement are obvious. It is in the interest of the pool operator to maintain account balances a high as possible, trade the accounts for commissions and to have at least some profits.

Assume that a pool operator established two limited partnerships for trading commodities, that he was general partner of both partnerships, and that he was to be compensated as previously described. The general partner, who has trading authority, then buys 100 contracts of December Corn for Pool A, establishing a long market position, and at the same time sells 100 contracts of December Corn for Pool B, establishing a short market position. (If these transactions occurred in the same account they would offset each other.)

Over time one of the pools will suffer a loss while the other will enjoy a gain. For the general partner things haven't changed much. The amount of equity in the two pools combined will be about the same with the loss in one pool being offset by the gain in the other pool. This preserves the basis for general partner's management fee while the profitable pool will owe him a percentage of the gain.

In the long run, one of the investment pools will dissolve because of trading losses while the other will enjoy handsome profits. This then takes on some of the characteristics of a Ponzi scheme when the pool operator creates a new limited partnership, advertises his success from the results of the profitable pool, and participants in the successful pool tell their friends. The trick here is to ensure that participants in the original two pools don't know each other.

Supervisors and compliance managers of brokerages should be on the lookout for this type of activity. They can do little, however, if the general partner maintains the trading accounts at two separate brokerages. The CFE will need to acquire the trading records of all pools run by a pool operator in order to establish if such a trading scheme has occurred. The comparison of market positions over time is simple and the information is easily obtainable from the brokerages once it is discovered who they are.

The general partner would have committed a material breach of contract in that he failed in his fiduciary duties to the limited partners. There are also numerous violations of federal regulatory and SRO rules that prohibit this type of trading scheme.

Block Order Schemes

When several different accounts are combined on the same order it is called a block order. For example, a broker may wish to execute the same buy order for ten of his customers. To accomplish this he may write an order ticket such as: "For account 12345 and others, buy 100 contracts of December cattle at the market." The justification for this type of order is that time is of the essence. If the market is volatile, customers will need their order executed as quickly as possible. Writing ten separate order tickets for each account and calling the orders to the trading floor separately would take too much time. By combining all the orders on one ticket and providing one account number, time is saved and the other account numbers and quantities can be added to the order ticket when the executed order (fill) is reported back to the broker.

The potential for abuse is obvious. Prices move rapidly in volatile markets and the accounts the order has been executed for have not all been made known. The time from when the block order is placed and when the fill is reported back to the broker can take many minutes. On some busy days it can take an hour or more. During this time the market is moving and the executed order will either be in a loss or gain position by the time it is reported back. This is where fraud can occur.

For example, assume that 100 contracts of December cattle were bought at 80.00 (cents per pound) and that when the fill is reported thirty minutes later the market is at 81.00. This favorable change in market price (100 points) is equivalent to $400 profit per contract or $40,000 profit for the entire order. The broker then gives out the "other" account numbers to the floor clerk to complete the order with 55 contracts going to a favored account and 5 contracts going to the other nine accounts. The broker then immediately sells 55 December cattle contracts for the favored account realizing a $22,000 profit. Of course, if the market had moved lower by the time the fill was reported the favored account would not have been added to the order or the loss taken would have been minimal.

Proving such a scheme is easy. The CFE will need to obtain 1) the monthly brokerage recap of the salesman, 2) copies of all order tickets written by the salesman for the time period in question (brokerages must keep the hard copies for several years), 3) a copy of the telephone audio recording of the placement of the order and reported fill from the trading floor (all calls to the trading floor are recorded and archived), and 4) copies of the "daily equity statements" provided to the salesman by the brokerage firm detailing account numbers, account names, open positions and the cash value of all accounts represented by the salesman. A block order scheme will easily be detected by analyzing this information.

Market Manipulation

Market manipulation consists of a series of transactions designed to artificially raise/lower price or to give appearance of trading activity for the purpose of inducing others to buy or sell. This is especially common with "penny stocks" or "micro-cap" stocks. "Penny Stocks" are low-priced (usually less than $5), speculative securities that are registered but do not meet the listing requirements of an exchange. "Micro-cap" just means the stocks of companies with very small market capitalization. Once the price has been artificially inflated the stock is then sold to unsuspecting victims.

Insider Trading

Under the legal theory of misappropriation, the use of non-public information to profit from purchase or sale of securities may violate the insiders' fiduciary duty to their company or shareholders. Although not all courts accept this argument, criminal charges are not unusual in cases of this nature. Ivan Boesky and Michael Milken, indicted for insider trading in the late 1980s, both served time in prison.

EXAMPLE

A California psychotherapist, pleaded guilty to securities fraud after federal officials accused him of making a nice profit after trading on some inside information he learned during a counseling session with a client.

According to federal officials, the psychotherapist bought common stock in Lockheed Corp. hours after his client—a company executive undergoing marriage counseling—mentioned the secret and ultimately successful merger talks between Lockheed and Martin Marietta Corp.

Under a legal doctrine known as the "misappropriation theory," he was deemed to have violated securities laws because he stole information from a person who had assumed his trust and discretion, and then used the information to trade on the stock market.

PUBLIC DISCLOSURE REQUIREMENTS

Effective October 23, 2000, the SEC adopted new rules concerning public disclosure of information. Regulation FD (Fair Disclosure) was promulgated to eliminate "selective" disclosure by companies to certain groups (such as brokers and analysts) before such information was made available to the public.

The Regulation states that if a company, or someone on its behalf, discloses "material non-public" information to a particular group (primarily market securities professionals), it must make a public disclosure of the information. The timing of the disclosure depends on whether the disclosure was intentional or inadvertent. If the disclosure was intentional, then company must make the disclosure simultaneously. If the disclosure was inadvertent, then the company must make the disclosure "promptly."

The SEC provides three options for proper dissemination:
1. File the information with the SEC on a Form 8-K.
2. Disseminate the information through a press release.
3. Disseminate the information through any other method or combination of methods that are reasonably designed to provide broad public distribution of the information, such as an announcement at a press conference open to the public.

Regulation FD only applies to material communications between company executives or authorized spokespersons to analysts, institutional investors, and holders of the company's stock. Regulation FD also applies only to senior executives and excludes communications with the media, with ratings agencies, and with customers conducted in the normal course of business. Information is considered "material" if there is a substantial likelihood that a reasonable shareholder would consider it important in making an investment decision, or if it would have significantly altered the total mix of information available.

INSIDER TRADING RULES

In connection with Regulation FD, the SEC also issued Rule 10b5-1 and Rule 10b5-2. Rule 10b5-1 addresses the issue of when insider trading liability arises in connection with a trader's "use" or "knowing possession" of material non-public information. The rule provides that a person trades "on the basis of" material non-public information when the person purchases or sells securities while aware of the information. However, the rule also sets forth several affirmative defenses for traders if they can show that the information was not a factor in the trade decision.

Rule 10b5-2 addresses the issue of when a breach of a family or other non-business relationship may give rise to liability under the misappropriation theory of insider trading. Under the misappropriation theory, as defined by the Supreme Court case in *United States v. O'Hagan*, 521 U.S. 642 (1997), a person is liable for securities fraud if he or she:

- Misappropriates confidential information,
- For the purpose of securities trading,
- In breach of a duty owed to the sources, and
- Trades based on the misappropriated information.

The new Rule 10b5-2 seeks to provide further guidance regarding what types of relationships create a "duty" not to use the information received. For example, if a person agrees to keep the information in confidence, a duty of trust or confidence will exist. Similarly, if two persons have a "history, pattern, or practice of sharing confidences," such that the recipient reasonably should know that the other expects that the inside information will remain confidential, a duty of trust or confidence will exist.

Subsection (b)(3) also creates a presumption that any person who receives inside information from his or her spouse, parent, child, or sibling will owe that other person a duty of trust or confidence.

Disclosures (Misrepresentations and Omissions)

Securities laws require that the investor receive full and fair disclosure of all material information. Giving the investor or prospective investor false or misleading information is clearly a misrepresentation. An omission occurs where the issuer, in connection with the offer or sale of securities, omits to state a material fact necessary in order to make the statements made not misleading. Making misrepresentations to the investor or failing to inform the investor of certain facts (omissions) is a violation of both state and federal law only if the misrepresentation or omission is material.

It is important to show the *materiality* of misrepresentations or omissions. Even if representations made, for example in a prospectus, are clearly false, it is still necessary to show materiality. In a 1988 decision, the Supreme Court stated that a fact is material "if its disclosure would change the total mix of facts available and there is a substantial likelihood that a reasonable shareholder would consider the facts important to her investment decision." *See, Basic Inc. v Levinson*, 485 U.S. 224 (1988).

As a general rule, the examiner or investigator needs to determine the answer to the following question: Would a reasonable investor wish to know this information in order to make an informed decision? If the answer is "yes," then this information, or the lack thereof, has a high likelihood of being deemed material. (If an actual investor acted based on the misrepresentation, that clearly strengthens the case, but it is not essential that the false or misleading statement influenced an investor, merely that a reasonable investor could have been so influenced.)

The issuer of a biotechnology stock falsely claiming that the Food and Drug Administration has approved their new cancer drug would be an example of a misrepresentation which is clearly material to any prospective investor. Similarly, if the Chairman of the company had recently been released from prison after serving time for securities fraud, this fact should feature prominently in any offering document. Failure to disclose this fact would obviously constitute the omission of a material fact.

The SEC has adopted a so-called "safe harbor" provision whereby certain forward-looking statements and projections will not be held to be fraudulent. Issuers will not be held liable if these type of statements were believed true at the time and were accompanied by appropriate cautionary language.

Note also that federal and state laws usually prohibit the promoter from stating that the offering has government approval of some kind. For example, even if the offering is registered, the promoter cannot state that it is "SEC approved."

Securities Fraud by Unregistered Persons

In conducting investigations or examinations relating to alleged violations of the securities laws, the fraud examiner should always begin by seeking the answer to these crucial questions:

- Is the security registered? If not, does it meet an exemption?
- Is the person offering or selling the security registered? If not, is the transaction exempt?
- Are there indicators of fraud present?

Exemptions

Examples of exemptions under the 1933 Act include securities issued by the U.S. Government and those issued by state or local governments. Registration is also not required for limited offerings of securities issued pursuant to Regulation D of the Act.

Issuance of securities undertaken pursuant to Rules 501 through 508 of "Reg D" is fairly complex, but for these purposes the essential elements are as follows:

- Rule 501 defines "accredited investors" to include banks, insurance companies, certain charities, and individuals with a net worth exceeding $1 million or annual income of more than $200,000 ($300,000 including spouse).
- Rule 504 allows an issuer to sell up to $1 million in securities in a 12-month period to any number of purchasers. Rule 504 also allows general solicitation and advertising.
- Rule 505 increases the limit to $5 million, reduces the maximum number of non-accredited investors to 35, and does not allow general solicitation or advertising.
- Rule 506 allows the issuance of any amount of securities to any number of accredited and up to 35 non-accredited but sophisticated investors. Again no general solicitation or advertising is allowed.

The most relied upon exemption from registration where we are likely to see fraud is the so-called "private placement" exemption. In most states, this exemption is available where the security is sold to a small number of people and there is no general solicitation. In Florida, for example, there must be no more than 35 non-accredited investors in a 12-month period, they must receive full and fair disclosure of material information, and there is a prohibition on general solicitation or advertising. It is common to find that one or more of the conditions necessary for the claimed exemption are not present and/or that the offering is fraudulent.

Investigative Tips

Promotional Materials

Usually, but by no means on every occasion, the fraud examiner will discover that various written information has been provided to investors and potential investors. This disclosure is often in the form of documents entitled "prospectus," "offering memorandum," or "private placement offering memorandum." These documents can sometimes provide the "smoking gun" and should therefore be examined in detail. Do not overlook the information utilized in various advertising media to persuade the public to invest. How did the investor hear of this opportunity? Cold call, direct mail, newspapers, magazines, television, or the Internet?

A properly-prepared prospectus (usually indicates that the issuer claims the security is registered) or a private placement memorandum (the issuer claims the security is exempt) would normally be expected to contain detailed information concerning the issuer and the security being offered.

Such information should describe the type of security, the initial price, and the amount being offered for sale. The issuing company, its business, products, background, and the qualifications of its officers and directors should be described. Any legal problems involving the company or its officers should be disclosed. The financial condition of the issuer should be discussed with audited financial statements where applicable. Frequently, there will be projections or forecasts of expected future growth and development (see "safe harbor" provisions discussed earlier). Usually, there will be risk disclosures of various kinds in bold font stating that, for example, "these securities have not been registered" or "purchase of these securities involves a high degree of risk."

These documents should be examined thoroughly for misrepresentations, omissions, and downright lies. Look closely at the background of principals. If in doubt, conduct a detailed background investigation of the principal officers of the corporation. Look especially for any previous criminal or regulatory action relating to securities fraud or offenses involving dishonesty. Also check for lawsuits, bankruptcies, or other civil or administrative action against the entity or its principals whether allegedly resolved or not. Look not only for the disposition of the action, but also for potential evidence gathered during the course of the suit, for example, depositions. Do not forget to verify any claimed experience in the relevant industry or academic qualifications. Compare closely the information, if any, disclosed in advertisements and the offering document with the results of the background investigation.

A few other pertinent questions are:
- What promises are made regarding the viability of the product or service? Is a patent claimed? Does it exist?
- Is there a functioning business you can check out or is it in the "developmental stage"? Ascertain when and where the corporation was legally incorporated, or in the case of a partnership, where it was legally filed.
- Are investors promised guaranteed returns?
- Can financial statements concerning assets, liabilities, and income be verified?
- How will investor funds be used? Follow the money trail! Were the proceeds invested as represented or used for other purposes? Is the issue potentially oversubscribed?
- Are sales commissions paid to unregistered persons? Usually this is illegal. Also check to see if commissions paid are unusually high or concealed from investors.
- Are the insiders retaining a majority of the stock while the investors fund the company? Are there any other undisclosed benefits to insiders?
- Is there adequate risk disclosure? Investors may not have been made fully aware of a high percentage of failure, the degree of competition, or inexperience on the part of the principals.

Is it a Security or an Investment?

Some states include an investment fraud provision in their securities law. The advantage of this provision, if available, is that usually "investment" is much more broadly defined than "security." For example, in Florida, investment means the commitment of money or property principally induced by a representation that an economic benefit may be derived. In many cases, it is much easier to prove that there is an investment than to show there was a security sold. The violation, of course, would be the fraud in relation to the sale of the investment and would constitute a third degree felony in the State of Florida.

Investigative Resources
- *Central Registration Depository (CRD)* run by NASD is a national database of information on registered (and some unregistered) individuals and companies. Now available via the Internet to authorized users, it includes qualification, employment, and disciplinary actions in addition to basic biographical data.
- *North American State Securities Administrators Association (NASAA)* the organization of state securities regulators. (www.nasaa.org)
- *Federal Trade Commission* has bulletins regarding a number of investment and other securities (www.ftc.gov)

- *Securities and Exchange Commission.* The SEC home page is an excellent source of information and links. In addition to general information and details of enforcement actions, the public can also access the Electronic Data Gathering Analysis, and Retrieval System (EDGAR). EDGAR contains many of the documents that public companies are required to file with the Commission, including the annual report known as a 10-K. (www.sec.gov)

Self-Regulatory Organizations mentioned previously are all a good source of information and a useful resource for the investigator:
- National Association of Securities Dealers (www.nasd.com)
- Commodities Futures Trading Commission (www.cftc.gov)
- National Futures Association (www.nfa.futures.org)
- New York Stock Exchange (www.nyse.com)

Securities Fraud and the Internet

Of course, the very technology that gives us access to almost limitless information also gives the criminal greater opportunity to commit crime. Another factor that works in favor of the online scam artist is that there has traditionally been a culture of trust and benevolence on the Internet.

Using the Internet to promote fraudulent investment schemes is relatively easy and cheap. There is the potential to reach hundreds of thousands of people using equipment and software that are very inexpensive. There is such competition between providers of Internet access that the cost of maintaining a home page on the Web is very low.

The Internet is already being used to solicit investors. Many illegal pyramid schemes have excellent looking websites, for example. Use of e-mail and the Internet also makes it easier for the crooks to conceal their identities and operate anonymously from other countries.

Securities laws are based on geographic boundaries; on the Internet there are no boundaries. With the proliferation of "cyber cash" and various ways of exchanging payment for goods and services over the Internet, the fraud examiner can expect to see a huge rise in financial fraud committed online. Particularly prevalent online are the so called "pump-and-dump" schemes where promoters use Internet newsletters and bulletin boards to hype stocks they bought for little or no money so they can sell on a rising market.

Same Old Frauds, New Medium

Many of the fraudulent schemes proliferating in cyberspace are not new; rather, they are recycled and repackaged to appeal to a new generation of gullible consumers.

Newsletters

In this context, a "newsletter" is not an independent, objectively written article discussing the merits of a particular securities offering. Such objective analysis does exist but, more often than not, the slick marketing document is a far cry from the independent analysis that it purports to be. In reality, the company publishing the "newsletter" is often paid to hype a particular stock by the promoter. Consequently, there is a serious danger of misrepresentation to the investor. Usually the cozy relationship between the stock promoter and the "newsletter" publisher is not disclosed to the prospective investor. Neither is the fact that the promoter pays to have his particular offering receive prominent and flattering treatment.

The "newsletter" may take the form of an actual document mailed out to subscribers who may or may not pay for the privilege. Often, the information is imparted through a professional website designed to motivate investors to act on the great opportunity being offered.

Usually, information will be gathered on those who subscribe to such publications or view the website. This data is a rich mine of free leads to securities representatives or others who promote the securities being hyped in the "newsletter." The identity of investors who have shown some type of interest in a particular offering covered in the publication is a valuable source of new business.

Online Trading

A recent legal opinion has allowed a bulletin board to be used to buy and sell securities without registration. This bypassing of federal registration requirements may make the raising of venture capital easier, but it will reduce consumer protection and potentially create a regulatory nightmare.

Greater utilization of the Internet to promote both legitimate and fraudulent securities offerings will increasingly challenge the investigator or examiner. The fraud examiner will continue to face jurisdictional as well as technical issues as the Internet becomes the medium of choice for the financial criminal.

[Editor's Note: The Association would like to thank Chris Hancock, CFE, for his assistance in preparing this chapter. Mr. Hancock is the investigations manager for the State of Florida Department of Banking and Finance, Northwest Florida Region, and specializes in the investigation of financial crime with an emphasis on securities fraud.

We would also like to thank Richard J. Bobel, MBA, CFE, CPA, who authored the material on commodities, options, and derivatives. Mr. Bobel is a former commodity broker and college/university faculty member who specialized in derivative markets and worked for many years as a research economist for the Chicago Board of Trade where he designed commodity futures and options contracts. Richard was a contributing author to the CBOT Commodity Trading Manual *and the* CBOT Speculation Workbook. *He can contacted at 847-828-7417 or at RJB@RJBCPA.com]*

MONEY LAUNDERING

Introduction

Money laundering is the disguising of the existence, nature, source, ownership, location, and disposition of property derived from criminal activity. It is big business. The United Nations estimates that money produced by narcotics trafficking and other illegal activities might exceed $400 billion annually.

The "washing" of money includes all forms of illegal activities. In most instances the goal is to conduct transactions in cash (currency) in such a way as to conceal the true nature of transactions. Problems occur regarding large volumes of cash—transporting it, converting small denomination bills to larger denomination bills, and converting cash into assets which can be invested and/or spent.

Placement

Placement of funds into a financial institution is the initial step in the process. It is at this step that legislation has been developed to prevent launderers from depositing or converting large amounts of cash at financial institutions or taking cash out of the country. Money laundering schemes are most often detected at this stage.

Placement can take any number of forms. If the money launderer has a large amount of cash, he can move the money out of the country in a suitcase and deposit it in an off-shore bank. Another choice is to break up the money into smaller amounts and deposit it into bank accounts or purchase cashier's checks, traveler's checks, or money orders. The process of breaking transactions up into smaller amounts to evade the reporting requirements is known as *smurfing*. A sophisticated smurfing operation might involve hundreds of bank accounts in dozens of cities.

Once the funds have been deposited into a financial institution, a launderer can move the funds around by using layers of financial transactions designed to confuse the audit trail. The money can even be transported out of the country through wire transfers.

Integration

The final stage in the laundering process is the *integration* of the money back into the economy in such a way as to make it appear to be a legitimate business transaction. This stage of the process is also difficult to detect; however, if the integration process creates a paper trail such as deeds for real estate, invoices, loan documents, Currency Transaction Reports (CTRs), checks, etc., and if there is cooperation from informants or foreign entities, then the chances of detection are improved.

A money laundering scheme cannot be successful until the paper trail is eliminated or made so complex that the flow of illegal income cannot be easily traced. The number of steps used to launder funds depends on how much distance the money launderer wishes to put between the illegally earned cash and the laundered asset into which it is converted. A greater number of steps increases the complexity of tracing the funds, but it also increases the length of the paper trail and the chance that the transaction will be reported.

The object of money laundering is not only to disguise the source of illegal funds, but also to convert large stores of currency into other assets. In some cases, illegal funds are spent on personal assets: homes, cars, jewelry, furniture, etc. But the typical money launderer will not dispose of all his illegal currency in this manner; he will want to have a certain amount of liquid reserves for spending. Keeping large bundles of cash is inefficient because they are difficult to hide and transport. Therefore, money launderers will often convert substantial portions of their currency into negotiable instruments such as cashier's checks and money orders, which are routinely issued by financial institutions. Criminals prefer these negotiable instruments for two reasons. First, cashier's checks and money orders are bearer instruments, and the holder can use them or deposit them without having to prove the source of the funds. Second, they are "liquid" assets because the holder can use them immediately.

The following is an example of how a money laundering scheme operates.

EXAMPLE

Alberto Barrera, dubbed "Papa Smurf" by the federal agents investigating him, ran a rather sophisticated smurfing operation out of Miami involving bank accounts in cities all over the country. Barrera and his accomplices would fly to Phoenix, Denver, Omaha, Portland, and other cities. When they arrived they would immediately travel to various banks within each city. The scheme would begin with the purchase of cashier's checks and money orders in amounts less than $10,000 (to avoid federal reporting requirements). This would be repeated several times at different banks. The "Smurfs" would then travel to another city where some of the previously purchased check and money orders would be deposited in accounts controlled by Barrera. Then more purchases of cashier's checks and *money orders would be made before the group traveled on to the next city. Once the money was converted or deposited, much of it was transferred to off-shore banks.*

Using a Legitimate Business to Launder Funds

One of the most common methods of laundering funds is to filter the money through a legitimate business, otherwise known as a "front" business. A front business can be a very effective way to launder money because it provides a safe place for organizing and managing criminal activity, where the comings and goings of large numbers of people will not arouse undue suspicion. In addition, a front that does legitimate business provides cover for delivery and transportation related to illegal activity. The expenses from illegal activity can be attributed to the legitimate enterprise, and illegal revenues can be easily placed into the enterprise.

There are three methods that are most commonly used to hide assets or launder money through a front business: overstatement of reported revenues, overstatement of reported expenses, and balance sheet laundering.

Overstatement of Reported Revenues

Overstating revenues, also known as *income sheet laundering,* occurs when the money launderer records more income on the books of a business than is actually generated by that business. The fictitious revenue accounts for the illegal funds that are secretly inserted into the company.

EXAMPLE

ABC Used Cars encourages customers to pay with cash. If the customer pays in cash, he receives a discount which might be as high as 25%. The invoice, however, makes no mention of this cash discount. The company reports the full sales amount as income. Depending on the number of cars sold, the company can launder thousands of dollars in illegal income.

Overstatement of Reported Expenses

The disadvantage of overstating revenues is that taxes will be due on the income reported. Therefore, if a company overstates its revenue, it will also want to overstate its expenses to offset its tax liability. The fictitious expenses also enable the perpetrator to siphon money back out of the business in order to make payoffs, buy illegal goods, or invest in other criminal ventures.

Overstating expenses can be accomplished very easily by reporting payments for supplies never received, professional services never rendered, or wages for fictitious employees.

> EXAMPLE
>
> *ABC Used Cars reports wages for three mechanics and an assistant manager who do not exist. The company also reports payments of over $200,000 a year to several lawyers, accountants, and other "consultants" who do little, if any, actual work.*

Income statement laundering, which includes both overstated revenues and expenses, can be difficult to detect. When artificial price inflation is applied in moderate percentages to goods and services whose market value is difficult to establish (e.g., artwork, used cars, consulting fees, advertising expenses), detection is exceedingly difficult without inside information. Complete fabrication of transactions, on the other hand, or creation of "ghost" employees is somewhat easier to spot.

Depositing Cash and Writing Checks in Excess of Reported Revenues and Expenses (Balance Sheet Laundering)

Rather than attempting to disguise money as normal business revenue, excess funds can simply be deposited into the bank account of the business. This technique is known as balance sheet laundering because it is independent of the money that flows in and out of the business.

> EXAMPLE
>
> *ABC Used Cars deposits an additional $30,000 per month in its account although there are no recorded sales for this amount. At the end of the year, the company has an extra $360,000 in cash in its account.*

This type of scheme can be detected by examining the revenue records of the business. Every legitimate asset in a company's possession had to have come from somewhere— if not from revenues then from a limited number of other credible alternatives. The basic alternative sources are loans, sale of property or equipment, and capital investments from shareholders. All of these transactions require significant documentary evidence, which the examiner should seek out to explain any suspicious infusion of cash into a suspect business.

Favorite Businesses for Hiding or Laundering Money

In general terms, the businesses chosen for money laundering possess one or more of the following characteristics:

- *Revenue:* A revenue base that is difficult to measure because most revenue comes from cash transactions with a highly variable amount per customer. This allows extra money to be brought into the business and disguised as revenue.
- *Expense:* Expenses that are variable and difficult to measure can enable the launderer to extract money from the front business without giving rise to undue suspicion.
- *History:* Historical ties either with the ethnic base of a particular criminal group or with industries that have traditionally served as a base for criminal activity.

Bars, Restaurants, and Night Clubs

Businesses that are commonly used to front money laundering operations include bars, restaurants, and nightclubs. These businesses charge relatively high prices, and customers vary widely in their purchases. Sales are generally in cash, and it is notoriously difficult to match the cost of providing food, liquor, and entertainment with the revenues they produce. Fast food restaurants are also frequently used to front for money laundering operations. Although they tend to charge lower prices than other types of restaurants, most of their sales are made in cash, and expenses can be easily inflated.

Vending Machines

Vending machine operations also possess many characteristics favorable to a money laundering operation. They have a highly variable and difficult to measure volume of cash receipts, and in large operations there is a fair amount of flexibility with various transportation, installation, and promotion expenses, providing cover for the withdrawal of laundered funds.

Wholesale Distribution

Wholesale distribution businesses have historically been a prominent part of money laundering. The revenues in a wholesaling business are not typically as flexible as in food service and vending machine operations, but with a diverse product line and falsified invoices, it is still possible to inject a good deal of illegal cash into the business. More importantly, the industry is ideal for money laundering from the standpoint of expenses. The activities required to run this kind of business are so diverse and difficult to measure that expenses are easy to inflate. Furthermore, a wholesale business' buildings, warehouses, transportation fleet, and its contact with retail establishments are all attractive factors. Many of the classic criminal activities (drugs, fencing, contraband) are themselves nothing more than distribution operations and can hide behind this type of business cover.

Real Estate Purchases

Real estate purchases are also attractive because (at least historically) real estate increases in value. Also rental income can be altered on the books to launder more funds.

ATMs

Law enforcement officials are also reporting an increasing use of automatic teller machines (ATMs) to launder money. ATMs can be purchased for as little as $3,000. Money launderers purchase the machines and place them either in establishments they control or in legitimate businesses. The machines work the same as any other ATM machine, and all transactions are legitimate. The money launderer simply fills the machine with cash from illegal activities. The customer uses the machine and never realizes the source of the cash.

The ATM banking system debits the cardholders account and credits the ATM owner's bank account. At the end of the month, the launderer receives a bank statement showing funds being deposited from a legitimate financial institution.

This option is attractive for money launderers because there are currently no regulations governing the use and operation of privately-owned ATMS. There is no requirement to check the backgrounds of purchasers of the machines, and there are no mandatory reporting procedures and no rules for maintaining ATM sales records.

Calling in a Specialist

Converting ill-gotten gains into cashier's checks or money orders is not particularly difficult for even the most unsophisticated criminal. However because many launderers fear detection, they turn to more sophisticated specialists. *Couriers* arrange for the transportation of money to a site where it is converted into another form of currency. For instance drug traffickers will physically transport money to a foreign jurisdiction where it is deposited into a bank account or converted directly to checks or money orders. Since the courier has no apparent connection with the true owner of the funds, the money launderer retains his anonymity.

White-collar professionals, such as attorneys, accountants, and brokers, might also serve to launder illegal funds. Through investments, trust accounts, fund transfers, and tax avoidance schemes these professionals can manipulate the financial, commercial, and legal systems to conceal the origin and ownership of assets.

Federal and State Law

USA PATRIOT Act of 2001

On October 26, 2001, President George W. Bush signed into law the Uniting and Strengthening America by Providing Appropriate Tools Required to Intercept and Obstruct Terrorism Act (the USA PATRIOT Act). The USA PATRIOT Act was a response to the tragedies of September 11, 2001, and reflected Congressional concern with the money laundering activities of the terrorists who committed those attacks.

Title III of the Act is entitled the International Money Laundering Abatement and Anti-Terrorist Financing Act of 2001. Title III creates significant new requirements for financial institutions aimed at curtailing money laundering. The most significant anti-money laundering provisions of the new law include the following:

- Financial institutions are required to establish anti-money laundering programs.
- Financial institutions are required to establish programs for identifying customers.
- U.S. banks are prohibited from maintaining correspondent accounts with foreign shell banks.
- Securities broker-dealers are required to file suspicious activity reports.
- Financial institutions are required to adopt special due diligence procedures for foreign correspondent accounts and private banking accounts.
- Non-financial businesses are required to file currency transaction reports
- Financial institutions have increased authority to share customer information relating to money laundering.
- The government has greater power to obtain information from financial institutions.

Anti-Money Laundering Programs

Section 352 of the PATRIOT Act requires all financial institutions to establish anti-money laundering programs, which must include, at a minimum:

- The development of internal policies, procedures, and controls to prevent money laundering.
- The designation of a money laundering compliance officer.
- An ongoing training program for awareness of money laundering.
- An independent audit function to test the programs.

The Act defines the term "financial institution" broadly to include not only insured and commercial banks, but also securities brokers and dealers, investment companies, currency exchanges, issuers of cashiers checks and money orders, credit card companies, insurance companies, travel agencies, and a host of other businesses. The complete list can be found at 31, U.S.C., § 312 (a)(2).

Identification and Verification of Accountholders

Section 326 of the Act expands the Bank Secrecy Act (discussed below) by requiring financial institutions to implement Customer Identification Programs (CIPs). These CIPs are to be incorporated into financial institutions' money laundering programs, and at a minimum, they must include reasonable procedures for:

- Verifying the identity of any person seeking to open an account to the extent reasonable and practicable;
- Maintaining records of the information used to verify a person's identity, including name, address, and other identifying information; and
- Consulting lists of known or suspected terrorists or terrorist organizations to determine if the person seeking to open the account appears on any such list.

Prohibition Against Foreign Shell Bank Accounts

Pursuant to Sections 313 and 319 of the USA PATRIOT Act, the Treasury Department issued a far-reaching final regulation on September 18, 2002 which applies to over 9,000 foreign financial institutions that have correspondent accounts in the United States.

The rule prohibits foreign shell banks (those without a physical presence in any country) from maintaining correspondent accounts at any U.S. financial institution. It also requires U.S. financial intuitions to maintain the name and contact information of the owners of the foreign banks for whom they maintain correspondent accounts. The rule strongly encourages U.S. intuitions to obtain "certifications" from their foreign bank customers. The certification can be used by the U.S. institution to help assure that the customer is not a shell bank. (Although not required, obtaining the certifications and verifying the information can create a safe harbor from civil liability.)

U.S. institutions are also required to take "reasonable steps" to ensure that correspondent accounts provided to foreign banks are not used to provide services indirectly to foreign shell banks. Foreign banks that have accounts in the U.S. are required to appoint someone in the U.S. to accept service of legal process. The rule also gives the Secretary of the Treasury and the Attorney General the authority to issue a summons or subpoena to any foreign bank that maintains a correspondent account here and to request records relating to that account.

Suspicious Activity Reporting by Broker-Dealers

Pursuant to Section 356 of the Act, the Financial Crimes Enforcement Network (FinCEN) has announced a new rule requiring brokers and dealers in securities to report suspicious activity. This new reporting requirement will be discussed in more detail later in this section (see "Securities Broker-Dealers" under "Suspicious Activity Reports" below).

Special Due Diligence for Foreign Accounts

Section 312 of the USA PATRIOT Act requires financial institutions to establish due diligence policies, procedures, and controls that are reasonably designed to detect and report instances of money laundering through certain accounts held by non-U.S. citizens or their representatives. This provision applies to two types of foreign accounts:

- Private banking accounts
- Correspondent accounts

A *private banking account* is defined by the Act as an account (or combination of accounts) that: (1) requires a minimum aggregate deposit of funds or other assets of at least $1 million; (2) is established on behalf of one or more individuals who have a direct or beneficial ownership in the account; and (3) is assigned to or administered by an officer, employee, or agent of the financial institution acting as a liaison between the financial institution and the owner of the account.

For private banking accounts held by non-U.S. persons, the Act requires at a minimum that financial institutions take reasonable steps to:

- Ascertain the identity of the nominal and beneficial owners of the account, and the source of funds deposited into the account as needed to guard against money laundering and report any suspicious transactions; and
- Conduct enhanced scrutiny of any such account that is requested or maintained by, or on behalf of, a senior foreign political figure (or an immediate family member or close associate of such) that is reasonably designed to detect and report transactions that may involve the proceeds of foreign corruption.

A *correspondent account* is defined as an account established to receive deposits from or make payments on behalf of a foreign financial institution, or handle other financial transactions related to such an institution. Enhanced due diligence is required for correspondent accounts maintained by or on behalf of foreign banks that operate under off-shore banking licenses or for banks that are licensed by foreign countries that have either been designated as noncooperative with international anti-money laundering principles or that have been designated by the Secretary of the Treasury as warranting special measures due to money laundering concerns. Enhanced due diligence for these correspondent accounts consists of, at a minimum:

- Ascertaining the identity of the owners of any foreign bank whose shares are not publicly traded;
- Determining the nature and extent of each owner's interest;
- Conducting enhanced scrutiny of the account to guard against money laundering and report suspicious transactions; and
- Ascertaining whether the foreign bank provides correspondent accounts to other foreign banks and, if so, the identity of those foreign banks and related due diligence information.

Currency Reports by Non-financial Businesses

Section 365 of the PATRIOT Act requires persons engaged in *any trade or business* to file a report with FinCEN when, in the course of their business, they receive more than $10,000 in coins or currency. This reporting requirement is discussed in more detail later in this section under the reporting and recordkeeping provisions of the Bank Secrecy Act.

Sharing Information Between Financial Institutions

Pursuant to Section 314(b) of the USA PATRIOT Act, the Treasury Department issued a rule allowing financial institutions to share customer information with one another. The term "financial institution" includes any entity that is required to have an anti-money laundering program under the Bank Secrecy Act (see above). In order to share information with another financial institution, the sharing institution must follow these steps:

- File a prescribed notice form with FinCEN stating that it intends to share customer information with other financial institutions (the notice remains effective for one year);
- The institution may then share the information with another institution provided that it has verified that the other institution has also filed a notice with FinCEN (FinCEN will periodically release a list of institutions who have submitted notices; if an institution is on the list, then the sharing institution will be considered to have fulfilled its "verification" duty);
- The institution must ensure that the shared information is secure and not used for any purpose other than to identify and, where appropriate, report on money laundering or terrorist activities; determine whether to establish or maintain an account or conduct a

transaction; or assist the other sharing institution with its compliance of BSA regulations; and
- The institution must also file a Suspicious Activity Report if, based on the shared information, the institution suspects that the individual or entity may be involved in money laundering or terrorist activity.

Section 355 of the Act also permits insured depository institutions to share information in written employment references about known *or suspected* unlawful activity of their current or former directors, officers, employees, agents, or other persons affiliated with the institution. This provision, which is codified at 12, U.S.C., § 1828(w) does not make it mandatory for banks to disclose this information, but it does protect them from liability if they voluntarily make such disclosures, as long as the disclosures are not made with malicious intent.

New Government Access to Financial Information

On September 18, 2002, the Treasury Department issued new regulations that provide federal law enforcement agencies with greater power to obtain financial information. The two-part regulation is an amendment to the Bank Secrecy Act regulations and was mandated by Section 314 of the USA PATRIOT Act.

If a federal agency provides FinCEN with a "written certification" that a person, entity, or organization about whom information is sought "is reasonably suspected based on credible information to be engaged in…, terrorist activity or money laundering." FinCEN may then require any financial institution to search its records to determine if it "maintains or has maintained accounts for, or has engaged in transactions with" the subject.

The information reported is limited to the name or account number of each cited person, entity, or organization; the number of the matching account or transaction; and the Social Security number, taxpayer ID, passport number, date of birth, or other identifying information the subject gave when opening the account or conducting the transaction.

The institution may not disclose the information to anyone other than FinCEN or the requesting agency. The institution also cannot disclose that the information has been requested or provided. It may, however, use the information in the request to determine whether an account will be opened or a transaction conducted, and to comply with BSA regulations.

The term "financial institution" is defined as it is under the BSA and includes banks, broker-dealers, insurance companies, money services businesses, as well as car and airplane dealers, travel agents, and pawnbrokers.

Office of Foreign Assets Control (OFAC)

The Office of Foreign Assets Control (OFAC) is an office within the Department of the Treasury charged with administering and enforcing U.S. sanction policies against targeted foreign organizations and individuals that sponsor terrorism, and international narcotics traffickers. OFAC maintains a list of individuals, governmental entities, companies, and merchant vessels around the world that are known or suspected to engage in illegal activities. Persons or entities on the list, known as Specially Designated Nationals and Blocked Persons ("SDNs"), include foreign agents, front organizations, terrorists and terrorist organizations, and drug traffickers. The list contains over 5,000 variations on names of individuals, governmental entities, companies, and merchant vessels and is updated on a regular basis. On September 24, 2001, President George W. Bush issued an executive order imposing enhanced trade sanctions on 27 individuals and entities, including Osama bin Laden and Al Qaeda. The immediate effect of the order is to block all assets of these individuals and entities under U.S. control and ban all dealings with the listed parties.

On July 26, 2001, OFAC issued a bulletin specific to the insurance industry, including underwriters, brokers, agents, primary insurers, and reinsurers. The bulletin affirms that U.S. insurers may not insure SDNs or individuals or entities located in certain prohibited countries or make payments to beneficiaries who are designated as prohibited persons or entities. Examples of prohibited transactions include: (1) issuing an insurance policy or annuity contract to an SDN; (2) issuing a life insurance policy naming an SDN as a beneficiary; and (3) receiving premium payments for any such transactions.

The Bank Secrecy Act

The Bank Secrecy Act (BSA), which went into effect in 1970, was the first major piece of legislation aimed at detecting and preventing money laundering. The purpose of the law as stated in Section 5311 is "to require certain reports or records where they have a high degree of usefulness in criminal, tax, or regulatory investigations or proceedings." The BSA sets forth a system of reporting and recordkeeping requirements designed to help track large or unusual financial transactions.

The BSA consists of two titles. Title I contains provisions requiring that financial institutions and securities brokers and dealers keep extensive records of the transactions and accounts of their customers. It is codified in Title 12 of the United States Code (U.S.C.), Sections 1829b and 1951–1959. Title II of the BSA (originally entitled Currency and Foreign Transactions Reporting Act) requires banks, "financial institutions" (which include casinos, securities brokers and dealers, currency exchanges, and others), and, in some cases, individuals to report to the government certain transactions. Title II is codified at 31, U.S.C., §§ 5311–5330.

Title I — Recordkeeping

The regulations governing recordkeeping are set forth in Chapter 31 of the Code of Federal Regulations at Part 103, Subpart C. Recordkeeping requirements are set forth for banks, nonbank financial institutions, securities brokers, casinos, and currency dealers and exchangers. All institutions are required to keep a record of any financial transaction of more than $10,000.

These regulations provide, in part, that banks must keep for five years an original, microfilm, or other copy of certain documents relating to demand deposits and checking and savings accounts. The records that must be retained include:

- Signature cards
- Statements, ledger cards, or other records disclosing all transactions; that is, deposits and withdrawals
- Copies of both sides of customers' checks, bank drafts, money orders, and cashier's checks of more than $100 drawn on the bank, or issued and payable by it
- Identity of each purchaser of a certificate of deposit
- Each deposit slip or credit ticket reflecting a transaction in excess of $100

In addition to these requirements, financial institutions are required to capture, verify, and retain information on the identity of purchasers of monetary instruments (such as cashier's checks) in amounts of $3,000 or more, or any transmittal or transfer of funds involving $3,000 or more. These records are also required to be kept for five years.

Banks also must retain, for two years, all records necessary to reconstruct a customer's checking account. These records must include copies of customers' deposit tickets. They must also retain records necessary to trace and supply a description of a check deposited to a customer's checking account.

Although some of these requirements apply only to checks written or deposits made in excess of $100, most banks find it cheaper to microfilm all such items rather than sorting out those less than $100. The Bank Secrecy Act also requires financial institutions to retain a record of any extension of credit more than $10,000 as well as each transfer of $10,000 or more outside the United States.

The penalties for failure to comply with these recordkeeping requirements are severe. Any insured depository institution and any director, officer, or employee who willfully or through gross negligence violates any regulation can be subject to a $10,000 civil penalty. The statute further provides that a separate violation occurs for *each day* the violation continues and at each office, branch, or place of business at which the violation occurs. If a violation is committed in furtherance of a felony crime, criminal penalties can be imposed of up to five years in prison and/or a fine of not more than $10,000.

Title II — Reporting and Recordkeeping

Title II of the Bank Secrecy Act is codified as 31, U.S.C., §§ 5311–5330. The purpose of these Sections is to require certain reports or records to be filed or kept by "financial institutions." Section 5312(a)(2) defines "financial institution" very broadly to include not only banks, but also securities brokers; currency exchange houses; insurance companies; loan companies; travel agencies; telegraph companies; issuers or cashiers of checks or money orders; auto, boat, and airplane dealers; casinos; and persons involved in real estate closings and settlements. Only recently has the Treasury Department begun to reign in much of the non-financial institution transaction business in the U.S. by requiring registration of these diverse enterprises (see the "Money Services Business" excerpt below).

The regulations promulgated by the U.S. Treasury Department are contained primarily in Chapter 31 of the Code of Federal Regulations at Part 103, Subpart B and require the following reports:

CURRENCY TRANSACTION REPORT (CTR) — FINCEN FORM 104

Financial institutions are required to file a CTR for any transactions (deposits, withdrawals, exchanges of currency, or other payments or transfers) by or through the financial institution which involve more than $10,000 in currency (foreign or domestic) that circulates as a medium of exchange. The easiest way to summarize the filing requirement is to remember: if currency in excess of $10,000 is brought into a financial institution to conduct a transaction, or if as the result of a transaction, $10,000 in currency leaves the financial institution, a CTR must be filed.

FinCEN Form 104 (formerly named IRS Form 4789) is prepared by the financial institution and contains the name(s) of the individual(s) conducting the transaction(s) or the name(s) of the person(s) or organization(s) on whose behalf the transaction is being conducted, as well as all identifying data of these individuals or entities. It also requires the details of the transaction and identifying data of the financial institution preparing the form. For purposes of reporting, multiple transactions must be treated as a single transaction if the financial institution has knowledge that the transactions are by or on behalf of the same person and the amounts total more than $10,000 during any one business day.

Under Title 31, U.S.C., Section 5313, the Treasury Department publishes a "mandatory exemption" list that specifically identifies entities whose transactions with a financial institution are exempt from these reporting requirements. The exempted entities include banks, departments or agencies of state or federal government, and other businesses "whose reports have little or no value for law enforcement purposes." The exempt list must be published periodically in the Federal Register.

The Treasury Department can also provide "discretionary exemptions" for "qualified business customers" which are defined as businesses that: (1) maintain transaction accounts (as defined by the Federal Reserve Act) at the particular institution; (2) frequently engage in transactions with the institution that are subject to the reporting requirements; and (3) meet the guidelines and criteria established by the Treasury Department to ensure that the failure to file reports on these entities will not interfere with the purposes of the Act.

A copy of Form 104 is included at the end of this chapter.

CURRENCY REPORTS BY CASINOS — FINCEN FORM 102
Similar to the standard CTR, Form 102 (formerly named IRS Form 8362) is required to be filed by casinos licensed by state or local government and having an annual gross revenue in excess of $1,000,000. Nevada casinos are exempt from filing these forms because of a strict state law which requires reporting for currency transactions. The filing requirements and transaction details for this form are almost identical to Form 104.

CURRENCY REPORTS BY NON-FINANCIAL BUSINESSES — IRS FORM 8300
The USA PATRIOT Act created Title 31, Section 5331, of the U.S. Code, which requires persons engaged in *any trade or business* to file a report with FinCEN when, in the course of their business, they receive more than $10,000 in coins or currency, either in one transaction

or in two or more related transactions. For purposes of computing the amount of multiple related transactions, the recipient must aggregate all payments made within one year of the first payment. Transactions covered by this Section must be reported within 15 days of receipt of payments in excess of $10,000. The rules governing these reports are codified at 31, CFR, § 103.30.

This Section does not apply to financial institutions, which are already covered by 31, U.S.C., § 5313 as described above. It also does not apply to transactions occurring entirely outside the United States. In addition, the rules exempt certain loans, installment sales, and down payment plans.

The information required to be reported under 31, U.S.C., § 5331 is very similar to the information that was already required by the IRS under Section 6050I of the Internal Revenue Code. Because of the similarity between the two statutes, the reports are to be made on the same Form 8300, which is filed jointly with FinCEN and the IRS. Essentially, the new rule imposes no new record-keeping burden (since Form 8300 already had to be filed with the IRS).

Under the Internal Revenue Code, there are both civil and criminal penalties for failure to file Form 8300 or filing a false form. Criminal sanctions include imprisonment of up to five years (for a willful failure to file) and fines of up to $500,000 (for organizations knowingly filing a false return).

REPORTS OF INTERNATIONAL TRANSPORTATION OF CURRENCY OR MONETARY INSTRUMENT CUSTOMS (CMIR) — FINCEN FORM 105

Pursuant to Title 31, U.S.C., § 5316, a person shall file a report if he transports or is about to transport monetary instruments of more than $10,000 into or out of the United States at one time or if he receives by transport, mail, or shipment monetary instruments in excess of $10,000 at one time transported into the United Sates from a place outside the United States. FinCEN Form 105 (formerly named Customs Form 4790) is to be filed at the time of transportation or within 15 days of receipt.

For the purposes of this statute, the term "monetary instrument" means United States and foreign coin and currency; bearer instruments such as business, bank, or personal checks; money orders; promissory notes; bearer stocks; and bonds.

There are exemptions from the CMIR filing requirements which extend to banks for transfers of funds through normal banking procedures, the Federal Reserve, and certain common carriers.

A copy of this form is included at the end of this chapter.

REPORT OF FOREIGN BANK AND FINANCIAL ACCOUNTS (FBAR) — TREASURY FORM 90-22.1

Treasury Department regulations require citizens of the United States and resident aliens to file a report when they maintain a financial interest or signature authority over a foreign bank account with a balance of more than $10,000 during the calendar year. Accounts in different foreign countries have to be aggregated.

PENALTIES

Section 5321 of the BSA sets forth the civil penalties for noncompliance with the Act. A covered entity (including its partners, directors, officers, or employees) that willfully violates the reporting requirements can be hit with a penalty of up to the amount of the transaction (not to exceed $100,000) or $25,000, whichever is greater. A separate penalty can be imposed for each day the violation continues and at each branch or office. Civil penalties of up to $500 are also authorized for a negligent violation. If there is a pattern of negligent activity, the penalty limit increases to $50,000. This Section also sets forth other penalties applicable to structured transactions and foreign financial agency transactions.

Criminal penalties are set forth in Section 5322, which provides that a person willfully violating the statute or regulations can be fined up to $250,000 and/or imprisoned for up to five years. If the violation occurs while violating another federal law or as a pattern of illegal activity involving more than $100,000, the maximum fine increases to $500,000 and the maximum prison time increases to 10 years. As with the civil penalties, a separate violation occurs each day the conduct continues and at each location.

FORFEITURES

Section 5317(c) provides criminal and civil forfeiture penalties for violations of the currency reporting requirements in § 5313 (reports on domestic transactions), § 5316 (reports on exporting and importing monetary instruments), and § 5324 (structuring transactions to evade reporting requirements). A person convicted of an offense under any of these statutes, or of a conspiracy to violate any of these statutes, can be ordered to forfeit all property that was involved in the offense and any property traceable thereto.

Suspicious Activity Reports (SARs)
FINANCIAL INSTITUTIONS

Under Title 31, U.S.C., § 5318, financial institutions are required to report "any suspicious transaction relevant to a possible violation of law or regulation." For years, suspicious transactions were reported on the Currency Transaction Report (CTR). However, effective October 1, 1995, a new CTR form was issued by the Treasury Department which no longer requires suspicious activity reporting. Such activity is now reported using the Suspicious Activity Report (SAR).

Effective April 1, 1996, the Office of the Comptroller of the Currency (OCC) amended its regulations to require national banks to file the SAR with the OCC and the appropriate federal law enforcement agencies by sending the SARs to the Financial Crimes Enforcement Network (FinCEN) of the U.S. Department of Treasury. The new reporting requirements are found in Title 12, Part 353 of the Code of Federal Regulations. This is an enormous improvement on the old reporting systems because it establishes a centralized reporting system that is shared throughout government agencies simultaneously. The DEA, for instance, can now access the same information as the IRS when working on a suspicious report. The reporting procedure has also been simplified for banks, making the information much easier for the Department of the Treasury to obtain.

In 2000, the report form was modified to also require financial institutions to report incidents of computer intrusion. The term "computer intrusion" is defined as gaining access to the computer system to remove, steal, or procure customers' funds or other account information, or to access the institution's computer system with the intention of damaging or disabling any critical computer systems.

SARs are used to report a known or suspected criminal offense or a transaction that involves money laundering or violates the Bank Secrecy Act. More specifically, a SAR must be filed with FinCEN in each of the following instances:
- Any known or suspected criminal violation involving the financial institution when the institution has a substantial basis for identifying one of its directors, officers, employees, agents, or affiliated parties as having committed the act or aided in its commission.

- Any known or suspected criminal violation involving the financial institution and aggregating $5,000 or more when the institution has a substantial basis for identifying a possible suspect or group of suspects.
- Any known or suspected criminal violation involving the financial institution and aggregating $25,000 or more regardless of whether the institution has a substantial basis for identifying possible suspects.
- Any transaction conducted or attempted to be conducted through the financial institution when the institution has reason to suspect that: (1) the funds were derived from illegal activities, (2) the transaction is designed to evade any regulations under the Bank Secrecy Act, or (3) the transaction appears to have no business purposes or appears unusual in normal banking practice.

When a financial institution reports a suspicious transaction to a government agency, the Act (18, U.S.C., § 5318(g)(2)) makes it illegal for the financial institution to notify any person involved in the suspicious transaction that such a report has been made.

Section 5318(g)(3) of the Bank Secrecy Act also contains a safe harbor provision for financial institutions that report suspicious transactions or that make voluntary disclosures to a government agency of any other possible violation of a law or regulation. The Act provides that these financial institutions shall not be liable under any law, regulation, or contract to any person for making the report. Note that this safe harbor provision only applies to reports made to government agencies, not to self-regulatory organizations.

A copy of the SAR report form is included at the end of this chapter.

MONEY SERVICES BUSINESSES

Even before the passage of the USA PATRIOT Act, the Treasury Department was in the process of expanding its reporting guidelines to include businesses which did not fall under the traditional definition of *financial institutions* but nevertheless perform a myriad of financial services. One of these categories included "Money Services Businesses," (MSBs) which are comprised of various types of money transmitters, issuers of money orders and travelers checks, and check cashing businesses. MSBs have long been required to file CTRs, but otherwise very little government regulation has been required.

In August 1999, many of the reporting and registration obligations contained in the Bank Secrecy Act were extended to MSBs. These businesses are now required to register with

FinCEN under Chapter 31, C.F.R. part 103, subchapter D. Those that fail to register can incur substantial penalties.

Under the rules: (1) money transmitters, (2) issuers, sellers, and redeemers of money orders, (3) issuers, sellers, and redeemers of traveler's checks, and (4) the U.S. Postal Service (except with regard to the sale of postage or philatelic products) are required to report certain classes of transactions that meet certain dollar thresholds to the Department of the Treasury after January 1, 2002.

The reportable transactions include:
- Transactions involving funds derived from illegal activity or intended or conducted in order to hide or disguise funds or assets derived from illegal activity;
- Transactions designed, whether through structuring or other means, to evade the requirements of the BSA;
- Transactions that appear to serve no business or apparent lawful purpose; and
- Transactions that involve the use of a mutual fund to facilitate criminal activity.

The rule includes two different dollar thresholds depending on the stage and type of transaction involved:
- For transactions conducted or attempted by, at, or through a money service business or its agent, a threshold of $2,000 applies;
- For transactions identified by issuers of money orders or traveler's checks from a review of clearance records or other similar records of instruments that have been sold or processed, a threshold of $5,000 applies.

MSBs are given 30 days after becoming aware of a suspicious transaction to complete a Suspicious Activity Report by Money Services Business (SAR-MSB; Form TDF 90-22.56) and file it with FinCEN; in situations involving violations that require immediate attention, such as ongoing money laundering schemes, the MSB or MSBs are to notify the appropriate law enforcement authority immediately, by telephone, in addition to filing the required form. Supporting documentation relating to each SAR-MSB is to be collected and maintained by the reporting MSB for review as needed by law enforcement and regulatory agencies.

CURRENCY EXCHANGES

In a new rule issued February 10, 2003, U.S. currency exchanges would also be required to file Suspicious Activity Reports under the same rule that applies to money services businesses.

MUTUAL FUNDS

As part of the USA PATRIOT Act, mutual funds are also required to establish anti-money laundering programs. In May 2003, the Department of Treasury and the Securities and Exchange Commission (SEC) issued a regulation requiring mutual funds to implement "reasonable measures" to establish customer identification procedures and to verify whether customers appear on lists of any known or suspected terrorists.

In December 2002, the Treasury Department proposed new regulations that would also require mutual funds to report suspicious activities to FinCEN. Under the proposed rule, mutual funds would be required to report suspicious currency and non-currency transactions of $5,000 or more within 30 days after the mutual fund becomes aware of the transaction. The report would be filed on the new "SAR-SF" (Suspicious Activity for Securities and Futures Industries) form.

The rule states that four categories of transactions will require reporting. These are the same four categories that trigger reporting requirements for money service businesses and currency exchanges:
- Transactions involving funds derived from criminal activity, or intended or conducted to hide or disguise funds from criminal activity;
- Transactions designed to evade Bank Secrecy Act (BSA) requirements;
- Transactions appearing to serve no business or apparent lawful purpose; or
- Transactions involving the use of the mutual fund to facilitate criminal activity.

As of September 2004, no final rule had been issued on this proposal.

SECURITIES BROKER-DEALERS

In 2002, FinCEN announced a new rule requiring brokers and dealers in securities to report suspicious activity via the new Suspicious Activity Report by Securities and Futures Industries (SAR-SF; FinCEN Form 101). These firms are obligated to report suspicious transactions that are conducted or attempted by, at, or through a broker-dealer and involve or aggregate at least $5,000 in funds or other assets. This requirement took effect December 31, 2002.

Brokers and dealers in securities are required to report to FinCEN transactions that fall into one of the four categories below. Again, these categories are substantially similar to those that trigger reports by money service businesses and mutual funds (see above).

- Transactions involving funds derived from illegal activity, or intended or conducted in order to hide or disguise funds derived from illegal activity;
- Transactions designed, whether through structuring or other means, to evade the requirements of the Bank Secrecy Act;
- Transactions that appear to serve no business or apparent lawful purpose or are not the sort of transactions in which the particular customer would be expected to engage, and for which the broker-dealer knows of no reasonable explanation after examining the available facts; or
- Transactions that involve the use of the broker-dealer to facilitate criminal activity.

Broker-dealers are also required to establish anti-money laundering programs that, among other things, are designed to detect suspicious transactions, under recently promulgated self-regulatory organization (SRO) rules. The SEC has the authority to examine broker-dealers for compliance with the rule, and it is expected that the SROs will also be reviewing compliance as part of the enforcement of their rules.

A copy of SAR-SF is included at the end of the chapter.

CASINOS AND CARD CLUBS

Effective March 25, 2003, casinos and card clubs with gross revenue over $1,000,000 must file suspicious activity reports on the new form SAR-C. Under the new rule, casinos and card clubs must report suspicious activity if a transaction involves or aggregates at least $5,000 in funds and if it meets one of the four categories that generally trigger SARs. (See previous sections on Financial Institutions, Money Service Businesses, Mutual Funds, etc.)

Some possible examples of suspicious activity, according to FinCEN, include:
- Using wire transfers and cashier's checks to deposit funds into casino accounts and using the money for little or no gaming activity before cashing out; and

- Transferring chips to other individuals to cash out, or redeeming chips for casino checks that total "significantly more" than the amount deposited with "no apparent winnings to account for the excess amount."

Casinos are also required to file Currency Transaction Reports via FinCEN Form 103 or the Nevada state form (see above).

INSURANCE COMPANIES

Although insurance companies have always fallen under the definition of a "financial institution" under the BSA, the Treasury Department had never issued any rules pertaining to the industry. The USA PATRIOT Act, however, requires that all "financial institutions" must establish anti-money laundering programs, and it gives the Secretary of the Treasury the discretion to determine which institutions would be required to file SARs.

In September 2002, FinCEN published proposed rules for anti-money laundering standards for life insurance, annuity contracts, and certain other investment products that can store and transfer value to another person. A related proposal would also require these companies to file Suspicious Activity Reports.

The proposed rule is limited only to life insurance contracts, annuities, and any other product that has "stored value" that can be transferred to another person. It does not include property, casualty, or health insurers.

As of October 2004, no final rule has been issued.

Unregistered Investment Firms

As another part of the effort to reduce money laundering and the financing of terrorist activities, the Treasury Department proposed a new rule in September 2002 that would affect investment companies that are not registered with the SEC, including hedge funds, venture capital funds, commodity pools, and real estate investment trusts (REITs). To be covered under the rule, the investment company must have total assets over $1,000,000. The rule would exempt small investment companies, family-run companies, and employees' securities companies.

The proposal would require investment companies to file identifying information about the company with FinCEN as well as to institute anti-money laundering programs. The only

BSA requirement that currently applies to unregistered investment companies is the necessity to report the receipt of cash and certain non-cash instruments totaling more than $10,000 in one or more related transactions on the new FinCEN/IRS Form 8300. However, as of March 2004, no final rule has been issued.

Other Federal Laws Related to Money Laundering

The fraud examiner should be aware of the federal laws which are typically involved when prosecuting a money laundering transaction. Most such schemes will involve one or more of the following:

Title 31, U.S.C., § 5324 Structuring Transaction to Evade Reporting Requirements

If a person causes or attempts to cause a covered institution to fail to file a required report with the purpose of evading the reporting requirements, such person can be fined under the provisions of 18, U.S.C., § 3571 and/or imprisoned up to five years. If the violation occurs in the course of violating another federal law or as part of a pattern of illegal conduct involving more than $100,000 in a 12-month period, then the amount of the fine under § 3571 can be doubled and the prison time increased to up to 10 years.

Section 3571 of Title 18 provides for fines for individuals convicted of a felony of up to $250,000 and fines for organizations of up to $500,000. Alternatively, a fine can be imposed up to twice the amount of the ill-gotten gain to the criminal or twice the amount of the loss to the victim.

Title 31, U.S.C., § 5332 Bulk Cash Smuggling Into or Out of the United States

Section 5332, which was created by Section 371 of the USA PATRIOT Act, makes it illegal for anyone to knowingly conceal more than $10,000 in currency or other monetary instruments and transport or attempt to transport such currency into or out of the United States with the intent to evade a currency reporting requirement under 18, U.S.C., § 1956 (see below). Violators of these sections may be imprisoned up to five years and may be required to forfeit any property involved in the offense, or any property traceable thereto.

Title 18, U.S.C., § 1956 and § 1957 Money Laundering Statutes
TRANSACTIONAL MONEY LAUNDERING

Section 1956(a)(1) provides that anyone who, knowing that property involved in a financial transaction represents the proceeds of some form of unlawful activity, conducts a financial transaction:

- With the intent to promote the carrying on of "specified unlawful activity;"
- With the intent to violate Section 7201 (tax evasion) or 7206 (filing false return) of the Internal Revenue Code;
- Knowing that the transaction is designed to conceal or disguise the nature, location, source, ownership, or control of the illegal proceeds; or
- Knowing that the transaction is designed to avoid a reporting requirement, shall be fined up to $500,000 or twice the value of the monetary instrument or funds (whichever is greater) and/or imprisoned for not more than 20 years. "Specified unlawful activity" is defined in § 1956(c)(7) and includes a long list of federal crimes including RICO, fraud, embezzlement, theft, and false statements. Also, funds that are illegally transmitted in violation of this statute or any property traceable to those funds are subject to civil forfeiture under 18, U.S.C., § 981(a)(1)(A).

INTERNATIONAL TRANSPORTATION AND LAUNDERING OF FUNDS

Section 1956(a)(2) prohibits the transportation, transmission, or transfer of funds either into or out of the United States if the person knows the funds are the proceeds of unlawful activity and the transportation, etc. is done with the intent to promote the carrying on of "specified unlawful conduct"; is done to conceal the nature, location, source, ownership, or control of the funds; or is done to avoid reporting requirements. The penalties are the same as those set forth in subsection (a)(1).

STING OPERATIONS

Section 1956(a)(3) prohibits a person from engaging in financial transactions involving property the person *believes* to be the proceeds of illegal activity. This is intended to cover "sting" operations in which a suspect engages in money laundering activity with funds he believes to be illegally derived, even though the funds are actually supplied by government agents. The person can be imprisoned for up to 20 years and/or fined in accordance with 18, U.S.C., § 3571.

ENGAGING IN MONETARY TRANSACTIONS WITH MONEY DERIVED FROM SPECIFIED UNLAWFUL ACTIVITY

An offense occurs under Section 1957 if a person knowingly engages or attempts to engage in a monetary transaction with criminally derived property greater than $10,000 and which is derived from "specified unlawful activity." Section 1957 applies in situations where the offense takes place in the United States (or within its special maritime or territorial jurisdiction) or the offense takes place outside the U.S., but the defendant is a U.S. citizen or legal alien.

Violations of this statute are punishable by a fine under 18, U.S.C., § 3571 and/or 10 years in prison. In addition, the illegally transmitted funds can be forfeited under 18, U.S.C., § 981(a)(1)(A).

CIVIL PENALTIES

Section 1956(b) sets forth civil penalties for violations of §§ 1956 and 1957. Under this Section, those who violate either money laundering statute are liable to the United States for the value of the property, funds, or monetary instruments involved in the illegal transaction, or $10,000, whichever is greater.

LONG-ARM JURISDICTION OVER FOREIGN MONEY LAUNDERERS

Section 1956(b) also gives U.S. district courts jurisdiction over foreign persons or financial institutions when: (1) the foreign person commits a money laundering offense under § 1956(a) that occurs in whole or in part in the United States; (2) the foreign person converts to his own use property in which the United States has an ownership interest; or (3) the foreign financial institution maintains a bank account in the United States.

Under § 1956(b)(3), a U.S. court can issue restraining orders to freeze the assets of foreign money launderers described above prior to trial in order to ensure that the defendant's assets are available to satisfy a judgment. The court can also appoint a Federal Receiver to collect, marshal, and take control of the defendant's assets to satisfy a civil or criminal judgment for money laundering, or a civil or criminal forfeiture judgment.

Title 18, U.S.C., § 1960 Prohibition of Illegal Money Transmitting Businesses

This Section prohibits the operation of a business which transfers funds by any means (whether by wire, check, or courier) if the business does not have the appropriate state license or fails to comply with the registration requirements established under Title 31 of the U.S. Code, Section 5330. The offender can be fined under § 3571 of Title 18 and/or imprisoned not more than five years. Illegally transmitted funds can also be seized by the United States under 18, U.S.C., § 981(a)(1)(A).

Title 18, U.S.C., §§ 1961–1968 Racketeer Influenced and Corrupt Organizations (RICO)

Violations of the money laundering crimes statutes (18, U.S.C., §§ 1956 and 1957) and certain violations of the Bank Secrecy Act are predicate offenses constituting "racketeering activity." These acts can be prosecuted under the RICO statute, which includes criminal penalties of up to 20 years in prison and/or fines under § 3571 of Title 18. The statute also provides for a civil cause of action by "any person injured in his business or property" as a result of a violation of RICO. Remedies include treble damages and attorney's fees.

Title 18, U.S.C., § 981, et seq. Seizures and Forfeitures

Section 981 provides for the civil seizure and forfeiture of property involved in certain crimes including money laundering. Section 982 deals with criminal forfeitures. *Forfeiture* may be defined as "the taking by the government of property that is illegally used or acquired, without compensating the owner." These remedies are only available to the government and typically are used in connection with a criminal investigation and prosecution.

When a piece of property is forfeited, all right, title, and interest in the property vests in the government; consequently, all the defendant's ownership rights are extinguished. The transfer of rights dates back to the moment when the property became forfeitable; i.e., when the crime was committed. Any subsequent transfer by the defendant is of no effect. This is known as the *relation back doctrine*. In the eyes of the law, the subsequent judicial proceedings merely confirm that a forfeiture has, in theory, already taken place (although the government cannot claim any rights in the property until it receives a forfeiture judgment). Because the government's right to the property and related proceeds dates back to when the crime was committed, the government is legally entitled to any gain accruing from the proceeds of the illegal activity.

Criminal forfeitures are conducted in conjunction with a criminal trial. The proof necessary to perfect the forfeiture is the same as required to convict the individual of the criminal charge, that is, proof beyond a reasonable doubt. The criminal forfeiture is an action *in personam* (against the person). In such a proceeding the government has the same burden of proof as it does in a criminal case. If the government sustains a conviction, the judge will forfeit the property at time of sentencing, at which time the property can be seized.

Civil forfeitures are conducted independently from a criminal proceeding. A civil forfeiture is an action *in rem* (against the property). In response to perceived abuses on the part of the government, Congress passed the Civil Asset Forfeiture Reform Act of 2000 which drastically amended the laws concerning civil forfeiture.

Below are some of the highlights of the Act:
- Sets forth notification requirements with respect to seized property and civil forfeiture proceedings, including a requirement that the government notify interested parties as soon as practicable but within 60 days after the date of the seizure.
- Sets forth procedures for filing claims for seized property. After a claim is filed, the government has 90 days in which to file a complaint for forfeiture. If the government fails to do this, then it must return the property. In lieu of or in addition to filing a civil forfeiture complaint, the government may include a forfeiture allegation in a criminal indictment.
- Provides that the court appoint counsel to represent anyone with an interest in the property if the person is financially unable to afford counsel.
- Places the burden of proof on the government to establish, by a preponderance of the evidence, that the property is subject to forfeiture.
- Provides that if the forfeiture action is being prosecuted because the property was used to commit or facilitate the commission of a criminal offense, or was involved in such commission, the government must establish that there was a substantial connection between the property and the offense.
- Provides an "innocent owner's" defense to the forfeiture action. The owner must prove his innocence by a preponderance of the evidence.
- Authorizes a claimant to petition the court to determine whether a forfeiture was constitutionally excessive. Directs the court to compare the forfeiture to the gravity of the offense. Places upon the claimant the burden of establishing, by a preponderance of the evidence at a hearing conducted by the court without a jury, that the forfeiture is grossly disproportional to the offense upon the claimant.
- Amends the Federal Tort Claims Act to allow claimants to sue the government for any damage or loss of property while in possession of the government.
- Authorizes the use of forfeited property to pay restitution to any victim of the offense giving rise to the forfeiture, including, in the case of a money laundering offense, any offense constituting the underlying specified activity.
- Directs that all civil forfeitures of real property and interests in real property proceed as judicial forfeitures. Prohibits (with exceptions): (1) real property that is the subject of a

civil forfeiture from being seized before entry of a forfeiture order; and (2) the owners or occupants of the real property from being evicted from, or otherwise deprived of the use and enjoyment of, real property that is the subject of a pending forfeiture action.
- Provides for the forfeiture of the proceeds of "specified unlawful activity" under the money laundering statutes.

FORFEITURE OF FUNDS IN INTERBANK ACCOUNTS
Section 319 of the USA PATRIOT Act amended 18, U.S.C., § 981, expanding the United States' ability to seize the proceeds of money laundering activity by providing for forfeiture of funds held in United States interbank accounts. An interbank account is an account one financial institution holds at another financial institution.

If funds involved in a money laundering transaction or the proceeds of any "specified unlawful activity" as defined by the money laundering statute are deposited in a *foreign bank*, and if that foreign bank has an interbank account in the United States, then the tainted funds will be deemed to have been deposited into the U.S. account. In other words, the funds in the foreign bank's U.S. interbank account can be seized, even if the laundered money was not deposited in that account. The government does not have to trace the money in the U.S. interbank account to the money that was deposited in the foreign account. It is enough that the U.S. interbank account is held by the same financial institution in which the laundered money was deposited overseas.

Title 18, U.S.C., § 1001 False Statements
Persons who violate the Bank Secrecy Act and other reporting laws might also be guilty of violating of 18, U.S.C., § 1001. Because most of the obligations imposed by the BSA involve recordkeeping and reporting, many BSA violations might also constitute false statements. Section 1001 prohibits knowingly falsifying, concealing, covering up, or making a false, fictitious, or fraudulent statement or representation in any matter within the jurisdiction of any U.S. department or agency. Violations of this Section are often charged when an individual is stopped at the border with a large amount of unreported cash and responds falsely to the questions of customs officers or inspectors. It has been used to prosecute individuals for structuring a transaction so that it deceives a financial institution into filing a false report.

Title 18, U.S.C., § 37 Conspiracy to Defraud the United States

The federal conspiracy statute, 18, U.S.C., § 371, has two parts: (1) conspiracy to commit a crime, such as the failure to submit a CTR or violation of other criminal laws; and (2) conspiracy to defraud the United States. Several courts have upheld convictions based on the second prong of the statute solely for failure to file CTRs. Such prosecutions are based on the theory that the person deprived the IRS of accurate CTRs. In the case of *United States v. Richter*, 610 F.Supp. 480 (N.D. Ill. 1985), the court held that the division of large amounts of cash into smaller, nonreportable transactions by several individuals working as a team was a conspiracy to obstruct the government function of receiving CTRs. However, other courts have rejected this theory on the grounds that there is no duty on the part of the customer to inform the government or the bank of the nature of the transaction whether reportable or not.

Title 18, U.S.C., § 1952 Travel Act

The Travel Act is applicable if the offense involves the proceeds of illegal activity and interstate travel. The Act provides that it is an offense to travel in interstate or foreign commerce or use the mail with the intent to distribute the proceeds of any unlawful activity; commit any crime of violence to further unlawful activity; or otherwise establish, promote, or manage an establishment for the purposes of carrying on any unlawful activity. *Unlawful activity* is defined to include the reporting requirements under 31, U.S.C., Chapter 53 as well as the Money Laundering Statutes (18, U.S.C., §§ 1956 and 1957). The fines established under § 3571 can be imposed and/or up to five years imprisonment. If a crime of violence is involved, the term of imprisonment increases to a maximum of 20 years or life if someone was killed.

State Laws

Approximately 30 states have enacted statutes that criminalize money laundering, most of which apply to businesspeople and professionals. Some of the state statutes are broader than the federal statutes, and they are often enforced more aggressively than their federal counterparts.

Many states have criminalized *attempted* money laundering with the same penalties as the completed crime. Some states contain a "sting provision" which enables the prosecution of activity even though the laundered money is not actually derived from criminal activity, but rather supplied by government agents as part of a sting operation. Several states have also enacted legislation requiring financial institutions and businesses to file currency transaction reports that mirror the federal reports. Some require duplicate filing with the states; others are satisfied with the federal filing.

Enforcement and Prevention Strategies

Financial institutions, brokers, and insurance companies should be aware and should make their employees aware of situations which could indicate money laundering activity.

Bank Secrecy Act Compliance Programs

Most financial institutions are now required to have a Bank Secrecy Act compliance program in place. However, every business that has the potential for transactions dealing with significant amounts of cash should institute a compliance program and a money laundering awareness program. All employees should be made aware of the money laundering statutes and the serious implications of such laws on the institution and the employees. Employees should be educated to be aware of transactions which might suggest possible laundering activity. Procedures should be set out detailing what an employee should do if a customer or transaction appears suspicious.

Minimum Standards

Treasury regulations provide that, at a minimum, a written compliance program should be adopted that:

- Establishes a system of internal controls to ensure ongoing BSA compliance.
- Provides for independent testing of compliance by internal auditors and/or outside examiners.
- Designates a compliance officer(s) to ensure day-to-day compliance with BSA.
- Provides training on an ongoing basis for all personnel.

Compliance Officer

A business should select a person or team responsible for the day-to-day monitoring of the compliance program. The compliance officer should be given broad authority to monitor all aspects of the institution's compliance including the development and refinement of the program and the monitoring of employee training programs. Such individual should also have the authority to conduct regular and ad hoc audits to ensure that the program is functioning effectively and to hire outside consultants as necessary to investigate problems.

Policy Statement

All entities covered under the reporting and recordkeeping laws and regulations should have a written policy against handling the proceeds of drug trafficking or other criminal activity. The statement should provide that the institution requires its employees to operate with the highest moral and ethical principles. It should include a statement that the company refuses to do business with criminals and money launderers; a commitment to conduct business only with legitimate business organizations; a statement against doing business with organizations that fail to provide proper documentation of their identity and purpose; clear directions for referring all suspicious transactions to the appropriate department; and a commitment to comply with the provisions of the Bank Secrecy Act.

"Know Your Customer" Programs

Most financial institutions have "Know Your Customer" programs as part of their BSA compliance program. Such programs should provide for effective customer identification, account monitoring, and appropriate action in suspicious circumstances. Both the CTR reporting requirements and the recordkeeping requirements of the Bank Secrecy Act mandate the identification of customers using the institution's services.

NEW DEPOSIT ACCOUNTS

For individual deposit accounts, minimum identification standards should be established. The information to be obtained should include:
- Name
- Address
- Date of birth
- Social Security number (or for non-U.S. citizens, a passport, visa, or alien registration number)
- Current employer
- Business and residence telephone numbers

The customer should be required to submit some form of identification that includes a photo such as a driver's license or passport, and a copy should be made and kept in the customer's file. If there are any doubts or inconsistencies about the information provided, the employee should be instructed to notify the appropriate department.

Minimum standards for new business accounts should include:
- Business name and address

- Telephone number
- Taxpayer identification number
- Documents establishing the formation of the business entity (articles of incorporation, partnership agreement, etc.)
- Copies of all assumed name filings or d/b/a's
- A full description of the operations of the business
- Credit and banking references
- The identity of the officers, directors, or other principals

The account representative should also consider making a personal visit to the customer's place of business. Besides promoting good customer relations, a personal visit will help identify whether the business is legitimate or simply a front. The representative can also use this opportunity to get to know the principals of the business.

NEW LOAN ACCOUNTS

An institution should perform due diligence in establishing a new loan account because if the customer is engaged in money laundering, there is a risk of forfeiture of collateral pledged on the loans. Real or personal property that is traceable to drug sales or that is purchased with laundered funds is subject to seizure by the government. If the property seized is pledged as collateral, the financial institution must prove that it was an innocent lienholder of the property and had no knowledge of the illegal activity.

Minimum standards regarding the information to be gathered should include:
- Reliable identifying information similar to that required for new deposit accounts
- Reliable financial information such as financial statements, W-2s, and copies of tax returns
- The purpose of the loan
- Credit history and prior banking references
- Verifiable, legitimate means of repayment
- Assurance that the loan amount is consistent with the purpose of the loan and the nature of the business

SERVICES FOR NONACCOUNTHOLDERS

Banks often issue cashier's checks, money orders, and traveler's checks and perform currency exchanges, wire transfers, or check cashing services. Strict identification requirements should be established for transactions with persons who are not regular bank customers. In fact, regulations require that in some instances banks keep a record of the identity of persons who are not established customers. Such regulations usually require at a minimum the person's name and address, driver's license number (or other number of identifying document produced), and Social Security number or employer identification number.

MONITORING ACCOUNTS

While identification of customers is important, it is equally important to monitor the activity of accounts. The institution should identify unusual transactions that might not be consistent with the normal business of the customer. Unusual and dramatic changes in wire transfer, monetary instrument, and check transactions are important to identify. If unusual transactions or activities are noted, the institution should take some action to protect itself. The appropriate action in some cases might be to discuss the changes with the customer to find out the reasons. Increased transactions might be the result of an increase in sales or the result of a promotional activity. However, if the discussion leads to a reasonable suspicion that the transactions are illegitimate, the institution might be required to notify the appropriate government agency and/or file a Suspicious Activity Report.

Special Problems for Insurance Companies

Although financial institutions such as banks are primarily associated with money laundering activities, insurance companies have become major targets of money laundering operations because of the variety of services and investment vehicles they offer that can be used to conceal the source of funds.

The most common form of money laundering that insurance companies face involves single premium contracts or policies. Examples include purchases of annuities, lump sum top-ups to an existing life insurance contract, and lump sum contributions to personal pension contracts.

Insurance companies, like other financial institutions, should educate their employees to look out for transactions that appear to be inconsistent with a customer's known legitimate business or personal activities or the normal transactions for that type of account. To that end, insurance companies should institute "Know Your Customer" programs such as those described above.

Red Flags

The following transactions *might* indicate money laundering is taking place. The list should be used to identify those transactions and customers which *might* require further investigation.

- Large purchase of a lump sum contract where the customer typically purchases small, regular payment contracts.
- Use of a third-party check to make a purchase or investment.
- Lack of concern for the performance of an investment but great concern for the early cancellation of the contract.
- Use of cash as payment for a transaction which is typically handled by checks or other forms of payment.
- Lump sum payments made by wire transfer or with foreign currency.
- Reluctance to provide normal information when setting up a policy or account or providing minimal information.
- Purchase of investments in amounts considered beyond the customer's apparent means.
- Use of a letter of credit or other methods of trade finance to move money between countries where such trade is inconsistent with customer's usual pattern.
- Establishment of a large investment policy and within a short time period, customer requests cancellation of the policy and cash value paid to third-party.
- Use of wire transfers to move large amounts of money to or from a financial haven country such as the Cayman Islands, Colombia, Hong Kong, Liechtenstein, Luxembourg, Panama, or Switzerland.
- Request to borrow maximum cash value of single premium policy soon after paying for policy.

Detection

Insurance companies must file all appropriate reports and follow all the requirements of the Bank Secrecy Act, including the implementation of an effective BSA compliance program.

Certain other reports can help companies identify suspicious transactions. *Incoming and outgoing wire transfer logs* can help companies identify possible patterns suggestive of money laundering. *Account activity reports* generally show weekly and/or monthly balances, deposits, and withdrawals. Review of these statements can identify those accounts with large increases in average balances and numbers of transactions. *Policy cancellation reports* should identify policies canceled within a specific time period. Report details should include the amount of the cash surrender value, the identity of the sales agent, and the actual term of the policy.

The chapter on "Tracing Illicit Transactions" in the Investigation section provides more information about techniques for detecting illicit income and payments. Included in that chapter are details on analyzing financial records, financial and behavioral profiles, and net worth analysis.

FINCEN Form 104
(Formerly Form 4789)
(Eff. December 2003)
Department of the Treasury
FinCEN

Currency Transaction Report

▶ Previous editions will not be accepted after August 31, 2004.
▶ Please type or print.
(Complete all parts that apply—See Instructions)

OMB No. 1506-0004

1 Check all box(es) that apply: **a** ☐ Amends prior report   **b** ☐ Multiple persons   **c** ☐ Multiple transactions

Part I — Person(s) Involved in Transaction(s)

Section A — Person(s) on Whose Behalf Transaction(s) Is Conducted

2 Individual's last name or entity's name

3 First name

4 Middle initial

5 Doing business as (DBA)

6 SSN or EIN

7 Address (number, street, and apt. or suite no.)

8 Date of birth ___/___/_____ MM DD YYYY

9 City

10 State

11 ZIP code

12 Country code (if not U.S.)

13 Occupation, profession, or business

14 If an individual, describe method used to verify identity: **a** ☐ Driver's license/State I.D.   **b** ☐ Passport   **c** ☐ Alien registration
  d ☐ Other _____   **e** Issued by: _____   **f** Number: _____

Section B — Individual(s) Conducting Transaction(s) (if other than above).

If Section B is left blank or incomplete, check the box(es) below to indicate the reason(s)

a ☐ Armored Car Service   **b** ☐ Mail Deposit or Shipment   **c** ☐ Night Deposit or Automated Teller Machine   **d** ☐ Multiple Transactions   **e** ☐ Conducted On Own Behalf

15 Individual's last name

16 First name

17 Middle initial

18 Address (number, street, and apt. or suite no.)

19 SSN

20 City

21 State

22 ZIP code

23 Country code (If not U.S.)

24 Date of birth ___/___/_____ MM DD YYYY

25 If an individual, describe method used to verify identity: **a** ☐ Driver's license/State I.D.   **b** ☐ Passport   **c** ☐ Alien registration
  d ☐ Other _____   **e** Issued by: _____   **f** Number: _____

Part II — Amount and Type of Transaction(s). Check all boxes that apply.

26 Total cash in $ _____ .00

27 Total cash out $ _____ .00

28 Date of transaction ___/___/_____ MM DD YYYY

26a Foreign cash in _____ .00 *(see instructions, page 3)*

27a Foreign cash out _____ .00 *(see instructions, page 3)*

29 ☐ Foreign Country _____

30 ☐ Wire Transfer(s)

31 ☐ Negotiable Instrument(s) Purchased

32 ☐ Negotiable Instrument(s) Cashed

33 ☐ Currency Exchange(s)

34 ☐ Deposit(s)/Withdrawal(s)

35 ☐ Account Number(s) Affected (if any):

36 ☐ Other (specify)

Part III — Financial Institution Where Transaction(s) Takes Place

37 Name of financial institution

Enter Regulator or BSA Examiner code number ▶ *(see instructions)*

38 Address (number, street, and apt. or suite no.)

39 EIN or SSN

40 City

41 State

42 ZIP code

43 Routing (MICR) number

Sign Here ▶

44 Title of approving official

45 Signature of approving official

46 Date of signature ___/___/_____ MM DD YYYY

47 Type or print preparer's name

48 Type or print name of person to contact

49 Telephone number (___) ___ - ____

▶ For Paperwork Reduction Act Notice, see page 4.

Cat. No. 37683N

FinCEN Form **104** (Formerly Form 4789) **(Rev. 8-03)**

FinCEN Form 104 (formerly Form 4789) (Rev. 8-03)   Page 2

Multiple Persons
Complete applicable parts below if box 1b on page 1 is checked

Part I — Person(s) Involved in Transaction(s)

Section A--Person(s) on Whose Behalf Transaction(s) Is Conducted

2 Individual's last name or entity's name   3 First name   4 Middle initial

5 Doing business as (DBA)   6 SSN or EIN

7 Address (number, street, and apt. or suite no.)   8 Date of birth __/__/____ MM DD YYYY

9 City   10 State   11 ZIP code   12 Country code (if not U.S.)   13 Occupation, profession, or business

14 If an individual, describe method used to verify identity: a ☐ Driver's license/State I.D.   b ☐ Passport   c ☐ Alien registration

d ☐ Other _____   e Issued by: _____   f Number: _____

Section B--Individual(s) Conducting Transaction(s) (if other than above).

15 Individual's last name   16 First name   17 Middle initial

18 Address (number, street, and apt. or suite no.)   19 SSN

20 City   21 State   22 ZIP code   23 Country code (if not U.S.)   24 Date of birth __/__/____ MM DD YYYY

25 If an individual, describe method used to verify identity: a ☐ Driver's license/State I.D.   b ☐ Passport   c ☐ Alien registration

d ☐ Other _____   e Issued by: _____   f Number: _____

Part I — Person(s) Involved in Transaction(s)

Section A--Person(s) on Whose Behalf Transaction(s) Is Conducted

2 Individual's last name or entity's name   3 First name   4 Middle initial

5 Doing business as (DBA)   6 SSN or EIN

7 Address (number, street, and apt. or suite no.)   8 Date of birth __/__/____ MM DD YYYY

9 City   10 State   11 ZIP code   12 Country code (if not U.S.)   13 Occupation, profession, or business

14 If an individual, describe method used to verify identity: a ☐ Driver's license/State I.D.   b ☐ Passport   c ☐ Alien registration

d ☐ Other _____   e Issued by: _____   f Number: _____

Section B--Individual(s) Conducting Transaction(s) (if other than above).

15 Individual's last name   16 First name   17 Middle initial

18 Address (number, street, and apt. or suite no.)   19 SSN

20 City   21 State   22 ZIP code   23 Country code (if not U.S.)   24 Date of birth __/__/____ MM DD YYYY

25 If an individual, describe method used to verify identity: a ☐ Driver's license/State I.D.   b ☐ Passport   c ☐ Alien registration

d ☐ Other _____   e Issued by: _____   f Number: _____

Suspicious Transactions

This Currency Transaction Report (CTR) should NOT be filed for suspicious transactions involving $10,000 or less in currency OR to note that a transaction of more than $10,000 is suspicious. Any suspicious or unusual activity should be reported by a financial institution in the manner prescribed by its appropriate federal regulator or BSA examiner. (See the instructions for Item 37.) If a transaction is suspicious and in excess of $10,000 in currency, then both a CTR and the appropriate Suspicious Activity Report form must be filed.

Should the suspicious activity require immediate attention, financial institutions should telephone 1-800-800-CTRS. An Internal Revenue Service (IRS) employee will direct the call to the local office of the IRS Criminal Investigation Division (CI). This toll-free number is operational Monday through Friday, from approximately 9:00 am to 6:00 pm Eastern Standard Time. If an emergency, consult directory assistance for the local IRS CID Office.

General Instructions

Who Must File. Each financial institution (other than a casino, which instead must file FinCEN Form 103, and the U.S. Postal Service for which there are separate rules) must file FinCEN Form 104 (formerly 4789) (CTR) for each deposit, withdrawal, exchange of currency, or other payment or transfer, by, through, or to the financial institution which involves a transaction in currency of more than $10,000. Multiple transactions must be treated as a single transaction if the financial institution has knowledge that (1) they are by or on behalf of the same person, and (2) they result in either currency received (Cash In) or currency disbursed (Cash Out) by the financial institution totaling more than $10,000 during any one business day. For a bank, a business day is the day on which transactions are routinely posted to customers' accounts, as normally communicated to depository customers. For all other financial institutions, a business day is a calendar day.

Generally, financial institutions are defined as banks, other types of depository institutions, brokers or dealers in securities, money transmitters, currency exchangers, check cashers, and issuers and sellers of money orders and traveler's checks. Should you have questions, see the definitions in 31 CFR Part 103.

When and Where To File. File this CTR by the 15th calendar day after the day of the transaction with the:

IRS Detroit Computing Center
ATTN: CTR
P.O. Box 33604
Detroit, MI 48232-5604

Keep a copy of each CTR for five years from the date filed.

A financial institution may apply to file the CTRs magnetically. To obtain an application to file magnetically, write to the:

IRS Detroit Computing Center
ATTN: CTR Magnetic Media Coordinator
P.O. Box 33604
Detroit, MI 48232-5604

Identification Requirements. All individuals (except employees of armored car services) conducting a reportable transaction(s) for themselves or for another person, must be identified by means of an official document(s). Acceptable forms of identification include a driver's license, military and military/dependent identification cards, passport, state issued identification card, cedular card (foreign), non-resident alien identification cards, or any other identification document or documents, which contain name and preferably address and a photograph and are normally acceptable by financial institutions as a means of identification when cashing checks for persons other than established customers.

Acceptable identification information obtained previously and maintained in the financial institution's records may be used. For example, if documents verifying an individual's identity were examined and recorded on a signature card when an account was opened, the financial institution may rely on that information. In completing the CTR, the financial institution must indicate on the form the method, type, and number of the identification. Statements such as "known customer" or "signature card on file" are not sufficient for form completion.

Penalties. Civil and criminal penalties are provided for failure to file a CTR or to supply information or for filing a false or fraudulent CTR. See 31 U.S.C. 5321, 5322 and 5324.

For purposes of this CTR, the terms below have the following meanings:

Currency. The coin and paper money of the United States or any other country, which is circulated and customarily used and accepted as money.

Person. An individual, corporation, partnership, trust or estate, joint stock company, association, syndicate, joint venture or other unincorporated organization or group.

Organization. Entity other than an individual.

Transaction in Currency. The physical transfer of currency from one person to another. This does not include a transfer of funds by means of bank check, bank draft, wire transfer or other written order that does not involve the physical transfer of currency.

Negotiable Instruments. All checks and drafts (including business, personal, bank, cashier's and third-party), money orders, and promissory notes. For purposes of this CTR, all traveler's checks shall also be considered negotiable instruments whether or not they are in bearer form.

Foreign exchange rates. If completing items 26a/27a, use the exchange rate in effect for the business day of the transaction. The source of the exchange rate that is used will be determined by the reporting institution.

Specific Instructions

Because of the limited space on the front and back of the CTR, it may be necessary to submit additional information on attached sheets. Submit this additional information on plain paper attached to the CTR. Be sure to put the individual's or entity's name and identifying number (items 2, 3, 4, and 6 of the CTR) on any additional sheets so that if it becomes separated, it may be associated with the CTR.

Item 1a. Amends Prior Report. If this CTR is being filed because it amends a report filed previously, check Item 1a. Staple a copy of the original CTR to the amended one, complete Part III fully and only those other entries which are being amended.

Item 1b. Multiple Persons. If this transaction is being conducted by more than one person or on behalf of more than one person, check Item 1b. Enter information in Part I for one of the persons and provide information on any other persons on the back of the CTR.

Item 1c. Multiple Transactions. If the financial institution has knowledge that there are multiple transactions, check Item 1c.

PART I - Person(s) Involved in Transaction(s)

Section A **must** be completed. If an individual conducts a transaction on his own behalf, complete Section A and leave Section "B" BLANK. If an individual conducts a transaction on his own behalf and on behalf of another person(s), complete Section "A" for each person and leave Section "B" BLANK. If an individual conducts a transaction on behalf of another person(s), complete Section "B" for the individual conducting the transaction, and complete Section "A" for each person on whose behalf the transaction is conducted of whom the financial institution has knowledge.

Section A. Person(s) on Whose Behalf Transaction(s) Is Conducted. See instructions above.

Items 2, 3, and 4. Individual/Organization Name. If the person on whose behalf the transaction(s) is conducted is an individual, put his/her last name in Item 2, first name in Item 3, and middle initial in Item 4. If there is no middle initial, leave item 4 BLANK. If the transaction is conducted on behalf of an entity, put its name in Item 2 and leave Items 3 and 4 BLANK.

Item 5. Doing Business As (DBA). If the financial institution has knowledge of a separate "doing business as" name, enter it in Item 5. For example, Smith Enterprise DBA MJ's Pizza.

Item 6. SSN/ITIN or EIN. Enter the Social Security Number (SSN) or Individual Taxpayer Identification Number (ITIN) or Employer Identification Number (EIN) of the person or entity identified in Item 2. If none, write NONE.

Items 7, 9, 10, 11, and 12. Address. Enter the permanent address including ZIP Code of the person identified in Item 2. Use the U.S. Postal Service's two letter state abbreviation code. A P.O. Box should not be used by itself, and may only be used if there is no street address. If a P.O. Box is used, the name of the apartment or suite number, road or route number where the person resides must also be provided. If the address is outside the U.S., provide the street address, city, province or state, postal code (if known), and the two letter country code. For country code list go to www.fincen.gov/reg_bsaforms.html or telephone 1-800-949-2732 and select option number 5. If U.S., leave item 12 blank.

Item 8. Date of Birth. Enter the date of birth. Eight numerals must be inserted for each date. The first two will reflect the month, the second two the day, and the last four the year. A zero (0) should precede any single digit number. For example, if an individual's birth date is April 3 1948, Item 8 should read 04 03 1948.

Item 13. Occupation, Profession, or Business. Identify the occupation, profession, or business of the person on whose behalf the transaction was conducted. For example: secretary, shoe salesman, carpenter, attorney, housewife, restaurant, liquor store,etc. Do not use non-specific terms such as merchant, self-employed, businessman, etc.

Item 14. If an Individual, Describe Method Used To Verify Identity. If an individual conducts the transaction(s) on his/her own behalf, his/her identity must be verified by examination of an acceptable document (see **General Instructions**). For example, check box **a** if a driver's license is used to verify an individual's identity, and enter the state that issued the license and the number in items e and f. If the transaction is conducted by an individual on behalf of another individual not present or on behalf of an entity, enter N/A in Item 14.

Section B. Individual(s) Conducting Transaction(s) (if other than above). Financial institutions should enter as much information as is available.

However, there may be instances in which Items 15-25 may be left BLANK or incomplete. If Items 15-25 are left BLANK or incomplete, check one or more of the boxes provided to indicate the reasons.

Example: If there are multiple transactions that, if only when aggregated, the financial institution has knowledge the transactions exceed the reporting threshold, and therefore, did not identify the transactor(s), check box **d** for Multiple Transactions.

Items 15, 16, and 17. Individual's Name. Complete these items if an individual conducts a transaction(s) on behalf of another person. For example, if John Doe, an employee of XYZ Grocery Store, makes a deposit to the store's account, XYZ Grocery Store should be identified in Section A and John Doe should be identified in section B.

Items 18, 20, 21, 22, and 23. Address. Enter the permanent street address including ZIP Code of the individual. (See the instructions for Items 7 and 9 through 12.) Enter country code if not U.S. (Reference item 12).

Item 19. SSN/ITIN. If the individual has a Social Security Number, or Individual Taxpayer Indentifcation Number, enter it in Item 19. If the individual does not have an SSN/ITIN, enter NONE.

Item 24. Date of Birth. Enter the individual's date of birth. (See the instructions for Item 8.)

Item 25. If an Individual, Describe Method Used To Verify Identity. Enter the method used to identify the individual's identity. (See **General Instructions** and the instructions for Item 14.)

PART II - Amount and Type of Transaction(s)
Complete Part II to identify the type of transaction(s) and the amount(s) involved.

Items 26 and 27. Total Cash In/Total Cash Out. In the spaces provided, enter the total amount of currency received (Total Cash In) or total currency disbursed (Total Cash Out) by the financial institution. If foreign currency is exchanged, use the U.S. dollar equivalent on the day of the transaction (See "Foreign exchange rates"), and complete item 26a or 27a, whichever is appropriate.

If less than a full dollar amount is involved, increase that figure to the next highest dollar. For example, if the currency totals $20,000.05, show the total as $20,001.00.

Items 26a and 27a. Foreign cash in/Foreign cash out. If foreign currency is exchanged, enter the amount of foreign currency in items 26a and 27a. Report country of origin in item 29.

Item 28. Date of Transaction. Insert eight numerals for each date. (See instructions for Item 8.)

Item 29. Foreign Country. If items 26a and/or 27a are completed indicating that foreign currency is involved, check Item 29 and identify the country. If multiple foreign currencies are involved, check box 36 and identify the additional country(s) and/or currency(s) involved.

Determining Whether Transactions Meet the Reporting Threshold.

Only cash transactions that, if alone or when aggregated, exceed $10,000 should be reported on the CTR. Transactions shall not be offset against one another.

If there are both Cash In and Cash Out transactions that are reportable, the amounts should be considered separately and not aggregated. However, they may be reported on a single CTR.

If there is a currency exchange, it should be aggregated separately with each of the Cash In and Cash Out totals.

Example 1: A person deposits $11,000 in currency to his savings account and withdraws $3,000 in currency from his checking account. The CTR should be completed as follows:
Cash In $11,000 and no entry for Cash Out. This is because the $3,000 transaction does not meet the reporting threshold.

Example 2: A person deposits $11,000 in currency to his savings account and withdraws $12,000 in currency from his checking account. The CTR should be completed as follows:
Cash In $11,000, Cash Out $12,000. This is because there are two reportable transactions. However, one CTR may be filed to reflect both.

Example 3: A person deposits $6,000 in currency to his savings account and withdraws $4,000 in currency from his checking account. Further, he presents $5,000 in currency to be exchanged for the equivalent in French Francs. The CTR should be completed as follows:
Cash In $11,000 and no entry for Cash Out. This is because in determining whether the transactions are reportable, the currency exchange is aggregated with each of the Cash In and Cash Out amounts. The result is a reportable $11,000 Cash In transaction. The total Cash Out amount is $9,000, which does not meet the reporting threshold. Therefore, it is not entered on the CTR.

Example 4: A person deposits $6,000 in currency to his savings account and withdraws $7,000 in currency from his checking account. Further, he presents $5,000 in currency to be exchanged for the equivalent in French francs. The CTR should be completed as follows:
Cash In $11,000, Cash Out $12,000. This is because in determining whether the transactions are reportable, the currency exchange is aggregated with each of the Cash In and Cash Out amounts. In this example, each of the Cash In and Cash Out totals exceed $10,000 and must be reflected on the CTR.

Items 30-33. Check the appropriate item(s) to identify the following type of transaction(s):
30. Wire Transfer(s)
31. Negotiable Instrument(s) Purchased
32. Negotiable Instrument(s) Cashed
33. Currency Exchange(s)

Item 34. Deposits/Withdrawals. Check this item to identify deposits to or withdrawals from accounts, e.g. demand deposit accounts, savings accounts, time deposits, mutual fund accounts, or any other account held at the financial institution. Enter the account number(s) in Item 35.

Item 35. Account Numbers Affected (if any). Enter the account numbers of any accounts affected by the transactions that are maintained at the financial institution conducting the transaction(s). If necessary, use additional sheets of paper to indicate all of the affected accounts.

Example 1: If a person cashes a check drawn on an account held at the financial institution, the CTR should be completed as follows:
Indicate negotiable instrument(s) cashed and provide the account number of the check.

If the transaction does not affect an account, make no entry.

Example 2: A person cashes a check drawn on another financial institution. In this instance, negotiable instrument(s) cashed would be indicated, but no account at the financial institution has been affected. Therefore, Item 35 should be left BLANK.

Item 36. Other (specify). If a transaction is not identified in Items 30-34, check Item 36 and provide an additional description. For example, a person presents a check to purchase "foreign currency." Also list multiple foreign currencies from item 29.

PART III - Financial Institution Where Transaction(s) Take Place

Item 37. Name of Financial Institution and Identity of Regulator or BSA Examiner. Enter the financial institution's full legal name and identify the regulator or BSA examiner, using the following codes:

Regulator or BSA Examiner	CODE
Comptroller of the Currency (OCC)	1
Federal Deposit Insurance Corporation (FDIC)	2
Federal Reserve System (FRS)	3
Office of Thrift Supervision (OTS)	4
National Credit Union Administration (NCUA)	5
Securities and Exchange Commission (SEC)	6
Internal Revenue Service (IRS)	7
U.S. Postal Service (USPS)	8
Commodity Futures Trading Commission (CFTC)	9
State Regulator	10

Items 38, 40, 41, and 42. Address. Enter the street address, city, state, and ZIP Code of the financial institution where the transaction occurred. If there are multiple transactions, provide information of the office or branch where any one of the transactions has occurred.

Item 39. EIN or SSN. Enter the financial institution's EIN. If the financial institution does not have an EIN, enter the SSN of the financial institution's principal owner.

Item 43. Routing (MICR) Number. If a depository institution, enter the routing (Magnetic Ink Character Recognition (MICR)) number.

SIGNATURE

Items 44 and 45. Title and signature of Approving Official. The official who reviews and approves the CTR must indicate his/her title and sign the CTR.

Item 46. Date of Signature. The approving official must enter the date the CTR is signed. (See the instructions for Item 8.)

Item 47. Preparer's Name. Type or print the full name of the individual preparing the CTR. The preparer and the approving official may not necessarily be the same individual.

Items 48 and 49. Contact Person/Telephone Number. Type or print the name and telephone number of an individual to contact concerning questions about the CTR.

Paperwork Reduction Act Notice. The requested information is useful in criminal, tax, and regulatory investigations and proceedings. Financial institutions are required to provide the information under 31 U.S.C. 5313 and 31 CFR Part 103, commonly referred to as the Bank Secrecy Act (BSA). The BSA is administered by the U.S. Department of the Treasury's Financial Crimes Enforcement Network (FinCEN). You are not required to provide the requested information unless a form displays a valid OMB control number.

The time needed to complete this form will vary depending on individual circumstances. The estimated average time is 19 minutes. If you have comments concerning the accuracy of this time estimate or suggestions for making this form simpler, you may write to the **Financial Crimes Enforcement Network, P. O. Box 39, Vienna, VA 22183**. Do not send this form to this office. Instead, see **When and Where to File** in the instructions.

IRS Form 8300 (Rev. December 2001)
OMB No. 1545-0892
Department of the Treasury
Internal Revenue Service

Report of Cash Payments Over $10,000 Received in a Trade or Business

▶ See instructions for definition of cash.
▶ Use this form for transactions occurring after December 31, 2001. Do not use prior versions after this date.
For Privacy Act and Paperwork Reduction Act Notice, see page 4.

FinCEN Form 8300 (December 2001)
OMB No. 1506-0018
Department of the Treasury
Financial Crimes Enforcement Network

1 Check appropriate box(es) if: **a** ☐ Amends prior report; **b** ☐ Suspicious transaction.

Part I — Identity of Individual From Whom the Cash Was Received

2 If more than one individual is involved, check here and see instructions . . . . ▶ ☐

3 Last name | **4** First name | **5** M.I. | **6** Taxpayer identification number

7 Address (number, street, and apt. or suite no.) | **8** Date of birth ▶ M M D D Y Y Y Y (see instructions)

9 City | **10** State | **11** ZIP code | **12** Country (if not U.S.) | **13** Occupation, profession, or business

14 Document used to verify identity: **a** Describe identification ▶ ....
b Issued by .... **c** Number ....

Part II — Person on Whose Behalf This Transaction Was Conducted

15 If this transaction was conducted on behalf of more than one person, check here and see instructions . . . . . ▶ ☐

16 Individual's last name or Organization's name | **17** First name | **18** M.I. | **19** Taxpayer identification number

20 Doing business as (DBA) name (see instructions) | Employer identification number

21 Address (number, street, and apt. or suite no.) | **22** Occupation, profession, or business

23 City | **24** State | **25** ZIP code | **26** Country (if not U.S.)

27 Alien identification: **a** Describe identification ▶ ....
b Issued by .... **c** Number ....

Part III — Description of Transaction and Method of Payment

28 Date cash received M M D D Y Y Y Y
29 Total cash received $ _____ .00
30 If cash was received in more than one payment, check here . . . ▶ ☐
31 Total price if different from item 29 $ _____ .00

32 Amount of cash received (in U.S. dollar equivalent) (must equal item 29) (see instructions):

 a U.S. currency $ _____ .00 (Amount in $100 bills or higher $ _____ .00)
 b Foreign currency $ _____ .00 (Country ▶ _____)
 c Cashier's check(s) $ _____ .00 ⎱ Issuer's name(s) and serial number(s) of the monetary instrument(s) ▶ ....
 d Money order(s) $ _____ .00 ⎰
 e Bank draft(s) $ _____ .00
 f Traveler's check(s) $ _____ .00

33 Type of transaction
 a ☐ Personal property purchased
 b ☐ Real property purchased
 c ☐ Personal services provided
 d ☐ Business services provided
 e ☐ Intangible property purchased
 f ☐ Debt obligations paid
 g ☐ Exchange of cash
 h ☐ Escrow or trust funds
 i ☐ Bail received by court clerks
 j ☐ Other (specify) ▶

34 Specific description of property or service shown in 33. (Give serial or registration number, address, docket number, etc.) ▶ ....

Part IV — Business That Received Cash

35 Name of business that received cash | **36** Employer identification number

37 Address (number, street, and apt. or suite no.) | Social security number

38 City | **39** State | **40** ZIP code | **41** Nature of your business

42 Under penalties of perjury, I declare that to the best of my knowledge the information I have furnished above is true, correct, and complete.

Signature ▶ _____ Authorized official   Title ▶ _____

43 Date of signature M M D D Y Y Y Y
44 Type or print name of contact person
45 Contact telephone number ( )

IRS Form **8300** (Rev. 12-2001) Cat. No. 62133S FinCEN Form **8300** (12-2001)

IRS Form 8300 (Rev. 12-2001)   Page **2**   FinCEN Form 8300 (12-2001)

Multiple Parties
(Complete applicable parts below if box 2 or 15 on page 1 is checked)

Part I — Continued—Complete if box 2 on page 1 is checked

3 Last name	4 First name	5 M.I.	6 Taxpayer identification number
7 Address (number, street, and apt. or suite no.)		8 Date of birth (see instructions) ▶	M M D D Y Y Y Y
9 City	10 State	11 ZIP code	12 Country (if not U.S.)	13 Occupation, profession, or business

14 Document used to verify identity: **a** Describe identification ▶ ----------------
   b Issued by   **c** Number

3 Last name	4 First name	5 M.I.	6 Taxpayer identification number
7 Address (number, street, and apt. or suite no.)		8 Date of birth (see instructions) ▶	M M D D Y Y Y Y
9 City	10 State	11 ZIP code	12 Country (if not U.S.)	13 Occupation, profession, or business

14 Document used to verify identity: **a** Describe identification ▶ ----------------
   b Issued by   **c** Number

Part II — Continued—Complete if box 15 on page 1 is checked

16 Individual's last name or Organization's name	17 First name	18 M.I.	19 Taxpayer identification number
20 Doing business as (DBA) name (see instructions)			Employer identification number
21 Address (number, street, and apt. or suite no.)			22 Occupation, profession, or business
23 City	24 State	25 ZIP code	26 Country (if not U.S.)	

27 Alien identification: **a** Describe identification ▶ ----------------
   b Issued by   **c** Number

16 Individual's last name or Organization's name	17 First name	18 M.I.	19 Taxpayer identification number
20 Doing business as (DBA) name (see instructions)			Employer identification number
21 Address (number, street, and apt. or suite no.)			22 Occupation, profession, or business
23 City	24 State	25 ZIP code	26 Country (if not U.S.)	

27 Alien identification: **a** Describe identification ▶ ----------------
   b Issued by   **c** Number

Section references are to the Internal Revenue Code unless otherwise noted.

Changes To Note

- Section 6050I (26 United States Code (U.S.C.) 6050I) and 31 U.S.C. 5331 require that certain information be reported to the IRS and the Financial Crimes Enforcement Network (FinCEN). This information must be reported on **IRS/FinCEN Form 8300.**
- Item 33 box **i** is to be checked **only** by clerks of the court; box **d** is to be checked by bail bondsmen. See the instructions on page 4.
- For purposes of section 6050I and 31 U.S.C. 5331, the word "cash" and "currency" have the same meaning. See **Cash** under **Definitions** below.

General Instructions

Who must file. Each person engaged in a trade or business who, in the course of that trade or business, receives more than $10,000 in cash in one transaction or in two or more related transactions, must file Form 8300. Any transactions conducted between a payer (or its agent) and the recipient in a 24-hour period are related transactions. Transactions are considered related even if they occur over a period of more than 24 hours if the recipient knows, or has reason to know, that each transaction is one of a series of connected transactions.

Keep a copy of each Form 8300 for 5 years from the date you file it.

Clerks of Federal or State courts must file Form 8300 if more than $10,000 in cash is received as bail for an individual(s) charged with certain criminal offenses. For these purposes, a clerk includes the clerk's office or any other office, department, division, branch, or unit of the court that is authorized to receive bail. If a person receives bail on behalf of a clerk, the clerk is treated as receiving the bail. See the instructions for **Item 33** on page 4.

If multiple payments are made in cash to satisfy bail and the initial payment does not exceed $10,000, the initial payment and subsequent payments must be aggregated and the information return must be filed by the 15th day after receipt of the payment that causes the aggregate amount to exceed $10,000 in cash. In such cases, the reporting requirement can be satisfied either by sending a single written statement with an aggregate amount listed or by furnishing a copy of each Form 8300 relating to that payer. Payments made to satisfy separate bail requirements are not required to be aggregated. See Treasury Regulations section 1.6050I-2.

Casinos must file Form 8300 for nongaming activities (restaurants, shops, etc.).

Voluntary use of Form 8300. Form 8300 may be filed voluntarily for any suspicious transaction (see **Definitions**) for use by FinCEN and the IRS, even if the total amount does not exceed $10,000.

Exceptions. Cash is not required to be reported if it is received:

- By a financial institution required to file **Form 4789,** Currency Transaction Report.
- By a casino required to file (or exempt from filing) **Form 8362,** Currency Transaction Report by Casinos, if the cash is received as part of its gaming business.
- By an agent who receives the cash from a principal, if the agent uses all of the cash within 15 days in a second transaction that is reportable on Form 8300 or on Form 4789, and discloses all the information necessary to complete Part II of Form 8300 or Form 4789 to the recipient of the cash in the second transaction.
- In a transaction occurring entirely outside the United States. See **Pub. 1544,** Reporting Cash Payments Over $10,000 (Received in a Trade or Business), regarding transactions occurring in Puerto Rico, the Virgin Islands, and territories and possessions of the United States.
- In a transaction that is not in the course of a person's trade or business.

When to file. File Form 8300 by the 15th day after the date the cash was received. If that date falls on a Saturday, Sunday, or legal holiday, file the form on the next business day.

Where to file. File the form with the Internal Revenue Service, Detroit Computing Center, P.O. Box 32621, Detroit, MI 48232.

Statement to be provided. You must give a written statement to each person named on a required Form 8300 on or before January 31 of the year following the calendar year in which the cash is received. The statement must show the name, telephone number, and address of the information contact for the business, the aggregate amount of reportable cash received, and that the information was furnished to the IRS. Keep a copy of the statement for your records.

Multiple payments. If you receive more than one cash payment for a single transaction or for related transactions, you must report the multiple payments any time you receive a total amount that exceeds $10,000 within any 12-month period. Submit the report within 15 days of the date you receive the payment that causes the total amount to exceed $10,000. If more than one report is required within 15 days, you may file a combined report. File the combined report no later than the date the earliest report, if filed separately, would have to be filed.

Taxpayer identification number (TIN). You must furnish the correct TIN of the person or persons from whom you receive the cash and, if applicable, the person or persons on whose behalf the transaction is being conducted. **You may be subject to penalties for an incorrect or missing TIN.**

The TIN for an individual (including a sole proprietorship) is the individual's social security number (SSN). For certain resident aliens who are not eligible to get an SSN and nonresident aliens who are required to file tax returns, it is an IRS Individual Taxpayer Identification Number (ITIN). For other persons, including corporations, partnerships, and estates, it is the employer identification number (EIN).

If you have requested but are not able to get a TIN for one or more of the parties to a transaction within 15 days following the transaction, file the report and attach a statement explaining why the TIN is not included.

Exception: *You are not required to provide the TIN of a person who is a nonresident alien individual or a foreign organization if that person does not have income effectively connected with the conduct of a U.S. trade or business and does not have an office or place of business, or fiscal or paying agent, in the United States. See Pub. 1544 for more information.*

Penalties. You may be subject to penalties if you fail to file a correct and complete Form 8300 on time and you cannot show that the failure was due to reasonable cause. You may also be subject to penalties if you fail to furnish timely a correct and complete statement to each person named in a required report. A minimum penalty of $25,000 may be imposed if the failure is due to an intentional or willful disregard of the cash reporting requirements.

Penalties may also be imposed for causing, or attempting to cause, a trade or business to fail to file a required report; for causing, or attempting to cause, a trade or business to file a required report containing a material omission or misstatement of fact; or for structuring, or attempting to structure, transactions to avoid the reporting requirements. These violations may also be subject to criminal prosecution which, upon conviction, may result in imprisonment of up to 5 years or fines of up to $250,000 for individuals and $500,000 for corporations or both.

Definitions

Cash. The term "cash" means the following:
- U.S. and foreign coin and currency received in any transaction.
- A cashier's check, money order, bank draft, or traveler's check having a face amount of $10,000 or less that is received in a **designated reporting transaction** (defined below), or that is received in any transaction in which the recipient knows that the instrument is being used in an attempt to avoid the reporting of the transaction under either section 6050I or 31 U.S.C. 5331.

Note: *Cash does not include a check drawn on the payer's own account, such as a personal check, regardless of the amount.*

Designated reporting transaction. A retail sale (or the receipt of funds by a broker or other intermediary in connection with a retail sale) of a consumer durable, a collectible, or a travel or entertainment activity.

Retail sale. Any sale (whether or not the sale is for resale or for any other purpose) made in the course of a trade or business if that trade or business principally consists of making sales to ultimate consumers.

Consumer durable. An item of tangible personal property of a type that, under ordinary usage, can reasonably be expected to remain useful for at least 1 year, and that has a sales price of more than $10,000.

Collectible. Any work of art, rug, antique, metal, gem, stamp, coin, etc.

Travel or entertainment activity. An item of travel or entertainment that pertains to a single trip or event if the combined sales price of the item and all other items relating to the same trip or event that are sold in the same transaction (or related transactions) exceeds $10,000.

Exceptions. A cashier's check, money order, bank draft, or traveler's check is not considered received in a designated reporting transaction if it constitutes the proceeds of a bank loan or if it is received as a payment on certain promissory notes, installment sales contracts, or down payment plans. See Pub. 1544 for more information.

Person. An individual, corporation, partnership, trust, estate, association, or company.

Recipient. The person receiving the cash. Each branch or other unit of a person's trade or business is considered a separate recipient unless the branch receiving the cash (or a central office linking the branches), knows or has reason to know the identity of payers making cash payments to other branches.

Transaction. Includes the purchase of property or services, the payment of debt, the exchange of a negotiable instrument for cash, and the receipt of cash to be held in escrow or trust. A single transaction may not be broken into multiple transactions to avoid reporting.

Suspicious transaction. A transaction in which it appears that a person is attempting to cause Form 8300 not to be filed, or to file a false or incomplete form. The term also includes any transaction in which there is an indication of possible illegal activity.

Specific Instructions

You must complete all parts. However, you may skip Part II if the individual named in Part I is conducting the transaction on his or her behalf only. **For voluntary reporting of suspicious transactions, see Item 1 below.**

Item 1. If you are amending a prior report, check box 1a. Complete the appropriate items with the correct or amended information only. Complete all of Part IV. Staple a copy of the original report to the amended report.

To voluntarily report a suspicious transaction (see **Definitions**), check box 1b. You may also telephone your local IRS Criminal Investigation Division or call 1-800-800-2877.

Part I

Item 2. If two or more individuals conducted the transaction you are reporting, check the box and complete Part I for any one of the individuals. Provide the same information for the other individual(s) on the back of the form. If more than three individuals are involved, provide the same information on additional sheets of paper and attach them to this form.

Item 6. Enter the taxpayer identification number (TIN) of the individual named. See **Taxpayer identification number (TIN)** on page 3 for more information.

Item 8. Enter eight numerals for the date of birth of the individual named. For example, if the individual's birth date is July 6, 1960, enter 07 06 1960.

Item 13. Fully describe the nature of the occupation, profession, or business (for example, "plumber," "attorney," or "automobile dealer"). Do not use general or nondescriptive terms such as "businessman" or "self-employed."

Item 14. You must verify the name and address of the named individual(s). Verification must be made by examination of a document normally accepted as a means of identification when cashing checks (for example, a driver's license, passport, alien registration card, or other official document). In item 14a, enter the type of document examined. In item 14b, identify the issuer of the document. In item 14c, enter the document's number. For example, if the individual has a Utah driver's license, enter "driver's license" in item 14a, "Utah" in item 14b, and the number appearing on the license in item 14c.

Part II

Item 15. If the transaction is being conducted on behalf of more than one person (including husband and wife or parent and child), check the box and complete Part II for any one of the persons. Provide the same information for the other person(s) on the back of the form. If more than three persons are involved, provide the same information on additional sheets of paper and attach them to this form.

Items 16 through 19. If the person on whose behalf the transaction is being conducted is an individual, complete items 16, 17, and 18. Enter his or her TIN in item 19. If the individual is a sole proprietor and has an employer identification number (EIN), you must enter both the SSN and EIN in item 19. If the person is an organization, put its name as shown on required tax filings in item 16 and its EIN in item 19.

Item 20. If a sole proprietor or organization named in items 16 through 18 is doing business under a name other than that entered in item 16 (e.g., a "trade" or "doing business as (DBA)" name), enter it here.

Item 27. If the person is not required to furnish a TIN, complete this item. See **Taxpayer Identification Number (TIN)** on page 3. Enter a description of the type of official document issued to that person in item 27a (for example, "passport"), the country that issued the document in item 27b, and the document's number in item 27c.

Part III

Item 28. Enter the date you received the cash. If you received the cash in more than one payment, enter the date you received the payment that caused the combined amount to exceed $10,000. See **Multiple payments** under **General Instructions** for more information.

Item 30. Check this box if the amount shown in item 29 was received in more than one payment (for example, as installment payments or payments on related transactions).

Item 31. Enter the total price of the property, services, amount of cash exchanged, etc. (for example, the total cost of a vehicle purchased, cost of catering service, exchange of currency) if different from the amount shown in item 29.

Item 32. Enter the dollar amount of each form of cash received. Show foreign currency amounts in U.S. dollar equivalent at a fair market rate of exchange available to the public. **The sum of the amounts must equal item 29.** For cashier's check, money order, bank draft, or traveler's check, provide the name of the issuer and the serial number of each instrument. Names of all issuers and all serial numbers involved must be provided. If necessary, provide this information on additional sheets of paper and attach them to this form.

Item 33. Check the appropriate box(es) that describe the transaction. If the transaction is not specified in boxes a–i, check box j and briefly describe the transaction (for example, "car lease," "boat lease," "house lease," or "aircraft rental"). If the transaction relates to the receipt of bail by a court clerk, check box **i**, "Bail received by court clerks." This box is **only** for use by court clerks. If the transaction relates to cash received by a bail bondsman, check box **d**, "Business services provided."

Part IV

Item 36. If you are a sole proprietorship, you must enter your SSN. If your business also has an EIN, you must provide the EIN as well. All other business entities must enter an EIN.

Item 41. Fully describe the nature of your business, for example, "attorney" or "jewelry dealer." Do not use general or nondescriptive terms such as "business" or "store."

Item 42. This form must be signed by an individual who has been authorized to do so for the business that received the cash.

Privacy Act and Paperwork Reduction Act Notice. Except as otherwise noted, the information solicited on this form is required by the Internal Revenue Service (IRS) and the Financial Crimes Enforcement Network (FinCEN) in order to carry out the laws and regulations of the United States Department of the Treasury. Trades or businesses, except for clerks of criminal courts, are required to provide the information to the IRS and FinCEN under both section 6050I and 31 U.S.C. 5331. Clerks of criminal courts are required to provide the information to the IRS under section 6050I. Section 6109 and 31 U.S.C. 5331 require that you provide your social security number in order to adequately identify you and process your return and other papers. The principal purpose for collecting the information on this form is to maintain reports or records where such reports or records have a high degree of usefulness in criminal, tax, or regulatory investigations or proceedings, or in the conduct of intelligence or counterintelligence activities, by directing the Federal Government's attention to unusual or questionable transactions.

While such information is invaluable with regards to the purpose of this form, you are not required to provide information as to whether the reported transaction is deemed suspicious. No penalties or fines will be assessed for failure to provide such information, even if you determine that the reported transaction is indeed suspicious in nature. Failure to provide all other requested information, or the provision of fraudulent information, may result in criminal prosecution and other penalties under Title 26 and Title 31 of the United States Code.

Generally, tax returns and return information are confidential, as stated in section 6103. However, section 6103 allows or requires the IRS to disclose or give the information requested on this form to others as described in the Code. For example, we may disclose your tax information to the Department of Justice, to enforce the tax laws, both civil and criminal, and to cities, states, the District of Columbia, U.S. commonwealths or possessions, and certain foreign governments to carry out their tax laws. We may disclose your tax information to the Department of Treasury and contractors for tax administration purposes; and to other persons as necessary to obtain information which we cannot get in any other way in order to determine the amount of or to collect the tax you owe. We may disclose your tax information to the Comptroller General of the United States to permit the Comptroller General to review the IRS. We may disclose your tax information to Committees of Congress; Federal, state, and local child support agencies; and to other Federal agencies for the purposes of determining entitlement for benefits or the eligibility for and the repayment of loans. We may also disclose this information to Federal agencies that investigate or respond to acts or threats of terrorism or participate in intelligence or counterintelligence activities concerning terrorism.

FinCEN may provide the information collected through this form to those officers and employees of the Department of the Treasury who have a need for the records in the performance of their duties. FinCEN may also refer the records to any other department or agency of the Federal Government upon the request of the head of such department or agency and may also provide the records to appropriate state, local, and foreign criminal law enforcement and regulatory personnel in the performance of their official duties.

You are not required to provide the information requested on a form that is subject to the Paperwork Reduction Act unless the form displays a valid OMB control number. Books or records relating to a form or its instructions must be retained as long as their contents may become material in the administration of any law under Title 26 or Title 31.

The time needed to complete this form will vary depending on individual circumstances. The estimated average time is 21 minutes. If you have comments concerning the accuracy of this time estimate or suggestions for making this form simpler, you can write to the Tax Forms Committee, Western Area Distribution Center, Rancho Cordova, CA 95743-0001. **Do not** send this form to this office. Instead, see **Where To File** on page 3.

FinCEN Form **105**
(Formerly Customs Form 4790)
(Rev. July 2003)
Department of the Treasury
FinCEN

DEPARTMENT OF THE TREASURY
FINANCIAL CRIMES ENFORCEMENT NETWORK

REPORT OF INTERNATIONAL TRANSPORTATION OF CURRENCY OR MONETARY INSTRUMENTS

OMB NO. 1506-0014

▶ To be filed with the Bureau of Customs and Border Protection
▶ For Paperwork Reduction Act Notice and Privacy Act Notice, see back of form.

31 U.S.C. 5316; 31 CFR 103.23 and 103.27

▶ Please type or print.

PART I FOR A PERSON DEPARTING OR ENTERING THE UNITED STATES, OR A PERSON SHIPPING, MAILING, OR RECEIVING CURRENCY OR MONETARY INSTRUMENTS. (IF ACTING FOR ANYONE ELSE, ALSO COMPLETE PART II BELOW.)

1. NAME *(Last or family, first, and middle)*
2. IDENTIFICATION NO. *(See instructions)*
3. DATE OF BIRTH *(Mo./Day/Yr.)*

4. PERMANENT ADDRESS IN UNITED STATES OR ABROAD
5. YOUR COUNTRY OR COUNTRIES OF CITIZENSHIP

6. ADDRESS WHILE IN THE UNITED STATES
7. PASSPORT NO. & COUNTRY

8. U.S. VISA DATE *(Mo./Day/Yr.)*
9. PLACE UNITED STATES VISA WAS ISSUED
10. IMMIGRATION ALIEN NO.

11. IF CURRENCY OR MONETARY INSTRUMENT IS ACCOMPANIED BY A PERSON, COMPLETE 11a OR 11b

A. EXPORTED FROM THE UNITED STATES		B. IMPORTED INTO THE UNITED STATES	
Departed From: *(U.S. Port/City in U.S.)*	Arrived At: *(Foreign City/Country)*	Departed From: *(Foreign City/Country)*	Arrived At: *(City in U.S.)*

12. IF CURRENCY OR MONETARY INSTRUMENT WAS MAILED OR OTHERWISE SHIPPED, COMPLETE 12a THROUGH 12f

12a. DATE SHIPPED *(Mo./Day/Yr.)*	12b. DATE RECEIVED *(Mo./Day/Yr.)*	12c. METHOD OF SHIPMENT *(e.g. u.s. Mail, Public Carrier, etc.)*	12d. NAME OF CARRIER

12e. SHIPPED TO *(Name and Address)*

12f. RECEIVED FROM *(Name and Address)*

PART II INFORMATION ABOUT PERSON(S) OR BUSINESS ON WHOSE BEHALF IMPORTATION OR EXPORTATION WAS CONDUCTED

13. NAME *(Last or family, first, and middle or Business Name)*

14. PERMANENT ADDRESS IN UNITED STATES OR ABROAD

15. TYPE OF BUSINESS ACTIVITY, OCCUPATION, OR PROFESSION
15a. IS THE BUSINESS A BANK? ☐ Yes ☐ No

PART III CURRENCY AND MONETARY INSTRUMENT INFORMATION (SEE INSTRUCTIONS ON REVERSE)(To be completed by everyone)

16. TYPE AND AMOUNT OF CURRENCY/MONETARY INSTRUMENTS

		17. IF OTHER THAN U.S. CURRENCY IS INVOLVED, PLEASE COMPLETE BLOCKS A AND B.
Currency and Coins	▶ $	A. Currency Name
Other Monetary Instruments *(Specify type, issuing entity and date, and serial or other identifying number.)*	▶ $	B. Country
(TOTAL)	▶ $	

PART IV SIGNATURE OF PERSON COMPLETING THIS REPORT

Under penalties of perjury, I declare that I have examined this report, and to the best of my knowledge and belief it is true, correct and complete.

18. NAME AND TITLE (Print)
19. SIGNATURE
20. DATE OF REPORT *(Mo./Day/Yr.)*

CUSTOMS AND BORDER PROTECTION USE ONLY

COUNT VERIFIED Yes ☐ No ☐
VOLUNTARY REPORT Yes ☐ No ☐

DATE	AIRLINE/FLIGHT/VESSEL	LICENSE PLATE		INSPECTOR *(Name and Badge Number)*
		STATE/COUNTRY	NUMBER	

FinCEN FORM 105
(Formerly Customs Form 4790)

GENERAL INSTRUCTIONS

This report is required by 31 U.S.C. 5316 and Treasury Department regulations (31 CFR 103).

WHO MUST FILE:

(1) Each person who physically transports, mails, or ships, or causes to be physically transported, mailed, or shipped currency or other monetary instruments in an aggregate amount exceeding $10,000 at one time from the United States to any place outside the United States or into the United States from any place outside the United States, and

(2) Each person who receives in the United States currency or other monetary instruments In an aggregate amount exceeding $10,000 at one time which have been transported, mailed, or shipped to the person from any place outside the United States.

A TRANSFER OF FUNDS THROUGH NORMAL BANKING PROCEDURES, WHICH DOES NOT INVOLVE THE PHYSICAL TRANSPORTATION OF CURRENCY OR MONETARY INSTRUMENTS, IS NOT REQUIRED TO BE REPORTED.

Exceptions: Reports are not required to be filed by:

(1) a Federal Reserve bank,

(2) a bank, a foreign bank, or a broker or dealer in securities in respect to currency or other monetary instruments mailed or shipped through the postal service or by common carrier,

(3) a commercial bank or trust company organized under the laws of any State or of the United States with respect to overland shipments of currency or monetary instruments shipped to or received from an established customer maintaining a deposit relationship with the bank, in amounts which the bank may reasonably conclude do not exceed amounts commensurate with the customary conduct of the business, industry, or profession of the customer concerned,

(4) a person who is not a citizen or resident of the United States in respect to currency or other monetary instruments mailed or shipped from abroad to a bank or broker or dealer in securities through the postal service or by common carrier,

(5) a common carrier of passengers in respect to currency or other monetary instruments in the possession of its passengers,

(6) a common carrier of goods in respect to shipments of currency or monetary instruments not declared to be such by the shipper,

(7) a travelers' check issuer or its agent in respect to the transportation of travelers' checks prior to their delivery to selling agents for eventual sale to the public,

(8) a person with a restrictively endorsed traveler's check that is in the collection and reconciliation process after the traveler's check has been negotiated, nor by

(9) a person engaged as a business in the transportation of currency, monetary instruments and other commercial papers with respect to the transportation of currency or other monetary instruments overland between established offices of banks or brokers or dealers in securities and foreign persons.

WHEN AND WHERE TO FILE:

A. Recipients—Each person who receives currency or other monetary instruments in the United States shall file FinCEN Form 105, within 15 days after receipt of the currency or monetary instruments, with the Customs officer in charge at any port of entry or departure or by mail with the **Commissioner of Customs, Attention: Currency Transportation Reports, Washington DC 20229.**

B. Shippers or Mailers—If the currency or other monetary instrument does not accompany the person entering or departing the United States, FinCEN Form 105 may be filed by mail on or before the date of entry, departure, mailing, or shipping with the **Commissioner of Customs, Attention: Currency Transportation Reports, Washington DC 20229.**

C. Travelers—Travelers carrying currency or other monetary instruments with them shall file FinCEN Form 105 at the time of entry into the United States or at the time of departure from the United States with the Customs officer in charge at any Customs port of entry or departure.

An additional report of a particular transportation, mailing, or shipping of currency or the monetary instruments is not required if a complete and truthful report has already been filed. However, no person otherwise required to file a report shall be excused from liability for failure to do so if, in fact, a complete and truthful report has not been filed. Forms may be obtained from any Bureau of Customs and Border Protection office.

PENALTIES: Civil and criminal penalties, including under certain circumstances a fine of not more than $500,000 and Imprisonment of not more than ten years, are provided for failure to file a report, filing a report containing a material omission or misstatement, or filing a false or fraudulent report. In addition, the currency or monetary instrument may be subject to seizure and forfeiture. See 31 U.S.C.5321 and 31 CFR 103.57; 31 U.S.C. 5322 and 31 CFR 103.59; 31 U.S.C. 5317 and 31 CFR 103.58, and U.S.C. 5332.

DEFINITIONS:

Bank—Each agent, agency, branch or office within the United States of any person doing business in one or more of the capacities listed: (1) a commercial bank or trust company organized under the laws of any State or of the United States; (2) a private bank; (3) asavings association, savings and loan association, and building and loan association organized under the laws of any State or of the United States; (4) an insured institution as defined in section 401 of the National Housing Act; (5) a savings bank, industrial bank or other thrift institution; (6) a credit union organized under the laws of any State or of the United States; (7) any other organization chartered under the banking laws of any State and subject to the supervision of the bank supervisory authorities of a State other than a money service business; (8) a bank organized under foreign law; and (9) any national banking association or corporation acting under the provisions of section 25A of the Federal Reserve Act (12 U.S.C. Sections 611-632).

Foreign Bank—A bank organized under foreign law, or an agency, branch or office located outside the United States of a bank. The term does not include an agent, agency, branch or office within the United States of a bank organized under foreign law.

Broker or Dealer in Securities—A broker or dealer in securities, registered or required to be registered with the Securities and Exchange Commission under the Securities Exchange Act of 1934.

Identification Number—Individuals must enter their social security number, if any. However, aliens who do not have a social security number should enter passport or alien registration number. All others should enter their employer identification number.

Monetary Instruments— (1) Coin or currency of the United States or of any other country, (2) traveler's checks in any form, (3) negotiable instruments (including checks, promissory notes, and money orders) in bearer form, endorsed without restriction, made out to a fictitious payee, or otherwise in such form that title thereto passes upon delivery, (4) incomplete instruments (including checks, promissory notes, and money orders) that are signed but on which the name of the payee has been omitted, and (5) securities or stock in bearer form or otherwise in such form that title thereto passes upon delivery. Monetary instruments do not include (i) checks or money orders made payable to the order of a named person which have not been endorsed or which bear restrictive endorsements, (ii) warehouse receipts, or (iii) bills of lading.

Person—An individual, a corporation, a partnership, a trust or estate, a joint stock company, an association, a syndicate, joint venture or other unincorporated organization or group, an Indian Tribe (as that term is defined in the Indian Gaming Regulatory Act), and all entities cognizable as legal personalities.

SPECIAL INSTRUCTIONS

You should complete each line that applies to you. **PART II.** -Block 13; provide the complete name of the shipper or recipient on whose behalf the exportation or importation was conducted. **PART III.** — Specify type of instrument, issuing entity, and date, serial or other identifying number, and payee (if any). **PART IV.** — Block 22A and 22B; enter the exact date you shipped or received currency or monetary instrument(s). Block 21, if currency or monetary instruments of more than one country is involved, attach a list showing each type, country or origin and amount.

PRIVACY ACT AND PAPERWORK REDUCTION ACT NOTICE:

Pursuant to the requirements of Public law 93-579 (Privacy Act of 1974), notice is hereby given that the authority to collect information on Form 4790 in accordance with 5 U.S.C. 552a(e)(3) is Public law 91-508; 31 U.S.C. 5316; 5 U.S.C. 301; Reorganization Plan No.1 of 1950; Treasury Department Order No. 165, revised, as amended; 31 CFR 103; and 44 U.S.C. 3501.

The principal purpose for collecting the information is to assure maintenance of reports or records having a high degree of usefulness in criminal, tax, or regulatory investigations or proceedings. The information collected may be provided to those officers and employees of the Bureau of Customs and Border Protection and any other constituent unit of the Department of the Treasury who have a need for the records in the performance of their duties. The records may be referred to any other department or agency of the Federal Government upon the request of the head of such department or agency. The information collected may also be provided to appropriate state, local, and foreign criminal law enforcement and regulatory personnel in the performance of their official duties.

Disclosure of this information is mandatory pursuant to 31 U.S.C. 5316 and 31 CFR Part 103 (See Penalties).

Disclosure of the social security number is mandatory. The authority to collect this number is 31 U.S.C. 5316(b) and 31 CFR 103.27(d). The social security number will be used as a means to identify the individual who files the record.

An agency may not conduct or sponsor, and a person is not required to respond to, a collection of information unless it displays a currently valid OMB control number. The collection of this information is mandatory pursuant to 31 U.S.C. 5316.

Statement required by 5 CFR 1320.8(b)(3)(iii): The estimated average burden associated with this collection of information is 11 minutes per respondent or record keeper depending on individual circumstances. Comments concerning the accuracy of this burden estimate and suggestions for reducing this burden should be directed to the Department of the Treasury, Financial Crimes Enforcement Network, P.O. Box 39 Vienna, Virginia 22183. **DO NOT send completed forms to this office—See When and Where To File above.**

Suspicious Activity Report

July 2003
Previous editions will not be accepted after December 31, 2003

ALWAYS COMPLETE ENTIRE REPORT
(see instructions)

FRB:	FR 2230	OMB No. 7100-0212
FDIC:	6710/06	OMB No. 3064-0077
OCC:	8010-9,8010-1	OMB No. 1557-0180
OTS:	1601	OMB No. 1550-0003
NCUA:	2362	OMB No. 3133-0094
TREASURY:	TD F 90-22.47	OMB No. 1506-0001

1 Check box below only if correcting a prior report.
☐ Corrects Prior Report (see instruction #3 under "How to Make a Report")

Part I — Reporting Financial Institution Information

2 Name of Financial Institution

3 EIN

4 Address of Financial Institution

5 Primary Federal Regulator
a ☐ Federal Reserve   d ☐ OCC
b ☐ FDIC   e ☐ OTS
c ☐ NCUA

6 City

7 State

8 Zip Code

9 Address of Branch Office(s) where activity occurred   ☐ Multiple Branches (include information in narrative, Part V)

10 City

11 State

12 Zip Code

13 If institution closed, date closed ___/___/___ MM DD YYYY

14 Account number(s) affected, if any
a _____ Closed? ☐ Yes ☐ No
b _____ ☐ Yes ☐ No
c _____ Closed? ☐ Yes ☐ No
d _____ ☐ Yes ☐ No

Part II — Suspect Information   ☐ Suspect Information Unavailable

15 Last Name or Name of Entity

16 First Name

17 Middle

18 Address

19 SSN, EIN or TIN

20 City

21 State

22 Zip Code

23 Country

24 Phone Number - Residence (include area code)
( )

25 Phone Number - Work (include area code)
( )

26 Occupation/Type of Business

27 Date of Birth ___/___/___ MM DD YYYY

28 Admission/Confession?
a ☐ Yes   b ☐ No

29 Forms of Identification for Suspect:
a ☐ Driver's License/State ID   b ☐ Passport   c ☐ Alien Registration   d ☐ Other _____
Number _____   Issuing Authority _____

30 Relationship to Financial Institution:
a ☐ Accountant   d ☐ Attorney   g ☐ Customer   j ☐ Officer
b ☐ Agent   e ☐ Borrower   h ☐ Director   k ☐ Shareholder
c ☐ Appraiser   f ☐ Broker   i ☐ Employee   l ☐ Other _____

31 Is the relationship an insider relationship?   a ☐ Yes   b ☐ No
If Yes specify: c ☐ Still employed at financial institution   e ☐ Terminated
                   d ☐ Suspended   f ☐ Resigned

32 Date of Suspension, Termination, Resignation ___/___/___ MM DD YYYY

Part III Suspicious Activity Information

33 Date or date range of suspicious activity
From ___/___/_____ To ___/___/_____
     MM DD YYYY   MM DD YYYY

34 Total dollar amount involved in known or suspicious activity
$ _____.00

35 Summary characterization of suspicious activity:
- a ☐ Bank Secrecy Act/Structuring/Money Laundering
- b ☐ Bribery/Gratuity
- c ☐ Check Fraud
- d ☐ Check Kiting
- e ☐ Commercial Loan Fraud
- f ☐ Computer Intrusion
- g ☐ Consumer Loan Fraud
- h ☐ Counterfeit Check
- i ☐ Counterfeit Credit/Debit Card
- j ☐ Counterfeit Instrument (other)
- k ☐ Credit Card Fraud
- l ☐ Debit Card Fraud
- m ☐ Defalcation/Embezzlement
- n ☐ False Statement
- o ☐ Misuse of Position or Self Dealing
- p ☐ Mortgage Loan Fraud
- q ☐ Mysterious Disappearance
- r ☐ Wire Transfer Fraud
- t ☐ Terrorist Financing
- u ☐ Identity Theft
- s ☐ Other _____ (type of activity)

36 Amount of loss prior to recovery (if applicable)
$ _____.00

37 Dollar amount of recovery (if applicable)
$ _____.00

38 Has the suspicious activity had a material impact on, or otherwise affected, the financial soundness of the institution?
a ☐ Yes   b ☐ No

39 Has the institution's bonding company been notified?
a ☐ Yes   b ☐ No

40 Has any law enforcement agency already been advised by telephone, written communication, or otherwise?
- a ☐ DEA
- b ☐ FBI
- c ☐ IRS
- d ☐ Postal Inspection
- e ☐ Secret Service
- f ☐ U.S. Customs
- g ☐ Other Federal
- h ☐ State
- i ☐ Local
- j ☐ Agency Name (for g, h or i) _____

41 Name of person(s) contacted at Law Enforcement Agency

42 Phone Number (include area code)
(   )

43 Name of person(s) contacted at Law Enforcement Agency

44 Phone Number (include area code)
(   )

Part IV Contact for Assistance

45 Last Name

46 First Name

47 Middle

48 Title/Occupation

49 Phone Number (include area code)
(   )

50 Date Prepared
___/___/_____
MM DD YYYY

51 Agency (if not filed by financial institution)

Part V — Suspicious Activity Information Explanation/Description — 3

Explanation/description of known or suspected violation of law or suspicious activity.

This section of the report is **critical**. The care with which it is written may make the difference in whether or not the described conduct and its possible criminal nature are clearly understood. Provide below a chronological and **complete** account of the possible violation of law, including what is unusual, irregular or suspicious about the transaction, using the following checklist as you prepare your account. **If necessary, continue the narrative on a duplicate of this page.**

a **Describe** supporting documentation and retain for 5 years.
b **Explain** who benefited, financially or otherwise, from the transaction, how much, and how.
c **Retain** any confession, admission, or explanation of the transaction provided by the suspect and indicate to whom and when it was given.
d **Retain** any confession, admission, or explanation of the transaction provided by any other person and indicate to whom and when it was given.
e **Retain** any evidence of cover-up or evidence of an attempt to deceive federal or state examiners or others.
f **Indicate** where the possible violation took place (e.g., main office, branch, other).
g **Indicate** whether the possible violation is an isolated incident or relates to other transactions.
h **Indicate** whether there is any related litigation; if so, specify.
i **Recommend** any further investigation that might assist law enforcement authorities.
j **Indicate** whether any information has been excluded from this report; if so, why?
k If you are correcting a previously filed report, describe the changes that are being made.

For Bank Secrecy Act/Structuring/Money Laundering reports, include the following additional information:

l **Indicate** whether currency and/or monetary instruments were involved. If so, provide the amount and/or description of the instrument (for example, bank draft, letter of credit, domestic or international money order, stocks, bonds, traveler's checks, wire transfers sent or received, cash, etc.).
m **Indicate** any account number that may be involved or affected.

Tips on SAR Form preparation and filing are available in the SAR Activity Review at www.fincen.gov/pub_reports.html

Paperwork Reduction Act Notice: The purpose of this form is to provide an effective and consistent means for financial institutions to notify appropriate law enforcement agencies of known or suspected criminal conduct or suspicious activities that take place at or were perpetrated against financial institutions. This report is required by law, pursuant to authority contained in the following statutes. Board of Governors of the Federal Reserve System: 12 U.S.C. 324, 334, 611a, 1844(b) and (c), 3105(c) (2) and 3106(a). Federal Deposit Insurance Corporation: 12 U.S.C. 93a, 1818, 1881-84, 3401-22. Office of the Comptroller of the Currency: 12 U.S.C. 93a, 1818, 1881-84, 3401-22. Office of Thrift Supervision: 12 U.S.C. 1463 and 1464. National Credit Union Administration: 12 U.S.C. 1766(a), 1786(q). Financial Crimes Enforcement Network: 31 U.S.C. 5318(g). Information collected on this report is confidential (5 U.S.C. 552(b)(7) and 552a(k)(2), and 31 U.S.C. 5318(g)). The Federal financial institutions' regulatory agencies and the U.S. Departments of Justice and Treasury may use and share the information. Public reporting and recordkeeping burden for this information collection is estimated to average 30 minutes per response, and includes time to gather and maintain data in the required report, review the instructions, and complete the information collection. Send comments regarding this burden estimate, including suggestions for reducing the burden, to the Office of Management and Budget, Paperwork Reduction Project, Washington, DC 20503 and, depending on your primary Federal regulatory agency, to Secretary, Board of Governors of the Federal Reserve System, Washington, DC 20551; or Assistant Executive Secretary, Federal Deposit Insurance Corporation, Washington, DC 20429; or Legislative and Regulatory Analysis Division, Office of the Comptroller of the Currency, Washington, DC 20219; or Office of Thrift Supervision, Enforcement Office, Washington, DC 20552; or National Credit Union Administration, 1775 Duke Street, Alexandria, VA 22314; or Office of the Director, Financial Crimes Enforcement Network, Department of the Treasury, 2070 Chain Bridge Road, Vienna, VA 22182. The agencies may not conduct or sponsor, and an organization (or a person) is not required to respond to, a collection of information unless it displays a currently valid OMB control number.

Suspicious Activity Report
Instructions

Safe Harbor Federal law (31 U.S.C. 5318(g)(3)) provides complete protection from civil liability for all reports of suspicious transactions made to appropriate authorities, including supporting documentation, regardless of whether such reports are filed pursuant to this report's instructions or are filed on a voluntary basis. Specifically, the law provides that a financial institution, and its directors, officers, employees and agents, that make a disclosure of any possible violation of law or regulation, including in connection with the preparation of suspicious activity reports, "shall not be liable to any person under any law or regulation of the United States, any constitution, law, or regulation of any State or political subdivision of any State, or under any contract or other legally enforceable agreement (including any arbitration agreement), for such disclosure or for any failure to provide notice of such disclosure to the person who is the subject of such disclosure or any other person identified in the disclosure".

Notification Prohibited Federal law (31 U.S.C. 5318(g)(2)) requires that a financial institution, and its directors, officers, employees and agents who, voluntarily or by means of a suspicious activity report, report suspected or known criminal violations or suspicious activities may not notify any person involved in the transaction that the transaction has been reported.

In situations involving violations requiring immediate attention, such as when a reportable violation is ongoing, the financial institution shall immediately notify, by telephone, appropriate law enforcement and financial institution supervisory authorities in addition to filing a timely suspicious activity report.

WHEN TO MAKE A REPORT:

1. All financial institutions operating in the United States, including insured banks, savings associations, savings association service corporations, credit unions, bank holding companies, nonbank subsidiaries of bank holding companies, Edge and Agreement corporations, and U.S. branches and agencies of foreign banks, are required to make this report following the discovery of:

    a. **Insider abuse involving any amount.** Whenever the financial institution detects any known or suspected Federal criminal violation, or pattern of criminal violations, committed or attempted against the financial institution or involving a transaction or transactions conducted through the financial institution, where the financial institution believes that it was either an actual or potential victim of a criminal violation, or series of criminal violations, or that the financial institution was used to facilitate a criminal transaction, and the financial institution has a substantial basis for identifying one of its directors, officers, employees, agents or other institution-affiliated parties as having committed or aided in the commission of a criminal act regardless of the amount involved in the violation.

    b. **Violations aggregating $5,000 or more where a suspect can be identified.** Whenever the financial institution detects any known or suspected Federal criminal violation, or pattern of criminal violations, committed or attempted against the financial institution or involving a transaction or transactions conducted through the financial institution and involving or aggregating $5,000 or more in funds or other assets, where the financial institution believes that it was either an actual or potential victim of a criminal violation, or series of criminal violations, or that the financial institution was used to facilitate a criminal transaction, and the financial institution has a substantial basis for identifying a possible suspect or group of suspects. If it is determined prior to filing this report that the identified suspect or group of suspects has used an "alias," then information regarding the true identity of the suspect or group of suspects, as well as alias identifiers, such as drivers' licenses or social security numbers, addresses and telephone numbers, must be reported.

    c. **Violations aggregating $25,000 or more regardless of a potential suspect.** Whenever the financial institution detects any known or suspected Federal criminal violation, or pattern of criminal violations, committed or attempted against the financial institution or involving a transaction or transactions conducted through the financial institution and involving or aggregating $25,000 or more in funds or other assets, where the financial institution believes that it was either an actual or potential victim of a criminal violation, or series of criminal violations, or that the financial institution was used to facilitate a criminal transaction, even though there is no substantial basis for identifying a possible suspect or group of suspects.

    d. **Transactions aggregating $5,000 or more that involve potential money laundering or violations of the Bank Secrecy Act.** Any transaction (which for purposes of this subsection means a deposit, withdrawal, transfer between accounts, exchange of currency, loan, extension of credit, purchase or sale of any stock, bond, certificate of deposit, or other monetary instrument or investment security, or any other payment, transfer, or delivery by, through, or to a financial institution, by whatever means effected) conducted or attempted by, at or through the financial institution and involving or aggregating $5,000 or more in funds or other assets, if the financial institution knows, suspects, or has reason to suspect that:

   i. The transaction involves funds derived from illegal activities or is intended or conducted in order to hide or disguise funds or assets derived from illegal activities (including, without limitation, the ownership, nature, source, location, or control of such funds or assets) as part of a plan to violate or evade any law or regulation or to avoid any transaction reporting requirement under Federal law;

   ii. The transaction is designed to evade any regulations promulgated under the Bank Secrecy Act; or

   iii. The transaction has no business or apparent lawful purpose or is not the sort in which the particular customer would normally be expected to engage, and the financial institution knows of no reasonable explanation for the transaction after examining the available facts, including the background and possible purpose of the transaction.

   The Bank Secrecy Act requires all financial institutions to file currency transaction reports (CTRs) in accordance with the Department of the Treasury's implementing regulations (31 CFR Part 103). These regulations require a financial institution to file a CTR whenever a currency transaction exceeds $10,000. If a currency transaction exceeds $10,000 and is suspicious, the institution must file both a CTR (reporting the currency transaction) and a suspicious activity report (reporting the suspicious or criminal aspects of the transaction). If a currency transaction equals or is below $10,000 and is suspicious, the institution should only file a suspicious activity report.

2. **Computer Intrusion.** For purposes of this report, "computer intrusion" is defined as gaining access to a computer system of a financial institution to:

   a. Remove, steal, procure, or otherwise affect funds of the institution or the institution's customers;
   b. Remove, steal, procure or otherwise affect critical information of the institution including customer account information; or
   c. Damage, disable or otherwise affect critical systems of the institution.

   For purposes of this reporting requirement, computer intrusion does not mean attempted intrusions of websites or other non-critical information systems of the institution that provide no access to institution or customer financial or other critical information.

3. A financial institution is required to file a suspicious activity report no later than 30 calendar days after the date of initial detection of facts that may constitute a basis for filing a suspicious activity report. If no suspect was identified on the date of detection of the incident requiring the filing, a financial institution may delay filing a suspicious activity report for an additional 30 calendar days to identify a suspect. In no case shall reporting be delayed more than 60 calendar days after the date of initial detection of a reportable transaction.

4. This suspicious activity report does not need to be filed for those robberies and burglaries that are reported to local authorities, or (except for savings associations and service corporations) for lost, missing, counterfeit, or stolen securities that are reported pursuant to the requirements of 17 CFR 240.17f-1.

HOW TO MAKE A REPORT:

1. Send each completed suspicious activity report to:

   Detroit Computing Center, P.O. Box 33980, Detroit, MI 48232-0980

2. For items that do not apply or for which information is not available, leave blank.
3. If you are correcting a previously filed report, check the box at the top of the report (line 1). Complete the report in its entirety and include the corrected information in the applicable boxes. Then describe the changes that are being made in Part V (Description of Suspicious Activity), line k.
4. **Do not include any supporting documentation with the suspicious activity report.** Identify and retain a copy of the suspicious activity report and all original supporting documentation or business record equivalent for five (5) years from the date of the suspicious activity report. All supporting documentation must be made available to appropriate authorities upon request.
5. If more space is needed to report additional suspects, attach copies of page 1 to provide the additional information. If more space is needed to report additional branch addresses, include this information in the narrative, Part V.
6. Financial institutions are encouraged to provide copies of suspicious activity reports to state and local authorities, where appropriate.

FinCEN Form 101
January 2003

Suspicious Activity Report by the Securities and Futures Industries

▶ Please type or print. Always complete entire report. Items marked with an asterisk * are considered critical. (See instructions).

OMB No. 1506 - 0019

1 Check the box if this report corrects a prior report (see instructions, page 7) ☐

Part I — Subject Information

2 Check box (a) ☐ if multiple subjects   box (b) ☐ subject information unavailable

*3 Individual's last name or entity's full name

*4 First name

5 Middle initial

6 Also known as (AKA - individual), doing business as (DBA - entity)

7 Occupation or type of business

*8 Address

*9 City

10 State   *11 ZIP code   *12 Country (if not U.S.)   13 E-mail address (if available)

*14 SSN/ITIN (individual), or EIN (entity)

*15 Account number(s) affected, if any. Indicate if closed.
Acc't #_____ yes ☐   Acc't #_____ yes ☐
Acc't #_____ yes ☐   Acc't #_____ yes ☐

16 Date of birth ___/___/___ MM DD YYYY

*17 Government issued identification (If available)
a ☐ Driver's license/state ID   b ☐ Passport   c ☐ Alien registration   d ☐ Corporate/Partnership Resolution
e ☐ Other _____
f ID Number _____   g Issuing state or country _____

18 Phone number - work (___) ___ - ____

19 Phone number - home (___) ___ - ____

20 Is individual/business associated/affiliated with the reporting institution? (See instructions)
a ☐ Yes   b ☐ No

Part II — Suspicious Activity Information

*21 Date or date range of suspicious activity
From ___/___/___ MM DD YYYY   To ___/___/___ MM DD YYYY

*22 Total dollar amount involved in suspicious activity
$ ___,___,___.00

23 Instrument type (Check all that apply)

- a ☐ Bonds/Notes
- b ☐ Cash or equiv.
- c ☐ Commercial paper
- d ☐ Commodity futures contract
- e ☐ Money Market Mutual Fund
- f ☐ Mutual Fund
- g ☐ OTC Derivatives
- h ☐ Other derivatives
- i ☐ Commodity options
- j ☐ Security Futures Products
- k ☐ Stocks
- l ☐ Warrants
- m ☐ Other securities
- n ☐ Other non-securities
- o ☐ Foreign currency futures
- p ☐ Foreign currencies
- q ☐ Commodity type _____ (Please identify)
- r ☐ Instrument description _____
- s ☐ Market where traded ___|___|___ (Enter appropriate three or four-letter code.)
- t ☐ Other (Explain in Part IV)

24 CUSIP® number

25 CUSIP® number

26 CUSIP® number

27 CUSIP® number

28 CUSIP® number

29 CUSIP® number

*30 Type of suspicious activity:

- a ☐ Bribery/gratuity
- b ☐ Check fraud
- c ☐ Computer intrusion
- d ☐ Credit/debit card fraud
- e ☐ Embezzlement/theft
- f ☐ Futures fraud
- g ☐ Forgery
- h ☐ Identity theft
- i ☐ Insider trading
- j ☐ Mail fraud
- k ☐ Market manipulation
- l ☐ Money laundering/Structuring
- m ☐ Prearranged or other non-competitive trading
- n ☐ Securities fraud
- o ☐ Significant wire or other transactions without economic purpose
- p ☐ Suspicious documents or ID presented
- q ☐ Terrorist financing
- r ☐ Wash or other fictitious trading
- s ☐ Wire fraud
- t ☐ Other (Describe in Part VI)

Catalog No. 35349U

Part III — Law Enforcement or Regulatory Contact Information

31 If a law enforcement or regulatory authority has been contacted (excluding submission of a SAR) check the appropriate box.

- a ☐ DEA
- b ☐ U.S. Attorney (**32)
- c ☐ IRS
- d ☐ FBI
- e ☐ U.S. Customs Svc.
- f ☐ U.S. Secret Svc.
- g ☐ CFTC
- h ☐ SEC
- i ☐ NASD
- j ☐ NFA
- k ☐ NY Stock Exchg.
- l ☐ Other Registered Futures Assoc
- m ☐ Other registered entity-futures
- n ☐ Other state/local
- o ☐ Other SRO (PHLX, PCX, CBOE, AMEX, etc.)
- p ☐ State securities regulator
- q ☐ Foreign
- r ☐ Other (Explain in Part VI)

32 Other authority contacted (for Box 31 l through r) ** List U.S. Attorney office here.

33 Name of individual contacted (for all of Box 31)

34 Telephone number of individual contacted (box 33) (___) ___ - ____

35 Date contacted ___/___/____ MM DD YYYY

Part IV — Reporting Financial Institution Information

*36 Name of financial institution or sole proprietorship

*37 EIN / SSN / ITIN

*38 Address

*39 City

*40 State

*41 ZIP code

42 Additional branch address locations handling account, activity or customer.

43 ☐ Multiple locations (see instructions)

44 City

45 State

46 ZIP code

47 Central Registration Depository number

48 SEC ID number

49 Nat'l. Futures Ass'n. ID number

50 Has this reporting individual/entity coordinated this report with another reporting individual/entity? Yes ☐ (Provide details in Part VI) No ☐

51 Type of institution or individual- Check box(es) for functions that apply to this report

- a ☐ Agriculture trade option merchant
- b ☐ Affiliate of bank holding company
- c ☐ Commodity pool operator
- d ☐ Commodity trading advisor
- e ☐ Direct participation program
- f ☐ Futures commission merchant
- g ☐ Futures floor broker
- h ☐ Futures floor trader
- i ☐ Introducing Broker-Futures
- j ☐ Investment adviser
- k ☐ Investment company - mutual fund
- l ☐ Market maker
- m ☐ Municipal securities dealer
- n ☐ National Futures Assoc.
- o ☐ Registered Entity-futures
- p ☐ Other Registered Futures Assn.
- q ☐ Securities broker - clearing
- r ☐ Securities broker - introducing
- s ☐ Securities dealer
- t ☐ Securities floor broker
- u ☐ Securities options broker-dealer
- v ☐ Self regulatory organization (SRO)
- w ☐ Specialist
- x ☐ Subsidiary of bank
- y ☐ U.S. Government broker-dealer
- z ☐ U.S. Government interdealer broker
- aa ☐ Other (Describe in Part VI)

Part V — Contact For Assistance

*52 Last name of individual to be contacted regarding this report

*53 First name

*54 Middle initial

*55 Title/Position

*56 Work phone number (___) ___ - ____

*57 Date report prepared ___/___/____ MM DD YYYY

Paperwork Reduction Act Notice: The purpose of this form is to provide an effective means for financial institutions to notify appropriate law enforcement agencies of suspicious transactions that occur by, through, or at the financial institutions. This report is required by law, pursuant to authority contained in 31 U.S.C. 5318(g). Information collected on this report is confidential (31 U.S.C. 5318(g)). Federal securities regulatory agencies and the U.S. Departments of Justice and Treasury, and other authorized authorities may use and share this information. Public reporting and recordkeeping burden for this form is estimated to average 45 minutes per response, and includes time to gather and maintain information for the required report, review the instructions, and complete the information collection. Send comments regarding this burden estimate, including suggestions for reducing the burden, to the Office of Management and Budget, Paperwork Reduction Project, Washington, DC 20503 and to the Financial Crimes Enforcement Network, Attn.: Paperwork Reduction Act, P.O. Box 39, Vienna VA 22183-0039. The agency may not conduct or sponsor, and an organization (or a person) is not required to respond to, a collection of information unless it displays a currently valid OMB control number.

Part VI — Suspicious Activity Information - Narrative *

Explanation/description of suspicious activity(ies). This section of the report is **critical**. The care with which it is completed may determine whether or not the described activity and its possible criminal nature are clearly understood by investigators. Provide a clear, complete and chronological description (**not exceeding this page and the next page**) of the activity, including what is unusual, irregular or suspicious about the transaction(s), using the checklist below as a guide, as you prepare your account.

a. **Describe** conduct that raised suspicion.
b. **Explain** whether the transaction(s) was completed or only attempted.
c. **Describe** supporting documentation (e.g. transaction records, new account information, tape recordings, e-mail messages, correspondence, etc.) and retain such documentation in your file for five years.
d. **Explain** who benefited, financially or otherwise, from the transaction(s), how much and how (if known).
e. **Describe and retain** any admission, or explanation of the transaction(s) provided by the subject(s), or other persons. Indicate to whom and when it was given.
f. **Describe and retain** any evidence of cover-up or evidence of an attempt to deceive federal or state examiners, SRO, or others.
g. **Indicate** where the possible violation of law(s) took place (e.g., main office, branch, other).
h. **Indicate** whether the suspicious activity is an isolated incident or relates to another transaction.
i. **Indicate** whether there is any related litigation. If so, specify the name of the litigation and the court where the action is pending.
j. **Recommend** any further investigation that might assist law enforcement authorities.
k. **Indicate** whether any information has been excluded from this report; if so, state reasons.
l. **Indicate** whether U.S. or foreign currency and/or U.S. or foreign negotiable instrument(s) were involved. If foreign, provide the amount, name of currency, and country of origin.
m. **Indicate** "Market where traded" and "Wire transfer identifier" information when appropriate.
n. **Indicate** whether funds or assets were recovered and, if so, enter the dollar value of the recovery in whole dollars only.
o. **Indicate** any additional account number(s), and any foreign bank(s) account number(s) which may be involved.
p. **Indicate** for a foreign national any available information on subject's passport(s), visa(s), and/or identification card(s). Include date, country, city of issue, issuing authority, and nationality.
q. **Describe** any suspicious activities that involve transfer of funds to or from a foreign country, or transactions in a foreign currency. Identify the country, sources and destinations of funds.
r. **Describe** subject(s) position if employed by the financial institution.
s. **Indicate** whether securities, futures or options were involved. If so, list the type, CUSIP* number or ISID* number, and amount.
t. **Indicate** the type of institution filing this report, if this is not clear from Part IV. For example, an investment advisor that is managing partner of a limited partnership that is acting as a hedge fund that detects suspicious activity tied in part to its hedge fund activities should note that it is operating as a hedge fund.
u. **Indicate** in instances when the subject or entity has a CRD or NFA number, what that number is.
v. **If correcting a prior report (box 1 checked), complete the form in its entirety and note the corrected items here in Part VI.**

Information already provided in earlier parts of this form need not necessarily be repeated if the meaning is clear.
Supporting documentation should not be filed with this report. Maintain the information for your files.

Enter explanation/description in the space below. Continue on the next page if necessary.

CONSUMER FRAUD

Complaints of consumer fraud can be found as far back as the first century when Pliny the Elder told of the adulterated honey being sold in Rome and the mixing of wine with gypsum, lime, pitch, rosin, wood ashes, salt, sulphur, and other artificial additives.

Schemes against consumers range from home repair frauds to more sophisticated scams. In a nationwide solicitation, 100,000 people purchased light bulbs because they were persuaded that the profits were going to the disabled. They were, but the disabilities — certified by doctors — included such crippling disorders as acne, hay fever, nervousness, and obesity. Those "donating" paid about three times the going price for similar light bulbs.

Sometimes fraud occurs when the immediate victim cannot fight back: a Tennessee funeral director was charged with burying people without caskets and throwing trash in on top of the corpses.

Scandals involving the ministry, especially television evangelism, also have captured headlines. In 1988, U.S. evangelist Jim Bakker was indicted on mail fraud charges stemming from the television sale of lifetime "partnerships" in a vacation hotel at the Heritage USA theme park. Prosecutors were able to document that Bakker and his wife, Tammy Fay, received about $3.5 million in "bonuses" from the scheme. Bakker received a 45-year prison sentence, which later was reduced. He is now out of prison.

Fraud is notably common in the repair and service industries. Home repair fraud, frequently perpetrated against the elderly, ranges from the sale or use of substandard materials such as roofing to securing payment without doing any work at all. Automobile repairs often involve fraudulent acts. One study maintained that 53 cents of every "repair" dollar was wasted because of unnecessary work, overcharging, services never performed, or incompetence. A U.S. government survey concluded that American motorists are overcharged an average of $150 a car each year.

In Australia, John Braithwaite found that used car dealers rolled back odometers on a third of the cars they offer for sale. Interviews with the dealers in Australia illustrate the kind of reasoning that can buttress such illegal activity. One salesman said: "People pay too much attention to the mileage reading on a car. There might be a car with a low mileage reading but all sorts of faults, and another perfect car with a high mileage reading. It doesn't matter what the mileage reading is, but how good the car is. So if you turn the mileage reading back on a car in perfect order, you're encouraging people to buy a good car." There was no evidence, however, that it was only on "good" cars that the odometer was made to provide a lower reading.

Another Australian dealer said: "They think because you are a used car dealer you are a liar. So they treat you like one and lie to you. Can you blame the dealer for lying back?"[*]

Con Schemes

Confidence games involve a range of fraudulent conduct usually committed by professional "con artists" against unsuspecting victims. The victims can be organizations but more commonly are individuals. Con men usually act alone but they may group together for a particular complex endeavor.

These are some of the many kinds of confidence schemes. Telemarketing schemes and pyramid schemes are discussed in more detail at the end of the chapter.

Advance Fee Swindles and Debt Consolidation Schemes

Advance fee swindles are structured to obtain an illegal gain by falsely promising the delivery of a product or a service. In some schemes, the product is marketed to a large number of customers and then the operation is shut down prior to the delivery stage.

People who find themselves in debt sometimes turn to consolidation agencies for help. These agencies do not advance loans, but rather act as an intermediary between debtor and creditor. Some agencies are legitimate, many are not.

In a typical scenario, the debtor contacts the agency which compiles a list of the creditors and the amount of monthly payments owing. The agency usually writes letters to the creditors requesting a workout plan at lower monthly payments spread over a longer period of time. The creditors often will offer such an arrangement if they feel that the debt will thereby be paid or if the workout plan will forestall bankruptcy or default by the creditor.

Unscrupulous debt consolidation schemes often involve the agency collecting the money

---

[*]John Braithwaite, "An Exploratory Study of Used Car Fraud," in Paul R. Wilson and John Braithwaite (Eds.), Two Faces of Deviance. Brisbane: University of Queensland Press, 1978, pp. 101-122.

from the debtor but not forwarding it to the creditors. In some instances, considerable time can pass before the debtor finds out that his money has been misappropriated.

Another variation of the debt consolidation scheme occurs when a customer is "guaranteed" that he will receive a loan or a credit card regardless of his credit ratings. Typically, the victims have been rejected by legitimate financial institutions because their credit ratings are poor. The victim must pay a processing fee for the application to be accepted. After the victim pays the fee, the con artist disappears.

Directory Advertising Schemes

The essence of directory advertising schemes is the sale of advertising in a non-existent magazine or directory. A fake (or in some cases a real) directory is shown to the potential victim. The victim contracts and pays for display or classified advertising that is to appear some months in the future. By that time, the fraudster has disappeared.

Merchandising Schemes

Merchandising schemes run a wide gamut. If you have ever paid for an item and received less than what was advertised, you have been the victim of a merchandising scheme.

Personal Improvement Frauds

These frauds prey upon the desire of people to improve their education or job skills; in some instances, they appeal to a person's appearance.

Diploma Mills

For what often is a hefty fee, a "diploma" can be purchased by those who apply. The fraudster usually claims that the fee is for "processing" the application and/or for verifying the experience necessary for the degree to be awarded. The hallmark of the diploma mill is the ease with which the degree is obtained, though the degree, because the "school" is not accredited, is essentially worthless.

Correspondence schools also can operate with the same modus operandi as diploma mills. Investigators have at times submitted the scribblings of their infant children to schools that advertise that they will provide art lessons to persons who demonstrate talent: usually the infants' "drawings" are judged to show considerable ability, and the submitter is asked to send a fee to begin receiving the lessons.

Modeling Schools

Modeling schools appeal to the vanity of some people. In the typical scheme, the modeling school representative tells the prospective student that he will prepare a portfolio of portraits to be sent to potential customers who may employ the victim as a model. The victim is then charged an inflated price for the pictures. Con game modeling schools often claim—inaccurately—connections to famous people and maintain that they have been instrumental in starting the careers of successful models. The schools sometimes target parents and grandparents with lures of the money that can be earned by their "exceptionally pretty" infant children or grandchildren.

Direct Debit from Checking Accounts

When a customer decides to purchase an item (from a catalog or over the phone), he is told he can purchase it rapidly and simply by giving his bank's name and his checking account number for a direct debit from his account. This results in unauthorized withdrawals from the account.

Equity-Skimming Schemes

Falling for this scam can cost consumers their homes. Con men try to talk the mark out of the equity on their homes and may try to persuade them to borrow against their equity.

Fundraising, Non-profits, and Religious Schemes

Some groups use "cancer" or "AIDS" in their title to convince the consumer they are legitimate charitable organizations. Others offer a prize or award for the consumer as reward for their contribution.

Home-Based Businesses

A popular fad today, many companies marketing home-based businesses require one to buy materials for assembly-at-home products. The consumer is promised that the company will purchase the completed products, and when it does not, the consumer is left with a bad investment and a stock of cheap, worthless goods.

Home Improvements

A common scam involves phony repair people selling their services door-to-door. After paying them to fix a roof, window, or other item, the consumer is left with unfinished repair work and no workmen.

Money Manager or Financial Planner

These scams involve convincing marks to "invest" in low-risk, high-return opportunities. Of course, consumers who invest in this type of opportunity see no returns at all.

Phone Card Schemes

The con artist calls, claiming to be with the consumer's long distance company, and asks to confirm their card number. If the number is revealed, the consumer's next long distance bill will contain some expensive calls he did not make.

Scavenger or Revenge Scheme

This involves the company which initially conned the consumer. Using a different company's name, the outfit contacts the consumer again and asks if he would like to help put the unethical company out of business and get his money back. Naturally, an up-front fee is required to finance the investigation.

Sweepstakes, Giveaways, and Prizes

Many of these so-called "free gifts" require the consumer to pay a fee before collecting. This fee actually covers the cost of the merchandise deemed "free."

College Scholarship Services

This bogus service usually charges a front-end fee or advanced payment fee for finding a scholarship suitable for the applicant.

Credit Repair

Some of these firms may charge unnecessary fees to "fix" credit problems, knowing that the consumer could easily call the credit bureau and request a copy of his credit report himself.

Other Con Schemes

Block Hustle

So-called because purveyors of cheap stereo equipment, jewelry, and watches usually hawk their goods on street corners or at traffic lights. The items for sale are generally either "hot" or imitations of brand names.

Pigeon Drop

This is often used on middle-aged or elderly women deemed likely to have a savings account. Pretending to find a wallet full of money, the con men convince their mark that they should divide the "discovered" money. As a show of good faith, each should withdraw a sum of money from their bank and turn it over to a lawyer or another third-party for safekeeping. They agree to place an ad in a newspaper for the lost wallet. If it is not claimed within a certain amount of time, they will split the money. Naturally, when the designated time expires, the victim will find that the lawyer was part of the scam and that her money has vanished.

Bank Examiner Swindle

Bank examiner swindles are also perpetrated on older women, especially widows with access to their husband's life insurance policies. The con man impersonates a bank examiner investigating her bank. He asks her to withdraw a certain amount of cash from her account, place it in an envelope, and allow him to inspect the bills for counterfeits. Many con men use false IDs and dress to take on this role.

Jamaican Handkerchief or Envelope Switch

In this con, the criminal puts his money into an envelope with the mark's money and then unobtrusively trades this parcel for another that looks like the same thing but is instead bulked up with worthless paper.

The Obituary Hustle

Capitalizing on a bereaved person's grief, the con man, culling information from an obituary, poses as a delivery person collecting money for a package or other order the deceased supposedly made.

Three-Card Monte

An old card game that involves two people who fleece an unsuspecting onlooker into a rigged game.

Poker Bunco

This scam can involve poker, dice, pool, and other games. The con man is of course an expert and "hustles" the mark.

Missing-Heir Scheme

In the modern version of this scam, the con man poses as a probate investigator or other genealogist, charging fees to distribute the inheritance.

Gold Mine Swindle

Here, the con man claims to own a productive mine but requires money to start operation. The scheme involves selling shares to the mine.

Spanish Prisoner Game

This con can be traced back to the Spanish Armada of the sixteenth century. A businessman receives a letter purportedly from a hostage held prisoner in some foreign land. He needs money to bribe his captors or pay a ransom. As collateral, a treasure map or other "valuable papers" are often enclosed.

Murphy Game

Also known as "Miss Murphy," "paddy hustle," or "carpet game," the traditional con is played in places where prostitution occurs. The con artist plays a pimp but never delivers the prostitute.

Badger Game

A refined version of Miss Murphy, but in this con, the con woman or prostitute is in on the scam. The con artist robs the mark of his wallet through simple theft or pretense of blackmail.

Goat Pasture Scam

The mark receives a call from a person who says he's from an oil and gas service that is sponsoring a lottery on mineral rights. If the consumer invests a certain tax deductible sum, they can receive a percentage of the income in royalty payments.

Other common hustles occur in the privacy of one's own home or through telephone solicitations (i.e., boiler rooms).

Telemarketing Fraud

Victims of telemarketing fraud are swindled out of more than $40 billion a year. According to one survey, 92 percent of U.S. adults say they have received postcards or letters promising they had "definitely" been awarded a "guaranteed" prize. Of those responding, 69 percent never received the promised prizes. Telemarketers select victims deliberately, targeting the elderly and the unemployed. Over 5.5 million Americans said they had bought items by telephone in the past two years and were exploited in the process.

While the telephone, newspaper, and postal service remain the key tools of telemarketers, they are rapidly moving onto the Internet. The number one scam to be currently found on the Internet, says the National Fraud Information Center (NFIC), is fraudulent credit card offers making false promises of credit cards, even if credit is bad, for a fee paid upfront. Business opportunities and work-at-home schemes rank in the top ten schemes on the World Wide Web. A discussion of some of the specific Internet schemes can be found in the "Computer and Internet Fraud" chapter of this manual.

Telemarketing offenses are classified as consumer fraud, yet many businesses are affected by office supply and marketing services scams. The hit-and-run nature of phone rooms, the geographical distances between the crooks and their victims, and the resources and priorities of law enforcement agencies all make enforcement efforts difficult. Only about one in 100 victims ever files a complaint.

Top Ten Telemarketing Schemes of 2003 and 2002

2003	2002
1. Credit Card Offers	1. Credit Card Offers
2. Prizes/Sweepstakes	2. Work-At-Home Schemes
3. Work-At-Home Schemes	3. Prizes/Sweepstakes
4. Magazine Sales Scams	4. Advance Fee Loans
5. Advance Fee Loans	5. Magazine Sales Scams
6. Lotteries/Lottery Clubs	6. Buyers Clubs
7. Buyers Clubs	7. Telephone Slamming
8. Travel/Vacations	8. Lotteries/Lottery Clubs
9. Telephone Slamming	9. Travel/Vacations
10. Business Opportunities/Franchsises	10. Nigerian Money Offers

Of those who were contacted by fraudulent telemarketers, 57% were contacted by phone, 29% were contacted by mail, and 9% were contacted via print.

Telemarketing Terminology

Terms in the scammer's vocabulary include *banging*, or *nailing*, the customer, i.e., closing the deal. A salesperson's most effective skill is *puffing*, the ability to sound convincing while exaggerating the value of a business opportunity or gift. To make the puffing more persuasive, marketers hire *singers* or *criers* to tell potential victims what a great deal they are getting. Calls from angry customers who realize they have been swindled are known as *heat calls*. These are handled by someone claiming to be the company's manager or vice-president.

Boiler Room Staff

Work in a *boiler room* is shared by *fronters*, *closers*, and *verifiers*.

Fronters

The fronter calls victims and makes the initial pitch. This low-level worker is usually breaking into the business and reads from a script to the prospective customer. Fronters seldom see the merchandise or know the full extent of the operation. Keeping fronters in the dark, at least in theory, limits what they can tell investigators and protects them in the event of prosecution.

Closers

The closer is a veteran. Fronters pass an interested caller to their closer, identified as the firm's "manager," who convinces the person to buy.

Verifiers

Next, the caller is passed to a verifier, who reads some vague words about the deal and records the person's agreement. These recordings are intentionally vague, leaving out the pitch and key details, essentially recording only the customer's consent. Verifiers also stall customers who call back to complain (*heat calls*), finding reasons why a little more patience will solve the problem, and in some cases, convincing the person to send a little more money to help the process along.

Staff Exploitation

The customers of fraudulent telemarketing operations are not the only victims. Fronters are often poorly educated and easily taken advantage of by the career criminals who run the operations. Salespeople may face hidden costs in a work agreement, similar to the ones involved in the items they push on unsuspecting customers. For example, boiler room operators hold back parts of their phone lists and sell them to crew members as "hot leads."

Telescam veterans know how to operate a gift sting that bilks both the customer and the salesperson. Operators overstate the retail value of the gifts, so the customers get less than they paid for; then, by giving agents an inflated wholesale cost, the operators can pay these workers less commission, which is figured on the "profit margin" between wholesale and retail.

The salespeople in boiler rooms are sometimes as desperate as their victims. Most are unemployed, with little education or marketable skills. Telemarketing promises easy work and big pay without any experience. Many people who start out as fronters, however, are serving an apprenticeship in their criminal careers. They are wooed with cars, cellular phones, and other perks. Former workers have reported that supervisors sprinkled lines of cocaine along the phone bank table, and threw handfuls of money into the air, promising the proceeds to whoever made the next sale.

Naturally, there are no Social Security or payroll taxes deducted from paychecks, so employees can owe big tax bills at the end of the year. Fronters' commission payments are often shorted, or withheld. Paychecks frequently fail to clear the bank. Owners promise big profit shares for a month or two, then shut down the business. They tell the workers that their assets have been frozen by creditors or regulators. Workers lose their jobs and usually their last weeks' commissions. For the last few months, however, the owners have been taking in $25,000 to $30,000 a week.

Telemarketing Suppliers
The telemarketing industry relies on a number of sources to supply its phone scripts, mailing lists, merchandise, phone banks, and autodialers. Mailing lists and phone lists are sold for a few cents per name. Lists of people who have been stung before or who have bad credit records fetch between ten and fifteen cents per name. By supplying telemarketers with the tools of their trade, these companies make telescamming possible. Many of the suppliers are aware of telemarketers' criminal intentions and choose to ignore them.

Turnkeys
Turnkeys comprise an industry of their own by providing the collateral a telemarketing scam needs—turnkeys launder credit card receipts and checks, sell autodialers and phone lists, and provide the merchandise portrayed as valuable prizes.

Legitimate businesses, however, are routinely implicated in this scurrilous industry. The U.S. Postal Service, for instance, carries tons of telemarketing ads. In the early days of the industry, telemarketers used the Postal Service to deliver merchandise C.O.D., but when the postal service mounted an aggressive campaign against fraud, companies turned to credit card billings to avoid the scrutiny. They also use parcel delivery services or overnighters which are not subject to federal mail fraud laws. By keeping the value of the merchandise just below $300, telemarketers avoid the minimum amount at which postal inspectors are required to investigate fraud.

Independent Service Organizations

Telemarketers often have difficulty securing credit card services from reputable institutions. Many banks will not open credit-processing accounts for businesses who do a substantial amount of their business in phone sales because these accounts typically incur a high rate of "chargebacks." Federal law gives consumers 60 days to protest charges to their cards, and if successful, the issuer has to absorb the loss. MasterCard and Visa estimate their losses from phone fraud at $300 million a year.

Telemarketing operations have learned the difficulties they face when dealing directly with banks. To circumvent this obstacle, phone sales companies hire "independent service organizations," which approach banks on the telemarketer's behalf. The service company agrees with the bank to cover any chargebacks from the operation. The telemarketer is required to post a large bond to cover potential losses, so the service organization is also protected from loss. However, even with a half-million dollar bond, the reserve funds can be quickly depleted when customers start to realize they have been swindled, leaving the service company and/or the bank with enormous losses.

Factoring Companies

Telemarketing operations also commonly engage "factoring" companies. These groups buy credit card receipts from telemarketing concerns at a discount, then use their merchant bank accounts to convert the receipts into cash. Some factors charge as much as 30 percent of the receipts' gross value to launder the slips. Factoring is illegal in some states, though crooks find ways to slip through loopholes or disguise their alliances.

International Factoring Companies

Factoring through Asian and European merchants is becoming increasingly common. Factoring companies in these countries tend to charge a lower price for their services than some other countries: between nine and ten percent of the gross. Regardless of their locale, factors have the opportunity to make a great profit. They also, however, face the risk that banks will freeze their accounts or sue them for excessive chargebacks. In response to the losses suffered at the hands of dishonest telemarketers, banks and credit card companies have started reviewing their accounts to locate those businesses with inordinate numbers of chargebacks. The financial institution closes these accounts, and may file suit if the account holder can be located.

Check-Cashing Establishments

Another convenient tool at the telemarketer's disposal is the check-cashing store. If a boiler room operation wishes to avoid the risks of setting up a bank account which might be traced or seized, customers' personal checks are taken to a company which cashes them for a small fee. These establishments rarely require any identification to cash the checks. Customers may complain and try to stop payment on their checks, but they are ordinarily too late.

Common Telemarketing Scams

Senior Scams

Older people are the favorite prey of telescammers. In the U.S., they make up 11 percent of the population but constitute 30 percent of the victims of consumer fraud and 50 percent of all phone scam victims. Forty-five percent of senior citizens have been offered investments by a person unknown to them. Seniors own more than half of all financial assets in the U.S.

Fred Schulte, author of *Fleeced!*, relates the pitch delivered to an elderly woman in Philadelphia by Tim O'Neil. The woman told detectives about the more than $10,000 for which O'Neil and his lieutenants swindled her. O'Neil's call to mollify the woman's protests was recorded by the FBI. On the line, he insists the "collectibles" the woman bought, including "actual bullets excavated from the Civil War," are genuine and valuable.

> *Do you wear pendants? This is a beautiful, is a diamond. . . . I'm not gonna ask you to spend a penny. . . .*
>
> *How old are you? God bless you. . . 89 . . .*
>
> *We're gonna get that out to you. . . Look for it in the middle of next week, and then give us a call and then let us know how you like it. . . .*
>
> *Well I hope I put a little sunshine in your day. OK, honey and God bless you. Oh don't cry now, we're here to take care of you. . . . We'll be here and if you need to talk to anybody at any time you give us a call okay? Bye, bye, and God bless you.*

Telemarketers usually call in the evening. Nighttime calls find people of every age in more impulsive moods. Seniors may be more vulnerable to pitches promising them extra money and luxury goods because many live on fixed incomes. These lottery-style gambits can seem like an easy way for the elderly to improve their financial status.

Targeting the Unemployed

The unemployed are another favorite target for sweepstakes pitches and job search services. Whereas "the system" has left the jobless without hope, the telemarketer offers a way around official channels. People with bad credit pay telemarketers to "repair" their credit record or get a major card. Instead, they get a list of banks which offer credit cards, commonly published in newspapers, or an application for a card which requires a security deposit for activation, usually several hundred or a thousand dollars. These people are also targeted by advance-fee loan scams, which promise loans in exchange for a fee.

Affinity Fraud

Affinity fraud targets groups of people who have some social connection. Neighborhoods chiefly populated by racial minorities, especially immigrant groups, are often the site of affinity frauds. Religious and professional ties are often exploited. Marketing technology has made it possible for a company to buy targeted lists, not just by location, but according to buying habits, leisure time activities, and club memberships. The most expensive lists carry the names of people who have already fallen for a telemarketing scam. This is called *reloading*.

Chief among telescammers' tricks is obfuscation. Salespeople read off lists of prizes, emphasizing big-ticket items like jewelry and cars, not mentioning that the odds of actually winning anything besides a trinket are astronomical. Schulte relates an incident in which victims were told they had won a "Winnebago." Victims were asked to pay a handling fee of $2,900, a fraction of the cost of a new travel home. About two months later, victims found a delivery driver at their door with a "Winnebago tent."

Some operations actually encourage their marks to call and check with the Better Business Bureau (BBB) and with former customers, giving out the numbers for the person to call. These numbers ring at phony lines set up by the scammers which give out a glowing recommendation. Phone rooms have been known to set up reference arms with titles like "The Better Business Bureau of America" or "International Better Business Bureau" to recommend their ventures. If a potential victim does reach the Better Business Bureau, chances are the report will contain little or nothing of use. The information in these files is usually ambiguous and out of date.

Consolation

When irate customers call telemarketers back to complain, their calls are routed to professionals who placate the caller with more promises and obfuscations. Some boiler rooms have a prearranged communication route for leading complaints through four or five different "departments." This tactic causes many callers to eventually hang up without having spoken to anyone. In some instances, telemarketers confronted with furious callers threatening legal action do award something of value to the customer. Normally the item is worth far less than the person has paid out, however.

If obfuscation and consolation prizes fail to appease the caller, the con turns to threats and intimidation. This is a favorite method for dealing with senior citizens, especially elderly women. Threats are used not just to keep customers from filing complaints, but to cajole more money out of them. Some telemarketers have actually threatened callers' personal safety if they refused to pay.

The odds in favor of catching a boiler room operation in progress are usually poor. Operations can select a town, set up a room, make their haul, and leave again in a matter of weeks or months. When authorities raid a boiler room, the operation has typically already moved on. If the company owners registered with state regulators, they probably did so under an alias. By the time police arrive, the perpetrators have moved on—often just down the block or across the county line—but the chances of finding them are slim.

800 Numbers

Toll-free 800 numbers (or other toll-free prefixes such as 866, 877, 888, etc.) offered by phone service companies are used by some operations. The scam is a toll-free line, advertised in mailers, fliers and newspaper ads, to lure victims into making the call themselves. The toll-free number usually carries a recording which directs customers to a 900 number that charges the caller between $3 and $10 a minute to hear recorded messages. A favorite device of sellers is to insist that the offer being made is good for less than 48 hours. To secure the opportunity, the customer hands over a cashier's check to an overnight-delivery service. Even if the victim does have second thoughts, he will be unable to stop payment on a cashier's check.

Automatic Debits

The personal checking account is one of the most convenient tools for defrauding telemarketing customers, thanks to advances in electronic banking technology. Using computerized transfers, businesses can set up an automatic debit to the buyer's account. Telemarketing operations use this device to obtain payment before victims can change their minds about their purchases. Worse, telemarketers can simply use the information to drain the victim's account. This information is usually obtained by telling the victim that the account numbers are needed to "verify eligibility" for a giveaway or "biz op." Banks are not responsible for any losses customers suffer in this way, so there are no chargebacks and little recourse for the swindled customer besides filing a complaint. Even if an investigation of the complaint brings the scammer to court, the chances that the victim will receive restitution are poor.

According to the *2003 Telemarketing Fraud Report*, issued by the National Fraud Information Center, 37 percent of telemarketing fraud victims paid by automatic bank account debit, 21 percent paid by wire transfer, 13 percent paid by check, 11 percent paid by credit card, and 7 percent paid by money order.

Business Opportunities (Biz Ops)

Two of the top ten telemarketing frauds in the NFIC's rating are aimed at people starting their own business. Regulators put losses in fraudulent business opportunities at over $100 million a year, and most observers think the number is far higher. The NFIC points out that in just three recent cases, victims were taken for almost $64 million.

Work-at-Home Schemes

Besides franchise offers and other miscellaneous business scams, the most prevalent frauds involve Work-at-Home schemes and FCC-related investments. Victims of these phony offerings do not see themselves as part of the telemarketer's prey. They believe they are making a legitimate business investment.

"Biz op" promoters often use a team approach in their enterprises. The victim usually sees an ad and calls a *fronter*, who makes the introductory pitch and then passes the victim to a higher-up. Next, the caller is put through to a *crier* who endorses the opportunity and tells the victim of the profits he made. Finally, a *closer* seals the deal and gets the payment secured as quickly as possible.

Telemarketers use business-related terms such as *exclusive territory, annual gross revenues,* and *emerging markets* in these calls. This helps convince the mark that the biz op is legitimate. A Louis Harris poll found that 1 in 33 cold calls for investments were successful.

Some business-pitch operations are complete fabrications. They offer envelope stuffing or book-review enterprises which do not really exist. Scammers mail out postcards or buy cheap ads in magazines and newspapers. Some may not even take any phone calls. The ads convince the victims to send money to a mailbox. Unlike the U.S. Postal Service, which requires identification from renters and divulges this information to anyone who inquires, private companies will rent mail-drops to anyone for a few dollars a month and can refuse to say who paid for the box.

Fly and Buy

Some scams involve ventures such as vending machines, pay phones, and merchandise display racks. They often gain credibility by setting up a front operation and inviting investors for tours. This part of the ruse is known as the "fly and buy." For example, the Securities Division of the State of Washington prosecuted a case on behalf of a woman who traveled to Colorado and met with a promoter. The promoter offered to let her in on a deal for video pool and video bowling games. Thrilled with the demonstration and her tour guide's promises of quick profits, she paid $13,000 for machines which broke down in less than three months. When the woman complained to the promoter about the shoddiness of the machines, she was sent two new ones along with a bill.

Shoddy merchandise is a familiar element of the biz op scam. The scams are tailored for the targeted audience. A Maryland ring ran advertisements in *Income Plus* magazine and other investor-oriented publications for a solar-powered car battery recharger. "In seconds, you're off and running," the ad claimed. The offer stated that distributors were making over $200,000 a year with the revolutionary devices. But the machines were worthless. One investor took the recharger to an electrician, and was told it could recharge a battery but that it would take a few weeks.

Vending Machine and Payphone Scams

Buyers are promised exclusive territories, but find the same area has been sold to many people. Often, the machines do not work or they simply do not make any money. Sooner or later, the ruse is exposed. But in the short term, the operators can make substantial proceeds.

Entrepreneurial Enterprises

Telemarketers deal not only in machinery-oriented scams like those above. The raising of exotic animals like ostriches and emus for luxury items and for slaughter has been a popular scam for a while, including weekend retreats to a model farm for would-be ranchers. In the last ten years, the 900 telephone number service has been used to swindle those who set out to be swindlers themselves. People are convinced they can make a fortune charging between $3 and $10 a minute for recorded messages providing entertainment, psychic readings, or information available for free from other sources.

Scams involving computer technology are usually successful due to the layman's lack of knowledge in that field. Although 60 percent of Americans own some type of computer, few actually know how CD ROMs or fiber optics function. Whatever the nature of the opportunity, there are signs that indicate that it is not legitimate. Among the most common:

- Classified ads urging the prospect to call an 800 number.
- Wild, unsubstantiated claims about potential earnings.
- Promises about exclusive territories, assurances about good locations, or the assistance of a professional locator.
- References specified by the company.
- The lack of a complete disclosure document containing information about the promoter's experience, lawsuit history, audited financial statements, and substantiation for earnings assertions.

Inventions Schemes

In order to crack down on operations which offer fraudulent invention promotions, the FTC recently launched "Project Mousetrap." Using ads, these operations solicit inventors to submit their product ideas to the promotions firm, which supposedly specializes in bringing new products to the market. Inventions are supposedly evaluated and appraised, and nearly always endorsed. The firm offers to submit the product to manufacturers for a fee.

The U.S. Federal Trade Commission charged the American Institute for Research and Development, Inc. (AIRD) and its predecessor, American Inventors Corporation (AIC), with running a deceptive inventions-promotion scheme that bilked consumers nationwide out of thousands of dollars each over a 20-year time span. Promoters used print ads, in-person, and telephone sales presentations to offer two basic services: (1) a "feasibility report," priced from $250 to $495, to evaluate the patentability and marketability of the inventor's product, and (2) a "representation agreement" that promised to prepare, file, and prosecute a patent application, and to promote the product to industry representatives. The representation agreement cost from $5,490 to $11,990. The complaint alleged that the firms obtained design patents, which have little or no commercial value, instead of the utility patents they promised. Furthermore, people were told that only a select few inventions were accepted, when virtually every person who applied was brought into the program. AIRD and AIC also encouraged their customers to expect huge financial gains when, the Trade Commission charged, "in 20 years of business, perhaps no more than 13 customers have realized any financial gain at all" as a result of the companies' services.

Victims received a useless recommendation for their product and a coding from the U.S. Bureau of Standard Industrial Code (SIC). The code generates a list of manufacturers who make products similar to the inventors,' but regulators say the "lists of manufacturers that come from classifying your idea with the SIC usually are of limited value." Some victims thought they were securing a patent in their promotions deal, but instead received only a Disclosure Document from the U.S. Patent Office, available to the general public for $10. The document is not a patent but a statement of "evidence of the date of conception of the invention" and does not guarantee rights to any future products.

Employment Services

The phony employment service is similar in nature to the biz op. Preying on the unemployed, these scams promise good jobs, many of them overseas with the added enticement of "tax free" wages. Victims pay between $250 and $1,000 for the service. Some get lists of government jobs which are available free, or listings from classified ads. Most get nothing.

Credit Services

The simplest credit scam promises that the company will secure a loan for the applicant, regardless of credit history and references, if the person pays an upfront fee, usually between $35 and $75. Checking account debits are a favorite payment method, as are 900 numbers, which charge by the minute (up to $40 or $50 per call) to hear information widely available which provides no help in swaying a loan for the listener. Usually there are few or no loans made. Occasionally, loan information and applications may be mailed out to the victim, but usually, after the fee has been paid, the operators are not heard from again.

Credit Repair Scams

Similar to loan scams are those that promise to repair credit. Pitch-men like to say they can "wipe away" or "doctor" or "cosmeticize" blotches on credit, insinuating they have ways of changing or disguising a person's credit history. Despite the fact that there is really no way to erase bad credit, many people fall for this scam, paying hundreds of dollars to expunge their records.

Prime-Rate Credit Cards

In this scam, telemarketing companies assure customers they can get major cards for a small fee even if their credit report is poor. Victims receive an application for a MasterCard which they could obtain in any department store. Telemarketers also push "secured" cards, requiring a cash deposit (usually a $250–$300 minimum) in the issuer's bank to activate the card.

Gold Cards

A relatively new credit card sting on the Internet touts "gold card" status for customers, regardless of credit history. The advertisement claims applicants will be processed for a major credit card. In actuality, applicants are merely assisted in filing an application for a major credit card, a worthless service since applications are quite simple to complete and submit. For a large up-front fee, participants receive a "catalog card," which is only redeemable if the holder buys the company's over-priced, low-quality merchandise listed in the catalog as "discounted" for cardholders. Even then, an actual purchase may require paying additional fees or cash deposits before the customer is allowed to charge the remainder. Since the issuers do not report payment activity to any of the credit reporting bureaus, using the card does not improve the customer's credit rating.

Lotteries/Lottery Clubs

Consumers receive a false claim that they have won, or can get help to win, a lottery, often in a foreign country. Most lottery scams are perpetrated by con artists in other countries, sometimes using U.S. addresses to disguise their real locations. Sometimes the lottery actually exists, but invitations to play don't come from governments that operate legitimate lotteries or anyone connected to them. The consumer has no way of assuring that they will receive the tickets that they pay for or, in the unlikely event that they do win, will ever be able to collect their money. Potential victims need to remember that it is illegal to use the mail or telephone to play lotteries across borders, U.S. law prohibits it, not only across national borders but state lines as well. The consumer could be accused of illegal activities just by participating. Differences in legal systems, difficulties of conducting investigations in other countries, and expenses and other complications involved in pursuing cross-border fraud make the chances of a consumer getting his money back very, very slim.

Buyers Clubs

This scheme involves membership in discount buying clubs that consumers never agreed to join or were signed up for through free-trial offers. Consumers should beware of advertisements for products at incredibly cheap prices or free if the consumer pays for shipping, these offers may be designed to lure the consumer into a buyer's club membership. Another way to avoid being a victim of a buyer's club scheme is to understand how a "trial-offer" works. In many cases, the consumer will automatically be charged for a membership when the free-trial expires unless they contact the club to cancel. The consumer should ask for the details of all membership offers in writing before they agree to join. If unauthorized charges or debits are noticed on monthly statements, the consumer should contact their credit card issuer or bank and ask for their account to be credited for these unauthorized charges.

Travel/Vacation Schemes

Offers of free or discount travel that never materializes. Consumers need to be skeptical of offers for "free" trips. Airlines and other well-known companies sometimes operate contests for travel prizes; however, there are also companies that offer "free" trips to try to lure people into buying their products or services. Consumers also need to know what is included with the trip; a "free" or incredibly cheap trip may have hidden costs. For instance, the cruise may be free, but the consumer has to pay to fly to the departure point and stay in a hotel at their own expense. Or they may have to endure a long, high-pressure sales pitch for a timeshare or travel club membership as part of the trip. Often the best travel deals are only available for off-peak times, not during school vacations, holidays, or other popular travel dates.

To avoid being victims of travel/vacation schemes, consumers should confirm all travel arrangements. If transportation and hotel are included in the travel package, ask how to contact those companies and confirm with them directly that the reservations have been made. Consumers should do their own travel research; it's easy to get information from a local travel agent or other sources such as newspapers, books, and the Internet. When making travel arrangements, it is advisable to pay with a credit card. Fraudulent travel operators can take a consumer's money and run and even legitimate companies can go out of business. Paying with a credit card allows the consumer to dispute the charges if the promises that are made are not kept.

Telephone Slamming

Slamming occurs when a consumer's telephone service is switched from their current company to another one without their permission. Long distance is the most common target of slamming but it can also happen with local or local-toll service. Consumers should read the fine print on all contest entry forms, coupons, and other promotional materials as these might include an agreement to switch phone service. Federal law requires that written agreements to change phone service must be separate documents, not part of a prize package or other materials. If the company offers a check for the consumer to switch, the check must clearly state on the front and on the back, in the signature area, that the consumer is agreeing to change their service.

Consumers should always check their phone bills carefully. If the consumer notices a new company name, he should call the number that's listed on that portion of the bill and ask for an explanation. If he has been slammed, he should inform the company that he did not agree to use its service. He should then contact his original phone company and ask to be reinstated to his old calling plan. Under federal law, the consumer can switch back for free and they don't have to pay for the first 30 days of service from the slammer.

Real Estate

Real estate scams are easily recognized. There is almost always an element of time pressure, with the victims being convinced they are participating in a "once-in-a-lifetime, now-or-never" deal. The investors are led to believe there is no time to investigate the venture, and that if they hesitate, they will miss the opportunity to make a fortune. Promises of big profits for little or no involvement are the norm in real estate scams. The investor is also misled into assuming they are being let in on a special offer or an exclusive deal by the promoter.

Since the 1920s, when thousands of Americans bought swampland in Florida, real estate has served as a conduit for fraud. A modern-day variation has dispensed with the actual land entirely and simply sells information. Companies tout the riches available in real estate through seminars and books which claim to offer "secret" ways to cash in. The customer pays for the secret info and gets worthless tips in return.

Timeshares

Another scam sells timeshares in condominiums for vacationers. Telemarketers pass themselves off as brokers to condominium owners and purport to specialize in selling timeshares.

OPTIONS

Ads in the real estate section of newspapers coax investors into buying "options" on property. Supposedly, the option locks in a present-day price on behalf of the purchaser, who can exercise the option later if he wishes to buy the land or to sell it at a profit. Sometimes the investor has bought nothing but a piece of paper—the "agent" has no authority to make deals on the property. Occasionally, the option is only valid for a few months, or is too vaguely worded to be enforceable. Usually there is an actual plot of land, but in most instances it is undevelopable due to location or zoning restrictions, and is therefore worthless.

DEVELOPED PROPERTY

The General Development Corporation of Florida ran a legendary land fraud scam in which potential investors were shown lots and houses guaranteed to make them rich. In this rendering of the "buy-and-fly" sham, victims were shepherded, and their contacts restricted, until they signed a deal for a lot. The scam continued for approximately six years and cost victims millions.

Art/Rare Items

Land deals prey on the public's reverence for *real* estate. The con who deals in art objects preys on a similar impulse—the reverence for the rare. Paintings worth little more than their canvas and oil are tagged as "masterpieces" sure to grow in value. The victims who fall for these scams are art novices who seem to unquestioningly believe the "dealer's" appraisal of the object d'art.

This sort of willing victim will buy lithographic prints, mass-produced by the thousands, thinking they are purchasing a "limited edition." Any anxieties the victims may develop are calmed by a promised 30-day no obligation trial and with "certificates of authenticity." According to the FTC, the most popular artists to counterfeit are Salvador Dali, Pablo Picasso, Marc Chagall, and Joan Miro.

Collectibles and Memorabilia

Collectibles and household decorative items such as vases, bric-a-brac, and figurines are also commonly hawked by telemarketers. Again, these supposedly valuable objects are nothing more than cheap, shoddy merchandise. War memorabilia is especially popular, particularly items related to the World War II. Documents and keepsakes from any bygone era are on the fraudulent telemarketer's best-seller list. Stamps are sold as rare when they are in fact worthless.

Coins are another prime money-maker for telemarketers. "Certificates of authenticity" and "appraisals" are included with the merchandise to reassure customers, but needless to say these documents are usually produced by the sales company, or doctored from a legitimate original.

Precious Stones

Gems are generally regarded as items which will not lose their value. Telescammers exploit this mindset by offering "high-quality" gems for wholesale prices. Customers are told they are being offered a special deal due to fluctuations in the market or because their names are on an industry list.

The risk is minimal, victims are told. By acquiring the stones wholesale, the individual minimizes the investment exposure. The company even offers its own "brokerage" services, which can liquidate the stones at a moment's notice should the investor need the cash back quickly. The stones not only have a grading certificate and appraisal documents, but are also sealed in a plastic wrap to guarantee their condition remain flawless. The real purpose of the seal—which victims are told must not be broken if the gems are ever to be offered for sale—is to keep buyers from making a genuine inspection of the article.

Once a victim makes a buy, a company spokesperson calls a second time, saying that if the person buys more stones, his "gemstone portfolio" will be more attractive to prospective buyers and at auctions advertised in company literature. If the victim buys additional items, a company broker will inevitably call with "good news." The brokerage will have found a buyer for the victim's holdings, but before the transaction can go through, the customer must pay some "minor fees." These may be passed off as finders' fees, brokers' commissions, examination fees, international duties, or taxes. There may be a provision requiring the victim to buy more stones before making the sale.

A variation on the scheme targets those who have already bought gems from telemarketers and whose names are taken from insider lists. The caller claims to be a broker representing an "overseas buyer" ready to purchase the listener's portfolio. But, invariably, the buyer must have a few more stones in the portfolio—which the caller offers to supply— in order to make the sale, and there are fees and commissions to be paid.

Precious Metals

The precious metals market has traditionally been one of wide variances. Prices fluctuate constantly and even experts have trouble deciding what the next trend will be. Telemarketing operations play on this instability with offerings of gold, silver, and platinum. Once again, victims are told prices will never be this good again and that if they hesitate, they will miss a singular opportunity to make a fortune.

900 Numbers/800 Numbers/International Calls

900 numbers are usually associated with psychic hotlines, phone sex lines, and other dubious purposes. Using 900 numbers, customers can "dial a prayer" or even listen to the Easter Bunny. Some callers insist they did not know they were being charged for the service. By using a toll-free 800 number that then links the caller to the per-minute charges, promoters are able to surreptitiously begin charging customers for calls. 800 numbers are often used as a front in telemarketing operations to lead consumers to think that the call is free, when in fact there are hidden charges everywhere. A particularly vicious combination uses a toll-free number to make a presentation about communication services. Once the caller dials in, the computerized service automatically puts a monthly charge, sometimes labeled "voice mail," on the caller's phone bill.

Many operations familiar to law enforcement as traditional boiler rooms moved into the toll numbers when they became widely available in the 1980s. Victims dial in, thinking they will receive information on claiming funds from abandoned bank accounts or inheritances from long lost relatives. Credit repair offers and advance-fee loan services use 900 numbers extensively. Sweepstakes and prize give-aways are promoted this way, as are employment services, real estate education, information on government programs and auctions, and biz ops of every kind. The latest ruse uses a 900 number to convince people to invest in the 900 number business.

International Calls

An off-shore version of the 900 number scam uses international phone companies to reap big dollars. Callers believe they are dialing an international number for free information, usually about travel contests, discount fares, or overseas jobs. But the phone numbers, in Guyana and the Caribbean, charge up to $2.30 per minute for a recorded message that runs for 15 minutes. The promoters get a kickback from the phone company, in one case 37 cents per minute went to the scammers.

Selling Free Information

Companies involved in this kind of scheme take out ads in newspapers and magazines, or buy spots on talk radio, promising they can locate government jobs, get deals on liquidated equipment, or find student loans. All this information is available cheaply or free to the public, through government offices, on the Internet, and from other sources. One need only know where to look.

Scholarship Services

Maybe the most widely broadcast offering in the info racket is the college scholarship locator service. Student Aid Inc., a New York city firm, provides an example. SAI guaranteed students and their parents that for a $97 fee they would receive at least $1,000 in scholarships or grants. "In reality," government prosecutors showed, "the defendants almost never obtained scholarship money for consumers." SAI used a common clause in its contracts to keep from paying refunds "requiring students [to] produce letters of rejection from every scholarship on their search list even though the list included scholarships whose deadlines had passed or for which the students did not qualify."

Whatever information scholarship services do provide is available for little or nothing (at most, a $5 or $10 fee) from legitimate institutions. The perpetrators imply that they have insider connections, or that they actually administer the dispersal of monies, when in reality they merely provide lists of scholarships offered by foundations and universities.

In most cases, information scams sell freely available material. There is also a version that does offer the information for free but sticks a charge on anyway. The International Call scam promises "free information" on travel contests and discount fares. The information itself does not cost anything, but the call to get it costs from $3 to $6 a minute for a 15-minute call.

Charity Fronts

An increasing number of groups calling themselves non-profit, charitable concerns are not what they appear. Very little or no money goes to the advertised cause. Police and firemen's associations have in some cases lent their names to telemarketing fund drives which only give about 35 percent of their collections to the group. Some boiler room operators claim to call for these groups—or for drives against a disease or underprivileged children—when they are in no way affiliated with the charity.

A new twist to this scam is the impersonation of handicapped workers by boiler room operators. Phone pros call victims, claiming to be handicapped or disabled, and attempt to sell light bulbs and other household products. The merchandise is priced at three times its actual value. The money is, of course, pocketed by the operators.

Door-to-Door Promotions

Sweepstakes promoters using a charity front offer the possibility of new cars and cash prizes to contributors. The raffle approach—tying the number of "chances" to a set amount—helps drive up how much the victim is willing to give. A favored device of phony charities is to send school-age children door-to-door, saying they are raising money for antidrug programs or for a group that takes underprivileged kids on trips. Some of the children repeat what they are told in exchange for a few dollars. Others believe they will receive rewards and free trips when in fact they, too, are being scammed.

Prizes, Sweepstakes, Discount Services

The most common give-away is known as the "1-in-5." A postcard arrives in the mail telling the receiver they have already won a prize. A new Lincoln Continental tops the list, along with $5,000 in cash, a diamond necklace, a living room set, and $500 in gift certificates for clothing and household furnishings. The odds of winning any of the prizes are astronomical. Victims are given trinkets or coupons redeemable only for the company's own shoddy merchandise.

Winners who call back are often asked to stipulate how they intend to spend their winnings for the company's "records," or for "publicity materials." Then they will be asked to pay a processing fee or to prepay the taxes on their winnings. Sometimes winners pay immediately by dialing a 900 number which charges them for a 10-minute call even if they hang up immediately. This practice is a further violation of telemarketing laws, which require a toll number to disconnect no less than 30 seconds after the caller hangs up.

Magazine Subscriptions

A productive front for prize hawkers is the magazine subscription service. Prepaid subscription offers extract money from customers through credit cards and bank debits then never deliver the publication. In other instances, the processing fees far exceed the actual value of the subscriptions.

Office and Household Supplies

A scam which has recently become prevalent involves copy machine toner. An invoice for toner is sent to a company. The cons have usually called beforehand, gotten the name of the employee in charge of supplies, and addressed the invoice to that person. Although the office never ordered or received any toner, the con men are relying on poor communication to cover their ruse. The invoice will most likely be sent to the accounting department and paid. If the proper controls are in place at every level of business operations, this scheme should be detected. Too many businesses, however, are vulnerable to this kind of scam.

The caller may get the company's representative to accept a trial or promotional shipping of the product. He may claim to be a supplier for the company or a new salesman from a regular supplier. The product arrives and an invoice follows a couple of weeks later. If the company tries to send the product back, it is returned to them. To avoid further complications, the company will normally pay the bill just to put an end to the situation.

Any sort of office supply, from paper to shelving to cleaning products, can be part of a scam. Medical supplies shipped to doctor's offices and clinics are pushed in a similar fashion. Individual households can be the target of these ploys, as well. Water purifiers are often used in tandem with giveaway offers; the victim buys a filtering device, at an inflated cost, in order to qualify for the giveaway. Pyramid-style operations often use household products and health-related merchandise, such as vitamins or skin-care cream, as part of their machinations.

Recovery Rooms

Recovery room operations target those who have already lost money to a telemarketing scam. Posing as a consumer advocacy group or a law firm, telemarketers offer victims a chance to recover any funds they may have lost and bring the perpetrators to justice. Once the victim agrees, legal, investigative, and other fees will begin to emerge.

Ponzi and Pyramid Schemes

Definition

A Ponzi Scheme is generally defined as an illegal business practice in which new investors' money is used to make payments to earlier investors. A simple investment scam rakes in as much money as possible and then disappears. A Ponzi stays in business by turning some of the money back into the game. A few conspicuous rewards early on will whip up interest, the business will grow, and then, if they're smart and lucky, the operators will split.

Everyone involved pretends to mount a legitimate organization, but little or no commercial activity takes place. Payoffs are made from the pool of investor funds; the rest is siphoned into operators' pockets. Schemes may run for at least a year. Some Ponzis have flourished for a decade or more.

In accounting terms, money paid to Ponzi investors, described as *income*, is actually *distribution of capital*. It's like giving away the store. Instead of sharing profits, you're sharing cash reserves.

Approaching this crime analytically we can see into the mechanics of the fraud. Illegal cash is hidden in securities or other financial instruments. Promoters use phony accounts, phony books, and phony names. Successful prosecutions have to uncover these guises and track the funds. Plus, the inner workings of a Ponzi operation have to be summarized for a jury, whose members are probably not mathematicians or accountants.

Illegal Pyramid or Ponzi Scheme?

What's the difference between an illegal pyramid scheme and a Ponzi scheme? They both use new investors' money to make payoffs. But they're run very differently by their promoters, and legally they're prosecuted under different laws.

First we'll distinguish between legal and illegal pyramid schemes. Then we'll show how a Ponzi scheme and an illegal pyramid are the same thing, only different.

Pyramid Schemes, Legal and Illegal

> *Illegal pyramids generate revenue by continually recruiting new members. These operations may offer merchandise or services for sale, but the only significant revenues come from recruitment.*

Some legitimate merchandising companies use a pyramid structure to rank their employee-owners and to determine those people's compensation. But a pyramid structure becomes a pyramid scheme when the company makes its money by recruiting people. Instead of selling a product or service, the group deals primarily in new memberships. Joining the group allows the new member to profit by signing up new members. The process continues until the available pool of new members is drained, which happens sooner than one might think.

Usually there's a product or a cause that fronts the illegal pyramid scheme as a legitimate enterprise. Promoters shill beeswax supplements, or claim they're working to prevent youth crime. A favorite product front offers "courses" in areas like "investor education" or "self esteem." These materials usually convey very little pertinent information; in fact, they're nothing more than motivational tracts designed to make the victim a more enthusiastic participant in the pyramid.

In any case, regardless of the product front, an illegal pyramid emphasizes recruiting first and foremost. The product or service takes a back seat to getting new suckers signed up.

As a rule of thumb most courts apply the *70-Percent Rule*. This requires that at least 70 percent of distributor's profits come from retail sales. Of course this figure can be hard to verify. Distributors routinely sign falsified compliance statements because if they don't, promoters warn, the authorities will shut the whole thing down and everyone loses.

In the final assessment, legality rests on what the operators emphasize. If the company emphasizes the recruitment of new members over the sales of products, and if the only way to recognize promised riches is through recruitment, then the operation will likely be classified as an illegal pyramid.

What's the Difference between an Illegal Pyramid and a Ponzi Scheme?

> *Illegal pyramids are promoted as pyramids. Ponzi schemes are promoted as investment opportunities.*

The key element in a Ponzi scheme is that initial investors are paid with subsequent investors' money. There is little or no legitimate commerce.

The same thing occurs in an illegal pyramid. Nobody's selling the beeswax supplements; they're all coaxing new people to put up money. The original members of the pyramid get rich on subsequent investors' money. So: *A pyramid is a Ponzi scheme.*

How about the obverse? Is a Ponzi scheme a pyramid? The distinguishing factor of the illegal pyramid is the continual need for new investors. Each new member recruits two members, who each recruit two..., and so forth.

Ponzi schemes, like pyramids, require a steady march of new investor funds to pay dividends. This ever-growing pile of loot might look like a pyramid when graphed. So, in the sense that it requires exponential growth to avoid collapse, *A Ponzi scheme is a pyramid scheme.*

The difference between a Ponzi and a pyramid lies in how the operation is promoted.

Illegal pyramids announce themselves as pyramids: they hype levels or stages in their literature. The pyramidal structure helps draw new players, each believing that they will rise through the ranks of the pyramid to become "Golden," or "Fully Vested"—whatever hoaky titles the scammers have concocted.

A *Ponzi scheme*, on the other hand, masquerades as some type of investment—in financial instruments, mineral rights, or some other form of speculation. The participants believe they're buying mortgage-backed securities, or partial interest in an oil well. They have no idea they're funneling money into a bottomless pit. Certainly no one suggests moving on to the next level of the pyramid, because the pyramid isn't part of the pitch.

When an enterprise—Nu-Skin International, for example—promotes itself as an organization with levels or stages, and the only way to rise through the levels is to recruit new members, the promoters are running an illegal pyramid scheme. Before Tim and Melinda Rommel sued Nu-Skin, they were true believers, sprinkling Nu-Skin products across their bathrooms and kitchens, serving Splash, Nu-Skin's answer to Tang, for breakfast every day, and even redecorating their house at the behest of Nu-Skin consultants, all for the purpose of snaring new recruits. The Rommels sued because they were misled about their opportunities inside the organization. They knew all along they were joining a pyramid, they just thought it was a legal one.

When an enterprise promotes an investment opportunity that invests little or none of the participants' money, and which uses new investment dollars to make dividend payments, then the promoters are running a Ponzi scheme.

Distinguishing between Ponzis and pyramids seems a bit academic. But the differences become significant when perpetrators are brought to justice. To prosecute an illegal pyramid, the enforcement team needs to show that the offenders generated revenue mainly through recruitment—the company's pyramidal structure is an element of the charge. Pyramid schemes are sometimes charged as illegal lotteries because, prosecutors have successfully argued, the participants are totally dependent on the actions of others for any compensation.

In another prosecution strategy, operators are charged with falsely representing potential earnings, since the mathematical limits of the pyramid make the promised $10,000 a month impossible or extremely against the odds. Again, the pyramidal structure itself is an issue in the case.

In summary:

If operators make the bulk of participants' earnings dependent on recruiting, and emphasize levels and stages in their promotions, we call this an Illegal Pyramid.

If operators claim they're offering an investment opportunity, but conduct little or no commercial activity, we call this a Ponzi scheme.

Categories of Ponzi Schemes

Ponzi Schemes are classified according to the front used in their promotion. The categories are *Pure Cash* (which includes endless chain schemes and fill-and-split games) and *Product Fronts* (which includes financial instruments, MLMs, and speculations).

IDENTIFICATION OF PONZI SCHEMES

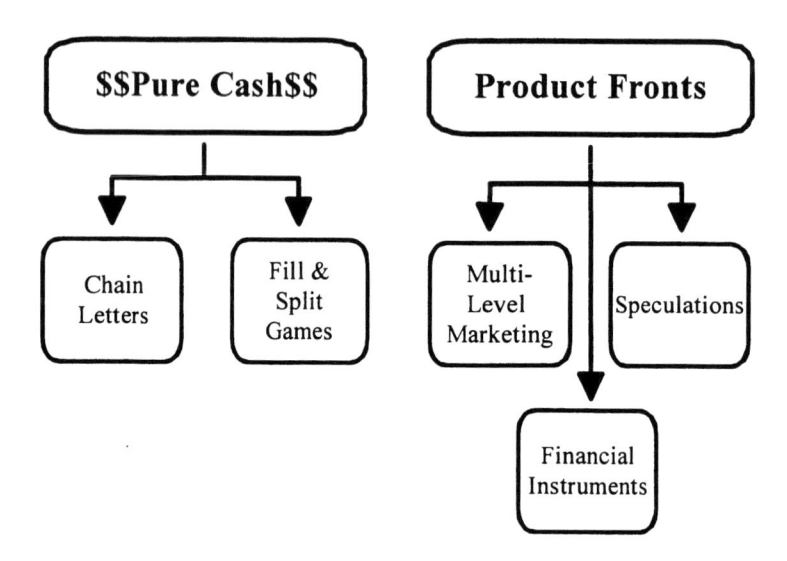

```
                    ┌─────────────────┐
                    │  Ponzi Schemes  │
                    │        &        │
                    │ Pyramid Schemes │
                    └─────────────────┘
                     /               \
          ┌──────────────┐      ┌──────────────┐
          │ $$Pure Cash$$│      │Product Fronts│
          └──────────────┘      └──────────────┘
            /       \            /      |      \
      ┌───────┐ ┌───────┐  ┌────────┐   |  ┌────────────┐
      │ Chain │ │ Fill &│  │ Multi- │   |  │Speculations│
      │Letters│ │ Split │  │ Level  │   |  └────────────┘
      └───────┘ │ Games │  │Marketing│  |
                └───────┘  └────────┘   ↓
                                 ┌────────────┐
                                 │ Financial  │
                                 │Instruments │
                                 └────────────┘
```

Pure Cash Schemes

There are two general types of pure cash schemes: Endless Chains and Fill-and-Split Schemes.

ENDLESS CHAINS

The most outrageous pyramid scams don't bother to hide their stripes. They don't use services or products to establish their legitimacy. Instead they use the "chain letter" approach. The recipient of the letter sends a sum of money ($5, $50, $100, the amount varies but isn't usually very large) to the person who mailed them the letter, then passes the letter on to three or four others.

Probability studies have shown that 93 to 95 percent of the players in a pyramid (everyone but those at the earliest initiation) will lose most of their money. Fully half can expect to lose everything they put in.

Some Internet chains have become known as "administered" pyramid schemes—every exchange in the chain is monitored by a central *administrator*, who makes sure everybody's playing (and paying) along. The *administrator* takes a cut of each transaction.

FILL-AND-SPLIT GAMES

The best way to launch a pure cash pyramid is to jazz it up with gaming elements, some kind of hook to keep players' attention focused on their riches and not how stupid their latest "opportunity" really is. These are sometimes called "Fill-and-Split Games." A popular version of this approach has been known as "Airplane." Each player buys a seat on a fictitious airplane, paying from $200 to $2,000 a seat, depending on the scale of the game. Initial players help recruit new "passengers" and move up through the ranks of "crew," "copilot" and "pilot." When a flight is fully booked—with something like 6 passengers, 4 crew members, a copilot and a pilot—the plane takes off, the pilots and crew are paid for the flight, and everybody moves up the ranks. Just like a real airline, a plane's investors are constantly looking to fill their seats.

Another variation of the fill-and-split game tries to capitalize on the phenomenal profits yielded over the last 15 years by the American stock market. Called "Financial Networking," "Market Climb," and other financial-sounding terms, these pure cash pyramids use a business metaphor in their pitch. A typical operation spreads 15 people over four levels. Eight investors buy into the network as "vice-presidents"; above them are four "presidents," just below two "co-chairman" positions; at the top, sitting pretty, is the "chairman." Every time the eight slots at the bottom are filled (average price $1,500 to $2,000), the pyramid splits. The chairman gets out of the game with a "golden parachute" and everyone moves up the corporate ladder, anxiously scanning for new recruits.

These games are usually predicated on what's become known as "affinity fraud." New players are recruited by their affinity with existing participants. People comb religious groups or community associations for fresh leads. Affinities may be racial or cultural. Financial networking, for example, has targeted a number of African-American communities. Churches, synagogues and other religious organizations offer fertile hunting grounds and great cover from promoters—an endorsement from a clergyperson is literally good as gold, and law enforcement authorities are often reluctant to meddle in religious affairs. Affinity frauds may also prey on social groups, like the swing-dance clubs so popular in recent years, or professional organizations.

Product Fronts

The category of product fronts is subdivided into Financial Instruments, MLMs, and Speculations.

FINANCIAL INSTRUMENTS

Financial instruments—such as stocks, borrower's certificates, currency exchanges, loan scams, and investment pools—are perfect tools for the Ponzi artist. Charles Ponzi's victims in 1920 thought they were investing in postal reply coupons which, Ponzi assured everyone, yielded whopping profits by playing off the exchange rates of international currency. In our own time, as legal tender in Mexico, Brazil, and Asia roller-coasters from one extreme to the next, the currency exchange still makes an ideal Ponzi front.

A stock market that gains 25 to 30 percent a year (and individual stocks quadrupling, sometimes in a matter of months) encourages the impression that all anyone has to do is put down their money and wait by the mailbox. Unscrupulous promoters like to tout new items like Internet stocks and biotechnology startups, but any product will do. Even in this wired age, commodities futures—from soybeans to pork bellies—are still numbered among the most common bait for Ponzi schemes.

Financial instruments are especially effective fronts because most people don't understand how legitimate financial operations take place. When Wall Street is set a-fluttering by *derivatives* of futures contracts, and hedge funds are betting that the market will rise at the same time they're betting it'll fall, how's an average investor with $20,000 supposed to understand his options?

MULTILEVEL MARKETING

When most people hear about a pyramid scheme, they think multilevel marketing, or MLM as it's often abbreviated. These organizations hawk nutrition supplements, household goods, cosmetics, television antennas, insurance, long distance phone service, everything from antiques to Zinc. Also among the offerings—*How to Make a Million Dollars in a MLM*. One of the industry's monster money makers is a string of "training materials" designed to pump the sales force into ever higher feats of hucksterhip.

Math remains the great enemy, as well as the prime tool, of MLMs. Promoters scratch *matrices* (never pyramids) on a chalkboard, and compute what 20 people mailing money to a distributor's house every month would amount to in a year's time. These shillers ignore other aspects of the equation. First, the market for any product outside those owned by large national brands is extremely small. Cashing in on a submarket requires an excess of savvy, finance, and luck, which most MLMers lack in spades. Then there's pyramidal mathematics—after a couple of levels, you run out of people willing to hear your spiel (which was already less than 5 percent of any area's population). In fact, between 90 and 95 percent of MLM operations fail in their first two years (compared to a 70-80 percent failure rate for small businesses in general).

As a rule of thumb, any organization which recruits distributors into a pyramid-style compensation plan, offers big payoffs for recruiting (say, more than $100 per recruit), and spends more time trumpeting its distributor levels than its product lines, is probably illegal.

SPECULATIONS

For the purpose of this course, the term *speculations* describes any investment proposition not covered as financial instruments or MLMs. This includes franchise offerings and business opportunities in general, work-at-home promotions, and investments in areas like real estate or mineral rights. These are good old-fashioned investments, except when they're Ponzi schemes.

Franchise scams hawk such opportunities as pay-phone businesses or vending machines. By their nature, such businesses are spread out geographically and don't involve much direct contact with the promoter and the franchise holder.

Work-at-home promotions are also favorite tools of the franchise scammer. Computer technology is a popular front, since thousands of people really are setting up businesses from their homes. ("Amazon.com doesn't need giant stores and mondo corporate offices, and neither do you!") A few early dividend checks, per the Ponzi playbook, are often enough to overcome a client's hesitation and provoke a more sizeable investment. Then the promoters can fold up and move to another state, or another coast.

Big-money speculations often base their high-flown claims in the ground beneath our feet. Land, and the minerals drawn from it like gold and coal and oil, has anciently been regarded as the ultimate commodity. The ground is literally the fundament of every human endeavor. Perhaps the land swindle is also the fundament of fraud. Someone somewhere, it seems, has always been selling flooded lots to homesteaders, salting gold mines with chunks of pyrite, or assuring a rich merchant the new aqueduct will cut across the thousand acres of desert he just bought for a song.

Obviously, a commercial environment that thrives on speculation is ripe for Ponzi fraud. Remember, the Ponzi element in a Ponzi scheme is only a technique—giving back a few dollars to sweeten the pot. Anything that can coax people to part with their money, from emu farms to underwater land developments, can be run as a Ponzi. All the name Ponzi really means is that a few marks get paid. This lends a competitive element to an otherwise run-of-the-mill fraud. Instead of everyone losing, some lucky players do make money.

Speculations frauds don't always start out as cons, but when their rollercoaster dips, many speculators find it too tempting to hang on and ride—they figure they can phony their way through the crisis, and pick up again later. Again, it's math that usually dooms these players. They simply can't make money fast enough to feed the deficits. They need a payoff so big nothing short of a miracle—or more fraud—will suffice.

Speculators can quickly get caught in a chain reaction, where each fraud demands more fraud. By the time these organizations are shut down, they're spending half of their resources or more just covering up their criminal acts.

Spotting Pyramid Schemes

Almost everyone knows what a pyramid scheme is. People see them exposed on television and read about them constantly in magazines and newspapers. So, if everyone is so well informed about the pyramid, how does it survive?

It could be that familiarity has lulled the public into a false sense of security. Pyramiders have several strong weapons at their disposal:

- They do pay off. Unlike a simple con game—which throws the ruse, grabs the cash, and exits—pyramiding builds up the take by paying initial investors. This makes for excellent testimonials. Early players circulate the word and bring in new marks. Initial payoffs also keep early players coming back. Payoffs make the enterprise look legitimate, and fuel the expansion process. Charles Phillip Elliot ran his investment business pyramid-style for 16 years, taking in more than $60 million from 1,100 investors. When Elliot was busted, a business associate quipped, "Elliot paid like a slot machine. He lulled everyone to sleep."[*]
- They operate mainly through preexisting affiliations. Community groups, religious organizations, and social clubs all make enticing targets for pyramiders. Any pyramid

---

[*] Holzman, Todd. *Business Dateline.* October 1987. Pages 16ff.

requires a healthy pool of participants, so a large group already gathered together is ideal. Besides that, pyramiders know how to manipulate the trust which people place in these groups.
- They use ingenuity and false logic in their pitches. The product fronts available for pyramiding are myriad, from bath soap to electronics. Fronts in financial instruments and real estate are especially effective because most people don't understand how those businesses work anyway. Pure cash games find clever metaphors—like a conceptual airplane, or a business executives' hierarchy—to make themselves attractive.

Pyramiders of every stripe use a seductive, though false, logic in their pitch: "Everybody has friends and associates; you only have to sign up three or four people below you." Of course the laws of mathematics spell doom to this logic. There simply aren't enough players to keep even a small pyramid running. Three people, each finding three people, will quickly play out their available friends and associates—if not mathematically, then socially. There's also a reasonable limit on how quickly money can grow.

The pyramid, then, is built to overcome people's most common misgivings about investment. Promoters offer far more than an "undertaking of great advantage, nobody to know what it is." They are very specific in their prospectus. The offer sounds good and (within its own logic) makes sense. The "opportunity" is usually pitched by someone familiar to the victim, or at least by someone with an affinity the victim trusts. Most importantly, the pyramid does return people's money, with the incredible profits attached as promised.

Speed is another potent weapon in the pyramid arsenal. Cons say, "Get in now, or regret it forever." They don't have time—because of market demand, or commitments elsewhere—for the person to check out the deal. That's because a moderate amount of due diligence research will expose the deal as a scheme.

The final factor is greed. A recent poll quoted in Charles Whitlock's Easy Money, revealed that when people received telephone calls from a bogus investment company, one in twenty took the bait. The victims had no prior contact with the salesperson or the company, but still, five percent of them bought. But there was a catch. The poll also reported that, considering all those stung by a telephone fraud, only two percent of those calling themselves trusting, and just two percent of those who called themselves open-minded, had been the victims of fraud. Simply put, persons with healthy lives, strong family ties, and an honest work ethic are not as likely to get burned as people who are lonely, desperate, and out to make a quick buck. Of course, as our examples have shown, the range of people caught in pyramid schemes has no bounds. Plenty of victims are experienced, careful professionals who have either let down their guard or become ensnared by the cleverest of shams.

Franchise Fraud*

Franchising is part of the American Dream. A gateway to business ownership for millions of Americans, franchising is estimated to account for more than 40 percent of all retail sales in the United States—a percentage that is expected to reach 50 percent in a few short years according to a report issued by the House Committee on Small Business. But the dream of business ownership can be easily shattered by fraud.

Franchise Regulation

In 1978, the U.S. Federal Trade Commission (FTC) entered the realm of franchise regulation by enacting "Disclosure Requirements and Prohibitions Concerning Franchising And Business Opportunity Ventures"—the "FTC Rule" (16 C.F.R. Part 436). As stated by the FTC, "the Rule is designed to enable potential franchisees to protect themselves before investing by providing them with information essential to an assessment of the potential risks and benefits, to meaningful comparisons with other investments, and to further investigation of the franchise opportunity." As this mission statement suggests, the FTC rule addresses the *disclosures* made by franchisers to potential franchisees, as opposed to ongoing issues in the *relationship* between franchisers and franchisees and other issues that arise in the *termination* of franchise relationships.

But the 1978 enactment of the FTC rule did not lead to the eradication of fraud claims in franchising relationships—among the rule's deficiencies, it does not create a private civil action. Many state legislatures have enacted laws that supplement the FTC Rule. Illinois is a good example of a progressive state in franchisee law.

The FTC Franchise Rule

The FTC Franchise Rule prohibits fraud in the initial sale of a franchise in which the franchise affects interstate commerce. Franchisors must furnish potential franchisees with written disclosures providing important information about the franchisor, the franchised

---

* The Editors wish to thank Carmen D. Caruso, J.D., for his assistance in preparing this section. Mr. Caruso is a Chicago attorney who specializes in franchise fraud litigation. More information about franchise law can be found at his website: www.cdcaruso.com.

business and the franchise relationship, and give them at least ten business days to review it before investing.

Franchisors may make the required disclosures by following either the Rule's disclosure format or the Uniform Franchise Offering Circular Guidelines prepared by state franchise law officials.

The Rule imposes six different requirements in connection with the "advertising, offering, licensing, contracting, sale, or other promotion" of a franchise in or affecting commerce:

- The Rule requires franchisors to give potential investors a basic disclosure document at the earlier of the first face-to-face meeting or ten business days before any money is paid or an agreement is signed in connection with the investment.
- If a franchisor makes earnings claims, whether historical or forecasted, they must have a reasonable basis, and prescribed substantiating disclosures must be given to a potential investor in writing at the same time as the basic disclosures.
- The Rule affects only ads that include an earnings claim. Such ads must disclose the number and percentage of existing franchisees who have achieved the claimed results, along with cautionary language. Their use triggers required compliance with the Rule's earnings claim disclosure requirements.
- The franchisor must give investors a copy of its standard-form franchise and related agreements at the same time as the basic disclosures, and final copies intended to be executed at least 5 business days before signing.
- The Rule requires franchisors to make refunds of deposits and initial payments to potential investors, subject to any conditions on refundability stated in the disclosure document.

While franchisors are free to provide investors with any promotional or other materials they wish, no written or oral claims may contradict information provided in the required disclosure document.

The FTC alone has jurisdiction to enforce the rule. However, any misrepresentations in a UFOC certainly could be used to support claims for fraud under state statutory and/or common law. The FTC rule preempts inconsistent state laws. As a practical matter, it creates a minimum disclosure standard, which many states have equaled or enhanced by statute.

State Laws

Fifteen states have enacted franchise disclosure laws that create a cause of action for failure to register a franchise with the designated state agency and/or failure to provide the franchiser's UFOC to the prospective franchisee in a timely manner. Those states are California, Hawaii, Illinois, Indiana, Maryland, Michigan, Minnesota, New York, North Dakota, Oregon, Rhode Island, South Dakota, Virginia, Washington, and Wisconsin.

The state statutes provide damages or rescission as the remedies available to the successful franchisee. These state laws give franchise purchasers important legal rights, including the right to bring private lawsuits for violations of the state disclosure requirements.

Other Remedies

COMMON LAW FRAUD

The failure of the FTC to outlaw fraud in franchising specifically beyond the disclosure phase does not leave a defrauded franchisee without remedies. Common law fraud is applicable, which requires proof of a knowing or recklessly false representation or omission of material fact, reliance, and injury. However, claims of fraud in the inducement (disclosure fraud) are often defeated by carefully drafted language in the franchise agreement.

RICO

The Racketeer Influenced and Corrupt Organizations Act (RICO), 18, U.S.C., § 1961 *et seq.*, is the most powerful anti-fraud statute available to civil litigants because it provides for automatic trebling (tripling) of damages plus attorneys' fees and costs—and RICO is highly relevant to franchising. There have been several cases where class action plaintiffs have established RICO claims based on the ongoing, system-wide fraud that had occurred concerning the advertising funds.

Overview of Franchising

Under the FTC rule, as well as the statutory and/or common law of all or almost all of the states, there are three prerequisites to apply the rule to a business format or product franchise:

Trademark

The franchiser offers the right to distribute goods or services that bear the franchiser's trademark, service mark, trade name, advertising, or other commercial symbol.

Significant Control or Assistance
The franchiser exercises significant control over, and/or offers substantial assistance to the franchisee in the operation of the franchised business.

Required Payment
The franchisee is required to pay the franchiser. These payments usually include initial franchise fees and ongoing royalties that are calculated as a percentage of sales, net of sales tax. Another typical fee is a transfer fee that is applicable on the sale of a franchise.

Fraud in franchising may occur at each stage of the franchise relationship, creating disclosure, relationship, and termination issues.

Disclosure Issues
"Disclosure issues" arise when the franchiser fails to communicate material information or discloses false information to induce the franchisee to purchase a franchise that he would not have otherwise purchased. Two prime examples of potentially misleading information are *earnings claims* and *success rates*.

Earnings Claims
Assume that a prospective franchisee relies upon *earnings claims* published by the franchiser as a key factor in his decision to buy the franchise, but those earnings claims are materially misleading, or even blatantly false. This is a prime example of disclosure fraud in connection with the franchiser's inducement of potential franchisees to buy the franchise.

Disclosure fraud historically has been the primary target of franchiser regulations. The FTC reported that from 1989 to 1992, 100 percent of its franchise enforcement cases were based on allegations that the franchiser had provided fraudulent or misleading earnings claims. But surprisingly, the FTC does not require franchisers to disclose earnings. The FTC rule provides for the disclosure of earnings claims regarding actual or potential sales. Income, costs, or profits — of either existing or prospective franchisees — is optional. But if a franchiser elects to make earnings claims, it must have a "reasonable" basis for those claims.

Absent published earnings claims, the prospective franchisee is vulnerable to non-written, boastful earnings claims made by franchise salespeople who make their living selling franchises instead of selling the underlying goods or services. Those non-written claims may turn out to be false but the franchiser may try to protect itself by including in the written franchise agreement a "no reliance" or "integration" clause that states in effect:

> *Franchisee acknowledges that this Agreement is the entire agreement of the parties, and that in entering into this Agreement, he or she is not relying upon any statements or representations that may have been made on or before the date of this Agreement, which are not expressly made a part of this Agreement.*

Clauses similar to this one often have been used to defeat claims of fraud submitted by franchisees who were induced to sign a contract based upon the franchiser's verbal representations.

Success Rates

Another important disclosure issue is a franchiser's claim that "X" percent (usually a high percentage) of its stores have been successful; in other words, they have remained in continuous operation from opening day to the present. But the franchise salesperson may not have told the franchisee that a number of stores were sold many times and in each sale the old franchisee sold the store back to the franchiser who re-sold it to a new franchisee. Would that additional information be material to the prospective franchisee? Would failure to disclose that information amount to fraud?

The FTC rule does not require franchisers to disclose re-sales or turnovers from one franchisee to the next.

Relationship Issues

Fraud in franchising is not limited to disclosure fraud. Once the franchising relationship is established, the franchiser and franchisee stand in a business relationship that typically involves the transaction of funds at several levels under a series of contracts:

- The payment of royalties under the franchise or license agreement for the right to use the franchiser's trademark, trade name, and business system.
- The payment of rent under a lease or sub-lease of real property and/or equipment.
- Contributions to an advertising fund.

All of these financial transactions may be subject to claims for breach of contract, fraud, or breach of a fiduciary duty. Of course, to determine the exact claims, you must consult the exact language in the franchise agreement.

Numerous issues also may arise in the course of the franchise relationship, each of which reflects an inherent tension between the interests of franchiser and franchisee:

- *Training and Support.* Has the franchiser provided the level of training and technical support that was promised?
- *Control.* What degree of control is the franchiser entitled to exercise over the franchisee's products, suppliers, and pricing? To what extent may the franchiser derive profit from the franchisee's supplier relationships?
- *New Products.* To what extent does the franchiser have a duty to introduce new products to keep ahead of the competition? Once the decision to introduce new products is made, is the franchiser held to any "standard of care" to ensure that the product is successful?
- *Expansion or Contraction of the System.* Does the franchiser's natural desire to expand the franchise system conflict with a franchisee's desire to maximize profits at his location? Conversely, what duties, if any, does a franchiser owe to franchisees in a particular market if the franchiser plans to withdraw from that market?
- *Encroachment.* To what extent does the franchiser have a duty to refrain from opening new outlets "too close" to existing units? How close is "too close" if the license agreement is silent?
- *Expansion by the Franchisee.* To what extent is an individual franchisee's desire to expand in conflict with what is best for the system as a whole?
- *Reinvestment.* May a franchiser require a franchisee to reinvest a portion of his revenue back into the business? Does it depend on whether the franchisee owns or leases the real estate?

Termination Issues

The end of a franchise relationship also may provide grounds for litigation:

- *Renewal.* Does a franchiser have a duty to renew a franchisee beyond the initial term of his license agreement?
- *Early Termination.* Under what circumstances may a franchiser terminate a franchise before the expiration of his contractual term?
- *Sale of a Franchise.* Under what circumstances may a franchiser veto a franchisee's proposed sale of his franchise to a third-party?
- *Post-Termination Restrictions on Competition.* To what extent may the franchiser restrict the franchisee's right to compete after termination? Even if a franchisee is allowed to compete after the franchise relationship is ended, the franchiser may sometimes validly demand that the franchisee leave his business telephone number to the franchiser as it departs the system.

Identity Theft

Identity theft is an increasingly frequent type of fraud that is non-discriminatory in nature. Anyone can be targeted; the victim might be a college student, a retiree, a schoolteacher, or a successful attorney. Even corporations are susceptible to identity theft. So quickly has this fraud scheme multiplied, that an estimated 27.3 million Americans have been victims of identity theft in the last five years, including 9.9 million people in 2003 alone. According to a survey conducted by the Federal Trade Commission, the 2003 identity theft losses to businesses and financial institutions totaled nearly $48 billion and consumer victims reported $5 billion in out-of-pocket expenses.

The survey reports that 52 percent of all identity theft victims, approximately 5 million people in 2003, discovered that they had been victimized by monitoring their accounts. Another 26 percent reported that they were alerted to suspicious account activity by companies such as credit card issuers or banks. Eight percent of all identity theft victims reported that they first discovered they were victims of identity theft when they applied for credit and were turned down.

Fifty-one percent of all identity theft victims say they know how their personal information was obtained. Nearly one-quarter of all victims said their information was lost or stolen, including lost or stolen credit cards, checkbooks, or Social Security cards. Stolen mail was the souce of information for identity thieves in 4 percent of all victims.

Repairing a credit record is where the victim's nightmare begins. It often takes victims years to clear their credit. It has been estimated that Americans spent almost 300 million hours resolving problems related to identity theft in 2003.

EXAMPLE

A California woman didn't have a clue that she had been a victim of identify theft until a bank in Delaware called and asked her why she hadn't paid on her $11,000 credit card balance. Not only did she not have a credit card from this bank, but she also had not been in a car wreck in a rental car for which she was receiving threatening letters from the rental agency for the damage done to the car. Perhaps the most troubling aspect of having her identity stolen was the felony record that she received because of the imposter being arrested. As a result, she has to carry around a police report in her wallet to prove that she isn't a felon.

Although there is no universal definition of identity theft, the Department of Justice offers the following definition:

> *Identity theft and fraud are crimes in which someone wrongfully obtains and uses another person's personal data in some way that involves fraud or deception, typically for economic gain.*

Personal identification data includes name, address, Social Security number, date of birth, mother's maiden name, or other identifying information. The perpetrator exploits this information by opening bank or credit card accounts, taking over existing accounts, obtaining loans, leasing cars or apartments, or applying for wireless telephone and utilities services in the victim's name without his or her knowledge.

Technological advancements that facilitate the electronic transfer of personal information and the transmission of financial transactions have greatly contributed to the recent increase in occurances of identity theft. As such technologies continue to develop, this type of fraud will likely remain a serious problem that affects many people.

The Profile
Unlike some fraudsters who steal as the result of a perceived need, most identity thieves make a living stealing identities for profit or at the very least, to supplement their incomes generously. Although it can be an employee, friend, or relative, generally the fraudster usually falls into one or more profiles:
- Been convicted, served time in prison, wishes to conceal his or her identity
- Been convicted, served time in prison and looking for a "safer" way to commit a crime and stay out of prison
- College student looking for an "easy" way to work his or her way through school
- Landlord
- Rental car agents
- Illegal aliens needing an identity
- Illegal telemarketers

Common Ways of Obtaining Information
While you might think that you are careful with your personal information, in reality, a lot of information can be easily found and acquired by identity thieves without you even realizing it. An innocent inquiry for the most basic of information, such as verifying an address or

mother's maiden name for a banker's files, can be the start of a financial nightmare. The most common ways information is obtained are:

- Sorting through discarded trash
- Shoulder surfing
- Rifling through co-worker's desk drawers
- Theft of mail — incoming or outgoing
- Using an accomplice within the organization
- Soliciting identifiers through false job application schemes
- Telephone companies, health clubs, and schools
- Certifications and licenses placed on workplace walls
- Using pretext, ruse, or gag calls
- Rental and loan applications
- Public records
- The Internet

Sorting Through Discarded Trash

Most people do not destroy their personal financial data; they simply throw it away with the rest of their trash for pick-up by the garbage collectors on their regularly scheduled day. Solicitations for pre-approved credit cards are some of the most valuable pieces of trash that an identity thief can steal. Additionally, "dumpster diving" as it is more popularly known as, can yield checks, credit card and bank statements or other records which bear your name, address and telephone number. In addition to targeting an individual's trash, dumpster divers target the trash at banks, insurance companies, hospitals, and other businesses — locations that an individual has no control over.

Shoulder Surfing

Shoulder surfing is another popular way that the identity thief obtains information. The person watches from a nearby location and listens to someone's telephone conversation or watches the numbers being punched for a calling card or credit card, thus obtaining enough information to use or procure a credit card. Identity theives also watch potential victims as they fill out bank deposit slips thus getting account information.

Rifling Through Co-Worker's Desk Drawers

When people leave for break, go to lunch, or take vacation or sick leave, many if not most, do not lock up their desks or offices. Many people also leave personal items in their desk drawers, such as bank statements, monthly credit card statements, mortgage coupon books, all of which have useful information for an identity thief.

Theft of Mail — Incoming or Outgoing

Theft of mail in either direction provides useful information to the fraudster. Outgoing checks left for the mail carrier to pick up provide bank account numbers and other information which can be used for illegal purposes.

EXAMPLE

Using just a driver's license number and bank account number, a thief was able to withdraw more than $30,000 from a security guard's checking account. In this case, the thief used the drive-through at the security guard's bank to deposit a series of stolen money orders and simultaneously make large withdrawals.

Using an Accomplice within the Organization

Sometimes the identity thief is able to compromise someone within an organization and obtain enough information where credit can be obtained. It may be a bank employee who has access to Social Security numbers and bank balances or an insurance clerk who has access to personal information such as name, address, Social Security numbers, and medical information — all useful when assuming someone's identity.

Soliciting Identifiers through False Job Application Schemes

Filling out a job application might also be the source of information to identity thieves. People believe that they are filling out a job application, when in reality they are only supplying personal information to a thief.

Utility Companies, Health Clubs, and Schools

Utility companies, health clubs, and schools all carry identifiers that a fraudster can make use of. Once again, the Social Security number is used on many applications and is a key to obtaining other information.

EXAMPLE

A California woman used a stolen Social Security number to obtain thousands of dollars in credit and then filed for bankruptcy in the name of her victim. She was sentenced to 16 months in federal prison. In addition to the prison term, she was ordered to pay restitution in the amount of $13,928 and pay a $5,000 criminal fine.

She admitted that she assumed the identity of another woman with a similar name in order to obtain loans that she was not qualified to receive. The FBI began investigating the case after it was contacted by the victim, an English professor at a university in Georgia. The professor had graduated from a college in Arizona that the defendant also briefly attended, and both women had received student loans that were administered through the same company.

Due to a computer mix-up, documents belonging to the professor — which included her Social Security number — were sent to the defendant. Shortly thereafter, the professor began receiving telephone calls from companies that she had never heard of claiming she owed them large sums of money.

Certifications, Diplomas, Licenses Placed On Workplace Walls

Something as innocent as a diploma, professional certification, or license can be the identifying information that a fraudster uses to obtain a false identity. In the case of a professional license, some states require that it be displayed in a prominent place. Consequently, information such as the name, address, and license number is readily available to the thief.

Using Pretext, Ruse, or Gag Calls

Using pretext, ruse, or gag calls claiming to be a person to whom personal information would normally be released is common in an identity theft. Since there is no way to verify the person on the end of a phone line with photo identification, having only a small amount of information can yield the additional data the fraudster seeks.

Rental and Loan Applications

Almost without exception, rental and loan applications yield enough information that can be used to establish a false identity. An applicant's name, Social Security number, previous address(es), employment history, telephone numbers, and credit history are required to complete the application. Once the thief gets a hold of that information, it is usually quite easy to establish an identity.

Public Records

Public records yield a wealth of personal data for the identity thief. Real estate records, tax liens, licenses, litigation records, and, in some states, drivers license numbers, all reveal enough information that can be used to steal a person's identity or least provide a start for the fraudster.

The Internet

The Internet offers many opportunities to the identity thief. It has made much information available to more people at a small cost. It has also been an attractive place for identity thieves to find their victim. Once you have logged on, information you thought was private might now be traced by anyone who is interested in finding personal information about you. Identifying information such as passwords, credit card numbers, and in some cases, banking information has been made available via the Internet. Spam, or unsolicited e-mail, is frequently responded to by many people who are unaware that the sole purpose of the email is to obtain personal information.

> EXAMPLE
> *A midwestern woman was accused of trying to get a $25,000 loan through an Illinois bank using personal information she found on the Internet. The victim, a college professor, called police when the bank sent the completed application to her home rather than to the home of the accused. The same woman reportedly obtained a MasterCard under another professor's name and ran up almost $3,000 in charges.*

In addition, some database companies sell information — your personal information — online to persons or organizations that you might not want to have that information, thus increasing the chance for fraud and abuse. For example, information you provide by responding to a questionnaire online might be collected and sold to insurance and drug companies without your knowledge. The same can be true when applying for a low-interest credit card or consumer loans. Do you know who is actually receiving the information that you provide online? There is no physical address to check out in most cases.

The Internet also is a source for "information brokering." For a fee, information brokers will reveal the most personal aspects of your life — from financial information to medical information. For fees as low as $40 per search, they will disclose everything from non-published telephone numbers to the location of your safety deposit box. Some of it is legal and can be found in public records, but some of it is illegal.

Tracking Down the Thief

There are many ways that the fraud examiner can track down an identity thief. Some require the assistance of law enforcement, while others do not. Examples of techniques that have been successfully used to catch an identity thief are:

- Establish surveillance of the address in question.
- Have overnight delivery services "flag" the address in question.
- Subpoena telephone records for the telephone(s) being used by the perpetrator.
- Contact credit bureaus and have them "flag" the true account holder's file.
- Contact the Social Security Administration to determine if the number is listed twice in the system.
- Obtain videos from retailers showing the perpetrator making purchases using the victim's identity.
- Obtain a copy of the perpetrator's picture on the fictitious driver's license.
- Track down addresses and telephone numbers that do not belong to the victim but show up in their file.
- Have the victim notify the fraud examiner when further breaches occur.
- Report the fraud to law enforcement.

Confronting the Fraudster

If the fraudster has been identified and is to be confronted, the fraud examiner should keep the following in mind:

- On initial contact, call the fraudster by the wrong name; generally he or she will then produce identification in the name of the victim.
- Try to establish the fraudster's true identity.
- For safety reasons, use caution when confronting the thief; never forget that the fraudster could be a convicted felon who does not want to go back to prison.

Federal Statutes

Identity Theft and Assumption Deterrence Act

In October 1998, Congress passed the Identity Theft and Assumption Deterrence Act (Identity Theft Act) to address the problem of identity theft. Specifically, the Act amended 18, U.S.C., § 1028 to make it a federal crime when anyone:

> *Knowingly transfers or uses, without lawful authority, a means of identification of another person with the intent to commit, or to aid or abet, any unlawful activity that constitutes a violation of Federal law, or that constitutes a felony under any applicable state or local law.*

It carries a maximum term of 15 years imprisonment, a fine, and criminal forfeiture of any personal property used or intended to be used to commit the offense. Identity theft schemes may also involve other violations such as mail fraud, wire fraud, credit card fraud, or financial institution fraud.

Violations of the Act are investigated by federal investigative agencies such as the U.S. Secret Service, the FBI, and the U.S. Postal Inspection Service and are prosecuted by the Department of Justice.

See the chapter on "The Law Related to Fraud" in the Legal Section for more information about the Identity Theft Act.

EXAMPLE

A Wisconson man was sentenced to 21 months imprisonment and three years supervised release after pleading guilty to identity theft. The defendant was also ordered to pay restitution totaling $62,850.

The perpetrator pled guilty to using another man's identity to obtain employment with a cleaning company, then using that employment to commit a burglary.

Through his job at the cleaning company, the fraudster gained access to the offices of the Wisconsin Supreme Court where he took six computer monitors owned by the State of Wisconsin. The monitors were recovered almost immediately following the burglary after the thief abandoned the vehicle that he was driving.

Gramm-Leach-Bliley Act

The Gramm-Leach-Bliley Act of 1999 includes a provision that prohibits "pretexting". This statute makes it illegal for anyone to obtain customer information from financial institutions by impersonating someone else or making false, fictitious, or fraudulent statements. It also prohibits soliciting someone else to engage in pretexting. Violations of this provision can result in a fine, imprisonment of up to 5 years, or both.

More information about other provisions of the Gramm-Leach-Bliley Act can be found in the "Sources of Information" chapter of the Investigation Section of the Manual.

State Laws

States have also passed laws related to identity theft. Below is a list of states that have passed such laws. Other states may be considering legislation in their next legislative session. In addition, where specific laws on identity theft have not been passed, there may be remedies under other state laws.

State	Statute
Alabama	Alabama Code § 13A-8-190 through 201
Alaska	Alaska Stat. § 11.46.565
Arizona	Ariz. Rev. Stat. § 13-2008
Arkansas	Ark. Code Ann. § 5-37-227
California	Cal. Penal Code § 530.5-8
Connecticut	Conn. Stat. § 53a-129a (criminal)
	Conn. Stat. § 52-571h (civil)
Delaware	Del. Code Ann. tit. II, § 854
Florida	Fla. Stat. Ann. § 817.568
Georgia	Ga. Code Ann. § 16-9-120, through 128
Hawaii	HI Rev. Stat. § 708-839.6-8
Idaho	Idaho Code § 18-3126 (criminal)
Illinois	720 Ill. Comp. Stat. 5/16 G
Indiana	Ind. Code § 35-43-5-3.5
Iowa	Iowa Code § 715A.8 (criminal)
	Iowa Code § 714.16.B (civil)
Kansas	Kan. Stat. Ann. § 21-4018
Kentucky	Ky. Rev. Stat. Ann. § 514.160
Louisiana	La. Rev. Stat. Ann. § 14:67.16
Maine	ME. Rev. Stat. Ann. tit. 17-A § 905-A
Maryland	Md. Code Ann. art. 27 § 231
Massachusetts	Mass. Gen. Laws ch. 266, § 37E
Michigan	Mich. Comp. Laws § 750.285
Minnesota	Minn. Stat. Ann. § 609.527
Mississippi	Miss. Code Ann. § 97-19-85
Missouri	Mo. Rev. Stat. § 570.223
Montana	Mon. Code Ann. § 45-6-332
Nebraska	NE Rev. Stat. § 28-608 & 620
Nevada	Nev. Rev. Stat. § 205.463-465
New Hampshire	N.H. Rev. Stat. Ann. § 638:26

New Jersey	N.J. Stat. Ann. § 2C:21-17
New Mexico	N.M. Stat. Ann. § 30-16-24.1
New York	NY CLS Penal § 190.77-190.84
North Carolina	N.C. Gen. Stat. § 14-113.20-23
North Dakota	N.D.C.C. § 12.1-23-11
Ohio	Ohio Rev. Code Ann. 2913.49
Oklahoma	Okla. Stat. tit. 21, § 1533.1
Oregon	Or. Rev. Stat. § 165.800
Pennsylvania	18 Pa. Cons. Stat. § 4120
Rhode Island	R.I. Gen. Laws § 11-49.1-1
South Carolina	S.C. Code Ann. § 16-13-500, 501
South Dakota	S.D. Codified Laws § 22-30A-3.1
Tennessee	TCA § 39-14-150 (criminal)
	TCA § 47-18-2101 (civil)
Texas	Tex. Penal Code § 32.51
Utah	Utah Code Ann. § 76-6-1101-1104
Virginia	Va. Code Ann. § 18.2-186.3
Washington	Wash. Rev. Code § 9.35.020
West Virginia	W. Va. Code § 61-3-54
Wisconsin	Wis. Stat. § 943.201
Wyoming	Wyo. Stat. Ann. § 6-3-901

Source: http://www.consumer.gov/idtheft/federallaws.html

Preventing False Identity Fraud

How do you protect yourself and your clients from identity theft? Some of the useful methods are:

- Before providing personal information, make sure the individual or business requesting it has a valid reason for requiring the information.
- Never write your credit card numbers or Social Security number on checks or on the outside of envelopes.
- Don't give account numbers over the telephone or to persons/companies you are not familiar with.
- Don't use cordless or cellular telephones or email to transmit financial or private personal information.
- Keep all financial documents in a secure place.

- If you have your drivers license information pre-printed on your checks, shred canceled checks before discarding them.
- Check your financial information regularly looking for what should and shouldn't be there.
- Obtain a copy of your credit report on a regular basis.
- Tear up or shred pre-approved credit applications.
- Have yourself taken off of "pre-screened lists."
- Mail bills from the post office or your business location
- Consider having your name and telephone number removed from the telephone directory or having the address removed.
- Don't provide personal information over the telephone unless you initiated the call and know who you are speaking with.
- If telemarketing companies call, tell them: "Under the federal Telephone Consumer Protection Act, I want to be on your 'do not call' list."
- Keep your birth certificate in a safe place.
- Place a fraud alert on your credit bureau lists.
- Close all unused credit card accounts.
- Choose passwords that will be difficult to crack and use different passwords for all accounts.
- Change passwords and PIN codes often.
- Don't put your Social Security number on any document that you aren't legally required to.
- Shred any papers with financial information and identifiers rather than simply throwing them in the trash.

In addition, insurance companies are now offering insurance for identity theft. For an annual fee, the policy covers the cost of clearing the policyholder's name and correcting their financial records including legal expenses, loan re-application fees, telephone and certified mailing charges, notary expenses, and lost wages for the time it takes to deal with the fraud.

What to Do If Your Identity Is Stolen
- Start keeping detailed records.
- Close all accounts that are affected by the fraudulent activity.
- Notify all creditors on your credit report.
- Check for and repair further breaches of your identity.
- Notify law enforcement agencies:

- Federal Trade Commission
- Federal Bureau of Investigation
- United States Secret Service
- Local and state agencies
- Notify the fraud units of the three principal reporting companies:
  - Equifax (800) 525-6285 or (888) 766-0008
  - Experian (formerly TRW) (888) 397-3742
  - Trans Union (800) 680-7289

COMPUTER AND INTERNET FRAUD

Over the last four decades, computer systems have improved dramatically. They are more powerful, smaller, cheaper, and more user-friendly. As they have advanced, computers have proliferated in our society, our businesses, and our personal lives. Most modern businesses and governments depend on their computer systems to support their operations, from personnel to financial management and everything in between.

Initially, computers used to support business and government processes were backed up with hard copies. If the computer went down, the hard copies were used and everyone went back to manual forms and processes. However in today's environment, most businesses and government processes could not survive without the computer—there are few hard copy backups.

Computers have become the mainstay of business and government processes. Without today's computers, entire businesses and government operations would almost cease to function. Imagine trying to manually process tax returns, use robotics, compile budgets, build automobiles, build weapons systems, check law enforcement files, or get cash from automated teller machines (ATM) without the aid of computers.

The proliferation of cheap, powerful, user-friendly computers has enabled more and more people to use them and more importantly, rely on them as part of their normal way of life. As businesses, government agencies, and individuals come to increasingly depend on computers as a necessary tool, so do the criminals. They use computers to support their illegal operations. Computer crimes and frauds are increasing and will no doubt continue to increase as more computers are networked internationally, thus giving global access to computer criminals.

The *2004 Computer Crime and Security Survey*, conducted by the Computer Security Institute in conjunction with the U.S. Federal Bureau of Investigation's International Computer Crime Squad, showed an alarmingly high number of businesses reporting difficulties with computer and Internet fraud. Among the findings:
- Of the organizations who acknowledged financial losses due to computer breaches, only 54% could quantify the losses.
- 53% of the respondents experienced incidents of unauthorized use of their computer systems during the last year.

- 66% reported incidents that originated from sources within the organization.
- 70% reported penetration from the outside.
- 17% reported denial of service attacks.
- 59% reported abuse of Internet privilieges by their employees.
- 49% reported theft of laptop computers and mobile devices.
- 78% detected computer viruses.
- 20% of the responding organizations had reported serious incidents to law enforcements in the past year; 48% did not report the incident at all.

In the area of e-commerce:
- All of the respondents experienced some sort of website incidents:
  - 89% of those acknowledging attacks reported one to five incidents.
  - 6% of those acknowledging attacks reported six to ten incidents.
  - 5% of those acknowledging attacks reported ten or more security breaches on their websites over the past year.
- 10% said they had experienced theft of proprietary information.
- 7% reported website defacement.
- 5% were victims of financial fraud.
- Losses due to computer security breaches totaled over $141 million in 2004, a figure that is down 30% from the over $201 million reported in 2003.

Unlike traditional fraud cases, computer fraud can be difficult for the fraud examiner because they:
- Lack a traditional paper audit trail.
- Require an understanding of the technology used to commit the crime.
- Usually require an understanding of the technology of the victim computer.
- Very often require the use of one or more specialists to assist the fraud examiner, even when the fraud examiner is computer literate.

Before exploring the specifics of high tech crime however, let us clarify the computer's function in the commission of these schemes. Computer crime is most often thought of as a crime that is committed with the aid of a computer. Yet the computer has various roles in high tech crime, both as tool and target. According to Donn B. Parker, a cybercrime authority and author, the function of the computer in crime is fourfold. In *Fighting Computer Crime*, Mr. Parker describes how the computer serves as an object, a subject, a tool, and a symbol.

- *Computer as an Object*—Computers and network systems are themselves often objects or targets of crime, subject to physical sabotage, theft, or destruction of information.
- *Computer as a Subject*—According to Parker, computers are the direct subjects of crime "when they are the environment in which technologists commit crimes." This category includes virus attacks.
- *Computer as a Tool*—Obviously, computers are used as the means to commit crime, whether embezzlement, theft of proprietary information, or hacking.
- *Computer as a Symbol*—Computers lend fraudsters an air of credibility and are often used to deceive victims into investment and pyramid schemes.

In these four capacities, common computer crimes include:
- Data alteration
- Unauthorized access and entry to systems and information
- Reading another's e-mail without permission
- Data destruction and sabotage
- Internet consumer fraud
- Sale of proprietary data
- Desktop counterfeiting
- Data extortion
- Disclosure of confidential data
- Identity theft
- Electronic letter bombing
- Software piracy
- PBX fraud
- Voice mail fraud
- Cellular telephone fraud
- Stolen long-distance calling cards

Computer Fraud vs. Computer Crime

A line that should be drawn is that between computer fraud and computer crime, terms that are commonly used interchangeably with little distinction made between the two. Some substantial differences exist between them, however, as we shall see.

A general definition of *computer fraud* is:

> *Any defalcation or embezzlement accomplished by tampering with computer programs, data files, operations, equipment, or media, and resulting in losses sustained by the organization whose computer system was manipulated.*

The distinguishing characteristic of computer fraud is that access occurs with the intent to execute a fraudulent scheme. Computer fraud statutes have established two very important principles:

- First, the statutes contain definitions of computer-related terms. These statutes allow the prosecutor to sidestep having to explain to the jury technical "computer speak" and its cumbersome fit with common law terminology.
- Second, the statutes create an offense based on proof of access with a particular intent. Success in carrying away property (money) does not have to be proven. Tracing the flow of proceeds is likely to be difficult without paper records and access might be the only provable event.

Most states have defined computer fraud as an attempt crime. By viewing the computer as a protected asset, the protection is independent of the actual loss to the owner as a result of the intrusion.

Computer Crime

Computer crime differs from computer fraud in two major ways. Employees who as a part of their normal duties have access to the computers are deemed to have authorized access and thus do not come under the law against access. Manipulation (alteration) or destruction of data (including computer software) is independent of fraudulent or other schemes. Such action does not fit into the normal vandalism crimes because the data is intangible.

Computer-Assisted Crime

It is sometimes said that most computer fraud is not "computer crime" but involves the use of computers instead of other means to break the law. In some cases these traditionally illegal acts can yield more loot by recourse to the high speed of the computer. These are in reality computer-assisted crimes and the existing criminal statutes can be appropriately applied to them. However, where detection and proof problems are exacerbated by the involvement of electronic media, computer fraud laws are invaluable for effective prosecution.

Information Crime

In some cases, the computer is an active weapon. These kinds of cases are termed *information crimes*; the crime would not be possible without computer technology. Examples of information crimes include the theft of computer time, software, and data.

Computer Hacking

As the number of computers and computer users increases, so does the number and types of hackers. A study by a mi2g, UK-based company that tracks computer attacks, reported that in 2003, there were over 217,000 successful hacker attacks, representing a 150 percent increase from the number of attacks in 2002. Further, according to the Business Software Alliance and Information Systems Security Alliance, almost two-thirds of IT professionals expect that their organization will be the victim of a cyberattack at some point during 2004.

Although the term *hacker* was originally used to describe a computer enthusiast, the term has now grown to mean someone seeking unauthorized access to computer systems and the information contained therein. It includes organizations' employees, members of hacker gangs, and hackers for profit. Motives vary according to the targeted system, information desired, and the perpetrator. While hacking was once commonly thought of as a precocious teenager's hobby, it has changed dramatically in the last twenty years to encompass a large and diverse group.

Definition

Hacking or "phreaking" is basically breaking into computers and telecommunications systems by learning the vulnerabilities of various hardware and software, and using a computer to systematically "guess" the telephone number, user's system identification, and password.

The more sophisticated hackers take advantage of the vulnerabilities of the system and exploit them through software programs, such as "war dialers". The term "war dialers" was coined from the movie *War Games* in which a teenager broke into a missile launching computer system by implementing a program that continuously sought out modem tones and tried guessing passwords.

Other hackers use "rogue" software applications, which can be installed surreptitiously or with the unwitting help of another. These programs can install a "backdoor," which usually consists of programming instructions that disable obscure security settings in an operating system and that enable future access without detection.

Another method commonly used by hackers is to send an e-mail which has covert code embedded within the attachment. Upon receiving the e-mail, most people will launch the attachment, which can lower the security settings on the target machine without the user's knowledge.

Still, the most direct way of gaining access to a computer is to use someone else's password or generate (without authorization) a password of one's own. Passwords are designed to keep computers safe. If you don't know the password, the machine won't run. However, most users choose passwords which, while not easy to crack, follow certain patterns. People usually pick something familiar and easy as their password. A deep-sea fisherman uses "marlin"; the man's secretary, who received a mug about "soaring with the eagles and working with turkeys" from her boss last Christmas, uses "turkey" as her password. There are lists circulated among hackers of the most likely passwords.

If the hacker knows or can learn something about his target, his job is even easier. That fisherman, for example, probably has a huge marlin mounted on his wall. It's located directly in the man's line of sight as he logs on each morning; it's a good guess this guy will have 'marlin' or 'reel' or something else fishy in his password. A simple lesson here: real-word passwords, even in variation, are not secure. The safest passwords combine letters, numbers, and other characters such as punctuation.

Social Engineering
Another means of gaining access to a system involves simple deception. The hacker uses his verbal skills to deceive victims into disclosing information they ought not to divulge, or convinces victims to commit acts that facilitate the hacker's scheme. Often posing as an employee or someone hired by the organization, the hacker easily deceives real employees into revealing information. In order to research his scheme, he may avail himself of documents in the company dumpster, such as internal telephone directories and correspondence.

The hacker may assume a number of different guises to accomplish this deception. He may pose as a new or temporary worker and ask information systems employees for a password so that he can begin work. He may also pose as someone in a position of authority and intimidate employees into revealing confidential information.

Sometimes overt deception is not required. In large corporations, hackers can take advantage of the anonymity among employees. By donning office attire, they can blend into the crowd and thus peruse the premises, perhaps gaining a password written down at an employee's desk in the process.

Hacker Computer Manipulation

War-Dialers

War-dialers are programs written by hackers to automate the hacking process. The program can be configured to call a series of telephone numbers to determine if any of the numbers are connected to a computer. These programs can also be configured to a dial a range of numbers to discover valid long-distance calling card numbers.

A hacker can program a war-dialer to dial hundreds of numbers in random patterns in an attempt to avoid detection. The war-dialer can recognize when a computer answers because of the unique tone of the answering modem. When the war-dialer finds a valid long-distance calling card number or the number of a computer, the program saves this information in a separate file.

Trojan Horse

A Trojan horse is the covert placement of instructions in a program that causes the computer to perform unauthorized functions but usually still allows the program to perform its intended purpose. This method is one of the most commonly used techniques in computer-based frauds and sabotage.

Trap Doors

When developing large programs, programmers insert instructions for additional code and intermediate output capabilities. The design of computer operating systems attempts to prevent this from happening. Therefore, programmers insert instructions that allow them to circumvent these controls. Hackers take advantage of these trap doors.

Salami Techniques

Salami techniques involve the execution of unauthorized programs used to steal small amounts of assets from a large number of sources without noticeably reducing the whole.

For example, in a banking system, the amount of interest to be credited to an account is typically rounded off. A fraudster might set up the system so that instead of rounding off the number, that fraction of it is credited to a special account owned by the perpetrator.

Logic Bombs

A logic bomb is a computer program executed at a specific time period or when a specific event occurs. For example, a programmer can write a program to instruct the computer to delete all personnel and payroll files if his name were ever removed from the file.

Data Diddling

Data diddling is the changing of data before or during entry into the computer system. Examples include forging or counterfeiting documents used for data entry and exchanging valid disks and tapes with modified replacements.

Scavenging and Dumpster Diving

Scavenging is obtaining information left around a computer system, in the computer room trashcans, etc. Dumpster diving refers to gleaning sensitive information from an organization's trash receptacles and dumpsters.

Data Leakage

Data leakage is the removing of information by smuggling it out as part of a printed document, encoding the information to look like something different, and removing it from the facility.

Piggybacking/Impersonation

Piggybacking and impersonation are frequently used to gain access to restricted areas. Examples include following someone in through a door with a badge reader, electronically using another's user identification and password to gain computer access, and tapping into the terminal link of a user to cause the computer to believe that both terminals are the same person.

Simulation and Modeling

Simulation and modeling is a computer manipulation technique using the computer as a tool or instrument to plan or control a criminal act.

Wire Tapping

Wire tapping into a computer's communications links is another technique used by hackers. This method enables perpetrators to read the information being transmitted between computers, or between computers and terminals

Network Weaving

This technique, more commonly known as "looping," involves using numerous networks in an attempt to avoid detection. For example, a hacker might dial into Company A's PBX system to obtain an outside line that can be used to dial into Company B's network. If Company B can track the origin of the hacker's call, it will lead them to Company A, not to the hacker.

The above is a relatively simple example. Hackers have been known to "loop" through 15 or 20 different networks before arriving at their final destination. Network weaving can make it extremely difficult for an investigator or fraud examiner to trace the point of origin for a specific telephone call or data transmission.

Altering the Way a System Generates Passwords

Not all passwords are supplied by users. Some are generated by a computer system's "randomizer" function. For example, many Internet Service Providers (ISPs) give first-time users a randomly generated password (and sometimes a random user name as well), which gets the person online. Then the user changes the log-on information to their own preference.

By learning how a certain system's randomizer works, the hacker can imitate the generation of valid passwords, or alter how the system operates. For example, with some tinkering, the randomizer can be set to give every new user the same, seemingly random, password: EVBDCL8. But that won't work for long. It's better to have the machine make a password built off some information about the user, which is publicly available. Using a relatively simple set of algorithms, a hacker can convert a user name, such as "halbfish" into an obscure looking string like "rueavzhr." (Letters are read as numbers by computers speaking ASCII code, so the algorithms are using sine values to convert the ASCII values into a new set of numbers.)

Here's a good example of how manipulating a randomizer works. Dennis Ritchie, who helped develop UNIX technology, reported how a hacker attacked one company's system.

Computer officials at the company had their system generate passwords, each eight characters long, mixing letters and digits. In a brute force attack, it should have taken 112 years to crack the nearly 3 trillion possibilities. However, the randomizer on the company system could only take 32,768 seeds for passwords. The hacker used his own machine to generate and test each of those combinations, using, according to Ritchie, "a total of only about one minute of machine time." In less time than the average commercial break runs on television, the hacker breached a seemingly impenetrable system.

Buffer Overflow Exploits

Buffer overflow exploits are one of the largest problems in computer security today. In all application programs, there are buffers that hold data. These buffers have a fixed size. If an attacker sends too much data into one of these buffers, the buffer overflows. The server then executes the data that "overflowed" as a program. This program may do any number of things, from sending passwords to Russia to altering system files, installing backdoors, etc., depending on what data the attacker sent to the buffer.

Privilege Escalation Exploits

Privilege escalation exploits grant administrator or root-level access to users who previously did not have such access. For example, an account exists on all Windows NT and 2000 servers called "Guest." This account, by default, has no password. Anyone can log-on to the server using this "Guest" account and then use a common privilege escalation exploit called "GetAdmin" to gain administrator-level access to the system. Many other privilege escalation exploits exist, such as HackDLL and others. These exploits are very useful, since they allow anyone who has any level of access to a system to easily elevate their privilege level and perform any activities they desire.

Backdoors

When attackers obtain root-level access to a server (using a buffer overflow exploit or a privilege escalation exploit, for example) they will want to do two things:
- Install a backdoor
- Cover their tracks

Backdoors allow attackers to remotely access a system again in the future. For example, the attacker may have used a particular security hole to get root-level access to a computer. However, over time, that particular security hole may be closed, preventing the attacker from accessing the system again. In order to avoid being shut out in the future, attackers install backdoors. These backdoors take different forms, but all allow an attacker to access the server again without going through the standard log-in procedures and without having to repeat the attack that gave them access in the first place. Many worms install backdoors as a part of their malicious payload. Code Red II, for example, installed a backdoor that provided access to the C and D drives of the compromised Web server from anywhere on the Internet. Other common backdoor programs are Netbus and BackOrifice, which allow attackers to remotely control a compromised server. Once a backdoor is established, the hacker retreats and covers his or her tracks to keep the initial attack unnoticed.

HTTP Exploits

HTTP exploits involve using the Web server application to perform malicious activities. These attacks are very common and are growing in popularity because firewalls typically block most traffic from the Internet to keep it away from corporate servers. However, HTTP traffic, used for Web browsing, is almost always allowed to pass through firewalls unhindered. Thus, attackers have a direct line to the Web server. If they can coerce the Web server into performing malicious activities, they can access resources that would otherwise be unavailable.

Anti-Hacker Measures

Because hackers require dial-in capability to gain access, the best prevention strategy is to eliminate as many dial-in ports as possible. Unfortunately, the trend today is to install more, not fewer, dial-in capabilities because telecommuting and customer connectivity are driving the demand for more dial-in capability. The following are some preventive measures that can be implemented:

- Welcome screens usually are proudly displayed at sign-on with a message, such as:

    Welcome to the XYZ Corporation Computer network.

    To discourage unauthorized use, such a screen might be replaced with one that informs the user that he is about to access a proprietary network. Additionally, the screen should warn that unauthorized access is prohibited and will be prosecuted under the law. The screen should not identify either the organization or the network.
- Security policies should be established and disseminated throughout the organization. These policies should include training for all employees, customers (who will appreciate the additional security), and others who have a need to access the network.

- Call-back modems should be used wherever practical. These modems will answer an incoming call and require the sender to enter a password. Once the caller has identified himself, the modem will terminate the connection, and dial a previously established phone number. When the prearranged number is called, the sender must again perform the sign-on procedure.
- Security software packages should be secured to the highest level possible. Most major software companies today have to release updates and patches to their software every so often. Check your software vendor's websites on a regular basis for new security patches or use the new automated patching features that some companies offer.
- Passwords should be used in accordance with sound security practices. For example:
  - Passwords should be changed periodically (every 90 days is suggested).
  - Passwords should be of sufficient length to deter "guessing" (minimum of 8 characters is suggested).
  - Passwords of transferred or terminated employees should be changed immediately.
- Most purchased software comes with a vendor supplied password that is used for installation and then deleted. All packages should be audited to ensure that these default passwords (which are widely known) have been changed.
- Encryption should be considered for sensitive data files, password files, and sensitive computer programs.
- Communications software should terminate any connection (whether dial-in or direct connect) after:
  - A reasonable number of unsuccessful attempts to enter a valid password (usually no more than three).
  - A terminal (direct connect or dial-in) has been connected for a period of time with no activity. This is called "timing-out."

  The terminated connection will require redialing into the network and/or re-performing the sign-on and verification process. Some companies require the data security officer to issue a new password before the user can sign-on again.
- Hacker publications and communications should be reviewed to learn the current jargon and hacker "handles," which are the names that hackers use in their online persona. Hackers have used the Internet quite efficiently to communicate with each other, while producing a significant amount of hacking documentation and programs. Almost any hacker website will contain a large number of text files that explain "how to hack," or how various systems operate. Many of these files will also explain the standard vulnerabilities of the systems, and the best methods to penetrate their security.

Hacker Detection Measures

An adequate hacker detection program contains three primary components:

- Almost all communication systems maintain a log file that records all successful and unsuccessful system access attempts. These also allow for the printing of reports containing sign-on and -off activity. These reports should be printed out regularly and reviewed by the data security officer. Where possible, special reports should be printed on the number of unsuccessful access attempts. These attempts at logging onto the system should be followed up by data security to determine their cause.
- The data security function should have sufficient resources and staff to administer passwords, maintain the security software, review system activity reports, and follow up on *all* potential security violations.
- Finally, periodic reviews of telecommunications security should be performed by consultants and/or internal or external auditors, if the latter have the necessary experience and qualifications.

Hacking Insurance

During the past three years, a handful of cyber-insurers have begun offering coverage specifically designed to address new forms of information age exposure. These e-commerce risks can include theft, damage or disclosure of data, denial of service attacks, theft of intellectual property, unauthorized access, loss of revenue, infringement of copyright and trademark, and the consequent damage to business reputation. These types of e-commerce risks are covered by what is known as first-party coverage.

Third-party coverage covers the company if it is being sued for problems caused by technology product errors and omissions; the pilfering, public release or misuse of sensitive or confidential information; the unwitting spread of disruptive viruses; hacker tampering to the information and advertising carried on websites; e-mail-facilitated sexual harassment; and privacy infringement.

Many businesses believe that their traditional business coverage will suffice, or failing that, their Web host or ISP will cover damages caused by any of the above. In both cases, they are probably wrong. Unless your business insurance policy or Internet service level agreement specifically includes language addressing e-commerce liability, any damages will probably not be covered.

Electronic Mail

E-mail has revolutionized the ability of businesses to interact swiftly and, indeed, global business has embraced the e-mail system wholeheartedly. Few organizations do not provide some form of internal electronic communications. Due to the speed at which businesses can now interact and conduct business, as well as the relative cost advantage e-mail enjoys over other means of communication, the number of new e-mail users will no doubt continue to boom.

E-mail does, however, also give organizations a degree of vulnerability. Aside from employees using it for personal correspondence, e-mail can be used to sabotage and crash organizations' networks. Forwarding viruses or even simple virus hoaxes are often enough to overload a system. Using e-mail through such systems as the Internet endows senders with identity protection—the original sender of the message can be disguised or obscured. Therefore, because a sender's identity can be concealed, sensitive business information can be safely forwarded to an unauthorized address.

Consider:
- Company employees now possess the ability to quickly disclose sensitive company materials to outside parties, increasing the opportunity for corporate espionage.
- Companies that employ a company-wide e-mail system can now be held responsible for any unethical or illegal activities conducted by employees on the e-mail system.
- Companies must now be concerned with the repercussions of the actions of any disgruntled or rash employees. The speed with which an e-mail can be "fired off" creates the opportunity for ill-advised communications.
- Once an e-mail message has left a company's system, it may travel through any number of "foreign" e-mail systems before reaching its destination. An e-mail transmission can quite easily be intercepted or compromised without the use of encryption software.
- Without a security-enhanced e-mail system, the receiver of an e-mail message has little assurance that the e-mail is authentic. E-mail addresses can be easily "spoofed" or cloned by a knowledgeable user.

E-mail can be delivered almost instantaneously anywhere the networks, computers, and software exist to handle its transmission and reception. In fact, one of the emerging security problems concerning e-mail is the huge volume of space required to archive old messages. In some organizations, people are regularly asked to cull through their old e-mail messages and delete those no longer needed. In addition, some organizations will delete any old e-mail messages left on the mail server machines after a certain amount of time (e.g., one or two months).

E-Mail Security Concerns

Since e-mail is quickly becoming a fact of life for most organizations, it is appropriate to discuss some e-mail security concerns from both a user-based and an organizational perspective. Organizations often fail to set boundaries for employees regarding e-mail and may later face legal ramifications as a result. Surveys have revealed several questions that are common to users and organizations alike concerning e-mail security.

E-mail Ownership

Who owns e-mail messages on an organization's system? This is the common question, but it is not necessarily the right question. An e-mail message that an employee wrote himself is a work of authorship and as such the rules of copyright apply. In general, if the employee wrote the message as part of his duties for his employer (i.e., "in the scope of your employment") the employer owns the copyright. If the e-mail was not part of the employee's duties (something personal or related to another activity, whether permitted by the employer or not), then the user has copyright, but the employer, as owner of the system on which it was created or passed through, may have some rights to the copy on the system. If an employee is forwarding a message written by someone else, the issue gets even more complicated. For instance, does the original author have the right or the intention to authorize any forwarding?

Organizational Liability

As with any communications media, legal issues of the Internet are emerging at a rapid rate, with a lot of discussion, but are of limited consensus so far. It can be said that employers do have some liability for how employees use a company's e-mail system. The issues are similar to an employee's use of the company telephone, the company postage meter, the company vehicle, and so on.

The best general advice is to exercise some caution when dealing with an e-mail system. Within the company, e-mail can become a vehicle for sexual harassment, for creating a hostile work environment, or setting up gambling pools. Outside the company, employees can use e-mail to operate their own businesses or to send out fabricated messages in the name of other employees or their employer. Some employers monitor their e-mail systems, which presents legal issues, such as invasion of privacy. E-mail has also been used to gather evidence against employers or employees. Of course, there are no more dangers and pitfalls of e-mail than there are of any form of communications, whether inside or outside the organization. The telephone and postal systems are just as capable of such problems.

As with any potential liability issue, employers must set guidelines for the proper internal and external use of e-mail, just as they would for the proper use of the company telephone, stationery and postage, vehicles, and so on. For instance, the organization should have a policy reminding employees in writing that e-mail must not be used to send inappropriate and unprofessional messages, including:

- Harassing other users of the system
- Consuming unreasonable amounts of available resources
- Intentionally sending other users viruses
- Evading software licensing or copying mechanisms
- Crashing/disrupting system services
- Impersonating another user anywhere on the Internet
- Bypassing system security mechanisms
- Translating encrypted material without authorization
- Eavesdropping on other e-mail interactions
- Using the system for any personal gain either monetarily or politically unless permitted by the organization

A number of prominent liability law firms recommend some monitoring of e-mail, but this decision should not be taken lightly and not just because of employee's privacy concerns. For instance, the fact that the company does try to monitor e-mail may be used against the company when something slips through that monitoring.

Due to rapid growth of the Internet and e-mail, there is a great deal of uncertainty in the law. Organizations may want to seek legal counsel in establishing proper use guidelines and before taking disciplinary action against employees because of alleged abuses.

Computer Viruses

Viruses are hidden computer programs that use all the computer's resources thereby shutting down the system or slowing it down significantly. Computer viruses range from the relatively harmless (displaying a message or greeting) to shut downs of entire computer networks for extended periods.

A computer virus is a program that contains instruction codes to attack software. The attack might erase data or display a message on the screen. The computer virus can copy itself to other programs. This copy ability can affect large networks. In recent years, viruses have disrupted large networks and caused the expenditure of millions of dollars in staff- and machine-hours to remove these viruses and restore normal operations.

Hoaxes

A massive amount of media attention in recent years has focused on computer viruses. Many of the virus scares that occur, however, are hoaxes. While that is, on one hand, fortunate, these phony warnings cause harm of their own. They slow down transmission of information and have been known to cause overloads of organizational e-mail networks. Most of these fraudulent warnings urge recipients to "forward this to everyone you know." Before forwarding a questionable warning, it is wise to consult a few of the authorities who track viruses. The following sites can be accessed to confirm or debunk virus notifications:

- www.symantec.com/avcenter/hoax.html
- www.vmyths.com
- www.fsecure.com/virus-info/hoax/

Types and Terminology of Computer Viruses

Macro Virus

A macro is an instruction that carries out program commands automatically. Many common applications (e.g. word processing, spreadsheet, and slide presentation applications) make use of macros. Macro viruses are macros that self-replicate. If a user accesses a document containing a viral macro and unwittingly executes this macro virus, it can then copy itself into that application's startup files. The computer is now infected—a copy of the macro virus resides on the machine.

Any document on that machine that uses the same application can then become infected. If the infected computer is on a network, the infection is likely to spread rapidly to other machines on the network. Moreover, if a copy of an infected file is passed to anyone else (for example, by e-mail or floppy disk), the virus can spread to the recipient's computer. This process of infection will end only when the virus is noticed and all viral macros are eradicated. Macro viruses are the most common type of viruses. Macro viruses can be written with very little specialist knowledge, and these viruses can spread to any platform on which the application is running. However, the main reason for their success is that documents are exchanged far more frequently than executables or disks, a direct result of e-mail's popularity and Web use.

The *I Love You* (also known as *LoveLetter*) virus is a type of macro virus. LoveLetter is a Win32-based e-mail worm. It overwrites certain files on your hard drive(s) and sends itself out to everyone in your Microsoft Outlook address book. LoveLetter arrives as an e-mail attachment named: LOVE-LETTER-FOR-YOU.TXT.VBS though new variants have different names including: Very Funny.vbs, virus_warning.jpg.vbs, and protect.vbs. The subject of the message containing the attachment varies as well. Opening the attachment infects your machine. This attachment will most likely come from someone you know. Don't open any attachments unless you are sure that it is virus free. If you're unsure, ask for the sender to confirm that the attachment was intended for you. You'll know you have the worm if you have difficulty opening MP3 and JPG files.

Boot Sector Viruses

The boot sector is the first logical sector of a hard disk or floppy disk. Seventy-five percent to 90 percent of viruses have been boot sector viruses. These viruses use system BIOS, replace the boot sector, and move the boot sector to another location. It then writes a copy of its own program code which will run every time the system is booted or when programs are being run. A boot sector cannot infect a computer if it is introduced after the machine is running the operating system. An example of a boot sector virus is *Parity Boot*. This virus's payload displays the message *Parity Check* and freezes the operating system, rendering the computer useless. This virus message is taken from an actual error message which is displayed to users when a computer's memory is faulty. As a result, a user whose computer is infected with the Parity Boot virus is led to believe that the machine has a memory fault rather than an disruptive virus infection.

Parasitic Viruses

Parasitic viruses attach themselves to programs, also known as executables. When a user launches a program that has a parasitic virus, the virus is surreptitiously launched first. To cloak its presence from the user, the virus then triggers the original program to open. The parasitic virus, because the operating system understands it to be part of the program, is given the same rights as the program to which the virus is attached. These rights allow the virus to replicate, install itself into memory, or release its payload. In the absence of antivirus software, only the payload might raise the normal user's suspicions. A famous parasitic virus called *Jerusalem* has a payload of slowing down the system and eventually deleting every program the user launches.

TSRAM Viruses

Terminate and Stay Resident (TSR) viruses usually hide in memory and cause system crashes, depending on their memory location. The TSR takes control of the operating system by passing its request to DOS each time DOS is executed. The virus *Cascade B* is a TSR virus which sometimes causes the system to crash. It also causes characters to fall down the screen.

Application Software Viruses

These types of viruses copy their virus code to a program file and modify the program so the virus code gets executed first. It does this by writing over the existing code or attaching itself to the program file. The more sophisticated types replicate themselves with a ".COM" extension each time the user accesses an executable program file. The virus *Vienna* is a type of application virus. It increases infected files by 648 bytes and destroys the system by making it reboot when running certain programs.

Multi-Partite Viruses

Multi-partite viruses share some of the characteristics of boot sector viruses and file viruses, which increases its ability to spread. They can infect .COM and .EXE files, and the boot sector of the computer's hard drive.

On a computer booted up with an infected diskette, a typical multi-partite virus will first reside in memory and then infect the boot sector of the hard drive. From there the virus can infect a PC's entire environment. This type of virus accounts for a large number of infections.

The *Tequila* virus is a type of multi-partite virus. Tequila is a memory resident master boot sector (partition table) and .EXE file infector. It uses a complex encryption method and garbling to avoid detection. When a program infected with Tequila is executed, the virus will modify the hard disk master boot sector, if it is not already infected. The virus also copies itself to the last six sectors of the system hard disk. When the workstation is later rebooted from the system hard disk, Tequila will become memory resident. Once Tequila is memory resident, it infects .EXE files when they are executed.

The CHKDSK command will indicate the system has 3,072 bytes less memory than what is installed. Infected .EXE programs increase in size by 2,468 bytes, though the file length increase cannot be seen in the disk directory listing because the virus hides it.

Tequila activates four months after the initial date of infection. At this time, and every month thereafter, the virus will display a graphic and the following message: "Execute: mov ax, FE03 / int 21. Key to go on."

Polymorphic Viruses

Polymorphic viruses create varied (though fully functional) copies of themselves as a way to avoid detection from antivirus software. Some polymorphic viruses use different encryption schemes and require different decryption routines. Thus, the same virus may look completely different on different systems or even within different files. Other polymorphic viruses vary instruction sequences and use false commands in the attempt to thwart antivirus software. One of the most advanced polymorphic viruses uses a mutation-engine and random-number generators to change the virus code and its decryption routine.

The *Spanska.4250* is a type of polymorphic virus. This virus infects program files (files with .EXE and .COM extensions). When one of the programs is infected, the virus hides in the computer's memory. Spanska.4250 remains in memory on the lookout to infect programs executed by users. Once Spanska.4250 carries out its infection the size of the infected programs will increase by 4250 bytes (the virus size). Moreover, the following message will be displayed: "(c) Spanska 97." This virus uses an "anti-tracing" technique to make more difficult to detect. In addition, it uses the system date to encrypt itself so it will be possible to find up to 366 different variants of this virus.

Stealth Viruses

The stealth viruses are the more sophisticated viruses. They constantly change their patterns in an effort to blend into the system like a chameleon. They attempt to avoid detection by bypassing DOS interrupt calls when they are installed, and remove their code from the infected files before the file is accessed by the requesting program.

The *4096* virus is a type of stealth virus. It increases the file size by 4096 bytes and decreases the memory by approximately 6kb. The message "FRODO LIVES" might appear in the middle of the screen. If the infected file is run on September 21, it causes the system to crash.

Mutation Engine Viruses

This "modern day" virus uses a special language-driven algorithm generator that enables it to create an infinite variety of original encryption algorithms. It avoids the checksum detection method like the stealth viruses by not changing the infected file size. Each time they replicate, they produce a new and different code.

The *Pogue* virus is a type of mutation virus. It only infects .COM files less than 61439 bytes long. If activated on May 1 or before 9 a.m. on any other day, it will make a variety of musical sounds. It contains the strings "TNX2DAV (Thanks to Dark Avenger) and "Pogue Mahone" in its code.

Network Viruses

It was just a matter of time before network-specific viruses were developed to attack the increased number of Local Area Networks (LANs) and other types of networks coming online. These viruses generally are developed to attack the file servers.

The boot sector and partition table viruses infect the boot operation of the file server. This virus does not spread from the workstation to the file server. However, if you are using NetWare it can cause the software to lose the location of its partition table on the file server if the file server is booted with an infected floppy.

Viruses that infect programs seem to be limited to infecting files on the server. However, because the files are continuously being accessed by workstations, this type of virus is difficult to contain.

At least two NetWare specific viruses have been discovered in Europe. One is the *GP1* (Get Password 1) virus. It was allegedly created to penetrate Novell security features and then spread throughout the network. The second, *CZ2986* virus, in Czechoslovakia. This virus places itself in memory and intercepts NetWare function calls when the workstations log into the server. After it collects 15 user name/password combinations, it saves them in an infected file and uses them to gain access to the network.

Worms

A worm is a self-replicating program which resides as a file on a system, executes an autonomous process, and deliberately moves from system to system. It looks for other nodes on the networks, copies itself to them, and causes the self-copy to execute on other nodes. These programs find network utilities showing node names, monitor network traffic, randomly select network identification codes as well as other mischief.

An example of a worm is the *SQL Slammer*, which raced across the globe and wreaked havoc on the Internet in January 2003. This worm doubled the number of computers it infected every 8.5 seconds in the first minute of its appearance. The worm, which exploited a flaw in Microsoft Corporation's SQL Server database software, caused damage by rapidly replicating itself and clogging the pipelines of the global data network. The worm did not erase or cause damage to desktop computers, but was designed to replicate itself so fast and so effectively that no other traffic could get through networks.

Virus Carriers

Viruses can infect computer systems from many sources. Some of the more common virus carriers are:

- Unknown or unchecked application software
- Software or media brought in by employees
- Programs downloaded from modem bulletin boards
- Unsolicited e-mails
- Vendors and suppliers with infected software
- Uncontrolled and shared program applications
- Demonstration software
- Freeware and Shareware

Virus Indicators

The following are some of the indicators that a computer might exhibit suggesting that it might be infected:

- A sudden and sometimes dramatic decrease of free space on your media.
- The system suddenly, and for no apparent reason, slows down its response time to commands.
- An increase in the size of some files.
- There has been a change in the length of executable files, a change in their content, or a change in their file date/time stamp.
- An unexpected number of disk accesses, especially to particular file(s).
- The operating system and/or other programs suddenly begin behaving in unpredictable ways for the first time. Sometimes disk files that should be there cannot be accessed or are suddenly erased with no warning.

- Unusual messages and graphics.
- Unable to boot-up the system.
- Unable to access files.
- Unexplained and repeated maintenance repairs.
- System or data files disappear or become fragmented.
- Unexplained changes in memory.
- Unexplained changes in program sizes.
- Resident antiviral software programs display messages that a virus has been encountered. Note that until the source of the virus has been identified and removed from the system, antiviral systems might continually inform the operator that a virus is being encountered and removed.

Virus Protection

Computer users should take measures to protect their computers against viruses. Some of the steps that can be taken are:

- Do not use a diskette to boot your system.
- If you must boot your system from a diskette, make sure it is properly labeled, and continuously protected.
- Don't install Shareware or other untested programs on your systems, but if you do, don't put them in the root directory.
- In a network environment, don't place untested programs on the server.
- If you are sharing information on diskettes, ensure they only contain information and no executable files.
- Use current antivirus software to detect potential viruses.
- Backup all programs and files.
- Write virus-free warranties and indemnities into your purchase orders and contracts.
- Always write-protect your systems and program disks.
- Teach computer users about computer viruses so that they can recognize them.
- Always use caution when opening e-mail attachments.

Antivirus Software Operation

Traditional Scanners

These programs work by looking for known viruses by checking for recognizable patterns and specific "strings" or virus "signatures."

Heuristic Scanners

These scanners inspect executable files for code using algorithms to identify operations that would indicate an unknown virus. They might also examine macros to detect virus-like behavior.

Behavior Blocking Scanners

These applications run continuously, looking for behavior that might indicate virus activity (for example, instructions to format a hard drive.)

Change Detection Scanners

Change detection scanners generate a database of characteristics for executable files and check for changes to these files that might signify a virus attack.

Investigating Virus Infections

Virus infections can be investigated by taking the following action:
- Isolate the system and all media
- Run antivirus software
- Document findings
- Interview the system custodian and all users, and determine:
    - Symptoms
    - Damage
    - Prior clean-up conducted
    - Access controls in place and working
    - System malfunction
    - Personal media used
    - Unauthorized media used
    - Virus identification
- Follow the audit trail of the infection
- Determine the source of the virus—person, system, and media
- Make users aware of protection policies and procedures
- Ensure countermeasures are in place and working
- Track costs of virus problems

Internet Fraud

A booming segment of computer fraud, internet fraud has become a growing concern to the law enforcement community. This type of fraud has proliferated and will continue to proliferate because of the ripe conditions which exist on the World Wide Web for fraudulent activities. The Internet is still a developing technology for much of international business and thus has not been subjected to much litigation or policing. The laws that do currently apply to the Internet are difficult to enforce, since the 'Net crosses virtually every international border on the planet. The lack of international laws and the difficulty enforcing those laws gives Internet fraudsters a better than average chance of avoiding capture and punishment.

Over 800 million people, or 12.5% of the world's population, were online in 2004 (www.internetworldstats.com). The Internet's increasing popularity has caused a tidal wave of businesses to enter cyberspace, hoping for a new business market. Unfortunately, many of these businesses do not understand how to properly safeguard themselves against Internet hackers, resulting in easy pickings for fraudsters.

Typical Internet Schemes

The majority of scams and schemes that have found new and lucrative homes on the Internet are similar to the conventional frauds which have plagued consumers for ages. A few scams, such as modem hijacking, are of an entirely new breed.

Modem Hijacking

According to the Federal Trade Commission, this scheme is a new incarnation adapted to exploit Internet users. While users are online, their computer modems are secretly disconnected from their ISP and reconnected to the Internet, only this time through an expensive international line. Victims have usually downloaded a special "viewer" program from a website offering free computer images. Once activated, the downloaded material began the hijacking disconnection and reconnection process. Long distance charges continued to mount until victims shut down their computers, even if their Internet connection had already been terminated.

Internet Commerce

Much has been made in the national media about the dangers of entering credit card numbers to companies on the Internet. And it is understandable that many businesses and individuals have apprehensions concerning Internet commerce; the Internet is the most impersonal form of communication and it is also the least well known to most. This concern, the feeling that a criminal might be "lurking in the shadows" of the Internet, scares many potential customers from making that initial transaction. There are some precautions to be made before purchasing online items, but conducting business transactions on the Internet is ultimately as safe as making an order from a company via the telephone.

Get Rich Quick

Entering the phrase *get rich quick* in an Internet search results in sites with names like *$50,000 First Ten Months, Secrets of the Millionaires,* and *Best Business Resource Center.* These types of sites hawk everything from home businesses to investment opportunities. Some push home and Internet based businesses; others' selling point is that telemarketers close all sales. The common denominator in these types of schemes is that consumers who spend money on them find themselves with worthless materials and information.

The medium through which victims are snared lends the scam a false appearance of credibility. Glossy websites give the operations an official air. But, as with all get rich quick schemes, victims' are sucked in through their desire to make easy money.

Pyramid Schemes

The tried and true pyramid has found a new high tech home on the Internet. As in most pyramid schemes, the initial participants of the scheme are rewarded handsomely, while the participants that join the scheme later are bilked out of their investment money.

Foreign Trusts

Information on this scheme is easily found on the 'Net. The set up caters to the desire to avoid taxes. For a fee, the company purports to be able to create a foreign trust to which taxpayers can transfer their assets. Since the trust is not within the taxpayer's country, the logic goes, the assets are not subject to taxation.

Naturally, the logic is faulty and for several reasons. First, if the taxpayer derives use from the funds in the trust, according to law those funds are considered taxable income. Thus, consumers who fall for this scam subject themselves to prosecution for tax evasion.

That is, of course, only if the trust is set up at all. Some of the operators of this scheme simply take consumer's money and disappear. And sadly, those are the consumers who get off lightly. Others who have fallen for this pitch find that they have transferred all of their assets to a trust of which they are not the beneficiaries. Their assets then legally belong to another entity and getting them transferred back to their control is virtually impossible.

Chain Letters
This fraud has once again become popular due to the Internet's e-mail capabilities. Instead of sending numerous letters through the mail, as fraudsters were forced to do in the past, the e-mail capabilities allow the fraudster to compose one letter and send thousands of copies to potential victims. The letter sent to unsuspecting targets generally forewarns of the grave dangers that await the target should he or she not reply to the letter. The letter asks for a small cash donation in exchange for the target's piece of mind that no bad tidings will be spread, providing examples of some of the unfortunates who did not heed the letter. The money should be sent to a P.O. box, the e-mail often instructs.

Investment and Securities Fraud
Websites that offer investment or securities advice are not in short supply. Many of these sites are reputable, but an illicit cottage industry has been born on many of these sites. A fraudulent website will claim to have insider information about the value of a given stock, suggesting that something unexpected will soon happen to that company. When the unknowing stock investor takes the advice of the supposedly knowledgeable investment advisor, the "advisor" manipulates the stock price to his advantage.

Spamming
Spamming involves sending e-mail to subscribers whose names appear on electronic versions of the phone list and posting ads to the plethora of discussion and chat groups using the Internet. These postings are often disguised to look like tips from individual citizens who are supposedly engaged in a lawful enterprise, when in fact they are part of an Internet boiler room.

Combating Internet Fraud
Conducting business on the Internet is generally a safe proposition that can be made even more so through a few additional safety precautions.
- *Encryption*—Any confidential information or credit card numbers should be encrypted in their entirety. An encryption system is comprised of a cryptographic function, which scrambles an electronic transmission, and an inverse decrypt function, which restores the transmission to its original state. Encryption hardware and software can be used to scramble any communication by utilizing a complex mathematical formula. The only way

to unscramble an encrypted message is to provide the unique answer "key," thus unlocking the message. Encryption is the best method to stymie would-be interceptors of company transactions.

- *Customer Validation*—Because the Internet offers users an additional layer of anonymity, businesses should install some form of a customer validation safeguard in their Internet purchasing system. This may include a customer code or password that the customer can identify himself with before purchasing a product. As well, the business should distinguish itself to the customer, ensuring that no one else can falsely assume the company's identity.
- *Internal Network Security*—Organizations that conduct business on the Web should never, under any circumstances, keep their financial information database on their Web server. A knowledgeable computer hacker can sometimes penetrate Internet websites, and financial information is the primary target of these hackers, for obvious reasons. Therefore, the database that maintains a company's financial information should be a completely internal system, untouchable from the Internet. This safeguard will help assure that the sensitive information is not compromised in any way.
- *Firewalls*—Firewalls are advanced software programs which effectively "lock up" access to an Internet sight or e-mail transmission. Firewalls are designed to control the interface between a network and the Internet. This technology surveys incoming and outgoing transmissions between the network and the Internet, stopping any questionable transmission attempt to access a sensitive area. While firewalls are not foolproof, they do provide an additional layer of protection against Internet attacks or breaches of security.

More information about scams perpretrated against businesses and individuals can be found in the previous chapter, "Consumer Fraud."

Electronic Commerce

Electronic commerce, or e-commerce, is becoming a major form of retailing, marketing, advertising, and inter-personal communications. The hardware infrastructure required for high-speed data, voice and video transmission to and from private homes is being introduced to residential streets everywhere.

We have all heard people talk about their fears about putting their credit card numbers, their personal identification numbers (PINs), their street addresses, phone numbers, and other personal information out on the Internet. A 2003 study by PaymentOne shows that 70% of U.S. consumers are hesitant to use a credit card online because they are concerned about security issues. Additionally, 73% of U.S. consumers have a great deal of concern about the information they provide in an internet purchase being sold to a third party, according to a 2003 Ipsos Public Affaris survey. In reality, there is very little difference between securing electronic commerce and securing any other kind of information system resource.

In addition to these traditional goals of information systems security, confidentiality, integrity, and availability, there are a few that are more directly related to networked transactions, which is exactly what e-commerce consists of:

- **Authentication.** This requirement addresses the problem of identifying the parties of an e-commerce transaction to each other. We want to make sure that we can determine with whom we (or our computers) are communicating.
- **Non-repudiation.** Non-repudiation can help assure that no party to an e-commerce transaction can later deny that the transaction occurred. We need some way to be able to recognize a "signature" between e-commerce parties just as we rely on written signatures on paper documents.

While recent years have seen an increase in the number of consumers and businesses willing to conduct transactions online, there still exists some hesitancy to fully embrace e-commerce technology. It is cases like the one described below which cause consumers to lose confidence in e-commerce. In the following example, a clever hacker crafted a sophisticated scam that completely duped many consumers.

EXAMPLE

One of the largest ISPs, America Online, has become a favorite mask for computer fraudsters. At one point, many of the company's subscribers found an e-mail message labeled "Important AOL Information." The text explained, "the No. 1 priority for all of us at America Online continues to be meeting our obligation to provide you with the best possible service." The latest effort included adding "a new server which offers a higher system capacity." The note then asked the reader to click on a highlighted section of text to "read in depth about the steps we have taken" and to "complete the required update of your information on our new servers." Clicking took customers to a website, where a letter from AOL Chairman Steve Case described the server project and instructed users to provide their name, address, home phone, and credit card number.

The whole thing was a hoax designed to grab credit card numbers and personal info. It's part of a barrage of e-mail attacks, and they're circulating throughout the Internet community, not just on AOL. Scammers offer free use of an ISP, or claim they need billing information to confirm a new payment plan.

ISP messages are also used to sneak "Trojan Horse" programs into a user's computer. The user is tempted with free pornographic pictures, or software that will boost their computer's performance. When the attached file is opened, it triggers a program that surreptitiously collects the subscriber's account name and password—which is then relayed to the hacker who sent the message.

Many experts say that it is currently possible to have secure transactions over the Internet because the latest encryption technologies and security protocols allow for this. However, fully-realized standards are not yet in place for all business-to-business or business-to-customer transactions. Some current security protocols do not permit non-repudiation of data, which is required if firms seriously want to conduct business over the Internet. However, the arrival of standards for using smartcard technology will transform Internet business and commerce as a whole. The smartcard technology offers a solution to the major secure transactions requirements, namely data integrity, user authentication and non-repudiation of data. Smartcard technology also involves the application of third-party trust relationships to the Internet.

Applying Encryption to E-Commerce Security
Generally speaking, the solutions offered by conventional and public-key encryption technologies are usually adequate to ensure that e-commerce transactions are as secure as the value of transactions requires.

The vast majority of transmissions over the Internet and the World Wide Web are not encrypted in any way. If there is no need to hide the contents of a message or communication, there is little need to expend resources on the encryption of such traffic and the decryption at the other end. Encryption can be an expensive solution, whether in terms of actual monetary cost or the cost in increased computational load on the user's machines. The needs of the organization to keep confidential transmissions secret should be weighed against the effort and cost of encryption.

Smart Cards

The cost and inefficiency of manually applying encryption techniques could prevent some organizations from fully engaging in e-commerce activities. Fortunately, a relatively inexpensive solution is available in the use of smart card technology.

A smart card is a credit-card sized plastic card embedded with an integrated circuit chip that makes it "smart." This marriage between a convenient plastic card and a microprocessor allows an immense amount of information to be stored, accessed, and processed either online or off-line. Smart cards can store several hundred times more data than a conventional card with a magnetic stripe. The information of application stored in the IC chip is transferred through an electronic module that interconnects with a terminal or a card reader. A contactless smart card has an antenna coil which communicates with a receiving antenna to transfer information. Depending on the type of the embedded chip, smart cards can be either memory cards or processor cards.

- **Memory Cards.** Any plastic card is made "smart" by including an IC chip. But the chip may simply be a memory storage device. Memory cards can hold information thousands of times greater than a magnetic stripe card. Nevertheless, its functions are limited to basic applications such as phone cards.
- **Processor Cards.** Smart cards with a full-fledged microprocessor on board can function as a processor device that offers multiple functions such as encryption, advanced security mechanisms, local data processing, complex calculation, and other interactive processes. Most stored-value cards integrated with identification, security, and information purposes are processor cards. Only processor cards are truly smart enough to offer the flexibility and multifunctionality desired in e-commerce.

The top three international markets in smart card production are (1) miniature subscriber identity modules (SIMs) that fit inside mobile phones, (2) banking cards, and (3) identification cards, specifically those used by governments and large corporations.

A 2002 study by SchlumbergerSema showed that while smart cards are more prevalent in Europe, the Middle East, and Africa (46%), Asia-Pacific (31%), and Latin America (19%), the United States, which only represented 4% of the smart card market, is expected to increase sales substantially. The smart card shipments in North America grew to around 58 million in 2002, and 85 million in 2003; this is a 79% growth from smart card sales in 2000. The United States represented a limited smart card market due to the availability of reliable and low cost online telecommunication services and the significant investment required for an extensive magnetic stripe-based infrastructure.

Most smart cards issued today are memory cards with limited processing capabilities; however, modern technology is constantly making advances toward increasing these capabilities.

Insider Threats

By far the greatest threat to information systems in terms of computer crime comes from employees inside an organization. It is not uncommon for operators, media librarians, hardware technicians, and other staff members to find themselves in positions of extraordinary privilege in relation to the key functions and assets of their organizations. A consequence of this situation is the probability that such individuals are frequently exposed to temptation.

A further complication is the tendency on the part of management to tolerate less stringent supervisory controls over information system personnel. The premise is that the work is not only highly technical and specialized but difficult to understand and control. As an example, systems software support is often entrusted to a single programmer who generates the version of the operating system in use, establishes password or other control lists, and determines the logging and accounting features to be used. In addition, such personnel are often permitted, and sometimes encouraged, to perform these duties during non-prime shift periods, when demands on computer time are light. As a result, many of the most critical software development and maintenance functions are performed in an unsupervised environment. It is also clear that operators, librarians, and technicians often enjoy a degree of freedom quite different from that which would be considered normal in a more traditional employment area.

Insiders typically are aware of the "holes" in the system of internal controls and often exploit weaknesses "just to see if they can get away with it." The most prevalent method of committing computer fraud probably is alteration or falsification of input transactions (and/or documents), including:

- Alteration of input
- Alteration of output
- Data file manipulation

- Communications systems
- Operating systems
- Computer operations

Characteristics

The characteristics of the traditional inside computer fraudster are very similar to those of the hacker or other computer criminal: intelligent, hard worker, seldom takes time off, bored with the routine of the job, and has very large ego. Many computer technicians have demonstrated a greater loyalty to the technology than to the organization for which they work. This technology loyalty can create an attitude that any behavior is acceptable if it is in the name of technology.

The following are indicators of insider computer fraud:
- Access privileges beyond those required to perform assigned job functions.
- Exception reports not reviewed and resolved.
- Access logs not reviewed.
- Production programs run at unusual hours.
- Lack of separation of duties in the data center.

Computer Security

Effective Security

Effective computer security ensures the availability of accurate data in time to meet an organization's needs at a cost that is commensurate with the risks involved. Key elements are:
- Protecting data and programs from intentional or inadvertent unauthorized alteration or destruction.
- Maintaining the confidentiality, integrity, and availability of data.
- Protecting the data center from physical threats such as fire, flood, and intentional destruction.
- Having the capability to restore data center operations in case of complete destruction.

The most important step is to obtain management support for effective security. Without such support, any security plan will falter.

Securing the Communications Network

Some communications networks are very large, very complex, and technically demanding. The task of effectively securing these networks is demanding and requires the close cooperation of both network and security administration. The objective of data and voice networks is to provide connectivity with acceptable response times, user-friendly access, and a secure mode at an acceptable cost to the organization.

Passwords

Passwords are the predominant form of authenticating valid users. Effective password administration is essential for maintaining security. Passwords should be of sufficient length (usually a minimum of eight characters) and a combination of letters, numbers, and other characters such as punctuation marks to avoid guessing. Group passwords and sharing of passwords should be prohibited so as to maintain individual accountability. Passwords of all terminated employees should be revoked immediately. Security administration often coordinates the notification of terminated employees with the personnel function. Employees who have changed job functions or transferred should have their old password canceled and a new one issued, if appropriate.

Other Network Security

Securing a computer network by means of logical controls is a difficult but necessary requirement for ensuring the safety of a computer system from attacks by outsiders. Logical controls include management security policies, user authentication systems, data access controls, network firewalls, security awareness training, encryption algorithms, penetration testing, intrusion detection software, and incident response plans.

Network security also can be provided by a combination of design, hardware devices, and software. Data encryption is carried out by a combination of hardware and software. Encrypted data is scrambled by a formula using a unique key and can only be unscrambled with the same formula and key at the receiving end. The decision to use encryption should be made in light of the risks and after a cost-benefit analysis. Drawbacks to encryption are the cost of the hardware and software, the cost of the administration, and the inherent delays incurred by the extra steps required for processing.

Digital signatures are becoming more common, in part because Congress and many states have passed legislation to legitimize the electronic "signing" of documents. On October 1, 2000, the Electronic Signatures in Global and National Commerce Act (E-SIGN Act) became effective. This federal statute basically provides a mechanism whereby any document that is required to be signed, can be signed "electronically." The E-SIGN Act does not require a party to use or accept electronic signatures, electronic contracts or electronic records, but rather seeks to facilitate the use of electronic signatures and documents by upholding their legal effect regardless of the type or method selected by the parties. The E-SIGN Act is also technology-neutral and does not require a specific type or method that businesses and consumers must use or accept in order to conduct their electronic transaction. The Act regulates any transactions involving interstate or foreign commerce. However, many states have enacted their own digital signature laws, which regulate purely intrastate transactions. Additionally, many state and federal agencies, including the Internal Revenue Service and the Securities and Exchange Commission, are encouraging the use of electronic filing and digital signatures as a means to speed up the collection and processing of information.

Biological access verification, long the favorite stuff of movie makers, is now available. This verification technique includes fingerprints, palm prints, voice prints, signatures, and retina scans.

Profiling software authenticates users by monitoring their statistical characteristics, such as typing speed and keystroke touch. Smartcard access devices are similar to an ATM card; like ATM cards, they are susceptible to loss and forgery.

The most effective components of internal security are education, reporting facilities, and vigorous disciplinary action for offenders, including prosecution of illegal acts. An enterprise-wide employee awareness program should be combined with formal training in the area of information security. For employees to fulfill their security responsibilities they should know what information needs to be kept confidential, how to recognize threats to security, and how to use backups and other aids for their desktop machines. Giving employees incentives such as bonuses to follow security guidelines, however, will be the most effective motivator.

Protecting the network from external threats requires some additional considerations. The less an external perpetrator knows about the technology environment (for example, type of hardware and software packages used), the harder it is to obtain fraudulent access. Part of the security policy should address how much and what kind of information regarding the technology of an organization should be made public.

Organizations should guard against providing too much access to third parties. There is pressure to establish connectivity by marketing, purchasing, research, and other branches. Connectivity should be granted only after it has been established that the benefits outweigh the risks and costs.

The Risk Assessment Process

As organizations grow, their information technology and data change both in type and quantity. Assumptions made about security need to be updated. The vehicle for updating is the risk assessment. This is a zero-based process that should be performed periodically. A risk assessment is an analysis of the security objectives of confidentiality, integrity, and availability.

Each data element should be examined to determine the impact if it is disclosed, lost, or entered incorrectly. Once this information is collected, the security measures in place should be reviewed to determine whether they provide necessary safeguards. The risk assessment process is a time-consuming process to undertake and many organizations employ outside security consultants to reduce its impact on day-to-day operations.

Internal Controls in the Data Center

In most instances, computer-related crimes are very difficult to detect. An intruder may be able to gain unauthorized access to a network or computer system, perpetrate whatever criminal activity was planned, and retreat without anyone being aware of the intrusion, much less the criminal activity that has taken place. So how does an organization become aware that its information resources have been compromised by someone—either inside or outside of the organization—with criminal intent? A few possibilities include:

- A strong set of policies and standards to define for employees and management what the company deems as unacceptable or unauthorized activities.
- Strong physical security to thwart those intent upon the theft of physical assets of the organization.
- Central Systems access control and data object protection.
- Strong security for the organization's application programs.
- Intrusion detection hardware and software for network and communications resources.
- Auditing of system and violation logs.

All of these mechanisms, if used correctly, will alert the organization of inappropriate actions. This all assumes, of course, that someone is keeping an eye out for exceptions and violations. All of the security policies and standards, the intrusion detection software, the violation logs, and the access controls will mean absolutely nothing if the organization is not committed to applying them properly and maintaining them adequately.

General controls over a data center are relevant for all applications. The general control categories include system maintenance, implementation of new systems (including development), computer operations, system software (including security and telecommunications software), and data files.

Systems Maintenance

All program and system changes should be approved in writing. Programmers should not have access to the production library, but only to "test" libraries. All programs that are to be modified should be moved into a test library by someone other than a programmer. All completed program changes should be tested and the results approved by both data center and user personnel before being placed into production. Adequate program documentation should be approved for all program changes. User personnel should be notified when modified programs will be placed into production.

Implementation Controls

Implementation controls are those controls over the development of, or purchase of, a new application. All new system requests should be made in writing. A system development life-cycle methodology should be used for developing and implementing in-house or purchased packages. All new systems requests should be approved by the appropriate management level. Users should be involved in the project from design through final testing. All test results should be approved by both data center management and user personnel. There should be an implementation plan for placing the new system into production.

Computer Operations

Computer operations controls are controls that govern the day-to-day operation of the computer system. There should be an approved schedule for all production runs. All system activity should be reviewed by data center management. Any unusual program executions should be investigated and resolved. A log of unusual events, such as *abends* (abnormal terminations of a program execution) or *reruns* should be kept by operations staff and also should be reviewed by data center management. Access to the computer room should be restricted to authorized personnel. All third parties, such as technicians, should be accompanied by a data center employee. Doors to the data center should be secured.

System Software

Controls over system software include those that govern the installation of the computer system, the communications software, and the security software. Data center management should approve the system software selection as well as the chosen options and parameters. System software should be tested before implementation in a production environment. (Note that this might not be possible for the operating system itself.)

Data Files

Controls over data files ensure that correct files are used for each production job and that adequate backup files exist. Data-file label bypass options should be disabled. A data-file management system should be used to record and locate all data files. Data-file backup copies should be made and stored in a secure facility. Off-site backup file copies should be maintained in case of a disaster in the data center. Utilities that can modify data files should be removed from the system and used only under management supervision. Live data files should not be used for testing.

Access and Telecommunication Controls

In the 1960s and 1970s, access controls meant ensuring that there was a lock on the computer room door. As online systems were implemented, the definition of access evolved to include logical access in addition to physical access. *Logical* access refers to any location where someone can sign on to the system. That sign-on access can be a direct connection or a dial-up. In today's online, real-time, and interconnected world, it is easy to forget physical guards over computer equipment. Computer equipment must be physically secured. This should include network servers, telephone system computers, communications controllers, and personal computers with sensitive data.

Access and telecommunications controls should achieve the following objectives:
- Provide physical security over equipment, users, and information
- Protect critical data from loss, damage, or unauthorized disclosure
- Ensure network reliability by using appropriate hardware and software
- Prevent unauthorized access and use of the network
- Ensure system availability
- Meet user requirements

Separation of Duties

Separation of duties is a key element in a well-designed internal control system. It also is fundamental to detecting and preventing fraud. Programmers should not operate the computer, have unsupervised access to production programs, or have access to production data sets (data files). Users should not have access to the production program code. Computer operators should not perform computer programming. Adequate supervision should be provided by personnel who do not actually perform the work.

Logs and History Files

Computer systems maintain a variety of history files or logs. These logs record activity in the following areas:

- Mainframe activity
  - Programs executed
  - Data files accessed
  - Date, time, and duration
  - User IDs that initiated a particular action
  - Error messages
  - Equipment malfunctions
- Communications activity
  - User ID
  - Terminal identifier
  - Dial-in port identifier
  - Date, time, and duration
  - Error messages
  - Equipment malfunctions
- Security software activity
  - User ID
  - Unsuccessful log-on attempts
  - Modifications to the password files and access capability

These logs originally were designed to help in troubleshooting the system and correcting errors. These files contain a very valuable audit and fraud examination trail of system activity, and are now used for internal control functions. The logs should be reviewed by a responsible data center official and evidence should exist of this review. Many of the history files have a limited capacity and can be forced into "wrapping" if not printed periodically.

Wrapping forces the software to record at the beginning of the file if the file is full and not printed out.

Security Software

There are a number of good security software packages on the market for all mainframes and most minicomputers. Security packages available for PCs are less numerous. Local area networks have some security packages available, but still rely primarily on the individual user in a stand-alone mode or the mainframe security in a connected mode. The purchase and installation of a security package might provide a false sense of security. Most of these packages are designed to be installed in a phased approach because of the complexity of the task.

These options and decisions about security software should be reviewed by management. For example, most mainframe security packages allow a minimum of three levels of security. *Log mode* merely logs all system access to defined programs and data files. *Warn mode* tells the user if he is accessing a program or file that is not authorized for the password he has employed. Activity also is logged. *Fail mode* will not allow a user to access defined data files and programs without the proper password. This is the highest level of security and the only one that provides adequate protection.

Another very important consideration involves the manual supervision of data provided by security packages, usually in the form of access logs. A security package needs consistent review to protect against possible violations.

Internal Controls in Computer Applications

Internal controls establish checks and balances to prevent one person from controlling the entire financial transaction. Competent and trustworthy employees are obviously a necessary element of a good internal control system. No employee with a known history of dishonesty should be hired.

Assets and records, which can easily be appropriated or destroyed, should be physically safeguarded. They should be safeguarded by locks, physical security, and other methods to ensure that they will not be misappropriated. All accounting systems rely on proper documentation. Missing documentation should be regarded as a red flag of possible fraud. Someone independent of the transaction must check the accounting controls. The knowledge that all work is checked is a powerful fraud deterrent. The elements of sound internal control do not change in a computerized environment. Objectives do not change, but techniques do.

Control Techniques

Control techniques commonly used in computerized systems are listed below.

- One-for-one checking consists of checking each source document against a detailed list processed by the computer. This technique normally is used for low-volume input because of the cost and time involved.
- Batch/control totals involve manually grouping transactions at the input stage and manually establishing a control total over the entire group. The methods used include document counts, item or line counts, dollar totals, and cash totals.
- In computer sequence checking, the computer verifies the preassigned serial numbers of input transactions and reports missing or duplicate numbers.
- Computer matching consists of the computer matching the input data to information held on the master file or suspense files. Unmatched items are reported for investigation.
- Programmed edit checks are computer program procedures that edit data. Examples include:
  - Reasonableness
  - Dependency
  - Existence
  - Format
  - Mathematical accuracy
  - Range
  - Digit verification
  - Prior data matching
- Prerecorded input is used to reduce errors during data entry.

Control Objectives

Well-designed computer applications have built-in controls for all functions. The major control objective is completeness of input.

Input completeness control techniques are one-for-one checking, batch control totals, computer sequence check, and computer matching. *Input accuracy controls* ensure that data is initially recorded correctly and converted correctly to machine-readable form. *Input accuracy control techniques* are one-for-one checking, batch control totals, computer matching, programmed edits, and prerecorded input.

Update accuracy ensures that the correct master file account is updated correctly with the correct transaction. *Update accuracy control techniques* are one-for-one checking, batch control totals, computer matching, and programmed checks. *Update control completeness* ensures that all data entered and accepted by the system updates the master file once and only once. *Update control completeness techniques* are one-for-one checking, batch control totals, computer sequence checks, and computer matching.

Authorization controls ensure that only valid transactions are processed, that all transactions processed are authorized by management, and that transactions represent events that actually occurred. *Authorization techniques* used are one-for-one checking and programmed checks.

Maintenance controls provide that data is kept up-to-date or identify unusual data requiring further action. They also ensure that data stored on file is not changed except through the normal processing cycle. *Maintenance control techniques* are used for one-for-one checking, batch control totals, and programmed checks.

Evaluating Application Controls

Evaluating internal controls in an application system requires a thorough understanding of the system. The first phase, information gathering, consists of collecting information about the industry and the risks associated with that industry; conducting ratio analysis and peer comparisons to identify aberrations; understanding how the management runs the business; and determining if there are strong budget-to-actual controls in the organization.

Evaluation is the second phase and consists of the use of questionnaires and/or matrices to evaluate the internal controls and to identify internal control weaknesses. Analyzing the results is necessary to determine if a weakness exists and/or the extent of any weaknesses. A results report should be prepared that includes recommendations.

End-User Computing Internal Control

End-user computing, or distributed processing, has emerged since the advent of microcomputers and provides end-users with equipment (PCs, etc.) and processing capability. Examples include microcomputer development tools such as spreadsheets, database programs, and downloading part of an application and its associated files for processing on a local area network either connected to the mainframe or in a stand-alone mode.

Several new control concerns have been identified as a result of end-user computing.
- Data center controls over the equipment itself (backups, access controls, local password administration, etc.) might not be implemented by the end-users.
- Locally developed spreadsheet or database applications might not have all the controls typically found in mainframe systems.
- Access can be compromised by the end-users by installing a modem and phone line connected to a local area network or stand-alone PC and not informing data security about the arrangement.

The advent of end-user computing raises new threats that should be evaluated as part of internal control evaluation.

Conducting an Investigation Regarding Computer Crimes

Once an organization has received an indication that a possible criminal violation has occurred by means of its information system resources, a preliminary investigation into the allegation should be conducted to achieve the following goals:

1) Determine if indeed a crime has been committed. This is the critical step in the internal investigation. The organization must be careful to differentiate between inadvertent computer misuse and deliberate criminal intent. The company's internal auditors, physical and information security specialists, and senior management should be involved in making this type of decision.

2) Determine the status of the crime. When did the incident begin? Where did the intrusion come from? Internal or external? Is the incident still occurring? If not still occurring, when did it stop?

3) Review the organization security and audit policies and procedures to determine the best method for continuing the investigation.

4) Determine the need for law enforcement assistance. The organization will have to decide if the violation is serious enough to call in the police or other law enforcement entities.

Most computer crimes are not reported to law enforcement due to several factors, including the organization's desire to keep its flaws and weaknesses from being exposed to its customers and stockholders. This is a difficult decision for the company to make. However, as we also mentioned earlier, if companies don't report computer crimes, then law enforcement will be powerless to help prevent and solve them and computer criminals will feel they have a free hand to continue their activities.

Handling the Evidence

One of the major differences between investigating computer-related crimes and conventional criminal activities is the volatility of the evidence that resides in the computers themselves. Indeed, the evidence of a computer intrusion might be erased or altered as part of the intrusion itself. It is therefore very important for the organization and/or law enforcement personnel to deal quickly and decisively with evidence of suspected computer-related criminal activities.

The admissibility of evidence obtained from computers in a court case is really no different from the admissibility of any other type of evidence. The evidence must be:

- Relevant
- Supported by a foundation for its introduction into court
- Legally obtained
- Properly identified
- Properly preserved

In the handling of computer data in criminal investigations, the examiner or investigators must be aware of some of the vulnerabilities of computer evidence:

- The investigator must ensure that turning off power to computer equipment will not destroy or erase evidence that is required for the investigation.
- The read/write heads of hard disk drives must be parked in a retracted position so that powering down the disk drive will not cause the read/write head to contact the surface of the disk platter.
- Be aware that magnetic storage media are vulnerable to magnetic fields and that evidence might be erased without the investigator being aware of the erasure if the media are brought close to a source of a magnetic field.
- Be aware that other equipment attached to the computer might be needed to complete the investigation into the data that resides in the computer.

- The investigator should write-protect all diskettes that are being used in the investigation so that they cannot be written upon inadvertently.

Integrity of Evidence

There are certain issues that must be considered when processing computer evidence. These areas should be considered regardless of whether the incident will be processed as a criminal offense for prosecution or possible civil litigation. Even if the organization decides to take no action at all, how a computer fraud examination is conducted might have potential civil liability implications for both the organization and/or the fraud examiner.

Should the fraud examiner discover evidence on a computer system, he or she must be able to state unequivocally that the evidence was not changed in any way by their actions. This requires that strict forensic methodologies be followed to satisfy the stringent evidentiary standards necessary to ensure the integrity of the evidence "beyond a reasonable doubt" for possible court presentation. Therefore, fraud examiners must be aware of the following issues that relate to the gathering of computer evidence.

Search & Seizure—Expectation of Privacy

The first question that should be asked in a computer fraud examination pertains to the expectation of privacy for any employee or outsider who might be involved in the incident.

For example, in one incident an employee was caught using a company computer for personal use. The company had never established computer use policies. The employee had never been formally notified that personal use of the computer was prohibited and that the company had the right to inspect the contents of the computer at any time. Therefore, when a supervisor discovered inappropriate personal files on the employee's computer, the employee protested the act as an invasion of his privacy.

This demonstrates that appropriate policies can be critical. In the above circumstances the company might have created a situation where they would actually need to obtain a court order or a search warrant through a law enforcement agency just to examine the contents of their own computers.

There is specific wording that should be used in the construction of a search warrant involving either computers or telecommunications equipment. How the equipment and magnetic media are described will be critical to the success of the court case.

Pre-Search Preparation

Obtaining as much intelligence as possible regarding the location of the potential evidence is very desirable before writing the search warrant affidavit. Questions that fraud examiners should consider might include:

- Determine the type of computer systems that will be involved in the search. What operating system is used? Are the computers networked together?
- Determine how many people will be needed to conduct the search. In one case, approximately 17 networked file servers were involved, with multiple routers and dial-up modems. A team of only two investigators would need at least four to six hours to complete a seizure of this magnitude.
- If expert witnesses with a specific expertise are required during the search, identify and clear them before the search warrant is written. Depending on the circumstances, their credentials should possibly be included in the warrant affidavit before they are approved by the magistrate issuing the search warrant. The time to discover that an "expert witness" has a criminal conviction is before the search warrant affidavit has even been written, not when the witness takes the stand to testify in a criminal proceeding.
- Determine the resources that will be required to successfully conduct the search. If a great deal of equipment is to be seized, consider how the equipment will be transported from the location. Obtain sufficient boxes, labels, bags, and other supplies at this time.
- Consider the timing of the search. In another case, an assistant district attorney requested assistance in the execution of a search warrant. When detectives arrived, they discovered that the DA wanted them to seize more than 30 computers, including 3 file servers. This was at 3 p.m., and the DA then told the detectives that the authority to execute the search warrant expired at 5 p.m. Naturally, the detectives could not possibly have conducted the seizure within that time frame and in this case, the evidence was lost. A better strategy would have been to time the execution of the search warrant for 5 p.m. on a Friday afternoon. This would give the entire weekend to conduct the search, if necessary.

Search Warrant Affidavit Construction

The construction of search warrants has been affected by both the new technology and the evolving nature of criminal law. Fraud examiners must now consider several problems not encountered before. For example, the fraud examiner must know how to write a warrant to seize tangible property that contains intangible evidence. Further, the fraud examiner must be allowed to convert that evidence into a human-readable form (i.e., computer storage devices such as floppy disks, which contain information that cannot be viewed without the aid of some electronic device).

The warrant must allow for such contingencies as the ability to seize data files pertinent to the case that are mixed with data files which have nothing to do with the case but reside on the same storage device. The warrant must be broad enough to defend the search and seizure of all computer evidence relevant to the investigation, but narrow enough to exclude all material that is not. This can be an extremely difficult standard to meet at times and might depend on the magistrate to whom the affidavit is presented.

To satisfy the "particularity" requirements of the Fourth Amendment, the fraud examiner must be able to justify each and every item that might contain evidence. For example, stating that "all printers" should be seized might be considered to be overly broad unless the fraud examiner can justify the need for each specific printer.

However, with some thought fraud examiners should be able to justify the search and seizure for everything that they need to complete the search for evidence. Items to be seized might contain any or all of the following, depending upon the nature of the fraud case:

- Computers
- Computer components
- Computer peripherals
- Word processing equipment
- Modems
- Monitors
- Printers
- Plotters
- Optical scanners
- Data storage devices
    - Magnetic
    - Laser
    - Optical
    - Tape
    - PCMCIA
    - ZIP or JAZ drives
        * Cables, wiring, cords
        * Storage media

- Floppy disks
- Hard disks
- Magnetic tape (reels)
- PCMCIA RAM cards
- CD-ROM
- Magnetic/Optical disks
- Digital Audio Tape (DAT)
- Personal data managers
- Flash RAM cards (consider digital camera storage)
  * Computer programs
- Operating systems
- Application software
- Utility programs
- Compilers
- Interpreters
  * Documents
  * Manuals
  * Printouts
  * File listings

All related documentation should be covered by the wording of the search warrant and seized along with the computer system. This documentation could be critical in the analysis of the system hardware and software. Documents could indicate changes that have been made to the system that will help the fraud examiner avoid damaging the system. The fact that access control products have been added to the system might be a helpful piece of information for the fraud examiner.

Processing Evidence for Removal

The search for and seizure of technical equipment requires specific procedures that must be followed by fraud examiners to guarantee the integrity of evidence, and to protect both the organization and the individual fraud examiner from civil litigation. These guidelines are written to satisfy the evidentiary requirements for criminal prosecution, and each step in the process is there for a reason. Fraud examiners who deviate from these guidelines should be able to justify their actions if called into question later.

1. If possible, before executing a search warrant where computer equipment and/or

magnetic storage media is to be seized, try to make sure that someone will be present who is familiar with computer equipment to assist in the identification of the various components.

2. It is critical that *anyone* not involved in the investigation be kept away from any computer equipment, and ***not be allowed to touch any of the equipment!*** This includes any person not directly involved in handling the computer and related equipment. It is possible for a suspect ***or any person*** touching only one key of a system keyboard (when a computer is operational) to destroy evidence. Limit the number of personnel responsible for processing computer-related evidence to maintain the integrity of this evidence.

3. If the person seizing the system has the appropriate training and expertise, it might be useful to observe the video display of the system. Information might be displayed that will be of value in the case. If this occurs, document with a close-up photograph of the video screen. (Take care if using a camera with a flash that the flash does not reflect back into the camera lens.)

4. If a computer or peripheral is not covered by the respective search warrant, leave it alone until a supplemental warrant can be obtained.

5. If the computer is to be removed from the location, do not enter anything via the system keyboard or attempt to read information from the system or any associated magnetic media.

6. Do not move the computer any more than is necessary until it is properly secured. Even then, extreme care should be taken, as sudden motion could cause the destruction of data or damage to the equipment itself.

7. Photograph the overall view of the computer system (wide view). Move the equipment as little as possible before taking this photograph to indicate how the equipment was originally positioned. Consider videotaping the confiscation procedure for complete documentation of all actions performed. However, caution is advised, since the video will capture everything that is said and done. Speculative statements or levity should be restricted.

8. Document the state of the computer when first observed (was it operational, what was displayed on the monitor screen, etc.).

9. Depending on the experience of the person seizing the system, it might be advisable to unplug the power from the Central Processing Unit (CPU) before taking any further action. Unplug the power at the wall outlet, if accessible. Even though this action will lose any data in Random Access Memory, it might prevent the computer from deleting or changing other data. ***NOTE: This applies to stand alone microcomputers only, and does not include computers connected to a Local Area Network (LAN).***

10. Turn off the power to all other components and/or pieces of peripheral equipment (such as printers, video display CRTs, or monitors, etc.). Be aware that many peripherals utilize Random Access Memory, which can contain evidence that will be lost when power is removed.

11. If possible, photograph all cable connections (usually in the rear of the system), before disconnecting.

12. Disconnect all components that are attached to an ***external power supply only*** (e.g., from an electrical wall socket, etc.).

13. Never connect or disconnect any of the cables of the system when the computer is operating. This could result in physical damage to the system components and/or peripheral equipment.

14. Label all cable connections, including any telephone cables that are connected to the system so that the system can be reconstructed at a later time for analysis.

15. Again, photograph all cable connections. Before photographing, try to arrange the cable connector labels in such a way that they will be visible in the photographs.

16. Label each item of equipment that will be confiscated. This includes the CPU, monitor, printers, etc. Each item that has a removable exterior case should be sealed with a tamperproof evidence tape (especially the CPU case). This will help to prevent later allegations that components were removed or altered.

17. Consideration should be given to separate close-up isolation photographs for each item to be seized. These close-up shots will serve the purpose of providing more specific identification of seized items, and responding to possible future allegations of physical damage to a seized item.

18. Document the location of all items seized (which room, specific location in the room, reference to photographs, the person who seized the item, serial numbers, special identification markings, etc.).

19. Check all floppy disk drives to determine if they contain a floppy disk. If so, remove the disk from the drive and place it in a disk sleeve. Write-protect the disk immediately. Label the particular disk drive to show which drive the disk came from, and then label a paper bag to indicate that the floppy disk was taken from the labeled drive. Place the disk in the paper bag and seal it.

20. Place a cardboard insert or a "throwaway" disk into the disk drive and secure the drive door shut to secure the drive heads for transportation. Cardboard inserts are specially made for this purpose. If none are available, a disk of the particular size that contains no data might be used (preferably a new, unused disk).

21. Check any other removable storage media drives, remove any storage media they contain, and label the media for identification purposes. (This includes components such as optical drives, external tape drives, IOMEGA drives, CD-ROM, etc.)

22. If there is any uncertainty as to what a piece of equipment is, do not speculate, just label the equipment with a unique identifying number and secure the item for later analysis. However, be prepared to justify the seizure of a component that might or might not be covered in the search warrant.

23. When all components and cables have been labeled and documented, disconnect the cables from their respective component and secure the cables.

24. If covered in the search warrant, confiscate all related manuals and other documentation, and all magnetic media. Also confiscate any other items that might be evidence in the case and that are covered by the terms of the search warrant.

25. If at all possible, after all equipment and magnetic media have been labeled and inventoried, each item should be stored in a paper bag or a cardboard box and sealed (to keep out dust). Large items, such as the CPU and/or printers could be stored in large paper bags or large boxes. Smaller items, such as floppy disks, could be stored in sandwich-bag sized paper bags. This practice will protect these items from unnecessary exposure to dust. An additional label should be attached to the bag identifying the contents of the bag, along with any identifying numbers, such as the number of an evidence tag. *Note: Plastic bags (such as garbage and sandwich bags) should not be used to store evidence!*

26. Ensure that adequate support is given to all items when they are being moved.

27. Thoroughly document the inventory of everything to be removed from the location. This will be required for the search warrant return (if applicable), but also serves to provide a measure of liability protection for the person seizing the system.

Basic computer procedures are essential when processing evidence. These precautions must be followed explicitly when working with computers:

- *Do not* eat, drink, or smoke close to the computer system or near any of the storage media (such as floppy disks). Crumbs, liquid, and/or smoke particles could all potentially damage the equipment or stored data. If this happens, it becomes very difficult, if not impossible, to recover the data (and evidence).
- *Do not* fold or bend floppy disks, or touch the magnetic media inside the disk cover.
- *Do not* write on a floppy disk, on a label of a disk, or on a bag that contains a disk. Write on a label and then place the label on the disk. If it is necessary to write on a disk, use a soft felt-tip pen.
- *Do not* place magnetic media near magnetic fields, as this could cause damage. Magnetic fields strong enough to damage data are more common than you might think.
- *Do not* expose magnetic media to either extreme heat or cold. Temperatures outside of the range from 40-90 degrees Fahrenheit can damage the data.
- *Do not* fingerprint magnetic media. The particles of fingerprint powder are almost impossible to remove from the media surface, and the drive will not be able to read the data contained on the media. Permanent damage to the drive equipment could also result.

Evidence Storage

After a computer system has been seized, most criminal justice agencies have a central evidence storage facility where the equipment is transported and stored until it is either processed further or needed in court. In the majority of cases, the special storage requirements of computer systems are not addressed.

The storage environment should be in a location that is:
- Relatively dust-free
- Both temperature and humidity controlled
- Free of magnetic and electronic fields

Possible Threats to Magnetic Media
- Telephones
- Radio speakers
- Radio transmitters
- Copy machines
- Plastic garbage or sandwich bags
- Degaussing equipment
- Electric fans
- Under-shelf lighting (heat)
- Leaving media in vehicle trunk during extreme temperatures (either hot or cold)
- Magnets
- Proximity to a radiator or an open heating vent

Evidence Analysis

The primary concern during the analysis of electronic evidence is to maintain the integrity of the evidence. This means that procedures must be developed to ensure that no allegations can be raised in court that the methodology used during analysis could have damaged or altered the hardware, media, or data that constitutes the evidence.

Currently, there are no specialized evidence analysis laboratories available to most criminal justice agencies to analyze computer, electronic, or magnetic evidence. The U.S. Secret Service and the FBI both have such capabilities, but unless the case is of critical importance these laboratories process only cases investigated by those agencies.

Understanding the Terms

To effectively analyze the data stored within a computer the fraud examiner must have a practical understanding of the basic operations of a computer and how it stores information. The fraud examiner must also have the expertise to access the data at the most basic level. Without this knowledge, information could be hidden from view or stored within other files or locations not usually accessed by the computer.

Each new development in technology brings with it new concepts and a new vocabulary. The modern fraud examiner must become familiar with such terms as HEX and ASCII code, switches, feature groups, DNR, memory maps, GUI's, and interrupts. An example of the need to be conversant with the new technology was pointed out when a fraud examiner, involved in a case based on a machine using the DOS Operating System, was asked by the defense attorney to explain the process by which DOS wrote files onto a floppy disk.

Fraud examiners must also be educated in the use of the various software utilities that will enable them to analyze the electronic data. Utilities such as Norton Utilities will be of great assistance in investigations involving personal computers. There are several new utility applications that now automate a great deal of the evidence analysis process. However, you should not use these programs unless you have been properly trained.

Evidence Inventory

Many times computers seized as evidence are only inventoried according to the information available on the outside of the CPU case—namely the make, model, and serial number of the particular unit. The components inside the CPU case are never examined. Fraud examiners must consider that there could literally be thousands of dollars of equipment inside this case. Inadequate inventories of computer equipment leave the organization, and possibly the fraud examiner, in a precarious liability position should any of this equipment be damaged or lost.

In analyzing and searching magnetic or optical media for potential evidence, the fraud examiner should consider the following:

- Mirror copies
- Virus detection
- Keyword search
- Hidden and deleted files
- File slack area

- File signatures
- Encrypted files

"Mirror" Copies

If possible, the fraud examiner should make an exact duplicate, or "mirror" copy, of any media that is to be analyzed. This will ensure that no changes or damage occurs to the original evidence. This will not be possible in all cases due to a lack of equipment or other resources, but should be considered as the "ideal" procedure.

When there is no alternative but to analyze the original of the seized evidence, consideration should be given to using utility software to "lock" the disk so that no information can be written to the disk. This will protect the integrity of the original evidence, and prevent inadvertent alteration of the original data.

Virus Detection

All data storage media should be examined for computer viruses. This will serve not only to protect the fraud examiner's own equipment, but also will protect the fraud examiner from possible allegations that he or she infected the seized media with a computer virus.

Keyword Search

Due to the tremendous storage capacity of contemporary computer media, it might be more cost effective for the fraud examiner to conduct a "keyword search" of the media, searching for key words, names, dates, account numbers, etc. that are material to the fraud case. This will minimize the amount of time used to complete the analysis, and also protects the fraud examiner from possible allegations that their search was overly broad.

"Hidden" and "Deleted" Files

Most computer operating systems allow files to be designated as "hidden" files. When so designated, the files might not be visible to normal search procedures, such as displaying a disk directory. Utility programs exist to show these "hidden" files. Fraud examiners should inspect these files to determine if they were intentionally hidden because they contain evidence.

In addition, many computer users do not realize that an initial command to "delete" a file does not necessarily mean that the file contents have been destroyed. With the appropriate utility programs, erased files can be "unerased" and reviewed by the fraud examiner.

File Slack Area

There is a difference in most operating systems between the "logical" size of a file and the "physical" size of the file. The logical size pertains to the size in the number of "bytes" that the file occupies. In a directory listing, this is the number that is displayed for "file size."

The physical size of a file depends on how the operating system stores files. In most operating systems, the disk is organized into designated blocks called clusters. Files occupy a whole number of clusters, even if the logical size of the file is smaller than the cluster size. In these cases, difference in space between the physical file space and the logical file space is called the file slack area. This area might contain data from previously-erased files that could contain evidence. Unless the fraud examiner has a special utility to identify and investigate the file slack area, potential evidence possibly located there could be missed.

File Signatures

When reviewing a directory listing in a file manager such as Windows Explorer, the "type" of file is one of the options that might display. This information might indicate that the file is an "application," or that it is a "Word Document," or some other type. However, this designation is usually based on the "extension" of the file, and might not be an accurate indication of the file contents.

For example, if a file were created in Microsoft Word, and saved with the file name of "Murder Confession.doc," the directory listing would correctly indicate that this file was a "Word Document." However, if the file were renamed as "Angel.exe," the directory listing would mistakenly indicate that the file was an "application," even though the contents of the file itself have not changed.

Inspecting each and every file on seized media would be tremendously tedious and very time-consuming. However, there are utility programs that can automate this process and report any discrepancies such as the one described above.

Encrypted Files

Should the fraud examiner come across files that have been encrypted during the analysis of seized computer media, several considerations arise.

First of all, utility programs exist to decrypt documents encrypted by many of the more common business software applications, such as Microsoft Word and WordPerfect. There are also several companies who specialize in this type of decryption.

Secondly, there is precedent for forcing the suspect to divulge the decryption code through a court order. Consider once again that the computer is only a container and that the encryption is an additional "lock" that is prohibiting the fraud examiner from reviewing the contents for potential evidence. If a valid search warrant exists authorizing the examination of the data, this would be no different than a court ordering a suspect to unlock a file cabinet to allow the inspection of its contents.

Computer Crime Laws

International Law
With a global communications network such as the Internet, the odds have dramatically increased that a crime may have been perpetrated in a foreign nation, or that records related to a portion of the communications transmission may have passed through another country. This can cause tremendous complications for a fraud examiner attempting to pursue his or her investigation.

Victims of scams originating overseas usually find themselves with virtually no recourse. Recent computer equipment and software scam operations in former communist nations have specifically targeted U.S. users. Language, communication, and distance obstacles are nearly insurmountable in working with foreign law enforcement officials to resolve such cases. In the future, greater international cooperation will be necessary to combat international high tech crime.

Federal Laws
There are many laws that can be used to prosecute computer crimes and frauds. In the United States, the basic laws used to prosecute computer and other high tech crimes are divided into the federal laws and state laws.

Computer Fraud and Abuse Act (Title 18, U.S. Code, Section 1030)
As is also explained in the *Law* section, computer crime is a somewhat nebulous term referring both to cases in which a computer is the instrument of a crime and those in which

it is the object. As the instrument, for example, a computer might be used to solicit fraudulent investments or gain unauthorized access to confidential information. As the object of a crime, the information contained in a computer might be stolen or destroyed. Most computer crimes are prosecuted under traditional fraud, theft, and embezzlement statutes. A statute enacted in 1984, Title 18, U.S. Code, Section 1030, makes certain computer-related activity a specific federal offense. The full text of Section 1030 is set out in the Law section of the *Manual*.

In brief, Section 1030 punishes any intentional, unauthorized access to a "protected computer" for the purpose of:
- Obtaining restricted data regarding national security.
- Obtaining confidential financial information.
- Using a computer which is intended for use by the U. S. government.
- Committing a fraud.
- Damaging or destroying information contained in the computer.

PROTECTED COMPUTER

Title 18, U.S. Code, Section 1030(a)(4) provides that a crime is committed if a person:

> *Knowingly and with intent to defraud, accesses a protected computer without authorization, or exceeds authorized access, and by means of such conduct furthers the intended fraud and obtains anything of value, unless the object of the fraud and the thing obtained consists only of the use of the computer and the value of such use is not more than $5,000 in any 1-year period.*

A *protected computer*, under this section, includes:
- A computer which is used exclusively by a financial institution or the United States government.
- Any computer the use of which affects a computer used by a financial institution or the federal government.
- A computer that is used in interstate or foreign commerce or communication.

The elements of the crime seem to include unauthorized access (or exceeding one's authority), an intent to defraud, and obtaining anything of value. Software as a thing of value would seem to be included. Certainly money is.

COMPUTER USED IN INTERSTATE OR FOREIGN COMMERCE OR COMMUNICATION

Section 1030 was recently amended to include computers used in interstate or foreign commerce or communication. Subsection (a)(5) now provides that a person commits a violation if he or she uses such a computer to knowingly transmit anything that causes damage to a protected computer. The conduct need not be intentional. A violation occurs if the person accesses a protected computer without authorization and causes damage as a result.

The penalty for violations of Section 1030 includes fines and up to twenty years of imprisonment. Subsection (g) provides a civil remedy for any person who suffers damage as a result of a violation of Section 1030.

Electronic Communications Privacy Act (Title 18, U.S. Code, Section 1029)

This federal law prohibits covert spying on voice and data communications. This law extends protection from eavesdropping on mail and telephone communications to include digital data communications, such as remote computing and electronic mail.

The act also defines privacy for electronic mail (e-mail) storage at off-site locations such as remote processing or time-sharing companies. These third-party rights protect the owner of the information from unauthorized access by government officials or employees of computer service firms.

In order to prosecute under this law, however, the data owner must prove that proper protective measures were taken to secure the computer system.

Unlawful Access to Stored Communications (Title 18, U.S. Code, Section 2701)

Whoever intentionally accesses without authorization a facility through which an electronic communication service is provided; or intentionally exceeds an authorization to access that facility; and thereby obtains, alters, or prevents authorized access to a wire or electronic communication while it is in electronic storage in such system is subject to a fine and up to two years in prison.

Wire Fraud (Title 18, U.S. Code, Section 1343)

Whoever transmits any writings, signs, signals, pictures, or sounds by wire, radio, or television communication, for the purpose of executing a fraud, will be fined or imprisoned a maximum of five years, or both. If the violation affects a financial institution, such person shall be fined not more than $1,000,000 or imprisoned not more than 30 years, or both.

The wire fraud statute is often used in tandem with mail fraud statutes in federal prosecutions. Courts interpret the *in furtherance* requirement under this statute similarly to the mail fraud statute. Unlike mail fraud, however, the wire fraud statute requires an interstate or foreign communication for a violation.

Limitations on Exclusive Rights: Computer Programs (Title 17, U.S. Code, Section 117)

Under this statute, the owner of a copy of a computer program is allowed to make additional copies of such program in two instances. First, whenever a program is run, it is generally necessary for a copy to be made onto the hard drive. Therefore, a copy may be made whenever it is necessary for the use of the computer program. Second, most users wish to make a copy for archival purposes, due to hard drive failures and the like.

Both of these copies are made with the authorization of law. However, there is one restriction. All copies must be destroyed when the possession of a computer program ceases to be deemed rightful. Furthermore, any copies made in accordance with this Section may be transferred but must be accompanied by the original program from which copies were made and with all rights in the program.

Criminal Infringement of a Copyright (Title 18, U.S. Code, Section 2319)

Any person who willfully reproduces or distributes, for commercial advantage or private financial gain, one or more copies of copyrighted works totaling in retail value $1,000 or more has committed copyright infringement. This Section imposes the criminal punishment for a copyright infringement conviction and is to be added to any other penalties imposed by other provisions or laws.

The Internet has spawned many criminal ventures. Violators have been known to copy a computer program and then post it on an electronic bulletin board accessible only to members. Users will then sign on to the bulletin board, find the software program, and download a copy for a cheaper price than the original.

Copyright Infringement: Criminal Offenses (Title 17, U.S. Code, Section 506)

This statute punishes the willful infringement of a copyright. Infringement is willful when performed for commercial advantage or private financial gain, or by the reproduction or distribution of copies valued in excess of $1,000. In addition to other penalties, a conviction shall order the destruction of all infringing copies and all devices used in the manufacture of such copies.

The placing of a copyright notice or similar notice that is known to be false will be fined when done with fraudulent intent. Likewise, the removal of a copyright marking will be fined when the alteration is performed with fraudulent intent. And, the false representation of a material fact will be fined when knowingly made in conjunction with the application for a copyright. Punishment for these acts shall be the imposition of a fine not to exceed $2,500.

Electronic Fund Transfers: Criminal Liability (Title 15, U.S. Code, Section 1693n)
This legislation was designed to allow consumers the ease and benefit of electronic fund transfer, while defining the rights and liabilities of the parties involved in such transactions. In particular, this statute attaches criminal liability to the acts of:
- Giving false or inaccurate information under the banking laws and regulations; or
- Failing to provide information required under the banking laws and regulations.

It also prohibits certain actions affecting commerce, including:
- Using, attempting to use, or conspiring to use any fraudulently obtained debit instrument, with knowledge of fraudulent character, to obtain anything with an aggregating value of at least $1,000 within a one-year period; or
- Transporting, attempting to transport, or conspiring to transport a fraudulent debit instrument with unlawful or fraudulent intent, and knowledge; or
- Selling or transporting in interstate or foreign commerce of any fraudulent debit instrument, with knowledge; or
- Receiving, concealing, using, or transporting anything which is proceeds from a fraudulent activity and has a value exceeding $1,000 within any one-year period; or
- Receiving, concealing, using, selling, or transporting of one or more tickets for interstate or foreign transportation which have a value aggregating $500 or more and were obtained by use of a fraudulent debit instrument; or
- Furnishing money, property, services, or anything else of value, aggregating $1,000 or more within a one-year period, in conjunction with the use of a fraudulent debit instrument.

A "debit instrument" as used in this statute means a card, code, or other device (other than a check, draft, or similar paper instrument) which can be used to initiate an electronic fund transfer.

State Laws

At the state level, statutes that might be of use in prosecuting computer crimes would include the penal code violations of larceny (in its many forms), false pretenses, forgery, fraud, embezzlement, vandalism, property destruction, malicious mischief, proprietary information, theft, commercial bribery, and extortion. But most states now expressly provide penalties for crimes perpetrated by use of computers or perpetrated against computers. See the *Law* section for a complete listing of state computer fraud statutes.

Government Information on Cybercrime

The Computer Crime and Intellectual Property Section (CCIPS) of the Criminal Division of the U.S. Department of Justice provides a number of excellent resources regarding computer and Internet fraud.

Their web address is www.cybercrime.gov. On that site, the CCIPS has information about computer crimes, encryption, electronic commerce, hacking, legal issues relating to computer crimes, privacy issues, and international issues, among others.

They also have some superb information regarding the search and seizure of computers, including the CCIPS's manual entitled, *Searching and Seizing Computers and Obtaining Electronic Evidence in Criminal Investigations*. Additionally, they have set forth the federal criminal code sections relating to searches, as well as materials about the Fourth Amendment and the Internet. The materials on search and seizure can be accessed directly at the following site: www.cybercrime.gov/searching.html.

PUBLIC SECTOR FRAUD

Government Fraud Auditing Standards

Standards for audits of government organizations, programs, activities, and functions, and of government assistance received by contractors, non-profit organizations, and other non-government organizations have been developed by the Comptroller General of the United States, General Accounting Office (GAO). These standards are by and large taken from generally accepted auditing standards as established by the AICPA. However, *Government Auditing Standards (2003 Revision)*, also known as the *Yellow Book*, go beyond the AICPA standards. Generally accepted government auditing standards (GAGAS) are required to be followed by auditors and audit organizations when required by law, regulation, agreement, contract, or policy. These standards are classified as follows:

- General Standards
- Fieldwork Standards for Financial Audits
- Reporting Standards for Financial Audits
- Field Work Standards for Performance Audits
- Reporting Standards for Performance Audits

General standards apply to both financial and performance audits and relate to:
- Qualifications of the staff
- Independence of the audit organization and the individual auditor
- Exercising due professional care
- Quality control

Financial statement and financial-related audits:
- Provide reasonable assurance about whether financial statements are presented fairly in all material respects in conformity with generally accepted accounting principles (GAAP), or with a comprehensive basis of accounting other than GAAP.
- Other objectives of financial audits, which provide for different levels of assurance and entail various scopes of work, may include:
    - Providing special reports for specified elements, accounts, or items of a financial statement;
    - Reviewing interim financial information;
    - Issuing letters for underwriters and certain other requesting parties;
    - Reporting on the processing of transactions by service organizations; and

- Auditing compliance with regulations relating to federal award expenditures and other governmental financial assistance in conjunction with or as a by-product of a financial statement audit.

Performance audits:

- Provide information to improve program operations and facilitate decision making by parties with responsibility to oversee or initiate corrective action, and improve public accountability.
- Encompass a wide variety of objectives, including objectives related to assessing program effectiveness and results; economy and efficiency; internal control; compliance with legal or other requirements; and objectives related to providing prospective analyses, guidance, or summary information.

Summary of GAO Standards Relating to Fraud

Field Work Standards for Financial Audits — Chapter 4

GAGAS field work standards for financial audits include the three AICPA generally accepted standards of field work and five other standards specific to government financial audits covering auditor communication, considering the results of previous audits, detecting material misstatements from violations or abuse, developing elements of a finding, and audit documentation.

Detecting Material Misstatements Resulting from Violations of Contract Provisions or Grant Agreements, or from Abuse

4.17 GAGAS require the following:

   a. Auditors should design the audit to provide reasonable assurance of detecting material misstatements resulting from violations of provisions of contracts or grant agreements that have a direct and material effect on the determination of financial statement amounts or other financial data significant to the audit objectives. If specific information comes to the auditors' attention that provides evidence concerning the existence of possible violations of provisions of contracts or grant agreements that could have a material indirect effect on the determination of financial statement amounts or other financial data significant tot eh audit objectives, auditors should apply audit procedures specifically directed to ascertain whether violations of provisions of contracts or grant agreements have occurred or are likely to have occurred.

b. Auditors should be alert to situations or transactions that could be indicative of abuse, and if indications of abuse exist that could significantly affect the financial statement amounts or other financial data, auditors should apply audit procedures specifically directed to ascertain whether abuse has occurred and the effect on the financial statement amounts or other financial data.

4.18 AICPA standards and GAGAS require the following:

a. Auditors are to assess the risk of material misstatements of financial statement amounts or other financial data significant (the terms "material" and "significant" are synonymous under GAGAS. "Material" is used in the AICPA standards in relation to audits of financial statements. "Significant" is used in relation to other types of audits governed by GAGAS, such as performance audits, where the term "material" is generally not used) to the audit objectives due to fraud and to consider that assessment in designing the audit procedures to be performed. (Two types of misstatements are relevant to the auditors' consideration of fraud in an audit of financial statements—misstatements arising from fraudulent financial reporting and misstatements arising from misappropriation of assets. The primary factor that distinguishes fraud from error is whether the underlying action that results in the misstatement in the financial statements is intentional or unintentional.).

b. Auditors are also required to design the audit to provide reasonable assurance of detecting material misstatements resulting from direct and material illegal acts (violations of laws and regulations) and to be aware of the possibility that indirect illegal acts (indirect illegal acts are violations of laws and regulations having material but indirect effects on the financial statements) may have occurred. (Whether a particular act is, in fact, illegal may have to await final determination by a court of law or other adjudicative body. Thus, when auditors disclose matters that have led them to conclude that an illegal act is likely to have occurred, they should not imply that they have made a determination of illegality.)

The additional compliance standard for financial statement audits is:

Auditors should design the audit to provide reasonable assurance of detecting material misstatements resulting from direct and material violations of provisions of contracts or grant agreements. If specific information comes to the auditors' attention that provides evidence concerning the existence of possible violations of provisions of contracts or grant agreements that could have a material indirect effect on the financial statements or significant indirect effect on other financial data needed to achieve audit objectives, auditors should apply audit procedures specifically directed to ascertain whether violations have occurred or are likely to have occurred.

Auditors are responsible for:

- Designing audits to provide reasonable assurance of detecting fraud that is material to the financial statements.
- Designing audits to provide reasonable assurance of detecting material misstatements resulting from direct and material illegal acts as well as other types of noncompliance such as noncompliance with provisions of contracts or grant agreements.
- Being aware of the possibility that indirect illegal acts might have occurred and of the characteristics and types of potentially material fraud.
- Understanding the possible effects of laws and regulations that have a direct and material effect on the financial statements.

4.19 Abuse is distinct from fraud, illegal acts, and violations of provisions of contracts or grant agreements. When abuse occurs, no law, regulation, or provision of a contract or grant agreement is violated. Rather, abuse involves behavior that is deficient or improper when compared with behavior that a prudent person would consider reasonable and necessary business practice given the facts and circumstances. Auditors should be alert to situations or transactions that could be indicative of abuse. When information comes to the auditors' attention indicating that abuse may have occurred, auditors should consider whether the possible abuse could affect the financial statement amounts or other financial data significantly.

4.20 Auditors should exercise professional judgment in pursuing indications of possible fraud, illegal acts, violations of provisions of contracts or grant agreements, or abuse, in order not to interfere with potential investigations, legal proceedings, or both. Under some circumstances, laws, regulations, or policies require auditors to report indications of certain types of fraud, illegal acts, violations of provisions of contracts or grant agreements, and abuse to law enforcement or investigatory authorities before extending audit steps and procedures. Auditors may also be required to withdraw from or defer further work on the engagement or a portion of the engagement in order not to interfere with an investigation.

Developing Elements of a Finding

4.21 Audit findings, such as deficiencies in internal control, fraud, illegal acts, violations of provisions of contracts or grant agreements, and abuse, have often been regarded as containing the elements of criteria, condition, and effect, plus cause when problems are found. However, the elements needed for a finding depend entirely on the objectives of the audit. Thus, a finding or set of findings is complete to the extent that the audit objectives are satisfied. When problems are identified, to the extent possible, auditors should plan audit procedures to develop the elements of a finding to facilitate developing the auditors' report.

Audit Documentation

4.22 The standard related to audit documentation for financial audits performed in accordance with GAGAS is:

Audit documentation related to planning, conducting, and reporting on the audit should contain sufficient information to enable an experienced auditor who has had no previous connection with the audit to ascertain from the audit documentation the evidence that supports the auditors' significant judgments and conclusions. Audit documentation should contain support for findings, conclusions, and recommendations before auditors issue their reports.

4.23 AICPA standards and GAGAS require auditors to prepare and maintain audit documentation. The form and content of audit documentation should be designed to meet the circumstances of the particular audit. The information contained in audit documentation constitutes the principal record of the work that the auditors have performed in accordance with professional standards and the consclusions that the auditors have reached. The quantity, type, and content of audit documentation are a matter of the auditors' professional judgment.

4.24 Audit documentation serves to (1) provide the principal support for the auditors' report, (2) aid auditors in conducting and supervising the audit, and (3) allow for the review of audit quality. The preparation of audit documentation should be appropriately detailed to provide a clear understanding of its purpose and source and the conclusions the auditors reached, and it should be appropriately organized to provde a clear link to the findings, conclusions, and recommendations contained in the audit report. Audit documentation for financial audits performed under GAGAS should contain the following additional items not explicitly addressed in the AICPA standards or elsewhere in the GAGAS:

a. The objectives, scope, and methodology of the audit.
b. The auditors' determination that certain additional government auditing standards do not apply or that an applicable standard was not followed the reasons therfor, and the known effect that not following the applicable standard had, or could have had, on the audit.
c. The auditors' consideration that the planned audit procedures are designed to achieve audit objectives when evidential matter obtained is highly dependent on computerized information systems and is material to the objective of the audit and that the auditors are not relying on the effectiveness of internal control over those computerized systems that produced the information. The audit documentation should specifically address (1) the rationale for determining the nature, timing, and extent of the planned audit procedures; (2) the kinds and competence of available evidential matter produced outside a computerized information system and/or plans for direct testing of data produced from a computerized information system; and (3) the effect on the audit report if evidential matter to be gathered does not afford a reasonable basis for achieving the objectives of the audit. (This documentation requirement does not increase the auditors' responsibility for testing internal control but is intended to assist the auditors in ensuring that audit objectives are met and audit risk is reduced to an acceptable level.)
d. Evidence of supervisory review, before the audit report is issued, of the work performed that supports findings, conclusions, and recommendations contained in the audit report.

4.25 Underlying GAGAS audits is the premise that federal, state, and local governments and other organizations cooperate in auditing programs of common interest so that auditors may use others' work and avoid duplication of audit efforts. Auditors should make arrangements to make audit documentation available, upon request, in a timely manner to other auditors or reveiewers. Contractual arrangements for GAGAS audits should provide for full and timely access to audit documentation to facilitate reliance by others on the auditors' work.

4.26 Audit organizations need to adequately safeguard the audit documentation associated with any particular engagement. Audit organizations should develop clearly defined policies and criteria to deal with situations where requests are made by outside parties to obtain access to audit documentation, especially in connection with situations where an outside party attempts to obtain indirectly through the auditor information that it is unable to obtain directly from the audited entity. In developing such policies, audit organizations need to consider applicable laws and regulations that apply to audit organizations of the audited entity.

Field Work Standards for Performance Audits — Chapter 7

GAGAS has adopted four field work standards for performance audits. The field work standards for performance audits relate to planning the audit; supervising staff; obtaining sufficient, competent, and relevant evidence; and preparing audit documentation.

Designing the Audit to Detect Violations of Legal and Regulatory Requirements, Contract Provisions, or Grant Agreement, Fraud, and Abuse

7.17 When laws, regulations, or provisions of contracts or grant agreements are significant to the audit objectives, auditors should design the audit methodology and procedures to provide reasonable assurance of detecting violations that could have a significant effect on the audit results. Auditors should determine which laws, regulations, and provisions of contracts or grant agreements are significant to the audit objectives and assess the risk that illegal acts or violations of provisions of contracts or grant agreements could occur. Based on that risk assessment, the auditors design and perform procedures to provide reasonable assurance of detecting significant instances of illegal acts or violations of provisions of contracts or grant agreements. Auditors should include audit documentation on their assessment of risk.

7.18 It is not practical to set precise standards for determining whether laws, regulations, or provisions of contracts or grant agreements are significant to audit objectives because government programs are subject to many laws, regulations, and provisions of contracts or grant agreements, and audit objectives vary widely. However, auditors may find the following approach helpful in making that determination:

  a. Reduce each audit objective to questions about specific aspects of the program being audited.

b. Identify laws, regulations, and provisions of contracts or grant agreements that directly relate to specific aspects of the program included in questions that reflect the audit objectives.
c. Determine if violations of those laws, regulations, or provisions of contracts or grant agreements could significantly affect the auditors' answers to the questions that relate to the audit objectives. If they could, then those laws, regulations, and provisions of contracts or grant agreements are likely to be significant to the audit objectives.

7.19 Auditors may find it necessary to rely on the work of legal counsel to (1) determine those laws and regulations that are significant to the audit objectives, (2) design tests of compliance with laws and regulations, or (3) evaluate the results of those tests. Auditors also may find it necessary to rely on the work of legal counsel with audit objectives require testing compliance with provisions of contracts or grant agreements. Depending on the circumstances of the audit, auditors may find it necessary to obtain information on compliance matters from others, such as investigative staff, other audit organizations or government entities that provided assistance to the audited entity, or the applicable law enforcement authority.

7.20 In planning tests of compliance with significant laws, regulations, and provisions of contracts or grant agreements, auditors should assess the risk that violations could occur. That risk may be affected by such factors as the complexity or newness of the laws, regulations, and provisions of contracts or grant agreements. The auditors' assessment of risk includes consideration of whether the entity has controls that are effective in preventing or detecting violations of laws, regulations, and provisions of contracts or grant agreements. If auditors obtain sufficient evidence of the effectiveness of these controls, they can reduce the extent of their tests of compliance.

7.21 In planning the audit, auditors should consider risks due to fraud that could significantly affect their audit objectives and the results of their audit. The audit team should discuss potential fraud risks, considering fraud factors such as individuals' incentives or pressures to commit fraud, the opportunity for fraud to occur, and the rationalizations or attitudes that could allow individuals to commit fraud. Auditors should gather and assess information necessary to identify fraud risks which could be relevant to the audit objectives or affect the results of their audit. For example, auditors may need to obtain information through discussion with officials of the audited entity or through other means to determine the susceptibility of the program to fraud, the status of internal controls the entity has established to detect and prevent fraud, or the risk that officials of the audited entity could override internal control. Auditors should exercise professional skepticism in assessing these risks to determine which factors or risks could significantly affect the results of their work if fraud has occurred or is likely to have occurred.

7.22 When auditors identify factors or risks related to fraud that they believe could significantly affect the audit objectives or the results of the audit, auditors should respond by designing procedures to provide reasonable assurance of detecting fraud significant to the audit objectives. Auditors should prepare audit documentation related to their identification and assessment of and response to fraud risks. Auditors should also be aware that assessing the risk of fraud is an ongoing process throughout the audit and relates not only to planning the audit but also to evaluating evidence obtained during the audit.

7.23 Auditors should also be alert to situations or transactions that could be indicative of fraud. When information comes to the auditors' attention indicating that fraud may have occurred, auditors should consider whether the possible fraud could significantly affect the audit results. If the fraud could significantly affect the audit results, auditors should extend the audit steps and procedures, as necessary, to (1) determine if fraud likely has occurred and (2) if so, determine its effect on the audit results.

Obtaining Information About Laws, Regulations, and Other Compliance Requirements

7.24 Auditors' training, experience, and understanding of the program being audited may provide a basis for recognizing that some acts coming to their attention may be indicative of fraud. Whether an act is, in fact, fraud is a determination to be made through the judicial or other adjudicative system and is beyond auditors' professional expertise and responsibility. However, auditors are responsible for being aware of vulnerabilities to fraud associated with the area being audited in order to be able to identify indications that fraud may have occurred. In some circumstances, conditions such as the following might indicate a heightened risk of fraud:

a. Weak management that fails to enforce existing internal control or to provide adequate oversight over the control process;
b. Inadequate separation of duties, especially those that relate to controlling and safeguarding resources;
c. Transactions that are out of the ordinary and are not satisfactorily explained, such as unexplained adjustments in inventories or other resources;
d. Instances when employees of the audited entity refuse to take vacations or accept promotions;
e. Missing or altered documents, or unexplained delays in providing information;
f. False or misleading information; or
g. History of impropriety, such as past audits or investigations with findings of questionable to criminal activity.

Abuse

7.25   Abuse is distinct from fraud, illegal acts, or violations of provisions of contracts or grant agreements. When abuse occurs, no law regulation, or provision of a contract or grant agreement is violated. Rather, abuse involves behavior that is deficient or improper when compared with behavior that a prudent person would consider reasonable and necessary business practice given the facts and circumstances. Auditors should be alert to situations or transactions that could be indicative of abuse. When information comes to the auditors' attention indicating that abuse may have occurred, auditors should consider whether the possible abuse affects the audit results significantly. If indications of abuse exist that significantly affect the audit results, the auditors should extend the audit steps and procedures, as necessary, to (1) determine whether the abuse occurred and, if so, (2) determine its effect on the audit results. However, because the determination of abuse is subjective, auditors are not expected to provide reasonable assurance of detecting it. Auditors should consider both quantitative and qualitative factors in making judgments regarding the significance of possible abuse and whether they need to extend the audit steps and procedures.

7.26   Auditors should exercise professional judgment in pursuing indications of possible fraud, illegal acts, violations of provisions of contracts or grant agreements, or abuse in order to not interfere with potential investigations, legal proceedings, or both. Under some circumstances, laws, regulations, or policies require auditors to report indications of certain types of fraud, illegal acts, violations of provisions of contracts or grant agreements, or abuse to law enforcement or investigatory authorities before extending audit steps and procedures. Auditors may also be required to withdraw from or defer further work on the audit or a portion of the audit in order not to interfere with an investigation

7.27 An audit made in accordance with these standards provides reasonable assurance of detecting illegal acts, violations of provisions of contracts or grant agreements, or fraud that could significantly affect the audit results; however, it does not guarantee the discovery of illegal acts, violations, of provisions of contracts or grant agreements, or fraud. Nor does the subsequent discovery of illegal acts, violations of contracts or grant agreements, or fraud committed during the audit period necessarily mean that the auditors' performance was inadequate, provided the audit was made in accordance with these standards.

Evidence

7.48 The field work standard related to evidence for performance audits performed in accordance with GAGAS is:

Sufficient, competent, and relevant evidence is to be obtained to provide a reasonable basis for the auditors' findings and conclusions.

7.49 A large part of auditors' work on an audit concerns obtaining and evaluating evidence that ultimately supports their judgments and conclusions pertaining to the audit objectives. In evaluating evidence, auditors consider whether they have obtained the evidence necessary to achieve specific audit objectives. When internal control or compliance requirements are significant to the audit objectives, auditors should also collect and evaluate evidence relating to controls or compliance.

7.50 Evidence may be categorized as physical, documentary, testimonial, and analytical.

PHYSICAL EVIDENCE
Physical evidence is obtained by auditors' direct inspection or observation of people, property, or events. Such evidence may be documented by memoranda, photographs, drawings, charts, maps, or physical samples.

DOCUMENTARY EVIDENCE
Documentary evidence consists of created information such as letters, contracts, accounting records, invoices, and management information on performance.

TESTIMONIAL EVIDENCE

Testimonial evidence is obtained through inquiries, interviews, or questionnaires.

ANALYTICAL EVIDENCE

Analytical evidence includes computations, comparisons, separation of information into components, and rational arguments.

Tests of Evidence

7.52   Evidence should be sufficient, competent, and relevant to support a sound basis for audit findings, conclusions, and recommendations:

   a. Evidence should be sufficient to support the auditors' findings. In determining the sufficiency of evidence, auditors should ensure that enough evidence exists to persuade a knowledgeable person of the validity of the findings. When appropriate, statistical methods may be used to establish sufficiency.
   b. Evidence is competent if it is valid, reliable, and consistent with fact. In assessing the competence of evidence, auditors should consider such factors as whether the evidence is accurate, authoritative, timely, and authentic. When appropriate, auditors may use statistical methods to derive competent evidence.
   c. Evidence is relevant if it has a logical relationship with, and importance to, the issue being addressed.

7.53   The following presumptions are useful in judging the competence of evidence. However, these presumptions are not to be considered sufficient in themselves to determine competence. The amount and kinds of evidence required to support auditors' conclusions should be based on auditors' professional judgment.

   a. Evidence obtained when internal controls are more effective is more competent than evidence obtained when controls are weak or nonexistent. Auditors should be particularly careful in cases where controls are weak or nonexistent and should, therefore, plan alternative audit procedures to corroborate such evidence.
   b. Evidence obtained through the auditors' direct physical examination, observation, computation, and inspection is more competent than evidence obtained indirectly.
   c. Examination of original documents provides more competent evidence than do copies.

d. Testimonial evidence obtained under conditions where persons may speak freely is more competent than testimonial evidence obtained under compromising conditions (for example, where the persons may be intimidated).
e. Testimonial evidence obtained from an individual who is not biased or has complete knowledge about the area is more competent than testimonial evidence obtained from an individual who is biased or has only partial knowledge about the area.
f. Evidence obtained from a credible third-party may in some cases be more competent than that secured from management or other officials of the audited entity.

7.54 Auditors may find it useful to obtain written representations concerning the competence and completeness of certain evidence from officials of the audited entity. Written representations ordinarily confirm oral representations given to auditors, indicate and document the continuing appropriateness of such representations, and reduce the possibility of misunderstandings concerning the matters that are the subject of the representations. Written representations can take several forms, including summary documents prepared by the auditors and signed by the entity's management. If officials of the audited entity refuse to provide a written representation that the auditors have requested, the auditors should consider the effects of the refusal on the results of the audit.

7.55 The auditors' approach to determining the sufficiency, competence, and relevance of evidence depends on the source of the information that constitutes the evidence. Information sources include original data gathered by auditors and existing data gathered by either officials of the audited entity or a third-party. Data from any of these sources may be obtained from computer-based systems.

7.56 *Data gathered by auditors.* Data gathered by auditors include the auditors' own observations and measurements. Among the methods for gathering this type of data are questionnaires, structured interviews, direct observations, and computations. The design of these methods and the skill of the auditors applying them are the keys to ensuring that these data constitute sufficient, competent, and relevant evidence. When these methods are applied to determine cause, auditors are concerned with eliminating conflicting explanations.

7.57 *Data gathered by management.* Auditors can use data gathered by officials of the audited entity as part of their evidence. However, auditors should determine the validity and reliability of data that are significant to the audit objectives and may do so by direct tests of the data. Auditors can reduce the direct tests of the data if they test the effectiveness of the entity's internal controls over the validity and reliability of the data and these tests support the conclusion that the controls are effective. The nature and extent of data testing will depend on the significance of the data to support the auditors' findings. How the use of unaudited data gathered by officials of the audited entity affect the auditors' report depends on the data's significance to the auditors' findings.

7.58 *Data gathered by third parties.* The auditors' evidence may also include data gathered by third parties. In some cases, these data may have been audited by others, or the auditors may be able to audit the data themselves. In other cases, however, it will not be practical to obtain evidence of the data's validity and reliability. How the use of unaudited third-party data affects the auditors' report depends on the data's significance to the auditors' findings.

7.59 *Validity and reliability of data from computer-based systems.* Auditors should obtain sufficient, competent, and relevant evidence that computer-processed data are valid and reliable when these data are significant to the auditors' findings. This work is necessary regardless of whether the data are provided to the auditors or auditors independently extract them. Auditors should determine if officials of the audited entity or other auditors have worked to establish the validity and reliability of the data or the effectiveness of the controls over the system that produced the data. If the results of such work are current, auditors may be able to rely on that work. Auditors may also determine the validity and reliability of computer-processed data by direct tests of the data.

7.60 Auditors can reduce the direct tests of the data if they test the effectiveness of general and application controls over computer-processed data and these tests support the conclusion that the controls are effective. If auditors determine that internal controls over data that are significantly dependent upon computerized information systems are not effective or if auditors do not plan to test the effectivesss of such controls, auditors should include audit documentation regarding the basis for that conclusion by addressing (1) the reasons why the design or operation of the controls is ineffective, or (2) the reasons why it is inefficient to test the controls. In such circumstances, auditors should also include audit documentation regarding their reasons for concluding that the planned audit procedures, such as direct tests of the data, are effectively designed to achieve specific audit objectives. This documentation should address:

a. The rationale for determing the types and extent of planned audit procedures;
b. The kinds and competence of available evidence produced outside a computerized information system; and
c. The effect on the audit report if the evidence gathered during the audit does not allow the auditors to achieve audit objectives.

7.61 When the auditors' tests of data disclose errors in the data, or when they are unable to obtain sufficient, competent, or relevant evidence about the validity and reliability of the data, they may find it necessary to:

a. Seek evidence from other sources,
b. Redefine the audit's objectives to eliminate the need to use the data, or
c. Use the data, but clearly indicate in their report the data's limitations and refrain from making unwarranted conclusions or recommendations.

Audit Documentation

7.66 The field work standard related to audit documentation for performance audits performed in accordance with GAGAS is:

Auditors should prepare and maintain audit documentation. Audit documentation related to planning, conducting, and reporting on the audit should contain sufficient information to enable an experienced auditor, who has had no previous connection with the audit, to ascertain from the audit documentation the evidence that supports the auditors' significant judgments and conclusions. Audit documentation should contain support for findings, conclusions, and recommendations before auditors issue their reports.

7.67 The form and content of audit documentation should be designed to meet the circumstances of the particular audit. The information contained in audit documentation constitutes the principal record of the work that the auditors have performed in accordance with standards and the conclusions that the auditors have reached. The quantity, type, and content of audit documentation are a matter of the auditors' professional judgment.

7.68 Audit documentation serves to (1) provide the principal support for the auditors' report, (2) aid auditors in conducting and supervising the audit, and (3) allow for the review of audit quality. Audit documentation should be appropriately detailed to provide a clear understanding of its purpose and source and the conclusions the auditors reached, and it should be appropriately organized to provide a clear link to the findings, conclusions, and recommendations contained in the audit report. Audit documentation for performace audits should contain the following items not explicitly addressed elsewhere in GAGAS:

   a. The objectives, scope, and methodology of the audit, including sampling and other selection criteria used;
   b. The auditors' determination that certain standards do not apply or that an applicable standard was not followed, the reasons therefor, and the known effect that not following the applicable standard had, or could have had, on the audit;
   c. The work performed to support significant judgments and conclusions, including descriptions of transactions and records examined (auditors may meet this requirement by listing file numbers, case numbers, or other means of identifying specific documents they examined. They are not required to include copies of documents they examined as part of the audit documentation, nor are they required to list detailed information from those documents); and
   d. Evidence of supervisory reviews, before the audit report is issued, of the work performed that supports findings, conclusions, and recommendations contained in the audit report.

7.69 Audit organizations should establish reasonable policies and procedures for the safe custody and retention of audit documentation for a time sufficient to satisfy legal and administrative requirements. Audit documentation allows for the review of audit quality by providing the reviewer with documentation, either in written or electronic formats, of the evidence supporting the auditors' significant judgments and conclusions. If audit documentation is only retained electronically, the audit organization should ensure that the electronic documenatation is capable of being accessed throughout the specified retention period established for audit documentation and that it is safeguarded through sound computer security.

7.70 Underlying GAGAS audits is the premise that federal, state, and local governments and other organizations cooperate in auditing programs of common interest so that the auditors may use others' work and avoid duplication of effort. Auditors should make arrangements to make audit documentation available, upon request, in a timely manner to other auditors or reviewers. Contractual arrangements for GAGAS audits should provide for full and timely access to audit documentation to facilitate reliance by others on the auditors' work.

7.71 Audit organizations need to adequately safeguard the audit documentation associated with any particular engagement. Audit organizations should develop clearly defined policies and criteria to deal with situations where requests are made by outside parties to obtain access to audit documentation, especially in connection with situations where an outside party attempts to obtain indirectly through the auditor information that it is unable to obtain directly from the audited entity. In developing such policies, audit organizations need to consider applicable laws and regulations applying to the audit organizations of the audited entity.

Reporting Standards for Financial Audits — Chapter 5

For financial statement audits, GAGAS incorporate the AICPAs' four generally accepted standards of reporting. In addition, GAGAS has adopted six additional standards: reporting auditors' compliance with GAGAS, reporting on internal control and on compliance with laws, regulations, and provisions of contracts or grant agreements; reporting deficiencies in internal control, fraud, illegal acts, violations of provisions of contracts or grant agreements, and abuse; reporting views of responsible officials; reporting privileged and confidential information; and report issuance and distribution.

Reporting Auditors' Compliance with GAGAS

5.05 The standard related to reporting auditors' compliance with GAGAS for financial audits performed in accordance with GAGAS is:

Audit reports should state that the audit was performed in accordance with GAGAS.

5.06 When the report on the financial audit is submitted to comply with a legal, regulatory, or contractual requirement for a GAGAS audit, or when GAGAS are voluntarily followed, the report should specifically cite GAGAS and may also cite AICPA standards.

Reporting on Internal Control and on Compliance with Laws, Regulations, and Provisions of Contracts or Grant Agreements

5.08 The second additional reporting standard for financial statement audits is:

When providing an opinion or a disclaimer on financial statements, auditors should include in their report on the financial statements either a (1) description of the scope of the auditors' testing of internal control over financial reporting and compliance with laws, regulations, and provisions of contracts or grant agreements and the results of those tests or an opinion, if sufficient work was performed, or (2) reference to the separate report(s) containing that information. If auditors report separately, the opinion or disclaimer should contain a reference to the separate report containing this information and state that the separate report is an integral part of the audit and should be considered in assessing the results of the audit.

5.09 For audits of financial statements in which auditors provide an opinion or disclaimer, auditors should report the scope of their testing of internal control over financial reporting and of compliance with laws, regulations, and provisions of contracts or grant agreements including whether or not the tests they performed provided sufficient evidence to support an opinion on the effectiveness of internal control over financial reporting and on compliance with laws, regulations, and provisions of contracts or grant agreements.

5.10 Auditors may report on internal control over financial reporting and on compliance with laws, regulations, and provisions of contracts or grant agreements in the opinion or disclaimer on the financial statements or in a separate report or reports. When auditors report on internal control over financial reporting and compliance as part of the opinion or disclaimer on the financial statements, they should include an introduction summarizing key findings in the audit of the financial statements and the related internal control and compliance work. Auditors should not issue this introduction as a stand-alone report.

5.11 When auditors report separately (including separate reports bound in the same document) on internal control over financial reporting and compliance with laws and regulations and provisions of contracts or grant agreements, the opinion or disclaimer on the financial statements should state that the auditors are issuing those additional reports. The opinion or disclaimer on the financial statements should also state that the reports on internal control over financial reporting and compliance with laws and regulations and provisions of contracts or grant agreements are an integral part of GAGAS audit and should be considered in assessing the results of the audit.

Reporting Deficiencies in Internal Control, Fraud, Illegal Acts, Violations of Provisions of Contracts or Grant Agreements, and Abuse

5.12 The third additional reporting standard for financial statement audits is:

For financial audits, including audits of financial statements in which the auditor provides an opinion or disclaimer, auditors should report, as applicable to the objectives of the audit, (1) deficiencies in internal control considered to be reportable conditions as defined in AICPA standards, (2) all instances of fraud and illegal acts unless clearly inconsequential, and (3) significant violations of provisions of contracts or grant agreements and abuse. In some circumstances, auditors should report fraud, illegal acts, violations of provisions of contracts or grant agreements, and abuse directly to parties external ot the audited entity.

REPORTING DEFICIENCIES IN INTERNAL CONTROL

5.13 For all financial audits, auditors should report deficiencies in internal control considered to be reportable conditions as defined in AICPA standards. The following are examples of matters that may be reportable conditions:

a. Absence of appropriate segregation of duties consistent with appropriate control objectives;
b. Absence of appropriate reviews and approvals of transactions, accounting entries, or systems output;
c. Inadequate provisions for the safeguarding of assets;
d. Evidence of failure to safeguard assets from loss, damage, or misappropriation;
e. Evidence that a system fails to provide complete and accurate output consistent with the control objectives of the audited entity because of the misapplication of control activities;
f. Evidence of intentional override of internal controls by those in authority to the detriment of the overall objectives of the system;
g. Evidence of failure to perform tasks that are significant part of internal control, such as reconciliations not prepared or not timely prepared;
h. A weakness in the control environment at an entity such as the absence of a sufficient positive and supportive attitude towards internal control by management within the organization;

i. Deficiencies in the design or operation of internal control that could result in violations of laws, regulations, provisions of contracts or grant agreements; fraud; or abuse having a direct and material effect on the financial statements or the audit objectives; and

j. Failure to follow up and correct previously identified deficiencies in internal control.

5.14 When reporting deficiencies in internal control, auditors should identify those reportable conditions that are individually or in the aggregate considered to be material weaknesses. Auditors should place their findings in proper perspective by providing a description of the work performed that resulted in the finding. To give the reader a basis for judging the prevalence and consequences of these findings, the instances identified should be related to the population of the number of cases examined and be quantified in terms of dollar value, if appropriate.

5.15 To the extent possible, in presenting audit findings such as deficiencies in internal control, auditors should develop the elements of criteria, condition, cause, and effect to assist management or oversight officials of the audited entity in understanding the need for taking corrective action. In addition, if auditors are able to sufficiently develop the findings, they should provide recommendations for corrective action. Following is guidance for reporting on elements of findings:

a. Criteria: An audit report is improved when it provides information so that the report user will be able to determine what is the required or desired state or what is expected from the person or operation. The criteria are easier to understand when stated fairly, explicitly, and completely, and the source of the criteria is identified in the audit report.

b. Condition: The audit report is improved when it provides evidence of what the auditors found regarding the actual situation. Reporting the scope or extent of the condition allows the report user to gain an accurate perspective.

c. Cause: The audit report is improved when it provides persuasive evidence on the factor or factors responsible for the difference between condition and criteria. In reporting the cause, auditors may consider whether the evidence provides a reasonable and convincing argument for why the stated cause is the key factor or factors contributing to the difference as opposed to other possible causes, such as poorly designed criteria or factors uncontrollable by program management. The auditors also may consider whether the identified cause could serve as a basis for the recommendation.

d. Effect: The audit report is improved when it provides a clear, logical link to establish the impact of the difference between what the auditors found (condition) and what should be (criteria). Effect is easier to understand when it is stated clearly, concisely, and, if possible, in quantifiable terms. The significance of the reported effect can be demonstrated through credible evidence.

5.16 When auditors detect deficiencies in internal control that are not reportable conditions, they should communicate those deficiencies separately in a management letter to officials of the audited entity unless the deficiencies are clearly inconsequential considering both quantitative and qualitative factors. Auditors should refer to that management letter in the report on internal control. Auditors should use their professional judgment in deciding whether or how to communicate to officials of the audited entity deficiencies in internal control that are clearly inconsequential. Auditors should include in their audit documentation evidence of all communications to officials of the audited entity about deficiencies in internal control found during the audit.

Reporting Fraud, Illegal Acts, Violations of Provisions of Contracts or Grant Agreements, and Abuse

5.17 AICPA standards and GAGAS require auditors to address the effect fraud or illegal acts may have on the audit report and to determine that the audit committee or others with equivalent authority and responsibility are adequately informed about the fraud or illegal acts. GAGAS further require that this information be in writing and also include reporting on significant violations of provisions of contracts or grant agreements and significant abuse. Therefore, when auditors conlude, on the basis of evidence obtained, that fraud, an illegal act, a significant violation of a contract or grant agreement, or significant abuse either has occurred or is likely to have occurred, they should include in their audit report the relevant information.

5.18 When reporting instances of fraud, illegal acts, violations of provisions of contracts or grant agreements, or abuse, auditors should place their findings in proper perspective by providing a description of the work performed that resulted in the finding. To give the reader a basis for judging the prevalence and consequences of these findings, the instances identified should be related to the population or the number of cases examined and be quantified in terms of dollar value, if appropriate. If the results cannot be projected, auditors should limit their conclusion to the items tested.

5.19 To the extent possible, auditors should develop in their report the elements of criteria, condition, cause, and effect when fraud, illegal acts, violations of provisions of contracts or grant agreements, or abuse is found.

5.20 When auditors detect inmaterial violations of provisions of contracts or grant agreements or abuse, they should communicate those findings in a management letter to officials of the audited entity unless the findings are clearly inconsequential considering both qualitative and quantitative factors. Auditors should refer to that management letter in their audit report on compliance. Auditors should use their professional judgment in determing whether and how to communicate to officials of the audited entity fraud, illegal acts, violations of provisions of contracts or grant agreements, or abuse that is clearly inconsequential. Auditors should include in their audit documentation evidence of all communications to officials of the audited entity about fraud, illegal acts, violations of provisions of contracts or grant agreements, and abuse.

Direct Reporting of Fraud, Illegal Acts, Violations of Provisions of Contracts or Grant Agreements, and Abuse

5.21 GAGAS require auditors to report fraud, illegal acts, violations of provisions of contracts or grant agreements, and abuse directly to parties outside the audited entity in two circumstances, as discussed below. These requirements are in addition to any legal requirements for direct reporting of fraud, illegal acts, violations of provisions of contracts or grant agreements, or abuse. Auditors should meet these requirements even if they have resigned or been dismissed from the audit prior to its completion.

5.22 The audited entity may be required by law or regulation to report certain fraud, illegal acts, violations of provisions of contracts or grant agreements, or abuse to specified external parties, such as a federal inspector general or a state attorney general. If auditors have communicated such fraud, illegal acts, violations of provisions of contracts or grant agreements, or abuse to the audited entity and the audited entity fails to report them, then the auditors should communicate such an awareness to the governing body of the audited entity. If the audited entity does not make the required report as soon as possible after the auditors' communication with the entity's governing body, then the auditors should report such fraud, illegal acts, violations of contracts or grant agreements, and abuse directly to the external party specified in the law or regulation.

5.23   Management of the audited entity is responsible for taking timely and appropriate steps to remedy fraud, illegal acts, violations of provisions of contracts or grant agreements, or abuse that auditors report to it. When fraud, illegal acts, violations of provisions of contracts or grant agreements, or abuse involve awards received directly or indirectly from a government agency, auditors may have a duty to report directly if management fails to take remedial steps. If auditors conclude that such failure is likely to cause them to depart from the standard report on the financial statements or resign from the audit, they should communicate that conclusion to the governing body of the audited entity. Then, if the audited entity does not report the fraud, illegal act, violation of provisions of contracts or grant agreements, or abuse as soon as possible to the entity that provided the government assistance, the auditors should report the fraud, illegal act, violation of provisions of contracts or grant agreements, or abuse directly to that entity.

5.24   In these situations, auditors should obtain sufficient, competent, and relevant evidence, such as confirmation from outside parties, to corroborate assertions by management that it has reported fraud, illegal acts, violations of provisions of contracts or grant agreements, or abuse. If they are unable to do so, then the auditors should report such fraud, illegal acts, violations of provisions of contracts or grant agreements, or abuse directly as discussed above.

5.25   Laws, regulations, or policies may require auditors to report promptly indications of certain types of fraud, illegal acts, violations of provisions of contracts or grant agreements, or abuse to law enforcement or investigatory authorities. In such circumstances, when auditors conclude that these types of fraud, illegal acts, violations of provisions of contracts or grant agreements, or abuse either have occurred or are likely to have occurred, they should ask those authorities and/or legal counsel if publicly reporting certain information about the potential fraud, illegal acts, violations of provisions of contracts or grant agreements, or abuse would compromise investigative or legal proceedings. Auditors should limit their public reporting to matters that would not compromise those proceedings, such as information that is already a part of the public record.

Reporting Views of Responsible Officials

5.26   The fourth additional reporting standard for financial statement audits is:

If the auditors' report discloses deficiencies in the internal control, fraud, illegal acts, violations of provisions of contracts or grant agreements, or abuse, auditors should obtain and report the views of responsible officials concerning the findings, conclusions, and recommendations, as well as planned corrective actions.

Reporting Privileged and Confidential Information

5.31 The fifth additional reporting standard for financial statement audits is:

If certain pertinent information is prohibited from general disclosure, the audit report should state the nature of the information omitted and the requirement that makes the omission necessary.

Report Issuance and Distribution

5.34 The sixth additional reporting standard for financial statement audit is:

Government auditors should submit audit reports to the appropriate officials of the audited entity and to appropriate officials of the organizations requiring or arranging for the audits, including external funding organizations such as legislative bodies, unless legal restrictions prevent it. Auditors should also send copies of the reports to other officials who have legal oversight authority or who maybe responsible for acting on audit findings and recommendations and to others authorized to receive such reports. Unless the report is restricted by law or regulation, or contains privileged and confidential information, auditors should clarify that copies are made available for public inspection. Nongovernment auditors should clarify report distribution responsibilities with the party contracting for the audit and follow the agreements reached.

Reporting Standards for Performance Audits — Chapter 7

According to GAGAS, the reporting standards for performance audits relate to the form of the report, the report contents, report quality, and report issuance and distribution.

The report contents reporting standard includes the following requirements:

8.16 The audit report should include any significant deficiencies in internal control, all instances of fraud and illegal acts unless they are inconsequential, significant violations of provisions of contracts or grant agreements, and significant abuse.

Fraud, Illegal Acts, Violations of Provisions of Contracts or Grant Agreements, and Abuse

8.19 When auditors conclude, based on evidence obtained, that fraud, illegal acts, significant violations of provisions of contracts or grant agreements, or significant abuse either has occurred or is likely to have occurred, they should include in their audit report relevant information.[93] Abuse occurs when the conduct of a government program or entity falls far short of behavior that is expected to be reasonable and necessary business practices by a prudent person.

8.20   When reporting instances of fraud, illegal acts, violations of provisions of contracts or grant agreements, and abuse, auditors should place their findings in proper perspective by providing a description of the work conducted that resulted in the finding. To give the reader a basis for judging the prevalence and consequences of these findings, the instances identified should be related to the population or the number of cases examined and be quantified in terms of dollar value, if appropriate. If the results cannot be projected, auditors should limit their conclusion to the items tested.

8.21   When auditors detect violations of provisions of contracts or grant agreements; or abuse that is not significant, they should communicate those findings in a separate letter to officials of the audited entity unless the findings are clearly inconsequential, considering both qualitative and quantitative factors. If the auditors have communicated instances of fraud, illegal acts, violations or provisions of contracts or grant agreements, or abuse in a separate letter to officials of the audited entity, auditors should refer to that letter in the audit report. Auditors should use their professional judgment in determining whether and how to communicate to officials of the audited entity fraud, illegal acts, violations of provisions of contracts or grant agreements, and abuse that are clearly inconsequential. Auditors should include in their audit documentation evidence of all communications to officials of the audited entity about instances of fraud, illegal acts, violations of provisions of contracts or grant agreements, and abuse.

Direct Reporting of Fraud, Illegal Acts, Violations of Provisions of Contracts or Grant Agreements, and Abuse

8.22   GAGAS require auditors to report fraud, illegal acts, violations of provisions of contracts or grant agreements, and abuse directly to parties outside the audited entity in certain circumstances, as discussed below. These requirements are in addition to any legal requirements for direct reporting of fraud, illegal acts, violations of provisions of contracts or grant agreements, and abuse. Auditors should meet these requirements even if they have resigned or been dismissed from the audit.

8.23 The audited entity may be required by law or regulation to report certain fraud, illegal acts, violations of provisions of contracts or grant agreements, or abuse to specified external parties, such as a federal inspector general or a state attorney general. If auditors have communicated such fraud, illegal acts, violations of provisions of contracts or grant agreements, or abuse to the audited entity and it fails to report them, then the auditors should communicate their awareness of that failure to the governing body of the audited entity. If the audited entity does not make the required report as soon as possible after the auditors' communication with the entity's governing body, then the auditors should report such fraud, illegal acts, violations of provisions of contracts or grant agreements, or abuse directly to the external party specified in the law or regulation.

8.24 Officials of the audited entity are responsible for taking timely and appropriate steps to remedy fraud, illegal acts, violations of provisions of contracts or grant agreements, or abuse that auditors report to them. When fraud, illegal acts, violations of provisions of contracts or grant agreements, or abuse involves assistance received directly or indirectly from a government agency, auditors may have a duty to report such fraud, illegal acts, violations of provisions of contracts or grant agreements, or abuse directly to that government agency if officials of the audited entity fail to take remedial steps. If auditors conclude that such failure is likely to cause them to report such findings or resign from the audit, they should communicate that conclusion to the governing body of the audited entity. Then, if the audited entity does not report the fraud, illegal act, violation of provisions of contracts or grant agreements, or abuse as soon as possible to the entity that provided the government assistance, the auditors should report the fraud, illegal act, violation of provisions of contracts or grant agreements, or abuse directly to that entity.

8.25 In these situations, auditors should obtain sufficient, competent, and relevant evidence, such as confirmation with outside parties, to corroborate assertions by officials of the audited entity that the officials have reported fraud, illegal acts, violations of provisions of contracts or grant agreements, or abuse. If the officials are unable to do so, then the auditors should report such fraud, illegal acts, violations of provisions of contracts or grant agreements, or abuse directly as discussed above.

8.26 Laws, regulations, or other authority may require auditors to report promptly indications of certain types of fraud, illegal acts, violations of provisions of contracts or grant agreements, or abuse to law enforcement or investigatory authorities. In such circumstances, when auditors conclude that these types of fraud, illegal acts, violations of provisions of contracts or grant agreements, or abuse either have occurred or are likely to have occurred, they should ask those authorities or legal counsel if publicly reportingcertain information about the potential fraud, illegal acts, violations of provisions of contracts or grant agreements, or abuse would compromise investigative or legal proceedings. Auditors should limit the extent of their public reporting to matters that would not compromise those proceedings, such as information that is already a part of the public record.

False Claims and Statements

Intentionally false statements (such as false eligibility declarations for government benefits and false claims) may be offenses themselves or could be part of broader schemes involving misappropriation, contract or procurement fraud, and corruption.

Federal Laws Prohibiting False Claims

There are a number of federal statutes related to false claims and statements made to the federal government. Among the most useful are:

- Conspiracy to Defraud the Government with Respect to Claims (18, U.S.Code, § 286)
- False, Fictitious, or Fraudulent Claims (18, U.S. Code, § 287)
- False Statements (18, U.S. Code, § 1001)
- Major Fraud Against the United States (18, U.S. Code, § 1031)
- Obstruction of Federal Audit (18, U.S. Code, §1516)
- Racketeer Influenced and Corrupt Organizations (RICO) (18, U.S. Code, § 1961, et. seq.)
- Federal Corruption Statutes (18, U.S. Code, § 201, et. seq.)
- Anti-Kickback Act of 1986 (41, U.S. Code, §§ 51–58)

These statutes are discussed in greater detail in the Law section. There are also a number of civil remedies discussed in the Law section including the Civil False Claims Act, Program Fraud Civil Remedies—Public Law 99-509, and the Civil Monetary Penalty Law (CMPL).

Generally, a false statement can be oral, written, sworn or unsworn, signed or unsigned. The person must make the false statement knowingly and willfully and the statement must be made to a government agency or a government contractor or fiscal intermediary. The false statement must be a material fact that influences the outcome of the agency action. The plaintiff (government) does not have to prove that the false statement led to a favorable agency action, but only that the government relied on the statement and it was capable of influencing a decision, that the government suffered a loss, and that the false statement was made directly to the government.

The false statement does not have to be presented to the government directly or indirectly. If it remains part of the contractor's business records, such as altered employee time cards as part of a scheme to mischarge labor costs to the government, a § 1001 violation is possible if the records were to be made available for inspection by the government agency.

Examples of False Claims

Some examples of false claims and statements include:
- Falsified contractor qualifications
- False certifications or assurances
- False records or invoices
- Invoices from nonexistent companies
- Claims made in duplicate or altered invoices
- Billing for fictitious employees
- Billing for goods and services not provided
- Inflated costs or substitution of cheaper goods

Other examples of false claims and statements might include false statements about employees, fictitious transactions, and falsified documents.

False Statements Concerning Employees

EXAMPLE

A meat packing company in Nebraska pled guilty to SSN misuse, Social Security benefits fraud, harboring aliens, and filing false employment documents. The company was fined $103,000. The settlement came after federal agents raided the plant, arresting more than 300 people. Of those arrested, most agreed to deportation without hearings. The company admitted to harboring aliens, but it claimed that illegal workers were never hired knowingly.

Fictitious Transactions

EXAMPLE

A former supervisory accountant in the Environmental Protection Agency pled guilty to defrauding the EPA of $28,000. She admitted that she entered false information into the EPA's Integrated Financial Management System resulting in her receiving 23 U.S. Treasury checks which she later deposited into her credit union account. After receiving the *funds, she then made entries into the financial reporting system which balanced the accounts.*

False Documentation

EXAMPLE

A former real estate salesperson was indicted and arrested for submitting false statements to a mortgage corporation in an attempt to qualify a veteran for a VA-guaranteed loan. The indictment charged that the individual deposited funds into a credit union account belonging to the veteran, then submitted a document to the mortgage corporation reflecting the false and fictitious account balance. The loan defaulted and resulted in a loss to the VA of $44,708.

Detection

The ultimate detection method for false statements is the examination of source documents. This auditing approached is termed "Inside-Out," that is, from the source document out to the report or financial statement.

However, the auditor might be alerted to the possibility of false statements if any of the following red flags are present:
- Failure to produce documents in a timely manner
- Failure to respond to inquiries in a timely manner
- Inadequacies in reporting requirements (for example, untimely reports, incomplete reports, and others)
- Failure to have an adequate information gathering and retrieval system
- Altered or missing documents
- Photocopied or duplicate documents
- Failure to have adequate supporting documentation for reports and summary data

Failure to Produce Documents in a Timely Manner

This might be an indication that there are no source documents to substantiate the summary data. For example, if costs are submitted for reimbursement, and the costs have not been incurred, then there will be no supporting data.

Failure to Respond to Inquiries in a Timely Manner

This might also be an indication that there is no source documentation. It can also be an indication that the information is not readily retrievable. This area should, however, be approached with caution. If new and different information is requested, the contractor or agency might have to redesign its system in order to retrieve the requested information, causing an unanticipated time delay. It is important the requests for proposals include adequate specifications for responding to data requests.

Inadequacies in Reporting Requirements

If the required reports are consistently late, incomplete, or unsatisfactory, this might be an indication that the source data is either unavailable, nonexistent, or it cannot be retrieved. Source data is derived from source documentation. If the source documentation is false, then summarizing the corresponding data becomes an increasingly more difficult problem.

Failure to Have Adequate Information Gathering and Retrieval Systems

This, along with the red flags concerning the source documents, assists the auditor in determining whether or not the scope of the audit should be increased, and if so, in what areas.

Altered or Missing Documents

Frauds are often concealed by altering or "misplacing" the supporting documentation. The tenacity of the auditor to obtain and examine the source documentation will go a long way in proving false statements.

Photocopied or Duplicate Documents

Transactions should be authorized and recorded based on original documentation, not duplicates. Duplicates or photocopied documentation is subject to alteration and manipulation.

Failure to Have Adequate Supporting Documentation for Reports and Summary Data

In order for supporting documentation to be adequate, it must be sufficient, competent, and relevant. In addition, the auditor must apply common sense to the source document. For example, are the amounts too high or too low, do they include odd times, places, and/or people?

These are all indicators that there might be false statements. Therefore, these red flags might alert the auditor to select a larger sample of source documents for examination.

Beneficiary Fraud

Beneficiary frauds tend to be perpetrated by individuals, without collusion or bribery. The motive for this type of fraud is personal gain (or reduction of loss) by the perpetrator.

An example of this type of fraud might include a taxpayer who claims an unearned tax credit on his federal income tax return. This person has perpetrated a fraud against the government.

Some reported cases typifying these frauds are:
- Social Security frauds
- False claims for benefits
- Supplemental Security Income fraud
- Fraudulent Social Security numbers
- Improper billing procedures
- False Medicare claims
- Kickbacks

Schemes
Social Security Frauds

> EXAMPLE
>
> *An Indiana woman was sentenced to 5-1/2 years incarceration, suspended, ordered to make restitution of $40,800, and fined $10,000 for concealing her mother's death and forging and cashing her Social Security benefits checks. An out-of-state relative had told police it was difficult to believe that her mother, who was in her seventies, was always indisposed when they called. Police found the woman's remains in a padlocked mobile home next to the woman's house.*

> EXAMPLE
>
> *A Washington D.C. woman was found to have wrongfully converted 34 Social Security widow's benefit checks made payable to her deceased mother, thereby improperly receiving $13,400 from the Social Security Administration. Aggravating circumstances were found in that she wrongfully converted an additional 190 Social Security checks and attempted to*

conceal her misconduct by lying to the SSA field representative regarding the whereabouts of her deceased mother. The Administrative Law Judge found that the woman was liable under the Program Fraud Civil Remedies Act for having submitted claims she knew were false. She therefore had to pay the maximum amount of penalties and assessments, which totaled $196,800.

False Claims For Benefits

EXAMPLE

A Michigan man was sentenced to 5 months in prison, 5 months of house arrest, and 2 years supervised probation for disability fraud. He was also fined $20,000 and ordered to make restitution of more than $39,999 to SSA. A building contractor, he began receiving disability benefits from SSA in 1979. After bragging to friends and family about ripping off the system, he came under investigation which led to his conviction.

Supplemental Security Income Fraud

EXAMPLE

A California woman was convicted of murdering three of seven SSI beneficiaries found buried in the yard of her boarding house. She had been charged with murdering all seven boarders, plus two found elsewhere, for their benefits. The OIG investigators who assisted in identifying the victims and the theft of their benefits checks also proved that the woman had impersonated one of the victims in attempting to obtain Dalmane, a drug found in seven of the bodies. She was sentenced to life imprisonment without possibility of parole.

Fraudulent Social Security Numbers

EXAMPLE

Nine individuals were sentenced to prison in Illinois for terms ranging from 2-½ to nearly 5 years for a series of schemes through which they defrauded several insurance companies. They obtained approximately $500,000 by submitting false claims under fraudulent SSNs in 27 incidents in several cities throughout the United States. The claims were based on automobile and slip-and-fall accidents that were either staged or never occurred. In addition, three of the defendants, two of whom were insurance company employees, stole blank checks from an insurance company and cashed them on forged endorsements for

$68,000. The group moved from city to city using false names and SSNs' which made them difficult to find or identify.

Improper Billing Procedures

EXAMPLE

A Utah physician was convicted on 32 federal counts of mail fraud, submitting false claims, and aiding and abetting. Although he was excluded from participating in the Medicare and state health care programs in 1987 for similar crimes, he continued to submit claims under the names and provider numbers of physicians who performed services at his clinic. He also upcoded claims and billed for services not rendered. He was sentenced to 56 months in prison and 3 years probation upon release, fined $50,000 and assessed a special victim's assessment fee.

False Medicare Claims

EXAMPLE

A speech therapist was sentenced in Minnesota to 16 months incarceration for causing the submission of false Medicare claims. He contracted with a therapy company to bill Medicare and Medicaid for his work in several nursing homes. The company reported that he overstated time spent with patients, claiming up to 20 hours a day. He claimed to provide speech therapy to a patient several days after the patient's death, and to nursing home residents he had never met. He was also observed using flash cards with a blind resident. He was ordered to pay restitution of $40,000 and a fine of $25,000.

Kickbacks

EXAMPLE

The former billing clerk and 14 former patients of a Georgia chiropractor were sentenced in a kickback scheme costing Medicare and more than 30 insurance companies millions of dollars. All were incarcerated and ordered to pay fines and restitution. The chiropractor and his office manager wife had paid employees 10 percent of each week's revenues, and patients 33 percent of whatever the carriers paid on their claims. Claims were submitted for patients and their families regardless of whether they were treated. In one instance, bills were submitted for 169 persons supposedly treated in one day. More than 40 persons have *been sentenced thus far, including the chiropractor and his wife, who earlier received lengthy jail sentences and were ordered to pay $2.2 million in restitution.*

Detection

As with false statements perpetrated by management, the best detection methods for beneficiary fraud will require the examination of source documents or developing computer programs to identify fraudulent patterns.

In either a performance audit or a financial audit, the fraud examiner should include some steps to determine if there is a high occurrence rate for beneficiary fraud. By selecting a random sample of recipient beneficiaries and examining the documentation supporting the benefits, the auditor might be able to estimate the potential of beneficiary fraud schemes.

Government Initiatives to Reduce Fraud

The Department of Defense (DoD)

This department, long notorious for its waste and abuse, has dramatically increased its fraud detection and prevention efforts in the last decade. A full complement of auditors and investigators are assigned to detect and prevent fraud. Contract officers are trained to recognize and required to promptly report any possibly fraudulent situations. Major government contractors are assigned a DoD auditor who works on-site, increasing the chances of possible procurement fraud being reported. The measures taken to combat fraud in this agency have proven quite effective, with increased prosecution and recovery.

DoD investigative agencies exist for all branches of the armed services:
- Air Force Office of Special Investigations (OSI)
- Army Criminal Investigation Command (CIC)
- Naval Investigative Services (NIS)

In addition to their other investigative duties, each of these agencies pursues fraud cases involving military personnel, civilian employees, and contractors.

Defense Contract Audit Agency (DCAA)

The DCAA is essentially an audit agency that reviews procurement contracts. It has the authority to subpoena contractors' records, if fraud is suspected. Government suppliers with large contracts usually are assigned their own DCAA auditor. The *Defense Contract Audit Manual* explains fraud reporting procedures for DCAA auditors. Reports of fraud are passed to DCAA Counsel and the Assistant Director and from there, to the appropriate DoD or federal investigative branch. DCAA auditors are trained to look for:

- Poor internal controls
- Bad financial situations
- Inadequate accounting records
- Poor timekeeping system
- A mix of commercial, fixed-price, and cost-type contracts
- A background of fraud
- Management dominated by one or a few individuals
- Individuals with lavish lifestyles beyond their incomes
- No or few internal and external audits

Defense Logistics Agency (DLA)

Larger government contractors have staff from this agency stationed in their facilities. Their purpose there is to serve as contract administrators and inspection personnel. If a DLA employee working in this capacity suspects contract or procurement fraud, a report is made to DoD legal personnel. Cases are investigated by the appropriate branch's Inspector General personnel.

The Justice Department

According to a report issued by the Office of the Attorney General in 1980 ("National Priorities for the Investigation and Prosecution of White Collar Crime"), procurement fraud is the primary area of investigative efforts by the Justice Department. Since the publication of that report, priorities do not appear to have changed. The Department of Defense and the General Services Administration seem to be the two governmental entities with the highest incidences of corruption and fraud.

> *Procurement fraud by contractors was described in the report as including 1) inflated payrolls and other costs, (2) substitution of inferior goods, (3) collusion among contractors, developers, and suppliers resulting in rigged-bidding or overbilling, (4) nonperformance of contracted services, (5) exaggerated weights and measures, and (6) diversion of federal funds to personal use.*

Criminal prosecution of government fraud has dramatically increased since the 1980 report. The government's message is clear: offenders will be prosecuted and punished to the full extent of the law.

Criminal Division

Within the Justice Department's Criminal Division, two offices are primarily occupied with white-collar crime: the Public Integrity Section and the Fraud Section. The Public Integrity Section reviews anti-fraud programs involving white-collar crimes by public officials. The Fraud Section's duties include:

- Investigating and prosecuting complex, sensitive, or multi-district cases involving major white-collar crimes either developed by the Section or as requested by U.S. Attorney's offices
- Providing training to federal, state, and local investigators and prosecutors
- Developing and implementing national white-collar crime enforcement policies

Voluntary Disclosure

The Voluntary Disclosure Program was begun by DoD in 1986, and allows contractors to inform DoD of irregularities. While the program does not state that voluntary disclosure will exempt contractors from prosecution or suspension, it does note that voluntary disclosure and full cooperation "are strong indications of an attitude of contractor integrity even in the wake of disclosures of potential criminal liability."

Certain criteria exist for contractors to claim they made a voluntary disclosure. While voluntary disclosure of wrongdoing may not exempt a corporation from prosecution, it certainly is a contributing factor in the decision of whether to prosecute.

- The admission must come from the corporation, not an individual employee.
- Any disclosure precipitated by the knowledge that news of the fraud may soon leak out and cause a government investigation would not allow the contractor to claim voluntary disclosure.
- After the disclosure has been made, the corporation must take immediate steps to correct the damage done the government and discipline the offending parties.
- Full cooperation with the government investigation is essential.

Prosecution: The Government Employee's Role

The government employee will frequently work with investigators from the appropriate government agency. Some of the investigators will be specialists, while others handle a great variety of cases. In addition, some investigators are assigned to civil cases, while others will specialize in criminal activity.

Common Problems of Investigators
Regardless, they all face common problems, as set forth below.

Lack of Familiarity with Terminology
Many investigators assigned to fraud and white-collar crime cases lack a business background. This is both a strength and weakness. It is a strength in that they will normally ask the same questions and be confused on the same issues as a lay jury. It is a weakness in that many investigators are confused over accounting concepts, and the auditor must explain these concepts in nontechnical language.

Wide Variety of Case Assignments
The typical investigator for a government agency must investigate a wide variety of cases, and therefore might not be intimately familiar with your type of case.

Case Loads
Like auditors, most government investigators have more cases than they can handle. They therefore look for the most egregious violations, or the ones in which proof is easily at hand. For that reason, investigators tend to place more reliance on witnesses than on documents.

Reluctance of Government Prosecutors
An investigator will not investigate cases that prosecutors will not accept. Although not prosecutors themselves, investigators tend to develop a "sixth sense" for what will be prosecuted and what will not. This issue is addressed below.

Key Issues Facing Investigators
Investigators are looking to maximize the cost-benefit relationship of their resources. In general, they believe that auditors are too ready to place undue reliance on documentation, and do not understand the concept of "jury appeal" which is detailed in the next section.

The typical investigator asks:
- What is the evidence? Is it clear and convincing?
- Who are the witnesses? Are they credible?
- What is the amount of the loss? Can it be proven?
- What is the intent of the perpetrator? Can it be demonstrated that there was malice aforethought?

- How difficult is the case to investigate? Is it necessary to review reams of documents looking for evidence?

Overcoming the Reluctance to Investigate

The auditor can best overcome reluctance of the investigator to work a case by good salesmanship. In this regard, the following suggestions are helpful:

- Present your case in person, not over the telephone.
- Spend a little time establishing a relationship with the investigator if you do not know him.
- Summarize your case in one sentence. If you cannot, there is little realistic hope of prosecution.
- After summarizing the case, fill in the details. Do not overwhelm the investigator with minutia.
- Pledge the resources of your agency in helping provide backup.
- Follow up periodically with the investigator after the case has been referred, but be careful of making a pest of yourself.
- Offer an expert witness if necessary. Remember, though, if you testify in a criminal case, you might be excluded from sitting in on your own case due to rules concerning witnesses.

Interviewing Government Officials

More and more frequently, high government officials find themselves the subjects of investigations into allegedly fraudulent activities. In today's climate of complaints and accusations, a high official may be questioned intensely on subjects ranging from misallocating parking spaces or personal use of frequent traveler miles on the trivial end to bribery and conflict of interest on the serious side.

Regardless of the seriousness of the allegations, the accusation will trigger an all-out investigation/audit into the matter. This is true whether the source of the allegation is a reliable one or an anonymous tipster. The issue is not the lack of discretion in deciding what "cases" to investigate, but how to conduct interviews of senior officials.

Assigning the Interview

People assigned to interview high officials will find that there are both similarities and differences with "normal" interviews.

The first rule is to ensure that the interviewer is not subordinate to the subject of the interview. This is no problem for outside entities such as an independent counsel or even an inspector general, but where auditors or investigators need to interview someone far up in their own chain of command, problems may arise.

If there is any possibility that the high official could presently or in the future influence the career of the interviewer, someone else should be chosen. Agencies should be able to call on outside entities to conduct such interviews where appropriate. In any event, any hint by the official of help (or harm) to the interviewer should be documented and reported.

The term "high official" appears to encompass a homogenous group, but, in reality, anyone from a naive or brash political appointee to a grizzled and canny veteran civil servant with many such interviews under his belt may be encountered. The best method of interviewing will therefore depend on a number of factors:
- Is the interviewee suspected of wrongdoing?
- Is he likely to be cooperative? (Are there files or previous interviewers who can be consulted?)
- Is he likely to be embarrassed by the results of the inquiry even though not personally culpable?

These and other factors will determine whether the interviewer should be humble, deferential, apologetic, matter-of fact, or aggressive. Obviously, no one mode fits all subjects or all situations. However, the interviewer should not be cowed by the subject's position, although feigning humility may be appropriate.

The Warning Dilemma
A crucial element in interviewing a high official as with the interview of any public employee is proper regard for the Constitutional rights of the subject. A series of cases in the 1960s such as *Murphy v. Waterfront Commission of New York Harbor*, 378 U.S. 52 (1964), *Garrity v. New Jersey*, 385 U.S. 493 (1967) and *Gardner v. Broderick*, 392 U.S. 273 (1968) are instructive. In a nutshell, the United States Supreme Court held that a public employee cannot be compelled to answer job-related questions concerning his own possible criminal conduct under threat of disciplinary action, e.g., removal, without violating his rights under the Self-Incrimination Clause of the Fifth Amendment. The choice between job forfeiture and self-incrimination, said the Court, is inherently coercive and, in effect, a choice "between the rock and the whirlpool." Put another way, a public employee cannot be put in a position wherein he will incriminate himself if he tells the truth, will subject himself to perjury prosecution if he lies,

or will set himself up for a removal action if he refuses to cooperate. Thus, the issue of what warning(s), if any, to give the subject must be addressed.

If the high official is *reasonably* believed to be merely a third-party witness, no warnings are required, and he is obligated to respond to the questions. In fact, most agencies have a provision in their policies and procedures manual that mandates cooperation. The following is typical:

Requirement to Cooperate

> *Employees must furnish testimony, or fully disclose information in their knowledge or possession, concerning any matter of official interest, to any federal court, board, panel, tribunal, agent, or official authorized to conduct a particular inquiry, investigation, hearing, trial or other proceeding, or to act upon such testimony or information, when directed to do so by proper authority. In this regard, employees must answer any proper questions, under oath or affirmation if required, including furnishing or authorizing the release of information related to their financial affairs, which has reasonable relationship to matters of official interest.*

An agency's table of offenses and penalties then delineates the punishment for failure to cooperate.

However, before these rules can be utilized in a case where the official is suspected of wrongdoing, a threshold determination of whether or not the violation is potentially criminal (and not whether a prosecutor would in fact accept it), must be made. If the allegation is inherently administrative, i.e., noncriminal, in nature, such as misuse of vehicles or giving the appearance of a conflict of interest, the Fifth Amendment does not come into play and the official must cooperate in the same fashion as if he were a third-party witness. Instructive is the Merit Systems Protection Board's 1981 decision in *Ashford v. Bureau of Prisons*, 6 MSPB 389, MSPR 458, 81 FMSR 7044.

Administrative Warnings

The official should be advised of his obligation to cooperate via the agency's so-called "administrative warning" which will read similar to the following:

> *Under [the applicable agency policies and procedures manual] you are required to disclose any information in your possession pertaining to the matter which I am investigating and answer any proper questions which might be put to you.*
>
> *You may be subject to disciplinary action for your failure or refusal to answer proper questions relating to the performance of your duties as an employee. You may also be subject to criminal prosecution for any false answer that you give to any of my questions. Do you understand this?*

It should be noted that there is never a right to lie, even if incorrect warnings or no warnings were given. Only silence would be acceptable.

Criminal Investigations

If, on the other hand, the high government official is the subject of an actual or potential criminal investigation, a totally different situation arises. As noted above, a public employee cannot be compelled to cooperate or face loss of his job. The first step may well be attempting to secure the *voluntary* cooperation of the individual with clear and full knowledge on his part of the possible consequences. Many agencies have developed their own wording, but the "Beckwith" or "Civiletti" warning is often used:

> *You have the right to remain silent if your answers may tend to incriminate you.*
>
> *Anything you say may be used as evidence both in an administrative proceeding or any future criminal proceeding involving you.*
>
> *If you refuse to answer the questions posed to you on the grounds that the answers may incriminate you, you cannot be discharged solely for remaining silent. However, your silence can be considered in an administrative proceeding for its evidentiary value that is warranted by the facts surrounding your case.*

This warning clearly discloses its voluntary nature and the possible adverse consequences of cooperation. But in reality, adverse consequences for failing to cooperate under these circumstances are negligible.

Declination of Prosecution

If the interviewee declines to cooperate voluntarily, the interviewer must make an election. If he absolutely needs the statement of the official to ascertain what occurred, he must forego any use of the statement (or of any evidence derived from the statement) in a subsequent criminal prosecution. In fact, the interviewer must secure a declination of prosecution from a prosecutor and thus eliminate the Fifth Amendment problem. (The United States courts and most state courts confer "only" use immunity on an official who must cooperate pursuant to an agency's regulations, although at least one state's supreme court has mandated transactional immunity). In any event, a heavy burden is imposed on the government to show that its subsequent criminal case was not tainted by the compelled statement, and a decision to compel an interview will ordinarily preclude the option of criminal prosecution.

To ensure that the interviewee has been advised of his obligation to cooperate in a declined criminal case, the "Kalkines" warning must be given immediately following the above-mentioned administrative warning:

> *You are further advised that the answers you give to my questions pertaining to the matter presently under investigation or any information or evidence which is gained by reason of your answers, cannot and will not be used against you in any subsequent criminal proceedings, except that you may be subject to criminal prosecution for any false answer that you give to any questions. Do you understand this?*

Failure to comply with this elaborate and complex array of warning requirements can and unfortunately does ruin otherwise well-run investigations of senior officials. Two additional cases worth reading are *Kalkines v. United States*, 473 F.2d 1391 (CtCl, 1973) and *Weston v. Department of Housing and Urban Development*, 724 F.2d 943 (CAFC, 1983). A final key point to remember is that a failure to give a proper warning by *any* interviewer, with or without official authority to bind the government, will in fact do so.

Legal Counsel

The higher the official to be interviewed, the more likely he is to be cognizant of his right to the presence of counsel and his ability to afford one. High officials are also frequently shocked by the fact that they may not be entitled to representation. In fact, government employees are more often than not in a position where no right to counsel in an interview exists. Simply put, if the official is being interviewed as a witness only (and not as a suspect) or if the matter is strictly administrative, or if, although criminal in nature, a decision has been made not to prosecute, there is simply no right to the presence of an attorney (or any other personal representative).

Miranda warnings, of course, are limited to those situations where the interviewee is "in custody or otherwise deprived of his freedom of action in any significant way," i.e., is in jail, under arrest, or in a situation that has all the trappings of a formal arrest. Such situations will rarely arise. See *Beckwith v. United States*, 425 U.S. 341 (1976); *Howard v. Office of Personnel Management*, 86 FMSR 5342 (1986); *Ashford v. Bureau of Prisons, supra.*

Only where criminal liability is a possibility and the interview is thus voluntary in nature will the official be able to insist on the presence of a lawyer as a condition of his cooperation. It is important to remember, however, that even though an official may not have the *right* to counsel, the decision as to whether or not to allow it is a tactical one and, in a particular case, may be the quickest and most efficient means to secure the desired information.

Obstructing the Investigation

An official who declines to be interviewed or to answer certain questions acts at his own peril if under orders from his own superior or on the advice of counsel. In fact, a superior who tells his employees of whatever rank that they do not have to cooperate with investigations commits actionable misconduct. Often overlooked is the ability of high officials to influence underlings to be less than forthcoming or to "misplace" key documents.

When appropriate, the high official should be reminded of all public employees' obligation to assist in the fact-finding process. Interviewers should make no assumption in advance of any high official's integrity or lack thereof. Finally, the high official who offers the "I was conducting my own investigation" story usually gets no further than did the "Abscam" defendants.

Rules of Procedure

Those who interview high officials must avoid extremes of procedure and should, as a general rule, neither act overly belligerent nor kowtow to them. Basic rules of procedure in the areas of warnings and representation apply to these people as much as to the general population of public employees. What is different is the high official's ability to influence others and their particular susceptibility to embarrassing publicity, and a good interviewer will turn these traits to his own advantage in his quest for a truthful recitation of what did in fact occur.

CONTRACT AND PROCUREMENT FRAUD

The detection and proof of fraud in contract and procurement areas require expertise in the law of contracts, in company or agency policies and rules, and about industry standards and practices.

Elements of a Contract

A contract is a mutual agreement, oral or written, between two or more parties which must contain the following elements:
- Competent parties
- Lawful subject matter or objective
- Legal consideration(s)
- Mutual promises
- Mutual obligations

To be successful in detecting and proving fraud, the fraud examiner must establish objective criteria to evaluate the contract. The fraud examiner must have an understanding of proper contracting procedures at the presolicitation, solicitation and negotiation, and performance and administration phases.

Presolicitation Phase

The activities typically involved during presolicitation are:
- Need recognition
- Notice of intent to contract
- Development of specifications
- Award criteria

The fraud examiner should look for variations from standard or accepted procedures and the absence of proper documentation.

The most prominent schemes involved at this phase of contracting or procurement are:
- Determining needs
- Bid specifications

Determining Needs

The typical fraud in the need recognition phase of the contract negotiation is collusion between the buyer and contractor, where the buyer's employee receives a gratuity or kickback for recognizing a "need" for a particular product or service.

Bid Specifications

Bid specifications and statements of work detailing the types and amounts of goods and services to be provided are prepared to assist in the selection process. They are intended to provide both potential bidders and the selecting officials with a firm basis for making and accepting bids.

A well-written contract will contain specifications, standards, and statements of work which clearly detail the rights and entitlements of the contractor. Carelessly written specifications, standards, and statements of work make it easier for a contractor to claim at a later time that he is entitled to more money than the buyer intended to pay.

Sometimes, the buyer's personnel and the contractor deliberately collude to write vague specifications. At other times, there is an agreement to amend the contract to increase the price immediately after the award. One contractor actually developed a "cost enhancement plan," which identified all the changes he would make in order to double the cost of the contract, before it was even signed.

POORLY WRITTEN SPECIFICATIONS

In some instances, the fraud is committed solely by the contractor based on poorly written specifications. In the instance of poorly written specifications, it is easy for the contractor to deliver a product or service that is priced higher than what was ordered.

VAGUE SPECIFICATIONS

In other instances, vague specifications are deliberately written by the buyer in collusion with the contractor, so that more money can be claimed later.

AGREEMENT TO AMEND CONTRACTS

In situations where there is collusion between the buyer and supplier, there is sometimes an agreement to award the contract based on skimpy specifications, and then increase the price later once the contract has been awarded through amendments to the contract.

DETECTION

The following is a list of potential red flags for frauds involving specifications:

- Providing the contractor with information or advice on a preferential basis
- Using statements of work, specification or sole source justifications developed by, or in consultation with, a contractor who will be permitted to bid
- Permitting consultants who assisted in the preparation of the statements of work, specifications, or design to perform on the contract as subcontractors or consultants
- Splitting costs into separate categories to avoid review
- Writing specifications not consistent with past similar procurement

Solicitation and Negotiation Phase

Fraud schemes involved during this phase typically involve collusion between the buyer and contractor and contractors of competing companies in the bidding process. Schemes in this phase also involve defective pricing.

Bid Submission Schemes

Schemes involving bid submissions can take on many forms. It can involve anyone in the contracting cycle such as a buyer or contracting official, engineer, technical representative, quality or product assurance representative, subcontractor liaison employee—anyone who can *influence* the awarding of a contract.

Examples of bid submission schemes are:
- Premature opening of bids
- Altering bids
- Unjustifiable extension of bid opening dates
- Controlled bid opening
- Falsifying bid logs and documents

DETECTION

To detect bid submission schemes the fraud examiner should be aware of:
- Acceptance of late bid
- Falsification of documents or receipts to get a late bid accepted
- Change in bid after other bidders prices are known
- Change in bid dates
- Receipt of late bids
- Last bid usually receives the bid

Bid-Rigging Schemes

Most bid-rigging fraud schemes involve collusion between contractors of competing companies during the bidding process.

BID ROTATION

Collusive bidding occurs when a group of prospective vendors exchanges information on contract solicitations, taking turns at submitting the "low bid."

BID SUPPRESSION

In this type of scheme, one or more competitors agrees with at least one other competitor to refrain from bidding or agrees to withdraw a previously submitted bid so that a contractor's bid will be accepted. Other forms of this activity involve agreements by competitors to fabricate bid protests or to coerce suppliers and subcontractors not to deal with nonconspirators who submit bids.

A variation of bid suppression occurs when competitors make arrangements to refrain from competing in a designated portion of a market. This might be accomplished based on customer or geographic area. The result of such a division is that competing firms will not bid or will submit only complementary bids (discussed below) when requests for bids are issued in the competitor's unassigned area.

COMPLEMENTARY BIDS

Complementary bidding, also known as "protective" or "shadow" bidding, occurs when competitors submit token bids that are too high to be accepted (or if competitive in price, then on special terms that will not be acceptable). Such bids are not intended to secure the buyer's acceptance, but are merely designed to give the appearance of genuine bidding.

PHANTOM BIDS

Several companies have been caught creating dummy companies to submit a variety of bids on a single contract. That way, they give the appearance of vigorous competition while actually bidding against themselves.

DETECTION

To detect these types of fraud, the fraud examiner must be alert for:
- "Unsuccessful" bidders who later become subcontractors
- Wide disparity in bid prices

- Same contractors who bid on all projects with rotating low bidders
- Other qualified vendors who fail to submit bids
- Bid protests from losing, qualified bidders
- Splitting up requirements so contractors can each get a "fair share," and can rotate bids
- A rotational pattern to winning bidders
- A geographical pattern to winning bidders
- Joint venture bids by firms who could have bid individually

Defective Pricing Schemes

Defective pricing occurs during the negotiated contracting process when contractors fail to disclose accurate cost or pricing data in their price proposals, resulting in an increased contract price.

Examples of defective pricing schemes generally involve the submission of inflated labor costs and inflated material/parts costs. Other schemes involve:
- The use of vendors other than the one proposed
- Not disclosing documents on vendor discounts
- Changing make or buy decisions
- Not disclosing residual material inventory
- Inflating costs by channeling work under contract through a dummy company
- Withholding information on batch purchases

DETECTION

To detect defective pricing schemes, the fraud examiner should be alert for the following:
- Failure to update cost or pricing data even though it is known that past activity showed that costs or prices have decreased
- Failure to correct known system deficiencies which can lead to defective pricing
- Repeated denial by the contractor of the existence of historical records
- Delay in the release of data to the buyer to preclude possible price reductions
- Altered supporting data

Contract Performance and Administration Phase

Contract performance activities include change orders; timely review of completed portions prior to sign-off and release of monies; and assessment of deliverables for compliance with the terms of the contract, including quality control. There are two basic schemes perpetrated during the performance phase: product substitution and mischarges (accounting, material, and labor).

Product Substitution

In order to increase profits, the contractor might employ a product substitution scheme, failing to meet the contract specifications in the areas of either quantity or quality of products. Examples of schemes involving product substitutions include:

- Delivery of inferior/substandard material
- Delivery of materials that have not been tested
- Falsification of test results
- Delivery of used, surplus, or reworked parts
- Delivery of counterfeit products
- Submission of false certifications (Certifications are statements that parts or materials are new, domestically manufactured, and meet the contract specifications concerning quality and quantity or that the company is minority-owned.)
- Delivery of commercial equivalents hardware
- Passing off or specially creating samples for inspection
- Surreptitious movement of inspection tags to uninspected goods
- Substitution of look-alike goods

DETECTION

The following is a list of potential red flags for product substitution schemes:

- High percentage of product returns to vendor for noncompliance with specifications
- Product compliance certificate missing
- Compliance certificates signed by low-level employee with no quality assurance responsibilities
- Materials testing done by supplier, using his own personnel and facilities
- Laboratory test reports are identical as to sample descriptions and test results, varying only as to date and lot number tested
- Highest profit product lines have the highest number of material return authorizations or reshipments

In order to detect these types of frauds, the fraud examiner should consider the following audit procedures:

- Conduct both routine and unannounced inspections and testing
- Carefully review the inspection and testing reports
- Request assistance from outside technical personnel to conduct after-the-fact tests
- Interview personnel and others for indications of noncompliance
- Review correspondence and contract files for indications of noncompliance

Mischarges

ACCOUNTING MISCHARGES

Accounting mischarges are defined as knowingly charging unallowable costs to the buyer, concealing or misrepresenting them as allowable costs, or hiding them in accounts (such as office supplies) which are not usually audited closely. Another common variation involves charging types of costs or independent research and development to other cost categories.

MATERIAL MISCHARGES

Material mischarges are usually limited to raw materials which can be used on many different contract products or diverted for personal use. Numerous cases have been discovered where the buyer-owned material, which was used on a similar contract (for example, commercial), shows up on the accounting records as being used in the manufacturing process for the subject contract (for example, government).

DETECTION

Material mischarges can be detected by examining material cost transfers. These might include transfers:

- From government contracts to commercial
- Via any type of suspense or holding account
- From ongoing jobs to jobs not scheduled for delivery until far into the future
- From prior lot work orders to current or future work orders
- To inventory write-off accounts
- To scrap accounts
- Of materials ordered and charged in excess of contract requirements
- Of seemingly unrelated materials charged on routing slips
- In which material standards are not updated over periods of time when the contractor recognizes improvements in manufacturing technology or product design
- In which a significant variance exists between proposed versus negotiated vendor prices

LABOR MISCHARGES

Labor costs are perhaps more susceptible to mischarging than are material costs, because employee labor can readily be charged to any contract. The only way to ensure that labor costs are charged to the correct account is to actually observe the work of each employee (to determine the contract on which he is working), then determine from the accounting records that the employee's cost is charged to the proper contract.

There are several schemes involving mischarged labor costs. Some of the more prominent ones are:
- Transfer of labor costs
- Time and charges do not agree with contractor billing
- Fictitious time cards
- Changes made to individual time cards
- Time card charges by supervisors

DETECTION

Labor mischarges can sometimes be detected by examining the following:
- Distinctive labor-charging patterns on research and development
- Significant increases in charging to overhead accounts (for example, idle time, down time, and nonapplied time)
- Reclassification or reorganization of employees from indirect to direct charges
- Changes in the labor-charging relationships between certain tasks or types of labor
- Decrease in indirect expense pools
- Increased labor hours with no corresponding increases in materials used or units shipped
- Actual hours and dollars consistently at or near budgeted amounts

COMPUTER PROGRAMS

The computer can have a tremendous impact on fraud examinations. Generally, programs can be easily written which will identify suspicious activity without having to manually review a voluminous amount of data. This is more conducive to detecting fraud as well as being a more efficient use of a fraud examiner's time. Computer programs can be written to identify the following:
- Vendors with post office box addresses
- Vendors with addresses in common with employee addresses
- Contractors who were unsuccessful bidders who are now subcontractors
- Payments to a particular vendor over a specified period of time

- Vendor payments that were initiated or paid outside the normal system (for example, hand carried or approved)
- Employees who are assigned to more than one contract on any given day